MANCELONA TWP. LIBRARY
MANCELONA, M...

W9-AQX-229

780.92 LANDON, H.C. ROBBINS
MOZ   THE MOZARD COMPENDIUM

Mancelona Township Library
202 W State Street
P.O. Box 499
Mancelona, MI 49659

DEMCO

Mancelona Township Library
37 10000119355

THE
MOZART
COMPENDIUM

THE MOZART COMPENDIUM

A GUIDE TO MOZART'S LIFE AND MUSIC

EDITED BY H.C. ROBBINS LANDON

SCHIRMER BOOKS
A Division of Macmillan, Inc.
New York

FRONTISPIECE: Detail from oil painting of Mozart by Barbara Krafft (1819).

Copyright © 1990 by Thames and Hudson, Ltd.
All rights reserved. No part of this book may be reproduced or transmitted in any form or
by any means, electronic or mechanical, including photocopying, recording, or by any
information storage and retrieval system, without permission in writing from the Publisher.

First American edition published in 1990 by
Schirmer Books
A Division of Macmillan, Inc.
866 Third Avenue, New York, N.Y. 10022
Collier Macmillan Canada, Inc.
1200 Eglinton Avenue East, Suite 200
Don Mills, Ontario M3C 3N1
First published in Great Britain by Thames and Hudson Ltd., London
Library of Congress Catalog Card Number: 90-9071
printing number
3 4 5 6 7 8 9 10

Library of Congress Cataloging-in-Publication Data
The Mozart compendium / edited by H.C. Robbins Landon.
   p. cm.
   Includes bibliographical references (p.   ) and index.
   ISBN 0-02-871321-4
   1. Mozart, Wolfgang Amadeus, 1756–1791. I. Landon, H. C. Robbins
(Howard Chandler Robbins), 1926–
ML410.M9M6995   1990
780′.92—dc20   90-9071
                                                                           CIP
                                                                           MN

CONTENTS

Readers' Guide

THE AIM OF THIS BOOK is to provide a compendium of information on every significant aspect of Mozart and his music. Our team of some two dozen contributors has covered the entire range of Mozart studies – historical and musical background, Mozart as an individual, the sources of the works, their reception, the musical style and performance practice – to offer, in each section, a clearly presented, accessible and thoroughly up-to-date summary of the most authoritative thinking on the subject. The volume also includes a calendar of Mozart's life, work and related events, a Mozart–Weber family tree, a glossary of names, a full listing and discussion of the works by genre, a bibliography and a detailed index (with a list of Mozart's music).

A compendium is of necessity diverse, but that diversity can, and indeed ought to, be a virtue. Part of the purpose of a compendium on a figure of Mozart's stature is to enable two dozen authorities to examine facets of the composer's life and music and to present two dozen different views. In the light of this, we have not obliged the contributors to adhere to one 'standard' translation of Mozart's letters; on the contrary, we have translated anew from the now standard German-language edition by the late O.E. Deutsch and others. Some of the translations are by the contributors, some by the general editor: it was not thought necessary to indicate the translator. Between various contributions there were overlappings, which in some cases we have allowed to stand, as we have also differences of opinion. We have, then, tried to keep our editorial hand as light as possible. (The 'we' is not *pluralis majestatis*, but consists of the general editor, his assistant Frau Dr Ulrike Hofmann, and the managing editor – formerly with Thames and Hudson – Barry Millington.)

It is hoped that the list of contents and the index together will lead the reader swiftly to the desired information. Cross-references have therefore been kept to a minimum. Bibliographical references have likewise been minimized. Where an opinion has been generally accepted, references have not been included; rather they serve to indicate controversial opinions, or recently discovered, and as yet little-known, scholarly facts. Such references are shown as follows: 'Einstein, 1945'. Or, in cases where two or more publications emanate from the same year: 'Deutsch, 1961a', 'Deutsch 1962b'. In the last decade, a great deal of scholarly investigation has been undertaken (notably by Alan Tyson and Wolfgang Plath) regarding chronology, with occasionally spectacular results. In such cases the appropriate references have been indicated.

References to Mozart's music cite the Köchel catalogue as follows. Where only one Köchel number is given, it is identical in *Köchel 1* and *Köchel 6*. Two numbers indicates *Köchel 1* followed by *Köchel 6* (in parentheses). Where *Köchel 3* differs from *Köchel 6*, the order is *Köchel 1*, followed by *Köchel 3* and *6* (in parentheses). *Anh.* = *Anhang* (Appendix).

For quotations from Mozart's letters, we have cited the date of the letter rather than a page reference, to enable the reader more easily to locate the letter in question in English, German or (in the case of foreign-language editions of the *Compendium*) other editions.

H.C.R.L
CHÂTEAU DE FONCOUSSIÈRES
Christmas, 1989

Acknowledgments

We would like to single out one of our contributors for a special word of thanks: John Arthur, who read with scrupulous care the entire music section, with associated work-lists. In addition to his own substantial section on the fragments and sketches, he added much new and unpublished information on such material, together with datings revised by recent scholarship, to the work-lists of other contributors. Dr Alec Hyatt King and his wife Eve were of invaluable help to us throughout the planning and writing of the book and the correction of proofs. Ingrid Grimes brought a meticulous and expert eye to the reading of the proofs. Else Radant (Mrs H.C. Robbins Landon) also read the entire book in typescript and proof, and weeded out many inconsistencies and errors. We wish to thank Albi Rosenthal for allowing us first publication of his newly discovered portrait, believed to be of Mozart, and David Cummings for assistance with the opera documentation. The map on page 100 was drawn by Hanni Bailey. Peter Branscombe's chapter 'Mozart and the Theatre of his Time' is a revised version of the Cramb Lecture delivered at the University of Glasgow in February 1987.

Section 1

CALENDAR OF MOZART'S LIFE, WORKS AND RELATED EVENTS

Mozart's life and works

1756
27 Jan Mozart born in Salzburg at 8 o'clock in the evening.
28 Jan Baptized Joannes Chrysost[omus] Wolfgangus Theophilus.

1761
24 Jan Learns his first piece on the piano, a Scherzo by G.C. Wagenseil, between 9 o'clock and 9.30 in the evening.
1 Sept Appears the first time as a performer at the university in Salzburg in a musical drama by J.E. Eberlin.

1762
12 Jan L. Mozart travels with both children to Munich. They play before the Elector Maximilian Joseph III.
18 Sept The family travels to Vienna, where they arrive 6 Oct.
13 Oct The children play at court, performing nearly every day.
21 Oct Wolfgang ill with erythema nodosum.
5 Nov They play for Dr von Bernhard, who had looked after Wolfgang during his illness.

Other musical events

1756
L. Mozart: *Versuch einer gründlichen Violinschule*; *Musikalische Schlittenfahrt*. C.P.E. Bach: Symphony in E minor (Wq.178). J. Haydn: Organ Concerto in C (Hob.XVIII:1); *Salve Regina* in E (Hob.XXIIIb:1). B. Galuppi: *La cantarina*, Rome. N. Piccinni: *L'astrologo*, Bologna; *Zenobia*, Naples.

1757
J.C. Bach: Requiem. J.P. Rameau: *Les surprises de l'Amour*. P. Guglielmi: *Lo solachianello 'mbroglione*, Naples. J. Haydn: string quartets (Hob.III: 1–4, 6, 7, 8, 10, 12). N. Piccinni: *L'amante ridicolo*, Naples.

1758
J.C. Bach: Dies Irae. A.M.G. Sacchini: *Fra Donato*, Naples. J. Haydn: *Der neue krumme Teufel* (lost), Vienna. N. Piccinni: *Alessandro nell'Indie*, Rome; *Gli' uccellatori*, Naples.

1759
J. Haydn: Symphonies nos 1–5, 10, 15, 18, 27, 32, 33, 37 and 'A' (-1761). G.F. Handel dies (b.1685).

1760
N. Piccinni: *La Cecchina, ossia La buona figliuola*, Rome. C.P.E. Bach: *Sechs Sonaten für Clavier mit veränderten Reprisen* (Wq.50). L. Boccherini: Six String Trios, op.1, Vienna. 1760–1842 Luigi Cherubini, Italian composer.

1761
T. Arne: *Judith* (oratorio), London. J.C. Bach: *Artaserse*, Milan. Ch.W. Gluck: *Don Juan*, Vienna. J. Haydn: Symphonies nos 6–8 (*Le Matin, Le Midi, Le Soir*). N. Piccinni: *Olimpiade*, Rome.

1762
J.C. Bach: *Alessandro nell'Indie*, Naples. Ch.W. Gluck: *Orfeo*, Vienna. T. Arne: *Artaxerxes*, London. C.P.E. Bach: *Versuch über die wahre Art das Clavier zu spielen* (part 2). J. Haydn: Symphony no.9.

Other arts and current events

1756
F.M.A. de Voltaire: *Essai sur les moeurs*. A.B.L. de
Mirabeau: *L'Ami des hommes*. E. Burke: *On the
Sublime and Beautiful*. First chocolate factory
opened in Germany. N. Jardot's new university
building opened in Vienna. 1756–1823 H.
Raeburn, Scottish painter.

1757
D. Diderot: *Entretien sur le fils naturel*. J.J. Bodmer
edits *Das Nibelungen-Lied*. C.F. Gellert: *Geistliche
Lieder und Oden*. *The London Chronicle* issued.
Damien tries to kill Louis XV in Paris. Order of
Maria Theresa for outstanding bravery founded
in Austria. 1757–1822 A. Canova, Italian
sculptor.

1758
D. Diderot: *Le Père de famille*. J.J. Rousseau: *Lettre
à l'Alembert*. S. Johnson publishes his weekly *The
Idler*. Duke of Bridgewater begins construction of
a canal from his coal mines in Worsley to
Manchester. 1758–1823 P. Prud'hon, French
painter. 1758–1840 J. Hoppner, English painter.

1759
F.M.A. de Voltaire: *Candide*. *The Public Ledger*, a
daily paper, appears in London. British Museum
opens in Montagu House (London). 1759–1805
F. von Schiller, German dramatist. 1759–1796 R.
Burns, Scottish poet. 1759–1825 J.T. Serres,
English painter.

1760
J.J. Rousseau: *Julie ou La Nouvelle Héloise*. J.
Macpherson: *Ossian* (famous fraud). F. von
Knaus constructs the first typewriter
(*Schreibautomat*). 1760–1836 C.J. Rouget de Lisle,
French poet and composer.

1761
G. Goldoni: *Una delle ultime sere di Carnevale*.
Porcelain manufactory opened in Nymphenburg
(Bavaria). Austrian doctor L. Auenbrugger
publishes *Inventum Novum*, his method of
recognizing chest diseases by percussion. 1761–
1807 J. Opie, English painter. 1761–1819 A.F.
Kotzebue, German dramatist.

1762
J.J. Rousseau: *Émile ou de l'éducation*; *Du contract
social*. C. Wieland translates Shakespeare into
German. Madame de Pompadour is given Le
Petit Trianon. First paper money (*Bancozettel*)
appears in Austria. Sorbonne library opened in
Paris. J. Wedgwood's cream-coloured pottery,
'Queens-ware', commissioned by Queen
Charlotte. 1762–1814 J.G. Fichte, German
philosopher.

History

1756
Seven Years' War. Austria and France against
England and Prussia. British driven by the
French from the Great Lakes in America. W. Pitt
the Elder becomes Secretary of State. 1756–1836
A. Burr, US statesman. 1756–1818 H. Lee, US
general.

1757
Prussians invade Bohemia, but are defeated by
the Austrians. Russia, Austria's new ally, invades
East Prussia. Frederick of Prussia receives English
subsidies.

1758
Frederick defeats the French and Russians but is
routed by the Austrians at Hochkirch. British
defeated by Montcalm at Fort Carillon
(Ticondaroga), but Louisbourg surrenders. 1758–
1831 J. Monroe, fifth US president. 1758–1805 H.
Nelson, English admiral. 1758–1794 M. de
Robespierre, French revolutionary.

1759
Prussians are defeated by the French, Russians
and Austrians. 13,000 Prussians surrender at
Maxen. British take Quebec, Canada under
English rule.

1760
Russians burn Berlin. Frederick defeats the
Austrians at Torgau. George II dies; his grandson
George III succeeds him. England taxes the
colonists to finance the war against the French in
America. 1760–1794 C. Desmoulins, French
revolutionary.

1761
W. Pitt resigns. Subsidies to Frederick cancelled,
English war debt £127 million (state budget
annually £8 million). French propose peace to
the English.

1762
Russia ends war with Prussia, but Tsar Peter is
deposed by his wife Catherine. English financial
reforms create ill-will in colonies. Austria and
Prussia agree to armistice. 1762–1831 J. Hoban,
American architect.

Mozart's life and works

1762 *(cont.)*
11 Dec   The family travels to Pressburg
(Bratislava), but returns to Vienna and back to
Salzburg (31 Dec).

1763
5 Jan   They arrive home and the boy stays a
week in bed with rheumatic fever.
9 June   First journey through Europe in own
coach and with a servant, Sebastian Winter. First
stop is Munich, where they play at court (13
June) from 8 till 11 o'clock at night. After four
concerts they leave (22 June) for Augsburg (three
public concerts) and go on to Frankfurt-am-
Main. Goethe's father pays 4 gulden 7 kreuzer to
hear the children play (18 Aug). In Oct the
family stays in Brussels.
18 Nov   They are in Paris, rue St Antoine, with
Count von Eyck.

1764
1 Jan   Concert before King Louis XV. The
Mozarts stay five months; Wolfgang publishes his
first music.
27 Apr   George III receives the family in
London. For a concert they receive 24 Guineas.
The children give many concerts, but Leopold
falls ill. They move to Chelsea (6 Aug) and stay
there till Sept. J.C. Bach befriends the Mozarts.
Wolfgang composes his first symphonies, some
given at a concert in London (21 Feb 1765).

1765
18 Jan   Wolfgang dedicates his Opus III sonatas
to the Queen. To earn some money after
Leopold's illness, the children play daily concerts
for a week, from 12 to 3 o'clock at 'The Swan
and Harp' before leaving London (7 July).
1 Aug   Arrival in Calais, where their coach
waits. In Lille father and son are ill (angina). In
The Hague Nannerl catches intestinal typhoid
(12 Sept) and Wolfgang plays the first concert
alone. A week after Nannerl's recovery, Wolfgang
is infected (15 Nov) and is ill for two months.
During their stay in Holland, Wolfgang publishes
six sonatas for keyboard and violin (K.26–31).

1766
May   After concerts in Utrecht, Amsterdam and
Antwerp, they journey via Brussels to Paris (10
May). They stay two months. Wolfgang is
painted by M.B. Ollivier playing the harpsichord
at a tea-party of the Prince de Conti.
18 July   In Dijon, where the children play, and
Wolfgang sings an aria of his own composition.
They travel, via Switzerland, to Munich.
9 Nov   Wolfgang plays at court, but is ill from
12 to 21 Nov. Both play again at court (22 Nov).
The Mozarts leave Munich and travel home.

Other musical events

1763
J.C. Bach: *Orione*, London. P. Anfossi: *La serva
spiritosa*, Rome. N. Piccinni: *Le contadine bizzarre*,
Venice. J. Haydn: *Acide* (Hob.XXVIII:1),
cantata 'Destatevi, o miei fidi' (Hob.XXIXa:2),
both Eisenstadt.

1764
G. Paisiello: *Il ciarlone*, Bologna. J. Haydn:
cantata 'Da qual gioja' (Hob.XXIVa:3),
Symphonies nos 21–24, cantata 'Qual dubbio'
(Hob.XXIVa:4), all Eisenstadt. J.C. Bach starts
concert series in London.

1765
J.C. Bach: *Adriano in Siria*, London; Symphonies
op.3. J. Haydn: Symphonies nos, 28–31; capriccio
'Acht Sauschneider' (Hob.XVII:1), all
Eisenstadt. P. Guglielmi: *Il ratto di sposa*, Venice.
1765–1838 T. Attwood, English composer.

1766
C.P.E. Bach: *Sechs leichte Clavier-Sonaten* (Wq.53).
A.M.G. Sacchini: *L'isola d'amore*, Rome. N.
Piccinni: *La pescatrice, ovvero L'erede riconosciuta*,
Rome. J. Haydn: *Missa Cellensis in honorem B.V.M.*
(Hob.XXII:5); Piano Sonata no.29
(Hob.XVI:45); intermezzo *La cantarina*
(Hob.XXVIII:2), all Eisenstadt.

Other arts and current events

History

1763
F.M.A. de Voltaire: *Traité de la tolérance*. G.E. Lessing: *Minna von Barnhelm* begun. F. Guardi paints *The Election of the Doge of Venice*. Boswell meets Johnson for the first time. Primary education compulsory in Prussia. Kärntnerthor theatre rebuilt after a fire and reopened in Vienna.

1763
End of Seven Years' War. Peace of Paris: France cedes India and the New World to England, Louisiana to Spain. Peace of Hubertusburg: Prussia keeps Silesia. 1763–1844 J.B.J. Bernadotte, French general and later King of Sweden. 1763–1820 J. Fouché, Napoleon's Minister of Police.

1764
C. Beccaria: *Tratto dei delitti e delle pene*. F.M.A. de Voltaire: *Dictionnaire philosophique*. O. Goldsmith: *The Traveller*. 'Spinning Jenny' invented by J. Hargreave in England. 1764–1823 A. Goblet, English sculptor.

1764
Archduke Joseph elected King of the Romans in Frankfurt. Catherine II frees 900,000 peasants in Russia and puts Stanislas Poniatowski on the Polish throne. British enforce Sugar Act in America.

1765
H. Walpole: *The Castle of Otranto* (birth of the Gothic novel). F. Boucher becomes chief painter to Louis XV. 'Victory', Nelson's flagship, launched in England. Place de la Concorde laid out in Paris. Schönbrunn Castle (Vienna) remodelled in Rococo style. Potatoes most popular food in Europe.

1765
Emperor Francis Stephen dies, his son Archduke Joseph succeeds as Joseph II. The Dauphin of France dies; his son Louis, later Louis XVI, inherits the title. Stamp Act leads to Congress in New York; nine colonies draw up a declaration of rights and liberties.

1766
D. Diderot: *Essai sur la peinture*. O. Goldsmith: *The Vicar of Wakefield*. G.E. Lessing: *Laokoon*. Freedom of worship granted in Russia. Joseph II opens his hunting domain (Prater) to the Viennese. 1766–1817 Madame de Stael, French writer. 1766–1834 T.R. Malthus, economist.

1766
W. Pitt English Prime Minister. British retract Stamp Act, but put tax on tea, paper and paint. Mason-Dixon line drawn up. Feudal dues in Hungary regulated. Old Pretender dies.

Mozart's life and works

1766 *(cont.)*
29 Nov Back in Salzburg; they stay nine months.

1767
12 Mar Wolfgang's cantata *Die Schuldigkeit des ersten Gebots* is performed at the archiepiscopal court; he receives a golden medal and 12 ducats for the work. Leopold asks for leave again. In Vienna there is a smallpox epidemic. They flee to Bohemia (23 Oct), but the boy contracts the disease there. He is treated in Olmütz (Olomouc) by Dr J. Wolff (26 Oct) and recovers. He rests until Christmas, but plays a concert (30 Dec) with his sister at a tavern in Brünn (Brno). Wolfgang is offended by the imprecise intonation of the trumpeters.

1768
10 Jan Back in Vienna, they are received at court ten days later.
Mar They give a concert at Prince Galitzin's.
Sept *La finta semplice*, a commissioned opera, is not performed in Vienna, because of intrigues, but in Salzburg, 1 May 1769. Mozart's second operatic work, the operetta *Bastien und Bastienne*, is given in Dr A. Mesmer's house (?Sept/Oct).
7 Dec Mozart conducts his new *Waisenhausmesse* and a lost trumpet concerto, K.47c, in the presence of the imperial family at the Orphanage Church (Waisenhauskirche) in Vienna. They travel back, via Lambach, to Salzburg.

1769
5 Feb Mozart's Missa Brevis K.65 is celebrated at the Collegienkirche in Salzburg. His serenatas in D, K.100 (62a), and G, K.63, are performed during the summer months at the university and Leopold prepares a second edition of his violin treatise. Mozart writes for his friend Father Dominicus Hagenauer the *Dominicus* Mass, which is performed at the abbey church of St Peter (15 Oct). Mozart's career advances: he is given the post of Konzertmeister (without pay) at the Salzburg court (27 Nov), but is given 120 ducats for a trip to Italy with his father.
13 Dec They leave the town and travel to Innsbruck, where Wolfgang plays at Count Künigl's house (17 Dec). They proceed to Verona (27 Dec), where they stay for nearly two weeks.

1770
6–7 Jan The painter Saverio dalla Rosa paints the young Wolfgang for the music lover P. Lugiati. Mozart gives two concerts, before he and his father leave for Milan, where they lodge at the Augustinian monastery of San Marco (23 Jan). The Mozarts attend opera performances at La Scala of works by Jommelli and Piccinni, and meet G.B. Sammartini at residence of Count

Other musical events

1767
Ch.W. Gluck: *Alceste*, Vienna. P. Guglielmi: *La sposa fedele*, Venice. N. Piccinni: *La notte critica*, Lisbon. J. Haydn: *Stabat Mater* (Hob.XX: bis), Symphony no.35, both Eisenstadt. J.C. Bach: *Carattaco*, London.

1768
G. Gazzaniga: *Il barone di Trocchia*, Naples. B. Galuppi: *Ifigenia in Tauride*, St Petersburg. J. Haydn: cantata *Applausus* (Hob.XXIVa:6), Zwettl; *Lo speziale* (Hob.XVIII:3), Eszterháza. N. Piccinni: *Li napoletani in America*, Naples; *La locandiera di spirito*, Naples.

1769
N. Piccinni: Flute Concerto in D, Rome; *Lo sposo burlato*, Rome. J. Haydn: Symphonies nos 41(?), 48 (*Maria Theresia*; date from MS copy by J. Elssler); Baryton Trio (Hob.XI:79). 1769–1832 B. Asioli, theorist.

1770
Ch.W. Gluck: *Paride ed Elena*, Vienna. J.C. Bach: *Gioas, rè di Giuda* (oratorio), London. L. Boccherini: Quartets op.9. A. Salieri: *Don Chisciotte alle nozze di Gamace*, Vienna; *Die Mode*, Vienna. A.M.G. Sacchini: *Armida*, Milan. N. Piccinni: *Cesare in Egitto*, Milan. 1770–1827 Ludwig van Beethoven.

Other arts and current events

History

1767
M. Mendelssohn: *Phaedon oder die Unsterblichkeit der Seele*. J.J. Rousseau: *Dictionnaire de musique*; he settles in England and gets a pension from George III. Veterinary school founded in Vienna. 1767–1855 J.B. Isabey, French painter. 1767–1845 A.W. von Schlegel, German poet.

1767
Jesuits expelled from Spain. Public meeting in Boston puts ban on imported English goods. 1767–1848 J.Q. Adams, sixth US president. 1767–1845 A. Jackson, seventh US president. 1767–1815 J. Murat, French general.

1768
J. Boswell: *Account of Corsica*. L. Sterne: *A Sentimental Journey*. James Cook starts his first circumnavigation. Church of City Orphanage (Waisenhauskirche) built by T. Karner in Vienna and consecrated with Mozart's music (7 Dec). Founding of the Royal Academy in London.

1768
Outbreak of Russo-Turkish war. Massachusetts Assembly dissolved for refusal to quarter troops and assist tax collection. 1768–1836 Archduke Francis, later Emperor Francis I (II).

1769
The Morning Chronicle issued in London. Royal Crescent in Bath completed. Watt patents his steam engine and J. Wedgwood opens new factory ('Etruria') in Staffordshire. 1769–1860 E.M. Arndt, German poet. 1769–1830 T. Lawrence, English painter. 1769–1859 A. von Humboldt, German naturalist.

1769
Spain occupies California, sends Don Galvez to Mexico to devise reforms. Virginia protests against colonial treason trials in London. 1769–1852 Duke of Wellington, English general and statesman. 1769–1821 Napoleon Bonaparte.

1770
O. Goldsmith: *The Deserted Village*. Gainsborough paints *The Blue Boy*. Cook lands in Botany Bay. First numbering of all houses in Vienna started. Paris gets its first public restaurant. Visiting cards introduced in England. 1770–1840 W. Wordsworth, English poet. 1770–1843 F. Hölderlin, German poet. 1770–1837 F. Gérard, French painter.

1770
Boston Massacre. British commander, defended by J. Adams, stands trial for the massacre. *Massachusetts Spy* issued. Marie Antoinette marries the Dauphin of France.

Mozart's life and works

1770 *(cont.)*
Firmian, Governor-General of Lombardy. At
another soirée at Firmian's (18 Feb) they meet
Beatrice d'Este, the future daughter-in-law of
Empress Maria Theresa, and her father. The
Mozarts travel on and reach Florence (30 Mar),
Wolfgang with a cold. Mozart plays before the
Grand Duke Leopold, later Emperor Leopold II
(2 Apr). They leave for Rome and arrive just
before Easter (11 Apr). At St Peter's they hear
Allegri's *Miserere*, which Wolfgang writes out from
memory. A month later they are in Naples (14
May). They are received by the British envoy, W.
Hamilton, at Prince Kaunitz's, and do some
sight-seeing, visiting Pompeii and Herculaneum,
before travelling back by express coach (27 hours)
to Rome (26 June). The Pope confers the Order
of the Golden Spur on Wolfgang, who appears in
full regalia (8 July), paid for by Leopold. Two
days later the Mozarts leave Rome to go north.
They are in Bologna (20 July) and decide to have
a rest, because Mozart senior has had an accident
during the trip from Naples to Rome. They stay
a few weeks at Count Pallavicini's estate near
Bologna (10 Aug to 1 Oct). Wolfgang is admitted
to the Accademia Filarmonica and is given a
diploma (10 Oct). Three days later they leave
Bologna and arrive in Milan (18 Oct). Mozart
starts work on the commissioned opera *Mitridate*
(74a), but finds time to play at Count Firmian's
(26 Nov). The opera is given at the Teatro Regio
Ducal (26 Dec) and is a great success. Mozart
conducts the first three performances.

1771
5 Jan Mozart receives another diploma, this
time from the Accademia Filarmonica in Verona.
During Carnival they are in Venice (11 Feb).
Mozart gives many concerts. From Milan arrives
a contract for another opera, *Lucio Silla*. After
more than fifteen months, they return to Salzburg
(28 Mar). In summer they set out again for Milan,
arriving in the evening (21 Aug). Mozart is given
the libretto for the opera *Ascanio in Alba*. A month
later rehearsals begin and the premiere is again at
the Teatro Regio Ducal (17 Oct), to celebrate the
wedding of Princess Beatrice d'Este to Archduke
Ferdinand. The day before, Hasse's last opera,
Ruggiero, was performed. Mozart is received by the
Archduke, who wants to engage him; but the
Empress is against the idea. Father and son return
to Salzburg, where they arrive (15 Dec) one day
before Archbishop Schrattenbach's death.

1772
14 Mar A new archbishop, Count Hieronymus
Colloredo, is elected. For the enthronement (29
Apr), Mozart composes *Il sogno di Scipione*.
21 Aug Colloredo confirms Mozart's post as

Other musical events

1771
A.M. Grétry: *Zémire et Azor*, Fontainebleau. G.
Gazzaniga: *La locanda*, Venice. L. Boccherini:
Symphonies op.12. A. Salieri: *Armida*, Vienna. J.
Haydn: *Salve Regina* in G minor (Hob.XXIIIb:2);
String Quartets op.17 (Hob.III:25–30);
Symphony no.42; Piano Sonata no.33 in C minor
(Hob.XVI:20).

1772
J.C. Bach: *Temistocle*, Mannheim. G.F. Handel:
Messiah, first German performance. G.
Gazzaniga: *L'isola di Alcina*, Venice. J. Haydn:
Missa Sancti Nicolai (Hob.XXII:6); Baryton Trio

Other arts and current events

History

1771
C. Wieland: *Der neue Amadis* (poem). G.F. Klopstock: *Odes*. H. Walpole: *Anecdotes of Painting*. L. Galvani discovers electrical nature of nervous impulse. New Assembly Rooms opened in Bath. First census in Austria. 1771–1832 W. Scott, Scottish novelist.

1771
Russian successes in Turkey alarm Prussia and Austria; Frederick offers mediation. New York Hospital founded.

1772
H.C.R. Mirabeau: *Essai sur le despotisme*. Capt. Cook starts his second voyage. 1772–1834 S.T. Coleridge, English poet. 1772–1829 F. von Schiller, German dramatist.

1772
First partition of Poland causes her to lose half her population. Colonial mob burns revenue boat in Narragansett Bay. Gustav III of Sweden re-establishes absolutism with French support.

Mozart's life and works

1772 *(cont.)*
Konzertmeister and pays him a yearly salary of
150 gulden. In Oct he and his father obtain leave
from the Archbishop to travel to Milan again.
They arrive (4 Nov) for the rehearsals of *Lucio
Silla*, which is performed the day after Christmas.

1773
17 Jan The famous castrato Venanzio Rauzzini
sings the motet *Exsultate, jubilate* at the Theatine
Church in Milan. In Mar they are back in
Salzburg. The family move in spring to their new
big flat at the Hannibal-Platz (now Makart-
platz). In July, Leopold and Wolfgang again
travel to Vienna. He hopes for a post there, but
an audience with the Empress (5 Aug) meets with
no success. Wolfgang gives concerts at Dr
Mesmer's and Dr Auenbrugger's, and plays in
churches, but they return to Salzburg (27 Sept)
empty-handed. First version of *Thamos, König in
Ägypten.*

1774
Mozart composes serenatas, concertos and very
condensed masses to please the reformist
Archbishop, until he receives another commission
from Munich for an opera (*La finta giardiniera*).
For the rehearsals they travel to Munich (6 Dec).

1775
The premiere (*La finta giardiniera*) is postponed
from 29 Dec to 5 Jan. Nannerl joins her father
and brother in Munich (4 Jan). She misses a
performance of Wolfgang's (K.125) and his
father's settings of *Litaniae de venerabili*; both
compositions are given on New Year's Day. The
opera is finally given at the Salvatortheater (13
Jan) and is a great success. Leopold conducts
Wolfgang's masses; *Misericordias Domini*, K.222
(205a), is performed, but the concerts bring no
appointment. The three Mozarts are soon back in
Salzburg (7 Mar). Archduke Maximilian visits
the Archbishop and Wolfgang provides the music
for his entertainment. He composes many
serenades, masses and violin concertos.

1776
3 Jan Performance of additional parts of
Thamos, König in Ägypten.
21 July Performance of *Haffner* Serenade, at
wedding celebrations of Marie Elisabeth Haffner.

1777
Aug Mozart is frustrated by Salzburg and
petitions the Archbishop for leave. The annoyed
Colloredo dismisses both Mozarts from his service.
In the end Leopold stays and Wolfgang sets out

Other musical events

1772 *(cont.)*
(Hob.XI:106); Symphony no.45 (*Farewell*). A.
Salieri: *La fiera di Venezia*; *La secchia rapita*, both
Vienna.

1773
C.P.E. Bach: Six symphonies ded. to G. van
Swieten (Wq.182). A.M. Grétry: *Le Magnifique*,
Paris. A. Salieri: *La locandiera*, Vienna. J. Haydn:
Hexenschabbas (Hob.XXIXa:2, marionette opera,
lost); *L'infedeltà delusa* (Hob.XXVIII:5); *Philemon
und Baucis* (Hob.XXIXa:1, marionette opera), all
Eszterháza.

1774
Ch.W. Gluck: *Iphigénie en Aulide*, Paris. N.
Piccinni: *I viaggiatori*, Naples. G. Gazzaniga: *La
dama soldato*, Vienna. A. Salieri: *La calamità de
cuori*, Vienna. J. Haydn: incidental music to
Regnard's *Le Distrait*, later adapted as Symphony
no.60; Symphonies nos 54–56, Eszterháza. G.
Paisiello: *La frascatana*, Venice.

1775
P. Anfossi: *Il geloso in cimento*, Vienna. A.M.
Grétry: *Céphale et Procris*, Paris. L. Boccherini:
Symphonies op.21. J. Haydn: *L'incontro improvviso*
(Hob.XXVIII:6); Divertimenti a otto voci
(Hob.X:2,3,5), all Eszterháza.

1776
J.C. Bach: *Lucio Silla*, Mannheim. P. Anfossi: *La
vera costanza*, Vienna. A. Salieri: *Daliso*, Vienna. J.
Haydn: *Dido* (Hob.XXIXa:3, marionette opera);
Symphony no.61; Piano Sonatas nos 42–47
(Hob.XVI:27–32).

1777
G. Gazzaniga: *La bizzaria degli umori*, Bologna. V.
Righini: *Il convitato di pietra*, Vienna. Ch.W.
Gluck: *Armide*, Paris. J. Haydn: *Il mondo della luna*
(Hob.XXVIII:7); insertion aria *D'una sposa*

Other arts and current events

History

1773
O. Goldsmith: *She Stoops to Conquer*. J.W. von Goethe: *Götz von Berlichingen*; *Urfaust*. G.A. Bürger: *Leonore*. Masonic lodge 'Grand Orient' opened in Paris. 1773–1853 Ludwig Tieck, German poet.

1773
Jesuits suppressed by the Pope. Tea Act leads to Boston Tea Party. Philadelphia Museum founded. 1773–1841 W.H. Harrison, ninth US president.

1774
J.W. von Goethe: *Die Leiden des jungen Werther*. J. Wesley: *Thoughts on Slavery*. W. Herschel builds his telescope and J. Wilkinson patents his precision cannon-borer in England. J.F. Pestalozzi opens in Zurich school for neglected children. 1774–1840 C.D. Friedrich, German painter.

1774
Louis XVI succeeds his grandfather Louis XV and starts reforms. Only military reforms carried through; these are responsible for the victories 1792–4. Virginia calls Continental Congress to meet in Philadelphia. Declaration of Rights and Grievances. British close Boston Harbour.

1775
P.A.C. de Beaumarchais: *Le Barbier de Séville*. R.B. Sheridan: *The Rivals*. S. Johnson: *A Journey to the Western Islands of Scotland*. P.S. Girard invents the turbine. 1775–1817 Jane Austen, English novelist. 1775–1836 A.M. Ampère, French physicist. 1775–1854 F.W.J. von Schelling, German philosopher.

1775
Peasants' revolt in Bohemia. Famine in Paris. Peasants' revolt in Russia under Pugachev's leadership crushed. War of Independence in America starts with battles of Lexington and Concord. Washington appointed Commander-in-Chief.

1776
E. Gibbon: *The Decline and Fall of the Roman Empire* begun. J.W. von Goethe: *Stella*. Concerts of Ancient Music start in London. 1776–1837 J. Constable, English painter. 1776–1822 E.T.A. Hoffmann, German author and composer.

1776
Washington relieves siege of Boston. Virginia Convention declares independence from England. Opposition to Marie Antoinette rises at French court. Necker called to reform French finances.

1777
R.B. Sheridan: *The School for Scandal*. J. Priestley: *Disquisition Relating to Matter and Spirit*. D. Bushnell, American engineer, invents the torpedo. *Journal de Paris* starts publication. 1777–1810 P.O.

1777
British plan three campaigns to crush American revolution; they occupy Philadelphia, but are beaten at Princeton and Saratoga. Joseph II visits his sister, the Queen of France. 1777–1825 Alexander, future Tsar of Russia.

Mozart's life and works

1777 *(cont.)*
(23 Sept) with his mother in their own carriage
(*chaise*). Travelling via Munich and Augsburg,
where Wolfgang finds his cousin, Maria Anna
Thekla, 'the Bäsle', very amusing, they arrive in
Mannheim (30 Oct). Wolfgang falls in love with
Aloisia Weber and spends nearly five months
there in the hope of finding an appointment.
Meanwhile, Leopold agonizes in Salzburg and
urges his son to proceed to Paris.

1778
23 Mar Finally Mozart tears himself away from
the Webers and leaves with his mother. It takes
them nine days to travel to Paris, where the battle
between the Gluckists and Piccinnists is at its height.
11 June Mozart's ballet music *Les Petits Riens* is
played at the Grand Opéra and a day later his
new Symphony in D, K.297, at the home of
Count Sickingen. At the Concert Spirituel the
symphony is again well received (18 June). But
his mother dies (3 July) and apart from
performing his compositions, there is no future for
the young man in Paris.
26 Sept After a stay of six months he leaves
Paris, stopping in Munich, where he lodges with
the Weber family (25 Dec), who have left
Mannheim. He presents the Electress with his
newly engraved violin sonatas K.301–306. His
father wants him back; the Archbishop has
promised not only to install Wolfgang again as
Konzertmeister, but also to appoint him court
organist with a generous salary.

1779
Mozart, who arrives at Salzburg in mid-Jan,
receives his new contract (25 Feb). For his salary
of 450 gulden, he has to play in church, at court
and in the chapel, instruct the choirboys and
compose the usual church and secular music
required in Salzburg. Then arrives a new opera
commission from Munich.

1780
5 Nov Mozart leaves Salzburg and travels to
Munich. A month later is the first rehearsal of
Idomeneo.

1781
27 Jan The general rehearsal is on his birthday.
His father and sister arrive for the successful
premiere. The Mozarts stay until early Mar and
visit their relatives in Augsburg. Archbishop
Colloredo, meanwhile established temporarily in
Vienna, orders Wolfgang to join him.
16 Mar He arrives in the morning and plays

Other musical events

1777 *(cont.)*
meschinella (Hob.XXIVb:2) for Paisiello's opera
La frascatana, Eszterháza. N. Piccinni: *Roland*,
Paris.

1778
A. Salieri: *L'Europa riconosciuta*, Milan; *La scuola de'
gelosi*, Venice. G. Gazzaniga: *La vendemmia*,
Florence. N. Piccinni: *Phaon*, Choisy. J. Haydn:
aria 'Quando la rosa' (Hob. XXIV b:3); *Die
bestrafte Rachbegierde* (Hob. XXIXb:3, marionette
opera, lost).

1779
L. Boccherini: Quintets op.27–29. J.C. Bach:
Amadis des Gaules, Paris. C.P.E. Bach: *Heilig* for
double choir (Wq.217); *Sechs Clavier-Sonaten für
Kenner und Liebhaber* (Wq.55). J. Haydn: *L'isola
disabitata* (Hob.XXVIII:9); Symphonies nos.75
and 70. D. Cimarosa: *L'italiana in Londra*, Rome.
Ch.W. Gluck: *Iphigénie en Tauride*, Paris. A.
Salieri: *Il talismano*, Venice; *La partenza inaspettata*,
Rome. L. Cherubini: *Il Quinto Fabio*, Alessandria.

1780
K. Dittersdorf: *Job* (oratorio). C.P.E. Bach: four
symphonies ded. to Friedrich Wilhelm of Prussia
(Wq.183). N. Piccinni: *Atys*, Paris. A. Salieri: *La
dama pastorella*, Rome.

1781
L. Boccherini: *Stabat Mater*. G. Paisiello: *La serva
padrona*, St Petersburg. J. Haydn: String
Quartets op.33 (Hob.III:37–42); Lieder
(Hob.XXXVIa: 1–12) publ. in two sets, 1781
and 1783. D. Cimarosa: *Il pittor parigino*; *Giannina
e Bernadone*, both Rome. A. Salieri: *Der
Rauchfangkehrer*, Vienna.

Other arts and current events

1777 *(cont.)*
Runge, German painter. 1777–1855 K.F. Gauss, German mathematician. 1777–1811 H. von Kleist, German poet.

1778
G.L.L. Buffon: *Époques de la Nature*. F. Burney: *Evelina* (novel). Dr F.A. Mesmer, an Austrian friend of the Mozarts, causes a sensation in Paris with cures by animal magnetism. La Scala opened in Milan. 1778–1829 Humphrey Davy, English chemist. 1778–1842 C. von Brentano, German poet. 1778–1827 U. Foscolo, Italian author.

1779
R.B. Sheridan: *The Critic*. J.W. von Goethe: *Iphigenie* (first version). G.E. Lessing: *Nathan der Weise*. Cook killed in Hawaii. Sir J. Banks recommends New South Wales as British penal colony. First velocipede seen in Paris.

1780
M. Claudius writes *Lieder für das Volk*. The *British Gazette* and *Sunday Monitor* issued in London. Screwdriver and circular saw invented. 1780–1867 J.A.D. Ingres, French painter.

1781
F. von Schiller: *Die Räuber*. I. Kant: *Die Kritik der reinen Vernunft*. P.A.F.C. de Laclos: *Les Liaisons dangereuses*. W. Herschel discovers planet Uranus. Construction of the Siberian Highway begun. 1781–1838 A. von Chamisso, German poet.

History

1778
France enters War of American Independence, its fleet supporting the colonists. British evacuate Philadelphia. Indians massacre inhabitants of Wyoming valley. War of Bavarian Succession between Austria and Prussia.

1779
Treaty of Teschen ends Bavarian War, Austria gains the Innviertel. British conquer Georgia and South Carolina; Congress sends troops against the Indians at Wyoming valley. Louis XVI abolishes serfdom in royal domains.

1780
Empress Maria Theresa dies and Joseph II initiates a series of reforms which shake the state's foundations. French troops arrive in America. Gordon Riots in London against Catholic Relief Act. British defeated in North Carolina.

1781
Louis XVI dismisses Necker, who publishes state deficit which shocks the public. French fleet cuts British communications with North America. British under Cornwallis surrender with 7000 men in Yorktown, evacuate Charleston and Savannah. Serfdom abolished in Bohemia (then part of Austria).

Mozart's life and works

1781 *(cont.)*
that afternoon at a concert. He is not content
with his position in the Colloredo retinue,
between the valets and the cooks. He is also not
allowed to earn money, and he misses – because
he has to play for the Archbishop's father (8 Apr)
– a concert which the Emperor attends at
Countess Thun's. He asks for his dismissal, which
is granted, and he is literally booted out of the
room (8 June) by *Oberküchenmeister* Count Arco.
Mozart takes lodgings with the Webers, who have
moved to Vienna, in St Peter's Square. Aloisia is
already married, but Wolfgang is very much
attracted to the younger sister, Constanze. He is
happy and very busy.
30 July   He is given the libretto for a new
opera, a German Singspiel, entitled *Die Entführung
aus dem Serail*. He has pupils and gives many
concerts. The well-known music publisher Artaria
agrees to publish his compositions.
24 Dec   Clementi and Mozart have their famous
piano contest in the presence of Joseph II and the
Russian Grand Duchess Maria Feodorovna.

1782
Apr   Mozart tries to win his father's consent to
marry Constanze, who writes a letter to her
future sister-in-law.
26 May   The concert series at the Augarten
starts. At the end of the month the third act of
the opera is ready. The premiere is two months
later at the Burgtheater (16 July) and is a great
success. Mozart earns 100 ducats.
29 July   For his Salzburg friend Siegmund
Haffner, Mozart writes a new symphony in D,
K.385, performed when Haffner is ennobled.
4 Aug   Wolfgang and Constanze are married at
St Stephen's with Leopold's grudging consent.
8 Oct   Mozart conducts *Die Entführung* at the
Burgtheater in honour of the Russian Grand
Duke and his consort. A month later he plays
together with his pupil Josepha Auernhammer at
a concert in the Kärntnerthor theatre (3 Nov). A
visit to Salzburg for his father's name-day is
postponed.

1783
3 Mar   During Carnival, Mozart and his friends
perform a 'Masquerade' with his music,
K.446(416d), in the interval of a masked ball at
the Redoutensaal. His sister-in-law Aloisia Lange
gives a concert at the Burgtheater with his music
(11 Mar). He plays the Piano Concerto in C,
K.415, and the Rondo in D, K.382.
23 Mar   Joseph II attends Mozart's academy
concert at the Burgtheater, where Wolfgang plays
the new Rondo (K.382) for his Piano Concerto in
D, K.175, and the Concerto in C, K.415.
9 May   For the first time a concert given by

Other musical events

1782
A. Salieri: *Semiramide*, Munich. L. Boccherini:
Symphonies op.35. J. Haydn: *Missa Cellensis*
(*Mariazellermesse*, Hob.XXII:8); Symphonies nos
76–78; *Orlando Paladino* (Hob.XXVIII:11),
Eszterháza. 1782–1871 D.F.E. Auber, French
composer.

1783
N. Piccinni: *Didon*, Fontainebleau. L. van
Beethoven: Drei Kurfürstensonaten (WoO 47). J.
Haydn: *Armida* (Hob.XXVIII:12); Cello
Concerto in D (Hob.VIIb:2), both Eszterháza.
A.M.G. Sacchini: *Renaud*, Paris.

Other arts and current events

History

1782
F. Burney: *Cecilia* (novel). W. Cowper: *Poems*. J. Priestley: *A History of the Corruption of Christianity*. A. Canova: monument to Pope Clement XIV begun. J. Watt patents the use of double action (steam and vacuum). 1782–1841 F.L. Chantrey, English sculptor.

1782
W. Pitt presses for economic reforms in England and starts peace talks with B. Franklin in Paris. Pope Pius VI visits Vienna. Joseph II puts clergy under supervision of the state. American Congress accepts peace preliminaries. 1782–1850 J.C. Calhoun, US statesman.

1783
G. Crabbe: *The Village*. F. von Schiller: *Fiesco*. G. von Vega publishes his table of logarithms. Joseph II issues civil marriage patent (divorce possible in Austria). In London, J. Broadwood patents piano pedal. 1783–1842 Stendhal (M.H. Beyle), French writer.

1783
Treaty of Versailles signed between France, Spain, Britain and United States. Britain recognizes the independence of its former colonies. Russia seizes the Crimea. 1783–1859 W. Irving, American author.

Mozart's life and works

1783 *(cont.)*
Mozart is reviewed in Cramer's *Magazin der Musik* in Hamburg.
17 June Mozart's first son Raimund Leopold is born and at the end of the next month the parents travel to Salzburg to visit Leopold.
19 Aug In Vienna the little Leopold dies. As early as Jan Mozart had worked on a votive mass – the Mass in C minor, K.427 (417a) – for Salzburg, which he never completes; but the torso is performed at the abbey of St Peter's (26 Oct). Constanze sings one of the solo soprano parts. On their way home the pair stop at Linz, where Wolfgang composes a new symphony, K.425, for a concert in the theatre (4 Nov). He returns ill.

1784
Jan The Mozarts move from the Judenplatz into a flat in the Trattnerhof and Wolfgang begins to keep a thematic catalogue of his works (*Verzeichnüss*) (9 Feb). During Lent, Mozart gives seventeen concerts and sends the subscribers' list to his father.
23 Aug In St Gilgen (near Salzburg) Nannerl marries Johann Baptist von Berchtold zu Sonnenburg. In Vienna Mozart attends the performance of Paisiello's opera *Il rè Teodoro in Venezia* at the Burgtheater (the same day); he has a severe attack of colic during the performance and is ill until Sept with a kidney infection.
21 Sept Carl Thomas, the second son, is born. Eight days later the Mozarts move to an expensive flat at Domgasse 5 (rent 450 fl.p.a.)
14 Dec Mozart joins the freemasons at the lodge 'Zur Wohlthätigkeit' ('Beneficence').

1785
15 Jan Haydn hears Mozart's quartets, K.387 etc. (the six later dedicated to Haydn), at the Domgasse. Mozart's father travels to Vienna to visit his son (11 Feb) and Wolfgang plays his new Piano Concerto in D minor, K. 466, at his first Friday concert in the 'Mehlgrube'. He thus misses Haydn's initiation into the freemasons at the lodge 'Zur wahren Eintracht' ('True Concord').
12 Feb Another quartet evening at the Mozarts': Haydn hears three of the six quartets later dedicated to him and compliments Leopold on his son's talents. Mozart plays five concerts in Feb, six in Mar.
13 Mar His new cantata *Davidde penitente* (arranged largely from the C minor Mass, K.427(417a)) is given at a concert of the Tonkünstler-Societät.
6 Apr Leopold becomes a freemason. Wolfgang composes the cantata *Die Maurerfreude* for the brethren and it is performed (24 Apr). The next day Leopold leaves Vienna.

Other musical events

1784
A.M. Grétry: *Richard Coeur de Lion*, Paris. D. Cimarosa: *La bella greca*, Rome; *Il mercato di Malmantile*, Florence. 1784–1859 Louis Spohr, German composer.

1785
N. Piccinni: *Pénélope*, Fontainebleau. A. Salieri: *La grotta di Trofonio*, Vienna. J. Haydn: Symphonies nos 83 (*La Poule*) and 87; Piano Trios nos 20–22 (Hob.XV:7–9); String Quartet op.42 (Hob.III:43). S. Storace: *Gli sposi malcontenti*, Vienna. D. Cimarosa: *Il marito disperato*, Naples.

Other arts and current events

History

1784
P.A.C. de Beaumarchais: *Le Mariage de Figaro*. F. von Schiller: *Kabale und Liebe*. J.G. Herder: *Ideen zur Philosophie der Geschichte der Menschheit* begun. First balloon ascent by V. Lunardi (England) and by Blanchard in France. Brighton Pavilion begun. Joseph II opens Europe's most modern hospital in Vienna, the Allgemeine Krankenhaus. 1784–1864 L. von Klenze, German architect.

1784
Independence war costs 70,000 lives; eleven states of the federation want amendments of the constitution. Pitt puts East India Company under governmental control. Joseph II revokes Hungarian constitution. 1784–1865 H.J. Temple, Lord Palmerston, English statesman.

1785
J.A. Houdon finishes bust of Washington. P. de Rozier crashes with his balloon trying to cross the Channel. Austrian East India Trade Company closed down. 1785–1873 A. Manzoni, Italian author.

1785
Joseph II's clerical reforms ill received in Belgium. Hungarian crown removed to Vienna. Marie Antoinette discredited by the 'Diamond Necklace Affair'. 1785–1795 Louis Charles.

Mozart's life and works

1785 *(cont.)*
17 Nov Mozart's *Maurerische Trauermusik* is performed at the lodge 'Zur gekrönten Hoffnung' ('Crowned Hope') to honour two dead brethren, Duke G.A. von Mecklenburg-Strelitz and Count F. Esterházy.
15 Dec The lodge gives a concert with music by Mozart and Wranitzky, in which Mozart's pieces for basset-horn are performed.
24 Dec Two new calendars appear in Vienna with portraits of Mozart by H. Löschenkohl.

1786
7 Feb Joseph II pays Mozart 50 ducats for the stage music to *Der Schauspieldirektor*, performed the same day at the orangery of Schönbrunn Castle, together with Salieri's little opera *Prima la musica, e poi le parole*. Both works are repeated at the Kärntnerthor theatre (11 Feb).
13 Mar Mozart conducts a performance of his opera *Idomeneo* at the palace of Prince Auersperg.
7 Apr He plays what is to be his last academy concert at the Burgtheater (Piano Concerto K.491) and rehearses his new opera *Le nozze di Figaro*, which is first performed at the Burgtheater to an enthusiastic public (1 May). A trip to England is contemplated, but Leopold refuses to take the little Carl.
18 Oct Constanze gives birth to third son, Johann Thomas Leopold; he lives only a month.

1787
17 Jan The Mozarts travel to Prague, where *Figaro* is a huge success. Mozart gives a concert in Prague (19 Jan), where the new Symphony, K.504 (*Prague*) is performed, and later conducts his *Figaro* in the theatre (22 Jan).
7 Apr Beethoven arrives in Vienna to study with Mozart. The family move to a cheaper flat in the Landstrasse; Mozart is ill and loses 300 ducats he loans to a friend. His father dies (28 May) and Mozart receives 1000 gulden from Leopold's estate.
4 Oct The Mozarts travel again to Prague, where *Don Giovanni* is rehearsed. *Figaro* is given to celebrate the wedding of Archduchess Maria Theresia to Prince Anton of Saxony.
29 Oct *Don Giovanni* has its premiere and Mozart conducts four performances.
7 Dec He is appointed *Kammermusicus* (chamber musician) to the court with a salary of 800 gulden; he had hoped for more. He is already in debt to M. Puchberg.

1788
7 May *Don Giovanni* has its unsuccessful premiere in Vienna. Mozart cannot raise enough subscribers to issue his three quintets (K.515 etc.). He gives his last academy concerts at the Casino.

Other musical events

1786
P. Anfossi: *L'inglese in Italia*, London; *Le gelosie fortunate*, Venice. J. Haydn: Symphonies nos 82, 84, 86; insertion arias for operas by Traetta and Gazzaniga. G. Gazzaniga: *Il finto cieco*, Vienna. A. Salieri: *Prima la musica e poi le parole*, Vienna. Martín y Soler: *Una cosa rara*, Vienna. S. Storace: *Gli equivoci*, Vienna. 1786–1826 C.M. von Weber, German composer.

1787
D. Cimarosa: *Missa pro defunctis*, St Petersburg. G. Paisiello: *Pirro*, Naples. C. Dittersdorf: *Die Liebe im Narrenhause*, Vienna. Martín y Soler: *L'arbore di Diana*, Vienna. J. Haydn: String Quartets op.50 (Hob.III:44–49); Symphonies nos. 88, 89; Six Allemandes for orchestra (Hob.IX:9). A. Salieri: *Tarare*, Paris.

1788
J. Haydn: String Quartets opp.54 and 55 (Hob.III:57–62) completed; Symphonies nos 90, 91. A. Salieri: *Il talismano, Axur, rè d'Ormus*, both Vienna. L. Boccherini: Quintets op.41 (*sic*).

Other arts and current events

History

1786
G.L.L. Buffon: *Histoire naturelle des oiseaux*. G.A. Bürger: *Gedichte*. Goya designs tapestries *The Seasons*. M.H. Klaproth discovers uranium. Balmant and Piccard climb Mont Blanc. Threshing machine invented.

1786
Pitt reforms government finances in England. First protests in Belgium against Joseph's reforms. Frederick of Prussia dies; his nephew Friedrich Wilhelm II succeeds. 1786–1868 Ludwig, later King of Bavaria.

1787
J.W. von Goethe: *Iphigenie auf Tauris*. F. von Schiller: *Don Carlos*. Plague in Algeria kills 17,000. First convicts arrive in Sydney. Joseph II prohibits children under nine years of age from working. 1781–1854 G.S. Ohm, German physicist. 1787–1824 G. Gordon, Lord Byron.

1787
Russia at war with Turkey (Austria sides with Russia from 1788). Capital punishment abolished in Austria, in favour of life sentences with hard labour; crimes committed by nobility carry humiliating punishments. Riots in Paris and Belgium. Parliament exiled. Notables assemble in France.

1788
J.W. von Goethe: *Egmont*. I. Kant: *Die Kritik der praktischen Vernunft*. *The Times* issued in London. J. Watt transfers piston action to rotary action in his steam engine.

1788
George III shows first signs of porphyria. W. Pitt calls for abolition of slave trade. Louis XVI demands a meeting of the French Estates General. Necker recalled to reform finances.

Mozart's life and works

1788 *(cont.)*
29 June His little daughter Theresia dies (b. 27 Dec 1787). Van Swieten and some of his aristocratic friends perform Handel's *Acis and Galatea*, arranged and conducted by Mozart. During Nov he conducts it at his own benefit concert at the Jahnscher Saal.

1789
2 Apr Mozart borrows money from F. Hofdemel and travels with Prince K. Lichnowsky to Germany (8 Apr). In Dresden his portrait is drawn by Doris Stock. He plays in Leipzig on the organ of the Thomaskirche and goes on to Potsdam (25 Apr). In May he is back in Leipzig and gives a concert (12th). He leaves again for Berlin, and plays for King Friedrich Wilhelm II (26 May). On his way home, he stops in Prague, but arrives in Vienna two days later (4 June).
16 Nov Constanze is pregnant again: another daughter (Anna Maria) is born and dies.
22 Dec At the concert of the Tonkünstler-Societät, Mozart's Clarinet Quintet is given. Private rehearsal of *Così fan tutte* in his flat (31 Dec); Haydn and Puchberg are invited.

1790
21 Jan First orchestra rehearsals at the Burgtheater for *Così*; Haydn and Puchberg are invited again. The premiere (26 Jan) is a success. Emperor Joseph II dies (20 Feb); his brother Leopold II is his successor and arrives in Vienna from Florence (13 Mar). Mozart hopes for the position of second Kapellmeister, but is confirmed in his former post.
12 June *Così fan tutte* is again performed at the Burgtheater and Mozart conducts. He works in the summer for Van Swieten's concert series and adapts Handel's *Alexander's Feast* and *Ode to St Cecilia*, K.591, K.592.
23 Sept For the coronation of Leopold II, Mozart and his brother-in-law Hofer travel to Frankfurt in their own coach. Constanze moves with little Carl into a flat in the Rauhensteingasse (30 Sept).
15 Oct In Frankfurt Mozart gives a poorly attended concert. He plays in Mainz, sees his first German *Figaro* in Mannheim (24 Oct) and arrives in Munich, where he plays before the King of Naples (4 or 5 Nov).

Other musical events

1789
C. Dittersdorf: *Hieronymus Knicker*, Vienna. P. Wranitzky: *Oberon, König der Elfen*, Vienna. A. Salieri: *La cifra, Il pastor fido*, both Vienna. J. Haydn: Symphony no.92; cantata *Arianna a Naxos* (Hob.XXVIb:2); pieces for musical clock (Hob.XIX:16 etc.); Piano Sonata no.58 (Hob.XVI:48).

1790
L. Boccherini: Quintets op.43. A.M. Grétry: *Pierre le grand*, Paris. N. Dalayrac: *La soirée orageuse*, Paris. J. Haydn: insertion arias for operas by Gassmann and Cimarosa; Piano Sonata no.59 (Hob.XVI:49); String Quartets op.64 (Hob.III:63–68). W. Müller: *Das Sonnenfest der Brahminen*, Vienna.

Other arts and current events

History

1789

W. Blake: *Songs of Innocence*. C. Burney: *A General History of Music* completed and published. J.W. von Goethe: *Torquato Tasso*. Mutineers of HMS Bounty settle on Pitcairn Island. 1789–1851 L. Daguerre, pioneer of photography.

1789

Estates General meets in Versailles. Third Estate constitutes itself the National Assembly. Oath of the Tennis Court. Storming of the Bastille. Washington first US president. Austrian troops take Belgrade.

1790

E. Burke: *Reflections on the Revolution in France*. J.W. von Goethe: *Versuch die Metamorphose der Pflanzen zu erklären*. A. de Chénier: *Avis au Peuple*. I. Kant: *Die Kritik der reinen Urteilskraft*. First lifeboat built. Vancouver explores North American coast of Pacific. 1790–1832 J.F. Champollion, first modern Egyptologist. 1790–1869 A.P. de Lamartine, French historian.

1790

Feudal rights in France abolished. Necker dismissed and finances reorganized. Radical clubs under Robespierre; Marat and Danton gain power. Joseph II dies; his brother Leopold succeeds. Philadelphia US capital.

Mozart's life and works

1791

4 Mar   Mozart participates in his last public
concert at the Jahnscher Saal, playing the Piano
Concerto K.595. Before 28 Apr he petitions the
magistracy of Vienna for the post of unpaid
assistant to L. Hofmann, Kapellmeister at St
Stephen's, with the promise to succeed him at his
death or retirement. The authorities agree (9
May).

4 June   Constanze goes with Carl to Baden,
which Mozart visits, writing there the *Ave, verum
corpus*. In July a messenger arrives to order a
requiem from the composer. Mozart's last child,
Franz Xaver Wolfgang, is born (26 July).

28 Aug   The Mozarts travel to Prague for the
coronation of Leopold II as King of Bohemia.
The Bohemian Estates had approached Mozart in
the summer to compose a festival opera: *La
clemenza di Tito*. He is pressed for time and works
in his coach with his pupil Süssmayr.

2 Sept   The Emperor attends a performance of
Don Giovanni and four days later the premiere of
Tito. Mozart visits the Prague lodge 'Zur
Wahrheit und Einigkeit' ('Truth and Unity'),
where his cantata *Die Maurerfreude* is performed.
Back in Vienna, Mozart finishes the opera *Die
Zauberflöte*, which E. Schikaneder had
commissioned in the spring. The premiere is
conducted by Mozart himself (30 Sept). It is soon
a great success and is given twenty times in Oct;
Mozart invites Salieri and his mistress, the singer
Cavalieri, to the theatre. Constanze is in Baden,
but returns in late Oct. Mozart, overworked
when he starts to compose the Requiem, suffers
from depression and delusions that he has been
poisoned. He is cheered by the success of his
Kleine Freimaurer-Kantate, which is performed at
the lodge 'Zur neugekrönten Hoffnung' (18 Nov).

20 Nov   Mozart takes to his bed and a week
later Dr Closset and Dr Sallaba discuss how to
treat his illness. He feels somewhat better in early
Dec and stages a rehearsal (4 Dec) of the still
unfinished Requiem. Süssmayr is given final
instruction how to finish the work. Friends from
the Freihaustheater sing parts of it, Mozart taking
the alto part. In the evening he is lucid; at five
minutes before one in the morning (5 Dec) he
dies.

Other musical events

1791

G. Paisiello: *La locanda*, London. L. Cherubini:
Lodoïska, Paris. J. Haydn: *L' anima del filosofo*
(*Orfeo ed Euridice*; Hob.XXVIII:13); Symphonies
nos 96, 95, 93, 94; Scottish Songs
(Hob.XXXIa:1–100 and 101–150). 1791–1857
Carl Czerny, Austrian pianist. 1791–1864
Giacomo Meyerbeer, German composer.

Other arts and current events

1791
J. Boswell: *Life of Samuel Johnson*. J.G. Herder:
Ideen zur Philosophie. *The Observer* published in
London. Blanchard flies to Vienna. N. Le Blanc
develops a soda-making process. 1791–1872 F.
Grillparzer, Austrian dramatist. 1791–1813 T.
Körner, German poet. 1791–1861 E. Scribe,
French dramatist.

History

1791
Louis XVI and his family intercepted at
Varennes and brought back to Paris. Guillotine
introduced in France. Washington D.C. founded.
Tax on foreign imports levelled to help US home
industry. 1791–1883 S.F.B. Morse, US inventor.

ELSE RADANT

Section 2

MOZART – WEBER FAMILY TREE

Johann Georg **Mozart** (1679–1736)
= (1) Anna Maria **Bannegger** [Peter]
    (d.1718)
(2) Anna Maria [Sulzer]
    (1696–1766)

┌ (Johann Georg) Leopold (1719–1787)
│   = Maria Anna [Pertl] (1720–1778)
│
├ Johann Christian (1721–1722)
│
├ Johann Christian (1722–before 1755)
│
├ Joseph Ignaz (1725–1796)
│
├ Franz Alois (1727–1791)
│   = Maria Viktoria [Eschenbach]
│   (1727–1808)
│
├ Maria Eleonora (1729–1806)
│
├ Maria Dorothea (1731–1751)
│
├ (Maria) Theresia Franziska (1734–1800)
│
└ Lorenz Anton (1735–1736)

Fridolin **Weber** (1691–1754)
= Maria Eva [Schlar] (1698–1776)

┌ (Maria Johanna) Adelheid (c1729–1807)
│
├ Franz Fridolin (1733–1779)
│   = Maria Caecilia [Stamm]
│   (1727–1793)
│
│
├ Franz Anton (1734–1812)
│   = (1) Maria Anna [Fumetti]
│   (1736–?1783)
│
│   = (2) Genovefa [Brenner] (1764–1798)
│
├ Maria Eva Magdalena (1739–1791)
│
└ Johann Nepomuk Fidel Felizian (b.1740)

A MOZART WEBER FAMILY TREE

Family names are shown in **bold** type,
maiden names in square brackets   [   ]

Compiled by MALCOLM BOYD

Johann Leopold Joachim (1748–1749)

Maria Anna Cordula (b./d.1749)

Maria Anna Nepomucena Walpurgis (b./d.1750)

Maria Anna Walburga Ignatia ('Nannerl')
(1751–1829)
=Johann Baptist Franz **von Berchtold
zu Sonnenburg** (1736–1801)

Leopold Alois Pantaleon (1785–1840)

Johanna (1789–1805)

Johann Karl Amadeus (1752–1753)

Marie Babette (1790–1791)

Maria Crescentia Francisca de Paula (b./d.1754)

(JOHANN CHRYSOSTOM) WOLFGANG
AMADEUS (1756–1791)
=

Maria Anna Barbara Josepha (1757–1758)

Maria Anna Thekla ('Bäsle') (1758–1841)

Raimund Leopold (b./d.1783)

son (d. c 1786)

Carl Thomas (1784–1858)

(Maria) Josepha (1758–1819)
=(1) Franz de Paula **Hofer** (1755–1796)
=(2) Friederich Sebastian **Mayer**
(1773–1835)

Johann Thomas Leopold (b./d.1786)

Theresia Constanzia Adelheid Friedericke
Maria Anna (1787–1788)

Johann Nepomuk (b.1760)

Anna (b./d.1789)

(Maria) Aloisia (Louise Antonia) (c1760–1839)
=Joseph **Lange** (1751–1831)

Franz Xaver Wolfgang (1791–1844)

(MARIA) CONSTANZE (CÆCILIA JOSEPHA
JOHANNA ALOISIA) (1762–1842)
=(1)
=(2) Georg Nikolaus **Nissen**
(1761–1826)

(Maria) Sophie (1763–1846)
=(Petrus) Jakob **Haibel** (1762–1826)

Ferdinand Joseph Fridolin Franz
(1765–1768)

Johann Baptist Anton (1769–1771)

Fridolin (Stephan Johann Nepomuk Andreas
Maria) (1761–1833)

(**Franz**) Edmund (Kaspar Johann Nepomuk)
Joseph Maria) (1766–1828)

Maria Caroline Friederika Auguste
(1818–1819)

Carl Maria von (1786–1826)
=Caroline [Brandt] (1794–1852)

Max Maria Christian Philipp (1822–1881)

son (b./d.1790)

Alexander Heinrich Victor Maria (1825–1844)

Section 3
WHO'S WHO

MOZART ENJOYED A WIDE CIRCLE of friends, acquaintances, relatives, colleagues and pupils – so wide, indeed, that one sometimes wonders how he found time to compose. The following alphabetical list includes only some of the more important names. It should be read in conjunction with the section on Mozart's patrons, pp. 96–9.

MBA = *Mozart: Briefe und Aufzeichnungen* (see Select Bibliography for full details)

Adamberger, Johann Valentin (b. Rohr bei Rottenburg, Lower Bavaria, 22 Feb 1740; d. Vienna, 24 Aug 1804) studied singing with Valesi (q.v.) and began his career in Venice. He was engaged by the German company in Vienna and sang Belmonte in *Die Entführung aus dem Serail* and Herr Vogelsang in *Der Schauspieldirektor*. Mozart also wrote for him the aria *Per pietà, non ricercate*, K.420, 'A te, fra tanti affanni', in K.469, and *Misero! o sogno*, K.431 (425b). A member of the masonic lodge 'Zur gekrönten Hoffnung' ('Crowned Hope'), he sang in Mozart's *Die Maurerfreude*, K.471. In 1780 he married Maria Anna Jaquet (1752–1804) of the Burgtheater in Vienna, who sang the role of Madame Krone in *Der Schauspieldirektor* (1786). Their daughter Antonie (1790–1867) was also a singer.

Adlgasser, Anton Cajetan (b. Inzell, 1 Oct 1729; d. Salzburg, 22 Dec 1777) was organist at Salzburg Cathedral and at court, and composed a good deal of liturgical music (including eight masses and two requiems) as well as oratorios and orchestral and keyboard works. After a visit to Italy in 1764–5 he set Metastasio's *La Nitteti* (his only opera), and in 1767 he collaborated with Mozart and M. Haydn (q.v.) on the oratorio *Die Schuldigkeit des ersten Gebots*. Mozart, who had a high regard for Adlgasser's music, succeeded him as organist at Salzburg Cathedral in 1777. Adlgasser's first marriage, in 1752, was to Maria Josepha, the daughter of his predecessor, J.E. Eberlin, at Salzburg Cathedral. Four years later he married Maria Barbara Schwab, and in 1769 the court singer Maria Anna Fesemayer (1743–82), who sang in *Die Schuldigkeit* and created the role of Ninetta in *La finta semplice*. Both Mozart and his father were witnesses to the third wedding.

Albert, Franz Joseph (1728–89) was landlord of the inn 'Zum schwarzen Adler' in the Kaufingerstrasse,

Munich, where Mozart lodged a number of times and where, in the winter of 1774–5, he engaged in competition with I. von Beecke (q.v.) Albert married Maria Anna Lechner (1724/36–82) in 1759 and had eight children, one of whom, Carl Franz Xaver (1764–1806), took over the inn in 1791.

Albertarelli, Francesco was engaged as a bass in the court theatre at Vienna from 1788 to 1790. He sang the title role in the first Viennese performance of Mozart's *Don Giovanni* and was active in London, 1790–92.

Albrechtsberger, Johann Georg (b. Klosterneuburg, 3 Feb 1736; d. Vienna, 7 Mar 1809) was a choirboy and later organist at Melk Abbey. In 1767 he moved to Vienna, where he became friendly with Mozart and succeeded him as assistant to Hofmann at St Stephen's Cathedral, becoming Kapellmeister there in 1793, a promotion previously promised to Mozart. He wrote voluminously in all the sacred and secular genres except opera, showing a predilection for contrapuntal structures, but he is remembered chiefly as the highly regarded teacher of Beethoven.

Amicis, Anna Lucia de (b. Naples, *c.* 1733; d. Naples, 1816) began her career as a soprano in comic roles, but turned to serious ones in 1763, when she sang in J.C. Bach's *Orione* in London. Mozart admired her performances in Venice and Naples and wrote the part of Giunia in *Lucio Silla* for her. She ended her brilliant public career in the first Italian performance (1778) of Gluck's *Alceste*. She was married in 1765/8 to a Florentine doctor, Francesco Buonsollazzi.

Antretter [Andretter]. Salzburg family. Johann Ernst von Antretter (d. 1792) was provincial chancellor and a councillor in the War Department.

Together with his second wife, Maria Anna Elisabeth (*née* Baumgartner), and his three sons, he was on friendly terms with Mozart, who composed the Divertimento K.205 (167A) for the family.

Attwood, Thomas (b. London, bap. 23 Nov 1765; d. London, 24 Mar 1838) was a chorister in the Chapel Royal. He studied in Naples (1783–5) and then with Mozart in Vienna (1785–7); his extant exercises throw valuable light on Mozart's teaching methods. On his return to England Attwood received a number of court appointments and in 1796 became organist of St Paul's Cathedral and composer to the Chapel Royal. He also established himself as a theatre composer and wrote extensively for the church. He married in 1793 and later enjoyed the friendship of Mendelssohn during the latter's visits to England.

Auernhammer, Josepha Barbara (b. Vienna, 25 Sept 1758; d. Vienna, 30 Jan 1820) was a pupil of Mozart in the 1780s; he dedicated to her the Artaria publication of the six violin sonatas K.376 (374d), 296, 377 (374e), 378 (317d), 379 (373a) and 380 (374f) in 1781, and also composed for her the two-piano Sonata in D, K.448 (375a). Josepha's love for her teacher was not returned, and in 1786 she married Johann Bessenig (1751–1837).

Bach, Johann Christian (b. Leipzig, 5 Sept 1735; d. London, 1 Jan 1782) was the youngest son of J.S. Bach. After his father's death he went to live with his elder brother Carl Philipp Emanuel (1714–88) in Berlin and then spent eight years (1754–62) in Italy, where he converted to Roman Catholicism, became organist at Milan Cathedral and wrote operas for Turin and Naples. In 1762 he went to London, where (apart from occasional visits to the Continent) he remained for the rest of his life, marrying the soprano Cecilia Grassi (probably in 1776) and collaborating with K.F. Abel (1723–87) in a famous series of subscription concerts. Mozart became friendly with Bach during his London visit of 1764–5 and greatly admired his music. The symphonies he composed there were largely modelled on Bach's, but Bach's influence is even more pronounced in Mozart's earliest original piano concertos, written after his return to Salzburg.

Baglioni, Antonio, a native of Rome, was active as a tenor in Venice, 1786–94, and also sang in Prague and elsewhere. He created the roles of Don Ottavio in Mozart's *Don Giovanni* and Tito in *La clemenza di Tito*, and was also in demand as a teacher. He married the daughter, Clementina, of Domenico Poggi, who had taken the part of the servant Simone in the premiere of *La finta semplice*.

Barisani. Family of medical practitioners originating in Padua. Silvester Barisani (1719–1810) was physician to the Archbishop of Salzburg. In 1749 he married Maria Anna Theresia Agliardi (1729–1802), who bore him nine children. One of these, Johann Joseph (1756–1826), was for a time Leopold Mozart's doctor; another, Sigmund (1758–87), became a close friend of W.A. Mozart and attended him professionally in Salzburg and Vienna.

Barrington, Hon. Daines (b. London, 1727; d. London, 14 Mar 1800), younger son of the first Viscount Barrington, was a barrister who gave up practising in 1785 to devote himself to the study of music and other pursuits. In 1765 he befriended the Mozarts in London and also subjected Wolfgang to a number of tests in score-reading, sight-singing and improvisation, reporting on them to the Royal Society in 1770.

Bassi, Luigi (b. Pesaro, 4 Sept 1766; d. Dresden, 13 Sept 1825), baritone, was a pupil of Morandi at Senigallia and Laschi at Florence. He went to Prague in 1784, sang in the first performance there of *Le nozze di Figaro* and created the title role in *Don Giovanni*. In 1806 he left for Vienna, but returned in 1814 and the following year moved to Dresden, where he continued to sing Mozart roles and was also engaged as an opera producer. During his last years he sang in oratorio in Italy.

Beecke, Notger Ignaz Franz von (b. Wimpfen am Neckar, 28 Oct 1733; d. Wallerstein, 2 Jan 1803) followed a military career but also took lessons in composition from Gluck. He became adjutant to Prince Krafft Ernst of Öttingen-Wallerstein and developed a virtuoso keyboard technique which he contested with Mozart's at the house of F.J. Albert (q.v.) in the winter of 1774–5. The two musicians met again in 1777 and 1790, when they played a concerto arrangement together. Beecke composed operas for Paris, Vienna and Mannheim, and a good deal of other vocal and instrumental music.

Beethoven, Ludwig van (b. Bonn, bap. 17 Dec 1770; d. Vienna, 26 Mar 1827), the greatest German composer of his time, knew and studied Mozart's music and was profoundly influenced by it. In April 1787 he played to Mozart in Vienna and may have had lessons from him, but it was not until after Mozart's death that he settled permanently in the Austrian capital. As a pianist he gave public performances of Mozart's Concerto K.466 and he also wrote cadenzas for it.

Benucci, Francesco (b. *c.* 1745; d. Florence, 5 Apr 1824) sang bass comic roles in 1778–9 at the Teatro San Samuele, Venice, where his wife Anna (*née* Carazza) was also engaged. From 1783 he sang at the Burgtheater in Vienna, where he created Figaro in *Le nozze di Figaro* and Guglielmo in *Così fan tutte*, and took the part of Leporello in the first Viennese performance of *Don Giovanni*. Except for a few months at the King's Theatre, London, in 1789, he remained in Vienna until 1795, when he returned to Italy.

Berchtold zu Sonnenburg, Johann Baptist Franz von *see* Mozart, Maria Anna (2)

Bernasconi, Antonia [*née* Wagele] (b. Stuttgart, 1741; d. 1803) was the stepdaughter of the composer Andrea Bernasconi (1706–84), in whose *Temistocle* she made her début as a soprano. In 1770 she was the first Aspasia in Mozart's *Mitridate* and she later sang in Venice, Naples and London, returning to Vienna in 1781, by which time her voice was on the decline.

Braunhofer, Maria Anna (b. 15 Jan 1748; d. 20 June 1819) was the daughter of F.J. Braunhofer, organist at Mondsee. She trained as a singer in Venice (1761–4) and was employed at the Salzburg court. She sang the part of Die göttliche Gerechtigkeit (Divine Justice) in Mozart's *Die Schuldigkeit des ersten Gebots* and was the first Giacinta in *La finta semplice*.

Bullinger, Franz Joseph Johann Nepomuk (b. Unterkochen/Württemberg, 29 Jan 1744; d. Diepoldshofen, nr Leutkirch/Württemberg, 9 Mar 1810) was a lifelong friend of the Mozart family. He trained as a Jesuit priest in Munich and was employed as a tutor in the household of Count Leopold Ferdinand Arco in Salzburg. It was to Bullinger that Mozart first confided the news of his mother's death in 1778.

Bussani. Francesco Bussani (b. Rome, 1743; d. after 1806) made his name as a *buffo* baritone in various Italian theatres before he was invited in 1783 to Vienna, where he stage-managed the premiere of *Der Schauspieldirektor* and sang a number of Mozart roles. He doubled as Bartolo and Antonio in the premiere of *Le nozze di Figaro* and as the Commendatore and Masetto in the first Viennese production of *Don Giovanni*, and was Don Alfonso in the first performance of *Così fan tutte*. He later sang in various Italian cities.

In 1807 he accompanied his wife, Dorothea (*née* Sardi, b. *c*. 1763), whom he had married in 1786, to Lisbon. She also was a singer, specializing in *buffa* roles. She was the first Cherubino in *Le nozze di Figaro* and the first Despina in *Così fan tutte*. After leaving Lisbon in 1809 she sang in London.

Calvesi, Vincenzo sang in Venice, and between 1785 and 1794 was a leading tenor in Vienna; during this time he also appeared at the King's Theatre, London. He sang in the quartet and trio, K.479, 480, that Mozart wrote for Bianchi's *La villanella rapita* (1785) and in 1790 was the first Ferrando in *Così fan tutte*.

Cambini, Giuseppe Maria Gioacchino (b. Leghorn, ?13 Feb 1746; d. ?Paris, 1825) moved from Italy to Paris in 1770 and made a reputation there as a composer of operas and instrumental music. Mozart found his quartets 'quite pretty', but suspected him of being behind Legros's failure to perform one of his symphonies concertantes at the Concert Spirituel in 1778.

Campi. Gaetano Campi was a bass who created the role of Publio in Mozart's *La clemenza di Tito*. His wife was the Polish soprano Antonia Campi (*née* Miclascewicz, 1773–1822), who sang in Warsaw, Prague (where she took major Mozart roles) and Leipzig before going to Vienna – from 1801 at the Theater an der Wien, from 1818 at the Hoftheater – and later Munich. They were married in 1791.

Cannabich. Family of musicians active at Mannheim and Munich. Christian Cannabich (b. Mannheim, bap. 28 Dec 1731; d. Frankfurt am Main, 20 Jan 1798) was a fine violinist and composer. By 1759 he was Konzertmeister and in 1774 director of instrumental music at the Mannheim court, and in 1778 moved with the court to Munich. He and his wife Marie Elisabeth (*née* de la Motte) were warmly hospitable to Mozart and his mother during their stay in Mannheim in 1777–8. Their daughter Rosina Theresia Petronella ('Rosa', b. 1764) became Mozart's pupil at this time; he wrote the Sonata K.309 (284b) for her.

Cavalieri, Catarina [Kavalier, Franziska Helena Appolonia] (b. Vienna, 19 Feb 1760; d. Vienna, 30 June 1801) was the daughter of J.C. Cavalier (1722–87), music director of the Redoutensaal at the Viennese court. She was trained as a soprano by Salieri (q.v.), whose mistress she became. She made her début at the Kärntnerthor theatre in 1775, and from 1778 was engaged at the Burgtheater. Mozart greatly admired her singing. She was the first Constanze in *Die Entführung aus dem Serail*, the first Mlle Silberklang in *Der Schauspieldirektor*, and sang Elvira in the first Viennese performance of *Don Giovanni* (1788) and the Countess in the 1789 revival of *Le nozze di Figaro*. She retired from the Burgtheater with a pension in 1793.

Clementi, Muzio (b. Rome, 23 Jan. 1752; d. Evesham, 10 Mar 1832) completed his musical education as a protégé of Peter Beckford (1740–1811) in Dorset. In 1774 he began to make his name as a pianist and composer in London. During a continental tour he engaged with Mozart in a famous contest of piano-playing, sight-reading and improvisation at the Viennese court of Joseph II on 24 December 1781; the Grand Duke and Duchess of Russia were also present. On his return to England Clementi added music publishing and piano manufacture to his other activities.

Consoli, Tommaso (b. Rome, 1753; d. after 1811) was a castrato singer engaged by the court at Munich from 1773 to 1777. He took the part of Ramiro in the first performance there of Mozart's *La finta giardiniera* (1775) and the same year visited Salzburg and played Arminta in *Il rè pastore*. In 1777 he returned to Italy and appeared in various opera houses, settling finally in Rome, where he joined the choir of the Sistine Chapel.

Da Ponte, Lorenzo (b. Ceneda, 10 Mar 1749; d. New York, 17 Aug 1838) was the librettist of Mozart's three finest comedies, *Le nozze di Figaro*, *Don Giovanni* and *Così fan tutte*. After being banished from Venice as an adulterer in 1779, he turned his poetic gifts to libretto writing and worked in various cities, including Vienna, London and New York; his move from one place to the next was usually marked by scandal or intrigue. Among other composers for whom he worked were Salieri (q.v.) and Martín y Soler (1754–1806).

Dauer, Johann Ernst (b. Hildburghausen, 1746; d. Vienna, 27 Sept 1812) sang tenor in Singspiels in Hamburg. After working in Gotha, Frankfurt am Main and Mannheim, he went to Vienna, where he was engaged in plays and Singspiels at the Burgtheater from 1779 to 1812, and appeared also at the Kärntnerthor theatre. He created the role of Pedrillo in Mozart's *Die Entführung aus dem Serail*. His divorced wife, Karoline, was also an actress at the Burgtheater from 1780 to 1822.

Demmler, Johann Michael (b. Hiltenfingen, nr. Mindelheim, bap. 28 Sept 1748; d. Augsburg, bur. 6 Jun 1785) was active as a pianist and composer in Augsburg, where, from 1774, he was also cathedral organist. Mozart supported his candidature for the organist's post at Salzburg Cathedral in 1778, and in October 1777 joined him and J.A. Stein (q.v.) in a performance of the Concerto for three pianos, K. 242.

Dittersdorf, Carl Ditters von (b. Vienna, 2 Nov 1739; d. Neuhof, Pilgram, Bohemia, 24 Oct 1799) succeeded M. Haydn (q.v.) as Kapellmeister to the Bishop of Grosswardein (1765–9) and served in a similar capacity the Prince–Bishop of Breslau, Count Schaffgotsch, at Johannisberg, near Jauernig (1770–95). He wrote operas and Singspiels for Vienna, Johannisberg and Oels, and was important in the early development of the Viennese symphony. According to Michael Kelly (q.v.), he played second violin in string quartets with Joseph Haydn (q.v.), Vanhal (q.v.) and Mozart.

Doles, Johann Friedrich (b. Steinbach, 23 Apr 1715; d. Leipzig, 8 Feb 1797), a pupil of J.S. Bach and Kantor at St Thomas's School, Leipzig (1756–89), was important as a teacher, choirmaster and composer of church music. He impressed Mozart with a performance of Bach's *Singet dem Herrn*, BWV 225, in Leipzig in 1789, manipulated the stops when Mozart played the organ in the Thomaskirche, and dedicated to him and J.G. Naumann (1741–1801) his cantata *Ich komme vor dein Angesicht* (1790).

Duschek. Franz Xaver Duschek (b. Chotěborky, bap. 8 Dec 1731; d. Prague, 12 Feb 1799) settled in Prague in 1770 and made his name as a pianist, teacher and composer, mainly of orchestral and instrumental music. In 1776 he married his pupil Josepha Hambacher (1754–1824), a singer, and the following year the couple became close friends of the Mozarts. It was at their villa near Prague that Wolfgang completed the score of *Don Giovanni*, and for Josepha he wrote the concert aria *Bella mia fiamma*, K.528, in 1787.

Épinay, Louise-Florence-Petronille Tardieu d'Esclavelles, Marquise d' *see* Grimm, F.M. von

Esterházy family. Through his Vienna lodges, Mozart was on close terms with many members of the Esterházy family (see Landon, 1989 for details), but one of his principal patrons in the 1780s was Johann Baptist, Count Esterházy (1748–1800), m. 1772 Maria Anna Countess Pálffy (1747–99), who supported a private orchestra (led by violinist Paul Wranitzky, a member of Mozart's lodge 'Zur gekrönten Hoffnung' ('Crowned Hope')) in their various Hungarian castles. Count Johann Baptist was the host of many Mozart concerts in Vienna from 1784 to 1790, e.g. the *Messiah* arrangement on 6 March 1789.

Eybler, Joseph Leopold (b. Schwechat, nr Vienna, 8 Feb 1765; d, Vienna, 24 July 1846) was a pupil of Albrechtsberger (q.v.) and a protégé of Haydn. He became a close friend of Mozart, whom he assisted in rehearsing the first production of *Così fan tutte*. Mozart's widow commissioned him to complete her husband's Requiem, but after working on the instrumentation of the Dies Irae he felt unable to finish the task. After directing the choir at the Carmelite Church and the Schottenkloster in Vienna, he succeeded Salieri (q.v.) as Kapellmeister of the Austrian court, but was forced to resign in 1833, when he suffered a stroke while conducting Mozart's Requiem.

Ferrarese del Bene, Adriana [*née* Gabrielli] (b. Ferrara, *c.* 1755; d. Venice(?), after 1798) studied with Sacchini in Venice. In 1783 she married a Roman, Luigi del Bene, and two years later sang in opera and concerts in London. In 1787 she was back in Italy, at La Scala, Milan, and she spent the years 1788–91 in Vienna, where her roles included Susanna in *Le nozze di Figaro* and Fiordiligi in the premiere of *Così fan tutte*; Mozart composed two new arias, K.577 and 579, for her to sing in *Figaro*. Intrigues involving Da Ponte (q.v.) led to her dismissal by Leopold II, and she subsequently appeared in Warsaw, Venice, Trieste and Bologna.

Fesemayer, Maria Anna *see* Adlgasser, Anton Cajetan

Fischer, Johann Ignaz Ludwig (b. Mainz, 18 Aug 1745; d. Berlin, 10 July 1825) studied with Anton Raaff (q.v.) in Mannheim and was engaged as a bass singer at the court there. He later taught at the Seminario Musico in Mannheim, but moved to Munich with the court in 1778, and the following year married the singer Barbara Strasser (1758–1825). In 1780–83 they both met with great success in Vienna: Fischer sang the part of Osmin in the first performance of *Die Entführung aus dem Serail*, and Mozart composed for him the scena *Alcandro lo confesso*, K.512, and probably also *Così dunque tradisci*, K.432 (421a). Between 1783 and 1812 he sang in most of the European centres and, with his wife, was in the service of the Prince of Thurn und Taxis at Regensburg (1785–9). Their son Joseph (1780–1862) and daughters Josepha (b. 1782) and Wilhelmine (b. 1785) were also singers.

Fränzl, Ignaz Franz Joseph (b. Mannheim, bap. 4 June 1736; d. Mannheim, 3 Sept 1811) was a violinist and (from 1774) joint leader in the court orchestra at Mannheim; he married Antonia Sibilla de la Motte, the sister-in-law of Cannabich (q.v.). After the court moved to Munich in 1778, Fränzl remained in Mannheim to found the civic Akademie-Konzert, for which Mozart, who admired Fränzl's playing, planned the incomplete concerto K.Anh.56 (315f).

Freysinger. Munich family with whom Mozart become friendly in 1777. The father, Franziskus Erasmus Freysinger, a privy councillor, had been at school in Augsburg with Leopold Mozart (q.v.) Wolfgang admired the beauty of his two daughters, and seems to have felt special affection for the younger, Josepha, for whom he wrote a keyboard sonata, possibly K.311 (284c).

Gabrielli, Adriana *see* Ferrarese del Bene, Adriana.

Galitzin, Prince Dmitry Michailovich (b. Åbo, now Finland, 15 May 1721, d. Vienna 30 Sept 1793), Russian Ambassador in Vienna and one of Mozart's principal patrons in 1784.

Gerl. Franz Xaver Gerl (1764–1827) was a pupil of Leopold Mozart (q.v.) in Salzburg and studied logic and physics at university (1782–4). He began his career as a bass singer in 1785 and joined Schikaneder's company at Regensburg, and later Vienna, for which he also composed. He sang several Mozart roles in Vienna and was the first Sarastro in *Die*

Zauberflöte; the concert aria *Per questa bella mano*, K.612, was also written for him, and he took part in the read-through of the unfinished Requiem at the composer's deathbed. He left Vienna with his wife in 1793 and sang at Brno (1794–1801) and Mannheim (1802–26). He retired in 1826 and married his late wife's sister, Maria Magdalena (1768–1839), widow of Georg Dengler, the theatre director at Mainz. Gerl's first wife, Barbara (*née* Reisinger, 1770–1806), sang with Georg Wilhelm's troupe before joining Schikaneder's company in 1789. She created the role of Papagena in *Die Zauberflöte*. In 1793 she went with her husband to Brno, where she died shortly after their second child was born.

Gilowsky von Urazowa. Salzburg family of medical practitioners with whom the Mozarts were on friendly terms. Wenzel Andreas Gilowsky (1716–99) was a surgeon at the Salzburg court. In 1749 he married Maria Anna Wagner (d. 1782). Their daugher Maria Anna Katharina (1750–1802) was a close friend of Nannerl Mozart; their son Franz Xaver Wenzel (1757–1816) was a witness at Mozart's marriage in 1782, when he signed himself 'Magister chirugiae et anatomiae'; their other children were Maria Josepha Johanna (1753–1814) and Maria Anna Barbara (1756–82). It was probably to Wenzel Andreas's nephew, Franz Anton Gilowsky (1756–after 1800), who bankrupted himself running a postal service in Vienna, that Mozart lent 300 gulden in 1786.

Girelli, Maria Antonia is first known from 1756 as a dancer at the Teatro San Samuele, Venice, and from 1759 as a singer. She participated in new operas by Gluck in Bologna and Parma, and in 1771 was the first Silvia in Mozart's *Ascanio in Alba*. She appeared in London in 1772–3, but by then her voice was on the decline. She was married to a Spanish oboist called Aquilar (or Aguilar).

Goldhahn, Joseph Odilo was a Viennese ironmerchant who became somewhat mysteriously involved in Mozart's financial affairs during the composer's last years and witnessed the inventory of his effects after his death. He is often referred to in the Mozart correspondence as 'N.N.' (*non nominato*).

Gossec, François-Joseph (b. Vergnies, Hainaut, 17 Jan 1734; d. Paris, 16 Feb 1829) settled in Paris in 1751, where he played in La Pouplinière's orchestra, founded the Concert des Amateurs (1769) and became director of the Concert Spirituel (1773) and the École Royale de Chant (1784). He was later professor of composition at the newly-founded Conservatoire, and one of the leading composers during the period of the French Revolution. Mozart made his acquaintance in 1778, when he described him to his father as 'a very good friend and at the same time a very dull fellow'.

Gottlieb, Anna (b. Vienna, 29 Apr 1774; d. Vienna, 4 Feb 1856) was the daughter of Johann Christoph Gottlieb (1737–98) and his wife Anna Maria (*née* Theiner, 1745–97), both members of the Burgtheater in Vienna. When only twelve she took the part of Barbarina in the premiere of Mozart's *Le nozze di Figaro*, and she was also the first Pamina in *Die Zauberflöte*. After leaving Schikaneder's company in 1791, she worked until 1828 as a singer and actress in the Leopoldstadt theatre, but during her last fifteen years there her singing and acting suffered a sharp decline. In 1842 she was present at the unveiling of the Mozart monument in Salzburg.

Graf, Friedrich Hartmann (b. Rudolstadt, 23 Aug 1727; d. Augsburg, 19 Aug 1795) was a flautist who, after some years in a Netherlands regiment, found employment as soloist and concert director in Hamburg, Augsburg and (in 1783–4) London. He composed mainly orchestral and instrumental music and was honoured with a doctorate from Oxford University and membership of the Royal Swedish Academy of Music. Mozart made his acquaintance in 1777 and admired his industry and his dressing-gown, but not his music.

Grimm, Friedrich Melchior von (b. Regensburg, 25 Dec 1723; d. Gotha, 19 Dec 1807), a diplomat and man of letters, was employed as secretary to Count Friese of Saxony and later to the Duke of Orléans in Paris, where he was Mozart's most influential champion in 1763–4, 1766 and 1778. Accounts of Mozart's youthful genius were contained in Grimm's *Correspondance littéraire*, a manuscript journal which he compiled in collaboration with friends among the Encyclopedists and circulated in Germany and other north European countries. After his mother's death in July 1778, Mozart lodged with Grimm and his mistress, Mme d'Épinay (1726–83), but shortly afterwards he reported to his father that 'M. Grimm may be able to help *children*, but not grown-up people . . . Do not imagine that he is the same as he was'.

Haibel, [Maria] Sophie [*née* Weber] (b. Zell, Oct 1763; d. Salzburg, 26 Oct 1846), Mozart's sister-in-law, was the youngest daughter of Fridolin Weber (q.v.) In 1807 she married the composer and singer Jakob Haibel (1762–1826). After his death she went to live in Salzburg with her sister Constanze (Mozart's widow), whose second husband, G.N. Nissen (q.v.) died the same year.

Haina, François-Joseph *see* Heina, François-Joseph

Hamm, Joseph Konrad von (1728–95) was a secretary in the War Department at Munich with whom Mozart and his mother became acquainted in 1777. Mozart persuaded his father to accept Hamm's daughter, Maria Anna Josepha Aloysia (b. 1765), as a pupil, but Hamm failed to respond to Leopold's offer to provide her with board and lodging as well as tuition for 200 gulden a year.

Hasse, Johann Adolf (b. Bergedorf, nr Hamburg, bap. 25 Mar 1699; d. Venice, 16 Dec 1783) was the most successful opera composer of his time. He wrote operas for Naples, Venice and other Italian cities, and married the singer Faustina Bordoni (1700–81) in 1730. From 1731 to 1763 he served (with frequent leaves of absence) as Kapellmeister to the electoral court at Dresden, and in 1764 moved to Vienna, where Mozart made his acquaintance in 1769. Hasse furnished Mozart with a letter of introduction to Giovanni Maria Ortes (1713–99), a lay priest and wealthy patron of opera in Venice, and the two composers came into contact again in Milan in October 1771, when Mozart's serenata *Ascanio in Alba*, K.111, followed Hasse's *Ruggiero* in the festivities to celebrate the marriage of Archduke Ferdinand and Maria Beatrice d'Este, and, according to Leopold Mozart, 'was an extraordinary success and . . . killed Hasse's opera'. *Ruggiero* was Hasse's last stage work. He spent his last years in retirement in Venice, but continued to compose and teach.

Hässler, Johann Wilhelm (b. Erfurt, 29 Mar 1747; d. Moscow, 29 Mar 1822) travelled widely as a pianist and organist. On 15 April 1789 he competed with Mozart on the organ of the Hofkirche, Dresden, and afterwards on the piano at the residence of the Russian ambassador. The following year he went to London, and in 1792 to Russia, where he spent the rest of his life. His compositions are mostly for keyboard.

Hatzfeld, Count August Clemens Ludwig Maria (b. 1754; d. Düsseldorf, 30 Jan 1787) got to know Mozart early in 1786. He was a good violinist; in March that year Mozart wrote for him the violin solo in the scena *Non più, tutto ascoltai*, K.490, for a performance of *Idomeneo* in the private theatre of Prince Auersperg, in which Hatzfeld's sister-in-law, Maria Anna Hortensia (*née* Countess Zierotin), sang the role of Elettra. When Hatzfeld died the following year Mozart lamented him as 'this noble man, dearest, best of friends and preserver of my life'.

Haydn, Joseph (b. Rohrau, 31 Mar 1732; d. Vienna, 31 May 1809) spent most of his working life in the service of the Esterházy family, first at Eisenstadt and then (from 1766) at the new palace of Eszterháza in the Hungarian marshes. He probably first met Mozart in 1781 (or later?), and the two men became firm friends and admirers of each other's music. Haydn played the violin at quartet meetings with Mozart, Vanhal (q.v.) and Dittersdorf (q.v.), and it was to his 'most dear friend' Haydn that Mozart dedicated his six quartets K.387, 421 (417b), 428 (421b), 458 and 464–5.

Haydn, Michael (b. Rohrau, bap. 14 Sept 1737; d. Salzburg, 10 Aug 1806) was, like his brother Joseph (see above), a chorister at St Stephen's Cathedral in Vienna. In 1757 he was appointed Kapellmeister to the Bishop of Grosswardein (Oradea Mare, Romania), and in 1763 Konzertmeister to the Archbishop of Salzburg, where he was a colleague of Mozart; in 1781 he took over from Mozart the post of cathedral organist as well. After Mozart's move to Vienna the two men remained in touch, and in 1783 Mozart apparently fulfilled a commission on Haydn's behalf by composing the duets for violin and viola, K.423–4, and he also wrote a slow introduction, K.444 (425a), for Haydn's Symphony in G, P.16. In 1768 Haydn married the singer Maria Magdalena Lipp (1745–1827), who the previous year had sung the part of Die göttliche Barmherzigkeit (Divine Mercy) in the first performance of *Die Schuldigkeit des ersten Gebots* (Act I by Mozart, Act II by M. Haydn). In 1769 she created the role of Rosina in *La finta semplice*.

Heina [or Haina], François-Joseph (b. Mieschitz, nr Prague, 20 Nov 1729; d. Paris, Feb 1790) was, by 1764, a horn player in the service of the Prince de Conti in Paris; he later served as trumpeter in the king's light cavalry. After his discharge in 1775, he and his wife Gertrude (*née* Brockmüller) ran a publishing firm in Paris which first issued seven of Mozart's works: K.179 (189a), 180 (173c), 254, 309 (284b), 310 (300d), 311 (284c) and 354 (299a). Heina's friendship was invaluable to Mozart at the time of his mother's last illness and death, and he was present at her burial.

Heufeld, Franz Reinhard von (b. Mainau, bap. 13 Oct 1731; d. Vienna, 23 Mar 1795) was director of the German Theatre in Vienna in 1769 and again in 1773–5, during which time he became acquainted with the Mozart family. In 1776 he married Maria Anna Zach von Hartenstein (d. 1803), by whom he had seven children. In 1778 Leopold Mozart requested his help in securing a post for Wolfgang as Kapellmeister of the German Opera. Heufeld held out little hope of this, suggesting instead that Wolfgang should compose an opera and send it to the emperor – a suggestion which the young Mozart treated with contempt, calling Heufeld 'a Viennese booby'.

Hofdemel. Franz Hofdemel (b. *c.* 1755; d. Vienna, 6 Dec 1791) held a post in the law courts in Vienna. In 1789 he made Mozart a loan of 100 gulden. His wife Maria Magdalena (*née* Pokorný, b. 1766) was a pupil of Mozart's. The day following Mozart's death Hofdemel attacked his wife with a razor and then committed suicide, giving rise to suspicions (now discounted) that Mozart was the father of Maria's son Johann Alexander Franz (b. Brno, 10 May 1792) and that Hofdemel had poisoned Mozart.

Hofer. Franz de Paula Hofer (1755–96) was a violinist at St Stephen's Cathedral, Vienna, from October 1780 and in the court orchestra from 1787. In 1790 he accompanied Mozart on a visit to Frankfurt am Main, Mainz, Mannheim and Munich, and sang tenor in the read-through of Mozart's unfinished Requiem at the composer's deathbed.

In 1788 Hofer married Mozart's sister-in-law, Josepha, eldest daughter of Fridolin Weber (q.v.) She had begun her career as a soprano in the 1780s, and from 1790 sang with Schikaneder's company in Vienna, where she created the Queen of Night in *Die Zauberflöte*. Mozart also wrote for her the aria *Schon lacht der holde Frühling*, K.580. In 1797 she married the singer and actor F.S. Mayer (1773–1835), and in 1805 she retired.

Holzbauer, Ignaz (b. Vienna, 17 Sept 1711; d. Mannheim, 7 Apr 1783) worked in Vienna and Stuttgart before being appointed Kapellmeister at Mannheim in 1753. There he composed symphonies, chamber music and operas, one of which, *Günther von Schwarzburg* (1776), was important in the revival of the German Singspiel. Mozart heard it in 1777 and admired the music; the following year he adapted one of Holzbauer's Miserere settings for performance at the Concert Spirituel in Paris. Holzbauer, for his part, was friendly and helpful towards Mozart. When the Mannheim court moved to Munich in 1778, Holzbauer remained behind, devoting himself to teaching and composing.

Hübner, Beda was librarian at the Benedictine abbey of St Peter's in Salzburg and secretary to the abbot, Beda Seeauer (1716–85), his uncle. He wrote a diary in which he recorded his impressions of the Mozart family and the exploits of Wolfgang and his sister.

Hummel, Johann Nepomuk (b. Pressburg [Bratislava], 14 Nov 1778; d. Weimar, 17 Oct 1837) was a pupil of Mozart in 1786–8, during which time he lived with the Mozart family in Vienna. He later studied with Albrechtsberger (q.v.), Salieri (q.v.) and J. Haydn (q.v.), whom he in effect succeeded as Kapellmeister to Prince Nikolaus Esterházy in 1804, although his official title was that of Konzertmeister. After his contract was terminated in 1811, he held similar posts in Stuttgart and Weimar. He is remembered mainly for his piano music (he was himself a piano virtuoso), but he composed voluminously in practically every musical genre. Towards the end of his life he made a sketch for a Mozart biography. His death was marked in Vienna by a performance of Mozart's Requiem.

Ippold, Franz Armand d' (b. Doxan, nr Leitmeritz, 1729/30; d. Salzburg 25 Feb 1790) was, from 1775, director of the Collegium Virgilianum, a school for court pages and the sons of noblemen situated near the Mozarts' dwelling in Salzburg. In 1781 he was in love with Mozart's sister, Nannerl, but their marriage plans, which Mozart supported, came to nothing.

Jacquin, von. Viennese family with whom Mozart was on friendly terms. Nikolaus Joseph von Jacquin (1727–1817) was a famous botanist and professor at the University of Vienna. He married Katharina Schreibers (c. 1735–91) and had three children. Joseph Franz (1766–1839) was, like his father, a botanist and, from 1797, university teacher; on 24 April 1787 Mozart wrote the double canon, K.228 (515b), in his album. Emilian Gottfried (1767–92) was employed in the Austro-Bohemian chancellery; he was a pupil of Mozart, some of whose songs were published as Jacquin's own with the composer's consent. Franziska (1769–1853) was also a pupil of Mozart, who wrote the piano part of the Trio with clarinet and viola, K.498, for her; in 1792 she married Leopold von Lagusius (d. 1828).

Jautz, Dominik Joseph (1732–1806), born in Prague, was a member of the Burgtheater, Vienna, from 1772 to 1793. He played minor roles, such as that of Horatio in the first Viennese production of Shakespeare's *Hamlet* (1773), and created the part of Pasha Selim in Mozart's *Die Entführung aus dem Serail*. His daughter Therese married (in 1796) Friedrich Baumann, an actor and singer at Leopoldstadt.

Kavalier, Franziska Helena Appolonia *see* Cavalieri, Catarina

Kelly, Michael (b. Dublin, 25 Dec 1762; d. Margate, 9 Oct 1826) appeared in operas in Dublin before taking the advice of his teacher, Rauzzini (q.v.), to study in Italy. Between 1779 and 1783 he made a reputation as a tenor in various Italian cities and was engaged by Count Durazzo for the court opera in Vienna. There he became friendly with Mozart and created the roles of Don Curzio and Basilio in *Le nozze di Figaro*. He left for London in 1787, along with Mozart's other British friends, the Storaces (q.v.) and Attwood (q.v.), and spent the rest of his life there as a singer and stage manager at the King's Theatre. His *Reminiscences* (London, 1826) contain much valuable information on Mozart and on musical life in Vienna.

Kirchgässner, Maria Anna Antonia [Marianne] (b. Bruchsal, 5 June 1769; d. Schaffhausen, 9 Dec 1808) was blind from the age of four. She played the glass armonica on tours in Germany and abroad. Mozart became acquainted with her in Vienna in 1791 and composed two works for her: an Adagio in C, K.356 (617a), and an Adagio and Rondo, K.617, with flute, oboe, viola and cello.

Kymli, Franz Peter Joseph (c. 1748–c. 1813) studied painting in Paris and became court painter at Mannheim, where Mozart got to know him in 1778 through their mutual friend, Anton Raaff (q.v.) Kymli was also known to the Weber family (q.v.), and this contributed to Mozart's interest in the friendship.

Lange, Aloisia [*née* Weber] (b. Zell, c. 1760; d. Salzburg, 8 June 1839) was the second daughter of Fridolin Weber (q.v.) and a talented singer. Mozart met her during a visit to Mannheim in 1777–8, wrote several arias for her and fell in love with her. She, however, rejected him, and in October 1780 married Joseph Lange (q.v.) in Vienna; two years later Mozart married Aloisia's sister, Constanze. Aloisia and her husband remained close friends of the Mozarts in Vienna; the role of Madame Herz in *Der Schauspieldirektor* was composed for her, and she also sang the part of Donna Anna when *Don Giovanni* was first given in Vienna two years later. She parted from her husband in 1795.

Lange, Joseph (b. Würzburg, 1/2 Apr 1751; d. Vienna, 17 Sept 1831) was an actor and a painter. He was engaged at the Burgtheater, Vienna, from 1770 to 1810 and again from 1817 to 1821 (with guest appearances between these two periods). He studied painting with J.M. Schmutzer (1733–1811); his unfinished portrait of Mozart now hangs in the Mozart Museum in Salzburg, and that of Constanze Mozart in the Hunterian Art Gallery, Glasgow University. In 1775 he married the singer Anna Maria Elisabeth Schindler (1757–79), by whom he had three children. His second wife, Aloisia Weber (see previous entry) bore him three sons and three daughters; after their separation he lived with his chambermaid Theresia Vogel (d. 1851), who bore him three more children.

Laschi-Mombelli, Luisa (b. Florence, c. 1766; d. c. 1790) was the daughter of the Signor Laschi for whom Mozart wrote the part of Fracasso in *La finta semplice*. She was engaged as a soprano at the court theatre in Vienna, 1784–90. She was the first Countess in *Le nozze di Figaro* and sang the part of Zerlina in the first Viennese performance of *Don Giovanni*. She spent most of the 1785–6 season in Naples, where she met and later married the tenor Domenico Mombelli (1751–1835). She presumably died by 1791, when Mombelli remarried.

Leutgeb, Joseph (b. ?Salzburg, 8 Oct 1732; d. Vienna, 27 Feb 1811), the horn player, was friendly with Mozart for almost the whole of the composer's life. By 1763 he was a member of the court orchestra at Salzburg and married to Barbara Plazerian (c. 1733–85). In 1777 they moved to Vienna, where Leutgeb ran a cheesemonger's shop and continued his musical career. In 1786 he married Franziska

Hober (*c.* 1734–1828); Mozart often stayed with them during Constanze's absence in Baden in 1791. The music that Mozart wrote for Leutgeb (including the concertos K.412 (386b), 417, 447 and 495 and the Quintet K.407 (386c)) bears testimony to his artistry as a horn player, and the frequent jocular remarks included in the autograph parts point to the friendship that existed between the two men.

Linley, Thomas (b. Bath, 5 May 1756; d. Grimsthorpe, 5 Aug 1778) came from a musical family. His father, also called Thomas, directed concerts and oratorios in Bath before moving in 1776 to London, where he shared direction of the oratorio seasons with John Stanley (and later with Samuel Arnold) and wrote operas for the London theatres. At least eight of his twelve children were musicians. Thomas the younger was a child prodigy like Mozart, whom he met and became friendly with in Italy when they were both fourteen. Linley was then studying the violin with Pietro Nardini (1722–93). He subsequently began a promising career as a violinist and composer in Bath and London, which was cut short when he was drowned in a boating accident while on holiday in Lincolnshire.

Lipp, Maria Magdalena *see* Haydn, Michael

Lugiati, Pietro (1724–88) was a revenue official at Verona. He played host to Mozart and his father when they visited the city in 1770–73, admired the boy's precociousness and had his portrait painted by Saverio dalla Rosa (1745–1821).

Mandini. Stefano Mandini (1750–*c.* 1810) sang baritone in Venice and Parma in 1775–6. Together with his wife Maria (*née* Soleri de Vesian), a soprano, he was engaged in the Italian opera in Vienna in 1783. They both took part in the first performance of Mozart's *Le nozze di Figaro*: he as Count Almaviva, she as Marcellina. Nothing is known of Maria's subsequent career, but Mandini later sang in Paris, Venice and St Petersburg.

Manzuoli, Giovanni (b. Florence, *c.* 1720; d. Florence, 1782) was a castrato who, during a career which lasted until 1771, sang opera in various Italian cities, as well as Madrid, Lisbon, London and Vienna. He met the Mozart family in London in 1764–5, when Wolfgang took singing lessons from him. They were together again in Florence in 1770, and in Milan the following year Manzuoli sang farewell to his public in the title role of *Ascanio in Alba*.

Marchand, Heinrich Wilhelm Philipp (b. Mainz, 4 May 1769; d. after 1812) was the son of Theobald Hilarius Marchand (1741–1800), director of the German National Theatre at Mannheim and (from 1778) Munich. Heinrich and his sister Maria

Margarethe (1768–1800) lived with the Mozart family in Salzburg from 1781 to 1784 as pupils of Leopold. Heinrich was employed as a violinist and pianist at the Salzburg court, where in 1786 he performed Mozart's Piano Concerto in D minor, K.466, from the score, Michael Haydn (q.v.) turning the pages; he was active later at Regensburg and Paris. Margarethe made her name as a singer, and in 1790 married the composer Franz Ignaz Danzi (1763–1826).

Martini, Giovanni Battista (b. Bologna, 24 Apr 1706; d. Bologna, 3 Aug 1784) was a Franciscan monk and *maestro di cappella* at the church of San Francesco, Bologna, from 1725 until his death. He composed voluminously, was a gifted and revered teacher, amassed an extensive library and collection of portraits (including Mozart's), published an unfinished history of music and left an enormous and important correspondence. Mozart studied with him during his visit to Bologna in 1770, and in 1776 sent him a copy of his offertory, *Misericordias Domini*, K.222 (205a), ending the accompanying letter with: 'I never cease to grieve that I am far away from that one person in the world whom I love, revere and esteem most of all . . .'.

Meissner, Joseph Nikolaus (b. *c.* 1724; d. Salzburg, Mar 1795), a bass singer of uncommon ability, was employed at the Salzburg court from 1747. He was with Mozart at Donaueschingen in 1766 and at Rome in 1770. In 1757 Meissner's voice was said to possess 'the high pitch of a good tenor' as well as the low pitch of a bass (see Deutsch, 1961), and he sang tenor in *Die Schuldigkeit des ersten Gebots* (1767) and in *La finta semplice* (1768, in the role of Fracasso). His sister Maria Elisabeth Sabina (1731–1809) was also a singer at the Salzburg court from 1759.

Mesmer, Franz Anton (b. Iznang am Bodensee, 23 May 1734; d. Meersburg, 5 Mar 1815) studied in Dillingen and Ingolstadt, went to Vienna in 1759 and became a Doctor of Medicine in 1766. In 1768 he married a wealthy widow, Maria Anna von Bosch (*née* von Eulenschenk, b. 1724), and in 1775 he began to practise his method of healing by 'animal magnetism' (parodied by Mozart and Da Ponte (q.v.) in *Così fan tutte*). After unsuccessfully treating the blind pianist M.T. von Paradis (q.v.) he left Vienna in 1778 and lived until 1785 in Paris and later in Constance. He was a keen music-lover, sang tenor and played the piano, cello and glass armonica. Mesmer was a close friend of the Mozarts. In the garden of his home in Vienna stood a theatre in which Mozart's first Singspiel, *Bastien und Bastienne* (1768), was first performed.

Meuricofre, Jean Georges (1750–1806) was a merchant whom Mozart and his father got to know during their visit to Lyons in July–August 1766. He befriended them again in Naples in 1770, by which time he had joined his uncle's bank in that city. In 1792 he married the singer Celeste Coltellini (1760–1828), the daughter of Mozart's librettist for *La finta semplice*, Marco Coltellini (*c.* 1719–77).

Mölk, von. Salzburg family friendly with the Mozarts. Franz Felix Anton von Mölk (1714–76) was born in Buxheim, near Memmingen in Swabia, and became court chancellor in Salzburg. He married Anna Wasner von Wasenau (*c.* 1718–99) and had six children. One of his five sons, probably the eldest, Franz (*c.* 1748–1800), was in love with Mozart's sister Nannerl in 1770, while the following year Mozart himself was on affectionate terms with the daughter, Maria Anna Barbara (1752–1823).

Mozart, Carl Thomas (b. Vienna, 21 Sept 1784; d. Milan, 2 Nov 1858) was Mozart's second son (the first, Raimund Leopold, died in infancy). He went to Leghorn in 1797 to serve a commercial apprenticeship, and then to Milan in 1805, where, after a period of study with the composer Bonifazio Asioli (1769–1832), he gave up music and secured a position in the service of the viceroy.

Mozart, Constanze [*née* Weber] (b. Zell, 5 Jan 1762; d. Salzburg, 6 Mar 1842) was the third daughter of Fridolin Weber (q.v.) After being rejected by her sister Aloisia (*see* Lange, Aloisia, above) and despite opposition from his father, Mozart married Constanze in 1782. Of their six children only two survived infancy. After Mozart's death, Constanze organized and sang in several performances of his works, and she disposed responsibly of his estate. In 1809 she married G.N. Nissen (q.v.), whom she assisted in writing Mozart's biography. After Nissen's death in 1826 she was joined in Salzburg by her younger sister, Maria Sophie Haibel (q.v.)

Mozart, Franz Xaver Wolfgang (b. Vienna, 26 July 1791; d. Carlsbad, 29 July 1844) was the last of Mozart's six children. He studied music in Prague and with Hummel, Salieri and others in Vienna, and was, like his father, a prodigious child; he published a piano quintet when he was only eleven. He spent most of the years 1807–38 in various posts in or near Lemberg [L'vov] in the Ukraine, after which he settled in Vienna. His compositions include piano concertos, a good deal of chamber and solo piano music, and several songs.

Mozart, Leopold (b. Augsburg, 14 Nov 1719; d. Salzburg, 28 May 1787), Mozart's father, was destined for a career in the church and enrolled in the Benedictine University in Salzburg, but in 1739 he turned his energies to music and four years later entered the service of the Archbishop of Salzburg as a violinist, rising eventually to be vice-Kapellmeister (1763). In 1747 he married Maria Anna Pertl (see next entry); of their seven children, all but two, Maria Anna (q.v.) and Wolfgang Amadeus, died in infancy. The years 1762–75 were spent largely in travelling with these two prodigiously gifted children throughout Germany, France, England, Holland and Italy, the long absences causing considerable friction with Leopold's employer in Salzburg. His compositions, which include several masses and other church pieces, numerous symphonies and concertos, and a good many chamber works, have been overshadowed by those of his son, but his *Versuch einer gründlichen Violinschule* (1756) remains one of the most important instrumental treatises ever written.

Mozart, Maria Anna (1) [*née* Pertl] (b. St Gilgen, bap. 25 Dec 1720; d. Paris, 3 July 1778), Mozart's mother, was the daughter of Wolfgang Nikolaus Pertl (1667–1724) and Eva Rosina Barbara (*née* Altmann, ?1688–1755). In 1777 she accompanied Mozart on a tour, staying at Munich, Augsburg and Mannheim *en route* for Paris, where they arrived in March 1778. She fell seriously ill there in May and died shortly afterwards.

Mozart, Maria Anna (2) (b. Salzburg, 30/31 July 1751; d. Salzburg, 29 Oct 1829), Mozart's sister (known as 'Nannerl'), was a brilliantly gifted keyboard player, and in her youth she travelled with the family, displaying her artistic prowess in the courts and salons of Europe. In 1784 she married the magistrate Johann Baptist Franz von Berchtold zu Sonnenburg (1736–1801) and lived at St Gilgen, where her son and two daughters were born. After her husband's death in 1801 she returned to Salzburg, where she made her living as a piano teacher.

Mozart, Maria Anna Thekla (b. Augsburg, 25 Sept 1758; d. Bayreuth, 25 Jan 1841), Mozart's cousin (known as 'the Bäsle'), was the daughter of Leopold Mozart's brother Franz Alois (1727–91). Mozart struck up a playful and affectionate friendship with her when he and his mother visited Augsburg in 1777, and he subsequently addressed several letters to her which are notorious for their scatological references and lavatorial vocabulary. In February 1784 she bore an illegitimate daughter, Josepha; the father was later identified as Abbé Theodor Franz von Reibeld (1752–1807), a canon at Augsburg Cathedral. Josepha married in 1802, and the 'Bäsle' accompanied her and her husband, Franz Joseph Streitel (1771–1854), to Kaufbeuren and (in 1814) to Bayreuth.

Mysliveček, Joseph (b. nr Prague, 9 Mar 1737; d. Rome, 4 Feb 1781) studied in Prague and, from 1763, with Pescetti in Venice. He composed operas for several Italian cities, as well as oratorios, symphonies and chamber music. Mozart met him in Bologna in 1770 and was with him in Milan in 1772–3; he admired his music and was influenced by it. In 1777 Mysliveček contracted venereal disease in Munich; Mozart visited him there and found him 'full of fire, spirit and life' but facially disfigured. He returned to Italy, but his last operas there were failures and he died in poverty and neglect.

Nissen, Georg Nikolaus (b. Haderslev, 22 Jan 1761; d. Salzburg, 24 Mar 1826) went to Vienna in 1793 as a diplomat. He became friendly with Mozart's widow, Constanze (q.v.), in 1797 and married her in 1809. They lived in Copenhagen until 1820, when they moved to Salzburg and began collecting material for Nissen's *Biographie W.A. Mozarts*, which he left unfinished. It was completed and seen through the press by Constanze with the help of J.H. Feuerstein, and published in 1828 (with supplement, 1829).

Nouseul, Johann Joseph (b. Vienna, 1742; d. Vienna, 9 Dec 1821) was an actor at the Burgtheater in Vienna, 1779–81 and 1800–04. Between these two periods he appeared in plays and Singspiels put on by Johann Friedel and Emanuel Schikaneder (q.v.) at the Theater an der Wien, and in 1791 he created the role of Monostatos in Mozart's *Die Zauberflöte*. His wife Maria Rosalia (*née* Lefebre, 1750–1804), whom he married in 1779, was also an actress at the Burgtheater, 1779–1804. They separated in 1788.

Paradi(e)s, Maria Theresia von (b. Vienna, 15 May 1759; d. Vienna, 1 Feb 1824) was blind from an early age. Her teachers included Koželuch and Salieri (q.v.) She composed stage works, songs and instrumental music, but made her reputation as a concert pianist. She visited the Mozarts in Salzburg in 1783 at the start of a concert tour which extended as far as Paris; Mozart wrote a concerto (probably K.456) for her to play there.

Pichler, Karoline [*née* Greiner, 1769–1843] was the daughter of Franz Sales von Greiner (1730–98), councillor in the Austro-Bohemian chancellery, and his wife Charlotte (*née* Hieronymus, 1739–1815), at whose home in Vienna Mozart was often a guest. Karoline was a musician and a prolific writer. Although not a formal pupil of Mozart, she received instruction from him, and left valuable reminiscences of him in her *Denkwürdigkeiten aus meinem Leben* (Vienna, 1844; ed. E.K. Blümml, Munich, 1915).

Ployer, Barbara von was the daughter of Gottfried Ignaz von Ployer, court councillor and agent of the Salzburg court in Vienna. She was a pupil of Mozart and took part in concerts with him. Mozart wrote two piano concertos (K. 449, 453) for her.

Poggi, Domenico *see* Baglioni, Antonio

Puchberg, Johann Michael (b. Zwettl, 1741; d. Vienna, 1822) went to Vienna and in *c.* 1768 joined the firm of Michael Salliet, for whom he worked as textiles manager. In 1780 he married Salliet's widow, Elisabeth (*née* Rusterholzer, 1748–84). After her death he ran the firm with his brother Philipp Anton and lived in the home of Count Walsegg-Stuppach (*see* 'Mozart's patrons', p. 96–9). In 1787 he took as his second wife Anna Eckart. He got to know Mozart as a freemason, and between 1787 and 1791 lent him at least 1,415 florins. He made no claim to this after Mozart's death (it is not impossible that Mozart had in fact repaid at least some of it) and indeed continued to advance furthers sums to Mozart's widow, which she later repaid. Puchberg himself died in poverty. Mozart dedicated to him the String Trio, K.563, and possibly the Piano Trio, K.542.

Punto, Giovanni [Stich, Johann Wenzel] (b. nr Čáslav, 28 Sept 1746; d. Prague, 16 Feb 1803) was a protégé of Count Thun, who sent him to Prague, Munich and Dresden to study the horn. He returned to Count Thun in 1763, but absconded three years later; it was then that he adopted his Italian name. Mozart met him in Paris in 1778 and wrote the horn part in the unperformed Sinfonia Concertante, K.Anh.9 (297B) for him. He travelled a great deal throughout Europe and was everywhere acclaimed the finest horn player of his time. In Vienna in 1800 Beethoven composed his Horn Sonata, op.17, for him.

Raab, Maria Anna (b. *c.* 1710; d. Salzburg, 5 Apr 1788), commonly referred to as 'Mitzerl', was a close friend of the Mozart family. In 1767 her cousin F.K.G. Speckner (1707–67) left her the 'Tanzmeisterhaus' ('Dancing-master's house') in the Hannibal-Platz, Salzburg, and in 1773 she let the first floor to Leopold Mozart. After his death she made the house over to her cousin, Dr Ignaz Raab (1743–1811).

Raaff, Anton (b. nr Bonn, bap. 6 May 1714; d. Munich, 28 May 1797) entered the service of the Elector of Cologne in 1736 and then trained as a singer in Munich and Bologna. He returned to the Elector's service, 1741–9, and then made his name as a leading tenor in Vienna, Madrid, Lisbon and the major Italian cities. From 1770 he was in the service of the Elector of Mannheim (and later Munich). Mozart met him in 1777 in Mannheim, where he wrote for him the aria *Se al labbro mio*, K.295, and again in Paris, where their friendship deepened despite Mozart's poor opinion of Raaff's voice, which by then was past its best. Raaff was instrumental in securing the commission for Mozart to compose *Idomeneo* for Munich, and he sang the title role at the premiere.

Ramm, Friedrich (1744–1811) was an oboist in the court orchestra at Mannheim, and a close companion of Mozart there. He was with Mozart and Wendling (q.v.) in Paris in 1778 and was to have played in the cancelled performance of a sinfonia concertante there (*see* Cambini, above). Mozart was with him again in 1780–81 in Munich, where he composed for him the Oboe Quartet in F, K.370 (368b).

Rauzzini, Venanzio (b. nr Rome, bap. 19 Dec 1746; d. Bath, 8 Apr 1810) studied in Rome and made his operatic début there as a castrato in 1765. From 1766 to 1772 he was in the service of the Elector at Mannheim, where he was active as a composer as well. Mozart, who had heard him in Vienna in 1767, composed the part of Cecilio in *Lucio Silla* (Milan, 1772) for him, and the following month the brilliant solo motet, *Exsultate, jubilate*, K.165 (158a). From 1774 to 1777 Rauzzini was active as a singer and composer at the King's Theatre, London. He then moved to Bath, where he added concert management and teaching to his other activities. During his retirement he received many visitors, including Joseph Haydn (q.v.) in August 1794.

Ritter, Georg Wenzel (1748–1808) was a bassoonist in the court orchestra at Mannheim from 1764, and in 1778 transferred with other players to Munich. In 1788 he joined the Kapelle of Friedrich Wilhelm II in Berlin. In 1778 he was in Paris, where he was to have played in a new sinfonia concertante by Mozart, but the performance was cancelled (*see* Cambini, above).

Rodolphe [Rudolph], Jean Joseph (b. Strasbourg, 14 Oct 1730; d. Paris, 12/18 Aug 1812) studied in Paris with Leclair and in Parma with Traetta. In *c.* 1760 he joined the court orchestra at Stuttgart, where he also studied with Jommelli and composed ballets. By 1767 he had settled in Paris, where he was known as a violinist, horn player and composer (especially of operas and ballets). He became friendly with Mozart in Paris in 1778 and offered to secure him a post as organist at Versailles; but Mozart, despite his father's urgings, was not interested.

Rumbeke, Marie Karoline, Countess Thiennes de (1755–1812) was the cousin of Count Johann Philipp Cobenzl, court and state chancellor in Vienna; she was Mozart's first pupil in Vienna, and he wrote a set of piano variations for her (probably K.352 (374c)) in 1781.

Salieri, Antonio (b. Legnagno, 18 Aug 1750; d. Vienna, 7 May 1825) was orphaned when he was fifteen and taken to Venice, where he studied with Pescetti and Pacini, but a year later Gassmann took him to Vienna and supervised his education there. When Gassmann died in 1774, Salieri was made court composer and conductor of the Italian opera, and the following year he married Theresia Helferstorfer (1755–1807); they had eight children. In 1788 he was appointed Kapellmeister at Vienna, but his most successful opera, *Tarare*, was written for Paris in 1787. Most of his numerous church pieces were composed for the Viennese court, and he also wrote a great deal of chamber music. Many famous musicians, including Beethoven, Schubert and Liszt, were among his pupils. Salieri and Mozart were frequently in contest with each other, but, while it seems certain that Salieri was jealous of Mozart's superior gifts, the admission he supposedly made during his final illness – that he poisoned Mozart – is unsubstantiated and now discredited.

Salomon, Johann Peter (b. Bonn, bap. 20 Feb 1745; d. London, 28 Nov 1815) was a violinist at the Bonn court, and then music director to Prince Heinrich of Prussia at Rheinsburg. In 1781 he settled in London, and spent the rest of his life there as a violinist and impresario. He arranged Haydn's visits to London in 1791–2 and 1794–5; his efforts to secure a similar visit from Mozart did not reach fruition.

Saporiti, Teresa (b. 1763; d. Milan, 17 Mar 1869) sang soprano with her elder sister, Antonia, in Pasquale Bondini's company in Leipzig, Dresden and Prague in the 1780s. She was often seen in castrato roles, as the company included too few men. In 1787 she created the role of Donna Anna in Mozart's *Don Giovanni* and shortly afterwards appeared in various Italian cities. It was probably at this time that she married a certain Codecasa. From 1795 she was employed as the leading soprano at St Petersburg.

Schachtner, Johann Andreas (b. Dingolfing, 9 Mar 1731; d. Salzburg, 20 July 1795) studied at Ingolstadt University and then with the trumpeter, Caspar Köstler, at Salzburg. In 1754 he was appointed court and field trumpeter to the Archbishop of Salzburg and married Maria Franziska Rosalia Stain (*c.* 1731–1794). They were survived by only two of their nine children. Schachtner was later appointed 'Spielgraf' in Salzburg. He played the violin and cello, as well as the trumpet, and was also a writer. He translated into German the libretti of *La finta giardiniera* and *Idomeneo* and wrote the text of the Singspiel *Zaide*. He was a close friend of the Mozart family and in 1792 supplied valuable reminiscences of Mozart's childhood at Nannerl Mozart's request.

Schack, Benedikt Emanuel (b. Mirotice, 7 Feb 1758; d. Munich, 10 Dec 1826) was a chorister at the Jesuit school in Prague, and from 1776 studied philosophy and singing in Vienna. In 1780 he was appointed Kapellmeister to Prince Heinrich von Schönaich-Carolath in Gross-Glogau, Silesia. In 1786 he joined Schikaneder's theatre company, for which he composed a number of Singspiels. In Vienna he became very friendly with Mozart, who assisted him with his compositions and wrote for him the tenor role of Tamino in *Die Zauberflöte*; Schack's wife, Elisabeth (*née* Weinhold), sang the part of the Third Lady in the same premiere. Schack himself took part in the read-through of Mozart's unfinished Requiem at the composer's deathbed. He later sang at Graz and Munich, where his daughter Antonie (1784–1851) was also employed. After he retired from singing in 1814 he took to composing sacred music, including two masses (one of them possibly includes material by Mozart), two requiems and a set of Lamentations.

Schi(e)denhofen, Johann Baptist Joseph Joachim Ferdinand von (b. 20 Mar 1747; d. 31 Jan 1823) was educated at the gymnasium in Kremsmünster and at Salzburg University. He became a court councillor, later chancellor, in Salzburg. In 1778 he married Anna Daubrawa von Daubrawaick (1759–1818). He and his sister Maria Anna Aloisia Walburga Thekla (1760–1831) were close friends of the Mozarts; Schiedenhofen's diary for the years 1774–8 contains frequent references to both Leopold and Wolfgang, and documents performances of their music.

Schikaneder, Emanuel (b. Straubing, 1 Sept 1751; d. Vienna, 21 Sept 1812) was educated at the Jesuit school in Regensburg and joined the company of F.S. Moser as an actor in 1773/4. In 1777 he married a member of the company, Maria Magdalena Arth (1751–1821), and in 1778 took over direction of the troupe. After years of travel and association with other companies, he rented the Freihaustheater in Vienna for the production of (mainly) Singspiels and operas, including Mozart's *Die Zauberflöte*, for which he wrote the text and in which he took the part of Papageno. His brother Urban (1746–1818), also a member of the company, sang the role of the First Priest. In 1801 Schikaneder opened the new Theater an der Wien, but sold the licence the following year. From 1806 to 1809 he directed the Brno theatre and in 1812 he would have taken charge of a new theatre in Budapest, but mental illness forced him to return to Vienna, where he died.

Schmith, Anton was a doctor of medicine, an amateur violinist and a friend of Mozart in Vienna. He made an entry in Mozart's album (31 October 1789) and Mozart presented him with the autograph score of *Ein musikalischer Spass* (*A Musical Joke*), K.522. In 1815 he was a committee member

of the Gesellschaft der Musikfreunde and later settled in Kiev.

Spitzeder, Franz Anton (b. Traunstein, 1735; d. 1796) was educated in Salzburg, where in 1759 he found employment as a tenor in the court Kapelle. The following year he married Maria Elisabeth Payrhuber (or Bayerhuber) – in 1764 Archbishop Siegmund Christoph stood godfather to a son of theirs – and in 1770 he took as his second wife Maria Anna Englhart. He sang the part of Der Christgeist (The Christian Spirit) in the premiere of *Die Schuldigkeit des ersten Gebots* and created the role of Don Polidoro in *La finta semplice*.

Stadler, Anton Paul (b. Bruck an der Leitha, 28 June 1753; d. Vienna, 15 June 1812) and his brother Johann Nepomuk Franz (1755–1804) were both excellent performers on the clarinet and bassethorn. In 1781 they were employed in the court orchestra in Vienna. Anton was known particularly for his playing in the low (chalumeau) register of the clarinet and devised a downward extension of his instrument. It was for this modified clarinet that Mozart composed his Quintet K.581 and Concerto K.622; the clarinet and basset-horn solos in *La clemenza di Tito* were also written for Stadler. A.P. Stadler was pensioned from the court orchestra in 1799, but he continued to perform until 1806, and also composed for his instruments.

Stadler, Mathias Franz de Paula (b. Schnaitsee, nr Wasserburg-Obb, *c.* 1744; d. Salzburg, 20 Apr 1827) studied rhetoric and music in Salzburg. By 1766 he was employed as a tenor in the court Kapelle, and in 1787 he succeeded L. Mozart (q.v.) as violin teacher to the choristers there. In 1767 Stadler had sung the part of Oebalus in the premiere of W.A. Mozart's intermezzo *Apollo et Hyacinthus*. His wife (*née* Wilhelmseder) was landlady of the 'Goldener Hirsch'.

Stein, Johann Andreas (b. Hildesheim, 6 May 1728; d. Augsburg, 29 Feb 1792) was a maker of keyboard instruments. After learning the craft from his father he worked for a time with the organ-builder J.A. Silbermann (1712–83) in Strasbourg and then (1749–50) with F.J. Spaeth in Regensburg. In 1750 he settled in Augsburg. Between 1755 and 1757 he built the organ in the Barfüsserkirche there, probably assisted by his brother Johann Georg (1735–67), and was appointed organist. In 1760 he married Maria Regina Burkhart (1742–1800), who bore him fifteen children. He became acquainted with the Mozart family in 1763, when Leopold bought a practice piano from him, but Wolfgang's first personal contact came in 1777, when he praised Stein's pianos in letters to his father (14 and 17 October). Stein also experimented with new instruments, including the 'Melodika' and a 'clavecin organisé' which combined features of the organ and the piano.

Stephanie, Johann Gottlieb (b. Breslau, 19 Feb 1741; d. Vienna, 23 Jan 1800) studied law at Halle, and in 1761 enlisted in the Austrian army. Encouraged by Anton Mesmer (q.v.), he joined the National-Schaubühne theatre company in 1768, and from 1769 was a member of the Burgtheater in Vienna, acting mainly comic parts (including Polonius in Shakespeare's *Hamlet*) and writing or adapting plays and Singspiels. He was friendly with Mozart and prepared the libretti of *Die Entführung aus dem Serail* and *Der Schauspieldirektor* for him. In 1771 he married Anna Maria Myka (1751–1802), an actress at the Burgtheater.

Stich, Johann Wenzel *see* Punto, Giovanni

Stoll, Anton (1747–1805) was a schoolteacher and choirmaster at Baden, near Vienna. He was friendly with Mozart, performed his music in the church and found rooms for Constanze during her visits to Baden. He possessed the autographs of the motet *Ave, verum corpus*, K.618, which was composed for him, and of other sacred works by Mozart: K.193 (186g), 194 (186h), 260 (248a) and 337.

Storace. Family of musicians. Stephen Storace (*c.* 1725–*c.* 1781), a double bass player, was born in Torre Annunziata. He went to Dublin before 1749 and thence to London, where he was engaged at the King's Theatre and directed the music at Marylebone Gardens. In 1761 he married Elizabeth Trusler. Their son Stephen (1762–96) became a composer, mainly of stage works, and their daughter, known professionally as Anna, though more generally as Nancy (1765–1817), a leading soprano. Stephen studied in Italy and Nancy started her singing career there. Between 1783 and 1787 they were in Vienna, where they were on close terms with Mozart; Stephen may have taken lessons from him and Nancy sang his music. She was the first Susanna in *Le nozze di Figaro* (1786), and Mozart wrote the concert aria *Ch'io mi scordi di te*, K.505, for her. They were both married: Stephen in 1788 to Mary Hall, the daughter of an engraver; and Nancy (unhappily) in 1784 to the violinist and composer John Abraham Fisher (1744–1806).

Strinasacchi, Regina (b. nr Mantua, 1764; d. Dresden, 11 June 1839) studied the violin at the Ospedale della Pietà, Venice, and possibly also in Paris. Mozart admired her playing; he shared a concert with her in Vienna in 1784 and wrote for her the Violin Sonata in B♭, K.454. The following year she married the cellist Johann Conrad Schlick and went to live in Gotha. After his death in 1825 she went to Dresden and lived with her son.

Süssmayr, Franz Xaver (b. Schwanenstadt, 1766; d. Vienna, 17 Sept 1803) was educated at Kremsmünster and went to live in Vienna in 1788. Mozart, and later Salieri, taught him composition. He became a successful opera composer, and from 1794 until his death he worked at the National Theatre in Vienna. He may have assisted Mozart with *La clemenza di Tito* by composing the simple recitatives and he completed the Requiem and the Horn Concerto in D major that Mozart left unfinished at his death. According to Sophie Haibel (q.v.), he received instructions about the former from Mozart himself on his deathbed.

Tenducci, Giusto Ferdinando (b. Siena, *c.* 1736; d. Genoa, 25 Jan 1790), the castrato singer, was trained in Naples, probably at the Conservatorio della Pietà dei Turchini. From 1758 to 1786 he lived mainly in London, where the Mozart family made his acquaintance in 1764. Mozart met him again in Paris in 1778 and wrote for him a scena with solo parts for piano, oboe, horn and bassoon (K.Anh.3 (315b), now lost). Tenducci himself was a composer of operas (for Dublin) and songs. Unusually for a castrato, he married (three times according to some accounts) and was even taken to court for adultery.

Teyber. Viennese musical family on friendly terms with the Mozarts. Matthäus Teyber (*c.* 1711–1785), a violinist, was born in Weinzettel and joined the court orchestra in Vienna in 1757. In 1741 he married Therese Ried(e)l. Their first child, Elisabeth (1744–1816), made her name as an operatic soprano, especially in Italy, where she married a certain Marchese Venier. Matthäus's eldest son, Anton (1756–1822), studied with Padre Martini (q.v.) in Bologna and was active elsewhere in Italy and in Madrid and Lisbon before returning to Vienna in 1781; he was court organist at Dresden, 1787–91, and in 1793 succeeded Mozart as court composer in Vienna. He was a quite prolific composer of stage works, sacred music, symphonies, concertos and chamber music. His brother Franz (1758–1810) studied with G.C. Wagenseil (1715–77) and became a member of Schikaneder's company, for which he wrote Singspiels, and later organist at St Stephen's Cathedral and at the Viennese court. Therese (1760–1830), his younger sister, was a soprano at the Vienna court theatre, and also sang at performances of the Tonkünstler-Societät; she took the role of Blonde in the premiere of Mozart's *Die Entführung aus dem Serail*. She married the tenor Ferdinand Arnold about 1786 and accompanied him on concert tours.

Tibaldi, Giuseppe Luigi (b. Bologna, 22 Jan 1729 (MBA: 1719); d. after 1789) was a pupil of Padre Martini (q.v.) in Bologna and began his career as a singer and composer before deciding to specialize as an operatic tenor. He sang the role of the priest

Aceste in the first performance of Mozart's *Ascanio in Alba*.

Trattner, Maria Theresia von [*née* von Nagel] (1758–93) was the daughter of the mathematician Joseph Anton von Nagel. In 1776/7 she married the widowed Johann Thomas von Trattner (1717–98), an important publisher, printer and bookseller in Vienna; of their ten children only one reached maturity. Mozart lived in their fine building, the Trattnerhof, in 1784 and put on subscription concerts there. The Trattners remained on friendly terms with Mozart until his death, and stood godparents to four of his children. Maria Theresia was his pupil; he dedicated the Fantasia and Sonata in C minor, K.475 and 457, to her.

Valesi, Giovanni (b. Unterhattenhofen, 28 Apr 1735; d. Munich, 10 Jan 1816 (MBA:1811)) was a German tenor, born Johann Evangelist Wallishauser. In 1756 he entered the service of Duke Clemens Franz at Munich and was sent to Italy for training. From 1770 to 1798 he was a member of the court Kapelle at Munich and took part in the first performances of Mozart's *La finta giardiniera* and (as the High Priest of Neptune) *Idomeneo*. He afterwards took up teaching, his pupils including J.V. Adamberger (q.v.), C.M. von Weber, and his five children, born from his marriage in 1775 to Leni Mindl.

Vanhal, Johann Baptist [Jan Křtitel] (b. Nové Nechanice, 12 May 1739; d. Vienna, 20 Aug 1813), a Czech composer, went to Vienna *c.* 1761 and studied with Dittersdorf (q.v.). He then worked in Italy and Hungary before settling again in Vienna *c.* 1780. Despite periods of mental illness, he composed voluminously in virtually every musical genre. According to Michael Kelly (*Reminiscences*, 1826), he played the cello in string quartets with Mozart, J. Haydn (q.v.) and Dittersdorf.

Villeneuve, Louise may have been a sister of Adriana Ferrarese del Bene (q.v.). In 1787–8 she sang soprano at the Teatro San Moisè in Venice and in 1789 joined the company at the Burgtheater in Vienna, where Mozart composed the aria *Alma grande*, K.578, for her to sing in Cimarosa's *I due baroni* and two further arias, K.582–3, which she sang in *Il burbero di buon cuore* by Martín y Soler. She was also the first Dorabella in *Così fan tutte*.

Vitásek, Jan Matyáš Nepomuk August (b. nr Mělnik, 22 Feb 1770; d. Prague, 7 Dec 1839) was a pupil of F.X. Duschek (q.v.) and through him got to know Mozart. He was a gifted pianist and was much admired as a soloist in Mozart's concertos. In 1814 he was appointed choirmaster at St Vitus's Cathedral, Prague, where he wrote a good deal of church music, as well as symphonies, concertos and chamber music.

Wallishauser, Johann Evangelist *see* Valesi, Giovanni

Weber. Family of musicians. Franz Fridolin Weber (1733–79) held an official position in Zell until 1763, when he moved to the Mannheim court as a violinist, singer and copyist. In 1756 he had married Maria Caecilia Stamm (1727–93). The first two of their four daughters, Maria Josepha (*see* Hofer) and Maria Aloisia Louise Antonia (*see* Lange, Aloisia) both became singers. The third, Constanze, married Mozart (*see* Mozart, Constanze) and the fourth, Maria Sophie, became the wife of Jakob Haibel (*see* Haibel, Maria Sophie).

Fridolin's brother, Franz Anton Weber (1734–1812), was also a court musician at Mannheim. He was later active at Lübeck and Vienna, where his two sons, Fridolin (1761–1833) and Edmund (1766–1828) studied with Haydn. Their mother, Maria Anna (*née* Fumetti, b. 1736), died about 1783. In 1785 Franz Anton took as his second wife Genoveva Brenner (1764–98); the composer Carl Maria von Weber (1786–1826) was their son.

Weidmann, Joseph (b. Vienna, 1742/3; d. 1810) was employed in the theatre from *c.* 1762, and appeared at Prague, Graz and Linz before going to Vienna, where he was active from 1773 to the early years of the 19th century as an actor, writer and singer of small parts at the Burgtheater and the Kärntnerthor theatre. He played the role of Herz in the premiere of Mozart's *Der Schauspieldirektor*.

Weiser, Ignaz Anton von (b. Salzburg, 1 Mar 1701; d. Salzburg, 26 Dec 1785) was a friend of the Mozart family in Salzburg, where he was a textile merchant and councillor, and mayor in 1772–5. He was the grandfather of Josepha Duschek (q.v.). He wrote the texts of two cantatas by Leopold Mozart (q.v.) and of *Die Schuldigkeit des ersten Gebots*, set by Mozart, M. Haydn (q.v.) and Adlgasser (q.v.).

Wendling. Family of musicians, colleagues and friends of Mozart in Mannheim and Munich. Johann Baptist Wendling (1723–97) was for a time flautist in the court orchestra at Mannheim. Mozart met him there and enjoyed his bohemian companionship; in 1777 he assisted him in orchestrating one of his flute concertos, and the following year Wendling was to have been a soloist in the cancelled performance of Mozart's Sinfonia Concertante, K.Anh.9 (297B) (*see* Cambini, above). In 1752 Wendling married the singer Dorothea Spurni (1736–1811), for whom Mozart wrote the part of Ilia in *Idomeneo* and the concert aria *Basta vincesti*, K.486a (295a). Their daughter, Elisabeth Augusta (1752–94), was also a singer; Mozart composed two French songs with piano, K.307 (284d) and 308 (295b), for her.

Johann Baptist's brother, Franz Anton Wendling (1729–86), played violin in the Mannheim orchestra. In 1764 he, too, married a singer, Elisabeth Augusta (*née* Sarselli, 1746–86). She also was employed at the Mannheim court and in 1778 moved with her husband to Munich. The role of Elettra in *Idomeneo* was written for her, and possibly also the concert aria *Ma che vi fece*, K.368. Their daughter, Dorothea (1767–1839), remained in Mannheim as a singer, but moved to Munich after the death of her husband, Johann Melchior Güthe (1753–1812), a medical officer, whom she had married in about 1789.

Willmann, Maximiliana Valentina Walburga (b. Bonn, 18 May 1769; d. Mainz, 27 June 1835) was a member of a large family of musicians who were of particular importance in the life of Beethoven (q.v.). She was reputedly a piano pupil of Mozart, and in 1787 was the soloist in a Viennese performance of one of his concertos (possibly K.503). Süssmayr (q.v.) was present when she married F.X. Huber (1755–1814), the librettist of Beethoven's *Christus am Ölberge*, in 1797.

Yppold, Franz Armand d' *see* Ippold, Franz Armand d'

MALCOLM BOYD

Section 4
HISTORICAL BACKGROUND

Church and State

MOZART'S BIRTHPLACE, SALZBURG, was the principal city and residence of a prince–archbishop, a part of the Holy Roman Empire which had been established in 800 under Charlemagne, and which from the 16th century was referred to as the 'Holy Roman Empire of German Nations' to differentiate it from the Roman empire of antiquity. It consisted from the middle of the 18th century until its dissolution in 1806 of approximately the German-speaking countries from the North and Baltic Seas to the Alps (excluding Switzerland): today's Belgium and Luxemburg as well as the mixed-language areas of Bohemia and Moravia. Its structure included two kingdoms, dukedoms, principalities, counties and independent imperial cities. The emperor was chosen by vote of the Electors (hence the name) and crowned at Frankfurt am Main. At his election he received the title 'king' and at his coronation the title 'emperor', an historical precedent which was, however, of no political importance for the period under consideration.

From 1508 to 1806, with one exception – Charles VII, formerly Elector of Bavaria, who reigned 1742–5 – only members of the house of Habsburg were elected. From the first half of the 17th century they resided only in Vienna, which was therefore officially the imperial principal residence and city. Although there was a whole series of central departments and central institutions for this Empire, the individual kingdoms, dukedoms, principalities, etc. and their rulers felt themselves to be quite autonomous within the Empire. But even when some of them indulged in local politics to an extent that might be damaging to other parts of the Empire, the emperorship as a traditional institution was never placed in jeopardy. There was always a strong sense of homogeneity.

The principality of Salzburg was ecclesiastical, which meant that the Salzburg archbishop exercised not only ecclesiastical authority but also, as prince of the land (*Landesfürst*), governmental and political. He ruled the principality of Salzburg, and was elected by the cathedral chapter there. His court also included a *Kapelle*, which provided music for both court and cathedral functions. Politically this Salzburg archishop was a reigning prince like many others in the Holy Roman Empire of German Nations. From the standpoint of ecclesiastical law he enjoyed a special position: he held the title 'Primas Germaniae'. That meant that he was recognized by pope and emperor as the highest ranking archbishop of the entire Empire – and this was a title whose importance was not restricted to a protocol.

The Habsburgs – from 1736 properly the house of Habsburg–
Lorraine – supplied the emperors for the *Reich* in the period under
consideration. As princes they reigned as heirs over a number of
countries, some of which belonged to the Empire and some not.
Among those of the first kind were the so-called Austrian
Netherlands (today's Belgium and Luxemburg), various parts of
south Germany, present-day Austria, Bohemia and Moravia and
Krain (now Yugoslavia). The following were not part of the
Empire but were Habsburg fiefs: Hungary, parts of northern and
central Italy, the Banat (now Yugoslavia) and Transylvania (now
Romania), from 1772 Galicia (now Poland), and from 1775
Bukovina (now Russia).

On the whole Mozart lived in peaceful times. The Seven Years'
War (1756–63), which was fought to decide if Silesia were to belong
to Prussia or the Habsburgs, did not affect life in Salzburg,
although Salzburgian troops fought on the Habsburg side. The
War of the Bavarian Succession (1778–9), which was concerned
with the Wittelsbach domains, led to some excited comments in the
Mozart family correspondence, but in fact there was not a real war
at all and the problems were solved at the conference table. When,
because of a treaty with Russia, Austria was drawn into a war with
Turkey, the effects felt in Vienna were not entirely negative: rather
it led to a big display of patriotism which, after the victories of
Field-Marshal Gideon Freiherr von Laudon and *Feldzeugmeister*
Josias Prince of Coburg, resulted in a series of occasional works by
Mozart.

'Austria' was at that time a not entirely correct shortened
description of all the Habsburg lands, which should properly have
been called 'the Austrian hereditary lands'. Originally they were
independent, for example the Archduchy of Austria, the Kingdom
of Hungary, the Kingdom of Bohemia, etc., which were gradually
united under the Habsburgs, centrally managed and, after the
'Pragmatic Sanction' of Emperor Charles VI (1713), considered a
unified state, even if the long series of titles of the Habsburg princes
and many details in the execution of the central government took
into consideration the historical independence of every single land
in this confederation of countries. This unity was also regarded as
such from the outside. The fact that some of these countries
belonged to the Holy Roman Empire of German Nations and some
did not may seem confusing to us, but represented in those days an
independence achieved historically.

In these partly overlapping systems of government, Mozart lived
under the following regents: in Salzburg under the Prince–
Archbishop Siegmund, Count von Schrattenbach (reigned 1753–
71), and Prince–Archbishop Hieronymus, Count von Colloredo
(reigned 1772–1801). As regents of the Habsburg lands ('Austrian
hereditary lands') were: Maria Theresa (reigned 1740–80), first
with her consort Francis Stephen (1740–65), then with her son
Joseph II, who succeeded her (1780–90). As Emperor there
reigned in Mozart's lifetime: Francis I (as Emperor he did not use

his other Christian name, Stephen), the consort of Maria Theresa (reigned 1745–65); he was able to arrange – the only time it ever occurred – for his son to succeed him in a vote of 1764, and Joseph II then reigned from 1765 to 1790. The successor to Joseph II as regent of the Habsburg lands and as Emperor was his brother Leopold II (reigned 1790–92).

The period in which Mozart lived was one of transition for both state and church. The old order of society was changing, with results of considerable significance. In the state and in government, the old division between ruler and ruled was placed in question, the boundaries between nobility and the middle class began to be eroded, as were those between city and country dwellers since the peasantry was now emancipated. In the Habsburg lands, this process took place slowly and continually and saved all parties concerned from the fate of the French Revolution.

In the little archbishopric of Salzburg, both ruler and ruled acknowledged the new order. Nothing was more significant than the opening up of the small, enclosed court town by the construction of the 'New Gate' through the rocks of the Mönchberg, which took place on the orders of the Archbishop during the years 1764–7. The town became more open, and for everyone. In 1772 street lights were introduced by the reigning Archbishop, and they were important not for him but for the citizens. Three years later the Archbishop placed his former *Ballhaus* at his citizens' disposal as a public theatre and opera house. The townspeople could attend theatrical performances at court or at the University, but it was more than a gesture to provide them with their own theatre. When they celebrated in 1782 the 1200th anniversary of the Christianization of Salzburg, the Prince–Archbishop donated the huge sum of 12,000 gulden for the madhouse, the infirmary and the old age home (all under the town's supervision). The money was saved as a result of a deliberately simple celebration of the jubilee.

In the Habsburg lands the new relationship between rulers and ruled – always a very cordial one hitherto – entered the year 1765 with a dramatic turn of events: Empress Maria Theresa and her son Joseph II turned over the private fortune of their consort and father Francis Stephen to the Austrian hereditary lands so as to pay off the state debts (thus avoiding the usual methods of new taxes or other fiscal measures). And not only was money given: hunting estates and gardens were turned over to the public (in 1766 the Prater and in 1775 the Augarten, both in front of the city of Vienna). General schooling was introduced in 1774, torture in conjunction with judiciary procedures abolished in 1776 and the whole judiciary system reorganized in 1781 and 1787. In the year 1781 religious toleration was introduced and serfdom abolished in Bohemia, where it was most firmly entrenched. In 1783 there was introduced along with the ecclesiastical marriage ceremony the so-called civil marriage, according to which marriage was a citizens' contract, thus enabling divorce and the possibility of a divorcé(e) to remarry.

On 10 February 1789 – half a year before the storming of the Bastille and the beginning of the French Revolution – a new tax law was introduced, being based on the principles of equality and against the old feudal system.

The ecclesiastical reforms of these years derived from the sober, rational thinking of the Enlightenment. The number of holidays in Salzburg was curtailed in 1773, for example; the amount of ornament in churches (including the number of candles burning at the altar) and the way in which the service was to be given (including the amount of Latin church music permitted) were limited in 1782; in 1783 the singing of German-language hymns by the congregation was required not for all, but for many church services (this reform was hardly put into practice); and in 1784 processions were reduced to a minimum. In several respects, the Salzburg archbishop set an example for the Austrian hereditary lands in terms of ecclesiastical reforms (only a selection has been included): in the hereditary lands, the number of holidays was reduced in 1771, and from 1773 several German church songbooks were published (though here no attempt was made to enforce their use). In 1782 processions and pilgrimages were reduced to a minimum, and in 1783 a new ritual was promulgated, which also included reductions in the church music. In 1782 the authorities began to shut down the monasteries, especially those not concerned with teaching or hospital work, i.e. those which were not 'useful' to public life in any obvious sense. At the same time new parishes were established so that everyone could reach a church easily. All these reforms were initiated by the state and put into effect by and with the church. But against these dissolutions of the monasteries came serious objections from Rome, which in the end led to a fruitless journey by Pope Pius VI to Vienna in 1782.

In the musical sphere, these ecclesiastical reforms meant less work and fewer positions for the musicians, but also new tasks for the composers, even for Mozart (who composed two German church songs) in a peripheral way; his Salzburg successor Michael Haydn, on the other hand, not only wrote German church songs, but between 1783 and 1790 composed nearly 100 Latin church works for the new liturgy. We also find composers in Vienna who accommodated themselves to the new requirements for church music (such as Johann Georg Albrechtsberger) and others (like Joseph Haydn and Mozart) who paid no attention whatever to the reforms.

It is not only in these ecclesiastical reforms that we find a corresponding echo in music, but also in the governmental and political situation. It was the latter that provided the possibilities for the musical scene to develop. Mozart's desire to be an independent and unfettered artist – he was in fact without a permanent position between 1781 and 1787 – was reflected in the intellectual spirit of the times. The emancipation and the newly won self-confidence of the bourgeoisie ended the former exclusive importance of aristocratic and court music within the general musical scene. Nobility and bourgeoisie attended public concerts together, such as those in which Mozart appeared as performer and composer. Operatic productions were the responsibility of the court theatres, freely open to the general public and paid for by the court as a public service: the public included regent, prince, count and housewife. There were also theatrical impresarios whose houses were privately financed. Mozart worked for both.

Such examples as these show that a wide range of governmental and ecclesiastical developments in this period are reflected not only in Mozart's biography but also in his artistic life.

OTTO BIBA

Currency

THE PRINCIPAL UNIT of currency circulating in the Austrian Empire in Mozart's time was the silver florin (fl) or gulden, divided into 60 kreuzer (itself consisting of 4 pfennig). The ducat was a gold coin worth about $4\frac{1}{2}$ florins. 2 florins were equivalent to a common thaler. Discussion of Mozart's finances is complicated by the fact that 10 Viennese florins were worth 12 Salzburg florins. Internationally, there were 8 to 9 florins to the English pound sterling, $7\frac{1}{2}$ florins to 1 French louis d'or (or pistole), while the Venetian zecchino was worth about 5 florins. For further details, see Bruford (1959) and Dickson (1987).

Economics

THE CHIEF STATES of the Empire in Mozart's maturity were Austria itself, Hungary, Galicia and Siebenbürgen (Transylvania) to the east, Styria, Carinthia, Carniola, Croatia and Slavonia in the south, and Bohemia and Moravia to the north. More remote were the Austrian Netherlands, the County of Falkenstein, and the Duchies of Milan and Tuscany. Salzburg was a separate state governed by the Prince–Archbishop, but its geographical and cultural proximity to Austria restricted its independent activity. The population of Austria was 1.5–1.6 million in the 1780s, with 2.5 million in Bohemia. Both were dwarfed by Hungary with its vast acreage and some 9.5 million inhabitants. The people were predominantly rural, and there were few substantial towns or cities. It has been estimated that during the 1780s, the population of Vienna was 206,000 and Prague 80,000. Apart from these, only Graz could boast more than 20,000 inhabitants.

Any account of economics during this period must recognize that war and the threat of war dominated society, affecting patterns of finance even in peacetime (Dickson, 1987). Maria Theresa and Joseph II maintained large standing armies, and these were augmented at times of conflict. During the War of the Bavarian Succession in 1778–9, the army grew from 163,000 to more than 308,000. Similarly, the Turkish wars of 1788–90 caused the complement of about 214,000 in the 1780s to rise to 315,000. Mobilizations of this magnitude had a major impact on economic and social life, as even skilled craftsmen were pressed into service. Special taxes were also imposed to pay for the army. Thus in September 1778 a tax of 10 per cent was levied on all state salaries and on the incomes of lawyers, merchants and others. A 7 per cent war tax was also introduced at the end of 1788. Military expenses led to the curtailment of Imperial patronage. It is likely, for example, that the costs of the Turkish wars caused Joseph II to withdraw from sponsorship of the Italian Opera in 1788 (not, as Lorenzo da Ponte would have it, a letter of complaint from the soprano Celesta Coltellini).

The revenue of the government derived from direct taxes, in particular the 'Contribution' which was supposed to finance the military system, and a number of indirect taxes such as customs and excise and taxes on salt and tobacco. In addition, the state was obliged to borrow substantial sums from Christian and Jewish finance houses in the Empire and elsewhere. The considerable assets of the Society of Jesus (dissolved in 1773) were also put to good use by the state. As far as personal wealth was concerned, the most striking impression is of massive discrepancies between the rich and poor. At the top of the hierarchy were the landowning aristocracy and religious houses. In Bohemia, for example, families such as the Schwarzenberg, Kinsky, Waldstein, Lobkowitz, Colloredo, Auersperg and Thun had vast incomes (mostly over 100,000 fl), yet appalling poverty and squalor were found among the lower orders, even in Prague. In Hungary, Prince Esterházy's annual income was estimated at 700,000 fl in the 1760s, and he ruled over 45,000 houses and 10 million acres. At the opposite extreme, the annual income of peasants with relatively large holdings averaged 200–300 fl, 45 per cent of which was lost in taxes and lord's dues. Most people in the country earned well below this level. In Vienna itself, it has been estimated that 75 per cent of the population had taxable incomes of less than 50 fl, while 20 per cent of the inhabitants controlled over 80 per cent of the assets (Dickson, 1987).

It is difficult to generalize about how much people earned, since within any occupation there were wide variations with experience and location. At the lowest level, bricklayers, builders and other artisans received 15–30 kreuzer per day. Domestic servants might earn between 10 and 30 fl annually; Mozart and Constanze paid their servant Liserl Schwemmer 12 fl in 1784. Higher in society, minor administrators, tradespeople and middle-class professionals would receive 200–1000 fl, while large merchants and senior government officials would have earned between 1,000 and 10,000 fl.

The incomes of musicians were as variable as those of other categories, and are difficult to compute since many payments were made in kind. Joseph Haydn, for example, received much of his income in the form of provisions, wine, firewood and candles. In the

Esterházy household, the average salary of orchestral musicians was less than 400 fl, with an additional income of about 120 fl in clothing allowances and goods. This is comparable to the 450 fl paid to Dittersdorf's friend Pichel, who played the violin in a Vienna theatre. Salaries in Salzburg were less generous. Mozart received only 450 fl (fewer than 400 Viennese florins) in the comparatively senior post of court organist, while Leopold was paid 350 fl as deputy Kapellmeister. In other centres, leading musicians earned a good deal more. Thus Christian Cannabich, the Kapellmeister in Mannheim at the time of Mozart's visit in 1777, was paid 1,800 fl, the Konzertmeister Franzl took 1,400 fl, while the composer and Kapellmeister Ignaz Holzbauer was paid 3,000 fl. Dittersdorf's salary in Johannisberg rose to 2,700 fl over his years of service to the Prince–Bishop of Breslau.

Equally important as far as Mozart is concerned were the high salaries paid to singers and actors. Even in parsimonious Salzburg, the castrato Ceccarelli was paid 800 fl at the time Mozart was earning 450 fl. When Aloisia Weber was invited to sing in Munich in 1778, she was offered 1,000 fl. The leading actors at the Burgtheater received between 1,400 and 2,500 fl. At the upper extreme the soprano Nancy Storace was so popular in Vienna that the Emperor instructed the directorate of the opera to offer her 4,500 fl in 1787. As for the celebrated buffo Francesco Benucci, Joseph II ruefully noted that three such singers would cost as much as one hundred grenadiers. To these large salaries was added the opportunity of earning substantial fees for private appearances and special performances. On some occasions, performers received as much as 450 fl for a single event.

These incomes can be placed in perspective by considering the cost of living. The author Friedrich Schiller stated that a single man could live decently in Jena on 400 fl in 1790, and on 600 fl in Dresden or Weimar. The poet Wieland apparently lived comfortably with a large family on less than 1,500 fl per annum. However, while these costs are relevant to Salzburg, Vienna was a different matter. The cost of lodgings was high in the inner city; various Burgtheater actors who were friends of Mozart paid 500–700 fl in rent alone. Clothing was also expensive, with a man's suit costing 30–50 fl, and a good lady's dress up to 100 fl (Leopold Mozart was delighted in 1781 when Nannerl had a black dress made up for only 70 fl). Men's silk stockings cost five florins a pair, and shoes and pommade were also costly. The clothes that were sometimes required for special occasions could only be obtained at a premium. Thus when Dittersdorf attended the coronation of Joseph II, his two suits of clothes cost 700 fl. Food, on the other hand, was relatively cheap for the most part, although the cost of grain (and bread) increased markedly in the 1780s, reaching such heights in 1788 that there were riots in Vienna when bakeries and granaries were looted. Schiller recollected that he could dine well in Jena for less than ten kreuzer, and the entire Mozart family stayed in Vienna in 1762 on one ducat a day.

Mozart's style of work demanded that he paid particular attention to his appearance, since he was obliged to present himself as an independent artist without the protection of a livery. Nor could he be taken as a gentleman on the basis of his name or background. His day to day expenses were therefore considerable. It is also clear that in choosing to live in Vienna, Mozart was obliged to accept a more costly existence than was possible elsewhere. One reason why he elected to stay in Vienna may lie in the special mood of intellectual licence that was prevalent during the reign of Emperor Joseph II.

Enlightenment and revolution

MOZART LIVED THROUGH a period of great political turmoil, in which the forms and conventions of the established hierarchy were challenged by the rising tide of 'rationalism' and enlightened reform. Assertion of the rights of the individual against an entrenched social order led to revolution in some countries (notably France and America), while other régimes defused the threat to stability by absorbing the urban middle classes into the ruling structure. The Austrian Empire was in a unique position, since it was here that an attempt was made to impose Enlightenment reforms from above, through the efforts of Emperor Joseph II. Mozart experienced at first hand not only the liberation from intellectual constraints promoted by the Emperor, but also the repression in the face of dissent and rebellion that followed Joseph's retractions at the end of his reign.

The structure of the society in which Mozart grew up was dominated by the distinction between the ruling nobility and the remainder of the population. The nobility were favoured in terms of taxes and rates, legal rights and punishments, promotion in military and religious careers, and numerous other aspects of life. Few ordinary citizens were likely to be successful in any dispute with the nobility. However, membership of this privileged class was not immutable, and one of the first indications of social change in the Empire was the advancement into the ranks of the nobility of officers and civil servants who supported Habsburg policies. In part this transformation was forced on the rulers by the decline of the old nobility during the Thirty Years' War. In Bohemia, for example, only 100 of the 600 knightly families established before 1620 still survived in 1750. Ennoblement was also a valuable source of revenue, and both Joseph II and his mother Maria Theresa raised thirty to forty officials, military officers and industrialists each year. Many of these individuals subscribed to the beliefs of the Enlightenment, since the tenets underlying reform first became established among the urban intelligentsia.

The Enlightenment is an amorphous term covering a multitude of beliefs and practices, some of which were mutually contradictory. In the late 18th century, the main targets for rational reform included established religion, education and censorship, the penal system and the regulations governing land ownership and taxation. The Enlightenment first took root in Austria with the importation of foreign influences, not only from France and England but from the Northern German states where writers such as Gellert, Lessing and Wieland were prominent (see Wangermann, 1973). Joseph von Sonnenfels (born 1733), an economist and professor at the University of Vienna, was highly influential in introducing rationalist ideas, through lectures, societies and his periodical *Der Mann ohne Vorurteil* (*The Man without Prejudice*). Sonnenfels was also a leading figure in Viennese freemasonry, and Mozart owned copies of his writings. Other publications such as the *Volkskalender* were also important in disseminating enlightened views, so that they even penetrated artisan households.

Maria Theresa was crowned Empress in 1740, and her son Joseph II became co-regent in 1765. Mother and son ruled the Empire jointly until her death in 1780. Then came the 'Josephinian' decade, in which the 'enlightened despot' was able to turn many of the theories of 18th-century thinkers into practical reality (see Macartney, 1968). The co-regency was often uneasy, since Joseph's reforming zeal far outstripped the vision of Maria Theresa and the Chancellor Prince Kaunitz. As early as 1765, Joseph admitted that his approach was autocratic:

> Great things have to be accomplished at one stroke. All changes arouse controversy sooner or later. The best way of going about it is to inform the public of one's intention at once, and, after having made one's decision, to listen to no contrary opinion, and resolutely to carry it out.

Nevertheless, one issue on which they did agree was the need for ecclesiastical reform. The opulence and immense wealth of the church, the large number of monks, and frequency of saints' days impeded economic development. Religious practices were rife with superstition and sentimentality, although not incompatible with pleasure, as the diplomat Nathaniel Wraxall noted:

> The superstition of an Austrian woman, however characteristic, habitual and excessive, is by no means inconsistent . . . with gallantry: she sins, prays, confesses and begins anew; but she never omits her Masses, not even for her lover. (Wraxall, 1799, vol. 2)

Maria Theresa dissolved the wealthy Society of Jesus in 1773, curtailed clerical privilege, and reduced the independent power of the Catholic church. After his mother's death, Joseph went further, and with the Toleranzedikt of 1781 ended discrimination against Lutherans, Calvinists and the Greek Orthodox churches. The operatic grandeur of church services was also restrained, and in 1786 Joseph decreed that loud singing in church be replaced by quiet prayer; this may be one reason why Mozart's output of religious works was so modest in his later years. Educational reforms were put into operation at both primary and secondary levels, stimulated by the fact that in the 1780s over 30 per cent of the population of Austria was under eighteen. Legislation to prohibit child labour, institute poor relief, permit civil marriage and abolish the death penalty was also put in train.

Important as these changes were, the most tangible effect of the Enlightenment for people in the middle stratum of society was the freedom of thought and relaxation in censorship that were encouraged by Joseph II. The Emperor believed that openness in speech and publications would favour reform and egalitarianism. Over the early years of the Josephinian decade, the intellectual licence of salon debate in Vienna became renowned throughout Europe. The promotion of freemasonry during this period was one product of this atmosphere. Equally significant was Joseph's informality and dislike of ceremony. Unlike other absolute rulers of the period who isolated themselves in protocol, the Emperor liked to mingle in society and was unaffected in his manner. This unusual behaviour was described by Dr John Moore, a Scottish physician:

> His manner . . . is affable, obliging and perfectly free from the reserved and lofty deportment assumed by some on account of high birth. Whoever has the honour to be in company with him, so far from being checked by such despicable pride, has need to be on his guard not to adopt such a degree of familiarity as would be highly improper to use. (Moore, 1779, vol. 2)

The combination of pleasure, intellectual stimulation and informality that characterized Vienna in the Josephinian decade was remembered with great fondness by contemporaries such as Wraxall:

> I shall always . . . esteem the time which I have passed here among the best employed as well as most pleasing moments of my life.

However, the air of reform was not to last. The later part of Joseph's reign (which coincided with Mozart's final years) saw a series of dramatic political retractions and the introduction of a repressive society in which freethinking was met with deep suspicion. The reasons for this abrupt *volte face* originated both within and outside the Empire. Internally, many of Joseph's reforms elicited a hostile response from the establishment. The land reforms threatened the wealth of the nobility. The Emperor's standing with the people at large was damaged by legislation such as the tax on alcohol that was imposed in 1780 and repealed three years later after popular opposition. The Turkish Wars of 1788–90 caused further hardship in terms of recruitment and taxation. The intelligentsia became disillusioned by the lack of support for the sciences and for the arts apart from music. The liberal censorship policy rebounded against the Emperor when reactionary forces began to use pamphlets to propagate their views. Opposition to reforms led to open revolt in the Austrian Netherlands and in sections of Hungary.

But the event that precipitated retrenchment was the news of revolution from France. The enlightened circles of Vienna were delighted by the developments in Paris. Yet when the Emperor heard about the fall of the Bastille in July 1789, the British chargé-d'affaires reported that:

> It excited a transport of passion, and drew from him the most violent menaces of vengeance in case any insult had been, or should be offered to the person of his sister (Marie Antoinette).

Three months later, Louis XVI and Marie Antoinette were forcibly transported from Versailles to Paris by the mob; the heads of two Swiss guards were carried in triumph in the procession.

The effects in the Empire were dramatic. New laws were repealed wholesale. Within a short period, Joseph II reversed the policies that he had been promulgating for decades. Censorship was taken out of the hands of Mozart's patron Gottfried van Swieten, and the Ministry of Police under Court Pergen established control. Newspapers were suppressed, people were detained without trial, and freemasonry was curtailed. The freedom of thought that was so characteristic of Vienna almost disappeared. Joseph died early in 1790, but there were few changes during the short reign of his brother Leopold. It is interesting to see how closely the ascent and decline of Mozart's popularity in Vienna mirrored the political fate of Enlightenment thought in the Habsburg Empire.

Patronage and the place of the musician in society

THE SECOND HALF of the 18th century witnessed major changes in the status of artists in society. At the time of Mozart's birth, the Baroque order was still in place in many parts of Europe, and the position of the artist was fixed in the lower echelons of the social hierarchy. For members of Leopold Mozart's generation, there were few alternatives, even for talented musicians and composers, to a post as a servant musician in an aristocratic or ecclesiastical court.

Independent careers were rarely successful. Joseph Haydn, for example, eked out a fragile existence in Vienna as a teacher until the age of twenty-seven, when he was appointed Kapellmeister to Count Morzin, moving to the Esterházy household two years later in 1761. Carl Ditters (born 1739) also embarked on an independent career as a young man. He toured Italy under the patronage of Gluck as a virtuoso violinist, but soon found that it was necessary to enter service. He worked for the Bishop of Grosswardein, but this worldly cleric earned the censure of Empress Maria Theresa by permitting performances of operas on fast days, and his orchestra was disbanded. Ditters (later Ditters von Dittersdorf) was subsequently employed by the Prince–Bishop of Breslau, and distinguished himself as much by his skill on the hunting field as on the concert platform. Many of Mozart's contemporaries also worked in the households of the nobility. Johann Schenk (born 1753) was employed by Count Auersperg, Joseph Schuster was Kapellmeister in Dresden, while the Moravian Anton Wranitzky (born 1761) was in the service of Prince Lobkowitz.

Life in an aristocratic household had advantages, notably in terms of security of employment. In some cases, provisions were generous. At Eszterháza, for example, widows and orphans of employees were awarded pensions, medical care was available, and retired servants were given lodgings. On the other hand, there were many drawbacks to this feudal existence. Musicians employed as Kapellmeisters were expected to work very hard, not only composing and performing in chapel, hall and opera house, but coaching singers and instrumentalists, teaching members of the household, adapting or editing music by other composers for the forces available, and maintaining discipline among the players. Secondly, the status of the individual within the household was modest. Throughout his years in the service of Prince Esterházy, Haydn was obliged to wear uniform, and he was not permitted to travel without his employer's approval. In his earlier post with Count Morzin, Haydn's contract had specifically forbidden him to marry. Servant musicians were frequently expected to fulfil other menial duties in addition to performing; as late as 1798, this advertisement was placed in the *Wiener Zeitung*:

> *Musical valet-de-chambre wanted*
> A musician is wanted, who plays the piano well and can sing too, and is able to give lessons in both. This musician must also perform the duties of a *valet-de-chambre* . . .

At a time when the expectations of the urban bourgeoisie were expanding through the teaching of the Enlightenment, the social status of servant must have appeared miserable. A further constraint on the life of servant musicians was that they were expected to spend a substantial segment of each year in the often remote country seats of their employers. Haydn's despondency at Eszterháza is well known. Dittersdorf passed most of his adult life at Johannisberg in Silesia, while Anton Wranitzky resided at the castles of Roudnice and Jezeří in Bohemia for at least six months every year.

By the time Mozart reached his maturity, the possibilities for careers outside the exclusive service of an aristocratic household were becoming greater (see Steptoe, 1988). There were two directions in which Mozart's talents might have led him. The first was to live as a composer without allegiance to one court or city. The only musicians to manage this with any consistency were the composers of Italian opera. The late 18th century saw a convergence of taste in opera throughout Europe, so that instead of being satisfied with local work, houses offered their *scrittura* to a handful of composers who travelled extensively to fulfil their commissions. Although a few of these individuals (notably Gluck and Mysliveček) were of central European origin, the majority were Italian. The most popular during Mozart's time was probably Giovanni Paisiello (born 1740). Paisiello began his career in 1764, and worked throughout Italy composing both *seria* and *buffa* works. In 1776, he was invited by Catherine the Great to St Petersburg, where for the next eight years he produced one or two operas annually. Paisiello passed through Vienna on the way back to Italy in 1784, pausing to compose *Il rè Teodoro* to a libretto by Giambattista Casti. His payment for this work was an astonishing 300 ducats (1,350 fl), testifying to the esteem in which he was held. He spent his declining years in Naples, working not only for the theatres there but also composing operas for other houses.

Such an existence may have held some appeal for a composer with Mozart's predilection for opera, but again it had its disadvantages. Composers during this period were paid no royalty when their music was performed, so did not benefit directly from successful work. Instead they earned a single fee from the commissioning body, after which the music could be played, adapted or edited for presentation elsewhere with impunity. The survival of an operatic composer depended on an ability to secure commissions, and this involved travelling, diplomacy and continuous popularity. Such a peripatetic existence may not have been congenial to Mozart, who both for emotional and ideological reasons remained strongly attached to Vienna.

The other career open to musicians at the time also involved considerable travel: it was to earn a living as a virtuoso performer, giving concerts and lessons, and possibly publishing popular pieces for the instrument. Several virtuosi of Mozart's time carved out successful existences in this fashion, including the blind pianist Maria Theresia Paradies, for whom Mozart wrote a concerto (generally supposed to be K.456), and Johann Samuel Schroeter, who studied in Leipzig but eventually retired when he eloped and married a pupil from the English gentry. This type of career is exemplified by Muzio Clementi (born 1752), an Italian who was brought to England at an early age by Peter Beckford and spent his youth in ruthless training for pianistic dexterity. After some successes in London, he embarked on a long continental tour in 1780, giving concerts and taking on a select group of pupils in cities such as Paris, Munich, Vienna and Strasbourg. His popularity in Paris was marked by the publication of five sets of piano pieces. Later he settled back in England, but repeated his continental forays on other occasions.

It is clear that when Mozart settled in Vienna in the early 1780s, he intended to earn his living primarily as a virtuoso. Indeed, for several years he was successful. Unfortunately, the taste of the nobility and public for his keyboard performances waned in the second half of the decade. There is a strong possibility that had Mozart moved to another major city at this time (as he was probably encouraged to do by his friends), he would have been able to maintain a high standard of living as a pianist. By this time, however, his own musical ambitions had also shifted (see 'Mozart's income and finances' (pp. 127–30)).

It is evident that the opportunities open to talented musicians evolved considerably over Mozart's lifetime. There was a progressive release from patronage as the facilities for independent careers became established. In his adult life, Mozart was prepared to work for the church or the imperial household, though not to enter the service of the nobility. But this decision was not so radical as it was sometimes painted by the early Romantics, who perceived Mozart as a tragic figure, rejecting the constraints of social hierarchy and aristocratic patronage, only to suffer ignominious consequences. Mozart could see that other composers such as J.C. Bach in London and Johann Baptist Vanhal in Vienna were able to survive without entering service, and that celebrated virtuosi and opera composers were often successful both socially and financially. Musicians during this period were beginning to move towards the working arrangements already developed by painters and architects. Jean-Baptiste Greuze in Paris, Robert Adam in London and Franz Anton Maulpertsch in Vienna were not contracted exclusively to one court or household, but accepted commissions from a range of aristocratic, ecclesiastic and secular clients. In this fashion, the social (and sometimes financial) status of musicians rose towards the levels enjoyed in the 19th century.

ANDREW STEPTOE

Section 5

MUSICAL BACKGROUND

The origins of Mozart's style

Opera

Opera in the 18th century was not a homogeneous art-form. Its features varied according to its subject matter and the language in which it was sung. The dominant genres were serious and comic opera in Italian (commonly referred to nowadays as *opera seria* and *opera buffa*). Only in France was a systematic attempt made (for political and chauvinistic reasons) to keep the influence of the Italians at bay and foster a national French opera with its own distinctive features. Elsewhere efforts to combat the overwhelming influence of the Italians were desultory and ineffective. After the mid-century, as we shall see, efforts were made in the German-speaking world to popularize comic opera in that language. Nonetheless a young German of Mozart's generation who had ambitions to become an internationally famous opera composer had few realistic choices. He could conceivably go to Paris to write opera in French (a difficult task for all sorts of reasons, but Gluck managed it in the 1770s). A better alternative, however, was to join the ranks of Italian composers and learn to write as they did.

Italian serious opera (*opera seria*) was unashamedly élitist. Its plots were loosely based on ancient history and its characters (kings, generals, etc.) chosen from that period. However, leading librettists of this genre (notably Pietro Metastasio, 1698–1782) distorted history where necessary in order to give their upper-class heroes/heroines those particular attributes (steadfastness, loyalty, generosity, etc.) thought to depict nobility of character. The librettists' intention was to bolster the position of the contemporary upper class by demonstrating on stage its worthiness to rule. Complementary to *opera seria* was the *festa teatrale*, a genre occasionally promoted by European courts (notably the Viennese) to celebrate a particular event, e.g. a royal wedding. Its usual function was to praise royalty and/or draw a flattering picture of its role in the world by means of a simple allegory; dramatic plot in this case was limited or non-existent.

Italian comic opera (*opera buffa*) served a different function. It started by satirizing certain human foibles (incredulity, miserliness, lechery, etc.) held to be typical of the lower social orders. Many early *opere buffe* therefore contained casts of exclusively middle- and servant-class characters. By the mid-century, however, *opera buffa* was beginning to offer a broader picture of the world by enlarging its repertoire of characters to include the lower ranks of the aristocracy. This mixing of different social groups was perhaps the single most important development within comic opera of the time. It allowed among other things for the appearance of 'middle' or 'mixed' characters (*mezzi caratteri*) whose attributes crossed the normal dividing lines of what was considered suitable for different groups. Quite common in comic opera of Mozart's time, in fact, is the upper-class hero/heroine who knowingly or unknowingly acts below his/her social station. The upper-class male who falls for, or flirts with, ladies of inferior rank is one type of character who belongs to this category. (The Count in Mozart's *Le nozze di Figaro* is an obvious example.)

It might be expected that a genre with many types of character (*opera buffa*) would contain a greater variety of music than a genre with high-class characters only (*opera seria*), and this is indeed the case. As it developed, *opera buffa* borrowed several of the styles previously found in *opera seria*, but there was little borrowing the other way round. The musical quality of *opera seria* was determined by the fact that, because it was patronized by the social élite and financially well supported, it attracted the best singers. This meant that 'serious' music, the sort normally associated with high-class characters in *opera seria*, tended to have vocal lines demanding superior technique, i.e. it included long sustained passages, embellishments and vocalizations. 'Comic' music, the sort normally associated with lower-class characters in *opera buffa*, was sung in many cases by singers with moderate vocal skills. It tended therefore to have shorter phrasing, to be less virtuoso and possess the simpler tunes. Patter song was another characteristic of the 'comic' style. By the mid-century, both serious and comic styles were occurring in *opera buffa* because both upper- and lower-class characters were present. No such coexistence of style occurred in *opera seria*, for the obvious reason that there were no comic characters in it and thus no pretext for comic music.

The structural layout of a mid-century *opera seria* or *festa teatrale* was simple and repetitive. *Secco* recitatives (accompanied by keyboard only) and da capo arias alternated as often as was necessary to give all singers the number of arias appropriate to their position in the cast (in *opera seria* there were generally four or five arias for a leading singer, perhaps one for the least important). Each da capo aria gave the singer extensive possibilities to show his/her technique by varying the repeat. Only occasionally within an opera was the pattern broken by the inclusion of an accompanied recitative, short arietta, ensemble or chorus. Reasons why opera developed this way have to be sought long before Mozart's birth. Suffice it to say that a repetitive (recitative followed by da capo aria) pattern superimposes on opera a kind of geometric design which has analogies with the rectangular and square shapes of the 17th- and early 18th-century formal garden. There is an obvious relationship here to the Cartesian belief that nature (i.e. everything outside the self) is best illustrated and explained by mathematical formulae.

The layout of a mid-century *opera buffa* was very similar – which means that there, too, singers expected varying numbers of arias according to their rank. But it had one peculiarity: an ensemble finale for all or most of the cast at the end of each act. Around 1750 the great Venetian playwright and librettist Carlo Goldoni (1707–93) introduced a new type of lengthy 'action' finale during which characters moved freely on and off stage. The historical importance of this is that composers, setting an action finale to music, had to write without preconceptions about the musical form. The form, in other words, was determined by what happened on stage and by the fluctuating numbers of characters that were present at any one time.

The appearance of the action finale is the first sign of that loosening of the conventions regarding structure that gradually affected all aspects of opera during Mozart's lifetime. The aria forms were affected first of all. Da capo form was abandoned in *opera buffa* during the 1750s and early 1760s; it disappeared from serious opera about fifteen years later. The aria forms that now became fashionable included: binary, rondo, bipartite (slow–fast), also free forms which, like those in action finales, must be described as 'dramatically ongoing'. The relaxation of the old formal conventions ultimately had its effect, too, on the numbers of ensembles, which rose as the numbers of arias (correspondingly) fell. The 1750s, in other words, is the period during which rigid structural uniformity started to give way to structural diversity. This development created the possibility of presenting the dramatic action to the audience in a more naturalistic way. An analogy with 18th-century gardens can be drawn here too. The changes in opera paralleled the changes in late-century landscape design in favour of more irregular, supposedly 'natural' arrangements (as exemplified by the English country park).

This discussion has so far concentrated on Italian opera because so many of Mozart's stage works are Italian. But it is also necessary to consider the characteristics of French and German opera of the mid-18th century, both to explain some unusual features of one particular Italian opera by Mozart (*Idomeneo*) and secondly to provide the background to his operas in German. Francesco Algarotti's 'Essay on opera' (*Saggio sopra l'opera in musica*) published in 1756 offers us a useful starting point. Dissatisfied with the way in which *opera seria* had evolved as a showcase for singers, Algarotti declared in his book that musical interests should no longer be paramount and that librettists should have greater control over the artistic result. He suggested, too, that much of a practical nature could be learnt from contemporary French grand opera (*tragédie lyrique*). French grand opera was different from *opera seria* in a number of ways. Its plots were based on classical myth rather than on ancient history; it placed greater emphasis than Italian opera did on the element of magic and the *merveilleux*; it included ballets and choruses within the mainstream of the action. Partly because it had these dances and choruses, and partly because its solo songs were not overwhelmingly cast in one structural mould, French opera contained a greater variety of music than *opera seria* did.

Unfortunately it was so badly sung by French singers that most foreigners found it unbearable to listen to.

Algarotti's ideas about operatic reform along French lines had few immediate results. The notion that, in effect, Italian-style music (minus its extreme showcase element) and Italian words should be superimposed upon a French dramatic plan met with favour only among that minority of patrons who had particular reason to be francophile. A few hybrid operas of this type were produced at the instigation of the Minister of State, G.-L. du Tillot (a Frenchman), at the court of Parma in 1758–9. Gluck's well-known 'reform' operas *Orfeo ed Euridice* and *Alceste*, produced in Vienna in the 1760s when the Austrian court was pursuing a policy of friendship with France, also come into this category. Examples of this reform genre were also staged elsewhere in Germany, including the Bavarian court of Munich. It was for this court that Mozart composed his *Idomeneo*, replete with a plot based on an old *tragédie lyrique* and with ballets and choruses, in 1781.

The cross-fertilization of ideas was felt as much in France as in Italy and in the German states. One of the most important events affecting opera in the mid-century was the arrival of an Italian company in Paris in 1752 to perform a selection of Italian comic operas and intermezzi. The impact of these intermezzi upon the French public was considerable. Although the comparison Frenchmen drew between on the one hand Italian comic opera and on the other French grand opera was not exactly between like and like, their dispute about which nation had the superior opera grew into a short-lived yet bitter public row sometimes called the Guerre des Bouffons.

The Guerre had little effect upon either genre in the long term. But it did have an influence on another genre which until then had rarely had major artistic pretensions, namely French comic opera (*opéra comique*). Prior to the mid-century, *opéra comique* had been in practice a farcical or rustic play with musical insertions (many of these consisting of popular tunes to new words). The excitement created by the Italians gave the French the incentive to change *opéra comique* from musical play to true opera by introducing into it the modern, 'naturalistic' features of *opera buffa*: the realistic characters drawn from different walks of society, the sophisticated musical gestures associated with them, the large number of musical items in an increasing variety of forms. *Opéra comique* remained distinctive, however, not just because its texts were in French. It continued to use spoken dialogue. Many of its melodies retained the simple tunefulness characteristic of the popular songs that once upon a time had been its chief musical feature. Furthermore, it was not affected, as all Italian opera was, by that peculiar Italian preoccupation with distributing musical arias and ensembles in the right order and number to please the singers. It was not more theatrically effective than *opera buffa*, but its plots, unaffected by any predetermined position and order of the musical items, were often more obviously coherent.

Mozart never composed an opera in French. But French developments affected his work. The emergence of comic opera in German, of which Mozart completed four examples (one short work early in his career and three – one small and two full-length – after he reached maturity), owed much to the wide dissemination not only of *opera buffa* but also of Italianized *opéra comique* throughout the German-speaking world in the 1750s and 1760s. The evolution of German musical comedy into comic opera followed the same artistic course as the French, but it occurred more slowly and at a slightly later date. It has been suggested that the Leipzig production in 1752 of Johann Standfuss's *Der Teufel ist los* is the starting point of German comic opera (Bauman, 1985). But it was not till after the Seven Years' War, i.e. the mid-1760s, that regular productions of this genre began in Saxony and then elsewhere in Germany.

It was fortunate that Mozart grew to manhood at a time of change. It was not an age in which the hegemony of the Italians was being seriously challenged (the fact that the majority of operas Mozart wrote were in Italian is itself proof of this). But there was a new concept in the air that the best features of operas of different nations could be assimilated within a single work. One way of doing this was to join 'serious' Italian music with a French dramatic plan (as Algarotti suggested). Another way was to transfer the musical techniques of Italian comic opera, in which the number of styles and structures was increasing for the sake of a more naturalistic manner of dramatic presentation, to comic opera in French and German. There were of course practical constraints upon composers of Mozart's generation being able to develop these possibilities to their ultimate extent. But in so far as he was given the opportunity, he took it and gave to the world not only the greatest Italian operas of the late 18th century, but also, some would say, the first true operatic masterpieces in the German language.

MICHAEL F. ROBINSON

Instrumental

As well as the birth of Mozart, the 1750s saw the deaths of Johann Sebastian Bach and George Frideric Handel, two figures that had dominated the music of the earlier period. In Salzburg and southern Europe generally, their music was virtually unknown and, although a few of their works did circulate in manuscript in Austria (e.g. Bach's '48' preludes and fugues and Handel's *Acis and Galatea*), Mozart did not make sustained acquaintance with the music of these composers until the 1780s. Indeed, to composers working in Salzburg in the 1750s the music of Bach and Handel would have appeared entirely alien in spirit and technique: Protestant rather than Catholic, overwhelmingly vocal rather than instrumental and prone to complexity rather than simplicity; for

Austria, together with Italy and southern Germany, had been for some decades nurturing a style that was quite different. Though the changes that were affecting contemporary opera were sweeping and exciting enough, even more radical changes were taking place in instrumental music. The new Classical style produced several major new genres, principally the keyboard sonata, quartet and the symphony, all of which were to figure prominently in Mozart's output. The composers of these pioneering sonatas, quartets and symphonies are, with the notable exception of Joseph Haydn, all composers of the second, even third rank, but it is to these people and not to Bach and Handel that we have to turn to gain any understanding of the formative background to Mozart's instrumental music.

Although the sonata for one player seated at a keyboard was a new genre, it shared one crucial feature with older keyboard music and Baroque chamber music in general: it was a form of music making almost entirely associated with amateurs – music played by individuals, typically ladies, for private amusement, rather than by professionals for the entertainment of others. Naturally, these keyboard amateurs varied greatly in accomplishment, from the ham-fisted beginner to the polished artist, and the enormous quantities of keyboard sonatas composed and published in the 18th century reflect this diversity. Some composers were employed as keyboard teachers to aristocrats or royalty, such as Georg Wagenseil (1715–77) in the court of Maria Theresa, and Domenico Scarlatti (1685–1757) in the court of Maria Barbara in Spain; publications were often described as being 'pour le beau sexe'; and, occasionally, the word 'sonata' was replaced by something that signalled a didactic purpose, for instance 'Lessons' in England and 'Essercizi' for some of Domenico Scarlatti's sonatas. For a fledgling composer anxious to gain recognition, publishing a set of sonatas as his op. 1 was a routine course. In Mozart's case his first published music was to be a set of keyboard sonatas with the optional accompaniment of a violin (K.6 and 7, Paris 1764); the well-known Sonata in C major (K.545), called 'A little keyboard sonata for beginners' by the composer, is only a late example of the practice of writing very simply when necessary.

The predominant texture of the well-known first movement of Mozart's C major Sonata – melodic line over a broken-chord accompaniment – was already commonplace by 1760; it is often termed 'Alberti bass' after Domenico Alberti (c. 1710–40), a Venetian composer of some three dozen sonatas which feature the texture. Its use by Alberti and others may appear relentless to modern ears, but it enabled the slow harmonic rhythms of the new style, and its tuneful, sometimes melancholy melodies, to acquire much needed momentum and atmosphere; for the amateur player, of course, it had the advantage also of being easy to play.

Not all keyboard sonatas of the mid-century are of this insipid kind. Leopold Mozart (1719–87) in his three sonatas published in Nuremberg (1762/3) and Wagenseil in his op. 1 published in

Vienna (1753) strove after a keyboard style that was less reliant on routine texture. But two other names dominated the period as composers of keyboard sonatas: Domenico Scarlatti and C.P.E. Bach (1714–88). The former spent most of his working life in Portugal and Spain and, though his individuality in over 500 sonatas was recognized at the time, his influence is much less than this individuality would seem to deserve. Certainly Mozart's music seems unaffected by Domenico Scarlatti. On the other hand, C.P.E. Bach's music is much more of an influence, not that Mozart's music very often sounds like C.P.E. Bach – it is more generally akin to that of J.C. Bach – but in the sense that C.P.E. Bach was the first composer to demonstrate that the principal quality of the new style, its simplicity, could be combined with sentiment and rhetoric. It is in this sense that Mozart's alleged tribute (first reported in 1832) should be understood: 'He is the father, we are the children. Those of us who know anything at all learned it from him . . .'. By 1760, C.P.E. Bach had served as first harpsichordist in the court of Frederick the Great for nearly twenty years and had published four sets of keyboard sonatas, works noted for their seriousness, range of emotion, inventive keyboard texture and questing structures. This laid the foundation of a popularity and esteem that were maintained until his death in 1788.

Not surprisingly, given C.P.E. Bach's temperament, his favoured keyboard instrument was the clavichord, where the touch of the player directly controlled the volume of sound. The piano shared this ability with the clavichord but, even though it had been invented at the turn of the century and was ideally suited to the nuanced expression of the Classical style, it was not to replace the harpsichord as the most common keyboard instrument until well into the second half of the 18th century.

The Classical symphony had its origins in the overture to a dramatic work, such as an opera, oratorio or, especially common in Salzburg in the first half of the 18th century, the school play. In anything from one to three movements, the 'sinfonia', once liberated from its original function as an introduction, was free to gather outside influences and to develop its own identity. Nevertheless, there remained a close link between the independent symphony and the opera house in particular, and Mozart, like many other composers, often converted overtures into symphonies.

Statistically, by 1760 most symphonies had three movements in the order fast, slow and minuet or fast, but there were plenty of examples, especially emanating from Austria, of the four-movement pattern (fast, slow, minuet and fast) which later in the century became the dominant one. Also, slow introductions indicating the ambition and scope of the work were beginning to feature, for instance in the symphonies of Leopold Mozart and the Viennese composer Leopold Hofmann (1738–93). As regards scoring, symphonies of the middle years of the century could be scored for an orchestra as small as three-part strings (first and second violins and bass instruments), as in the symphonies of the

Italian Sammartini (1700/01–75) and the Austrian Georg Matthias Monn (1717–50). At the other extreme, a group of composers led by Johann Stamitz (1717–57) and based at the Mannheim court had developed a highly characterful love of orchestral sonority involving the full range of instruments, including clarinets. Several times in his career Mozart was to experience at first hand the special qualities of the Mannheim orchestra, 'this army of generals' as Dr Burney called it, and the richness, depth and colour of Mozart's orchestration owes much to Mannheim.

Within Austria, however, the trend was to write symphonies for a smaller orchestra, typically two oboes, two horns, two bassoons and strings, with other instruments (excepting clarinets, which were very rare before c. 1780) regarded as extras. There had already emerged in the symphonies of the Haydn brothers, Leopold Mozart, Carlo d' Ordonez (1734–86) and Johann Baptist Vanhal (1739–1813) a predilection for movements featuring one or more solo instruments; it is a trait found occasionally in the younger Mozart's symphonies but more consistently in his orchestral serenades. Symphonies with trumpets and timpani were normally restricted to two keys, D major and C major. While the former were to be found throughout Europe, the latter were more distinctively Austrian, the essential background against which Mozart's *Linz* and *Jupiter* symphonies were to be composed. Most Austrian church masses of the time were also in C major and this association of C major, trumpets, church music and symphonies was a potent one, more easily made then than today, since symphonies were as likely to be played in religious services in churches and monasteries as in the halls of the aristocracy.

Stimulating sonorities and attractive invention had ensured that the symphony by the time of Mozart's birth had supplanted the concerto as the leading instrumental genre. It had, too, formulated a schema that was to be the basis of its development for the next two hundred years: the first movement was the most lengthy and ambitious and lent itself to contrasts of mood; the slow movement and minuet were less dynamic, the former lyrical and relaxed, the latter energetic but formal; and the last movement was brisk and lighthearted. One major resource remained to be discovered after 1760, the sonority of the minor key; minor-key symphonies are conspicuously rare before Mozart's birth, perhaps because the sound of the minor was regarded as being incompatible with the easy attractiveness of the Classical style.

Of the major new genres associated with the Classical style, the string quartet was the last to establish itself; to all intents and purposes it was invented by Joseph Haydn (1732–1809) in his ten early quartets, dating from c. 1757 to c. 1759. In many parts of Europe, notably England, France and north Germany, the chamber music of the earlier epoch, based firmly on the presence of a continuo, had prevented the growth of a four-part ensemble without keyboard continuo. In Austria, however, the continuo tradition was not as strong as elsewhere and, as early as the second decade of the 18th century, composers such as Franz Asplmayr (1728–86), Monn and Giuseppe Porsile (1680–1750) were composing chamber music without keyboard. Such works soon acquired the title of divertimento which, as James Webster (1974) has demonstrated, had specific connotations in 18th-century Austria. It always meant chamber music, never orchestral music and did not carry implications of music in a lighter vein, as in the 19th and 20th centuries. Thus, works that were later described as sonatas, trios, quartets, quintets, octets etc. were usually called divertimentos. One of the most common divertimento media was that of a trio for two violins and bass instrument (Leopold Mozart and the young Joseph Haydn both composed many such works) and it was inevitable that one day a viola would be added to make a divertimento for string quartet. Although Haydn's earliest quartets had been preceded by a few examples by Franz Xaver Richter (1709–89) and Ignaz Holzbauer (1711–83), the true history of the quartet does not begin until Haydn's first examples.

In addition to the divertimento tradition, quartet playing would have arisen naturally from the frequent practice of playing symphonies of the period with one player per part rather than with several players per part, either out of choice, or simply because local resources, for instance in the poorer churches, did not permit doubling. Thus a symphony for strings in three parts by the Salzburg composer Johann Ernst Eberlin (1702–62) would have sounded like a trio, one in four parts like a quartet. In the orchestral music of Mozart's predecessors in Salzburg, divided violas are often encountered, making a five-part texture; played with one player per part this music would have yielded the quintet combination of two violins, two violas and cello that Michael Haydn (1737–1806) and Mozart were to use in their specially composed quintets.

One of the few major instrumental genres to survive the transformation of musical style in the middle decades of the century was the concerto, not the concerto grosso, which was quickly forgotten – though its spirit was to be rekindled in the sinfonia concertante – but the solo concerto. In most European centres composers wrote large quantities of concertos featuring violin, cello, flute, oboe, horn, trumpet and, increasingly common, keyboard. As the new Classical style developed its distinctive qualities, for the composer of concertos it became a question of pouring new wine into old bottles, the structures of the Baroque being maintained and little attempt made to incorporate the dramatic eloquence of the new Classical style. Consequently, the concertos of Leopold Mozart, Stamitz, C.P.E. Bach and even the young Joseph Haydn sound not only inconsequential in comparison with the mature works of Mozart, but inert in comparison with other instrumental works by the same composers; it seems that only the timeless love of solo display kept the genre alive at all in the middle of the century. Its survival, however, did ensure the development of chamber music with piano, since concertos too were often performed with one player per part, effectively forming piano quartets or quintets; in 1783 Mozart was to indicate that his latest concertos (K.413–15) could be played in this manner.

For any composer born in the 1750s, the new era of musical style provided major opportunities: there was no longer any doubt that the new style would displace the old, even in conservative areas such as England, France and north Germany; leading composers had already probed and developed some of its distinctive qualities; and musicians and public were particularly excited by the new genres of instrumental music that had been evolved. All that was needed, in instrumental music especially, was a creative imagination of the first rank to realize works of lasting individuality.

DAVID WYN JONES

Sacred

Though it never produced a composer of Mozart's genius, the imperial court in Vienna, with its august historical associations, would have seemed to any contemporary observer the most important musical centre in Austria and comparable with any in Europe. Much of its reputation was based on the magnificence of the dramatic spectacles mounted at court, but it also boasted a solid tradition of church music. Many Viennese churches, above all St Stephen's Cathedral, boasted lively and distinguished musical traditions, but the imperial court chapel (Hofkapelle) outshone them all. The period of its greatest magnificence began as early as the reign of Maximilian I, a lavish spender and cultivator of the arts, whose chapel included musicians of the distinction of Heinrich Isaac (d. 1517) (though he spent part of his career living away from the court in Florence), Ludwig Senfl and Paul Hofhaimer. A lasting monument to the splendour of the ritual and also to the early history of music printing in Vienna, is the *Choralis Constantinus*, a huge collection of Mass Propers according to the local Constantine Use begun by Isaac and completed, after his death, by Senfl. In Vienna as elsewhere, Flemish singer–composers were much sought after, and it is therefore no surprise to find a number of important Flemish polyphonists working in the Hofkapelle during the 16th century, among them Arnold von Bruck, Jacobus Vaet and Philippe de Monte.

Early in the 17th century there was a pronounced change of taste at court in favour of Italian Baroque culture, initially under the influence of Ferdinand II but also maintained by his successors. All the Austrian emperors of this period supported the arts with lavish generosity, and practised music themselves (Ferdinand III, Leopold I, Joseph I and Charles VI were all composers). Especially after Ferdinand II's marriage to Eleonora Gonzaga in 1622 the court's cultural relations with Italy flourished, and envoys secured the service of musicians from Florence, Mantua and Rome. Monteverdi's relationship with the imperial court also dates from this period. Italian composers who worked in Vienna included Giovanni Priuli, Giovanni Valentini and Orazio Benevoli, the first two as Hofkapellmeister. Of more direct relevance to Mozart is the 18th-century Hofkapelle tradition. Under Charles VI (reigned 1711–40), when the tradition of Baroque magnificence reached its culmination, the Kapellmeister was the celebrated Johann Joseph Fux (1660–1741), whose works include masses and other church works in both the Baroque concerted style and the Italian-derived learned or *stile antico* tradition. Fux's great counterpoint treatise *Gradus ad Parnassum* (1725) was and long remained the prime model for students of ecclesiastical or 'Palestrina style' counterpoint, though in an impure 18th-century form. The disciplines of species counterpoint, canon and fugue which it teaches were passed on by Mozart (who also probably drew on his lessons with the great Italian counterpoint pedagogue Padre Martini) to the young Englishman Thomas Attwood, who was Mozart's pupil from 1785 to 1787, and whose surviving workbook is still preserved in the British Library. An equally distinguished contemporary of Fux's was the Italian Antonio Caldara (*c.* 1670–1736), the composer of a large body of church music and opera. Other prominent musicians resident in Vienna during this period included Attilio Ariosti, the singing teacher Piero Francesco Tosi and Giuseppe Porsile.

After the death of Charles VI the activities of the musical establishment suffered temporary reverses as a result of the Austrian War of Succession (1740–49) and more long-lasting damage under the influence of political problems and Enlightenment attitudes to church music. Prominent composers of church music in the new *galant* form of the concerted style (see MacIntyre, 1984) included Florian Gassmann (1729–74), whose main direct connection with Mozart is the fact that the Kyrie of his incomplete Requiem setting has strong thematic links with Mozart's own and presumably influenced it. Mozart, in his later Vienna years, also copied out church works by another prominent Viennese musician, Georg Reutter the younger (1708–72). Mozart's own musical relationships with Vienna were oddly unfruitful as regards church music, despite a famous occasion from his childhood in which one of his early masses K.139 (47a, the *Waisenhausmesse*) was performed before the Viennese court on 7 December 1768. When he actually took up residence there in the spring of 1781 he must have been aware that Joseph II's 'rational' attitude to church music – a product of the Enlightenment – was unlikely to give him many opportunities in this direction. Mozart did not hold a church post for the last ten years of his life, except for his appointment on 9 May 1791, at his own suggestion, as unpaid assistant to the sick and aging Kapellmeister of St Stephen's, Leopold Hofmann – an appointment which was never to benefit Mozart financially, since Hofmann outlived him, dying in 1793.

Naturally, the long-standing tradition of church music at the archiepiscopal court in Salzburg also played an important part in Mozart's early development as a church composer. The musical tradition of the Salzburg court lacked the distinction of the imperial court in Vienna, and many of Mozart's predecessors and colleagues in the musical establishment were more or less obscure local musicians (together with some Italians) who looked to Vienna, Innsbruck, Munich or northern Italy for their inspiration. When the new cathedral was consecrated on 24 September 1628 the musical side of the accompanying festivities was largely entrusted to Italians, whose activity in Salzburg was part of the close relationships with northern Italian culture fostered by successive archbishops. Chief among the works performed was a Te Deum (now lost) by the court Kapellmeister, Stefano Bernardi, for twelve choirs placed in each of the twelve side-chapels, four of which were later destroyed by rebuilding. This was presumably a tribute to the sumptuous Venetian polychoral tradition. Another early Kapellmeister, Peter Gutfreund (also known as Pietro Bonamico), is said to have been influenced by the music of Lassus, who had spent his working life in Munich. Following the need for new music created by the liturgical reforms instituted by Pope Urban VIII (d. 1644) adaptations of works by Lassus and Victoria by two local musicians, Georg Moser and Abraham Megerle, long continued in use in the cathedral. In general, the early years were an undistinguished period in Salzburg musical life. The deprivations of the Thirty Years' War, which almost reached the gates of Salzburg, and the consequent impoverishment of the local economy, tended to produce a turning-away from German models in favour of Italian ones. Cultural links with Italy had already been forged by one of the early archbishops, Marcus Sitticus von Hohenems (reigned 1612–19), and had made Salzburg a centre of Italian Baroque art.

More distinguished musicians returned to Salzburg in the second half of the 17th century. They included two major figures in Baroque music, Georg Muffat and the violin virtuoso Heinrich Ignaz Franz Biber (1644–1704). Biber, who was active as a church composer, may have been the real composer of the famous 53–part *Missa Salisburgensis*, once attributed to Orazio Benevoli and wrongly supposed to have been performed at the consecration of the cathedral in 1628. A local musician, Andreas Hofer, who was choir director from 1654 to 1666 and Kapellmeister to 1684, is thought to be the earliest Salzburg musician whose works Mozart knew in their original form. All three composers were also active in the production of music for Benedictine school dramas. The last generation of Baroque composers was somewhat less distinguished. Although the famous Antonio Caldara, then deputy director of the Hofkapelle in Vienna, worked intermittently at the Salzburg court during 1716 and 1717, he was primarily concerned with dramatic music. The provision of church music was left in the hands of less gifted local figures, principally Carl Biber (son of Heinrich) and Matthias Sigismund Biechteler; these two composers are now credited with 98 and 105 church works respectively. Music by both these composers was still performed in Salzburg in the 1780s and could thus have been known to Mozart, though the technical shortcomings of Biechteler's work in particular suggests that Mozart would have had little to learn from it. Other major events from this period were the installation of a carillon (still working today) in 1702 and of the new cathedral organ in the following year.

With the second quarter of the 18th century we reach a group of musicians who have a more direct bearing on Mozart. Chief among these was Johann Ernst Eberlin (1702–62), who was influential in changing Salzburg taste from Baroque to Rococo. He was also the earliest Salzburg Kapellmeister whom Mozart could have known personally and the first in whose music he took any interest. Some of Mozart's copies of church music by Eberlin have survived, and have in the past given rise to mistaken attributions to Mozart himself; he studied Eberlin's keyboard fugues, describing them as 'the length of extended versets'. However, scholars who have worked on Eberlin's music have rejected the theory that he was a major influence on Mozart's early style. Another church musician who knew Mozart well in his early years was Anton Cajetan Adlgasser (1729–77), who was first organist in Salzburg. Mozart, though not apparently influenced by him, praised him in a letter to Padre Martini as 'a very good contrapuntist' (*bravissimo contrappuntista*).

A much more important figure in Mozart's early development was Johann Michael Haydn (1737–1806), younger brother of Joseph, who served the court from 1763 until his death. Haydn (the name refers to Michael Haydn throughout this section) was a considerable composer with a close working relationship with Mozart, and it is therefore not surprising that despite making occasional rude remarks about him in his letters, Mozart was undoubtedly impressed with his work. In March 1767 Haydn, Adlgasser and Mozart each composed one act of the oratorio *Die Schuldigkeit des ersten Gebots*. Haydn's strong influence can also be found in a number of Mozart's early church works. They include Mozart's Te Deum, K.141 (66b) and the doubtful Offertory *Sub tuum praesidium*, which is closely related to Haydn's *Offertory in Honour of the Most Blessed Virgin* (also known with the text *Schöpfer der Erde*). The Gloria of his *Missa sancti Hieronymi* has been related to the main theme of the overture to *La clemenza di Tito*. This Mass seems to have made a great impression on both Mozart and his father, who recommends it for study in his letters. Many of Haydn's Graduals and Offertories are too late to have influenced Mozart, but the evidence of the Mozart family letters show that he continued to take an interest in Haydn's music after moving to Vienna in 1781. Mozart was not professionally involved with church music after the move to Vienna, but about the period of the C minor Mass we find him writing to Leopold to ask him to send 'some of Haydn's fugues' (the reference is to Michael) and another letter indicates that he intended to have music by him (together with Leopold Mozart and Eberlin) performed at the 'learned' music society which met regularly at the house of Baron van Swieten. Other performances are also mentioned. Finally, one of the most often cited models for Mozart's Requiem is Haydn's well-known setting, composed on the death of Archbishop von Schrattenbach in 1771, though it should be added that much of what Mozart is alleged to have borrowed from Haydn can be described as common stock.

Eberlin and Michael Haydn were two of the three Salzburg musicians who were of most immediate concern to Mozart as a church composer. The third was his father. Although far less talented in composition than Michael Haydn, Leopold Mozart played a key role in his son's development, both in training him and in building his early career. As regards church music, it has been shown that the most ambitious of Wolfgang's juvenile Mass settings, K.66 and K.139 (47a), are both indebted to Masses by Leopold. The same applies to Wolfgang's Sacramental Litany K.125, as Walter Senn's comparatively recent discovery of the autograph of a setting of the litany by Leopold has demonstrated. Two Mass fragments, K.115 (166d) and K.116 (90a), which were formerly attributed to Wolfgang, are now known to be by Leopold (Klafsky, 1915, Senn, 1971–2).

DAVID HUMPHREYS

Musical life in Europe

Salzburg (1756–83)

In his letters Mozart often makes derogatory remarks about Salzburg and its musical life. Salzburg was 'hateful' to him, the condition of the court music 'crude, mean and slovenly'. But it would be an unjust conclusion to read into these words a valid judgment of Salzburg's musical life during the Mozart era. Mozart's words reflected at that juncture his deep bitterness over the petty treatment from the Archbishop Colloredo and at the same time the realization – perfectly justified – that in the long run Salzburg was not the place for his talents.

In fact, it was precisely during Mozart's lifetime that Salzburg's musical life reached the apex of its long and rich history: a history intimately attached to that of the ecclesiastical principality – something difficult for our age to appreciate. Salzburg archbishops were also the ruling sovereigns of the land, and followed precisely the pattern of European principalities with their own courts and all the requisite forms of worldly display. In this pattern the court music played a special role: the archiepiscopal band was responsible for a variety of duties: in the church (music for services) and at court (*Tafelmusik*, chamber music, 'academies' or, as we would call them, concerts). The Salzburg court band was held in high repute and was a centre of attraction for numerous artists, among them many Italians. Also of the greatest importance to Salzburg was the musical theatre, the 'azione sacra' or ecclesiastical-cum-secular opera.

In earlier times Salzburg's reputation had generally rested on the skills of particular individuals, but by the end of the 18th century an astonishing array of talent had assembled there: the Mozarts (father and son), the important church composer Johann Michael Haydn, and excellent musicians such as Kapellmeister Giuseppe Maria Lolli, Domenico Fischetti and Giacomo Rust, as well as instrumental virtuosi on the level of Joseph Fiala (oboe), Joseph Otto (violin) or Anton Cajetan Adlgasser (organ and harpsichord); there were also many excellent singers (including castrati). The availability of such exceptional talents is reflected in Mozart's own scores: some demand such a high degree of virtuosity that their performance today is often very problematical.

With the rise of the bourgeoisie after the middle of the 18th century, many features of court etiquette began to be reflected in the life of the lesser nobility and non-aristocratic members of Salzburg's society. Private bands and both larger and smaller instrumental and vocal ensembles began to figure in bourgeois circles. Among Leopold's and Wolfgang's compositions of this period are many written for such occasions: serenades, symphonies, chamber music; works for balls, masquerades and sleigh rides, and for family celebrations. The names of several of these patrons – Haffner, Antretter, Lodron – have been immortalized in the dedications of works of Mozart.

In Mozart's output during his Salzburg years – interrupted by many trips abroad – the so-called *Gebrauchsmusik* (occasional works) dominated. A special place was occupied by religious pieces: litanies, offertories, vespers, church sonatas and, especially, masses (among them the famous *Coronation* Mass of 1779). There were also a large number of secular pieces: sonatas, symphonies, concertos for diverse instruments, etc.; and also dedicatory works and others which were performed at court festivals. Theatrical works were already plentiful at this period, as witness, *inter alia*, *Il sogno di Scipione* (1772), *Il rè pastore* (1775) and *Zaide* (1779). As Mozart matured, a process determined by many foreign experiences (not least that of Mannheim in 1778), we may notice his clear determination to absent himself from Salzburg's stereotyped musical life. To the final period belongs the decisive success of *Idomeneo* (Munich, 1781) – an occurrence which may have strengthened Mozart's decision to concern himself in the future particularly with opera.

Mozart served under two Salzburg rulers. Siegmund, Count von Schrattenbach (reigned 1753–71), was a prince whose mentality and sympathies were rooted in the Baroque, a great protector of the arts, and well disposed towards the young Mozart. His successor was Hieronymus, Count von Colloredo (reigned 1772–1801), also a great music-lover – he himself played violin in musical evenings at the Residenz – but, as a man of the Enlightenment and a dedicated follower of Emperor Joseph II, he severely curtailed the lavish ceremony, and with it the court band. Mozart often came into conflict with this prince, and in May 1781 came the final break between the artist and his patron. Mozart's Salzburg years were at an end.

CLEMENS HÖSLINGER

France (1764–6 and 1778)

Mozart's visits to France took place in dramatically different circumstances. In 1764 and 1766 he was a *Wunderkind*, whose talent opened doors even at court; in 1778 he was a reluctant rival to established composers, native and foreign. He had professional friends in the Mannheimers, but it is hardly surprising if, for instance, such a well-established Italian as Cambini did not want to help him (see Mozart's letter of 1 May 1778). The attitude of Baron Grimm, 'to whom we owe everything' (1764), naturally altered with circumstances; at twenty-two, Mozart was just another ambitious visitor, and the extent to which he outclassed his contemporaries was never less apparent than at this time.

Parisian music centred on opera, but was by no means lifeless in other respects. Church music was perhaps its weakest point, although in 1764 Leopold praised the choral singing; otherwise, in common with most Italian and German musicians, he considered French music 'not worth a sou', and this attitude undoubtedly rubbed off on his son. They attended Mass at Versailles in 1764 and probably heard the old-fashioned *grand motet* there or at the Concert Spirituel.

In 1764 the question of Mozart's writing for the theatre did not arise. He was received in the highest circles; the children displayed their talents before an audience of no particular discrimination but eager for novelty. Exceptionally they were allowed to give a public concert (such matters were controlled by royal privilege). They also met the keyboard masters of Paris, mainly expatriate countrymen such as Johann Schobert and J.G. Eckard, by whom Wolfgang was influenced. He composed sonatas for keyboard with violin accompaniment, suitable for the cultivated amateur and published as op. 1 with a royal dedication.

In 1778 Mozart's aim was to become established, which had ultimately to be through opera. But musical Paris was far too embroiled in the Gluck–Piccinni problem to welcome him. In certain circles 'German' was almost a term of abuse, although J.C. Bach was commissioned by the Académie Royale de Musique (Opéra) for 1779. The epoch of Lully and Rameau was over; the repertoire was dominated by Gluck and his Italian rival whose first French opera, *Roland*, was given in 1778. Mozart's experience of this and other recent works influenced the composition of *Idomeneo*, but his only commission from the Opéra was a ballet divertissement, *Les Petits Riens*. The Opéra-Comique was dominated by native composers, notably Grétry: Mozart was to work in a related style soon afterwards, in the unfinished *Zaide*.

Mozart's least miserable Paris experiences in 1778 concerned instrumental music, in which the orientation of the French capital was more towards Germany. The orchestras were large and excellent, and well used to Haydn's music (he was soon to be commissioned to write his six *Paris* symphonies). Mozart's Mannheim friends performed at the Concert Spirituel, where he achieved one solid success, the *Paris* Symphony. Despite the Comte de Guines and his daughter, for whom Mozart wrote the Flute and Harp Concerto, he was no longer fascinating to the rich and influential; but he published another op. 1, again sonatas for piano with violin accompaniment, and three sets of variations on popular melodies aimed at an amateur market drawn increasingly from middle as well as upper ranks of society.

JULIAN RUSHTON

England and the Netherlands (1764-6)

Measured only by the importance of native composers, England and the Netherlands in the 1760s might seem musical backwaters. But all kinds of musical life flourished, and in England by no means all of it represented a hangover from the age of Handel (d. 1759). Mozart was a child when he visited these countries, but there is no reason to doubt his powers of assimilation, even at the age of nine. Later he was to be well acquainted with English musicians: Linley in Italy, Storace and Attwood in Vienna.

Handel's influence remained, with revivals of his works and the composition of new oratorios (composers active in the decade include Smith, Stanley and Arne). Although the first volume of Boyce's historical anthology of cathedral music had appeared in 1760, the Catholic Mozarts were probably little exposed to this long sacred tradition. Yet Wolfgang contributed to the *genius loci* with a 'chorus', *God is our Refuge*, commissioned by the trustees of the British Museum and presented to them (see King, 1984b).

The 1760s saw the composition of several new operas in English (e.g. by Arne), but the Mozarts will have regarded London as an outpost of the operatic empire of Italy. At the King's Theatre the principal composer was the Italian-trained J.C. Bach (b. 1735), who became almost a role-model; Mozart was far too young for the labour of writing for the theatre, but when he demonstrated his powers of affective improvisation to Daines Barrington (who delivered a report to the Royal Society in 1769), it was with Italian words, an intrinsic part of the internationally understood musical language in which he was already fluent. His first known concert aria was written in London, to a Metastasio text.

London was socially the most advanced city the Mozarts ever

visited. The genuinely musical King George III and his Queen were remarkably accessible; there was relatively more mingling of aristocratic and mercantile classes than elsewhere. Musicians relied mainly on the patronage of the former, but the latter class was more numerous, more influential, and no less cultured, than its continental counterparts. This situation favoured instrumental music and song, which were popular in the pleasure gardens (Vauxhall, Ranelagh), and concert series such as the one recently established by J.C. Bach and his countryman K.F. Abel. Mozart acquainted himself with their music and quite naturally composed his first symphonies in London. The large amateur market for instrumental music induced Leopold to publish a set of six sonatas for keyboard with violin accompaniment in 1765 as op. 3, with a dedication to the Queen.

Holland was a major publishing centre and encouraged further production in these genres. Despite the illness of both Mozart children in The Hague, they were welcomed as performers, and for local consumption Mozart published the sonatas op. 4, again with a royal dedication, and an aria. He produced his first divertimento, the *Gallimathias musicum*, and wrote keyboard variations on two Dutch melodies. Leopold remarked upon the wealth of these mercantile nations and might have followed the example of many Germans in settling there; but he was too much disturbed by what he saw as atheism in England, and by Calvinism in Holland, to contemplate such a step.

JULIAN RUSHTON

Germany (1763–81)

The musical scene encountered by Mozart between 1763 and 1781, on his travels through those lands which today we call Germany, was characterized by a fading tradition. From Baroque times (and it was still true) the courts had been the true representatives of public music culture. Each court was a cultural centre in itself, independent politically and culturally from either a more highly placed ruler or some other ideal. The bourgeoisie occasionally took part in the musical productions of the courts – particularly as far as operas were concerned, but also in church music, hardly in concerts – yet it scarcely showed the same initiative and was hence less attractive for performers or composers. Perhaps it was more open for a *Wunderkind*, but here one must consider not what Mozart gave to the musical scene but what it could offer him as an artist.

Mozart did actually give a concert in 1777 in Augsburg – not a court town but one dominated by middle-class citizens. If we recall that he appeared wearing the insignia of the papal Order of the Golden Spur, we realize that the occasion, in the birthplace of his father, was a social rather than a musical event. And none of his compositions was written in or for the patrician town of Augsburg.

He was stimulated by the courts at Munich and Mannheim, but both were dominated for some length of time in Mozart's career by one and the same person – a man who was more important for the composer than the places in themselves. Three months after Mozart's visit to Munich in the autumn of 1777 occurred the death of Maximilian III Joseph, Elector of Bavaria, for whom Mozart had already composed *La finta giardiniera* in 1774–5. That meant that two months after Mozart's arrival in Mannheim, the Elector Karl Theodor of the Palatine, who resided there, and from whom Mozart rightly expected much, left Mannheim to take up residence in Munich, combining the two electoral positions in his own person. With him, singers and musicians who were important to Mozart left for Munich, which now, until the commission of *Idomeneo* (1780), became the only artistically important German court for him: Mannheim without the Elector was devoid of artistic interest. Returning to Munich from Paris in the autumn of 1778, he witnessed the first attempt on the part of the bourgeoisie to form a musical establishment, an 'académie des amateurs'. With this in mind he began work on a double concerto for piano and violin, K.Anh.56 (315f), which he soon abandoned, since the project did not develop as expected.

Visits to other courts (such as that of Prince Krafft Ernst von Öttingen-Wallerstein or of Princess Caroline von Nassau-Weilburg), or to monasteries with similarly flourishing musical cultures (Heilig Kreuz in Augsburg, Kaisheim near Donauwörth), brought him recognition but were no inspiration artistically. Other cities were only interesting to Mozart as a tourist. What stimulated Mozart in Frankfurt in 1790 was neither the city nor its citizens but the coronation of Leopold II and the many visitors who arrived for the occasion.

Such observations must not be understood negatively. The standard of the musical forces in many a court was exceptionally high, the ability of the Kapellmeister and composers working there most remarkable and in part (as was the case of Christian Cannabich in Munich) recognized as such by Mozart. Considering all this in a broader context, it must be admitted that more was received by Mozart than was given. It is also the case that by the time Mozart came into contact with the Mannheim court band, the era in which it had set the tone for the whole of Central Europe had passed.

The centuries-old domination of the markets of south Germany and the Habsburg lands by south German music publishers had also ended. Leipzig, and its house of Breitkopf, with which Mozart – despite his father's efforts – never made the right contact, was still important. And the new music publishers founded in the 1770s at Mannheim, Speyer or Berlin had other interests than printing Mozart's music. When at Munich in 1779 Mozart presented to the Electress Maria Elisabeth the violin sonatas (K.301–306) which were dedicated to her, it was in the edition which had been printed in Paris.

It is clear, then, that the courtly and monastic musical tradition in Germany had begun to abate by this time, and new kinds of music making had not yet been developed to a similar extent. The Salzburg court musician Wolfgang Amadeus Mozart necessarily came into contact with what remained of the traditional courtly musical centres of Germany. It was not that he was incapable of relating to anything else or did not seek something different: quite simply, there was no alternative. In these centres he actually found less scope for his talents than in Salzburg, where he could compose and play not only at court but also for the university and artistically inclined bourgeois families and those of the minor nobility. These activities were supplemented by the possibility of opera commissions, such as he received from Munich.

OTTO BIBA

Italy (1770–74)

It is natural to regard musical life in Italy as dominated by opera, and the central events of the Mozarts' visits were indeed the Milan productions of *Mitridate, rè di Ponto, Ascanio in Alba* and *Lucio Silla*. Yet when they toured Italy in 1770–71 most of their activity had little to do with the theatre. Wolfgang quickly secured a commission (*scrittura*) to compose an *opera seria* for Milan; but while he witnessed many opera performances, he himself was mainly on display as a keyboard virtuoso (including organ) and improvisor, a musician of learning, and a composer of smaller-scale pieces.

Italy was not a nation, and much of it was under Austrian rule; Count Firmian, who befriended the Mozarts on all their visits, governed the Austrian province of Lombardy, and Tuscany was ruled by the future Emperor Leopold II in Florence. The Mozarts also visited the Papal states and the Kingdom of Naples. The family letters, like Burney's contemporaneous Italian diaries (1770), speak of manifold musical activities in every centre.

Modern sacred music resembled *opera seria*, with full orchestration, *galant* arias, and both dramatic and 'learned' (fugal) choruses. This was the style of Mozart's Salzburg Vespers and Litanies and C minor Mass. During his long stay with Count Pallavicini near Bologna in 1770, Mozart attended Vespers on the feast-day of St Petronio ('beautiful, but very long'), the instrumentation including trumpets. Only the Sistine Chapel, where Mozart wrote out Allegri's *Miserere* from memory, preserved a more ancient and 'purer' tradition of polyphony. A few months later Mozart sufficiently mastered the ancient style to gain the approbation of Padre Martini and membership of the Bologna Academy. It may be assumed that, although receiving no formal tuition, he assimilated all he might have learned from the most advanced pedagogical institutions of the day such as the Venetian 'Ospidali', orphanages which gave a high place to the musical training of their charges, and the Neapolitan Conservatorios (schools of music).

The letters are full of references to private music making: public concerts were comparatively rare. Wolfgang would improvise, accompany at sight, and present his own compositions (including arias), in the houses of patrons of the arts from the noble or merchant classes. Leopold remarked that it paid little; but the network of contacts contributed to the security of the Mozarts' position. It was the chance of performances which stimulated Mozart to write several symphonies in Italy, and on his second and third visits to Milan he composed divertimentos for strings and wind, and several string quartets.

Nevertheless the high points of Mozart's time in Italy were the Milan opera productions, two *opere serie* for the Carnival season and a serenata (*Ascanio*) for a court wedding. *Mitridate* (1770) is already a considerable achievement; *Lucio Silla* (1772) shows Mozart at sixteen the equal of his seniors. Among these was Hasse (b. 1699), whose *Ruggiero*, according to Leopold, was eclipsed by *Ascanio*; and the greatest Italian of his generation, Jommelli (b. 1714), whose *Armida*, heard in Naples, was dubbed by Mozart 'beautiful but too serious and old-fashioned for the theatre', an opinion apparently shared by the Neapolitans. In Milan the Mozarts met the symphonist Sammartini and Piccinni (b. 1728), whose *Cesare in Egitto* was deemed 'excellent': Piccinni was a leader of the sweet-singing style which Mozart had already learned from J.C. Bach in London, and which prevailed throughout Italy.

JULIAN RUSHTON

Vienna and the Habsburg Domains (1762–91)

The artistic highpoint attained by the Imperial Music Chapel in the Baroque period proved to be seminal. Just as the nobility sought to reproduce, in its estates in Austria, Bohemia, Moravia, Hungary and northern Italy, the imperial way of life, so it copied, with its musical forces, the Imperial Music Chapel, which in turn often engaged its musicians from the ranks of the aristocratic bands. This ambition and the artistic exchange which arose from it guaranteed a widespread high standard of the nobility's appreciation of music. Moreover, the fact that the 'middle' and 'high' aristocracy resided not only in country estates but also in a palace in Vienna meant that a regular artistic rivalry existed between the various orchestras; it also insured that from the artistic centre of Vienna new repertory and new impulses were received and passed on. Since these orchestras were showpieces, and music became associated with representation, or social display, music outside the court continued to flourish. That could even lead to a situation where the Batthyani band in Pressburg (now Bratislava) gave concerts in the open air.

The one place where everyone was confronted with music, whether they were interested or not, was in the church, at which regular attendance was considered a social obligation. It is true that church music degenerated when its production was regarded as an end in itself, and the Enlightenment accordingly objected to it. The situation led to reform by Emperor Joseph II, but the oft-repeated assertion that the Emperor forbade church music is incorrect. Throughout his reign (1780–90) church music was cultivated, but compared to earlier times restricted and disciplined.

The example of aristocratic and ecclesiastical cultivation of music also inspired the bourgeoisie. In those circles there arose, instead of the old tradition of private performance of music (which one might term drawing-room music), the so-called 'musical salon': music was made not for oneself, but for and in society; one was invited to listen or to participate. Thus this form of music making had a semi-public character; and since music making was no longer merely a personal source of pleasure, a different value was placed on musical education. To be able to sing or play an instrument became a social grace, music an intrinsic part of education. The most popular instrument was soon the piano, no doubt on account of its flexibility: 'this is surely piano country', wrote Mozart to his father in 1781.

The musical salon developed in Vienna during the 1770s. It was equally significant for the middle class and the lesser nobility, and soon spread to district capitals and other centres. Music itself, at least at the outset, did not develop in the salon; but it was produced there, and soon composers were taking it into consideration. As early as 1760 regular concerts were given by composers and performers, to present their products or abilities to the public. They came as guests to Vienna, and travelled abroad, so that these concerts soon came to be a typical part of city and town life.

Mozart himself appeared as a concert promoter in Vienna, Prague or Linz, and in Vienna he took an active part in the first professional attempts to organize subscription concerts. Concerts were also put on to support charitable causes, of which the most important were those of the Tonkünstler-Societät, or Society of Musicians, founded in 1772 to support the widows and orphans of their society. Mozart participated in several of these concerts, but through carelessness he neglected to become a member, just as he gave little thought altogether for his 'life insurance': otherwise he would not have been one of the first to live as an independent composer without any regular appointment.

The musical interests of the nobility and middle class converged not only when they attended public concerts but also in the opera houses, whether these were court, city or privately organized theatres. Such varied and numerous musical ambitions and interests required correspondingly active music publishers and copyists' firms, and music engravers began to establish themselves in Vienna in the 1770s; within the next decade Vienna became a European centre of music publishing. The manufacture of musical instruments also flourished. Piano-builders in Vienna introduced improvements and developments all through the 1780s. Stringed, woodwind, brass instruments and organs were manufactured in Vienna and in many cities of the Habsburg lands and were of an acknowledged high quality.

OTTO BIBA

Mozart's patrons

MOZART OCCUPIES A PIVOTAL POSITION in the history of musical patronage. He was born into a social structure in which, among composers, only those successfully engaged in opera could hope to make a comfortable living without some form of regular employment in the service of the church or of a princely court (and even opera was largely dependent on the support of aristocratic patrons, who were able both to call the tune and to vet the libretto). The changes in society that took place during Mozart's lifetime found their most violent expression, of course, in the events of the French Revolution, but the feudal ties that kept the composer under the control of an aristocratic patron had already been loosened in 1781, when Mozart provoked his own dismissal at the hands of Archbishop Colloredo; and the first performance of *Le nozze di Figaro* in Vienna in 1786 was as significant, in its way, as the events in Paris three years later.

Mozart was introduced to the workings of musical patronage by his father at an unusually early age, when, together with his sister Nannerl, he was exhibited as a child prodigy to the habitués of aristocratic salons in numerous European cities. Posterity can study one result of this early patronage in the form of Mozart's first published compositions, dedicated to some of those whose approval and support the family won on their travels. They naturally take the form of keyboard works, since it was as a keyboard prodigy that Mozart was received into society; the accompanying violin parts contribute little, though they may have increased sales. The earliest were the two sonatas op. 1, K.6 and 7, dedicated to the Princess Victoire (1733–99), second daughter of Louis XV, and published in Paris in 1764 together with two more sonatas (K.8 and 9) dedicated to Countess Adrienne-Catherine de Tessé (1714–1814), lady-in-waiting to the Dauphine. In London the following year there appeared a further six sonatas (K.10–15, this time with flute specified as an alternative to the violin, and with a cello part as well). The dedication to Queen Charlotte (1744–1818) flatters her as a constitutional monarch but at the same time hints at the writer's impatience with absolutism: 'Deign, Madam, to receive my poor gifts. You were from the first destined to reign over a free people; the children of Genius are so no less than the British People; free above all with their offerings, they take pleasure in surrounding Your throne.'

The fruits of the Mozarts' visit to the Netherlands in 1765–6, when Wolfgang played at the residence of Princess Caroline of

Nassau-Weilburg (1743–87), include six sonatas, K.26–31, dedicated to the princess and two sets of variations on Dutch songs, K.24 and 25. One of Mozart's most active and influential patrons during his visits to Italy (1770–73) was the Austrian Count Karl Joseph Firmian (1716–82), Governor General of Lombardy, who secured him the commission for the opera *Mitridate, rè di Ponto* (Milan, 1770) and provided introductions to well-placed Italian patrons, including Count Gian-Luca Pallavicini-Centurioni (1697–1773) in Bologna, who in turn wrote a letter of recommendation to his distant cousin in Rome, Cardinal Count Lazzaro Opizio Pallavicini (1719–85). It was no doubt Cardinal Pallavicini's influence that secured for Mozart the papal Cross of the Golden Spur in June 1770 and an audience with Pope Clement XIV the following month.

Mozart and his father enjoyed the patronage of some of Italy's most powerful Maecenases, but they left the country without securing for Wolfgang any permanent employment there. He had, in fact, already been taken onto the payroll at Salzburg by the newly-elected Archbishop Hieronymus, Count Colloredo (1732–1812). His position (which he had already occupied for some time in an honorary capacity) was that of *Konzertmeister*, and his duties included the composition of church music. During the years 1772–81 he wrote about a dozen masses, as well as litanies, vespers music, several shorter choral pieces and a series of single-movement sonatas, mostly for two violins and organ, to be played during the reading of the Epistle. The masses are relatively short, reflecting Colloredo's wishes in such matters; their scoring usually includes two trumpets (in K.167 there are four) but never violas, which were not available in the Salzburg church orchestra.

Mozart's official duties at Salzburg left him with sufficient time to fulfil commissions from individual patrons for works to celebrate particular occasions or to serve for family music making. Probably the best-known example of the former is the *Haffner* Serenade, K.250 (248b), commissioned by Siegmund Haffner (1756–87) for the marriage of his sister Marie Elisabeth (1753–84) in July 1776. From about the same time date also two divertimentos, K.247 and 287 (271b, 271H), composed for the name day of Countess Maria Antonia Lodron (1738–86); Mozart also wrote the Concerto in F, K.242, for the countess to play with her two daughters. Among his other Salzburg patrons was Count Johann Rudolf Czernin (1757–1845), whose father in Prague granted Mozart an annual settlement in 1776 (he died the following year).

After his break with Colloredo and his move to Vienna in 1781, Mozart held only one other salaried post – the relatively minor one of *Kammermusicus* (chamber musician) at the Viennese court, to which Emperor Joseph II appointed him in 1787. This entailed the composition of dance music for the court balls, and Mozart obliged with minuets, German dances and contredanses in considerable number and to a high standard. But he continued to depend on individual patrons for a substantial part of his livelihood. Among the most important of these were the Thun family and Baron van Swieten. Count Johann Joseph Anton Thun-Hohenstein (1711–88) divided his time between Linz and Prague; Mozart was his guest in both cities, and in 1783 dedicated to him the *Linz* Symphony, K.425. In 1761 Count Thun's son, Franz de Paula Joseph (1734–1800), married Maria Wilhelmine von Ulfeld (1747–1800), and Mozart was a frequent visitor at their home in Vienna. Baron Gottfried Bernhard van Swieten (1733–1803), who was in charge of the imperial library in Vienna, was something of a musical antiquarian. He held regular noonday gatherings at his house on Sundays, and it was probably for these that Mozart made his string quartet arrangements of keyboard fugues by Bach. Van Swieten also formed a Gesellschaft der Associierten for the performance of oratorios, and commissioned Mozart's arrangements of four Handel works: *Acis and Galatea, Messiah, Ode for St Cecilia's Day* and *Alexander's Feast*. After Mozart's death Van Swieten saw to the funeral arrangements and made provision for his children.

Van Swieten would occupy an honoured position in music history even if he had never known Mozart (he adapted the libretti for Haydn's two late oratorios and was active in promoting the music of C.P.E. Bach and Beethoven), but many of Mozart's patrons are remembered now only for their association with particular works by the composer. Thus, the names of a surgeon with the Dutch East India Company, Ferdinand Dejean, and of a minor French count, Adrien-Louis Bonnières de Souastre, Comte de Guines (1735–1806), will forever be linked with Mozart's flute music of 1777–9; the former commissioned two concertos, K.313–14 (285c–d), the Andante, K.315 (285e) and possibly the flute quartets K.285 and 285a, the latter the Concerto for Flute and Harp, K.299 (297c). Similarly, Friedrich Wilhelm II, King of Prussia (1744–97), is remembered, in musical circles at least, as the dedicatee of the three *Prussian* Quartets, K.575, 589 and 590, with their particularly prominent writing for the cello (the King's own instrument), while his daughter Friederike Charlotte Ulrike Katherine (1767–1820) is traditionally associated with a supposed commission of the same year (1789), resulting in the 'easy'(!) Piano Sonata in D, K.576.

Some idea of the nature and extent of the patronage Mozart enjoyed during his most successful years in Vienna may be gauged from his letter of 20 March 1784, in which he listed 174 subscribers to his concerts that year – a total which, as he proudly informed his father, exceeded those of G.F. Richter and J.A. Fisher together. The list includes the names of Prince Dmitry Michailovich Galitzin (1721–93), the Russian ambassador, and Count Karl Zichy von Vásonkyö (1753–1826), whose wife Anna Maria (*née* Khevenhüller-Metsch) was a pupil of Mozart's.

In his last year Mozart received two most unusual commissions from Austrian aristocrats. The first came from a Viennese count, Joseph Nepomuk Franz de Paula Deym von Stržitéž (1752–1804), who had been forced to leave the city after a duel, but returned under the name of Müller and set up a *Kunstgalerie*, an exhibition of *objets d'art*. In 1791 he opened a kind of mausoleum dedicated to the late Fieldmarshal Laudon, in which a mechanical organ played appropriate funeral music. It was for this machine that Mozart wrote the Adagio and Allegro, K.594, and possibly also two further pieces, K.608 and 616.

Probably the most famous musical commission of all time was that of Mozart's last, unfinished masterpiece, the Requiem, K.626. The 'grey messenger' who arrived on the composer's doorstep some time in the spring or summer of 1791 was a representative of Count Franz Walsegg-Stuppach (1763–1827), who delighted in commissioning works from well-known composers and passing them off as his own (the Requiem was to serve as a personal memorial to his young wife, who had died on 14 February 1791). The circumstances of this commission came to light only in 1964, when O.E. Deutsch discovered and published the very full account penned in 1839 by Anton Herzog, an official at Wiener Neustadt, near Vienna.

18th-century patronage was not often accompanied by deceit of this kind, even if it was frequently motivated by vanity in some form or other. But Herzog's final words on the Walsegg affair could apply equally to Mozart's other patrons, and could, indeed, serve as an epitaph on a whole tradition of aristocratic patronage to which Mozart was among the last important heirs: 'Peace be on the ashes of the great master, and also on his revered patron, to whose liberality we are indebted for this so valuable work of art.'

MALCOLM BOYD

Map of Europe in Mozart's time showing the chief places he visited
(see 'Mozart's journeys', pp. 135–6).

Section 6

MOZART AS AN INDIVIDUAL

MOZART AS AN INDIVIDUAL

*Family
background*

THE STARTING POINT for any consideration of Mozart's family background must be his father Leopold. Leopold Mozart had a profound influence on his son's development, and even in his maturity Wolfgang's ambivalent attitude to his father had an enduring impact on his personal and professional life. Leopold was born in November 1719, the son of an Augsburg bookbinder. His family had resided in the region of Augsburg for more than two hundred years, and were designated in contemporary documents by a number of variations on the name of Mozart, including Mozer, Mozarth and Mozhard. Leopold lived in Augsburg until 1737 when he moved to Salzburg to study philosophy and law. He showed some promise in these disciplines, but did not complete his studies, choosing instead at the age of twenty to enter the service of a canon of the cathedral as a musician and valet. In 1743 he became a violinist in the Salzburg Hofkapelle, and was soon appointed violin teacher at the choir school. He gradually progressed in the service of the Prince–Archbishop of Salzburg, reaching the rank of deputy Kapellmeister in 1763.

Leopold married Anna Maria Pertl in 1747. She was the daughter of a senior local administrator in nearby St Gilgen, and was a year younger than her husband. Over the next eight years, the couple had seven children, but only two survived infancy: the fourth child Maria Anna (Nannerl), and the seventh child who was Wolfgang. Mozart's mother Anna Maria remains a shadowy figure. She was the product of a society that made few attempts to educate women, preferring to instil the virtues of piety and duty to father, brothers and husband. Maria Anna was scarcely literate, and does not appear to have been influential in major family decisions. Although Leopold Mozart frequently expressed affection for her in letters, her status in the family was clearly secondary.

Leopold Mozart composed extensively during his early years in Salzburg, producing more than twenty-five symphonies in addition to sacred, chamber and incidental works. But it was his fame as a violin teacher that established his wider reputation. The year of Wolfgang's birth saw the publication of Leopold Mozart's other famous child, his *Versuch einer gründlichen Violinschule*. This treatise on violin playing was translated into several languages and reprinted many times. Yet within a few years, Leopold had relinquished his ambitions as a pedagogue and composer, devoting himself to the nurturing of his extraordinary children.

It soon became evident that, despite Nannerl's striking talents, her younger brother Wolfgang was the focus of their father's attentions. Leopold believed that his son was a divine miracle, whose God-given genius it was his duty to foster. The double standard became overtly apparent in 1767, when the family were temporarily settled in Vienna. Several children of their landlord contracted smallpox, so Leopold searched for new rooms. He failed to find anywhere that could accommodate the entire family, so decamped with Wolfgang to the house of a friend, leaving his wife and daughter in the infected lodging.

Leopold Mozart was a worldly man, well aware of the subtleties and intrigue of court life. He meticulously planned every development in his children's triumphant progress round Europe, weighing up the cost and likely profit of each engagement, placing judicious notices in the press and exploiting every contact for the advantage it might bring. He skilfully engineered his son's transition from child prodigy to adolescent composer, and it is probable (as Charles Burney noted) that much of Mozart's later professionalism was acquired through the discipline implanted by his father.

Leopold Mozart's astute behaviour is illustrated in the voluminous advice that he gave to Wolfgang in his letters. For example, during Mozart's stay in Munich in 1777, Leopold told him whom to cultivate and how to find out about the Elector's preferences, so as to be able to compose appropriate music:

> Possibly it would work if you only get the opportunity of showing the Elector everything you can do, and particularly in fugues, canons and contrapuntal music. You must pay assiduous court to Count Seeau, telling him that you will compose arias, etc., and ballets for his theatre without asking for any remuneration. . . . Should you have to write some gamba music for the Elector, [Wotschitka] can tell you what it should be like, and could show you the pieces which he [the Elector] likes best, so as to understand his taste. . . . (letter of 29 September 1777)

Yet Leopold paid an immense emotional price for living through his son, for he experienced frustration and anguish when Wolfgang matured as an independent being. In order to retain control, his affection became increasingly manipulative, as he blamed his own poor health and lack of success in Salzburg on his son's refusal to comply with his wishes. Here, for example, is his description of Wolfgang's departure for Munich, Mannheim and Paris in 1777:

> I made every effort to control myself when we said farewell, so as not to make our parting more painful; and in the tumult I forgot to give my son a father's blessing. I ran to the window and sent it after you; but I didn't see you both leaving through the gate, and thus we had to assume you had left already, since I had sat there beforehand for a long time without thinking of anything. Nannerl wept most bitterly and I had to make every effort to comfort her. She complained of a headache and stomach-ache and in the end she retched and vomited. . . . Poor Pimpes [the dog] lay next to her. I went to my room and said my morning prayers. (letter of 25 September 1777)

As he grew older, Mozart learned to ignore his father's advice, or else to misunderstand it to his own advantage, leaving Leopold to scribble off long letters of impotent rage. When Mozart moved to Vienna in 1781, Leopold remained at his post in Salzburg, and over the last six years of his life saw his son for only two periods. The first was in 1783 on the no doubt uncomfortable occasion on which Mozart took his new wife Constanze to Salzburg. The second time was in 1785, when Leopold stayed with his son in Vienna during the Lenten concert season. This visit was apparently more successful, since Leopold was treated with considerable respect by his son's Viennese friends. He was also able to observe Wolfgang's success with his own eyes, and assure himself that the household was managed properly. He died two years later, leaving a small estate that was divided between Wolfgang, who was in financial difficulties, and Nannerl, who had married Johann Baptist von Berchtold zu Sonnenburg in 1784 and was living in relatively comfortable circumstances.

Leopold Mozart was more typical of the Age of Rationalism than his son. He possessed an enquiring intellect, with interests in teaching, science and the arts coupled with a deeply inbred piety. He was a correspondent of Wieland and Gellert, and was described by a friend after his death as a man of 'wit and wisdom'. It is not difficult to feel sorry for Leopold in his later life, a lonely man still living through his son, straining to flesh out the scanty news brought from Vienna by irregular letters or itinerant acquaintances.

Mozart's appearance and character

ACCOUNTS OF MOZART's early life suggest that he was an attractive and affectionate child with an engaging lack of self-consciousness. When the family visited Paris in 1766, Friedrich Melchior Grimm noted in the *Correspondance littéraire* that 'one could talk interminably about this singular phenomenon. He is, moreover, one of the most lovable of creatures imaginable, who puts wit and spirit into everything he says and does, with all the grace and sweetness of his age'. Wolfgang's sister Nannerl felt that her brother's looks were permanently impaired by the bout of smallpox he contracted in 1767. Nevertheless, three years later, the celebrated composer Hasse described the boy as 'handsome, vivacious, graceful and full of good manners; and knowing him, it is difficult to avoid loving him'.

When Mozart matured, he remained small and pale, and frequently had an unhealthy appearance. His early Bohemian biographer Niemetschek ascribed these features to lack of exercise in his childhood, and the fact that from the age of six, Mozart spent most of his time in a sitting position! The singer Michael Kelly lived in Vienna from 1783 to 1787, and took the roles of Basilio and Don Curzio in the first production of *Le nozze di Figaro*. He remembered

Mozart as 'a remarkably small man, very thin and pale, with a profusion of fine fair hair, of which he was rather vain' (Kelly, 1826). In keeping with the fashion among the younger generation, Mozart did not wear a wig but had his own hair powdered.

Mozart emerged from his extraordinary childhood surprisingly undamaged psychologically. As a musical prodigy, he had been admired by the crowned heads and highest society in Europe. His youthful buoyancy coupled with exceptional talent had permitted an intimacy with rulers and aristocrats that was quite out of proportion with his social origins. When, for example, the family had an audience with Empress Maria Theresa at Schönbrunn in 1762, Leopold described how his six-year-old son 'jumped up on the Empress's lap, put his arms round her neck and kissed her heartily'. On such occasions, Mozart wore a lilac suit and moire waistcoat trimmed with gold braid; it was a cast-off from the Archduke Maximilian. A few years later, the adolescent Mozart was treated with equal courtesy by the Princes of the Church, had audiences with cardinals and even the Pope, and became a Knight of the Golden Spur (the only musician to attain this high rank since Orlande de Lassus).

This triumphal progress was abruptly halted when he returned to the mundane musical world of Salzburg. The Prince–Archbishop Count Hieronymus Colloredo, elected in 1772, was less indulgent than his predecessor in permitting Mozart leave of absence, and the young composer was left in no doubt about his lowly status in the court. Mozart's pride was seriously hurt, and he was disgusted by his position. His distaste was expressed to Leopold in a letter written during the visit of the Archbishop's household to Vienna in 1781:

> At about 12 noon – alas, a little too early for me – we go to table – our lunch party consists of the 2 valets, body and soul attendants to His Grace; the H[err] Contrôleur; H[err] Zetti, the pastry-cook; the two H[erren] cooks; Ceccarelli, Brunetti and – my modest self – NB: the two valets sit at the head of the table – whereas I at least have the honour to be placed above the cooks. . . .

He emerged from this demeaning position with an acute sensitivity to social nuance. The somewhat prickly personality described by contemporaries can be ascribed to Mozart's tendency to interpret the mildest condescension as a personal slight. This may have been one reason why he refused to accept the status of a servant–musician in an aristocratic household in his maturity, preferring an uncertain independent career. It is also likely to have influenced his decision to remain in Vienna during the last decade of his life. The atmosphere of egalitarianism and the absence of formality promoted by Joseph II allowed talented individuals like Mozart to achieve some personal dignity despite lowly origins and lack of wealth (see Steptoe, 1982, for a fuller discussion of this issue).

Another legacy of Mozart's unusual childhood was his inability to organize his professional life and behave diplomatically with patrons and fellow-musicians. It may be that Mozart failed to realize that his successful early career was the fruit not only of his own talent, but also of Leopold's careful planning and painstaking arrangements. Consequently, the adult Mozart assumed that he would be well received for his musical abilities alone, without exerting effort to promote himself. This trait was recognized by Baron Grimm, when Mozart was in Paris as a young man:

> He is too trusting, too inactive, too easy to catch, too little intent on the means that may lead to fortune. To make an impression here one has to be artful, enterprising, daring. To make his fortune I wish he had but half of his talent and twice as much shrewdness, and then I should not worry about him.

The result was that Mozart failed to capitalize on the opportunities that were available. This was particularly obvious when he set out on concert tours as an adult. Leopold had been quite definite on how matters should be arranged, as he told his son in November 1777:

> Enquire of your landlord who is *Capellmeister* or *Music Director*, or if there isn't any, who is the *most celebrated composer*. Arrange to be taken to him or, according to the circumstances of his rank, ask him to call on you and talk to him. In that fashion you will know straight away whether the costs of a concert are great, whether one can get hold of a good harpsichord – whether one can have an orchestra, whether there are many music-lovers . . . – You should do this in your travelling clothes, without unpacking anything: just put on a couple of rings, etc.; that is all that's needed in case during your visit you should find a harpsichord and want to play it.

Yet instead of taking these precautions, Mozart frequently alienated rather than cultivated local musicians and was not able to enlist their support. When, for example, he visited the court of King Friedrich Wilhelm at Potsdam near Berlin in 1789, Mozart might have anticipated a triumphal welcome. The King was an enthusiastic amateur, the court orchestra had a high reputation, and *Die Entführung* was being successfully performed in Berlin. Unfortunately, though, Mozart did not hide his contempt for the leading resident musicians. He prepared no new compositions in advance, and was not able to mount any public concerts in Berlin. Although after some difficulty he secured an audience with the Queen, the returns from the journey were meagre.

Much has been made of Mozart's coarse and vulgar character. Certainly, his family enjoyed scatological humour of a crude kind. There are numerous instances not only in Mozart's own correspondence, but in letters from other members of his family. Here, for example, is the greeting sent from Munich by his fifty-seven-year-old mother Maria Anna to her husband Leopold:

> Ad[d]io, ben mio, stay healthy, stick your arse in your mouth. I wish you good night, shit up your bed till it bursts.

This characteristic, thought by some contemporaries to be peculiar to Salzburg, was retained by Mozart in his adult life. His behaviour alienated the fastidious tastes of many contemporaries, leading them to conclude that although Mozart was musically gifted, he was in other ways boorish and unrefined. Karoline Pichler, daughter of the senior civil servant Franz Sales von Greiner and a member of the intelligentsia in Vienna, described Mozart and Haydn as 'persons who displayed in their contacts with others absolutely no other extraordinary intellectual capacity and almost no kind of intellectual training, of scientific or higher education. . . . Silly jokes, and in the case of Mozart an irresponsible way of life, were all that they displayed to their fellow men.' She and others also recalled Mozart's abrupt changes of mood, at one moment gripped with divine musical inspiration, while a minute later acting in a facetious and ridiculous fashion. Of all contemporary observers, it was perhaps Joseph Lange who had the greatest insight into these apparent inconsistencies. Lange was an actor with the Burgtheater company, and was the husband of Aloisia Weber, Mozart's early love and the elder sister of his wife Constanze. The two families were in regular contact, and Lange's late portrait of Mozart is thought to be one of the most faithful. He suggested that Mozart's inane, immature behaviour was a by-product of the creative intensity surrounding the process of composition:

> Never was Mozart less recognizably a great man in his conversation and actions, than when he was busied with an important work. At such time he not only spoke confusedly and disconnectedly, but occasionally made jests of a nature which one did not expect of him, indeed he even deliberately forgot himself in his behaviour. . . . Either he intentionally concealed his inner tension behind superficial frivolity, for reasons which could not be fathomed, or he took delight in throwing into sharp contrast the divine ideas of his music and these sudden outbursts of vulgar platitudes, and in giving himself pleasure by seeming to make fun of himself.

This temperamental polarity was allied with another characteristic that has frequently been noted – namely, Mozart's intellectual detachment, apparent most clearly in his ability to compose despite the emotional stresses impinging on him. Eric Blom (1955) termed this the 'callousness of genius', referring particularly to the story that in 1783 Mozart worked on the D minor Quartet, K.421 (417b), while Constanze gave birth to their first child in an adjacent room. The summer of 1788 was also remarkable for the manner in which the creative effort that produced the last three symphonies, a piano trio (K.542), keyboard sonata (K.545) and other major works within the space of three months coincided with extreme financial distress, the necessity to move to cheaper lodging and the death of his six-month-old daughter Theresia (see Steptoe, 1988). However, it should not be concluded that Mozart's work was entirely untouched by his personal life, for it is clear that the composer passed through periods (such as his stay in Paris in 1778, the early months of 1787 and 1789–90) during which he was mentally depressed and unable to complete works. Whether his depression caused, or was a product of his compositional and professional difficulties, is less certain. It seems likely that he was affected by both his own state of physical health, and that of his wife Constanze. For his relationship with Constanze was one of the major factors moulding his adult life and personality.

Despite these influences, perhaps the most remarkable facet of Mozart's character was his confidence in his own creativity. One searches in vain through his correspondence or the recollections of contemporaries for any hint of doubt about the value and quality of his compositions. Even during periods of acute poverty, loneliness or illness, Mozart's exultation in the creative process and delight in his work seem to have endured.

Marriage with Constanze

MOZART'S WIFE CONSTANZE has attracted considerable opprobrium from biographers. She has been portrayed as scheming in embroiling Mozart in the first place, then unsupportive in their life together, encouraging Mozart in feckless irresponsibility rather than providing a stable family background for his work. Alfred Einstein (1945) put it thus:

> She was not even a good housewife. She never looked ahead, and instead of making her husband's life and work easier by providing him with external comforts she thoughtlessly shared the bohemianism of his way of living. . . . She was wholly uneducated, and had no sense of the fitness of things.

Similar views were expressed by Hildesheimer (1977), who in addition suspected Constanze of a liaison with Mozart's pupil Süssmayr (a suspicion without foundation in fact, as Eibl, 1976, has demonstrated). Reading these comments, one has the impression that the writers do not simply object to Constanze, but resent the fact that Mozart deemed any woman worthy of his affection and companionship (for a rebuttal of these views, see Landon, 1988).

What does seem probable is that Mozart was to some extent manoeuvred into marriage with Constanze Weber by her mother. Mozart had been intimate with the Weber family during his stay in Mannheim in 1777–8, and fell in love with the second daughter, Aloisia. He travelled on to Paris seemingly confident that she returned his affection, and was bitterly disappointed by her indifference when they met again towards the end of the year. She was by this time a successful singer in Munich, and when she was engaged for the German Opera in Vienna in 1779, the entire family migrated to the capital. There she married the actor Joseph Lange, whose first wife Anna Maria Schindler had also been a member of the opera company. Although it has been asserted that Mozart retained his love for Aloisia for the rest of his life (Hildesheimer described her as 'the prima donna in life as on stage'), there is no evidence that this was the case. He and Constanze remained close to Aloisia and Joseph Lange throughout their years in Vienna, and Mozart worked with Aloisia on a number of musical projects without apparent heartache.

When Mozart broke with the Salzburg retinue in June 1781, he sought refuge in the widowed Frau Weber's house, and it was here that he became attached to Constanze, the third daughter. He became committed to such an extent that in December he was accused by Constanze's guardian of compromising her honour. Although Mozart denied this, he drew up a document stating that he would either marry Constanze within three years or pay her an annuity of 300 fl. Leopold Mozart's response to these disclosures has not been preserved, but he certainly opposed the union vigorously.

Despite this imbroglio, and the fact that Frau Weber was doubtless pleased to have matched her daughter with the promising young musician, Mozart's affection for Constanze seems to have been sincere and profound. Admittedly, the description of his future wife that he gave Leopold was not flattering:

> She is not ugly, but also far from beautiful. – Her whole beauty consists in two little black eyes and a pretty figure. She has no wit, but enough common sense to enable her to fulfil her duties as wife and mother ... – She understands housekeeping, and has the best heart in the world. ... (letter of 15 December 1781)

Mozart was deliberately emphasizing those aspects that he knew would appeal to Leopold, so as to appear not to have succumbed to superficial charms. In his correspondence with Constanze herself, Mozart wrote with intimate playfulness:

> If I could tell you everything I do with your dear *portrait*, you would often laugh. – For example, when I take it out of its cover, I say: 'God greet you, Stanzerl! – God greet you, God greet you; – little rascal; – pussy-kitty; – little turned-up nose – little bagatelle – schluck und druck!' – and when I put it back again, I let it slip in bit by bit, and always say, 'Stu! – Stu! – Stu!' but with that *certain emphasis* which such an important word requires; and at the very end, 'good night, little mouse, sleep well'. (letter of 13 April 1789)

Mozart became deeply reliant on Constanze, and was lonely and indecisive when away from her. There is no doubt either about his sexual passion for her:

> On the 1st of June I shall sleep in Prague, and the 3th: – the 4th? *With my darling little wife*: prepare your dear and loveliest nest very daintily, for my little piece has really earned it, he has behaved very well and wants only to possess your loveliest [...]. Imagine that rascal, as I am writing he is crawling on the table and looks at me questioningly, but I smack him down properly – that chap is still [raging] and I can hardly keep that villain in his place. (letter of 23 May 1789; the passages marked [   ] were deleted by Constanze or another hand)

The couple married in the summer of 1782, and between 1783 and 1791 Constanze gave birth six times. The contentment of their 'companionate marriage' and life together is illustrated by the comments of a Danish actor, Joachim Preisler, who visited Mozart one Sunday afternoon in August 1788:

> There I had the happiest hour of music that has ever fallen to my lot. This small man and great master twice extemporized on a pedal pianoforte, so wonderfully! so wonderfully! that I quite lost myself. He intertwined the most difficult passages with the most lovely themes. – His wife cut quill-pens for the copyist, a pupil composed, a little boy aged four walked about in the garden and sang recitatives – in short, everything that surrounded this splendid man was musical!

Mozart's emotional attachment to Constanze had another, less appealing feature. He transferred his acute concern for social proprieties and sensitivity about appearances to Constanze, and came to identify his personal honour with her actions. Constanze suffered a series of illnesses over the later years of Mozart's life, and from 1789 to 1791 spent several weeks at Baden, a spa near Vienna. Mozart's letters to her blend tender concern for her health with admonishments about her behaviour:

> Dearest little wife, I have many requests to make to you:
> 1 Please do not be sad;
> 2 Be careful of *your health* and *do not trust* the spring air;
> 3 That you do not go out alone, on foot – but preferably – do not *go out on foot at all*;
> 4 That you should be assured of my love; – I have not written a single letter to you without placing your dear portrait in front of me.
> 5 Please conduct yourself so as to take into consideration *your* and *my honour*, but also consider *appearances*.
> (letter of 16 April 1789)

The notion that Constanze was capricious and irresponsible is difficult to reconcile with her firm, businesslike organization of the family's affairs in later years. She was able to secure a state pension, even though Mozart's period of imperial service was not long enough for any entitlement. Over the decade following Mozart's death, she shrewdly collected and sold his remaining manuscripts in order to provide an income. She thereby avoided the extreme poverty that was all too common among families in the 18th century that had lost their main financial resource.

Mozart's social world

MOZART HAD AN EXTENSIVE acquaintance from many layers of society, ranging from the higher aristocracy to the humble shopkeeper and servant musician. That the spheres overlapped to an extent perhaps surprising in such an hierarchical social world was the result in part of the influence of freemasonry, and in part of the special privileges enjoyed by artists. Nevertheless, Mozart's social life can perhaps be divided into three elements: his relations with the nobility, associations with composers, and friendships with other men and women.

Plates 1–15

THE PORTRAITS

MOST OF THE KNOWN, authentic portraits of Mozart were made by artists of the second rank. No Hudson (Handel) or Hoppner (Haydn) graces these pages. The greatest and most poetic Mozart portrait is that by his brother-in-law Joseph Lange (15), but perhaps the most accurate likeness is the posthumous portrait by Barbara Krafft (10) – using *inter alia* a lost authentic miniature. That miniature may be identical with an earlier, smaller Lange painting of 1782, now lost; we have reproduced the frequently overlooked lithograph from Nissen's biography of 1828, which is presumed to have been made from the latter (12). The newly discovered 'Rosenthal' portrait (1) is curiously impressive, as is that by Doris Stock (14).

The plaster medallion by Leonard Posch (13) is one of many variants of that artist's work. Some have been included in Landon, 1988 and 1989; all except two (Hummel, Goethe Archives; La Scala Museum) are to be found in Deutsch, 1961a.

The well-known family portrait by Johann Nepomuk della Croce (9) of 1780–81 also seems to offer us realistic likenesses of the four figures (Mozart's mother, having died in Paris in 1778, is put into a picture hanging on the wall).

It should be stressed that in later life, when he moved to Vienna, Mozart liked to wear his own hair and had it dressed by a *friseur*. This modern fashion may be seen in (1) and (11–15).

There is, in addition, an appallingly large quantity of doubtful and spurious Mozart portraits, which may be studied in an appendix of Deutsch's book mentioned above.

H.C.R.L.

A new portrait of Mozart?

THE NOTORIOUS 'ANHANG' (Appendix) in Deutsch, 1961a, listing and reproducing all known 'supposedly authentic portraits' of Mozart, as well as the 'unauthentic portraits', is a salutary reminder that the discovery of hitherto unknown portraits of the composer rarely, if ever, passes the test of strict historical and art-historical investigation.

Nevertheless, a previously unknown original 18th-century profile drawing (reproduced opposite) deserves attention for its extraordinary likeness to what we perceive to be Mozart's features. The silverpoint drawing in the possession of the writer was sold at an Antiquarian Book Fair in Stuttgart in the early 1970s by the Joseph Fach Gallery of Frankfurt am Main, specialists in graphics and 16th- to 20th-century drawings. It had been found in the old Frankfurt Collection of old-master drawings assembled by Graf von Graimberg (1774–1865),

which had remained untouched and unknown until it was purchased, and its contents sold singly by its purchaser. The drawing was labelled by Joseph Fach 'German. Portrait of W.A. Mozart'.

The very strong resemblance to the small number of authentic portraits of Mozart of the 1780s is obvious. In the absence of corroborative evidence, the portrait is herewith presented for further study and discussion.

It does not appear to be a copy of any known effigy of Mozart: its vividness and precise duct make it likely that it is a drawing made from life. There is no reference to a sitting in Mozart's letters. The most likely period would be his visit to Frankfurt in September to December 1790, during which he also visited Mainz. This date would fit the paper and watermark, the style, and the costume of the sitter. The shading of the surround, with its rectangularly defined edges, could suggest that the drawing was intended to be engraved, though no engraving of it is known.

The features of the sitter should be compared with the drawing by Doris Stock (1789), with the painting by Joseph Lange (15), as well as with the several wax, plaster, and wood reliefs by, or after, Leonard Posch, the engraved version of the latter by Georg Mansfeld, and one by Klemens Kohl (1793). Another portrait by Lange is important for comparison with the present one: the lithograph in Nissen's 1828 biography of Mozart (12), which was specially favoured as a good likeness by Constanze. Deutsch refers to it thus: 'A smaller version, now lost, of the [earlier] painting by Joseph Lange seems to have been sent by Mozart to his father on 3 April 1783 . . . The lithograph in Nissen's biography was probably made from this smaller version.'

Several scholars who have examined the present portrait have, with varying emphasis, accepted it as most likely to be a portrait of Mozart. The art-historian Dr Erwin Rosenthal asked more cautiously: 'could Mozart have had a double?' The late Dr Joseph Heinz Eibl, the eminent specialist in Mozart iconography who was at work on a volume of Addenda and Corrigenda to Deutsch's NMA volume, wrote in 1981: 'I agree with you that the drawing is much more likely to be an effigy of Mozart than the numerous supposed portraits and the undoubtedly spurious ones. In my opinion there is quite definitely a strong likeness, indeed an identity of details with the drawing of Doris Stock (mouth and chin!). It seems to me to be essential to put the drawing up for discussion.'

The 'artist remains to be identified. May the publication of this portrait in *The Mozart Compendium* lead to the clarification of yet another Mozart mystery!

ALBI ROSENTHAL

1 The anonymous 'Rosenthal' portrait

2 Pietro Antonio Lorenzoni, Mozart as a boy, 1763, oil painting

3 Louis Carrogis de Carmontelle, Leopold Mozart with Wolfgang and Nannerl, November 1763, watercolour

4 Michel Barthélemy Ollivier, Tea at Prince Louis-François de Conti's residence in the 'Temple', summer 1766, oil painting

5 Saverio della Rosa, Mozart in Verona, January 1770, oil painting

6 Anonymous miniature of Mozart on ivory, ?1773

7 Anonymous miniature of Mozart on ivory, autumn 1777

8 Anonymous, Mozart as Knight of the Golden Spur, 1777, oil painting

9 Johann Nepomuk della Croce, Mozart family portrait, winter 1780–81, oil painting

10   Barbara Krafft, oil painting of Mozart, 1819

Wolfg: Amade Mozart

11 Hieronymus Löschenkohl, silhouette of Mozart, 1785, engraving

12 Joseph Lange, lithograph made probably from lost portrait of 1782

Mozart

13   Leonard Posch, plaster
medallion of Mozart, 1788/9

14   Doris Stock, drawing of Mozart,
April 1789, silverpoint

15 Joseph Lange, Mozart at the pianoforte, 1789/90

Nobility

As soon as Mozart arrived in Vienna in 1781, he was taken up by a number of patrons from the nobility. The first was *Countess Wilhelmine Thun*, the wife of Count Franz Joseph Thun. She was a former pupil of Haydn, later to be a supporter of Beethoven, and was regarded as one of the most cultivated ladies of Vienna. Mozart was captivated by her as early as March 1781:

> I've lunched twice already at Countess Thun's and go there almost every day – that's the most charming, dearest lady I ever saw in my life; and she entertains a high opinion of me too. Her husband is still the same odd but well-intentioned and honourable gentleman.

Countess Thun was quite innocently one of the causes of Mozart's decision to leave Archbishop Colloredo's service. In April 1781, Mozart was obliged to play at a concert for the Archbishop on the same night that Countess Thun had invited him to perform at her residence. To his chagrin, he discovered not only that the Emperor was present at the rival event, but that the performers had each received 50 ducats or 225 fl (equivalent to half his annual salary in Salzburg). Mozart had high regard for the Countess's musical taste, and played each act of *Die Entführung* to her as it was completed. She was the mother of three beautiful daughters, one of whom married Karl Lichnowsky, who was later to be Beethoven's friend and patron. Lichnowsky took piano lessons from Mozart, and later accompanied the composer on his journey to Prussia in 1789.

A second early patron was *Countess Marie Thiennes de Rumbeke*, who was Mozart's first pupil in Vienna. Mozart dedicated a set of keyboard variations to her in 1781, and frequented her house. More importantly, she was related to *Philipp Cobenzl*, a distinguished politician who held a series of influential posts within the Habsburg government, as well as being a member of the most intimate coterie surrounding Emperor Joseph. In the summer of 1781, Mozart went to stay at Cobenzl's estate on the Reisenberg near Vienna, where he commented enthusiastically on his rural surroundings. Cobenzl was a radical within the hierarchy, later admitting that he had even lost his religious faith at one time. Mozart's association with such people inevitably encouraged his development towards Enlightenment opinion.

Although Mozart was favoured by these nobles, it was clear that they were patrons rather than friends. In numerous letters to Leopold, Mozart excuses himself for failing to fulfil some promise on the grounds that he was called away by a message from one of these families (an explanation that was bound to appeal to its recipient). For Mozart each such invitation was in the nature of a ukase rather than a request. A few years later, Mozart developed bonds of genuine friendship with members of the younger generation of nobility. *Karl Lichnowsky* was one instance, and another was *August von Hatzfeld*. He was an exact contemporary of Mozart, and was the son of Count Karl von Hatzfeld, who played a prominent role in the financial and bureaucratic reforms of Maria Theresa and Joseph II. August was a violinist and studied with Mozart. He was involved in the private performance of *Idomeneo* that was mounted in 1786 at the private theatre of Prince Auersperg, at which his sister-in-law Countess Hortense Hatzfeld played the part of Elettra. He died a year later.

Gottfried von Jacquin was another young friend from the nobility, and the recipient of the famous letters from Prague in which Mozart described the reception of *Le nozze di Figaro* and *Don Giovanni*. He was the son of Baron Nikolaus von Jacquin, a celebrated botanist, and was also a competent musician. But perhaps the most loyal of all Mozart's acquaintances in the nobility was *Gottfried, Baron van Swieten*. Van Swieten (1733–1803) was the son of Maria Theresa's physician, and held a number of important diplomatic posts before becoming president of the Commission for Education and Censorship in 1781. In this position, he was instrumental in liberalizing, publishing and propagating enlightened views during most of Joseph II's reign. Van Swieten was himself a composer, and had a symphony performed at Mozart's Augarten concert in May 1782, when the C major Symphony (K.338) and E♭ Double Concerto, K.365 (316a), were also performed. He was devoted to the music of the early part of the century, and commissioned Mozart to produced four adaptations of Handel's works, beginning with *Acis and Galatea* in 1788. It is probable that as early as 1783, Mozart was familiarizing himself with the fugal styles developed in the first half of the century in preparation for Van Swieten's concerts, and that this interest of the Baron's influenced his own late work (see Tyson, 1987). After Mozart's death, Van Swieten supported his bereaved family, promoting the first performance of the Requiem in January 1793 for the benefit of Constanze. He is also said to have been one of the few witnesses to Mozart's funeral in St Stephen's Cathedral.

Composers

As was mentioned earlier, Mozart's relations with musicians were often uneasy. He was not slow to express his low opinion of the compositions or performances of others – as when he lambasted the music of Georg Vogler of Mannheim, or dismissed the virtuoso Muzio Clementi as a 'mere mechanicus'. On occasion, fellow musicians resented Mozart's youthful facility, and tended to underestimate his talents. This is how Mozart described his reception by the celebrated Mannheim orchestra in 1777:

> Some who know me by reputation were very civil and full of respect; but others, who had never heard anything of me, stared at me with round eyes, but in a certain sneering way. They think that because I am small and young, nothing great or mature is within me; but they will soon see. (letter of 31 October 1777)

The musical establishment in Salzburg was small and parochial. Throughout most of Mozart's childhood and adolescence the Kapellmeister was Giuseppe Francesco Lolli, with Leopold

Mozart being his deputy. Salzburg's most influential figure was *Michael Haydn* (1737–1806), who settled there when Mozart was six years old, and married the daughter of the court organist. Leopold privately regarded him as lazy and uncultivated, while admiring him as a composer. Nevertheless, the two families were on friendly terms, although a temporary bitterness arose when Haydn was appointed organist to the Dreifaltigkeitskirche (a position that Leopold Mozart considered to be due to his son).

Mozart of course came into contact with many of the leading musical figures of the day during his early travels. One to whom he seems to have become particularly attached was *Johann Christian Bach* (the London Bach). They first met in London during 1764–5, and Mozart was delighted to renew the acquaintance in the summer of 1778, when he was living alone in Paris shortly after the death of his mother. As Mozart told his father:

> . . . His joy, and my joy, when we saw each other again, you can easily imagine – perhaps his joy is not quite so sincere – but one must admit that he is an honourable man, and treats others with fairness. (letter of 27 August 1778)

Mozart also established warm friendships in Mannheim during his visit in 1777–8. It was here that he became acquainted not only with the Weber family, but with Kapellmeister *Christian Cannabich* and the composer *Ignaz Holzbauer*. Mozart and his mother dined regularly with Cannabich and his family, and Mozart composed a piano sonata for his daughter Rosa: K.309 (284b). Holzbauer was a composer of some distinction, achieving the high point of his career with the opera *Günther von Schwarzburg* in 1777. Mozart praised the work highly:

> Holzbauer's music is very beautiful. The poetry doesn't deserve such music. What surprises me most is that such an old man, as Holzbauer is, should still have such spirit; for it's unbelievable what fire there is in the music. (letter of 14 November 1777)

When Mozart moved to Vienna in 1781, the musical taste of the court was dominated by Italians. *Gluck* lived in semi-retirement, with a post at court that was more honorary than functional. He was complimentary of Mozart's operas, and dined with the younger composer more than once. The Kapellmeister was Giuseppe Bonno, while *Antonio Salieri* was a favourite of the Emperor and the dominant figure at the Italian Opera. There is only a modest foundation for the notion that Salieri was the *éminence grise* of Mozart's life. Certainly Mozart was suspicious of Salieri's machinations, believing that the Italian had foiled his attempt to become teacher to Princess Elisabeth of Württemberg, and had also tried to undermine the production of *Le nozze di Figaro*. As late as December 1789, Mozart promised to inform his friend Michael Puchberg of Salieri's designs against *Così fan tutte*:

> Then I'll tell you about all the cabals of Salieri, which however came to nothing. (letter of 29 December 1789)

Yet late in his life, Mozart apparently changed his opinion of Salieri. He invited the Italian, and his mistress, the singer Catarina Cavalieri, to *Die Zauberflöte* in October 1791, and was delighted by their reaction, as Constanze was informed the day after:

> You can't believe how nice both of them were, – how much they liked not only my music but the book and everything together. – They both said it was a grand opera. – worthy of being performed at the greatest festival for the greatest monarchs, – and they will certainly see it often, for they have never seen a more beautiful or pleasant production. – He listened and looked with the greatest attention and from the Overture to the last chorus there wasn't a piece which didn't call forth a 'bravo' or 'bello' . . . . (letter dated 14 October 1791)

Salieri also conducted several of Mozart's religious works during the coronation celebrations for Leopold II in Prague in 1791, seemingly having enough respect for the younger man to give him considerable prominence on this important occasion.

Mozart also made the acquaintance of other Italian opera composers as they passed through Vienna, including Giovanni Paisiello and Giuseppe Sarti. He seems nevertheless to have been more at home with composers and musicians of native extraction. Many of them were resident at aristocratic households in the country, and only came to Vienna for short periods each year. The most important friend of this kind was *Joseph Haydn*, who regularly met and played music with Mozart when he visited Vienna in the Esterházy suite. The tenor Michael Kelly described one such quartet party, held at the lodgings of Stephen Storace, the Anglo-Italian composer and brother of soprano Nancy Storace. The string quartet was made up of Haydn, Dittersdorf, the composer Johann Baptist Vanhal and Mozart. It was on an occasion of this type in February 1785 that Haydn heard three of Mozart's new quartets (K.458, 464 and 465), prompting him to make his famous remark to Leopold Mozart:

> I tell you before God, and as an honest man, that your son is the greatest composer I know, either personally or by reputation: he has taste and moreover the greatest possible knowledge of the science of composition. (letter from Leopold Mozart to his daughter of 16 February 1785)

Haydn last saw Mozart late in 1790, just before he left Vienna at Salomon's invitation to travel to London. Haydn later reported that Mozart was convinced that the two would never meet again; he attributed this remark to Mozart's concern about his relatively advanced age, rather than any premonitions of an early grave for Mozart himself.

Other friendships
Information concerning Mozart's friendships outside the circles of the nobility and musicians is unfortunately sparse, although as Eisen (1986) has pointed out, there is every reason to hope that additional information will surface as 18th-century archives are

investigated more thoroughly. It would seem, however, that Mozart's social life revolved around two groups – the class of merchants, professionals and higher civil servants in Vienna, and the companies of actors and singers working in the city.

The first group overlapped with the 'enlightened' section of the nobility, since many of the latter identified themselves with the mercantile virtues of thrift and hard work. Mozart's friendships stemmed initially from his activities as a keyboard teacher. One of his early pupils was *Josepha Auernhammer*, daughter of Councillor Johann Auernhammer. Although Mozart found her physically unappealing, he was impressed with her playing, and wrote the Sonata for Two Pianos, K.448 (375a) to perform with her at a concert at her father's house in November 1781. A few years later, *Therese von Trattner* became a pupil. She was the wife of *Johann von Trattner*, a self-made man who rose to the nobility through building a vast printing and papermaking empire centred on the Trattnerhof in the Graben. Mozart and Constanze rented an apartment in the Trattnerhof in 1784, and their friendly association with the Trattners seems to have continued for many years, with Johann standing godfather to three of their children.

Michael Puchberg had a similar background to Trattner, since he too rose from humble origins, marrying the widow of his employer in the textile industry. He was to play a prominent role in Mozart's life, since the composer frequently turned to him for small loans when in financial straits during his later years in Vienna.

Among the professional group associated with Mozart one can place such people as *Sigmund Barisani*, the son of Archbishop Colloredo's physician Silvester Barisani, and himself a doctor. Mozart also had contacts with the celebrated *Mesmer family* (see Steptoe, 1986). The link was probably first established in 1767–9 during the Mozarts' lengthy stay in Vienna, sometime before Franz Anton Mesmer had discovered the 'magnetic' cure that was to make him famous. Mesmer had married a rich widow, Frau Anna Maria von Posch, and they lived in a mansion in the Landstrasse suburb. Mozart spent much of his time there during his visit to the capital in 1773. However, by the time Mozart moved to Vienna for good in 1781, Mesmer had abandoned his family and set up his notorious practice in Paris. Consequently, Mozart found the Landstrasse household very subdued, as he told his sister:

> Concerning our old acquaintances I have to tell you that I've only gone out once to Frau von Mesmer's. The house is not what it once was. (letter of 15 December 1781)

He nevertheless maintained links with Mesmer's cousin Joseph, director of the Normalschule in Vienna who was a keen musician and friend of Gluck and Haydn.

Mozart was passionate about the theatre, and derived great pleasure not only from music but from spoken plays (see 'Mozart and the Theatre of his Time', pp. 357–8). Soon after his arrival in Vienna in 1781 he told his sister Nannerl:

> My only amusement is the theatre. I wish you could see a tragedy here: I know of no other theatre where all genres are *excellently* performed; but here it is the case with every role, the lowliest and poorest role is well done, and the cast doubled [in case of illness]. (letter of 4 July 1781)

The most prestigious theatre company shared the stage with the opera at the Burgtheater, and Mozart's friendships presumably emerged through his professional activities and his family connection with *Joseph Lange*. Lange was one of the leading players, taking heroic roles such as Hamlet and Prince Hal in *Henry IV*, as well as romantic leads in popular comedies such as *The West Indian* and *School for Scandal*. The other important players were *Johann Müller* (a former director of the Singspiel at the Burgtheater), *Gottlieb Stephanie* (librettist of *Die Entführung*) and his brother Christian, and for a period in the early 1780s, *Friedrich Schröder*. Schröder is sometimes known as the 'German Garrick', and was the most celebrated actor of the era, influential in introducing Shakespeare to the German stage. He remained a champion of Mozart's work when he moved to northern Germany later in the decade, producing a translation of *Don Giovanni* that was performed in Hamburg and Berlin.

Mozart's friendly relations with this group are documented as early as 1783, when he devised a Masquerade, K.446 (416d), for presentation during a carnival ball at the Redoutensaal. Mozart played Harlequin, Joseph Lange Pierrot and Aloisia Lange Columbine, with verses written by Müller. Two years later, Leopold Mozart's visit to Vienna was marked by dinners at the apartments of Müller, Gottlieb Stephanie, Lange and Trattner. It should not be overlooked that many of these people were also freemasons: Lange and Mozart's publisher Artaria belonged to the Craft, as did nobles such as Von Jacquin and Count Joseph Thun.

This group had close links with the singers in the Italian Opera company and with local musicians. Mozart's particular friends in this group included the sopranos *Nancy Storace* and *Josepha Duschek* and the instrumentalists *Anton Stadler* and *Joseph Leutgeb*. Nancy Storace was a young singer of mixed English and Italian parentage who came to Vienna in 1783 aged eighteen, remaining until 1787. She created the role of Susanna in *Le nozze di Figaro*, and Mozart dedicated the scena and rondo *Ch'io mi scordi di te – Non temer, amato bene* (K.505) to 'Mlle Storace und mich'. Josepha Duschek was based in Prague, where her husband *Franz Xaver Duschek* was a pianist and composer. Mozart first wrote an aria (K.272) for her in 1777 when she visited Salzburg, and the scena *Bella mia fiamma – Resta, o cara* (K.528) was composed with her voice in mind. Mozart stayed at the Duscheks' country house (the Villa Bertramka) at Smichov near Prague on a number of occasions when he was in Bohemia.

Both Stadler and Leutgeb were instrumental virtuosi. Mozart wrote the Clarinet Concerto and Quintet for Stadler, and the Serenade for thirteen instruments, K.361 (370a), was performed at

Stadler's benefit concert at the Burgtheater in 1784. Stadler has been dismissed as a scoundrel by many Mozart biographers, mainly because he borrowed money from the composer which he failed to repay. Mozart treated him with amused tolerance, but regarded the horn player Leutgeb as a buffoon. Leutgeb had been a member of the Salzburg orchestra before moving to Vienna to become involved in the cheese and sausage business of his wife's family. The four horn concertos were written for Leutgeb: one of the manuscripts is famed for the rude and facetious marginal comments and another for the different colours of ink with which Mozart teased the performer.

In his last years, Mozart's acquaintance in the theatrical world expanded to include the group surrounding *Emanuel Schikaneder*. Mozart had probably known Schikaneder since the late 1770s, when the impresario brought his troupe to Salzburg (see Heartz, 1983). Schikaneder was based not at the prestigious Burgtheater, but in the Theater auf der Wieden (Freihaustheater) in a working-class suburb of the city. He was of course the author of the text of *Die Zauberflöte*, and Mozart became more friendly during 1791 not only with him, but with *Benedikt Schack* and *Franz Xaver Gerl* (the first Tamino and Sarastro).

As might be expected, the social activities outside music and the theatre that Mozart enjoyed were typical of the urban bourgeoisie. Dancing, visiting the Prater, and playing billiards were all favoured pastimes of the composer, as was drinking punch. It is interesting in this respect to note that rates of alcohol consumption were very high in Mozart's time; in Vienna, it has been estimated that adults drank on average about half a gallon of wine per day (Dickson, 1987).

Mozart's income and finances

WHEN MOZART WAS A CHILD, his father Leopold was in charge of all practical matters, including the financial affairs of the family. The journeys through Europe in the 1760s and 1770s involved considerable outlay in terms of clothes and travel expenses, not to mention the loss of Leopold's salary, so they were frequently obliged to take out loans or rely on credit. Leopold was precise in financial as in other matters, and kept detailed records. Thus when Wolfgang was in Mannheim in 1777 projecting a journey through Belgium, Leopold was able to inform him of the exact cost of a lunch that the family had eaten at an inn in Louvain some fourteen years previously! Despite this care, the early concert tours did not generate great profits, so the Mozart family remained on the margin, with ambitions that frequently outstripped their modest resources.

Given this obsessional streak to Leopold's character, it is no surprise that he should react with such exasperation to his son's cavalier attitude to life and the pursuit of wealth. Leopold outlined his view of his son in a famous letter to the Countess Waldstätten:

... He is far too *tolerant* or *indolent*, too easy-going, perhaps sometimes too *proud* .... If he lacks for nothing, then he is at once satisfied and becomes *easy-going* and *lazy*. If he is forced into activity, he then bestirs himself and *wants to make his fortune at once*. (letter of 23 August 1782)

Leopold, however, was a salaried court musician with a reliable (though small) income. His perspective did not take account of the fact that his son's position in society was quite different. Mozart spent most of his adult life as an independent performer and composer without a fixed income. Moreover, he had a family to support, and elected to live in an expensive city. It was in the nature of this position that his earnings should be piecemeal, and that there was an element of uncertainty in his survival. Taking these factors into account, it can be seen that Mozart was relatively successful in his chosen path.

Mozart's income in his maturity derived from four principal sources (for more detailed accounts, see Bär, 1978, and Steptoe, 1984). Most important was the money he earned from performing in concerts and at the palaces of the nobility. Mozart was immensely popular during the first few years of his residence in Vienna, and was constantly in demand. The busiest time of year was Lent, since the theatres were closed and society turned more than ever to music. For several years, Mozart mounted orchestral concerts for his own benefit at the Burgtheater and elsewhere, the profits from which would typically have been in the range of 500–1,500 fl. His appearances for the nobility were so frequent that few details have survived. However, during March 1784 he listed his exhausting schedule for his father in a letter. Each week, he played on Monday and Friday nights at the palace of Count Johann Esterházy, on Thursdays at Prince Dmitry Galitzin's residence, and on Saturdays at the house of Georg Richter. In addition, he mounted three concerts, entrance for which was by subscription, and two concerts in the theatre.

Little is known about the payments Mozart received from the nobility, although on special occasions the gains were considerable. Thus when he took part in the piano joust with Muzio Clementi in 1781, he was given 50 ducats (225 fl). His high earnings certainly enabled him to marry, buy expensive items such as the modern fortepiano that cost 900 fl, and live in considerable style. Unfortunately his popularity as a pianist waned in the middle of the 1780s, and he was therefore obliged to fall back on other resources.

Piano and composition lessons provided a more reliable income. Early in his Vienna period, Mozart taught three or four pupils each day, with lessons taking up most of the morning hours. Many of his pupils were from the nobility or wealthy merchant classes, and would have several lessons a week. Mozart charged 6 ducats (27 fl) per month, but probably gave lessons for only part of the year, since most of society moved out of Vienna in the summer. One can only sympathize with the stultifying boredom of teaching amateurs, who were unlikely even to have practised between lessons, day in and day out. Lessons took valuable time away from composition, so that there may have been periods when Mozart preferred to forgo his fees for the pleasure of a less rigorous timetable. During the years in which he did teach, it is probable that Mozart received some 400–500 florins from his pupils.

His third important source of income was the payment he received for his compositions. Although concertos and symphonies were generally written for his own concerts, most of the chamber works were composed with publication in mind, since there was an insatiable demand for modern pieces suitable for domestic performance. For exceptional works the fees were high, such as the 450 fl the publisher Artaria gave for the six 'Haydn' quartets, but most of the payments were modest. The one class of composition from which large amounts could regularly be earned was opera. Composers were generally paid a flat fee for operas by the commissioning opera house, rather than a royalty, depending on the success of the work. Mozart earned 450 fl each for *Die Entführung*, *Le nozze di Figaro* and *La clemenza di Tito*, and rather more for *Don Giovanni*, *Così fan tutte* and *Die Zauberflöte*. Further profits were to be had if an astute composer made arrangements of popular operatic numbers for chamber ensemble, keyboard or wind band. Opera therefore compensated to some extent for the reduction in revenue from Mozart's public performances as a pianist.

The final regular supplement to his finances began in December 1787 with his appointment as imperial *Kammermusicus*. Since his departure from the Salzburg suite in 1781, Mozart had received no regular salary. Although the stipend of 800 fl was a great deal less than the 2,000 fl paid to the previous incumbent (Gluck), the obligations of the post were modest. Indeed, after Mozart's death, the position was abolished as being superfluous to the needs of the imperial household.

This brief survey of Mozart's finances suggests that for most of his years in Vienna he enjoyed a relatively comfortable annual income of somewhere between 2,000 and 6,000 fl. This level of earnings placed him moderately high in the economic hierarchy detailed on pp. 63–5. However, it is also true that he endured many episodes of acute shortage, to which the begging letters to fellow-mason Michael Puchberg bear eloquent testimony. Several commentators have concluded that such a state of affairs could only have arisen from extravagance or serious financial mismanagement, but two other factors were probably responsible. The first is that Mozart and Constanze moved in wealthy circles in an expensive city. Secondly, most of Mozart's revenue depended on his health and creative vigour. If he did not compose, teach or perform, no money would come in. The deterioration in his own health and preoccupation with Constanze's illnesses in the late 1780s may have brought about financial crises that could only be relieved by loans. These problems were transient, and when Mozart died his debts were modest. Mozart's reliance on his own efforts was the price he paid for an independent urban existence, outside the patronage of a single aristocratic or royal household.

Mozart as a performer

MOZART WAS KNOWN by his contemporaries as much as a virtuoso performer as a composer. In the course of his childhood travels, he astonished audiences throughout Europe by the dexterity of his piano playing, while the depth of his musical understanding was appreciated by connoisseurs. During this early period, he also performed on the violin and sang. The violin always took second place to the keyboard, and later he confined his string playing to private chamber concerts. The programmes for his early concerts indicate the way in which he was expected to display his talent. For example, the plan for his concert at the Teatro Scientifico in Mantua in 1770 included not only his own compositions but a concerto for harpsichord 'presented and performed by him at sight', a 'sonata for harpsichord performed at sight by the youth and variations of his invention extemporized and subsequently repeated in a key other than that in which it was written', a sonata and a fugue to be composed and performed on a theme provided extempore, and other prodigious feats. He also planned to sing one piece and improvise the violin part of a trio.

Despite the meretricious nature of this programme, it does point to the structure of Mozart's later concerts, almost all of which included not only works of his own composition but also improvisations. The benefit concert he promoted at the Burg-theater in March 1783 is typical. It included the *Haffner* Symphony (K.385), the piano concertos in D major (K.175) and C major (K.415/387b) and improvised solo variations and a fugue. Interspersed were arias or scenas sung by his friends Aloisia Lange, Therese Teyber and the tenor Adamberger. A later news report stated that the two concertos and 'other fantasies' were received with the loudest applause.

Mozart's keyboard style is best illustrated by his piano sonatas and concertos, most of which he wrote for his own use. More tantalizing are his improvisations, since these were particularly admired by contemporaries. The majority of reports that have survived are frustratingly vague and eulogistic, fulsome in their admiration without providing many particulars. However, Mozart's early biographer Niemetschek pinpointed the sensitivity and grace of his playing combined with great technical proficiency:

> His admirable dexterity, which particularly in the left hand and the bass were considered quite unique, his feeling and delicacy, and beautiful expression, . . . were the attractions of his playing, which together with his abundant ideas and his knowledge of composition must have enthralled every listener and made Mozart the greatest pianist of his time. (Niemetschek, 1798)

This view is echoed by Muzio Clementi, who had an opportunity to study Mozart's playing from the viewpoint of a professional when the skills of the two men were pitted against each other in the presence of Joseph II and the Grand Duchess Maria Feodorovna of Russia in 1781. Clementi later admitted to a pupil that:

> Until then I had never heard anyone perform with such spirit and grace. I was particularly astonished by an Adagio and some of his extemporized variations. (Plantinga, 1977)

The cadenzas Mozart wrote for his piano concertos perhaps come closest to reflecting his improvisatory style. The balance and coherent structure of his improvisations led some listeners to doubt that they were really invented extempore. The Abbé Maximilian Stadler, a friend of both Mozart and Haydn, later recalled how these reservations were once brought to the test:

> His improvisations were as well-ordered as if he had had them lying written out before him. This led several to think that, when he performed an improvisation in public, he must have thought everything out, and practised it, beforehand. Albrechtsberger (the composer and organist) thought so too. But one evening they met at a musical soirée; Mozart was in a good mood and demanded a theme of Albrechtsberger. The latter played him an old German popular song. – Mozart sat down and improvised on this theme for an hour in such a way as to excite general admiration and shew by means of variations and fugues (in which he never departed from the theme) that he was master of every aspect of the musician's art.

Mozart was almost as adept on the organ as the harpsichord or fortepiano, even though he had fewer opportunities to practise or display his skill. In a letter written to Leopold in 1777, Mozart described how he played the organ in the court chapel at Mannheim during a Sunday service attended by the Elector Karl Theodor:

> I entered during the Kyrie and played the end of it; and after the priest had intoned the Gloria, I played a cadenza. Because this was all so different from what they are accustomed to here, they all turned round. . . . The people had enough to amuse them. Now and then was a pizzicato, and each time I just brushed the keys. I was in the best of spirits. Instead of the Benedictus [the organist] has to play throughout. I took the subject of the Sanctus and treated it as a fugue. Everybody stood there and stared. The pedal is different from ours; that put me off at first, but I soon understood how it worked. (letter of 13 November 1777)

The impression that lingers is the sheer enjoyment Mozart had in playing, and the sense of exultation he experienced when he performed. The exhilaration he felt when exercising his talent can still be sensed in his music after two hundred years.

ANDREW STEPTOE

Freemasonry

AFTER THE FOUNDATION of the Grand Lodge of England (1717), freemasonry developed among all strata of 18th-century European society – except among the peasantry and lower classes – as a reaction to the prevalent religious intolerance and political absolutism. The use of symbolic rituals, deriving from those of the medieval guilds, allowed men of different social origin to share in a common experience, and strengthened their sociable feelings. The main characteristics of the Craft were conviviality and charity, but its membership was open to every ideological trend, including those of a heterodox kind, and it was soon condemned by Pope Clement XII (1738). English lodges had already been penetrated by rationalist ideas when Newton's secretary, Désaguliers, was elected a Grand Master (1719). This trend led to the blossoming of academic lodges, such as 'Les Neuf Soeurs' ('The Nine Muses') in Paris, and 'Zur wahren Eintracht' ('True Concord') in Vienna.

The last-named lodge was founded at the time Mozart settled in the Austrian capital, when Emperor Joseph II had just begun to carry out his programme of reforms in the spirit of the Enlightenment. In his struggle against the zealous adherents of conservative traditions in a hierarchical society, Joseph II found his strongest support among freemasons, especially among the members of the lodges 'Zur wahren Eintracht' and 'Zur Wohlthätigkeit' ('Beneficence'). Other lodges, such as 'Zur gekrönten Hoffnung' ('Crowned Hope'), were more concerned with conviviality, or with mysticism of an unorthodox nature, as in 'Zum heiligen Joseph' ('St Joseph').

Mozart had been in touch with members of the Craft for a long time, especially during his residence in Vienna, and in his visits to Germany and France (1777–8); thus he was well aware of the variety of Viennese freemasonry when he decided to enter one of the lodges there. Although the minutes of the two lodges to which he belonged have not been preserved, there is ample documentation of his involvement with masonry through numerous events and compositions. (Datings etc. in the following chronology are from Autexier, 1984, 1986 and 1987a.)

Chronology of masonic events and compositions

1772–4

Mozart composes his first masonic song, *O heiliges Band*, K.148 (125h) (for alternative dating, see p. 331), and two choruses for *Thamos*, K.345 (336a), a play by the freemason Tobias Philipp Gebler.

1777

End Becomes acquainted with Theobald Marchand, one of the founders of the Mannheim lodge, and with Otto von Gemmingen, another prominent mason living there.

1783

11 Feb Gemmingen establishes his own lodge in Vienna, 'Zur Wohlthätigkeit', and invites Mozart to enter it as a musician. His feelings of hesitation are echoed in the Andante con moto of the String Quartet in E♭, K.428 (421b).

1784

22 Apr The lodges of the Habsburg monarchy create a National Grand Lodge, and adopt a unified rite.
Nov Sends letter of candidature to 'Zur Wohlthätigkeit'.
14 Dec Admitted into Gemmingen's lodge. Karl Lichnowsky also belongs to 'Zur Wohlthätigkeit'.
24 Dec Attends the reception of Count Apponyi at the lodge 'Zur wahren Eintracht'.

1785

7 Jan Is passed to the Fellow-Craft Degree at 'Zur wahren Eintracht'.
10 Jan Completes the String Quartet in A, K.464, the Andante of which refers to the ceremony of reception.
13 Jan Made a Master Mason at 'Zur wahren Eintracht'.
14 Jan Completes the String Quartet in C, K.465, which refers to his progression to the Second Degree, and attends the reception of Anton Tinti at 'Zur wahren Eintracht'.
28 Jan Attends the meeting at 'Zur wahren Eintracht' for the reception of Joseph Haydn, but the candidate is not present.
11 Feb Haydn is admitted into 'Zur wahren Eintracht'. Mozart cannot attend the ceremony because of his concert at the Mehlgrube.
9 Mar Completes the Piano Concerto in C, K.467, the Andante of which refers to the Third Degree.
26 Mar Completes the *Lied zur Gesellenreise*, K.468, most likely written in connection with his father's candidature at that time.
6 Apr Leopold Mozart is admitted into 'Zur Wohlthätigkeit'.
16 Apr He is passed to the Fellow-Craft Degree at 'Zur wahren Eintracht'. Puchberg attends the ceremony.
20 Apr Mozart completes the cantata *Die Maurerfreude*, K.471, in honour of Ignaz von Born, the Worshipful Master of 'Zur wahren Eintracht'.

24 Apr *Die Maurerfreude* is sung for the first time at the lodge 'Zur gekrönten Hoffnung' by the tenor and member Johann Valentin Adamberger.

1 May *Die Maurerfreude* is sung at 'Zur wahren Eintracht'. . .

7 May . . . and at Puchberg's lodge 'Zum Palmbaum' ('Palm Tree') and 'Zu den drey Adlern' ('Three Eagles').

July Mozart composes the *Master Music*, K.477, for male chorus and orchestra, and two responsory songs, *Des Todes Werk* and *Vollbracht ist die Arbeit* (K.desunt).

12 Aug On the occasion of Karl von König's elevation to the Third Degree at 'Zur wahren Eintracht', Adamberger sings the two songs, and the *Master Music* is performed with David playing the basset-horn.

17 Aug *Die Maurerfreude* is published by Artaria, a member of 'Zur gekrönten Hoffnung', for the benefit of the poor.

27 Sept Mozart probably attends the reception of Anton Stadler at Puchberg's lodge.

20 Oct Mozart and Stadler take part in a concert of the latter's lodge for the benefit of two basset-hornists, the masons David and Springer.

17 Nov At 'Zur gekrönten Hoffnung', the *Masonic Funeral Music*, K.477 (479a) (= *Master Music* without chorus), is played in honour of two lately deceased masons.

7 Dec At 'Zu den drey Adlern', the *Masonic Funeral Music* is performed in a new version with other wind instruments.

11 Dec The Emperor orders the lodges in Vienna to be reduced from eight to two or three.

15 Dec Mozart plays a piano concerto and extemporizes at 'Zur gekrönten Hoffnung' for the benefit of David and Springer. Adamberger sings *Die Maurerfreude*.

19 Dec 'Zur Wohlthätigkeit' is dissolved: Gemmingen and Mozart become members of 'Zur gekrönten Hoffnung'. They attend a meeting at 'Zur wahren Eintracht'.

1786

Jan: beginning Mozart sets two responsory songs to music, *Zerfliesset heut'*, K.483, and *Ihr unsre neuen Leiter*, K.484.

14 Jan Cannot attend the installation of the new 'Zur gekrönten Hoffnung' for which he has written the two songs because he feels unwell.

Spring Works at the cantata *Dir, Seele des Weltalls*, K.429 (468a), for St John's Feast (24 June), but does not complete it. (For more information on dating, see p. 321.)

1787

30 Mar Writes an inscription in the album of Kronauer, a member of his lodge.

27 Apr Born writes an inscription in the composer's album.

1788

12 Jan Mozart plays at an academy (concert) of 'Zur gekrönten Hoffnung' in honour of Archduke Francis and his wife Elisabeth.

1789

Mar: end Writes to Hofdemel that he will soon be admitted into 'Zur gekrönten Hoffnung'.

1790

Jan Attends a reception at 'Zur gekrönten Hoffnung'. A painting of this ceremony has been preserved.

1791

Sept: first half On his visit to the lodge 'Zur Wahrheit und Einigkeit' ('Truth and Union') in Prague, he is welcomed with a performance of *Die Maurerfreude*.

28 Sept Completes *Die Zauberflöte*.

30 Sept Conducts its first performance at Schikaneder's theatre.

15 Nov Completes *Eine kleine Freimaurerkantate*, K.623 (published in 1792 with an appendix of questionable authenticity, *Lasst uns mit geschlungnen Händen*, K.623/623a).

18 Nov *Eine kleine Freimaurerkantate* sung for the inauguration of the new premises of 'Zur gekrönten Hoffnung'.

Masonic symbols in music

Most of the music performed in 18th-century lodges is not specifically masonic: new texts were set to well-known tunes, such as religious hymns, national anthems, and popular songs. The *ad notam* device enabled every member of the lodge to participate in the performance without any training or knowledge of musical notation. Traces of that practice appear in *Die Zauberflöte*, when Papageno (no. 20) and the two armed men (no. 21) sing the melodies of the Lutheran chorales *Errett' dein armes Leben* and *Ach Gott, vom Himmel sieh' darein!* Papageno's first aria (no. 2) may be based on a Venetian tune.

The songs and cantatas written especially for the lodges generally end with a chorus, which only repeats the last phrase of a section previously sung by a soloist. Mozart had already made use of this device in the song *O heiliges Band*, but the most characteristic examples of it are to be found in *Die Maurerfreude* and in Sarastro's aria 'O Isis und Osiris' (no. 10 of *Die Zauberflöte*). To make responsory singing easier, the composer uses a distinctive trait of popular tunes, which are based mainly on seconds and thirds (see the last twelve bars of *Die Maurerfreude*, or the responses to Tamino's interrogations in the first finale of *Die Zauberflöte*). The second, being the smallest interval, symbolizes close fraternity; the third is one of the many examples of triads which evidently refer to freemasonry, but generally have no particular significance.

Tonality and rhythm are, indeed, the main features of Mozart's masonic language. The number of flats – not sharps – in the key correspond to the degree, although E♭ major does not always refer to the degree of Master Mason. The march (no. 9) and song (no. 10), which form the musical frame of the priests' decision to initiate Tamino, are in F; the *Lied zur Gesellenreise*, composed for the ceremony of promotion to the Second Degree, is in B♭; *Die Maurerfreude* for the Master Mason Born is in E♭.

The ritual used in Viennese lodges in Mozart's time contained characteristic rhythms for each degree: – ∪ – for the Entered Apprentice, ∪ – – for the Fellow-Craft, and ∪ ∪ – for the Master Mason.

The significance of a rhythm is determined by the position of its first long knock. (The same formula may have a different meaning in other kinds of ritual, making its interpretation difficult even for freemasons.) These knocks appear in many works by Mozart, e.g. in the overture to *Die Zauberflöte* (bars 1–3, 97–102, and 225–6), or in the first piece he completed after his reception at 'Zur Wohlthätigkeit', the String Quartet in A: in the last variation of the Andante, one can hear the violin playing the rhythm of an Entered Apprentice, while the cello imitates the hammer of the Worshipful Master. During this section the candidate's eyes are bound. The high G in the first violin part (bar 160) denotes the moment when he is permitted to see again: he can read the letter G inscribed in the blazing star (which is also present in the frontispiece of the original libretto for *Die Zauberflöte*).

Mozart employs these symbols, and many others of a more complex nature, in concertos, in symphonies, and in chamber music not written for the lodges (but apparently not in works for solo piano). They play an even more important part in the so-called profane repertory than in compositions for masonic occasions. This makes the study of Mozart's masonic world indispensable for a better knowledge of his musical expression in general.

From fraternal to mixed masonry

The attention of biographers and scholars has hitherto been focused on a supposed conflict between Mozart's Catholic faith and his masonic involvement. In fact this is a false assumption, since the papal condemnations of the Craft were not pronounced *ex cathedra*, and consequently had no theological importance. Furthermore, they were not published in Austria, in France, or in several other Catholic states. In 1784 Mozart chose to join one of the lodges where the trend was rationalist, contrasting strongly with the conservative attitude of most of the clergy in Vienna. But his decision had no direct connection with his opinions on religious matters. On the other hand, there is no reason to assert that freemasonry strengthened his faith, since the rationalist lodges were not especially concerned with it. According to contemporary sources such as the *Journal für Freymaurer*, published by 'Zur wahren Eintracht', the significance of the ceremonies and their symbols was in no way mystical. The aim was rather to produce an experience which all the members of the Craft could share, creating an exceptional relationship between them. This sort of friendship may have had more significance for Mozart than for his brethren, because nowhere else in Vienna did all those present participate in the performance of his music, as was the case in the lodges, on account of the responsory device of the compositions.

On 27 November 1800, Constanze Mozart sent to Härtel in Leipzig a plan written by her husband for a new secret society he wanted to found under the Rousseauist name of 'The Grotto'. Since the manuscript (now lost) was incomplete, it can be considered as contemporary with *Die Zauberflöte*, the libretto of which shows the same Rousseauist trends, and with *Eine kleine deutsche Kantate*, K.619, on a text by Ziegenhagen. Neither the opera nor the cantata is a work intended for the use of the lodges, but they are closely related to Mozart's idea of freemasonry and of society. Ziegenhagen's thought was far more revolutionary than Rousseau's. In particular he promoted the idea of equality between men and women. This is not only a social question, but one which refers to masonry: regular lodges were exclusively composed of men. The debate on the problem of feminine initiation was very acute among German and Austrian freemasons. A special initiation for women, called 'Adoption', had developed in France since 1744, but even there women could not be accepted in regular lodges. The misogynist attitude of the priests in *Die Zauberflöte* (e.g. in no. 11) alludes to the prevalent opinion in Mozart's own lodge as well as in others. But he, like Ziegenhagen, stood for the equality of women, and he believed them to be worthy of initiation: in the second finale, Pamina and Tamino undergo the trials of initiation hand in hand. Apparent contradictions in works like *Die Zauberflöte* (no. 11 versus no. 21) are not due to any lack of attention to detail, as has often been said; they are inherent in the central questions dealt with in these pieces. Realism, after all, is a natural consequence of Enlightenment.

PHILIPPE A. AUTEXIER

Mozart's journeys

c = concert(s), *o* = played the organ

MOZART SPENT ABOUT 250 days of his short life travelling. The carriages he took were either privately hired or post vehicles. The journeys were bumpy and slow, and the inns were often cold, damp and dirty. At nearly every stopping-place Wolfgang was expected to perform, on the clavier, violin or the local organ. The child prodigy returned after his foreign trips with his luggage full of trinkets given to him by admiring dignitaries.

Munich (1762)
12 Jan for approx. 3 weeks (*c* for Elector of Bavaria)

Vienna (1762–3)
(Leopold, Nannerl and 6-year-old Wolfgang) 18 Sept 1762 to PASSAU(*c*) (arr. 20 Sept), then by post-boat down the Danube to LINZ (26th) where Wolfgang gave his first public concert on 1 Oct. On via MAUTHAUSEN (4th), YBBS(*o*) and STEIN (5th) to VIENNA (6th). Then to PRESSBURG (Bratislava) by Danube boat (11 Dec 1762). Back to VIENNA by private carriage (24th). 31st via LINZ (arr. 2 Jan 1763) to SALZBURG (arr. 5th).

The Great European Journey (1763–6)
Leaving SALZBURG on 9 June 1763, the Mozart family travelled in their own carriage, accompanied by a servant (Sebastian Winter). They went via WASSERBURG (arr. 10 June) *o* to MUNICH (12 June) *c*. The next stop was AUGSBURG (22 June) *c* where Leopold bought a travelling clavier from Johann Andreas Stein. Then via ULM (6 July) *o*, and LUDWIGSBURG (9th), where they met Jommelli, to BRUCHSAL (12th), SCHWETZINGEN (arr. 14th) *c*, HEIDELBERG (after 19th) *o*, and MANNHEIM (3 days) to WORMS. The itinerary is uncertain until MAINZ (arr. 3 Aug) *c*. To FRANKFURT by market boat (arr. 10th) 5*c* and back to MAINZ (31st). To COBLENZ by private boat (17 Sept) *c*. then BONN (27th), by mail coach via BRÜHL to COLOGNE (arr. 28th), AACHEN (30th), LIÈGE (2 Oct), TIRLEMONT (3rd), via LOUVAIN to BRUSSELS (5th). Via MONS (15 Nov) BONAVIS (16th) and GOURNAY (17th) to PARIS (18th). VERSAILLES from 24 Dec to 8 Jan 1764 *o*/*c*. 10 Apr they left PARIS for CALAIS (19th). They were all rather seasick on the crossing to DOVER from where they went straight on to LONDON (arr. 23rd) where they stayed until July 1765. Apart from a short trip to TUNBRIDGE they did not leave the London area during their English sojourn.

The return journey began via CANTERBURY (24 July 1765) where they went to the races on the 31st. After a calm channel crossing DOVER–CALAIS (1 Aug), they picked up their carriage again. Then they went on via DUNKIRK (3rd?), LILLE (5th?) and

GHENT (4–6 Sept) *o*, to ANTWERP (arr. 7th) *o*, where they left the carriage. On via MOERDIJK to ROTTERDAM (10th) and by canal boat to THE HAGUE (arr. 11th) *c*. Here Mozart was dangerously ill with intestinal typhoid from 15 Nov for two months. They went on to AMSTERDAM (?26 Jan 1766), THE HAGUE (early Mar) *c*, and UTRECHT in their own carriage (18 Apr) *c*. Then via MOERDIJK, ANTWERP *c*, MALINES, BRUSSELS (arr. 8 May), VALENCIENNES (9 May), and CAMBRAI to PARIS (arr. 10th). VERSAILLES (28 May–1 June). They left PARIS on 9 July and travelled via DIJON (arr. ?12th) *c*, LYON (arr. ?26th) *c*, GENEVA (arr. 20 Aug) *c*, LAUSANNE (arr. 14 Sept) *c*, BERNE (19th/20th) *c*, BADEN to ZÜRICH (arr. ?28th) *c*. The next part of the journey took them via WINTERTHUR (12 Oct) *o*, SCHAFFHAUSEN (11th-16th), DONAUESCHINGEN (17th-31st), MESSKIRCH, ULM, GÜNZBURG, DILLINGEN (arr. 4/5 Nov) *c*, BIBERACH (*o* contest with Sigmund Bachmann), AUGSBURG (6th), MUNICH (arr. 8th) *c*, arriving home in SALZBURG on 29 Nov.

Family journey to Vienna (1767–9)
VÖCKLABRUCK (11th Sept). Via LAMBACH to LINZ (12th). Via MELK to ST PÖLTEN (14th). Via PURKERSDORF to VIENNA (15th). To BRÜNN (Brno) (23 Oct), OLMÜTZ (Olomouc) (26th), BRÜNN (24 Dec), POYSDORF (9 Jan 1768), VIENNA (10th) *c*. and back to SALZBURG (arr. 5 Jan 1769).

Italy (Dec 1769 – Mar 1771)
(Leopold and Wolfgang with a servant) Via ST JOHANN in Tyrol to WÖRGL (14 Dec), SCHWAZ, INNSBRUCK *c*, STEINACH (19th), STERZING, BRIXEN (Bressanone) (20th), ATZWANG, BOZEN (Bolzano) (21st), EGNA (23rd), ROVERETO (24th) *c*/*o*, VERONA (27th), where Mozart gave his first Italian concert on 5 Jan 1770, *o*, MANTUA (10th) *c*, BOZZOLO (19th), CREMONA (20th), MILAN (23rd) *c*, LODI, PIACENZA, PARMA and MODENA (15–23 Mar), BOLOGNA (24th), FLORENCE (29th–30th) *c*, SIENA, ORVIETO and VITERBO (7–10 Apr), ROME, famous visit to the Sistine Chapel to hear the Allegri *Miserere* (11th) *c*, MARINO (8 May), SESSA (11th), CAPUA, (12th), NAPLES (arr. 14th) *c*; visits to VESUVIUS, POMPEII, HERCULANEUM, CASERTA and CAPODIMONTE (18 and 19 June), ROME (25th/26th), CIVITÀ CASTELLANA *o*, TERNI, SPOLETO, FOLIGNO, LORETO (arr. 16th), ANCONA, SENIGALLIA, PESARO, RIMINI, FORLÌ, IMOLA (arr. 19th), BOLOGNA (20 July). Stay in the country outside Bologna 10 Aug – 1 Oct. PARMA (14 Oct), PIACENZA (16th), MILAN for *Mitridate* (18th). TURIN (14 Jan 1771), MILAN (31st), CANONICA, BRESCIA, VERONA, VICENZA, PADUA, VENICE (4–11 Feb) *c*, PADUA by boat (12 Mar) *o*/*c*, VICENZA (14th), VERONA (16th) *c*, ROVERETO, BRIXEN, INNSBRUCK, SALZBURG (arr. 28 Mar).

Italy (Aug – Dec 1771)
1769 route taken from SALZBURG (13–17 Aug) to

ROVERETO, then ALA, VERONA (18th), BRESCIA (20th), CANONICA, MILAN (arr. 21st) for *Ascanio in Alba*. Return to SALZBURG taking the same route (5–15 Dec).

Italy (24 Oct 1772 – 13 Mar 1773)

MILAN for *Lucio Silla* and back by route taken in 1769 and 1771.

Vienna (14 July – 26 Sept 1773)

Mozart and his father arrived in Vienna on 16 July and returned home, leaving Vienna on 24 Sept, via ST PÖLTEN, LINZ and LAMBACH.

Munich (6 Dec 1774 – 7 Mar 1775)

Mozart travelled with his father, via FRABERTSHAM to WASSERBURG (6th), then on to MUNICH for the production of *La finta giardiniera* (7th).

Paris (23 Sept 1777 – 15 Jan 1779)

Travelling with his mother, he went first via WAGING, STEIN, FRABERTSHAM and WASSERBURG to MUNICH (arr 24th) *c*. On to AUGSBURG (11 Oct) *c*. They visitied HOHEN-ALTHEIM (26th) *c* and continued on to MANNHEIM. Mozart visited KIRCHHEIM-BOLANDEN for several days with Herr Weber and Aloisia (23 Jan 1778–?) He then left MANNHEIM with his mother on 14 Mar, arriving in PARIS on the 23rd via CLERMONT (19th). Maria Anna Mozart died there on 3 July. Mozart left PARIS on 26 Sept and travelled alone to NANCY (?3 Oct), STRASBOURG (?14th–3 Nov) *c*, and MANNHEIM (arr. 6th). He set off again on 9 Dec, travelling via HEIDELBERG, SCHWÄBISCH-HALL, CRAILSHEIM, DINKELSBÜHL, WALLERSTEIN, NÖRDLINGEN, the Monastery at KAISHEIM (13th–24th), NEUBERG and INGOLSTADT to MUNICH. ?13 Jan 1779 he returned to SALZBURG with his cousin, the 'Bäsle'.

Via Munich to Vienna (1780–81)

Mozart went to MUNICH on 5 Nov 1780 for the first production of *Idomeneo*. His father and sister returned to Salzburg when he left to live in VIENNA on 12 Mar 1781 (arr. 16th).

Travels from Vienna

July 1783, Wolfgang took Constanze to SALZBURG. They left there on 27 Oct and returned to VIENNA via VÖCKLABRUCK, LAMBACH, EBELSBERG and LINZ *c*, where they stayed from the 29th until the end of Nov.

8 Jan 1787, to PRAGUE for *Figaro*; returned ?12 Feb. 1 Oct 1787, to PRAGUE for *Don Giovanni*; returned ?16 Nov.

On 8 Apr 1789 Mozart set off from VIENNA with Prince Karl Lichnowsky and travelled via PRAGUE (arr. 10th) to DRESDEN (arr. 12th) *c*. Leaving on the 18th he went via MEISSEN, OSCHATZ and WURZEN to LEIPZIG (arr. 20th) *o*. He left on ?23rd and travelled to POTSDAM (arr. ?25th). He arrived back in LEIPZIG

with the Prince on 8 May, leaving again on 17th for BERLIN (arr. 19th). On 28th he left Berlin and stayed in PRAGUE from 31st–2 June. He arrived back in VIENNA on the 4th.

On 23 Sept 1790 Mozart set out with his brother-in-law, Hofer, and went via EFERDING, REGENSBURG, NUREMBERG, WÜRZBURG and ASCHAFFENBURG to FRANKFURT for the coronation of Leopold II. They arrived on the 28th. On 16 Oct he went by river to MAINZ, going on to MANNHEIM on the 21st (arr. 23rd). On the 25th he went via BRUCHSAL, CANNSTATT, GÖPPINGEN, ULM, GÜNZBURG and AUGSBURG (arr. ?28th) to MUNICH (arr. 29th). He was there until 6/7th and arrived back in VIENNA on 10th.

On ?25 August he set out for PRAGUE with Constanze and Süssmayr, arriving on 28th for the coronation of Leopold II and *La clemenza di Tito*. They returned in mid-Sept.

The only other occasions when Mozart left Vienna were to visit BADEN, where Constanze went several times for health reasons.

AMANDA HOLDEN

Mozart's illnesses and death

MOZART'S THIRTY-SIX YEARS of life were wracked by a series of illnesses, the most serious of which are enumerated below.

1. On the evening of 21 October 1762, in Vienna, Mozart became ill. Two physicians diagnosed scarlet fever, but from Leopold Mozart's detailed description he was probably suffering from a condition now known as erythema nodosum, and probably related to the catarrh he had been suffering from earlier in the month at Linz. (letters of 16, 19, 30 October and 6 November 1762)

2. Shortly after the Mozart family's return to Salzburg early in January 1763, he suffered the first of what seem to have been two infantile bouts of rheumatic fever. (letters of 15 and 22 November 1766)

3. On the morning of 16 February 1764, in Paris, he was stricken by 'a violent sore throat and catarrh' and was so ill during the night that he was in danger of suffocating. He recovered after four days. (letter of 22 February 1764)

4. On 15 November 1765, at The Hague, he suffered an attack of typhoid fever. He was recovering by 12 December. (letter of 12 December 1765)

5. He became ill, in Munich, on the evening of 9 November 1766 and was better by the 22nd. The second bout of rheumatic fever (see illness 2 and reference).

6. On 26 October 1767, at Olomouc, he went down with smallpox. The illness lasted about a fortnight and left him permanently scarred. (letter of 10 November 1767)

7. In later years Mozart's sister recollected he had suffered a serious illness on his Italian journey of 1771 (letters of 24 November 1799 and 2 July 1819), leaving his skin a yellow colour, although the correspondence of the period offers no support for this.

8. In a newly discovered letter from Constanze Mozart to Leopold of November 1783 (Sotheby's auction of 17 May 1990), Constanze records that Mozart had been extremely ill (probably a viral infection) and that he had been bled by Dr Gilowsky; but see p.434.

9. In 1784 (late August/early September) Mozart, living in Vienna, suffered a serious illness. His physician Sigmund Barisani diagnosed rheumatic fever, and Mozart described having repeated attacks of colic at the same hour, four days in succession. (letter of 14 September 1784) He was well enough to resume writing to his father before 14 September.

10. Another serious illness, again treated by Barisani, and mentioned by him in an inscription in Mozart's album of 14 April 1787. No dates or details are known.

11. Quite certainly the area of greatest interest and greatest controversy concerns the illness leading to Mozart's death in December 1791. There is no reliable evidence that Mozart displayed signs of illness in 1791 before the end of the month of August. According to Niemetschek, on his visit to Prague (28 August to around the middle of September) he 'was sickening and taking medicine incessantly, his colour was pale and his countenance sad', and although often manifesting his customary good humour was so melancholy on finally leaving his friends 'that he burst into tears'. But whatever else Mozart was suffering from at this juncture, given his work schedule of the previous weeks, simple nervous exhaustion cannot have been very far off.

It is uncertain whether he showed continued signs of illness on his return to Vienna, but events seem to have taken a decisive turn in the latter part of October. On 'a beautiful autumn day' Mozart declared to his wife in the Prater, where they had gone for a drive, that he believed that he had been poisoned. According to the Novellos, 'he felt a great pain in his loins and a great languor spreading over him by degrees'. Both the Novellos state, in fact, that this incident occurred six months before Mozart's death (May/June 1791), but in order for their account to square sensibly with Niemetschek and Nissen, it would be plausible to suppose that this was a mistake for six weeks, placing the event around 24 October. The weather records for Vienna suggest 20 or 21 October. The belief that he had been poisoned was to pursue Mozart intermittently as his health got worse.

Mozart became bed-ridden around 20 November. Nissen writes:

> His final illness, in which he became confined to bed, lasted 15 days. It began with swelling in the hands and feet and almost complete immobility: after which followed sudden vomiting, which illness was diagnosed as miliary fever. Up until two hours before his death he retained complete understanding.

Sophie Haibel, his sister-in-law, recalled making him a nightshirt which could be put on from the front, 'since because of the swelling he could not turn himself over'. Two days before the day of his death (Saturday 3 December) he seemed to feel better. But when Sophie returned the following day her sister told her: 'he was so ill last night I thought he would die today. If he becomes so again, he will die tonight.' Mozart himself was resigned to the fact that he would die that night: 'I have the taste of death on my tongue.'

The Novellos give the following detailed account from an interview with Sophie Haibel:

> Towards evening they sent for the Medical person who attended Mozart, but he was at the Theatre and, on receiving the message, merely said that he would come 'as soon as the opera was over'. On his arrival he ordered Madame Haibl to bathe the temple and forehead of Mozart with vinegar and cold water. She expressed fears that the sudden cold might be injurious to the sufferer, whose arms and limbs were much inflamed and swollen. But the Doctor persisted in his orders and Madame Haibl accordingly applied a damp towel to his forehead. Mozart immediately gave a slight shudder and in a very short time afterwards he expired in her arms.

Mozart died around 1 am on the morning of Monday 5 December 1791, and the cause of death given in the register of deaths was 'heated miliary fever'. Further light is shed on the diagnosis given by Mozart's physician, Dr Closset, in a letter dated 10 June 1824 from the Austrian first physician Eduard Guldener to Giuseppe Carpani.

Guldener had not attended Mozart during his final illness, but he had been in close contact with Dr Closset, and he had seen Mozart's body. He is at great pains to stress the commonplace – almost epidemic – nature of Mozart's symptoms, which had not only led Closset to a confident diagnosis, but also to predict with accuracy the manner and time of Mozart's death. According to Guldener Mozart had an inflammatory rheumatic fever that developed into a condition he refers to as 'deposit in the head', which Carl Bär (1972) has demonstrated was believed at the time to be the terminal phase of a rheumatic fever. The term 'heated miliary fever' found in Nissen and on the death register is not contradictory, being a non-specific term for an inflamed fever with rash – a rash being a normal symptom of a rheumatic fever. As a sufferer from a diagnosed 'inflammatory fever' Mozart would certainly have been subject to substantial blood-letting by his physician, which could only have further hastened his demise.

The diagnosis of rheumatic fever may not accommodate Mozart's illness of early September, but growing 'languor' and pains in the lower abdomen ('loins') in October are plausible symptoms for the onset of an attack. Although the childhood attacks of rheumatic fever (illnesses 2 and 5) are perhaps too far back to be considered contributory, Mozart had at least one diagnosed adult attack of rheumatic fever – a recurrent and cumulatively weakening condition – in illness 9.

The most scholarly extended account of the circumstances surrounding Mozart's death is Bär (1972). The recent writings of Peter J. Davies (1983,

1984, 1987 and 1989) must also be listed if only for the amount of scholarly patronage they have received. Davies argues amongst other things that Mozart at the time of his death had an underlying condition known as Henoch-Schoenlein syndrome, which had led to renal malfunction and failure, and caused neurological damage, partial paralysis and a fatal stroke. This explanation is dependent on an amalgam of sources, several of which are contradictory or of questionable provenance. Notably Davies has argued that Mozart's letters of 1791 are evidence of 'emotional lability' resulting from neurological damage, although latterly (1987) he has portrayed Mozart as a congenital manic-depressive, citing the same correspondence. The condition of 'partial paralysis' does not appear in the literature until the English edition of Jahn in 1891, a mistranslation for 'almost complete immobility'. The 'fatal stroke' is drawn, probably via Jahn, from the novellettish memoirs of a 'man of the people', first published in the Vienna *Morgen-Post* in 1856.

JOHN STONE

Section 7
MOZART'S OPINIONS AND OUTLOOK

Religion and politics

IN ORDER TO EXAMINE the views of the adult Mozart it is necessary to examine his origins, his family background, and most particularly the exceptional personality of his father. (For more on Leopold and his career, see under 'Family background' (pp. 102–4).) Whatever the levels of psychological friction which came to exist between them, the set of attitudes and ambivalencies which had obtained in Mozart's childhood could only leave a profound mark. As time went on he was to find it increasingly difficult to sustain Leopold's poised mixture of deference to authority, combined with scepticism about those in whom it was invested. In their personal dealings Leopold was self-possessed and calculating while Mozart remained impulsive; nevertheless Leopold provided the grounding for Mozart's developing attitudes.

Leopold's education at the Benedictine university in Salzburg implanted in him a marked tendency towards Catholic piety, and the family correspondence even in the face of the most terrible catastrophe continues to invoke divine providence. In the 1760s, touring Europe with his talented children, he continually arranged with his Salzburg correspondent, his landlord Lorenz Hagenauer, for Masses to be said for the recovery of his children from the series of appalling illnesses which beset them during these years – requiring that they be said at his expense in various multiples and at certain specified shrines. (Indeed, his son was to follow the tradition years later in penning the great C minor Mass, K.427 (417a), for performance at Salzburg for the recovery of his wife from illness.)

On one occasion we learn in a letter to Hagenauer that the Mozart family broke their journey in order for Leopold to persuade a lapsed Catholic from Salzburg back into the fold. In 1770 in Italy, while showing impatience with the fast days which prevented him and his son from eating properly, he is an eager visitor to the 'uncorrupted' remains of St Catherine of Bologna and St Rosa of Viterbo, bringing away relics and 'fever powder'. And when for the first time separated from his son, who as a young adult in the years 1777–8 travelled through Germany and to Paris accompanied by his mother in the search for a court appointment, he worries for the young Mozart's soul:

I must wish you a happy nameday! but what can I wish you which I do not always wish you? – I wish you the grace of God, that it accompanies you everywhere, that it will never leave you, and never will it, if you practise the duties of a true Catholic Christian diligently. You know

me. I am no pedant, no begging friar, not in the slightest bit
sanctimonious; but would you really reject your father's request? –
That is that you will take care for your soul, that you will cause your
father no anguish in the hour of his death . . . (23 October 1777)

This was not the only such entreaty, and the young Mozart was
generally quick to offer reassurance; nevertheless the remark 'I am
no pedant, no begging friar, nor in the slightest bit sanctimonious'
suggests that Leopold's mind was not entirely taken over by
heavenly pursuits. Indeed, there had always existed a great degree
of ambivalence, in terms of both intellectual interest and,
particularly in later years, scepticism about the dignitaries of the
Catholic church.

Certainly piety had not prevented the Mozart family from
accepting hospitality, in the 1760s, from some of the most notable
(and notorious) figures of the French Enlightenment. On their first
visit to Paris they lodged with Baron Grimm and Madame
d'Epinay, and in 1778 Leopold mentions that he must send his son
letters for Diderot and d'Alembert (23 February 1778). On their
second Paris visit of the 1760s Leopold subscribed to an edition of
an engraving sold by Grimm for the rehabilitation of the Huguenot
family Calas, whose reputation had recently been defended before
the French nation by Voltaire (Grimm, 1877–82). Voltaire,
however, at the time of his death in 1778 is singled out for some
opprobrium by both father and son, apparently on the grounds of
his irreligion. Possibly they were simply piqued at not having
gained an audience with him when staying at Geneva in
September 1766, Voltaire having apparently been ill at the time.

But Leopold was perhaps more generally inclined to take people
at their individual worth, or at least, their potential usefulness. At
the beginning of Mozart's 1777–9 journey, while he was staying at
his father's native Augsburg, Leopold wrote to him savouring the
possibility that a triumph amongst the Protestant community of
that town might spite his feudal master, the Catholic Archbishop of
Salzburg:

> If you see that you are greatly applauded and highly esteemed, I would
> like afterwards, when you have left Augsburg, that a special article in
> your praise appear in the Augsburg newspapers, which my brother or
> Herr Glatz could deliver to Herr Stein, and Herr Stein can arrange.
> You know already why: it would fill someone here with gall. Herr Stein
> and other Evangelicals themselves would derive pleasure from it. N.B.
> You must be well aware that one must call the Lutherans Evangelicals,
> for they will not be called Lutherans, and not the Lutheran Church,
> just as the Calvinists desire to be Protestants, and not Calvinists. It has
> occurred to me to mention this subject, as one can often enrage
> troublesome people through a single such word, although the sensible
> pass it over. (15 October 1777)

This lack of respect for a prince of the Catholic church may have
been personally motivated, but it was typical of Leopold's attitude
not to be intimidated by people of rank or power whether secular or

spiritual. Thus writing from Rome in April 1770 he describes how he and his son achieved admittance to the Vatican apartments:

> . . . on the 12th we attended the Function, and the Pope at his table administered alms, so close to see, that we stood above and next to him. It is even more to be wondered at, since we had to get through two doors with armoured Swiss guards, and press our way through at least a hundred people, and NB still without being known to anyone. Only our good clothes, our German speech, my customary freedom with my servant, who, in German, commanded the Swiss to let us pass, soon helped us through everywhere. They took Wolfgang for a German knight, or otherwise even for a prince, and my servant left them in this happy belief; and I was thought his tutor . . . (14 April 1770)

In addition, a note of conventional popular anti-clericalism is to be discerned when in 1777 he jokingly reproaches his niece – Mozart's 'little cousin' (Bäsle) Maria Anna Thekla Mozart – for having 'too much acquaintance with the clergy'. Leopold also evinced a contempt, which Mozart was to echo, for military parading, although it is not clear whether this represented part of a thoroughgoing dislike of military aggrandizement, or just an irritating municipal hazard of the petty German states which they visited.

The grand progress of the infant Mozart through Europe as 'the prodigy of Salzburg' was to have serious consequences when as a young man he had to confront the world no longer as a charming, and much indulged, freak, but as a supreme artist. The difficulty was to be exacerbated by the succession of a new Archbishop of Salzburg. The acceptance of feudal authority (with, in Salzburg, its confusion between spiritual and temporal claims) could be sustained while the Archbishop of Salzburg was prepared to regard the talented and socially emancipated Mozart family as his ambassadors, bringing by their ceaseless tours honour and fame to his principality. It could not so easily be sustained when, with the death of Archbishop Siegmund Schrattenbach (14 December 1771) and the subsequent election of Hieronymus Colloredo (14 March 1772), Mozart and his father were increasingly expected to resume their role as household servants.

Already at the time of Mozart's first break with the court of Salzburg in 1777, an overtly political theme is present. His petition to the Archbishop asking for his discharge – almost certainly dictated by Leopold – is a stilted mixture of the theology and the jurisprudence class; if not intended to cause the maximum possible offence, it certainly succeeded in doing so:

> Most gracious Prince, and glorious Lord! Parents strive to place their children in the position to earn their own bread: and this they owe to themselves, and the service of the state. The greater the talents children have received from God, the greater their obligation to make use of them, for the betterment of their own and their parents' circumstances, to support their parents, and look after their own advancement and future. In this way we are taught to benefit from our talents in the Gospel . . . (1 August 1777)

The prince, presumed to be cognisant of his power, is reminded of his responsibility. The argument conforms to a mode of political theory which had evolved amongst the absolutist states of 18th-century Europe, and particularly in Austria. The authority of the prince can only be derived from his devotion to the well-being of his subjects. Such thoughts are the commonplace of operatic texts of Metastasio – the Austrian Imperial Poet, still living at the time – and notably of his *La clemenza di Tito*, a text already elevated by Voltaire for its noble sentiments, and which Mozart turned his hand to in the last months of his life.

This is, however, to look ahead. Already in 1777 Mozart's sense of *amour propre* was well developed, even if it is questionable how global his sense of human affairs was. Vienna in the early 1780s, with the accession of Joseph II, was a city alive with new-found political freedoms and hopes for further reform, and it is evident that Mozart was ultimately to acquire a degree of political commitment. Writing to his father in 1781 after his final brutal dismissal from the employment of the Archbishop of Salzburg at the boot of the court chamberlain, Count Arco, he declared:

> The heart ennobles the man; and if I am assuredly no count, I have perhaps more honour in me than many a count; and lackey or count, as soon as he insults me he is a scoundrel . . . (20 June 1781)

The statement is one of individual pride, but it is not clear that the democratic implications inherent in the phrase 'the heart ennobles the man' are realized in an identification with any more general cause. And although he had already made the acquaintance of the two most politically influential figures of Austrian Enlightenment, Joseph von Sonnenfels (professor of political science and councillor of the court chancellery) and Gottfried van Swieten (the imperial censor), it must be uncertain whether he regarded them at this stage as anything other than well-disposed Viennese court dignitaries.

The decisive step can, however, be seen in his enrolment in freemasonry in December 1784 – an institution in the forefront of political activity in contemporary Vienna, and openly campaigning for the systematization of law upon natural foundations; universal education and the advance of knowledge; and the extension of freedom of political and religious expression. Mozart's enthusiasm at this stage seems reflected in the fact that within weeks of his joining, both his father – who was visiting him in Vienna – and Joseph Haydn – who was becoming around this time his closest friend – were also admitted to the brotherhood. The Mozarts joined the minor lodge 'Zur Wohlthätigkeit' ('Beneficence'), where Mozart's friend the dramatist Otto von Gemmingen was master, and Haydn the prestigious 'Zur wahren Eintracht' ('True Concord') lodge at which Sonnenfels was a leading member. Mozart is known, nevertheless, to have visited 'Zur wahren Eintracht' on five occasions before its suppression at the end of 1785.

The notion of the 'enlightened society' was to hold Mozart's imagination in much more adverse political circumstances till the end of his life – his last public appearance being at a masonic meeting on 18 November 1791. The greatest monument to his devotion is *Die Zauberflöte*. In his last but one surviving letter he tells his wife of the fury he felt at an acquaintance who had made fun of the work's solemnity during a performance. He dismisses him to his face as 'a Papageno' (i.e. as a non-initiate too foolish to comprehend), although his own humour was to return sufficiently later in the performance to sabotage the magic bells in 'Ein Mädchen oder Weibchen'.

Related to *Die Zauberflöte* is a broadsheet that Mozart put together and distributed as a masquerader at a ball at the Hofburg Assembly Rooms during the Carnival season of 1786. The document, of which only a part survives, is entitled *Bruchstücke aus Zoroastens Fragmenten* (*Pieces from the Fragments of Zoroaster*). Alluding to the Persian magus and proponent of dualist philosophy from whose name that of Sarastro is derived, and also to the traditions of ancient wisdom invoked in masonic lore, Mozart compiled a series of riddles and aphorisms of a broadly humorous and satirical nature. Along with the characteristic jokes about horns and cuckoldry, censorious remarks about social pretension and hypocrisy, is the following barbed, rather coarse, parody of the social system:

> If you are a poor numskull – then become a *K—r*. If you are a rich numskull – then become a farmer. If you are a noble, but poor numskull – then, become what you can, for bread. If you are however a rich, noble numskull, then become, what you will; only not a man of sense – that I pray you. (19 February 1786)

> ['K—r', on grounds of typecasting, is presumably *Kleriker* (cleric), although Mozart might have been expected to use *Pfaff*. 'Farmer' (*Pächter*) perhaps signifies a farmer of taxes.]

Leopold Mozart was sufficiently pleased with the *Fragments* to have the surviving extracts reprinted in a Salzburg newspaper.

Sexual morality

On 1 February 1764 Leopold Mozart wrote from Paris to Maria Theresia, wife of his landlord, Lorenz Hagenauer:

> One must not always write to male persons, but also remember the fair and devout sex. Whether the women in Paris are beautiful, I cannot with certainty say; for they are, against all nature, painted like Berchtesgaden dolls, that even a naturally beautiful person, through such horrid daintiness becomes to the eyes of an honest German intolerable. As for the piety, I can assure you, that one has not the least difficulty investigating the miracles of the French women saints; the greatest wonders are performed by those who are neither virgins, nor wives or widows; and these wonders all take place with living bodies. We will speak in more detail of these things in good time. Enough! one has trouble enough here to distinguish, who the woman of the house is. Everyone lives as they like, and (if God is not peculiarly gracious) then

the French state will go the way of the former Persian empire. (1 February 1764)

And in the following letter to her husband he remarks of the death in Paris of a Salzburg dignitary:

One dies nowhere with pleasure, only here for an honest German, if he falls ill, or even dies, the grief is double. (22 February 1764)

It is true that Leopold was also offended by the filth, disease, and poverty of France's capital city – true also that he latterly became somewhat acclimatized to it all, for years later he was to express no specific anxiety about his son seeking employment there – nevertheless the level of disapproval and sexual disgust is impressive. To be German in this context is more important than being a Catholic, and the contrast is between the order and probity of one nation and the dissoluteness and frivolousness of another.

The requirements of seriousness and propriety were in their turn to determine Mozart's attitudes. In 1778 Mozart is alarmed at the possibility of travelling from Mannheim to Paris in the company of the Wendling family, who prefer the theatre to the church, and one of whom had been a mistress of the Elector of Mannheim: 'for in a word, I have no proper trust in them. Friends without religion, are not long-lasting.' (letter of 4 February 1778) And for once father and son are in agreement over a matter of policy.

Three days after this communication Mozart is found inveighing against the corrosiveness and frivolousness of aristocratic values:

Herr von Schidenhofen could properly have given me news long since through you, that he soon intended to hold a wedding. I would have composed him new minuets for it. From the heart I wish him luck. It is nevertheless a money match, nothing more. I would not marry in this way; I will make my wife's fortune, and not my fortune through her. For which reason I'll let things remain, and enjoy my golden freedom, until I am in a good enough position to support a wife and children. To Herr von Schidenhofen it was necessary to choose for himself a rich wife; his noble birth required it. Noble people must not marry according to inclination and love, but only for advantage, and all sorts of peripheral things; it would also scarcely be proper for such high born persons by chance to still love their wife, after they had no doubt done their duty, and brought a bouncing male heir into the world . . . (7 February 1778)

Mozart is always keen to rebut charges of loose behaviour, and often in tones which suggest a level of priggishness. A fortnight later he writes in ironic terms:

People believe it impossible to love a poor girl without having base intentions; and that beautiful word *maîtresse*, in German h–re [*hure*: 'whore'], is I think quite beautiful! I am no Brunetti and no Misliwetcek! I am a Mozart, but a young and virtuous minded Mozart . . . (22 February 1778)

By the time of the great Da Ponte comedies, however, there seems to be an increasing recognition that not all feeling can be circumscribed by such exacting moral standards. Mozart and his wife had become during these years intimate with the family of the imperial botanist Nikolaus von Jacquin, and particularly his son Gottfried, who had just turned twenty. Mozart is plainly seduced, if not entirely deceived, by the latter's character – amongst other things presenting him with compositions to pass off as his own, including, rather backhandedly, *Als Luise die Briefe ihres ungetreuen Liebhabers verbrannte* (*When Luise burnt the letters of her faithless lover*). On the first of his visits to Prague, where *Figaro* had just become a brilliant success, he writes to Jacquin:

> At 6 o'clock I went with Count Canal to the so-called Breitfeld ball where the kernel of Prague beauty likes to assemble. – It was something for you to have been at, my friend. – I believe I see you after all the young girls, and women. – Hot on their heels you trust? – no lumbering behind! I did not dance and did not try my luck. – The first, because I was too tired, and the last out of my native shy stupidity . . . (12 February 1787)

Despite this piece of self-revelation, censoriousness remains. In a letter some months later reporting the successful first performances of *Don Giovanni* in Prague – even as he makes over to Jacquin yet another composition, the song *Das Traumbild* – he turns to lecture him:

> Are you not daily more convinced of the truth of my little sermons? Is the pleasure of a fluttery, whimsical love, not a heaven's breadth distinct from the happiness which a true, sensible love secures? You thank me well often enough in your heart for my instruction! – You will yet come to make me completely proud. – But, without any joke – you still owe me a bit of thanks at bottom, if you otherwise have become worthy of Fräulein N., because after all I played in your reform or conversion certainly no insignificant role . . .

At this point Mozart is taken over by a sense of embarrassment and concludes the letter with an awkwardly elaborate joke concerning familial wisdom. Undoubtedly his position is, though entirely earnest, uneasy.

Ultimate beliefs

On 3 July 1778, at twenty-one minutes past ten in the evening, Mozart's mother died in Paris. In the hours which followed Mozart penned two letters. One to his father sought to prepare him by telling him that she was simply very ill, before going on to talk about other matters including the death of Voltaire (actually some weeks before):

> Now I give you a piece of news that you perhaps already have, namely that the godless arch-rogue Voltaire so to say dropped dead like a dog – like an animal – that is his reward! (11 June 1778)

The other letter to the Mozart family's ecclesiastical friend Abbé Bullinger revealed the full truth of the situation, and the circumstances of his mother's death. In both letters he seeks comfort – apparently denied in the case of Voltaire, whom he perhaps wrongly supposes not to have received the Catholic church's absolution – in subjection to the will of God:

> I am solaced, come what may – because I know that God, who arranges all (however arbitrary it stills appears to us) for the best, has so willed; for I believe (and this I will not be dissuaded from) that no doctor, no man, no misfortune, no accident, gives life to man, nor takes it away, but God alone. (3 July 1778)

To Bullinger, and in a later letter to his father, he repeatedly describes her death as happy ('how much happier she now is, than we') and he expresses the expectation that: 'she is not forever lost from us – joyous and happy the reunion to come; only the time is unknown to us.' (9 July 1778)

This view of death is repeated in later years. On 3 September 1787 he records the death of his friend and physician Sigmund Barisani: 'He is content – but to me – us – and all who knew him closely, – we will never be content – until we happily are to see him in a better world – once more – and *never to part*.' According to Dies, Haydn's biographer, on Haydn's departure for England on 15 December 1790 Mozart told the older composer: 'We are probably saying our last adieu in this life.'

To his father, on first learning of the illness of which the latter was to die, he writes: 'as death (to consider it closely) is the true end and purpose of our life, I have thus made myself acquainted for a couple of years with this true, best friend to mankind, that his image not only is not longer frightening for me, but properly most soothing and consoling.' (4 April 1787) There is a great gap between the 18th-century rhetoric of death and the attitudes of the modern world; nevertheless there are few grounds for doubting the sincerity of this passage, and certainly no basis for the claim by Hildesheimer (1977), following the notes from the standard edition of the letters, that it was plagiarized from Moses Mendelssohn's *Phaedon*. (Nor, for that matter, if it had been, would it have proved the cynicism that Hildesheimer believes it does.) Yet it is also true that Mozart was unable to retain this equanimity when little more than four years later he approached the reality of his imminent death with a mixture of paranoia, sorrow and frustration.

Reading matter

IT IS HARD TO RECONSTRUCT Mozart's reading. There is, indeed, a posthumous inventory of his library (Deutsch, 1961b, Appendix II), but we cannot be sure that all the books in it had his attention, or that there were not many others that he read but did not possess. From his letters, for example, we know that he enjoyed reading an Italian edition of the *Arabian Nights* – the opening of which, via Ariosto's tale of Giocondo in Canto XXVIII of *Orlando Furioso*, is a distant ancestor of the plot of *Così fan tutte* – in Bologna in 1770. He also read at this time Fénelon's *Télémaque*. Again not a single work by Goethe is to be found in the library, but it is interesting to note that when uniquely among his song texts he set one of great literary quality – Goethe's *Das Veilchen* – he paid the poet the tribute of acknowledging his authorship at the head of the sheet, something which he omitted to do on other occasions. (Arthur and Schachter, 1989)

Mozart's widow told the Novellos that he was well acquainted with Shakespeare in translation. How far this knowledge actually extended is not clear. *Hamlet* alone of Shakespeare's works is referred to in the letters. On one occasion, while struggling to cut back the vocal intervention of Neptune in *Idomeneo* he complains that the ghost scene in the play is too long to make a strong effect (letter of 29 November 1780) – a perhaps rather temporary opinion, for he was to provide one of equal length in *Don Giovanni*. On another occasion he repeats a widespread comparison of Grand Duke Paul of Russia to Shakespeare's prince. (10 November 1781) It must, however, remain doubtful how much else he knew, apart perhaps from Da Ponte's libretto for Stephen Storace's *Gli equivoci*, based on *The Comedy of Errors*.

We can be sure that Mozart looked at a parallel Latin/German text of Ovid's *Tristia*, listed amongst his possessions, because he adapted a well-known passage from it in his dedication of the 'Haydn' string quartets, made in 1785. His late paranoid fantasy that he had been poisoned by Salieri with 'acqua toffana' may owe something to a novel he owned by a fellow Viennese freemason, Johann Pezzl – *Faustin, oder das aufgeklärte philosophische Jahrhundert* – in which the hero flees from Naples under fear of death by the same means. A three-volume edition of the minor poet Christian Felix Weisse provided the text of four songs. An edition of Metastasio published in Venice in the early 1780s served for occasional wordsetting – concert arias, and the *notturni* for the Von Jacquins – though he was likely to go to texts which he knew for other reasons. Thus, for example, an aria text from Metastasio's *Il natale di Giove* pointed out to Mozart by the tenor Raaff in 1780 for possible use in *Idomeneo*, is used to help cobble together the text of *Davidde penitente* in 1785.

We cannot know what attention he paid to the volumes of pastoral prose and poetry by Salomon Gessner presented to the Mozart family by the author in 1766, or the Molière given him by Fridolin Weber in 1777. He may very well have read his copy of Moses Mendelssohn's popular adaptation of Plato's *Phaedo* (*Phaedon*) with its rationalist reassurances about death. Rather more unusual is the compilation of occultist data *Die Metaphysik in der Konnexion mit der Chemie* by Friedrich Christoph Oetinger, the presence of which in his collection may be related to the alchemical strand of freemasonry. If he attended to its numerological account of musical elements he might have concluded that it was impossible to compose more than two bars without a host of spurious significances.

From the residue of the library certain patterns emerge: travel books, numerous educational works for children, and books concerning contemporary history and politics, including the first four volumes of Sonnenfels' collected works. Mozart's widow also mentioned to the Novellos that amongst his favourite reading was a nine-volume work, the title of which she was unwilling to divulge, possibly because of its Jacobin tendencies. Harder to account for are the now entirely forgotten plays – Mozart possessed the complete six-volume edition – of Johann Gottfried Dyk (Leipzig, 1786–8), but given the date, and the state of Mozart's finances during that period, it was most likely a gift. Or did he contemplate composing a historical tragedy and consider also Hannah Moore's *Percy* which he possessed in the original English?

With two volumes on his shelves by Wieland – his epic poem *Oberon* and the novel *Diogenes von Sinope* – we do at least approach, with a degree of uncertainty, an area which has some relation to Mozart and his work. Mozart had met Wieland in Mannheim late in 1777, and gave a rather detached description of him to his father, who was a steadfast admirer of the north German writer. Mozart's commitment is less, but allows that 'he is as we all know, an excellent mind'.

Between the writings of Wieland, however, and the two late operas *Così fan tutte* and *Die Zauberflöte* there are definite affinities. *Diogenes von Sinope*, presented as the thoughts and reminiscences of the cynic philosopher who lived in a barrel, and recovered in secrecy from a manuscript in a monastic library, recasts Diogenes' philosophy along Epicurean lines. Speaking in a calm, lyrical tone, Diogenes celebrates the pleasure of a simple life lived away from the corrupting and insidious influence of human civilization. In the last section of the book, 'The Republic of Diogenes', he conjures a vision of an island – beyond the reach of the existing world and peopled by beautiful youths and maidens. In his expectations of them he speaks in similar terms to Don Alfonso in *Così fan tutte*:

> Is eternal love possible? – That I know not. So much is certain, that it would be reckless to swear to one another eternal love, as one is inclined to at sixteen; but *to be made* to swear eternal love? – No, my children, I will give you no cause the sooner to be weary of one another.

Even closer to *Così fan tutte* perhaps – although not in Mozart's library – is Wieland's comic verse tale *Aurora und Cephalus* adapted from Ovid's *Metamorphoses* (Book VII), in which Cephalus, challenged by the jealous goddess Aurora concerning the faithful character of his wife Procris, seduces the latter in magical disguise and then consoles himself in Aurora's arms. The tale was prefaced in its original edition – although it was later suppressed – with the Latin motto adapted from Ovid's *Ars amatoria* (Book II, l.366): '– quod faceret quaelibet, illa facit' ('– what any woman would do, she does'). In each of these instances – *Aurora und Cephalus*, *Diogenes* and *Così fan tutte* – the point lies in virtue being circumscribed by human dimensions.

In the case of *Die Zauberflöte* two of Wieland's projects lie in the background: *Oberon*, and the collection of prose tales which appeared under his editorship, *Dschinnistan*. The notion of a fairy tale opera was not, of course, necessarily dependent on Wieland's contribution to fairy tale literature, but in fact a whole popular operatic genre was being created in Vienna at the time – and mainly under the auspices of the Schikaneder company – based on these works. With *Die Zauberflöte* the amalgam of sources had grown beyond these texts, but the title at least is derived from the *Dschinnistan: Lulu, oder Die Zauberflöte*. The mixture of popular and lofty tone – the employment of folk material with its alluring use of the fantastic in order ultimately to serve higher reason – is close to Wieland's expressed design in the preface to *Dschinnistan*.

Attitude to environment

GIVEN MOZART'S CEASELESS musical labours it is unsurprising that his knowledge of, or concern for, other cultural matters was partial. Unlike his father who expressed an enthusiasm for Rubens, he never refers to painting or sculpture; nor at the time of his death did the inventory of his estate list a single picture. It would not, however, be right to conclude that he was indifferent or oblivious to his visual surroundings. Alfred Einstein's speculation, for example, that Mozart never 'wasted a glance' on the elaborately stuccoed ceiling which graced the apartment he lived in during the years 1784–7 cannot really be credited. Visiting the apartments of the Electress of Bavaria in January 1779, he remarks: 'she lives here entirely as I would certainly one day wish to live – pretty and neat, except for the miserable outlook, just as a private person might live.' (letter of 8 January 1779) And when in 1782 his friend at court, Johann Valentin Gunther, is placed under house arrest, although incensed on his behalf, he questions 'if it is a misfortune', for him 'to have been detained 2 months in a beautiful room, with continued use of all his books, his forte piano etc.' (11 September 1782)

A few scattered statements suggest that Mozart retained a family prejudice for classical order. From Rome he writes: 'I wish my sister had come to Rome, for to her this city would certainly be pleasing, because St Peter's church and a lot of other things in Rome are *regular*'. (14 April 1770) From Venice he writes in Italian 'Venice pleases me much'. (13 February 1771) Father and son both disparage medieval Bozen (now Bolzano) at the beginning of their third visit to Italy – for Leopold it is 'mournful', for Mozart a 'sow-hole'. (26 October 1771) Returning from Paris in 1778 Mozart finds praise for Nancy: 'the town is indeed charming – beautiful houses, broad streets, and superb squares'. (3 October 1778) Two months later the largely Gothic abbey of Kaisheim seems to him unimpressive compared to the predominantly Baroque Krems-münster, which he must have remembered from a journey to Vienna. (18 December 1778) A similar prejudice is probably involved in an unfavourable comparison between Nuremberg and Würzburg in September 1790. (28 September 1790)

Mozart virtually never refers to the scenery which accompanies his travels, but he takes pleasure in the estate of Count Cobenzl outside Vienna where he is a guest in July 1781: 'the little house is nothing, but the environs! – the wood – in which a grotto is built, as if it was thus through nature. It is splendid and very delightful'. (13 July 1781) And while staying in Mannheim in late October 1790 he intends to make a special trip to visit the gardens at Schwetzingen. (23 October 1790) There is perhaps no need to be sceptical about Vincent Novello's report from his conversations with Constanze Nissen that Mozart took pleasure in the picturesque scenery of Salzburg, 'especially the romantic grounds at Aigen'. He notes again that Mozart was 'especially fond of flowers' and 'extremely fond of the country and a passionate admirer of everything that was beautiful in nature – liked little excursions and [they] passed much of their time out of town'.

Composers and composition

IN A LETTER FROM AUGSBURG IN 1777, Mozart gives an account of an incident which establishes much of his attitude at the time to the craft of composing. He had been introduced to the composer Friedrich Hartmann Graf and taken part in an impromptu performance of a double flute concerto by the latter, and then performed himself:

> The concerto is thus. Not sufficiently good in the ear. Not natural. He marches through the keys far too – clumsily; and this all without the least magic. When it was over I praised him very properly; for he earned it too. The poor man would have had to work hard enough. He would have studied enough. Finally a clavichord was brought forth from the private quarters (of Herr Stein's manufacture), very good but full of muck and dust. Herr Graf, who is director here, stood there as one who had always believed his journey through the keys to be wholly special, and now finds that one can be yet more special, and without offending the ear. In a word, all were astounded. (14 October 1777)

Four years later, writing to his father, Mozart gives a more specific indication of his requirement for key relation and his sense of what is permissible in musical composition. He is describing Osmin's aria 'Solche hergelauf'ne Laffen' from *Die Entführung*, and it is his only surviving detailed account of the rationale behind a particular composition:

> You have here only the beginning of it, and the end, which should make a very good effect – through it the rage of Osmin is rendered comical, because the Turkish music is brought in at this point. – In writing the aria I have (in spite of the Salzburg Midas) allowed his beautiful low notes to shine. – The *drum beym Barte des Propheten* etc: is indeed in the same tempo, but with quick notes – and here his rage continues to increase, so must – here one believes the aria to be already at an end – the allegro assai – wholly in another measure, and in another key – make just the very best effect; for, a man who finds himself in so violent a rage, overstepping all orderliness, measure and limit, does not know himself – so must the music also no longer know itself – but because the passions, violent or not, must never be pressed to the extent of [exciting] disgust, and the music in the most tremorous

situation, never offend the ear, but nevertheless be pleasing, remaining as a consequence always music, I have therefore chosen not a key strange to the F (the key of the aria) but one friendly to it, yet not the nearest, D minor, but the more distant A minor. (26 September 1781)

In both the above quotations the avoidance of tonal disjunction, even in the most extreme contexts, is seen as a necessary constituent of an absolute demand for aural beauty – and with the relinquishment of such aural beauty, in Mozart's view, music ceases to be, properly speaking, music.

An allied requirement would be the precise matching of instrument to musical idea and vice versa. Mozart only ever raises the topic in relation to the human voice, remarking famously in February 1778: 'I like an aria to suit a singer as accurately as a well made garment'. (letter of 28 February 1778) At around this time the composer Schweitzer, Wieland's collaborator, is held out for particular censure in this respect. Mozart writes of Aloisia Weber's chances of impressing in Schweitzer's *Rosamunde*, raising not simply the issue of matching the specific voice, but also of more general vocal idiom:

> She has one aria, which judging by the ritornello could close well, but the singing part is alla Schweizer like the bark of a dog; she has a single sort of a rondeau, in the 2nd act, where she can sustain her voice a little and consequently show it off; yes, unhappy is the singer, man or woman, who falls into the hands of Schweizer; for he will never learn to write in a singable manner as long as he lives! (11 September 1778)

This kind of ineptitude could never be acceptable. Briefly, however, in 1778–9 Mozart became interested in a theatrical form – the melodramas of Georg Benda – in which beauty of effect was eschewed, and music itself became entirely subsidiary to dramatic force. The intention of such a piece as Benda's *Medea*, which excited Mozart in Mannheim in November 1778, in which music accompanied and heightened a spoken recitation, was clearly related to the emotionally disruptive ambitions of the literary *Sturm und Drang*. It is interesting that even as he became exercised by this harsh theatrical medium, projecting in collaboration with Otto von Gemmingen the melodrama *Semiramis*, he continued to complain about the poor quality of Schweitzer's vocal writing. But it was not an ambivalence which Mozart could eventually sustain. *Semiramis*, though lost, was probably completed, but *Zaide* – the opera in which he incorporated melodramatic fragments in place of accompanied recitatives – was abandoned, and the procedure not taken up in *Idomeneo* or subsequently.

Mozart began his compositional career in an epoch, the 1760s, when little of the music being composed was to retain a long-term foothold in the performing repertory, and when the music of the great composers of the Baroque had fallen into almost complete neglect. Against this background his first efforts were derived not so much from the example of his father's music, or that of Michael Haydn, who became resident in Salzburg in 1763, but from the music of Johann Christian Bach, whose friendship the Mozart family had gained in London in 1764–5.

Years later Mozart retained a deep attachment both to the man – they met again in Paris in 1778 – and his music. Earlier that year, while still in Mannheim, he had paid him a particular tribute by resetting the text of a favourite aria by him 'Non so d'onde viene':

> which is so beautifully composed by Bach, because, I know the one by Bach so well, and because it so pleases me, and is ever in my ears; that I have attempted to see whether I could not, notwithstanding all this, write an aria quite unlike it . . . (28 February 1778)

He describes Bach's death four years later as 'Misfortune for the musical world!' (10 April 1782)

Mozart had from his youth been acquainted with the grand Baroque style of church music, but it is not until 1782 – in fact in the very same letter as he remarks on the death of J.C. Bach – that we learn of his excitement, under the influence of Baron van Swieten, with the works of Johann Sebastian Bach and Handel, and with the possibilities of contrapuntal style. He writes that he is making a collection of fugues by the Bach family and he asks his father to send him fugues by Handel and Eberlin with the intention of introducing those of Eberlin at one of Van Swieten's Sunday midday gatherings. Ten days later, however, writing to his sister he has come to realize that the Eberlin pieces are unworthy of comparison with Bach and Handel. He forwards in the same letter his own prelude and fugue for piano (K.394/383a), remarking:

> I have intentionally written Andante Maestoso on it, so that one should not play it too quickly – for if a fugue is not played slowly, one cannot bring out the entry of the subject distinctly and clearly, and it is consequently of no effect. (20 April 1782)

A project to write a set of six such pieces was never completed, but on 31 December 1782 Mozart finished his first great string quartet, K.387, with its contrapuntal finale. Probably from this time also date arrangements of Bach fugues for string quartet (K.405) – no doubt for Van Swieten's salon, and it was also in association with Van Swieten that in the years 1788–90 Mozart made a series of arrangements of Handel's English choral works. Perhaps, however, his most beguiling and spontaneous tribute to a Baroque master is the comic gigue for piano (K.574), written in evident tribute to Bach on a visit to Leipzig in 1789.

Gluck seems, from the letters, to have been held in artistic respect if personal suspicion by the Mozart family (9 and 12 February 1778), until the 1780s when both composers were resident in Vienna. Gluck gave Mozart a friendly reception and even requested a repeat performance of *Die Entführung*. (7 August 1782) Mozart showed consistent interest, in his Viennese letters, in the church music of Michael Haydn (4 January 1783, 12 March 1783, 29 March 1783, 2 August 1788, 12 July 1791), and also invited the latter to come and stay in Vienna at the time of Leopold Mozart's death.

Mozart's greatest artistic friendship, however, must quite certainly have been with Joseph Haydn. It was late in commencement – a letter of Mozart to his father of April 1784 suggests both that at the time they were not as yet closely acquainted, and that Mozart, while manifesting a degree of respect, had not yet fully recognized Haydn's importance:

> There are now quartets by a certain Pleyel; who is a pupil of Haydn. If you do not yet know these, then try to obtain them; it is worth the trouble. They are very well written, and very agreeable; you will realize too like his master. Good – and happy for music, if Pleyel in his time, replaces Haydn for us!

It was a strange and rather shallow judgment that Haydn's art could be interestingly replicated by another composer. In strong contrast, Mozart's first biographer Niemetschek recounts an anecdote in which Mozart acknowledged Haydn's ability to envisage musical possibilities unavailable even to himself. It is noteworthy that the object of Mozart's reproof on this occasion – presumably Leopold Koželuch – was, with his strategic position in the music publishing world, someone he could ill afford to alienate:

> At a private gathering it happened once that a new work of Joseph Haydn was performed. Several musicians were present with Mozart, among others one L.K., who had never yet praised anyone, as he did himself. He placed himself by Mozart and faulted now one thing, now the other. He listened to this for a time with forbearance, so long as he was able to endure it, and the fault finder finally once more cried out at a passage with self-satisfaction: 'That I would not have done!' – Mozart rejoindered: 'I also not. But do you know why? Because neither of us would have hit upon anything so good!'

Opera

IN A LETTER TO the Abbé Bullinger of August 1778, Mozart becomes humorously exercised over the possibility of an opera to be mounted in Salzburg in which the Archbishop's new castrato Ceccarelli takes alternately the parts of a pair of lovers of such extraordinary virtue that they never appear together in public. Metastasio, he suggests, might be persuaded from Vienna to furnish a 'few dozen' texts of this kind. (7 August 1778) No such opera, of course, was ever composed, but nevertheless the sense of rigidity, of stiltedness, communicated here is something which Mozart evidently associates not only with castrati but with the theatre of Metastasio. The period from which this letter dates is not so much a period of coherent thought with regard to the operatic theatre, as simply of impatience. Soon afterwards Mozart became involved with the melodramas of Georg Benda, in which traditional forms of musical and theatrical decorum were traded in for enhanced emotional verisimilitude, and in which the spoken word was dramatically heightened by musical accompaniment. 'Do you know what my thought was?' he wrote to his father. 'One should treat most recitative in opera in this way – and only occasionally *sing* the recitative if the words *are to be well expressed in music*'. (12 November 1778) Something of the mood which led him to espouse the melodrama was undoubtedly still left when he set to work on *Idomeneo* – with its sustained, almost breathless, intensity – in the latter part of 1780, even though the melodrama project had been put aside.

No greater contrast in dramatic values could be imagined than that between *Idomeneo* and *Die Entführung*, although the latter was being planned within months of the completion of the former. If *Idomeneo* forcibly resists the conventions of operatic pacing, *Die Entführung* contentedly plays to the audience. In describing the music of the opera to his father, he repeatedly stresses his wish to elicit, even to the point of cynicism, a quick popular response. For instance, writing of the rationale behind the trio finale in the first act, he says: 'the noisier, the better; – the shorter the better – so that people will not be slow to clap'. (26 September 1781)

Coupled with this are a lack of commitment to the theatrical subject matter and a carelessness towards the literary quality of the text. He delegates the finding of a libretto, and allows the librettist Stephanie to write bad verses:

> And I know not – with an opera the poetry must simply be the submissive daughter of the music. – Why then do the Italian comic operas please everywhere? – With all the wretchedness of the libretto! – even in Paris – of which I myself was witness – because there the music reigns – and beyond that one forgets everything else. (13 October 1781)

Admittedly this is the preamble to an extraordinary attack on the poverty of invention and restrictive rhyme schemes of poetry, and the contemplation of a form of opera which he never realized, in which music would adapt itself to free, rhymeless, verse. Nevertheless, he is unabashed by the level of artistic compromise which in these terms *Die Entführung* represents.

In arguing the opposite case to Mozart's ambivalently expressed view that the text should be subservient to the music, the popular essayist Francesco Algarotti, like Gluck in his dedication of *Alceste*, was attempting to place dramatic integrity above the frivolous requirements of singers and audience, and neither, writing in the 1750s and 60s, would have seen the potential that Mozart did in the 1780s for incorporating text into the design of the music. Gluck, indeed, who lived to take pleasure in the musical versatility of *Die Entführung*, would surely nevertheless have been alarmed at Mozart's negligent attitude to poetic content as it is expressed in the passage quoted above and through much of the earlier part of Mozart's Viennese correspondence.

If *Die Entführung* proved a viable project – saved at a dramatic level, perhaps, by its simple sentimental outlines – Mozart was nevertheless to come adrift. Writing to his father in May 1783 he proposes that Varesco, the librettist of *Idomeneo*, should be encouraged to provide a comic libretto:

but it is necessary that it should be properly comic throughout, and if then possible introduce two equally good female roles. – The one must be serious, but the other *mezzo carattere* [ie. a character somewhere between comic and serious] – but it is important that both roles be completely equal. – The third female role can however be completely *buffa*, as also all the male ones if need be.

The path is hazardous – this is an opera without a subject and Mozart soon found himself at work on two operas, *L'oca del Cairo* (in collaboration with Varesco), and *Lo sposo deluso* (librettist unknown), neither of which he apparently found sufficiently compelling to finish.

If there is a shortage of information concerning the genesis of the later operas, what information there is suggests that Mozart's attitude was by no means so casual. According to Da Ponte's usually self-promotional testimony, it was Mozart who proposed the subject of Beaumarchais' *Le Mariage de Figaro* as the basis of an opera, and Mozart again who chose the subject of *Don Giovanni*, seeing potential in the inferior libretto of Bertati offered him by the Prague opera company (Da Ponte, 1819). In the original printed libretto of *Figaro*, Da Ponte goes so far as to indicate the ambitious intent behind the work:

> the opera will not be one of the shortest to have been exhibited in our theatre for which we hope sufficient of excuses the variety of threads from which is woven the action of this drama, the vastness and size of the same, the multiplicity of musical pieces which had to be made in order not to keep the actors excessively idle, in order to reduce the boredom and monotony of the long recitatives, in order to express on occasion with diverse colour the diverse passions which there stand forth, and our desire particularly to offer a virtually new kind of spectacle to a public of such refined taste, and such informed judgement. (Sonneck, 1914)

Mozart and Da Ponte make a historical claim for the opera: that it is an attempt to expand the scope of the operatic theatre, and by implication that of public taste as well. If this had been the effect of *Die Entführung*, Mozart's intention had always been more modest. In 1788 with *Figaro* and *Don Giovanni* behind him, on receiving praise from an emissary of the Danish court for *Die Entführung*, Mozart could only dismiss it in retrospect as 'a trifle'.

In his catalogue Mozart categorizes the three Da Ponte operas unpretentiously as 'opera buffa'. This should probably be understood as a description of musical genre – works written in the mode of Italian comic opera, and probably with particular reference to their extended act finales – rather than an interpretation of their evidently serious dramatic content. Latterly *Die Zauberflöte* was simply described by him with the German 'Oper'. The most interesting of his catalogue entries is that for *La clemenza di Tito*, described by him as '*opera seria* . . . reduced to true opera by Signor Mazzolà'. What Mazzolà, the Saxon court poet, had done was to cut Metastasio's original libretto to a fraction of its original length, to produce texts for ensemble, and at the end of the first act facilitate the absorption of the dramatic action into the musical structure. Thus Mozart's words imply that what has taken place is a transposition from a medium which is primarily literary to one which is primarily musical, in which the old, literary mode is not recognized by him as being properly operatic.

How would Mozart have regarded the other generic titles applied to the operas in his lifetime – some of which have latterly given rise to misunderstanding? The libretti of *Don Giovanni* and *Così fan tutte* are published with the description 'dramma giocoso' which is an abbreviation of the term 'dramma giocoso per musica' meaning 'a humorous play for music', which is probably not intended to signify anything very different from the designation 'commedia per musica' or 'comedy for music' received by the libretto of *Figaro*. Indeed, Da Ponte (1819) repeatedly uses the word 'drama' as a synonym for 'libretto'. All three Da Ponte works are advertised in original posters as 'Singspiel', which is employed simply as a German word for 'opera' rather than specifying a genre of German opera in which *Die Entführung* and *Die Zauberflöte* were subsequently supposed to have been written.

Mozart's Italian operas were soon translated into German and performed in that language, and indeed *Die Entführung* and *Die Zauberflöte* rapidly also found their place in the repertoire of Italian companies. The expectations of different stages were by no means rigid. This is an important consideration in relation to the formal evolution which *Die Zauberflöte* represents. Certainly in a broad theatrical sense *Die Zauberflöte* is a product for the popular Viennese theatre, but in finding sophisticated musical procedures which were quite different from those deployed in his Italian comedies, Mozart went a long way to creating almost from scratch a sense of a fully formed German operatic style, based on the peculiar mixture of solemnity and vernacular humour present in the verbal text. In particular there are the finales, which move in an entirely different way from those of the Italian model – based as the latter are on theatrical movement and the creation of mounting tension and confusion. Was it purely the stimulus of writing for the vernacular theatre which led Mozart in this direction, or was he also beginning to feel constrained by the musical–dramatic formulas of *opera buffa*, and seeking as much for this latter reason to evolve in an entirely new way?

JOHN STONE

Section 8

SOURCES FOR MOZART'S LIFE AND WORKS

Family letters

THE MOZART FAMILY LETTERS are the most extensive and richly detailed surviving correspondence of any composer of the 18th century or earlier. All together, almost twelve hundred letters survive from the period 1755–91, by Mozart, his father, his mother, and his sister. Another four hundred letters, most of them by Mozart's widow and sister, date from after 1791.

Only a few letters by Leopold Mozart from 1756 or earlier are known. Mostly they are addressed to his Augsburg friend and publisher Johann Jakob Lotter and concern the publication of the *Gründliche Violinschule* (1756). In one letter, dated 9 February 1756, Leopold wrote '. . . I must inform [you] that on 27 January, at 8 p.m. my dear wife was happily delivered of a boy. . . both child and mother are well. She sends her regards to you both. The boy is called Joannes Chrisostomus, Wolfgang, Gottlieb.'

The chief part of the correspondence begins with the family tour to Vienna in 1762 and continues with accounts of the grand tour of 1763–6 and the return to Vienna in 1767–8. The majority of these letters – which report not only on Wolfgang's activities but also on local events and personages as well as the business of conducting an 18th-century musical tour – are addressed to the Mozarts' Salzburg landlord, Lorenz Hagenauer. Although they sometimes transact left-over local business, many of them were intended for public circulation, to inform the Mozarts' friends of their activities and to impress the Prince–Archbishop of Salzburg with their successes. It is likely that Leopold expected the letters to be saved and that they were to form the basis of his projected biography of Wolfgang (see 'Documents').

The letters written from Italy between 1770 and 1773, when only Mozart and his father were on tour, are chiefly by Leopold and addressed to his wife, Anna Maria. They continue to report on Mozart's successes, and occasionally on Leopold's plans, often only cryptically described, to secure a position for his son; apparently Leopold wished to keep at least some of his dealings secret and he may have thought that the letters were read by the Archbishop's agents before being delivered. The letters from Italy also include the first correspondence by Mozart himself, usually humorous or nonsensical postscripts addressed to his sister. On occasion, however, when Leopold was too busy or too tired to write, Mozart would write more substantially, often imitating his father's tone.

Fewer letters are known from the period 1773–7 when the Mozarts were mostly in Salzburg. The only exceptions are letters deriving from the short journeys to Vienna in 1773 and Munich in 1774–5. Mozart's departure from Salzburg in 1777, however, and the subsequent trip to Munich, Augsburg, Mannheim and Paris, generated a substantial and intensely personal correspondence of almost two hundred revealing letters that have been much studied. Not only do they report on Mozart's frequent professional and personal failures – his inability to secure an adequate post or to make headway as a composer, as well as his unrequited love for Aloisia Weber – and the death of his mother in Paris in July 1778, but they are also among the chief witnesses to Mozart's troubled relationship with his father and its breakdown.

The Viennese letters from 1781 and later provide a remarkable record of Mozart's activities at the time of his greatest successes. In a letter of 3 March 1784, for example, Mozart reported on his commitments to perform more than twenty times between 26 February and 3 April; for many of these concerts he had to compose new works. They also continue to document Mozart's estrangement from Leopold: the letters are full of self-justifications, particularly with regard to his marriage to Constanze, a match Leopold Mozart considered disastrous. With Leopold Mozart's death in May 1787, however, the family correspondence comes to a virtual end. Leopold's estate was settled later that year and, as far as is known, Mozart did not write to his sister again after about August 1788. Most of the letters from the last years of Mozart's life are addressed to his wife and were written when he was on tour in Leipzig, Berlin and Dresden in 1789 and Frankfurt in 1790. Some well-known begging letters addressed to Mozart's fellow-mason Michael Puchberg also survive.

Finally, two important posthumous collections of letters, those of Mozart's widow, Constanze, and his sister, Nannerl, mostly concern the sale of Mozart's estate to the Offenbach publisher Johann Anton André in 1799 and Breitkopf & Härtel's attempts to collect Mozart's works for a projected complete edition. Neither collection has been studied sufficiently.

The surviving correspondence must be considered incomplete. Numerous letters and other documents make reference to correspondence that is now lost. In a letter of May 1789, for example, written at Berlin, Mozart mentions eleven letters, of which only seven survive. Similarly, there is convincing circumstantial evidence that Mozart must have corresponded with his English friends Anna (Nancy) and Stephen Storace after their return to London in 1787, although no such letters are known (see 'Dissemination of Mozart's music' and Anderson, 1985). Many letters no longer survive in the originals but only in copies. This is particularly the case with Leopold Mozart's letters written on the ground tour of 1763–6. The chief repositories for the correspondence are the Internationale Stiftung Mozarteum, Salzburg, the Staatsbibliothek Preussischer Kulturbesitz, Berlin, and the British Library, London, although many letters are owned by other libraries or are privately held.

A selection from the letters, sometimes bowdlerized or otherwise altered to suppress information Constanze Mozart thought to be damaging, was first published in Georg Nikolaus Nissen's *Biographie W.A. Mozarts* (1828). More comprehensive are editions by Ludwig Schiedermair (1914) and Erich Hermann Müller von Asow (1942). A complete edition, by Wilhelm A. Bauer and Otto Erich Deutsch, with extensive annotations and commentary by Joseph Heinz Eibl, has appeared under the auspices of the Internationale Stiftung Mozarteum (1962–75). An English-language translation of most of the letters – based primarily on Schiedermair and including Constanze Mozart's but not Nannerl Mozart's correspondence – was first published by Emily Anderson (1938); a second edition (1966) omitted Constanze's letters, while the third (1985) restored some passages omitted in the first edition.

The importance of the letters

The Mozart correspondence is a fundamental source of information concerning Mozart's biography and the authenticity, chronology and genesis of his works. Numerous details of Mozart's life are known only from the letters and much of the chronology of the family's tours, as well as Mozart's activities in Vienna in the 1780s, can be pieced together only from references in the correspondence. By the same token, Leopold's letters written when Wolfgang was on tour in 1777 and 1778 are the best surviving sources of information concerning musical life in Salzburg, though the opinions expressed are entirely one-sided (Eisen 1989b).

The letters also provide extensive information concerning Mozart's compositional activities. Many works, among them the Trumpet Concerto, K.47c (12 November 1768), the aria 'Misero tu non sei' from Metastasio's *Demetrio* (26 January 1770), additional wind parts for a flute concerto by J.B. Wendling (21 November 1777), the Rondo for keyboard K.284f (29 November 1777), and eight movements for a Miserere by Holzbauer (5 April 1778), are known only from the letters. Among the most important documents in this regard is the *Verzeichniss alles desjenigen was dieser 12jährige Knab seit seinem 7tem Jahre componiert, und in originali kann aufgezeiget werden* (*List of everything that this 12-year-old boy has composed since his 7th year, and can be exhibited in the original*) which was probably sent by Mozart to Emperor Joseph II together with a petition requesting the court's intervention against the Viennese cabal trying to prevent the production of *La finta semplice* in 1768. (Leopold's petition was, in the event, unsuccessful and the opera was not performed.) The list – the most comprehensive account of Mozart's earliest compositions – includes references to numerous lost works including the Stabat Mater, K.33c, six divertimentos for various instruments, K.41a, some solos for flute, K.33a, and the March, K.41c. Because it is non-thematic, the list has also been a source of controversy: the works described there do not always square with surviving compositions from the time, or cannot be accounted for adequately (Zaslaw, 1983).

Other letters – in particular those from 1780 and 1781 – give extensive accounts of Mozart's composition of opera and his concern for effective theatre. A letter to his father of 29 November 1780, concerning a scene in *Idomeneo*, is typical:

> . . . don't you find the speech of the subterranean voice too long? Consider it judiciously. Picture to yourself the theatre, and bear in mind that the voice must be frightening – must penetrate – that the audience must think that it really exists – how can this come to pass if the speech is too long, because the listeners will become increasingly persuaded that it means nothing? Were the speech of the Ghost in Hamlet not so long, it would be much more effective.

A detailed account of parts of *Die Entführung aus dem Serail* appears in a letter of 26 September 1781:

> The opera was supposed to begin with a monologue, but I asked H[err] Stephani[e] [the librettist] to turn it into a small arietta – and that instead of the dialogue which the two have after Osmin's little song, there should be a duet. Since we intended H[err] Fischer to sing the part of Osmin, and indeed he has an excellent bass voice . . . one has to make good use of such a man, especially since he has the public here totally on his side. – In the original libretto, however, Osmin had just that one single aria to sing, otherwise nothing except the trio and the finale. Now he's been given an aria in the first act, and will have another in the 2nd. I told H[err] Stephani[e] just how the aria should go; most of the music was finished before Stephani[e] knew anything about it. You have only the beginning and the end, which must create a good effect. Osmin's rage is transported into the comic through it, because the Turkish music is added. In composing the aria I allowed his fine, low notes . . . to shine through. His words, 'drum beym Barte des Propheten' etc. are in the same tempo but with quick notes, and as his rage increases steadily, one thinks the aria is already at an end, but the allegro assai – in quite another metre and in another key – will certainly be most effective; for a man who is in such a rage completely loses control and breaks all the rules, not being himself – and thus the music mustn't know what it's doing either. But since the passions, violent or not, must never be expressed in an offensive manner; and music, even in the most appalling situations, must never offend the ear and hence must always remain music; the key I have chosen is not foreign to F (the key of the aria) but related to it, though not the nearest, D minor, but the more distant, A minor. – Now, to Belmonte's aria in A major, 'O wie ängstlich, O wie feurig', do you know how that is expressed? Here, the heart, beating with love, is at once indicated – the two violin sections in octaves – this is the favourite aria with everyone who has heard it, also mine, and it's entirely tailored to Adamberger's voice; one sees the trembling – shaking –, one sees how his bursting breast swells, which is expressed by a crescendo; one hears his stuttering and sighing, which is expressed by the first violins using mutes and a flute in unison.

In addition to providing information concerning the genesis, authenticity and chronology of Mozart's works, the letters also give evidence concerning their performance. This is true not only of such performing practices as rubato and tempo (see letters of 18–20

July 1778 concerning K.395 (300g) and 7 August 1782 concerning K.385) but also with regard to sometimes uncertain questions of scoring. A letter of 13 April 1778, for example, documents the soloistic, as opposed to orchestral, performance of the Divertimento for strings and horns, K.287 (Webster, 1983), while others give specific information concerning the number of performers on particular occasions (see, for example, Leopold Mozart's letter of 12 April 1778 in which he names the orchestral performers at a private Salzburg concert).

Perhaps the most widely studied aspect of the letters, and in particular the letters of the Mannheim–Paris tour of 1777–8, has been the light they shed on Mozart's personality and his troubled relations with his father (see, for example, Hildesheimer, 1977, and Langegger, 1978 and 1987/8). In addition to showing that from Paris Mozart deliberately misled Leopold with regard to his compositional indolence and lack of success (Zaslaw, 1978 and Tyson, 1978), the letters have also been cited as evidence of Mozart's hypomania and cyclothymic depression, as well as his emotional insecurity (Davies, 1987 and 1989). Still broader conclusions have been drawn from the so-called 'Zoroastran Riddles' composed by Mozart for the Viennese Carnival of 1786 and sent by him to Salzburg shortly afterwards. The riddles confront Mozart's attempts to free himself from 'a lifelong paternal domination of overwhelming intensity' in which Leopold Mozart attempted to keep Wolfgang in a permanently dependent state (Solomon, 1985).

Documents

IN ADDITION TO MUSICAL SOURCES and the family letters, contemporary documents of various sorts also provide direct information concerning Mozart's biography and the genesis and dating of his works as well as their dissemination and reception. These documents are generally of three sorts: those that derive directly from Mozart and are, strictly speaking, not letters; private or semi-private documents, including the correspondence of individuals, court records, and catalogues of the music holdings of publishers, monasteries, and other similar institutions; and public documents intended for a broad circulation, chiefly reports in contemporary newspapers and journals of Mozart's public appearances, reviews of his published and performed works, and advertisements by music dealers.

Documents deriving from Mozart

The number of documents – as opposed to letters – deriving from Mozart is small but significant. They include entries in various private albums, such as those of his friends Joseph Franz and Gottfried von Jacquin, his fellow-mason Johann Georg Kronauer, and his pupil Barbara Ployer, now lost, which included the unique source for the *Marche funebre del Sig.r Maestro Contrapunto*, K.453a.

Mozart himself had several albums. A smaller one included entries by Karl Ludwig Fischer, the first Osmin in *Die Entführung*, Sigmund Barisani, son of the Salzburg physician-in-ordinary, and Ignaz Born, master of the lodge 'Zur wahren Eintracht' ('True Concord') and a leading Viennese intellectual; according to Constanze Mozart, another larger album was lost by Mozart on one of his journeys (see her letter of 30 July 1799). More substantial are three undated literary efforts: the poem *Der Kunstreiche Hund*; an outline for a stage work *Der Salzburger Lump in Wien*; and an incomplete draft of a libretto for a comedy in three acts, *Die Liebes-Probe*.

Perhaps the most important document to derive directly from Mozart is his *Verzeichnüss aller meiner Werke vom Monath Febrario 1784 bis Monath 1 . Wolfgang Amadé Mozart $\overline{m^{pia}}$* (*List of all my works from the month of February 1784 to the month 1 . Wolfgang Amadé Mozart by my own hand*), a chronological list of all his compositions, beginning with the Concerto K.449 of February 1784. The last work in the catalogue, *Laut verkünde unsre Freude*, K.623, was written in November 1791; it is a poignant reflection on the blanks in the list's title, a sure indication that Mozart expected to live at least until the 19th century.

The catalogue consists of unruled left-hand pages on which he wrote the date and title or description of his works and sometimes, in the case of the operas and vocal works, the names of the singers, and ruled right-hand pages lined with ten staves, collected into five systems, on which he wrote two-staff incipits of the works.

The chief importance of the catalogue is the evidence it provides concerning the dates and authenticity of Mozart's works. Almost every major work composed after February 1784 is listed there. The few works known to have been composed later but not listed in the catalogue are mostly small, occasional pieces. The catalogue also represents the only surviving evidence for the composition of some lost works, including the Andante for violin and orchestra, K.470, the March, K.544, the Contredanses, K.565, and the aria *Ohne Zwang, aus eignem Triebe*, K.569. Additionally, it sometimes provides otherwise unknown information concerning scoring. The Concerto, K.459, for example, is listed in the catalogue as including trumpets and timpani, although parts for these instruments are lacking in the autograph and do not otherwise survive; and the *Lied zur Gesellenreise*, K.468, presumed to have been composed for Leopold Mozart's induction in Mozart's Viennese lodge in March 1785, is described as having organ accompaniment in the autograph, but 'Klavier' (fortepiano) in the *Verzeichnüss*.

The catalogue is also a source of chronological problems, for the dates in it do not always square with the information on Mozart's autographs. The Concerto, K.467, for instance, is dated February 1785 on the autograph but 9 March in the catalogue. It may be that some entries in the catalogue were made from memory, later than the writing down of the autographs; at least this appears to be the case with the earliest works listed there (see Leeson and

Whitwell, 1973). And in numerous instances the incipits differ in details from the autographs and other sources.

Mozart's idea of a thematic catalogue of his works was not original. In a letter of 22 December 1777 to Padre Martini in Bologna, Leopold Mozart had written:

> I have [an] idea, which is to send you the beginnings of [my son's] compositions, beginning with the keyboard sonatas written for *Madame Victoire* [K.6–7] and printed in Paris *when he was seven years old* – then those [sonatas] he composed *when he was eight* for the Queen of England, printed in London [K.10–15] – then those he composed *at the age of nine* for the Princess of *Nassau-Weilburg*, printed at The Hague in Holland [K.26–31], etc., etc. I shall, moreover, add a short account of his travels and any noteworthy incidents.

Leopold's idea to create a thematic catalogue of his son's works, and to write his biography, was also not new, even in 1777. The non-thematic list of Mozart's compositions drawn up in 1768 for the Viennese court was already a step in that direction, and in the preface to the second edition of his *Violinschule* (1769) Leopold had expressed his intention to write a biography of Mozart:

> I might here take the opportunity of entertaining the public with a story such as probably appears but once in a century, and which in the domain of music has perhaps never yet appeared *in such a degree of the miraculous*; I might describe the wonderful genius of my son; circumstantially relate his unbelievably rapid progress in the whole extent of musical science from the fifth to the thirteenth year of his age; and I might, in so incredible a matter, call to witness the unanswerable testimony of many of the greatest masters, indeed even the testimony of envy itself. But since I am to write but a short preliminary notice and not a circumstantial story, I hope that after my return from Italy, where I now intend to go with God's blessing, I may . . . entertain the public with this story.

Private and semi-private documents

Numerous documents relating to Mozart derive from private or semi-private sources and were not intended for general dissemination. These include references in private correspondences or diaries, thematic catalogues compiled by various institutions, and the records of the courts where Mozart performed or where, as in the case of Salzburg, he was employed.

Because the Mozarts corresponded less when they were not on tour, and because many of Leopold Mozart's Salzburg letters are lost, the majority of references to Mozart in Salzburg derive from private sources. Many of them relate to his employment at court, although they fail to record his day-to-day activities (as they fail to report the day-to-day activities of the court music in general). Nevertheless, they provide extensive information concerning Mozart's various appointments, dismissals, resignations and leaves of absence, his remuneration for court services and for writing specially commissioned works, subsidies for his travels, and occasionally accounts of performances of specific compositions. A particularly important document is that relating to Mozart's appointment as court organist in 1779, which shows that composition was a secondary and non-specific condition of his employment: 'he shall . . . carry out his appointed duties with diligent assiduity and irreproachably, in the Cathedral as well as at Court and in the Chapel, and shall as far as possible serve the Court and the Church with new compositions made by him.'

Also important are several contemporary diaries, among them those of Beda Hübner, librarian at St Peter's, the important Benedictine monastery in the heart of Salzburg; Cajetan Hagenauer, son of the Mozarts' Salzburg landlord and from 1786 Abbot of St Peter's; and the Salzburg councillor Joachim Ferdinand von Schiedenhofen. Schiedenhofen's diary in particular provides numerous otherwise unrecorded details concerning the performance of Mozart's works in Salzburg between 1774 and 1778.

Private documents are plentiful from the Mozarts' many tours. The earliest independent references to Mozart's performances in Vienna in 1762 derive from the diaries of Count Johann Carl von Zinzendorf, a high state official (Zinzendorf's diaries also record Mozartiana for the 1780s), and numerous letters, by Voltaire and Johann Adolf Hasse among others, show the extent of the Mozarts' contacts and their importance in promoting Wolfgang's career. This is especially the case with a number of documents from the first Italian journey of 1770, including letters of recommendation by Count Carl Joseph Firmian, Governor-General of Lombardy, to Count Gian Luca Pallavicini of Bologna, an important patron of the arts, and Pallavicini's recommendations to his distant relation Cardinal Count Lazaro Opizio Pallavicini and Prince Andrea Doria Pamphili, both in Rome. Many other letters referring to Mozart are apparently lost. Wolfgang, writing to his father from Munich in 1777, mentions meeting the composer Mysliveček who showed him letters, now lost, 'in which', Mozart writes, 'I often read my name'. Not all of the letters referring to Mozart, however, were positive. On 12 December 1771, the Empress Maria Theresa wrote to Archduke Ferdinand at Milan:

> . . . you ask me to take the young Salzburger into your service. I do not know why, not believing that you have need of a composer or of useless people. If however it would give you pleasure, I have no wish to hinder you. What I say is intended only to prevent your burdening yourself with useless people and giving titles to people of that sort. If they are in your service it degrades that service when these people go about the world like beggars. Besides, he has a large family.

Institutional and other private documents also survive for the last decade of Mozart's life, when he had taken up permanent residence in Vienna. In addition to records of court payments for various works, other important documents include Mozart's marriage contract, papers concerning his involvement in various masonic lodges (see especially Autexier, 1984) his appointment as imperial chamber musician, and documents relating to the inventory and disposition of his estate, as well as Constanze Mozart's petition for a pension.

Mostly unknown but of potential importance are numerous thematic catalogues drawn up by courts, monasteries and other institutions and by late 18th-century publishers. These include the Lambach catalogue of 1768, which provides strong if still inconclusive evidence that the Symphony K.17 (Anh.C 11.02) is by Leopold Mozart, and the so-called *Quartbuch* of *c.* 1775, which shows that, contrary to the generally accepted view, Mozart's quartets K.168–173 circulated in central Austria, and possibly in Vienna, during the mid-1770s (Eisen, 1986). Also important is a catalogue of the Salzburg Cathedral holdings, drawn up in the late 1780s, which includes a number of Mozart's works but also suggests that not all of his sacred music was housed, or perhaps even performed, there (Senn, 1971/2b).

Perhaps the most important publisher's catalogue is the so-called Breitkopf & Härtel manuscript catalogue, an early 19th-century attempt to list titles and musical incipits of all works attributed to Mozart, organized by genre. Although the original of this catalogue is lost, copies made for Köchel and Jahn survive in the Gesellschaft der Musikfreunde, Vienna, and in the Staatsbibliothek Preussischer Kulturbesitz, West Berlin, respectively. In addition to listing a significant proportion of Mozart's authenticated works, the catalogue also includes entries for several compositions that are otherwise unknown, among them the symphonies K.Anh.222 (19b) and Anh.215, 217 and 218 (66c-e) and the solo sonatas K.Anh.199–202 (33d-g); sources for these works are lost. Their listing in the catalogue, however, is insufficient as otherwise unsupported evidence of Mozart's authorship, for although Breitkopf & Härtel's sources included printed editions by most of the major European music publishers of the time and manuscripts obtained from the original Breitkopf firm (taken over by Härtel in 1796), the Hamburg music dealer Johann Christoph Westphal, Mozart's widow Constanze, and his sister, Maria Anna, none of these sources is above suspicion.

Public documents
Whereas documents relating to Mozart's time in Salzburg derive mainly from private sources, many of those relating to his travels are found in widely circulated printed sources, primarily contemporary newspapers and periodicals. Between 1763 and 1766, substantial articles describing Mozart were published in the *Augsburgischer Intelligenz-Zettel* and *Ordentliche Wöchentliche Franckfurter Frag- und Anzeigungs-Nachrichten*, in Friedrich Melchior von Grimm's *Correspondance littéraire*, in the Paris *Avant-Coureur*, the *Oprechte Saturdagse Haerlemse Courant*, and the *Historisch-Moralische Belustigungen des Geistes oder ermunternde Betrachtungen über die wunderbare Haushaltung Gottes in den neuesten Zeiten*. The most important early descriptions of Mozart are articles published in *Aristide ou le Citoyen* (Lausanne, 1766) and Daines Barrington's 'Account of a very remarkable young Musician' published in the *Philosophical Transactions of the Royal Society* (London, 1771). Although these

articles generally report primarily on his precocity, they sometimes provide otherwise unknown biographical information; and much of our knowledge of Mozart's public concerts in London and Holland derives from advertisements in local newspapers.

Similar articles are plentiful for the first Italian journey (1769–71), but less common for subsequent trips and especially for the extended tour of 1777–9 to Mannheim and Paris, which is documented primarily by the Mozart family letters. Several explanations seem likely for this, among them that Mozart was no longer an exciting child prodigy, and, as has recently been established by the careful study of Mozart's scores and of the veracity of his letters, that by and large he was indolent and made few public appearances (Tyson, 1978, and Zaslaw, 1978).

With Mozart's move to Vienna, and his increased compositional and performing activity, published documents once again become common. Primary among several sources – including the *Wiener-blättchen*, *Wiener Kronik*, *Wiener Realzeitung* and *Provinzialnachrichten* – is the *Wiener Zeitung*, the court-sanctioned newspaper. Included in these periodicals are announcements and reviews of Mozart's public concerts and his operas, and in particular advertisements for his works, significant quantities of which became available for the first time. Some of the advertisements derive from Mozart himself, who often tried first to sell his compositions on a subscription basis, usually unsuccessfully. The majority, however, are by local dealers in manuscript and printed music, among them Johann Traeg, Lorenz Lausch, the court theatre copyist Wenzel Sukowaty, and such prominent firms as Artaria and Hoffmeister.

Also common are published reports of Mozart's trips during these years; his performances were regularly noted in local newspapers from Prague (1787 and 1791), Dresden, Leipzig and Berlin (1789), and Frankfurt (1790), where he attended the first coronation of Leopold II. And just as Mozart's personal appearances generated considerable local interest, so too did the appearance of his works in print and on stage. A remarkable number of articles testify to the widespread popularity of his operas, in particular *Die Entführung aus dem Serail*, and reviews of printed editions of his chamber and keyboard music appeared in journals published as distant from Vienna as Hamburg and London.

A final group of important public documents is the printed libretti for Mozart's stage works: examples survive for all of them except *Bastien und Bastienne* (1768), *Il sogno di Scipione* (1771–2), *La finta giardiniera* (1775), *Il rè pastore* (1775) and *Der Schauspieldirektor* (1786). Often these documents provide otherwise unknown information concerning the casts at the first performances.

Interpretation

Like the interpretation of the family letters, the interpretation of contemporary documents is not always straightforward. In most cases works are only vaguely described and their identification remains a matter of conjecture. By and large, documents cannot be interpreted in isolation: their evaluation often depends not only on other documents, but also on the evidence of the letters and musical sources.

It has been common to assume, for example, that works by Mozart offered for sale in Vienna during the 1780s were among his most recent compositions. Consequently three unidentified symphonies advertised by the Viennese dealer in manuscript music Johann Traeg in February 1785 are thought to be K.319 in B♭ major, K.338 in C major, and K.385 in D major (only the *Linz* Symphony, K.425, had been composed in the meantime). However, other evidence suggests that the symphonies were probably not among Mozart's most recent works. Striking parallels between Traeg's advertisement and a catalogue published in Hamburg by the dealer Johann Christoph Westphal suggest that the latter had direct connections with Viennese dealers and that three of the symphonies offered in Hamburg in the same year may be identical to those offered in Vienna. Westphal's catalogue provides the additional information that all three symphonies – listed as numbers 1, 2 and 3, respectively – were in D major. One of these works can be identified with certainty. For when Breitkopf & Härtel drew up their manuscript catalogue, they relied in part on Westphal; their source for the symphony based on the Serenade K.320 is listed there as 'Westphal No.2'. A second symphony can also be identified: among the recently discovered symphony manuscripts in Odense, Denmark, is a copy of a symphony based on the Serenade K.203 (189b) that very probably derives from Westphal; on its wrapper is the notation 'N: 1 D♯'. Consequently a more plausible interpretation for the original Viennese document is that in February 1785 Traeg offered for sale three D major symphonies by Mozart, K.320, K.203 (189b), and an as-yet-unidentified work (Zaslaw and Eisen, 1985/6).

The hypothesis that these symphonies were older works is strengthened by evidence from the letters and other sources. It is apparent, for example, that in Vienna Mozart performed several of his works from the 1770s. In a letter of 4 January 1783, he asked his father to send the symphonies K.182 (173dA), 183 (173dB), 201 (186a) and 204 (213a), all of them composed between 1773 and 1775; and copies from the mid-1780s by Traeg survive for K.181 (162b), 182 (173dA), 200 (189k), 201 (186a) and a symphony based on the Serenade K.204 (213a). Other Salzburg symphonies, including K.318, 319 and 338, survive in copies partly by Salzburg copyists and partly by Viennese copyists; these manuscripts apparently derive from Mozart's estate and were probably used by him to perform the works. That K.320 in particular circulated in the same year as Traeg's advertisement is documented by a copy in the Bartenstein collection which is dated 1785.

In short, the interpretation of documents also depends on the evidence of the family letters and contemporary manuscripts of Mozart's works. Further progress remains to be made in this area, for while the family letters are now available in a complete edition (a few recent discoveries notwithstanding) and sources for Mozart's works are by and large accounted for, documentary research is only partially complete. Some recent finds suggest that significant documents remain to be discovered and that their interpretation, in the light of previously known documents and other material, will provide valuable new insights into Mozart's biography and the genesis, dissemination and reception of his works (Eisen, 1986).

Autographs

History

Mozart's autographs are the primary musical documents transmitting his works. Although many compositions survive in manuscript copies or printed editions, these usually represent second- or later-generation sources. Autographs are generally the most reliable guides to the authenticity, chronology and texts of Mozart's works (but not exclusively: see 'Manuscript copies' and 'Editions').

Because Mozart held no significant church or court appointments during the last ten years of his life, it is fortunate that a large number of his autographs, more than four hundred, survive. After Leopold Mozart's death in 1787, Mozart's early autographs, the majority of which apparently had remained in Salzburg after 1781, were sent to him in Vienna, where they were carefully preserved, together with more recent scores. After Mozart's death, the collection passed to his widow, Constanze.

On several occasions Constanze attempted to sell parts of the collection, but unsuccessfully, and it remained with her throughout the 1790s. About 1799, however, she was approached by the Leipzig publishers Breitkopf & Härtel, who were collecting Mozart's works for a projected complete edition. Constanze suggested that they purchase the entire collection, but Breitkopf took only about forty autographs. In the same year, however, Constanze also had an offer from the publisher Johann Anton André, located in Offenbach am Main, not far from Frankfurt, and Constanze sold what was left of the collection to him – just under 300 autographs, as well as some copies.

Although it was André's original intention to publish new editions of Mozart's works based on the composer's autographs, he soon became more interested in studying the documents themselves. In particular he was concerned to distinguish Mozart's hand from others he found in the scores and to order the undated autographs chronologically according to the characteristics of their handwriting, a study now usually referred to as *Schriftchronologie* (see below). Some preliminary results of André's investigations appear in the foreword to a catalogue of his Mozart holdings drawn up in 1833 (Oldman, 1924). With few exceptions the autographs remained in his possession until his death in 1843. In 1811 or 1814, for example, twenty-two significant autographs, including the original manuscripts of the last ten quartets and other chamber and keyboard works, were sold to Johann Andreas Stumpff in London (these eventually became part of the British Museum, now the British Library). And in 1842 André offered the collection to the courts at Vienna, Berlin, and London, but was turned down. Consequently the collection was split among his heirs, although most of the autographs eventually found their way into the former Royal Library at Berlin.

Attacks on Berlin during World War II made it necessary to move the autographs, together with other treasures in the Berlin libraries, to secure hiding-places. After the war these items were largely split between East and West Germany except for a significant holding of more than 100 Mozart autographs stored at the convent of Grüssau in Silesia, which became a part of Poland. For many years these autographs were presumed lost. However, three of them surfaced in 1977 and shortly afterwards the recovery of almost the entire collection was publicly announced. Since 1980 this significant holding has been on deposit at the Biblioteka Jagiellońska in Kraków (Wilson, 1982/3). Other Mozart autographs are owned by numerous major and minor libraries, including the Internationale Stiftung Mozarteum, or are held by private collectors. The major holding in the Zweig Collection at the British Library was converted from a loan into an outright gift in 1987.

Evaluation

A significant proportion of Mozart's autographs are either signed or dated, or both. While in some cases the dates have been tampered with, or do not square with other evidence (see 'Documents'), in most cases they can be accepted as more or less accurate. Many of the autographs, however, are not dated, and in order to determine when they were written down, two techniques have recently proven particularly valuable: the study of the chronological development of Mozart's handwriting (*Schriftchronologie*) and the analysis of the types of paper on which the autographs are written.

Schriftchronologie documents changes in handwriting. When these changes can be shown on the basis of securely dated manuscripts to occur at particular times, they can serve as criteria for the dating of other, undated autographs (Plath, 1971/2). In Mozart's case, *Schriftchronologie* is uncertain for the period up to about 1770, prior to the first Italian tour. Insofar as can be judged from early dated autographs – of which there are, in fact, too few to construct a useful *Schriftchronologie* – Mozart's handwriting during the 1760s was fairly stable. By the same token, it is also consistent during the Viennese period after 1781 (although many more autographs survive from this time), and an exact chronology for the Viennese period is not yet possible, except to distinguish between pre- and post-*Figaro* works (Plath, 1984).

For the period 1770–80, however, *Schriftchronologie* has achieved striking results: many dated autographs survive from this time and the changes in Mozart's hand are readily identifiable. According to

Wolfgang Plath, three main periods can be distinguished: 1770–71 or 1772, 1772–4, and 1775–80 (Plath 1971/2, from which the following also derives). In the first of these, the chief signs to change are the shape of the treble clef, Mozart's notation of an abbreviation for quavers (eighth notes), his writing of the letter 'd' and the form of the crotchet (quarter) rest. In 1769 these symbols had appeared in Mozart's autographs relatively stabilized as: ♭, *q*, *∂* and *v* or *⌣*. During 1770, however, they change considerably: the vertical stroke of the treble clef now passes through the entire symbol and has a tail at the bottom ♭; the abbreviation for quavers becomes a stroke passing through the note-stem *q*; the earlier form of the letter 'd' gives way to *d*; and the crotchet rest, which formerly lay on its side, from now stands on its end *ſ*. Although these changes do not occur simultaneously or with rigorous consistency, they are nevertheless mostly present in later parts of the autograph to *Mitridate*, K.87 (74a), composed in late 1770, and – excepting the letter 'd' which continues to alternate between the older and newer forms – represent the normal state of Mozart's hand at this time.

About March 1772, in the autograph of the Litany, K.125, Mozart's hand again changes. The crotchet rest lies on its side, as formerly, and the treble clef is 'thinner'. The chief witness to the change in Mozart's hand, however, is the symbol for *piano*, which had previously taken the form *p:* or *pia:*, but now appears as *pia:* or *pia:*. This in particular characterizes the entire period from 1772–late 1774 or early 1775 although other less striking changes permit datings within more circumscribed times. The period 1775–80 can also be identified by changes in the *piano* sign: from 1775 it appears as *p:* and from the early summer of 1778 generally as *p:*. From 1780, in the autographs to the Symphony K.338 and *Idomeneo*, K.366, the dominant forms are *pia:* and *pia:*. Characteristic, too, is the symbol for *forte*: *for:* or *for:* prior to 1775; *for:* from 1775; and *for:* or *for:* beginning in late 1777 and early 1778.

A further result of Plath's investigations, with important implications for the authenticity of Mozart's works from before 1770, has been the establishment of criteria for distinguishing Mozart's hand from that of his father (Plath 1960/61). Numerous autographs previously thought to be by Wolfgang, including the Masses K.115 (166d) and 116 (90a, together with the related fragments 417B, Anh.A 18 and Anh.A 19), as well as the songs K.149–151 (125d–f), can now be shown to be by Leopold. Plath also articulated the important principle that an unsigned autograph does not guarantee the genuineness of the work it transmits. It is not the case, however, that significant problems of authenticity in Mozart are restricted only to works surviving in autographs said to be by Wolfgang or his father (see 'Manuscript copies').

The second principal means of evaluating Mozart's autographs is the study of the types of paper on which they are written, and in order to understand the techniques of paper analysis it is necessary to know how paper was manufactured during the 18th century (the following description is based on Tyson, 1987). All of the papers available to Mozart were hand-made. Two men, a vatman and a coucher, each worked with a rectangular sieve or mould, a rectangular frame with several wooden ribs. Across the bottom of the mould was a mesh made of two kinds of wires: many thin, closely-spaced wires running parallel to the long axis of the mould (laid wires) and fewer thicker wires, spaced farther apart, running at right angles to them (chain wires). Several additional ornamental wires attached to the laid and chain wires, forming a design, letters, or some combination of these, identified the maker and sometimes the size and quality of the paper.

The vatman would dip one of the moulds into a vat filled with a white liquid prepared from broken-down linen rags; excess water would drain through the wire mesh, leaving a layer of paper 'stuff'. The coucher then pressed the layer of paper 'stuff' onto a sheet of damp felt, to which it would adhere, free of the mould. Returning the mould to the vatman, who in the meantime had filled the other mould, the coucher would take the second mould and press it onto a new layer of felt, and so on. When the paper dried, the ornamental design sewn onto the mould produced a local thinning that is known as a watermark, which is visible when the paper is held up to light. Because two moulds were used in alternation, there are two watermarks in any single batch of paper; they are usually referred to as (sometimes fraternal, sometimes identical) twins.

By identifying paper-types in Mozart's autographs it is usually possible to determine where they were written (if the paper is characteristic of Salzburg, Vienna, or some other locality visited by Mozart) and when (if the same paper frequently occurs in other autographs). In this respect the principle underlying paper-studies is similar to that of *Schriftchronologie*: where a sufficiently large sample of securely dated autographs on a particular paper-type survives, the occurrence of the same paper-type in an undated autograph is strong evidence for its dating. A further refinement concerns details of staff-ruling. It is generally the case, for example, that when Mozart did not rule the staves himself, he could only obtain 10-staff paper in Salzburg; in Vienna he generally used 12-staff paper.

Because paper manufacturing in Salzburg was dominated by a single firm, that of the Hofmann family in Lengfelden, near Salzburg, and identical or very similar watermarks were in use for extended periods of time, paper-types are not always a reliable guide to the dating of Mozart's works before about 1772, although details of rastrology sometimes provide useful information (for example see Tyson, 1987). About that time, however, the Hofmann mill began producing paper with a different watermark (the initials 'ISH', which stand for Johann Sigismund Hofmann, were replaced by the intials 'AFH' for Anton Fidelis Hofmann), a useful guide to pre- and post-*c.* 1772 Salzburg manuscripts in general; and machine-ruled Italian papers became common in the

Archdiocese. The most important of the Italian papers are the so-called 'Klein-Querformat' papers distinguished primarily by their small dimensions (described and illustrated in Tyson). The five different types of this paper documented for the period 1773–9 (or possibly slightly earlier; see Eisen, 1989a) permit datings to relatively circumscribed periods for many autographs, and together with *Schriftchronologie* have important implications for the chronology of undated works.

The study of paper-types is most important for the period 1781–91. Undated Viennese autographs, generally on 12-staff Italian-made paper, can often be assigned to very exact periods on the basis of their watermarks and in particular their rastrology, or details of staff-ruling, for although some papers were common in Vienna throughout the 1780s, they often differ with regard to their total spans (the distance from the top of the uppermost staff to the bottom of the lowest staff). What is more, the careful study of watermarks and rastrology often shows that autographs were not written out at a single sitting; numerous works, among them the six quartets dedicated to Haydn, were apparently written over a considerable period of time.

The most immediate results of *Schriftchronologie* and paper-studies is a revised chronology for many of Mozart's works. Often the new datings differ by as many as five or more years from those given in the standard literature: the first movement of the Horn Concerto K.412, for example, usually thought to date from 1782, was probably started about 1786 and not finished until 1791; the Piano Sonata in B♭ K.333 (315c) was not composed in Paris in 1778 but probably in Linz about November 1783; and the contredanse 'Les Filles malicieuses', K.610, although it is entered in Mozart's own catalogue of his works under the date 6 March 1791, was possibly written down as early as 1783 (Tyson, 1987).*

Paper-studies and *Schriftchronologie* also have implications for Mozart's biography and his working methods. The commonly held notion that Mozart virtually abandoned church composition during the Vienna years – the only apparent exceptions are the unfinished C minor Mass, K.427 (417a), the *Ave, verum corpus*, K.618, and the Requiem, K.626 – is probably incorrect. A number of Kyrie and Gloria fragments, and two settings of psalm texts (K.93 and 93a, copies by Mozart of works by Georg Reutter the younger), are on paper used by Mozart only after about December 1787. These observations confirm the report of a Danish visitor to Vienna in 1788 who wrote that '[Mozart] is now working on church music'. Similarly, paper-studies show that numerous fragments are not drafts rejected by Mozart as unsatisfactory, but merely unfinished compositions. Mozart often began works but put them aside for completion later: the openings of the concertos K.449, 488 and 503, for example, are on paper from some years

---

*For a sceptical view of some of Tyson's assumptions, analogies and logical procedures, see King, 1989. (Ed.)

earlier than the paper in the rest of their autographs. Some other fragments should also be understood as 'works in progress'.

In addition to being the chief witnesses to the authenticity and chronology of Mozart's works, as well as some aspects of his working methods and biography, the autographs often represent the primary textual sources for his compositions. For many works they represent the only surviving, demonstrably authentic source and usually they are the basis for modern editions of the compositions; in particular they are the cornerstone of the *Neue Mozart-Ausgabe*. It is not the case, however, that the autographs always represent Mozart's last or most definitive thoughts and are in all cases to be preferred over other sources (see 'Manuscript copies').

Other features of the autographs, reflecting primarily on Mozart's compositional decision-making and performance practice, have been less thoroughly studied. Numerous crossed out passages or other changes in the autographs, as well as variations in ink or thickness of quill, show Mozart at work and may have important analytical implications (see for example Finscher, 1980, Flothuis, 1980b, Wolff, 1980, and Rosen, 1987). Similarly, the autographs have also proved important for questions of scoring, particularly in the chamber music, and for understanding Mozart's concepts of genre as well as the specific meaning of his terminology (Webster, 1983).

Manuscript copies

BEFORE 1780, the primary means of disseminating music in Austria and southern Germany was by manuscript copies. Even after 1780, when music printing became firmly established in Vienna, large-scale genres including symphonies, concertos, operas and sacred music, continued to be disseminated primarily (but not exclusively) by manuscript copies; the genres most commonly disseminated by printed editions included keyboard and chamber music.

After autographs, then, and in many instances where autographs do not survive, the chief sources for Mozart's music are manuscript copies. They range from copies made under Mozart's direct supervision and with his approval to copies of unknown provenance and date with no demonstrable connection to Mozart. In the first instance, copies must be considered as witnesses to the authenticity of the works they transmit. Additionally, they are important for questions of chronology, text and performance practice.

Salzburg copies
The most important early copies of Mozart's works, generally from before about 1780, derive from Salzburg. By and large they transmit accurate attributions and fairly reliable texts. Not all Salzburg copies, however, derive directly from the Mozarts and conflicting attributions among them are not uncommon. Leopold

Mozart's Mass Seiffert 4/1, for example, survives in three contemporary Salzburg copies, two of them attributed to Leopold Mozart (Salzburg, St Peter's, shelf-mark Moz 10.1 and Augsburg, Heiligkreuz, shelf-mark 77) and one, dated 1753, to Eberlin (Vienna, Nationalbibliothek, shelf-mark S.m. 22247). Similarly, in a letter of 4 August 1770 from Mozart to his sister, Wolfgang cites the openings of the Cassations K.63, 99 (63a) and 62/100 (62a), evidently in response to a comment by her from a now-lost letter that someone in Salzburg had passed off one of Wolfgang's compositions as his own: 'I find it difficult to believe that it is one of mine, for who would dare claim for himself a composition by the Kapellmeister's son, whose mother and sister are in Salzburg?' Consequently, Salzburg copies by themselves do not guarantee the genuineness of the works they transmit, nor are they necessarily authentic. In order to be considered reliable witnesses to authenticity, Salzburg copies of Mozart's works from before about 1780 must have title-pages or autograph corrections in the parts by Wolfgang or Leopold Mozart, be attested to by independent and unequivocal documentary evidence, or be by copyists whose direct connection to the Mozarts and reliability can be demonstrated.

Three copyists can be identified as 'Mozart' copyists: Maximilian Raab, Joseph Richard Estlinger and Felix Hofstätter, all of whom worked as official court copyists, by appointment or *de facto*, and privately for the Mozarts. Maximilian Raab (*c.* 1720–1780) first came to Salzburg in 1748. During the 1750s he was employed at the court as *Hofvioletist* and in 1766 he succeeded Johann Jakob Rott as court copyist. Raab was privately employed by Leopold Mozart as early as the 1750s and his hand is found in numerous authentic copies of Mozart's works from the 1770s. Joseph Richard Estlinger (*c.* 1720–1791), court double bassist from 1760, succeeded Raab as court copyist in 1780. But he had also worked privately for Leopold Mozart at least from 1752 and his hand is found more frequently than any other among authentic copies of Leopold's and Wolfgang's works; Estlinger was the Mozarts' preferred copyist. Felix Hofstätter (*c.* 1744–1814) was active in Salzburg as a tenor and violinist from the late 1760s and as a copyist from about 1773. Although he never received a fixed appointment as court copyist, he was *de facto* in charge of the court copying after Estlinger's death in 1791. Hofstätter worked privately for the Mozarts and for Michael Haydn. But although copies by him are reliable witnesses to authenticity, some of them may represent unauthorized copies produced without the permission or knowledge of the composer. On 15 May 1784, for example, Mozart wrote to his father from Vienna:

> Today I sent with the post coach the symphony that I composed in Linz for Graf Thun [K.425], together with four concertos [K.449, 450, 451 and 453]. I am not particular about the symphony, only I ask you to have the four concertos copied at home, for the copyists in Salzburg are as little to be trusted as those in Vienna – I am absolutely certain that Hofstetter copied Haydn's music twice.

Although it has been common to assume that Mozart's reference is to Joseph Haydn, there is no evidence to support this identification. More likely, because Mozart identifies the Salzburg copyist Hofstätter, he is referring to Michael Haydn, whose works are known to have circulated in Vienna in unauthorized copies.

Because a corpus of manuscripts and other documentary evidence sufficient to establish the identity and reliability of other scribes who may have worked for the Mozarts does not survive, the evaluation of other Salzburg copies is often problematic. In at least some cases, however, circumstantial evidence suggests that manuscripts, or parts of manuscripts, in certain hands may also be witnesses to authenticity, even if the copyists cannot be identified or their exact relationship to the Mozarts clarified. For example, a copy of the Litany, K.109 (74e) by a demonstrably Salzburg copyist whose work is accurate and who may have had access to other authentic copies, perhaps even court copies, transmits otherwise unknown parts for trumpets (Laufen an der Salzach, Stiftsarchiv). It was common practice in Salzburg, and elsewhere, for horn, trumpet and timpani parts to be added later to sacred music and frequently autographs of such parts do not survive. Consequently the Laufen trumpet parts to K.109 (74e) have a respectable claim to authenticity, although no conclusive evidence to prove it. The situation may be similar with other Salzburg copies, which to date have not been systematically studied.

Although the majority of authentic Salzburg copies of Mozart's works date from before c. 1780, some important copies were also made after Wolfgang's permanent move to Vienna in 1781. At least until 1785, Mozart continued to send his new works to Salzburg where they were copied and performed. A number of these copies survive, including important manuscripts of the *Linz* Symphony (Eisen, 1988a), and of the concertos K.449, 451 and 466. Similarly, when Mozart visited Salzburg in 1783, he brought with him Viennese copies of the concertos K.413–415 (387a, 385p, 387b) and had other works copied for performance there, among them the C minor Mass, K.427 (417a). With Leopold Mozart's death in 1787, however, the flow of authentic Salzburg manuscripts, and authentic manuscripts in Salzburg, apparently comes to an end.

Viennese copies

Despite the rapid growth of music publishing firms in Vienna after 1778, manuscript copies remained the primary means for the distribution of music, especially in the larger genres. Indeed, the number of copying shops was exceptionally large. When Charles Burney visited Vienna in 1772 he wrote:

> . . . as there are no music shops in Vienna, the best method of procuring new compositions is to apply to copyists. . . . I was plagued with copyists . . . they began to regard me as a greedy and indiscriminate purchaser of whatever trash they should offer; but I was forced to hold my hand, not only from buying bad music, but good. For everything is very dear at Vienna, and nothing more so than music, of which none is printed.

By the 1780s, music copying seems to have been dominated by three firms: Lorenz Lausch, Johann Traeg and Wenzel Sukowaty, the court theatre copyist.

In Vienna, Mozart used copyists to prepare parts for performance at his numerous concerts, and to provide copies for publishers. They are often mentioned in his correspondence. In the already-cited letter of 15 May 1784 to his father he wrote 'I myself have everything copied in my quarters and in front of me', and the autograph of the Andante cantabile of the String Quartet K.387 even has his instructions to the copyist scribbled in the margin, a rarity among the autographs. Moreover, in a letter of 4 August 1799, Mozart's sister Nannerl suggested not only that Mozart had regular Viennese copyists, but also that they had a more or less free hand with the composer: 'I have it from an eye-witness that at home his scores sat underneath the keyboard, and that the copyists could take them as needed.'

Nevertheless, not a single reliable Viennese 'Mozart' copyist has been identified to date, the survival of several Viennese copies with autograph entries in the parts notwithstanding. In fact, there is little documentary evidence for Mozart's dealings with any individual Viennese copyist or copying firm* and it may be that beyond providing copyists or copying firms with an original, Mozart did not take much interest in the subsequent dissemination of the works. In at least one instance, the sale of three symphonies and three concertos to the Donaueschingen court in 1786, Mozart seems to have acquired the copies from professional copying firms who already handled the works, not to have had new copies made from his own originals (Eisen, 1988a).

Consequently Viennese copies can be identified as authentic only when Mozart's autograph corrections appear in the parts, or when unequivocal documentary evidence testifies to the authenticity of a manuscript. Otherwise they are comparable to Salzburg copies in general: although most of them transmit genuine works, they do not themselves guarantee the authenticity of the works they transmit, nor are they necessarily authentic copies or copies prepared from other authentic sources. Among instances of Viennese copies misattributing works by Mozart is a copy from the early 1790s of the *Linz* Symphony, attributed to Joseph Haydn (Budapest, Széchényi National Library, shelf-mark IV.101).

Other copies

In addition to manuscripts from Salzburg and Vienna, copies of Mozart's works were made throughout Europe, especially during the 1780s and later. Some of these copies derive from printed editions, others from unidentified manuscript copies. In numerous instances they represent the earliest or only surviving copies of works attributed to Mozart, as in the case of the Symphony in

---

*As these proofs arrive, such evidence has been discovered, in Vienna, by the American scholar Dexter Edge (Ed.)

A minor listed in the Köchel catalogue as Anh.220 (16a). Yet although the manuscript is unique, and conflicting attributions are unknown, neither the source nor the style of the work suggest it was composed by Mozart (Zaslaw and Eisen, 1986). In general, lacking any reasonable claim to authenticity, other copies are of less value than generic Salzburg or Viennese copies as witnesses to the authenticity of the works they transmit and their texts.

A final group of copies from the 19th century deserves special notice: manuscripts prepared by or for the first important Mozart scholars, Otto Jahn, Aloys Fuchs and Ludwig Ritter von Köchel. For the most part these copies were based on Mozart's autographs, many of which were subsequently lost. Consequently, they sometimes represent the only surviving *potentially* authentic sources for Mozart's works. Although many previously lost autographs have now been recovered, a number of these copies transmit otherwise unknown works, sketches, or drafts.

Evaluation and Importance

The evaluation of manuscript copies of Mozart's works relies on the same general techniques as the evaluation of autographs, the study of handwriting and paper-types, albeit with modifications. The possibility of determining a *Schriftchronologie* for copyists, for example, seems unlikely. In most instances there is an insufficient number of manuscripts and, typically, the copies are not dated. Nevertheless, information about copyists, and in particular Salzburg copyists, often provides chronological boundaries for manuscripts or groups of manuscripts. It is the case, for example, that all manuscripts by Maximilian Raab date from not later than 1 February 1780, when he died; and significant changes in Estlinger's handwriting can be documented for the period 1760–65.

Similarly, watermarks also provide important evidence concerning the chronology of manuscripts in cases where an adequate sample of dated sources from a localized geographical area survives. This technique, which depends on the examination of large numbers of Salzburg and Viennese copies in particular, is often sufficient to date a manuscript within a one- or two-year span. For example, copies of the concertos K.449 and 451 mentioned in Mozart's letters to his father of 1784 can be identified not only because the surviving manuscripts have entries in the parts by Leopold and Maria Anna Mozart, itself insufficient as evidence for their time of copying, but also because they are written largely on paper that was available in Salzburg only during that year.

Like autographs, authentic copies provide direct evidence concerning the authenticity, chronology and texts of Mozart's works. Compositions such as the aria *Cara se le mie pene*, K. deest, known from a single source (Salzburg, Museum Carolino Augusteum, shelf-mark Hs. 1747), can be confirmed as authentic by the identification of the copyist, Estlinger. Similarly, it is arguable that the Offertory *Inter natos mulierum*, K.72 (74f), was composed somewhat later than *c.* 1771 as is usually supposed. Mozart's autograph of this work is unknown and the unique surviving authentic copy is on a type of paper that is found in Salzburg only from 1777 to about 1780. Since most authentic copies appear to be approximately contemporary with the composition of the works they transmit, it may be that the Offertory dates from the later 1770s. As for the texts of Mozart's works, a recent study of the *Linz* Symphony identifies a second, unquestionably authentic source which has significant implications for its text (Eisen, 1988a).

In some instances authentic copies provide information not found in Mozart's autographs. This is true not only of performance practice questions, such as the role of the keyboard continuo in the performance of Mozart's concertos (see, for example, Ferguson, 1984/5) or the number of players on a part, but also with regard to Mozart's revisions of his works. Numerous authentic copies transmit revised versions of Mozart's works, among them copies of *Così fan tutte* (Tyson, 1987), the Symphony K.Anh.221 (45a), and the motet *Exsultate, jubilate*, K.165 (158a).

First and early editions

During Mozart's LIFETIME, slightly more than 130 of his works appeared in printed editions published in Vienna, Prague, Speyer, Mainz, Paris, Amsterdam, The Hague and London. More than half of these editions are of works with keyboard, including solo and accompanied sonatas, piano trios and piano quartets. Others are of chamber works, including string quartets and quintets, dances (usually arranged for keyboard) and songs. Works for larger forces, such as operas, symphonies and piano concertos, which in south Germany and Austria were disseminated primarily by means of manuscript copies, are not so well represented. Before 1791, only two complete operas in vocal score (*Die Entführung* and *Don Giovanni*), three symphonies (K.297 (300a), 319 and 385) and six piano concertos (K.175+382, 413–415, 453 and 595) were published. By 1805, however, more than half of Mozart's works had appeared in print, including almost all of the major works in each genre.

First and early editions published during Mozart's lifetime

The majority of editions of Mozart's works published before 1780 – almost exclusively keyboard and chamber works – appeared under his direct supervision or with his consent, often as a result of his early travels. The sonatas and variations K.6–15, 24–25 and 26–31 were published during the grand tour of 1763–6, the songs K.52–53 in Vienna in 1768, and the variations and sonatas K.179–180, 301–306 and 354 in Paris in 1778. Often these editions bear dedications to royalty for whom Mozart composed or performed the works.

More of Mozart's works were published between 1781 and 1791, the majority of them in Vienna. Indeed, Mozart appears to have established connections with Viennese publishers shortly after taking up residence in the imperial capital. He was in touch with Artaria as early as August 1781 and in December they published the sonatas K.296 and 376–380. Only a few of these editions bear dedications and it is likely that Mozart had his works published primarily to secure some financial benefit and prestige in a rapidly developing market.

In some cases first and early editions represent the best surviving sources for Mozart's works. The juvenile sonatas K.9–15 and 24–31, for example, are not known in the composer's autograph or authentic manuscript copies. The same is true of some mature works composed during the Vienna period and published there during the 1780s, including the Piano Quartet K.493 and the songs K.552 and (in 1791) 596–598.

It is by no means sure, however, that the editions were carefully supervised or proof-read. A copy of the sonatas K.6–7 in the library of the Mozarteum, Salzburg, for example, has Leopold Mozart's autograph corrections. And when Mozart published the sonatas K.301–306 in Paris in 1778, he quit the city before the edition actually appeared. In Vienna, some of Mozart's sonatas and variations were seen through the press by his pupil Josephā Auernhammer. In fact, there is little evidence that Mozart actually supplied originals to publishers and it may be that they worked from second-generation sources.

Consequently it is uncertain whether numerous textual details in the first editions, details that differ from the autographs, actually derive from Mozart. The best-known example is the six string quartets dedicated to Haydn, published by Artaria in 1785 with a dedication by Mozart to his older colleague. The edition differs considerably from the autographs in matters of dynamics, phrasing and tempo indications. In this instance, at least, it is generally thought that the nature and extent of the changes show that Mozart proof-read the works, or was at least involved in some way in the production of them. The situation may be different, however, with other editions that differ from his autographs.

Mozart's satisfaction with Viennese editions of his works remains an open question. In a letter of 26 April 1783 he wrote, at least partly hyperbolically, to the Parisian publisher Sieber, who had published K.301–306 in 1778:

> You presumably know about my pianoforte sonatas with the accompaniment for one violin [K.296 and 376–380] which I have had engraved here by Artaria and Company; – but I'm not entirely satisfied with the standard of engraving here, and even if I were, I should like my fellow-countrymen in Paris to have some of my music once more. Hence I hereby inform you that I have three piano concertos ready [K.413–415], which can be performed with full orchestra, i.e. with oboes and horns, or merely *à quat[t]ro*. – Artaria wants to engrave them. But I give you, my friend, the first refusal. . . . Furthermore I am at work on six quartets for two violins, viola and cello [K.387, 421, 428, 458, 464 and 465, the six quartets dedicated to Haydn]. – If you want to engrave them as well, you can have them.

Sieber's answer to Mozart, if he did in fact answer, does not survive and eventually both the concertos and the quartets were published in Vienna by Artaria.

By the same token there is evidence that Viennese publishers were not entirely happy with Mozart and his often difficult music. According to Constanze Mozart's second husband, Georg Nikolaus Nissen, Mozart had a contract with Hoffmeister to publish three quartets for piano and strings. However, 'Mozart's first piano quartet, in G minor [K.478], was so little thought-of at first that the publisher Hoffmeister sent [Mozart] the advance on the honorarium on the condition that he not compose the two other agreed-upon quartets and Hoffmeister was released from his contract.' (Nissen, 1828) And a letter of Dittersdorf's from 1788, offering Artaria six new quartets, suggests that the Viennese firm did not do well with the six 'Haydn' quartets:

> I offer you the original manuscript or, more accurately, my own score [of the six quartets] for the same price you paid for Mozart's . . . and I am certain that you will do better with [them] than [you did] with Mozart's (which, indeed, I and still greater theorists consider to deserve the highest praise, but which because of their overwhelming and unrelenting artfulness are not to everyone's taste).

Although Mozart's income from these editions was significant, it was not exceptionally large. In his letter to Sieber he had asked for 30 louis d'or, or about 60 ducats, for the three concertos, and 50 louis d'or, or just over 100 ducats, for the quartets dedicated to Haydn (which he had not yet finished composing) – exactly the amount he received from Artaria when they published the quartets in 1785. These sums may be compared with the 100 ducats he received for the composition of *Die Entführung aus dem Serail* in 1782 and *Figaro* in 1786, or the 50 ducats for the composition of *Der Schauspieldirektor*, also in 1786. But it is worth noting that the four Italian singers in *Der Schauspieldirektor* also received 50 ducats each for a single performance, and that Mozart's annual salary as court chamber musician, about 175 ducats (800 florins), was considerably less than the 2000 florins Gluck had received when he held the same position.

In part because of a lack of documentation, Mozart's exact relationships with contemporary publishers remain unclear. Few of his letters to publishers survive and they do not always concern the publication of his works. Mozart's sole extant letter to Hoffmeister, for example, is a request for a loan (20 November 1785). It must be presumed that some letters are lost. Documents show that the firm of Breitkopf in Leipzig approached Mozart in 1786 (although they did not publish any of his works at this time, nor had they published any of his works during the 1770s, despite Leopold Mozart's regular offers) and that in 1790 the London publisher John Bland claimed to have settled a contract with Mozart, Haydn, Koželuch and Vanhal, among others. It may also be the case, however, that Mozart's relationships with contemporary publishers are clouded by his, and his father's, ambivalence concerning the dissemination of Mozart's works. For while it is clear that the Mozarts wished to have at least some of Wolfgang's works printed, the family letters also testify to a desire to withhold some of his compositions (see below, 'Dissemination').

Posthumous editions

The sudden availability in print after 1791 of a considerable number of Mozart's works was no doubt a result of the success of *Die Zauberflöte* and the composer's extraordinary popularity, which was fuelled in part by Romantic stories of his last days that began to circulate early in 1792. The *Teutschlands Annalen des Jahres 1794* reported that:

> In this year 1794 nothing can or may be sung or played, and nothing heard with approbation, but that it bears on its brow the all-powerful and magic name of Mozart. Operas, symphonies, quartets, trios, duets, piano pieces, songs, even dances – all must be by Mozart if they are to lay claim to general approbation. Nor have the music publishers, for their part, in any way failed to satisfy these whims of the dilettantes. By means of the great art of arrangement we already have this composer's *Die Zauberflöte* printed and engraved in all the above-named forms. Heaven alone knows how strangely many of these attempts have worked out, were indeed bound to work out, on account of the nature of the piece. Suffice it to say that what is played or sung is by Mozart, and more particularly from his *Zauberflöte*.

Presumably the appearance of these editions derived from Constanze Mozart's release of works from her husband's estate, at first by means of manuscript copies, many of which were advertised by Viennese firms in 1792 and 1793.

Even so, much of Mozart's music remained unavailable throughout most of the 1790s. About 1798, however, two important publishers, Breitkopf & Härtel in Leipzig and Johann Anton André in Offenbach am Main, made significant inroads into acquiring works from the composer's widow.

In fact, Breitkopf may have approached Constanze as early as 1795, although it was not until about 1798 that they managed to acquire a substantial number of works from her. Together with manuscript copies they already owned, and editions by other publishers, they began in 1798 to issue their *Oeuvres complettes*. Breitkopf's scheme was ambitious and although the edition remained far from complete, by 1806 they had published seventeen volumes of works for solo keyboard, chamber music with keyboard and some songs, the Requiem, *Don Giovanni*, the masses K.257 and 317, twelve quartets, twenty concertos and a number of arias.

More significant for the history of Mozart editions was Constanze Mozart's sale in 1799 of the bulk of Mozart's estate to the publisher Johann Anton André. It was André's intention to publish all of Mozart's works based on the composer's autographs, and several important publications, including many first editions, appeared in 1800 alone, among them the concertos K.246, 365

(316a), 482, 488 and 491, as well as the quartets K.168–173. However, progress on the editions was slow and it was not long before André became more interested in studying the autographs than in publishing them (see above, 'Autographs'). As a result, he published fewer works than Breitkopf; nevertheless, the importance of his editions is considerably greater. Some works published by André from the autographs, including the Concerto K.175, remain primary sources, for Mozart's original scores have, in whole or in part, subsequently been lost.

The standard reference work on Mozart first editions to 1805, with facsimiles of their title-pages, is Haberkamp, 1986.

Dissemination of Mozart's music

IT HAS ALREADY BEEN NOTED that during Mozart's lifetime music was disseminated principally by manuscript copies or printed editions. In order for a work to enter circulation, however, a composer must have sanctioned its reproduction – even if only by performing the work and not recovering the parts – and once a composition had fallen into other hands, there was little to prevent its being recopied or reprinted. Especially during the period before 1780, the unauthorized dissemination of Wolfgang's compositions was a special concern of the Mozarts, and on several occasions they described their attempts to prevent works from being copied without their approval. When Mozart was in Rome in April 1770, for example, he wrote to his sister that 'A symphony is being copied (my father is the copyist), for we do not wish to give it out to be copied as it would be stolen.'

One reason for preventing unauthorized copying was to secure whatever profits or credit might be made from a composition. Consequently the Mozarts considered it necessary for the copying arrangements to derive directly from them. Leopold alludes to this in a letter of 15 October 1777, written to Wolfgang at Augsburg:

> You must quickly look for a copyist, wherever you may be. . . . You can't wait until some amateur patron has them [your works] copied; *all you would gain by that is his gratitude*, nothing else.

It was important, too, to guarantee the quality of the copies, which could be accomplished only if Mozart or his father supervised a work's reproduction.

Leopold Mozart's concern to protect his son's interests may explain in part the restricted circulation of Mozart's early works, although it is clear that he also made attempts to have some of them published. On 7 February 1772 Leopold wrote to Breitkopf in Leipzig:

> If you should wish to print something by my son . . . they could include *keyboard compositions* or *trios* for 2 violins and violoncello, or *quartets* for 2 violins, viola and violoncello; or *symphonies* for 2 violins, viola, 2 horns, 2 oboes or transverse flutes and bass. In short, you can have any kind of composition which seems profitable to you, he will do anything . . .

A similar appeal was made in October 1775. However, Breitkopf did not publish any of Mozart's works during the 1770s, nor did they handle manuscript copies of his compositions. In fact, they seem not to have been interested, as a letter by Leopold Mozart of 12 February 1781 shows:

> For a long time I have hoped that you would want to print something by my son. Surely you will not judge him by the keyboard sonatas that he wrote as a child? Indeed, you will not have seen a note of what he has written for several years, perhaps only the 6 Sonatas for keyboard and a violin, which he had published in Paris [K. 301–306] . . . for we allow very little to appear. You could try a couple of symphonies, or keyboard sonatas, or quartets, trios, etc.

Leopold's comment 'we allow very little to appear' should probably be understood as an attempt on his part to make Wolfgang's works more attractive. But it may also have stemmed from an ambivalence on his part concerning the dissemination of his son's works. In an earlier letter of 24 September 1778 to Wolfgang, then at Paris, Leopold had written:

> . . . I've not issued any of your symphonies, because I know in advance that as you grow older and gain more insight, you will be glad that no one has them, even though when you composed them you were satisfied with them. One grows more fastidious.

Leopold's failure to have most of Mozart's early works published may have stemmed not only from the lack of music publishing in southern Germany and Austria before about 1780 and northern German publishers' apparent lack of interest, but also from a miscalculation on his part. Breitkopf did not publish large-scale works such as symphonies. Works of this sort, as well as operas and church music, generally circulated in manuscript copies. It may be significant that Leopold offered Breitkopf symphonies but not concertos, of which Mozart had already composed several. For concern with the prestige or importance of a particular genre was clearly a factor in Mozart's later decisions concerning the circulation of his works. In February 1784 he wrote to his father, 'Two gentlemen . . . are going to Salzburg in a few days. I will probably given them a sonata, a symphony and a new concerto to take along – the symphony in the original score, which you can have copied at your convenience and then send back to me; [you can] also give it away and have it performed, wherever you wish.' And in May, when he sent the Symphony K.425 and the concertos K.449–451 and 453, he wrote, 'I'm not particularly concerned about the symphony.' It must also be noted, however, that Mozart had tried to publish some of his earlier concertos in Paris in 1778.

In short, numerous factors including the genre of a work, the lack of music publishing in southern Germany and Austria and little interest on the part of northern German publishers for Mozart's music, attempts to prevent works from being stolen or otherwise circulated in unauthorized copies, and an ambivalence about publication on Leopold Mozart's part all contributed to the atypical dissemination of Mozart's early works. For unlike other well-known composers or performers whose music achieved a significant and broad distribution only a few of Mozart's works circulated in Europe during the 1760s and 1770s and generally in printed editions. For the most part these were the sonatas and variations issued under Leopold Mozart's supervision during the grand tour of 1763–6 and the works published by Mozart in Paris in 1778. Manuscript copies from before 1780 are rare, except for the sacred vocal music, which was widely performed in the Salzburg region but not elsewhere, and authentic copies of the instrumental works probably used by Mozart for concerts in Salzburg.

More of Mozart's works were disseminated during the 1780s. Not only had Vienna, unlike Salzburg, in the meantime become a centre of music copying and publishing, but Mozart, now on his own, seems to have been more concerned about securing his financial position and increasing reputation as a composer through publication. Vienna stands at the centre of the distribution of his mature works, which spread rapidly throughout much of Europe, so that by the time of his death in 1791 he was generally recognized as a composer with few if any equals other than Haydn.

Salzburg, Vienna and German-speaking Europe

Prior to 1781, Mozart's reputation in German-speaking Europe rested primarily on his accomplishments as a virtuoso child prodigy and the early sonatas and variations published on the grand tour of 1763–6. He is regularly mentioned in contemporary biographical and other works, among them Martin Gerbert's *De Cantu et Musica Sacra a prima ecclesiae aetate usque ad praesens tempus* (Monasterium Sancti Blasii, 1774), Christoph Gottlieb Murr's 'Entwurf eines Verzeichnisses der besten jetztlebenden Tonkünstler in Europa', published in the *Journal zur Kunstgeschichte und zur allgemeinen Litteratur* (Nuremberg, 1776), Johann Georg Meusel's *Teutsches Künstlerlexikon oder Verzeichnis der jetztlebenden teutschen Künstler* (Lemgo, 1778), and Christian Friedrich Daniel Schubart's *Leben und Gesinnungen* (written in 1779 but not published until 1791). Otherwise, however, few of his compositions were known although some of them did enter general circulation, probably as a result of Mozart's visits to Vienna in 1768 and 1773, Munich in 1775, and Munich, Augsburg and Mannheim in 1777–9. The song *An die Freude*, K.53 (47e), was published in the *Neue Sammlung zum Vergnügen und Unterricht* in Vienna in 1768, and the quartets K.168–173 are listed in the so-called *Quartbuch* of c. 1775 and may have had an independent distribution in the late 1770s. Similarly, early German or Bohemian manuscripts from before c. 1780 are known for the Symphony K.114 and for other symphonies of uncertain authenticity, including K.Anh.214 (45b), 81 (73l) and 84 (73q).

In Vienna Mozart established contacts with local publishers almost immediately after his arrival in 1781. Artaria published the violin sonatas K.296 and 376–380 in December of that year and the sonatas for piano four-hands K.381 (123a) and 358 (186c) in 1783. The work that made Mozart's reputation, however, was *Die Entführung aus dem Serail*, composed in 1781–2. By 1786 the opera had been performed in more than twenty cities, probably on the basis of unauthorized manuscript copies, for the entire opera was apparently not available commercially before 1785. Reports show that *Die Entführung* was a local favourite in Prague, Mannheim, Hamburg and Weimar. A review of a performance in Leipzig in 1788 stated that 'It is a veritable feast for the ear to hear a performance of such glorious music, made for the ear and the heart. Not a single sentiment remains unsatisfied when Herr Mozart is seen to paint and present passion after passion, and immediately afterwards the most droll humour'. And in his *Italienische Reise* of 1787 Goethe wrote that 'All our endeavours . . . to confine ourselves to what is simple and limited were lost when Mozart appeared. *Die Entführung aus dem Serail* conquered all.'

Most of the other mature operas were similarly successful. *Figaro* was widely performed, especially in German, and performances were mounted at Donaueschingen, Frankfurt, Hanover, Bonn, Stuttgart, Berlin, Mannheim, Munich and Augsburg by 1791. *Don Giovanni* was given at Mainz, Frankfurt, Mannheim, Bonn, Hamburg, Weimar, Munich and Augsburg, also in German, during the composer's lifetime. *Così* had numerous performances by 1793 and *Die Zauberflöte* was an almost instant success throughout most of German-speaking Europe. Only the *opere serie*, *Idomeneo* and *La clemenza di Tito*, were slower to gain public acceptance; generally they were not much performed before the early years of the 19th century, although Constanze had taken *Tito* on tour in the mid-1790s and performed the work, usually in a concert version, in Prague, Vienna, Graz, Leipzig, Berlin, Linz and probably Dresden, between 1794 and 1797.

The instrumental music, and in particular keyboard and chamber music, was also a cornerstone in the wider dissemination of Mozart's works. In Vienna, many of these were offered first in manuscript copies, either by Mozart himself on a subscription basis or through well-known dealers such as Lorenz Lausch and Johann Traeg. Other compositions were available in printed editions from Artaria, Hoffmeister and Torricella (see 'First and early editions'). Often they were shipped directly to other parts of German-speaking Europe. In 1784, for example, Torricella advertised his editions of K.333 (315c), 284 (205b) and 454 in a Hamburg journal, and in 1787 Artaria offered symphonies, concertos, quartets and sonatas with or without accompaniment in Dessau. Viennese manuscript copies also achieved a significant distribution and may have been available throughout Germany. Although there is no direct evidence to support this hypothesis, striking parallels between Lausch's and Traeg's advertisements and the published music catalogues of Johann Christoph Westphal in Hamburg suggest that this must have been the case (Zaslaw and Eisen, 1986).

A further stimulus to the dissemination of Mozart's works during the 1780s was the composer's tours of Leipzig, Dresden and Berlin in 1789 and Frankfurt in 1790. Almost certainly Mozart sold some of his compositions in Berlin; they then circulated throughout northern Europe and in Denmark (Eisen, 1986a). And probably as a direct consequence of these performances, as well as the diffusion of Viennese editions and manuscript copies, local publishers began issuing their own editions of Mozart's works during the mid-late 1780s. By the time of his death in 1791, many of the mature works were available throughout German-speaking Europe.

Almost certainly, this summary accounts for only part of the dissemination of Mozart's music in German-speaking Europe. Many more copies must have circulated than now survive, some printed editions are lost (Eisen, 1984), and more performances were given than can now be documented. A report published in the *Journal des Luxus und der Moden* (Weimar, 1788) is probably typical:

> Some time ago a single *Quadro* by [Mozart] (for pianoforte, 1 violin, 1 viola and violoncello) was engraved and published, which is very cunningly set and in performance needs the utmost precision in all the four parts. . . . The cry soon made itself heard: 'Mozart has written a very special new *Quadro*, and such and such a Princess or Countess possesses and plays it!' and this excited curiosity and led to the rash resolve to produce this original composition at grand and noisy concerts and to make a parade with it *invita Minerva*. . . . At nearly every place to which my travels led me and where I was taken to a concert, some young lady or pretentious middle-class *demoiselle*, or some other pert dilettante in a noisy gathering, came up with this printed *Quadro*.

France

In France, Mozart's reputation as a child prodigy lingered on well into the 1770s. When François-Joseph Darcis [d'Arcis, d'Arcy] (1759–c. 1783) performed a J.C. Bach concerto at the Concert Spirituel in 1771, the *Journal de Musique* noted that 'M. d'Arcy, who is nine or ten years old . . . plays the harpsichord, the piano-forte [and] the organ not only with the assurance of the masters, but also with their finesse and taste. To this merit he adds yet a greater one, that of composition. . . . We have not seen anything so astonishing since the little Mozart.' However, few – if any – of Mozart's works other than the early sonatas and variations were known in Paris before his return there in 1778.

The visit of 1778 brought several works, some of them composed earlier, before the Parisian public: the *Paris* Symphony, K.297 (300a), the ballet *Les Petits Riens*, the violin sonatas K.301–306 (published by Sieber) and the variations K.179 (189a), 180 (173c) and 354 (299a, published by Heina). Still others may have been left behind or sold to publishers, including the Divertimento K.254 and the sonatas K.309–311, which were published in Paris about 1781 at a time when Mozart is not known to have had active contacts there.

Regular if infrequent performances of Mozart's works in Paris can be documented throughout the early 1780s. Symphonies were given at the Concert Spirituel every year between 1779 and 1783, and according to *Les Spectacles de Paris ou Calendrier Historique & Chronologique*, Mozart held an official appointment, at least titularly, as *compositeur* to the Concert Spirituel during that same time. Because all of these concerts predate the appearance in print of Mozart's symphonies, the works probably reached Paris in manuscript copies. It is unlikely that all of them were left over from his visit there in 1778.

Beginning in 1784, most of Mozart's published works, primarily chamber and keyboard music, became available in Paris either in imported editions or in editions produced locally. Artaria's September 1785 edition of the six quartets dedicated to Haydn, for example, was available in Paris before the end of the year. In fact, publication in Vienna seems to have been a direct stimulus for Parisian reprints. The Piano Trio K.498, published in September 1788, was issued in a Parisian edition by Le Duc in December.

As elsewhere outside German-speaking Europe, the dissemination in Paris of Mozart's vocal music was slower than the instrumental works. Apparently the first vocal work performed there was the trio *Mandina amabile* K.480 (Vienna, 1785), which was included in a performance of the pasticcio *La villanella rapita* at the Théâtre de Monsieur in June 1789. A review published in the *Mercure de France* described the trio as '*charmant*'. Other vocal works followed later, including a pasticcio based on *Figaro* given at the *Académie de Musique* in 1793, and a travesty version of *Die Zauberflöte* performed in 1801 under the title *Les Mystères d'Isis*. The first Mozart operas to be given in Paris in their original forms were *Così* in 1809 and *Don Giovanni* in 1811 (Lesure, 1958).

England

It is traditionally thought that Mozart's music made little headway in England before the 19th century. About 1803, when Mozart's juvenile works including K.6–9 and 10–15 were still on sale in London, Charles Burney wrote in Abraham Rees's *Cyclopaedia* (not published until 1819) that 'In England we know nothing of [Mozart's] studies or productions, but from his harpsichord lessons, which frequently came over from Vienna; and in these he seems to have been trying experiments. They were full of new passages and new effects; but were wild, capricious and not always pleasing. We were wholly unacquainted with his vocal music till after his decease . . .' (Oldman, 1962/3). Credit for the appearance of some works during the later 1780s is usually given to Mozart's English friends and pupils Stephen and Nancy Storace, Thomas Attwood and Michael Kelly, who in early 1787 returned to London from Vienna, almost certainly bringing some of Mozart's works with them. Storace's *Collection of Original Harpsichord Music*, included the first English edition of the Piano Quartet K.493; it appeared only shortly after the first Viennese edition and is apparently based on an independent source.

Plates 16–30

MOZART'S HAND

THE FOLLOWING SELECTION of illustrations provides a representative cross-section of autograph manuscripts from the earliest period to the final weeks of Mozart's life. Also included is a page of Mozart's racy letter to his cousin, the 'Bäsle' (16), with whom he probably had sexual relations, and extracts from two further documents.

The first score (17) is the 'chorus' *God is our Refuge*. Wolfgang appears to have written the opening bars himself, though Leopold had to correct his son's misjudged spacing at the end of line one (King, 1984). Thereafter the manuscript is probably a joint effort, each trying to imitate the other's style.

The second manuscript (18) is a page from *Apollo et Hyacinthus* of 1767. Here, the 11-year-old Wolfgang's hand is much more poised and assured; the whole makes a thoroughly professional impression, as does the title-page of the String Quintet K.174 of 1773 (19), written under the influence of Michael Haydn's string quintets.

Ill. 20 is an interesting page from the autograph manuscript of the Concerto for Three Pianos in F (K.242), composed at Salzburg in February 1776. The uncrossed parts (first six lines) show the end of the cadenza to the first movement (bars 15–21[=252]) for the three piano parts. Then comes the cancelled cadenza to the second movement, following bar 62, entitled by Mozart 'Cadenza/per/*l'adagio*'.

Ill. 21 shows the first page of the Serenade in B♭ for 13 instruments, K.361 (370a). The superscription 'gran Partitta/Del Sigr. Wolfgang Mozart/ Eigne/Handschrift/1780' is in two strange hands. Concerning the correct dating of the work (Vienna, ?1781–2) see p.286. The autograph establishes that the thirteenth instrument is not a double bassoon but a 'Contra/Basso' or double (string) bass, as was the custom with large wind bands at that period.

The astonishing Mass in C minor, K.427 (417a), is the subject of the next illustration (22). It shows the entry of the soprano solo, presumably sung at the first performance at Salzburg in October 1783 by Constanze Mozart, at the words 'Christe eleison' from the middle of the Kyrie. It is one of the work's most sublime moments. In the left-hand margin Mozart noted 'NB Dieses Solo singt die Erste Sängerin' ('The first singer sings this solo'); there were two solo sopranos, the second of whom sang the 'Laudamus'. The melody of this 'Christe' comes from a collection of solfeggios 'per la mia cara Costanza' (K.393 [385b] no. 2, marked 'Solfeggio Adagio'), written in 1782, the time at which Mozart was composing the Mass.

The C minor Piano Concerto K.491 of 1786 (23, 24) has always been regarded as an extraordinary work, unique even among Mozart's piano concertos. The autograph shows signs of strain and haste, and the piano part was only sketched out, Mozart playing it from memory. Notice in the second of these two extracts, that the first version of the piano part had an 'outline' or skeleton right-hand part from bar 6 onwards, 'fleshed out' in the staff above. The illustrations show the second subject of the first movement (bars 200–228).

Ill. 25 shows the first page of *Der Schauspieldirektor* of 1786. Notice the economy with which the score is laid out: wherever possible, doubling instruments are not written out (e.g. the penultimate, cello, line is marked 'CoB', which means 'col basso', doubling the bass line at the very bottom). The C clarinets (line 6) are marked 'coll oboe'. As with most of Mozart's music composed in Vienna, the paper he used was manufactured in northern Italian mills; the watermarks are now carefully studied for establishing chronology in undated works, sketches or fragments.

Ill. 26 is a page of sketches for the majestic C major Piano Concerto K.503 of 1786, and some other unidentified works. The page is valuable because it shows graphically that, contrary to what has often been asserted, Mozart regularly made elaborate sketches prior to beginning the actual full score. The top section shows the first movement, bars 208–212 and 214, followed (staves 3–4) by bars 96–112 and bars 312–16.

The 6 German Dances K.509 for large orchestra (27) are inscribed by Mozart 'di W: A: Mozart *mpria* Praga 1787'. This set marks the beginning of the great series of dances composed by Mozart during the last five years of his life. K.509 was intended for a house ball in the Prague palace of Count Johann Pachta.

Ill. 28 shows what is possibly the last page of music Mozart wrote: the sketch for the Lacrimosa of the Requiem (1791). The two final bars of the soprano part are Eybler's continuation, immediately abandoned (see p. 314).

The last page of Mozart's thematic catalogue (29), omitting the incipits, shows the distribution of *Die Zauberflöte*, *La clemenza di Tito*, two additions to *Zauberflöte*, the Clarinet Concerto and, as the final entry, *Eine kleine Freymaurerkantate* of 15 November 1791, with (30) the signature and date on the autograph manuscript.

H.C.R.L.

16   A florid letter from Mozart to his cousin, the 'Bäsle', 10 May 1779

17   The 'chorus' *God is our Refuge*

18   *Apollo et Hyacinthus*, 1767

19   String Quintet in B♭ major, K.174 (1773)

20   Concerto for Three Pianos and Orchestra, K.242 (1776)

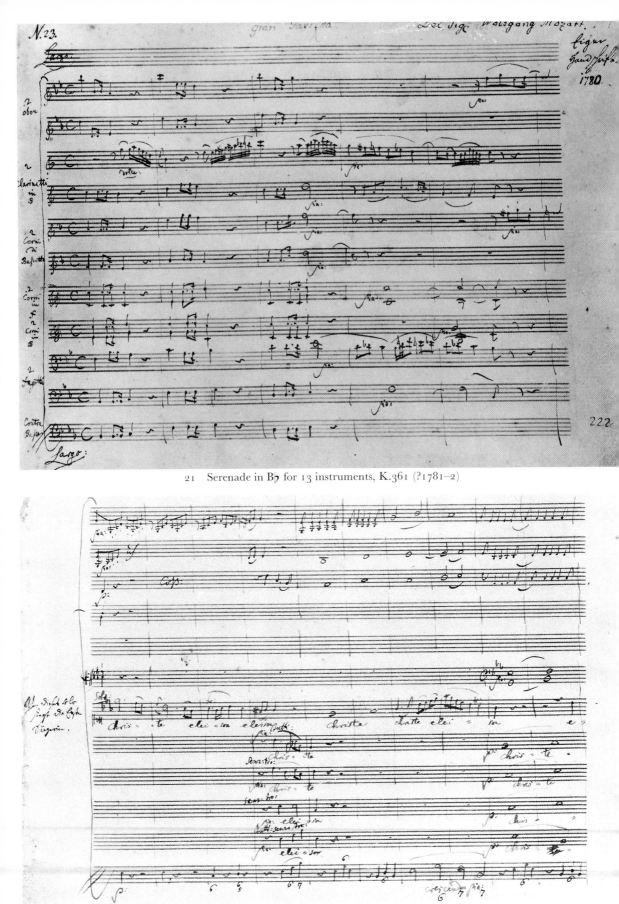

21 Serenade in Bb for 13 instruments, K.361 (?1781-2)

22 Mass in C minor, K.427 (417a), composed 1782-3

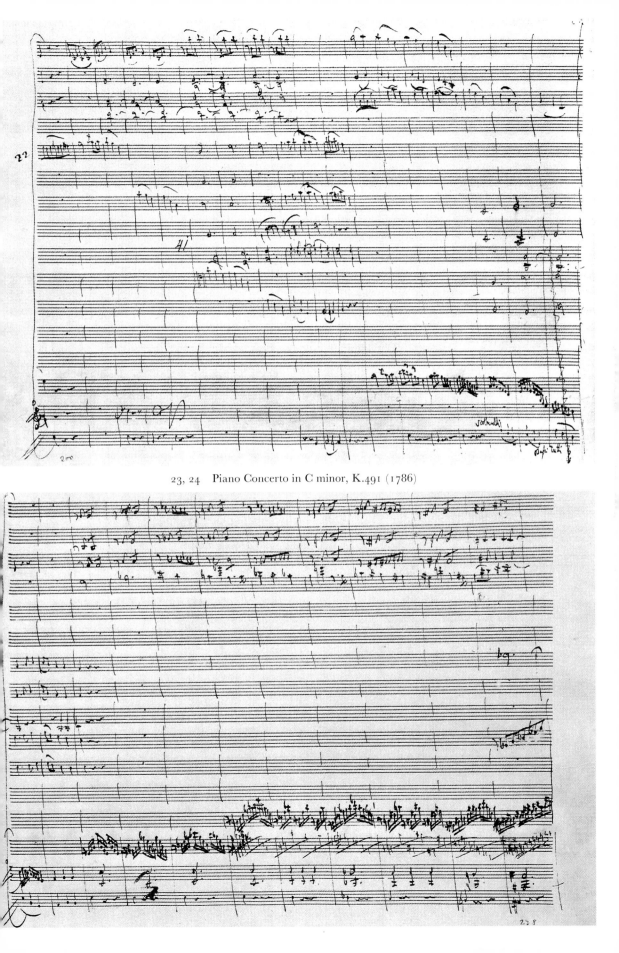

23, 24 Piano Concerto in C minor, K.491 (1786)

25   *Der Schauspieldirektor* (1786)

26   Sketches for Piano Concerto in C major, K.503 (1786), and other unidentified works

27   The first of the 6 German Dances, K.509 (Prague, 1787)

28   Last page of the 'Lacrimosa' from the Requiem (1791)

29 Final page of Mozart's thematic catalogue (*Verzeichnüss*)

30 Signature dated 15 November 1791 on first page of the *Kleine Freymaurerkantate*, K.623

Storace also published the first edition anywhere of the Piano Trio K.564, a work written only after his return to London; presumably it was sent to him by Mozart. The Storaces also used some of Mozart's music in their own compositions or performances. The chorus of the Turks in Stephen Storace's *The Siege of Belgrade* of 1791, for example, is an arrangement of part of the *Alla Turca* from Mozart's Sonata K.331 (300i), Anna Storace and Francesco Benucci sang the duet 'Crudel! perchè finora' from *Figaro* in a performance of Giuseppe Gazzaniga's *La vendemmia* given at the King's Theatre, Haymarket, in 1789, and when the pasticcio *La villanella rapita* was given in 1790 it included Mozart's *Dite almeno, in che mancai*, K.479, and *Mandina amabile*, K.480, as well as 'Deh vieni non tardar' from *Figaro* and 'Batti, batti' from *Don Giovanni*.

But it is not the case that Mozart's works began to be widely disseminated in London only during the last years of the 1780s. Ample documentation survives for performances of his works as early as 1784. In that year the subscription concerts sponsored by Lord Abingdon included three Mozart symphonies. Since none of Mozart's symphonies had been published by this time it seems likely that a number of them had already made their way to England in manuscript copies, possibly via Paris, where similar works were performed between 1779 and 1783. Certainly some printed editions had already arrived from Vienna, including copies of the concertos K.413–415 published by Artaria in 1785. Announcements in various London newspapers of January 1786 show not only that these works were available in London, but also that K.414 at least was performed by the pianist Johann Baptist Cramer the younger in the same month. Other works circulating in London about this time included the violin and piano sonatas K.296 and 376–380, the solo sonatas K.309–311, the C minor Fantasy and Sonata, K.475 + 457, and the variations K.264 (315d), 352 (374c), 353 (300f), 359 (374a), 360 (374b) and 455.

Burney's 1803 comments are, in any case, contradicted by his own earlier writings, for in a 1791 review of William Jackson's *Observations on the Present State of Music in London* he had written:

'The old Concerto (says he) is now lost, and modern full-pieces are either in the form of Overtures or Symphonies. The overture of the Italian opera never pretends to much; that of the English opera always endeavours to have an air somewhere, and the endeavour alone makes it acceptable.' . . . Richter's eternal repetitions, and Abel's timidity, are praised, for they are no more: – 'but later composers, to be grand and original, have poured in such floods of nonsense, under the sublime idea of being inspired, that the present Symphony bears the same relation to good music as the ravings of a bedlamite do to sober sense.' Now, might not the ingenious writer as well have said, at once, that the authors of these floods of nonsense are Haydn, Vanhall, Pleyel, and Mozart, and the admirers of them tasteless idiots, as leave us to guess who he means? (*The London Review*, October 1791, pp. 196–9).

In short, a significant number of Mozart's instrumental works were disseminated in England considerably earlier than has previously been supposed. As in France, however, the operas made a later appearance than the instrumental works. The first complete Mozart opera performance was *La clemenza di Tito*, given in 1806. *Così* and *Die Zauberflöte* followed in 1811, and *Figaro* and *Don Giovanni* were produced in 1812 and 1817, respectively. Selections from these operas had already appeared in various printed anthologies of the 1790s, usually with different English texts.

Italy, Iberia, Scandinavia and Eastern Europe
In other parts of Europe, Mozart's works generally achieved little distribution before about 1790, the evidence of a few early performances notwithstanding. For example, despite three successful tours, the composition of numerous instrumental works and arias, productions of *Mitridate, rè di Ponto*, *Ascanio in Alba*, and *Lucio Silla*, and continued contacts with important musicians such as Padre Martini, there is scant evidence that Mozart's works were widely performed or disseminated in Italy. One exception is an unidentified Mass copied out by Luigi Gatti, later Kapellmeister in Salzburg, during the Mozarts' visit to Mantua in January 1770 (Leopold Mozart, letter of 11 June 1778). Another is the March K.215 (213b), which survives in a very early Salzburg copy now in the Biblioteca del Conservatorio 'Giuseppe Verdi' in Milan.

Otherwise the earliest evidence for the dissemination south of the Alps of Mozart's works is a 'Report from Italy' published in Carl Friedrich Cramer's *Magazin der Musik* for 9 July 1784: 'Mozart's sonatas with obligato violin [possibly K.296 and 376–380, published by Artaria in December 1781] please me greatly. They are very difficult to play. Admittedly the melodies are not at all new, but the accompaniment of the violin is masterly.' Probably the technical demands of Mozart's works hindered their acceptance in Italy. An anecdote in Gotifredo Ferrari's *Aneddoti piacevoli e interessanti* suggests that this was the case with the six quartets dedicated to Haydn:

> My friend [Attwood] arrived in [Vienna] at the time when Mozart had just published his six quartets dedicated to Haydn. He made me a present of a copy, which he sent to me in Naples, with a letter in which he urged me not to pass judgment until I had heard them several times. I tried them with various *dilettanti* and teachers, but we could not play anything but the slow movements, and even these only with difficulty. (Saint-Foix, 1939)

And according to one of Mozart's early biographers, Niemetschek, a performance of *Don Giovanni* in Florence in 1798 was abandoned because the music was considered too difficult.

Nevertheless, at least some of Mozart's mature works were known in Italy during the composer's lifetime or shortly afterwards: *Figaro* was given in Monza in 1787 and Florence in 1788, and Viennese professional copies of K.338, 425 and 504 show that these symphonies circulated in Tuscany during the 1790s. Given the political connections between Vienna and northern Italy, other works must have circulated there as well, both in printed editions and manuscript copies. But the rest of the operas made a generally late appearance: *Don Giovanni* may have been performed in Florence as early as 1792, although the first securely documented performances of the work are Bergamo and Rome, 1811; *Così* was performed in Milan in 1807, *La clemenza di Tito* was given in Naples in 1809, and *Die Zauberflöte* was mounted at Milan in 1816 (in Italian). *Die Entführung aus dem Serail*, Mozart's first great operatic success, was not given in Italy until 1935.

As for Spain and Portugal, although works by Haydn and other Viennese composers circulated there during the 1780s, there is little evidence for the dissemination of Mozart's music there during his lifetime. A music inventory from 1787 of a collection in Madrid includes not a single work by Mozart, although it lists numerous symphonies, chamber works and keyboard sonatas by other Viennese composers (Subira, 1969). The operas were performed in Spain relatively late: *Così* in Barcelona in 1798 and *Figaro* in Madrid in 1802 are the only documented early performances.

Although the dissemination of Mozart's works in Scandinavia is poorly documented, the discovery of a copy of the Symphony in A minor, K.Anh.220 (16a), and subsequent research into its provenance, has uncovered the previously unexpected fact that at least some of Mozart's works were known in Denmark during the late 1780s and early 1790s. Vouchers and other documents deriving from the Odense Music Club show that by 1796 it owned manuscript copies of the symphonies K.203 (189b) (from the Serenade), 250 (248b) (from the Serenade), 504 and possibly 551, and printed editions of K.320 and 425. Between 1797 and 1799 the Club also purchased manuscript copies or printed editions of K.338, 543 and 550, as well as the overtures to *Figaro*, *Don Giovanni*, *La clemenza di Tito* and *Die Zauberflöte* (Wedin, 1987). The source for most of the manuscript copies was Hamburg (Zaslaw and Eisen, 1986) and it may be that during his visits to Berlin, Leipzig and Dresden in 1789 Mozart sold some of his works to local dealers who then disseminated them in northern Germany and Denmark (Eisen, 1986a).

The operas seem to have made their first appearances more or less simultaneously in Denmark and Sweden, but – again – somewhat later than the orchestral music. *Die Entführung* was produced in Copenhagen in 1813 and Stockholm in 1814 and *Figaro* was given in both cities in 1821. *Così* was mounted in Copenhagen as early as 1798 but *Die Zauberflöte* was not produced there until 1816; it had appeared in Stockholm a few years earlier, in 1812, as *Die Egyptiske Mysterierne eller Trollflöjten*.

In eastern Europe Mozart's music achieved a modest success. The Russian ambassador extraordinary to the Viennese court, Count (later Prince) Andrey Kyrillovich Rasumovsky, a well-known patron of the arts, was personally known to Mozart. In fact, Rasumovsky apparently attempted to secure Mozart's services for the Russian court. In September 1791 he wrote to Prince Grigory Alexandrovich Potemkin:

It was not for me, Sir, to send you the first keyboard player and one of the most gifted composers in Germany, named Mozart, who being somewhat discontented here [in Vienna] might be disposed to undertake such a journey [to St Petersburg]. He is in Bohemia at the moment, but will be back soon. If Your Highness will authorize me to engage him then, not for a long term, but simply to present himself to you for you to hear him and to attach him to your service, should you think fit.

Mozart had met another Russian, Alexandre Mikhailovich Beloselsky, in Dresden in 1789. A not entirely complimentary reference to the composer in Beloselsky's *Dialogues sur la musique* may date from this time: 'Mozzart is very learned, very difficult, and consequently very esteemed by instrumentalists: but he appears never to have had the good luck to love. Not a single melody emanates from his heart.'

Evidence for the early performance in eastern Europe of Mozart's music is rare, although there are some notable exceptions: *Die Entführung* was given in Warsaw in Polish in 1783 and *Don Giovanni* was given there in Italian in 1789 (Feicht, 1958). In St Petersburg the only relevant known document is a concert announcement published in a local newspaper on 15 October 1790 by a certain Frau Schulz, who performed a Mozart concerto and claimed to be his pupil. Nevertheless, beginning in the late 1780s some of Mozart's works became available in printed editions. Advertisements by various Russian music dealers in 1788 list sonatas for solo keyboard and for keyboard four hands, and some volumes of Hoffmeister's subscription series, to which Mozart contributed several works. In 1795 the firm Gerstenberg & Co. of St Petersburg offered a large number of Mozart's compositions, including symphonies, overtures, concertos, quintets, quartets, keyboard music and selections from the operas; during the same year they also published the first Russian-language biography of the composer.

It is from about this time, too, that the operas were first given in Russia. The court there had a long-standing interest in opera, and during the 1790s travelling troupes performed *Die Zauberflöte* and *Don Giovanni*. Excerpts from these operas, and from *Così fan tutte*, *Le nozze di Figaro* and *La clemenza di Tito* were then printed locally, in the *Giornale Musicale del Teatro Italiano di St. Pietroburgo, o Scelta d'Arie, Duetti, Terzetti, Overture, etc. delle Opere buffe, rappresentate sul Teatro Imperiale di St. Pietroburgo nell'Anno 1796 e seguenti* (Steinpress, 1964). Complete productions of the other operas came only later. *Die Entführung* was given in Moscow, in Russian, in 1810, and *La clemenza di Tito* was staged in St Petersburg in 1817.

CLIFF EISEN

Section 9

A CONSPECTUS OF MOZART'S MUSIC

A CONSPECTUS OF MOZART'S MUSIC

IN THIS CHRONOLOGICAL SURVEY, Mozart's music is discussed within four periods: 1762–74, the years of his European travels and intense study of diverse musical styles; 1775–80, when he was based mostly in Salzburg and produced the first works to establish his international reputation; 1781–8, when he settled in Vienna and was at his most prolific as a composer; and 1789–91, the time of his most visionary compositional experiments, of his exploration of the musical language he had forged during his earlier Viennese years. The terminology of formal analysis used in this chapter emerged in the 19th century, in reference to music of the Classical period, especially Beethoven's. The extent to which Mozart was aware of such formal categories is immaterial in the present context, where his music is interpreted in the light of its subsequent reception.

1762–74: apprenticeship and assimilation

Mozart's early works are often regarded as a reflection of the different musical styles he encountered in his native Salzburg and during his extensive travels. The degree to which this is the case must remain unclear, for the music of Mozart's lesser-known contemporaries is not widely available, and there is a lack of scholarly consensus on the very nature of musical influence.

Keyboard pieces, keyboard and violin sonatas, concertos, symphonies

In 1759, Leopold compiled a music book for his daughter, containing pieces of his own and by other composers, including Agrell, Tischer and Wagenseil. Mozart learnt some of this music before his fifth birthday, and his first surviving compositions – short, simple keyboard pieces, some written out by his father – are included in this manuscript. His earliest published pieces were keyboard and violin sonatas, emulating the general style of Schobert, Eckard and other Germans resident in Paris at the time of the Mozart family's visit. Symphonies of K.F. Abel and J.C. Bach, whom Mozart met in London, provided models for his own first symphonies (K.16 and K.19): both use Bach's favourite *forte/piano* contrast at the beginning, a 'singing', Italian-style slow movement and a light, presto finale in 3/8.

Also from the early years comes a group of keyboard concertos, based on sonatas by Eckard, Honauer, Raupach, Schobert and C.P.E. Bach. These concertos, like the later ones modelled on sonatas by J.C. Bach (K.107/21b), were probably intended for Mozart's own performance. His first original piano concerto,

K.175, was written in 1773; it is considerably longer than the preceding concertos and the first to use trumpets and drums. (The Violin Concerto, K.207, is now thought to have been composed before K.175.) In 1782, Mozart gave K.175 a new finale, the 'Rondo', K.382, more ornamental – it is closer to a set of variations than to a rondo – than the original. Towards the end of this early period come two serenades, K.185 (167a) and K.203 (189b), which both contain concerto-like movements for solo violin, the Concertone, K.190 (186E), for two violins and orchestra, and the Bassoon Concerto, K.191 (186e).

After his return to Salzburg from London, and probably during his visit to Vienna in 1767–8, Mozart wrote the symphonies K.43, 45 and 48, each with a minuet and trio as the third of four movements. K.48 begins with his earliest symphonic first movement to include an exact reprise of the opening melody immediately after a distinct 'development' section. This same development begins with a reference to the opening bars, a practice Mozart continued into his maturity. In all but the last symphonies of this period, *galant*, *buffo* ('Italian') and serious ('Viennese') styles emerge at appropriate chronological stages. Thus K.74, in G major, with its linked first and second movements and predominantly light textures, is probably from the first Italian journey, and K.114 in A major, with a sharper etching of inner voices and a Minuet and Trio, was composed in Salzburg at the end of 1771 – it was only from about 1770 that symphonies with the order of movements fast–slow–fast, or fast–slow–minuet–fast, became the norm in Salzburg (see Eisen, 1984). The symphonies K.183 (173dB) and 201 (186a), from 1773–4, stand out from their predecessors in terms of expressive range. The first and last movements of K.183 (173dB) are in minor-key, passionate *Sturm und Drang* style. The first surprise of the A major Symphony, K.201 (186a), is Mozart's reversal of the conventional *forte/piano* opening: the initial material is intimate, for strings only, in chamber music style, the *forte* repetition of this material has a fuller texture and added oboes and horns.

Other chamber music

Mozart's 'divertimentos' K.136–138 (125a–c) (probably for solo instruments) and K.80 (73f) (1770, though the finale was composed later), are his earliest contributions to the quartet repertoire. They were followed by six quartets, K.155–160 (134a, 134b, 157, 158, 159 and 159a), written in Italy and apparently intended as a group, for their keys (D–G–C–F–B♭–E♭) form a cycle of fifths. Two of these works finish with a substantial minuet and trio (in one of his earliest surviving letters, Mozart expresses an interest in the length and complexity of native Italian minuets). Four include a movement (slow, except for K.159) in a minor key, after Sammartini's style. In contrast, the six Viennese quartets, K.168–173, seem to take their lead from Haydn's quartets of the same period, which Mozart may have studied in Vienna during

1773. One of these quartets begins with a set of variations (K.170), two others have fugal finales (K.168 and 173); and all employ contrapuntal textures to a much greater extent than in his Italian quartets. Soon after these Viennese quartets, the String Quintet K.174 appeared, a pattern Mozart was to repeat – though probably not by design – during the Viennese years: the C major and G minor quintets are equidistant between the 'Haydn' and the 'Prussian' quartets, and the D major and E♭ major quintets were completed less than a year after the 'Prussian' works.

Sacred music

God is our Refuge, K.20, the chorus which Leopold presented to the British Museum during the London journey, generally described as Mozart's first sacred work, is in fact a secular composition (see King, 1984a and b). Unequivocally sacred works followed fairly regularly, including a Kyrie, masses, a Te Deum, and a fine Litany setting, K.109 (74e). Mozart copied out, and sometimes used as the basis of his own compositions, sacred music by Eberlin, Michael Haydn and his own father. These three Salzburg composers were, in turn, indebted to the Italian style of sacred music, especially that of Hasse. The Italian style is prominent in Mozart's two *Regina coeli* settings, K.108 (74d) and K.127, the first with large, busy orchestra, and both including expressive soprano solos. The Masses K.192 (186f) and 194 (186h) of 1774 are more concise: there are few instrumental interludes or text repetitions. Archbishop Colloredo (enthroned in 1772) expected a mass to last no longer than three-quarters of an hour, a restriction which, as Mozart sarcastically observed in a letter to Martini (4 December 1776), imposed 'an entirely new method of composition'. Around this time, and also during his later Salzburg years, Mozart contributed a series of church sonatas for performance during the mass. Each is a sonata form movement with minuscule development section, like the 'sonatina' movements of, for instance, Clementi. Most are for two violins, bass and organ continuo, but a few have more elaborate instrumentation – for example, K.329 (317a) (from ?1779) has additional oboes, trumpets, drums and solo organ part.

Dramatic music

At the age of 11, Mozart composed his first extended dramatic piece, one act of a sacred drama, *Die Schuldigkeit des ersten Gebots*, for the Salzburg palace. From then until 1772 he wrote music for a Singspiel, a Latin intermezzo, two serenatas, an *opera buffa* and two *opere serie*. Both *Die Schuldigkeit* and the intermezzo, *Apollo et Hyacinthus* (performed at Salzburg University in 1767), were genres of vocal entertainment well known to Salzburg audiences. The majority of arias and other tonally closed forms in these two works are in the usual tripartite, *da capo* form. Just two of the seven arias are in repeated binary form in *Die Schuldigkeit*; and two arias, a duet and a trio – out of a total of nine set pieces – in *Apollo* depart from the ternary format in various ways. *Apollo* includes evocative vocal writing and instrumentation (as in the pastoral music, with echoes, accompanying Apollo's appearance as a shepherd), but *Die Schuldigkeit* is on the whole more impressive, thanks to its brilliant *fioriture* singing, to the effective if traditional word-painting, and to the passages of impassioned recitative.

While the earliest dramatic works were of localized interest, the next had much wider appeal. *La finta semplice* is an *opera buffa* written for Vienna in 1768, to a libretto by Coltellini after Goldoni, but first performed in Salzburg in 1769. *Bastien und Bastienne*, a Singspiel based on Favart's parody of Rousseau's famous comedy, appeared in 1768, probably conceived in part during the composition of *La finta semplice*. The three-act *opera seria*, *Mitridate, rè di Ponto* was written for Milan (1770), to a libretto by Cigna-Santi, after Parini and Racine. Each act of *La finta semplice* concludes with a typical *buffa* finale, comprising several distinct sections; in the third finale, Rosina and Cassandro confirm their love for each other while Polidoro simultaneously expresses fury, an early example of Mozart's taste for complex ensemble characterization. *Bastien und Bastienne* is a pastoral story set simply. Colas, the magician, has the most striking aria: his fairly pedestrian vocal line in 'Diggi, daggi, shurry, murry', is accompanied by wild jumps in first and second violins, illustrating the force of his magic powers.

The arias of *Mitridate* are in conventional *seria* forms, including the 'dal segno' type, in which a repeated first section is abbreviated. Mozart shows his penchant for compositional richness by building a scene (Act III scene 4) from continuous *secco* recitative, accompanied recitative, an aria, and further accompanied recitative, rather than the conventional alternation of recitative and aria. He also aims for clear characterization, partly, no doubt, in response to the vocal abilities of his singers. Mitridate's arias, for instance, include wide and difficult leaps but forgo the ornamental passages found in the other roles. Musical characterization is developed still further in the last dramatic work of this period, Mozart's final *opera seria* for Italy, *Lucio Silla* (1772). Giunia's intricate, fiery *fioritura* contrasts with Celia's staccato *fioritura*, and both outshine Silla, with his more constrained vocal range. The orchestra plays an important part in underlining dramatic action, as in Silla's 'Il desio di vendetta', where an orchestral introduction represents the flames of which Silla later sings.

1775–80: compositional refinement

MOZART SPENT MOST OF THESE YEARS in Salzburg, where he was increasingly dissatisfied with his professional status. Not even his longest, sixteen-month journey to Paris, taking in Mannheim and Munich, led to any firm offer of employment away from his native city. Important operatic ventures occupied the beginning and end of these years. In between, he produced a series of major instrumental compositions and contributed fairly regularly to music for the church.

Solo piano and chamber music

The first surviving piano sonatas were probably written in early 1775: K.279–284 (189d–h and 205b), in C, F, B♭, E♭, G and D major. The closely related keys suggest that they may have been written as a set, like the Italian quartets mentioned above, but only the last was published during the composer's lifetime.

Though sometimes dismissed as insubstantial, these pieces contain many features which indicate the constantly restless creative imagination of a maturing genius. The first movement of K.279 (189d) is motivically fragmentary, with snatches of intense lyricism, and the second movement offers dramatic dynamic changes. The first movement of K.281 (189f) is a Haydnesque experiment in motivic permutation, and the memorable *cantabile* opening of K.283 (189h) was perhaps inspired by J.C. Bach's sonatas. The formal schemes of two movements of these sonatas are relatively unusual. In the opening exposition of K.280 (189e), Mozart repeatedly avoids settling on the dominant, the first subject being 13 bars long, and the transition no less than 31 bars. The first movement of K.282 (189g) is an Adagio with no return to the opening melody at the point of tonal reprise, but a diminution of that melody at the beginning of the second repeated section, and a restatement of the beginning of the opening melody to open the coda. The last sonata of the group, K.284 (205b) has an exciting, orchestral-style first movement, and a set of variations as the finale. These variations are rather more sophisticated in terms of harmonic language and overall design than most of the independent piano variations from the same decade, although the 'Lison dormait' set, K.264 (315d), is notable for the way some variations subtly extend the original proportions of the theme; and the eighth variation of 'Je suis Lindor', K.354 (299a), contains a cadenza, based on a diminished chord, which seems to have its origins not in some spontaneous, improvised flourish, nor in the theme, but in the subtle adaptation of thematic structure in variations 5 and 6.

The first two of the next three piano sonatas, K.309 (284b), 311 (284c) and 310 (300d) appeared at about the time of Mozart's visit to Mannheim in late 1777. The initial, *forte* idea of K.309 (284b) dominates the opening of the development, returns in an unexpected key at the end of the development, initiates a striking reformulation of the first subject eight bars into the recapitulation, and begins the brief coda. The first movement of K.311 (284c) has a 'reverse' reprise, where the second subject is recapitulated first; the first subject reappears at the end, like a coda. This symmetrical form was popular among the Mannheimers, and Mozart used it elsewhere, in the D major piano and violin Sonata K. 306 (300l) and the Symphony in G, K.318. The third sonata, K.310 (300d), written in Paris in 1778, is his first in the minor; the bold, 'tragic' style of the first movement has been likened to that of the *Sturm und Drang* style fashionable at the time, and to Schobert's 'fiery' keyboard writing. K.310 (300d) has been recognized by posterity as one of the early masterpieces of Mozart.

Around the time Mozart finished the A minor Piano Sonata, K.310 (300d), he also completed seven piano and violin sonatas, K.301–306 (293a–293c, 300c, 293d, 300l) and K.296. All but the last were published as his second op. 1 in Paris in 1778. Mozart, whom we tend to think of as the pianist *par excellence* of his day, was also a brilliant violinist, as might be expected of the son of Leopold. Yet, despite encouragement from his father, he was disinclined to follow the path of virtuoso violinist, and his violin sonatas seem to reflect that reticence, albeit very early in the history of a genre that was to be truly ennobled by Beethoven. The keyboard instrument for the op. 1 publication was specified as 'Clavecin ou Forté Piano', and for K.296 as 'Clavecin ou Pianoforte'. In the earlier keyboard and violin sonatas, the violin had mostly accompanied or doubled its partner. In these new works the two instruments are more equally balanced, with main thematic material usually stated by one instrument and imitated by the other. The keyboard part is the more demanding, however, especially in the D major Sonata, K.306 (300l), which has a written-out cadenza in the finale. In complete contrast to the extrovert D major work is the E minor Sonata, K.304 (300c). Its style is generally intimate and restrained, except at the point in the first movement where the end of the development dovetails into a slightly foreshortened and varied reprise, and when the 'missing' first part of the first subject appears in the coda. Other chamber music of this period includes the two flute quartets, K.285 and 285a. Mozart also wrote a Flute Concerto, K.313 (285c), an Andante for flute and orchestra, K.315 (285e) (possibly a substitute for the central movement of K.313 (285c), and a double concerto for flute and harp, K.299 (297c). He admitted that he did not enjoy composing for the flute.

Concertos

These years showed a rapid development in Mozart's concerto composition, beginning with the four violin concertos of 1775 (the first one having probably been written in 1773), followed by a series of piano (or harpsichord) concertos, including K.242, a *galant* three-piano work (later transcribed as a concerto for two pianos), his first masterpiece in the concerto genre, the Piano Concerto K.271 in E♭ major, and concluding with another important work, the Sinfonia Concertante for violin and viola, K.364/320d.

In the first and second violin concertos, K.207 in B♭ (from 1773) and K.211 in D major, occasional 'mechanical' figuration in the solo violin and neutral orchestral accompaniment recall similar textures in late Baroque concertos of Geminiani and Locatelli. The three following works, K.216, 218 and 219, are notable for their lyricism and freedom of form: the rondo finales of each include episodes contrasting sharply with the main theme (including a 'gigue' and 'gavotte' in K.218, and 'Turkish' music in K.219); the recapitulation of the first movement of K.216 is preceded by an unnotated cadenza; in K.218 the triadic beginning of the first-movement *tutti* and solo expositions never returns in the recapitulation, and in the first movement of K.219 the solo violin's first entry is an Adagio passage, after which the initial, faster tempo is resumed.

These violin works and the other piano concertos of 1776 are dwarfed by the E♭ major Piano Concerto, K.271, written in early 1777 for the French virtuoso Jeunehomme. The commanding, opening arpeggiation of the tonic chord in the orchestra is answered immediately and unexpectedly by the solo piano. This is a signal for further innovation: the piano enters with a trill just before the end of the orchestral exposition; and the piano exposition reformulates the orchestral exposition, a developmental process which is continued in the recapitulation. The muted canon between first and second violins at the beginning of the slow movement introduces music of unprecedented intensity, including lyrical melody, lush orchestration, quasi-recitative, and a cadenza. The relentless quavers of the finale are interrupted by a delicate minuet in the subdominant. Apart from providing a moment of repose, this minuet elaborates on the A♭ which is so prominent melodically at the beginning of the second movement.

The Sinfonia Concertante for violin and viola, in E♭ major, is Mozart's last completed concerted work of the late 1770s. Its instrumental medium was popular with the virtuoso Mannheim orchestra, and both the opening dotted rhythm, and the dramatic crescendo over a pedal point in repeated quavers which ends the first *tutti*, are Mannheim hallmarks. Mozart's masterly treatment of the soloists' sonority is apparent from their first entry, a high, sustained, E♭ octave, emerging from the climactic conclusion of the orchestral exposition and relaxing into thematic statement. Equally outstanding are the gradually intensifying dialogue between the two soloists in the central Andante, and Mozart's own concise, organic cadenzas. The solo viola part automatically sounds brighter than its orchestral counterparts, because its music is written in D major and the instrument tuned a semitone higher than usual.

Symphonies, cassations, serenades, divertimentos

During 1778–80, Mozart composed the *Paris* Symphony, K.297 (300a), and three symphonies for Salzburg, K.318, 319 and 338 (for discussion of Mozart's limited output of symphonies during the mid-1770s, see 'Symphonies', p. 257). The *Paris* Symphony is on a grander scale than his earlier symphonies, both stylistically and in terms of instrumental forces (flutes, oboes, clarinets, bassoons, horns, trumpets, drums and large string section). In a letter to his father, Mozart said: 'I haven't left out the the the *premier coup d'archet* . . . . 'What a fuss the oxen here make of this trick!' But the opening, unison flourish to which he refers is far more than a conventional gesture designed to show off the Paris orchestra's fine training and technique: it underpins the main points of formal articulation in the first movement, introducing the second subject, beginning the development, and appearing in the closing bars.

Mozart wrote two slow movements, a 6/8 Andante, and a simpler 3/4 movement. In the 20th century, there has been some controversy about which is the original; Mozart considered each 'appropriate in its own way'.

The C major Symphony, K.338, is also monumental in outline. The first movement's festive first subject seems almost bland, but twists towards F minor after twelve bars and towards the dominant minor just before the second subject. The logic of this particular elaboration of the underlying progression from tonic (first subject) to dominant (second subject) is clarified in the development, which has a *piano*, staccato section in A♭ major. Only the beginning of the first subject returns to initiate the reprise; a substantial section of it is reserved for the end of the movement. A similar procedure occurs in the one-movement Italian overture symphony, K.318. After the exposition and development, an Andante in the tonic substitutes for the expected return of the first subject. The second subject follows, transposed to the tonic, and then part of the first subject is adopted for the coda.

During these Salzburg years, Mozart wrote a series of pieces intended for entertainment of various kinds, usually called 'Cassation', 'Serenade' or 'Divertimento'. The instrumentation differed, from symphonic forces (he sometimes used or adapted serenade movements to form a symphony, as with the *Haffner* Symphony, K.385), to solo ensemble, including a series of divertimentos for wind instruments. (A detailed classification of these works, according to function and instrumentation, is included in 'Miscellaneous instrumental' and 'Harmoniemusik' (pp. 271–76 and 283–9).) Fine examples of the chamber-music style pieces are the divertimentos K.287 (271H) and K.334 (320b), both for two horns and strings. K.334 (320b) is preceded by the March K.445 (320c) (no march for K.287 (271H) survives), otherwise the two works follow virtually the same pattern – a brisk first movement, a set of variations, minuet and trio, slow movement with elaborate first violin part, second minuet and trio (and a further trio in K.334 (320b)) and fast finale (preceded in K.287 (271H) by an Andante introduction which is foreshortened and recast at the beginning of the coda). Among the most substantial orchestral works are the *Haffner* Serenade, K.250 (248b) and the *Posthorn* Serenade, K.320, which uses a posthorn in the second trio of the sixth movement. The *Haffner* has nine movements, which include violin concerto movements probably performed by Mozart himself, and three Minuets. Einstein thought that the first movement of the *Posthorn* (following one of the two marches, K.335 (320a)), reflected something of Mozart's relations with Colloredo, in view of a 'tense' introductory Adagio maestoso, the 'aggressive' first subject, with sudden dynamic contrasts, its 'pleading' second subject with interpolated *forte* dotted rhythms, and an 'impatient' Mannheim crescendo. In the *concertante* movements it is the winds that predominate, rather than the solo violin, with brief written-out cadenzas in the Andante grazioso and Rondo. Also from this period is the unusual Notturno, K.286 (269a), in which there are progressively shorter echoes of one ensemble of strings and horns in three other ensembles of the same instrumentation.

Vocal music

Towards the beginning of this period, while in Munich, Mozart finished the offertory *Misericordias Domini*, K.222 (205a), rich in Salzburg-style polyphony and incorporating material from a work by Eberlin. Other sacred works were written in connection with Mozart's duties at Salzburg. His masses, typically for the time, are mostly in operatic–symphonic style. One of the longest and most complex is K.262 (246a). It has elaborate vocal parts, fugues which conclude the Gloria and Credo, and trenchant instrumental ritornelli. The finest mass is often said to be the *Coronation*, K.317, which is thematically unified, and in which a lyrical Agnus Dei foreshadows (in a different metre and key) the Countess's aria in *Figaro*. Mozart wrote shorter sacred works too, during this period, probably including the *Regina Coeli*, K.276 (321b), with spirited violin writing against largely homophonic vocal parts; and his two complete settings of the vesper psalms, K.321 and K.339. The Requiem and C minor Mass aside, we do not think of Mozart as a liturgical composer, but here as in other particulars there is always a danger that his fecundity will blind us in relation to individual generic and social strands in his *oeuvre*.

With *La finta giardiniera*, premiered in January 1775, Mozart brought together many features that became typical of his later comic operas. The roles are musically well defined – servants have folk-like tunes, the tenor Belfiore has lyrical, wide-spanning melodies, and jealous Violante sings the most extrovert part. The orchestra sometimes offers commentary on events on stage, as in Podestà's aria, where the instruments he mentions play to him from the orchestra. And in the first- and second-act finales changes in dramatic situation and number of characters correspond to changes of key, tempo and metre. These finales, unlike the ones in Mozart's operas from *Die Entführung* onwards, do not begin and end in the same key. The main weakness of *La finta giardiniera* is its erratic libretto: it has two mad scenes, and stock features are lifted from the *commedia dell'arte* tradition. Nevertheless, critical hindsight cannot detract from its position as a watershed in Mozart's relations with theatre music.

Between *La finta giardiniera* and *Idomeneo* (completed in January 1781) Mozart wrote a series of arias for independent performance or for performance as parts of other composers' operas (for a survey of these, which Mozart wrote intermittently throughout his life, see 'Voice and orchestra', pp. 322–9). He also worked on three, possibly four, large-scale dramatic works: *Il rè pastore*, a work probably for concert or semi-staged performance after Metastasio; *Semiramis*, a lost, possibly never started 'duodramma per musica';

Thamos, König in Ägypten, a play by Gebler with incidental music by Mozart; and *Zaide*, an unfinished Singspiel (this was found, untitled, in Mozart's manuscripts after his death: Johann André named it after the principal female character). In *Zaide*, Mozart included one or more arias for each of the main characters, a duet, a trio, a quartet, and two *Melodramen*. The *Melodramen* consist of declaimed text with colourful orchestral accompaniment, the orchestra separating one section of the text from the next so as to avoid dominating the voice.

Mozart began *Idomeneo* (an *opera seria* to a libretto by Varesco, after Danchet) in the second part of 1780, in response to a commission by the Elector Karl Theodor at Munich. It was first performed there in January 1781. Correspondence between Mozart and his father during these months is a rich source of information on the composer's attitude towards opera composition, showing how he was prepared to alter the music and the libretto right up to the last moment in the service of the drama and to accommodate the needs and limitations of his singers. On 8 November 1780, for example, he wrote to Leopold about Ilia's second aria, saying that he wanted Varesco to take out 'what has always seemed to me to be unnatural – N.B., I mean in an aria – and that is a *spoken aside*. In a dialogue these things are quite natural – one says a few words quickly and aside; but in an aria, where the words have to be repeated, it creates a bad effect'. Varesco later complained that he had copied out the entire libretto four times, and then been asked to make further changes. His libretto was sent to press at the beginning of January, but Mozart continued to make revisions, all designed to improve dramatic and musical continuity. On 3 January 1781, for instance, he wrote that he was unhappy about Elettra's last aria, because 'it seems very stupid to me that [they] should hurry away so quickly – simply to allow Madam Elettra to be alone'. He subsequently replaced this aria with recitative.

In *Idomeneo*, certain keys have specific extra-musical associations: for instance, C minor is associated with moments of high drama, as in the chorus at nos 5, 17 and 24, and when the Oracle speaks. The two main tonal poles of the opera, D major/minor and C minor, are both represented in Elettra's D minor vengeance aria, no.4, with a recapitulation beginning in C minor. This aria starts with an unharmonized note A in bassoons and strings, which follows on from the E major chord concluding Elettra's preceding recitative, and which only resolves to an unambiguous D minor chord nineteen bars later. The aria ends on G^7, the dominant of the succeeding C minor chorus. Thus Mozart here, as elsewhere in *Idomeneo*, achieves musical continuity between what in conventional *opera seria* would be discrete numbers. As Heartz (1969) has observed, there are in fact very few opportunities in *Idomeneo* for audience applause.

1781–8:
productivity and
popularity

IN VIENNA, IN JUNE 1781, Colloredo released Mozart from his service. Mozart stayed in Vienna and began a career as freelance musician. There is no evidence that he wished to remain without attachment to a court or other institution, but he never subsequently found substantial, regular employment. During this period, especially from 1781 to 1786, he was at his most prolific as a composer, stimulated no doubt by the rich musical and intellectual life of Vienna, by commissions, by public performances, and possibly by his encounter with the music of J.S. Bach and Handel at Van Swieten's musical meetings, and his deepening connections with freemasonry.

Church music and serenades for wind

Away from Salzburg, Mozart had less reason to write music for the church, or divertimentos and serenades for mixed ensemble or orchestra. The Kyrie, K.341 (368a), an imposing and elaborate work in D minor, with large orchestra and voices *tutti* throughout, was thought to have been composed about the time of *Idomeneo*, though a much later date has recently been proposed (see 'Masses', p. 312). The C minor Mass, K.427 (417a), was left incomplete in 1783, as happened on other occasions with a number of non-commissioned works when other priorities intervened. The influence of J.S. Bach and Handel has been noticed in its choral writing, especially that of the highly chromatic 'Qui tollis', and in the double fugue of the 'Hosanna'; the lavish, Italianate 'Et incarnatus est' is a coloratura 'aria' with showy cadenza. In March 1785, Mozart gave two completed sections of the C minor Mass (Kyrie and Gloria) an Italian text (possibly by Da Ponte), and assembled them, together with two new arias, as an oratorio, *Davidde penitente*, K.469. After the C minor Mass, he completed no church compositions until the *Ave, verum corpus*, K.618, of 1791, although his masonic works, such as *Die Maurerfreude*, K.471, and the *Maurerische Trauermusik*, K.477 (479a) (its solemn tone anticipating the priest's music in *Die Zauberflöte*), arguably come into the category of sacred, or at least devotional music.

Three wind serenades date from the early Viennese years: K.375 (Mozart wrote this in 1781, but, in the following year, he added two oboes to the original six instruments); K.388 (384a), later to be arranged as the String Quintet, K.406 (516b); and K.361 (370a), for 12 winds and bass. K.361 (370a) is suite-like, in seven movements, with rich instrumental writing. K.375 has five movements, with more restrained instrumentation – Mozart said he wrote this work 'rather carefully'. K.388 has four movements and a chamber-music-like texture. This last work, in C minor, is remarkable for its thematic concision and its bold forms. The *forte*, unison opening outlines first a tonic chord, and then a diminished seventh, not unlike the main theme of the C minor Piano Concerto, K.491. The diminished interval recurs in the third movement Minuet and repeatedly in the finale. The Minuet and Trio are replete with contrapuntal devices: the Minuet offers a canon between the two outer parts; and the Trio has simultaneous canons *al rovescio* between the upper two and lower two parts. These three serenades are Mozart's last works for solo wind apart from a few shorter pieces, including the divertimentos K.Anh.229 (439b).

Piano concertos and symphonies

The frequency with which Mozart completed his Viennese piano concertos corresponds to the rise and fall of his popularity with the public. In 1782–3, he completed three, (K.414 (385p), K.413 (387a) and K.415 (387b)); in 1784, six (K.449, 450, 451, 453, 456 and 459); in 1785 and 1786, six (K.466, 467, 482, 488, 491 and 503); in 1787, none, and one each in 1788 and 1791 (K.537 and 595). Tyson has suggested that Mozart left some of these works in fragmentary form for several years, presumably finishing them when he needed a concerto for a specific purpose. The last finished concerto, K.595, for instance, was apparently begun on paper Mozart used in 1788.

Mozart's letter to his father of 28 December 1782 indicates that he wanted his first three Viennese concertos to be accessible to all types of listener:

> The concertos are in fact something intermediate between too difficult and too easy: they are very brilliant and fall pleasantly on the ear – without of course becoming vapid. Here and there only connoisseurs can derive satisfaction – but in such a way that the non-connoisseur will be pleased without knowing why.

Something of the unpretentious character of these works is indicated by their instrumentation: the wind parts can be omitted and the piano accompanied by solo strings. K.413 (387a) is the most restrained, with a lilting first-movement Allegro in 3/4 time and a minuet finale, and K.415 (387b) the most brilliant. K.414 (385p) is perhaps the finest, with its diverse melodic resources in the first movement, a delicate rondo finale, possibly replacing the Rondo, K.386, and a veiled Andante which opens with a theme by J.C. Bach, who died in the same year as this concerto was composed. Appropriately enough, if the movement was conceived as a valediction for Bach, the second part of the piano's first theme (bar 29) never returns in the reprise. Surviving sketches for the first movement of K.414 (385p) reveal the intense contemplation Mozart gave to the form and detail of his music. His revisions of the early drafts, both surgical and cosmetic, are ample testimony to the fact that hard and thoughtful work lies behind the fluency of his finished scores.

1784 to 1786 was Mozart's most concentrated period of concerto writing. In these years he completed the twelve works which established the piano concerto as one of the most serious and highly valued genres, where symphonic, chamber and operatic styles meet. The first six, all from 1784, are his most experimental in terms of form. K.449 (probably begun in 1782), like its three predecessors, can be performed as a piano quintet. Its slow movement has an unusual harmonic plan, including a repetition of the opening theme in the key of the flat leading-note; and the faintly Baroque-style first theme of the finale is varied by the solo piano (but not always by the orchestra) at each repetition. Mozart described the next two works, K.450 and 451, as concertos 'to make the performer sweat' (letter of 26 May 1784): they are virtuoso pieces, written for Mozart's own performance, the first including newly expressive wind writing, especially at the beginning and in the finale; the second in extrovert style. The wind writing is bolder in the following two works, K.453 and 456, and the chromaticism is more extreme – for example, in the central section of the second movement of K.453. Both works have a variation movement, the finale in K.453 – where the forward momentum of the increasingly elaborate variations is counterbalanced by a long, *buffa*-style coda – and the highly expressive slow movement of K.456. In the last concerto of 1784, K.459, the finale is the point of focus; it draws together 'learned' counterpoint, brilliant piano writing and *opera buffa* rhythmic drive, in a dramatic release from the preceding genteel, ornamental Allegretto.

The emotional range of Mozart's concertos was enhanced beyond precedent in the first two concertos of 1785, K.466 in D minor and K.467 in C major. In the restless opening Allegro of the D minor work, the piano and orchestra are opposed throughout, and there is no release of tension in the reprise, where the second subject is transformed – further than the harmony makes strictly necessary – into plaintive, tonic minor. The second movement Romance, in B♭ major, contains a highly-charged G minor episode, and the finale is a vigorous sonata rondo (anticipating the minor-key finale of Beethoven's Third Piano Concerto) with a luminous coda in the tonic major.

During the winter and spring of 1785–6, Mozart completed three further concertos, K.482, 488 and 491, all for his own concerts, and the first to use clarinets (K.488 was begun in about 1784, with oboes instead of clarinets). K.482 and K.488 are complementary, the former with elaborate piano writing, and saturated with woodwind colour, the latter more delicate and lyrical, with a smaller orchestra than K.482, and a slow movement in the unusual key of F♯ minor. The C minor Concerto, K.491, is even more sombre than the earlier D minor work. Its thematic integration, both within and between movements, has often been praised. For example, the melodic progression C, E♭, A♭, G, in the first three bars of the concerto, anticipates the two episodes of the E♭ Larghetto movement, in C minor and A♭ major respectively. The neighbour-note progression A♭–G reappears in the bass of the finale theme, and variations 1 through to 3; and the same progression is projected over a large span, by variation 4 (in A♭ major) and variation 5 (beginning with A♭ in the bass, resolving to G). The C major work, K.503 (December 1786) is the last of Mozart's 'monumental' concertos. The clarity of instrumentation and the first movement's unsettling minor-key inflections of tonic and dominant (contrasting with the exotic orchestral and harmonic palette of the 1784–5 concertos) are signs of a new compositional stringency, a move towards the terser style which characterizes the music of Mozart's later years. This line of development is even more pronounced in K.537, completed in 1788: blocks of melodic material are set in relief against almost bland, transitional passages, particularly in the finale. This work, where lyricism is contained within the clearest of formal outlines, has been described as the greatest of early Romantic piano concertos (Rosen, 1971).

Mozart composed few symphonies during the Viennese years, though he did revive some Salzburg works. The new symphonies written up to 1787 are the *Haffner*, K.385 (1782, but revised, probably in 1783), the *Linz*, K.425 (1783) and the *Prague*, K.504 (1786). The first two were apparently composed hastily: the *Linz* (his first symphony with a slow introduction) during his short stay in that city, when he had no other finished works to hand; the *Haffner* as a commission for the Salzburg family of that name – Mozart sent the music there as soon as it was written, and said some six months later, when he saw it again, 'My new Haffner Symphony has positively astonished me, for I had forgotten every single note of it' (letter of 15 February 1783). The *Prague*, in D major, again has a slow introduction. This section gravitates towards the tonic minor and then leads into a tonic major, sonata-form Allegro, remarkable for its intense motivic concentration and contrapuntal display. A gentle and curiously chromatic Andante follows, then an *opera buffa*-style finale, containing a reference to the duet between Susanna and Cherubino in *Figaro*, Act II which was popular in Prague at the time.

During the summer of 1788 Mozart completed his last three symphonies, K.543, in E♭ major, K.550 in G minor and K.551 in C major. It is unlikely that he composed these works without having specific plans for their performance. They were possibly intended for subscription concerts in autumn 1788 and he probably took them with him on his travels of 1789 and 1790. A Mozart symphony which can be presumed to be one of these three was performed at a public concert in Vienna in 1791 (Landon, 1988). Each symphony has a different scoring. K.543 has no oboes, and clarinets are prominent throughout, especially in the Trio. K.550 has no trumpets and drums – some time after its original composition clarinet parts were added and the oboe parts revised. K.551 has trumpets and drums in its brilliant outer movements and in the Minuet; in striking timbral contrast, the strings are muted in the Andante.

The first movement of each work is a sonata form with relatively regular recapitulation. K.543 begins with a slow introduction, with French-overture-style dotted rhythms. Einstein thought its repeated chords and the 'unusual' ties in the following Allegro had masonic significance. The first movement of K.551 has a 'false' reprise in the subdominant; Mozart used this device rarely – a similar example, where the false reprise leads on to further development rather than directly into the real reprise, appears in the overture of *Die Zauberflöte*. In the slow movements, radical recomposition of repeated formal sections is underlined by new orchestration. That of K.550 begins with an intense sequence of imitations, in a Classical assimilation of a typically Handelian texture. Each symphony has a minuet and trio; that of K.550 is decidedly untraditional, with its opening three-bar groups and jagged countermelody to the main theme in the central section.

The finales of the three works are strongly contrasting. K.551's is a grand, fugal-style sonata form with an elaborate coda in invertible counterpoint. The last movement of K.543 is monothematic: the monothematicism is not primarily a homage to Haydn, but rather an explicit version of a basic principle in all Mozart's mature instrumental music, the principle of underlying thematic unity. The codetta and coda of this movement begin with six-bar phrases which recall the literally arresting six-bar phrase at the beginning of the second subject (the latter is, in turn, derived from the four-bar phrases of the first subject). In the light of these six-bar phrases, the coda's closing pair of three-bar semiquaver flourishes offers an appropriate conclusion to the movement. The agitated finale of K.550 is notorious for the tonal disorientation at the opening of the development, which has been described as proto-serial, thanks to its radical chromaticism. As in an equivalent passage in the first-movement development section of the E♭ major Quartet, K.428 (421b), each note of the tonally disruptive gesture at the beginning of the development is subsequently harmonized in the development.

K.551 was Mozart's last work for orchestra, apart from numerous dances he composed in connection with his appointment at the Viennese court (from 1787). Many of these have colourful instrumentation and flashes of harmonic daring, but they are hardly what Mozart would have wished for in the way of commissions. He is said to have written on a receipt for such dance music: 'Too much for what I did, not enough for what I could do'.

Solo piano music
The dates of composition of Mozart's piano sonatas K.330 (300h), 331 (300i), 332 (300k) and 333 (315c) remain uncertain. (Köchel suggests 1779, Einstein 1778, and Tyson as late as the summer or autumn of 1783, when Mozart might have needed new works for teaching purposes (Tyson, 1987)). These sonatas include some of Mozart's most popular works for piano, especially the lyrical opening movements of K.332 (300k) and 333 (315c), and the much-analysed variation set which begins the A major Sonata, K.331 (300i). K.330 (300h) and 332 (300k) follow the same plan of outer movements in sonata form surrounding an aria-like slow movement (with different ornamentation in the autograph and first edition of K.332 (300k)). K.331 (300i) ends with an exuberant

Allegretto *alla Turca* and K.333 (315c) with a rondo, the beginning of which rehearses the outline of the opening bars of the first movement. The second movement of K.331 (300i) is a Minuet and Trio, the Trio notable for its metrically unsettling echo effects.

Mozart's other keyboard works of the early 1780s include a number of unfinished fugues, the Baroque-style Suite, K.399 (385i), and an elaborate C minor Fugue for two pianos, K.426: all presumably reflect his preoccupation at that time with the contrapuntal music of J.S. Bach and Handel. Also in the early 1780s, Mozart transcribed a series of keyboard fugues by J.S. Bach, and he later reorchestrated various vocal works by Handel, including *Messiah*. Einstein and other scholars believe Mozart's study of these Baroque composers (both little-known in Vienna at the time) had a decisive impact on his musical development and was an inspiration for the great contrapuntal finales of such works as the String Quartet K.387 and the *Jupiter* Symphony, as well as shorter passages of explicit or 'incidental' counterpoint in many of Mozart's other Viennese compositions. Sadie, on the other hand, regards the increased counterpoint in Mozart's music during this period as the natural corollary of a maturing style.

The next two piano sonatas are dated by Mozart in the thematic index which he began to keep in 1784: K.457 of October 1784, and K.533, which consists of two movements completed in January 1788, followed by a slightly revised version of the Rondo K.494 of June, 1786. He published K.457 together with the C minor Fantasia, K.475: other, incomplete fantasias by Mozart survive from the early 1780s. Thematic connections between the C minor Fantasia and Sonata are more than fleeting, and both share the same dramatic mood, yet they are highly contrasting in terms of form, the unpredictable and harmonically unstable Fantasia balanced by the traditional three movements of the Sonata. The second movement of K.533 is introspective and chromatically adventurous; the rondo finale has an expressive, tonic minor episode and exciting fugal build-up (not present in the original version of K.494) to the coda. At the time of writing his last symphonies, Mozart composed the Sonata K.545, in C major. He said this piece was 'for beginners', but the short rondo finale is technically finnicky and the first movement is a model of compositional ingenuity: it has a subdominant reprise, but rather than transposing the exposition exactly in the reprise, Mozart extends the recapitulatory transition and then varies the register of the second subject, beginning it a fifth lower than in the exposition but continuing it a fourth higher, so as to highlight the top E which is so important in the overall structure of the movement.

Further solo piano works during 1781–8 include several sets of variations, of which the most popular are those on a theme by Gluck, K.455, and, perhaps the finest, a set for piano duet on an original theme, K.501 (1786), where the thematic structure is not so much embellished as organically developed through each successive variation. Mozart completed two other piano duets during this period, the imposing Sonata K.497 (1786), with weighty slow introduction, and his last duet sonata, the brilliant K.521, from May 1787. Several remarkable short pieces for solo piano come from the end of this period, including a delicate and highly expressive Rondo, K.511 (1787), an emotionally charged Adagio, K.540 (1788), which rapidly becomes flooded with detailed figuration, and an inscrutably chromatic Minuet, K.355 (576b) (?1789–90).

Chamber music

In 1781, Mozart published a set of six piano and violin sonatas. Of these, K.296 had been written earlier, at Mannheim, and K.378 (317d) possibly originates from Salzburg. The others were composed in Vienna in the year of publication. A contemporary critic noted that 'these sonatas require just as skilful a player on the violin as on the clavier' and that they were 'rich in new ideas'. K.377 (374e) has a delicately mournful minor-key set of variations as the middle movement, in which the sixth, 'siciliano' variation strikingly prefigures the theme of the variation finale of the D minor String Quartet, K.421 (417b). K.379 (373a) is the only two-movement sonata of the set. The first movement comprises an Adagio in the tonic major, which is followed by a tonic minor Allegro. This Allegro begins as if it is in sonata form, and has two repeated sections, but the 'development' is of just twelve bars, and the first subject is radically revised towards the beginning of the reprise. The second movement, a set of variations in the major, reveals its organic connection to the first movement most explicitly after the double bar of variation 5, where the piano's broad chords in a low register evoke the character of the opening Adagio. The other two completed piano and violin sonatas from the first part of the decade are K.454, written for the violinist Strinasacchi, in 1784, with a slow introduction and an unusually lengthy, but light-textured, finale, incorporating brilliant writing for both instruments; and K.481, from late 1785. This last work is less popular than its predecessor, but equally striking, with the contrasting theme and texture in the development of the first movement anticipating both the first-subject coda and an internal section of the second movement. In the second movement, in A♭ major, Mozart – uncharacteristically – has to use enharmonic notation: the two sections marked with an A major key signature draw to a close with a chord on the flattened sixth degree of A♭ major (notated as E, not F♭), each of which ultimately resolves, Schubert-like, to the dominant of the main key.

Other chamber works with piano written between 1781 and 1786 include K.452, the Quintet for piano and winds, of 1784 (which Mozart considered at the time to be 'the best work I have ever composed'); the Piano Quartets, K.478 and K.493 (1785 and 1786); the Trios for piano and strings, K.496 and K.502 (1786); and the Trio for piano, clarinet and viola, K.498 (1786). In each of these works, the piano balances the other instruments, and it has particularly extrovert passages of concerto-like display in the stormy G minor Quartet, K.478, and the Trio, K.502. The publisher Hoffmeister apparently complained that the public found K.478 too difficult to listen to and would be unlikely to buy it. But, in an article on one of Mozart's piano quartets, from 1788, an anonymous writer observed that contemporary performance practice, where pieces were under-rehearsed and played by dilettantes at noisy gatherings, was hardly conducive to a proper understanding of challenging new music. 'What a difference', the writer continued, 'when this much-advertised work of art is performed with the highest degree of accuracy by four skilled musicians who have studied it carefully, in a quiet room where the suspension of every note cannot escape the listening ear, and in the presence of only two or three attentive persons'.

At least Mozart's crowning achievements in the chamber music up to the mid-1780s, his six quartets dedicated to Haydn, were indeed first performed in such ideal conditions. Haydn heard that first performance, in January 1785, and three of the quartets were repeated the next month, again with Haydn present. It was on the second occasion that Haydn remarked to Leopold: 'I tell you before God, and as an honest man, that your son is the greatest composer I know, either personally or by reputation; he has taste and moreover the greatest possible knowledge of the science of composition.'

Mozart called these works the 'fruits of long and laborious labour', and his unusually detailed alterations to the autograph manuscripts, his sketches and his revisions just before publication, seem to confirm that claim. The indebtedness of these works to Haydn's recently completed op. 33 quartets has often been observed, not only in terms of incidental thematic similarities, but also in the equal importance of the four instruments, the contrapuntal finales of K.387 and K.464, and in detailed motivic relationships within and between movements. The A major Quartet, K.464, offers a prime example of the latter. An opening chromatic motive returns, in various guises, in the first-movement transition, second subject and coda, in the slightly altered reprise of the first section of the Menuetto, in the bass when the variation theme returns to close the third movement, and throughout the finale. The 'dissonant' introduction to the first movement of K.465 has never failed to intrigue Mozart's audiences. His contemporary, Giuseppe Sarti, considered its apparent harmonic audacities a sign of Mozart's lack of compositional skill, while one 20th-century commentator is astonished that 'it does not fit in with the limpid style of the rest of the Quartet'. In fact, this introduction is a meditation upon ideas which recur throughout the work. For instance, the C minor references within these opening bars return just before the reprise of the first movement and foreshadow the key and eerie sonority of the third-movement Trio, as well as the C minor tinge at the beginning of the development in the finale. The repeated notes in the solo cello right at the beginning of the introduction reappear in various transformations to open the exposition, development, recapitulation and coda of the first movement. These repeated notes are subsequently embellished by the solo cello in the second subject of the second movement, just before the other instruments recall the imitative texture of the introductory Adagio. In this quartet, as in all the others of the set, every detail counts.

In 1786, Mozart composed a single quartet, K.499, in D major, notable for its clarity of texture, and passages where the first violin soars high above the other instruments. In the first-movement coda, F natural, supported by a diminished chord, is followed by F♯, as part of a cadential progression. This progression recalls the converging of F and F♯ at two earlier places in the work (towards the beginning of the development and during the recapitulation of the second subject), and it anticipates the dramatic augmented sixth climax of the slow movement (bars 82–9).

Mozart wrote two of his most outstanding chamber works during 1787. The String Quintet in C major, K.515, has expansive outer movements (the first of which has been described as 'the largest sonata allegro before Beethoven') and unusual phrasing in the Minuet (the beginning of the Minuet consists of eight bars expanded to ten, not two five-bar phrases, as at the opening of the first movement). The String Quintet in G minor, K.516, has a first movement characterized by developing variation in exposition and reprise (and a correspondingly concise development section), a relentlessly chromatic Minuet (a thematic outgrowth of the first movement), a muted slow movement, and a sombre Adagio introduction (offering a conspectus of the work's main harmonic and melodic material) to the finale. Soon after, Mozart completed the Piano and Violin Sonata K.526. This work has a Molto Allegro, sonata-form first movement, where the rapid changes of thematic material are shared equally between the violin and the right hand of the piano; a veiled Andante, with fragmentary melodic line and disconcertingly expressive accompaniment; and a virtuoso finale, where a distinction between melody and accompaniment is often suspended in Mozart's lean, contrapuntal texture.

Two works completed in the summer of 1787 are for solo instrumental groups, though neither is strictly classifiable as chamber music: the polished *Eine kleine Nachtmusik*, for string quartet and double bass, and the stylistic parody, *Ein musikalischer Spass* (*A Musical Joke*), K.522. Einstein has called the latter a negative 'key' to Mozart's whole aesthetic: incompetent performers are parodied, for instance, in the horn's excruciatingly wrong notes in the Minuet, the meandering violin cadenza of the third movement, concluding with an ascending scale that overshoots its mark by at least a tone, and the painfully multitonal final cadence. Mozart's compositional jokes include unusual bar lengths and tedious strumming on tonic and dominant at the beginning of the first movement, instrumental entries which seem to come in too soon or too late, and conspicuous lack of motivic development, especially in the outer movements. The danger, as Jahn has observed, is that 'it is only by context that we can be assured that no actual mistake has happened, and that the composer does not deserve to be hissed at on his own account'.

Of the three piano trios composed in 1788, the E major, K.542, is the most outstanding in terms of melodic felicity and long-range thematic reference – for instance, the falling-fifth motive, C♯–F♯/ B–E towards the end of the piano's opening solo returns two movements later, in the very last bars. Yet for all the compositional superiority of the E major Trio and its predecessor in B♭ major (K.502, 1786), there are some obvious, if superficial, points of similarity between these and the other piano trios of 1788, K.548 in C major and K.564 in G major. All four have the same overall design: first a sonata-form movement, always allegro and without a distinct coda, then a slower movement in the subdominant, and last a rondo, beginning with piano solo. Mozart never adopted in his other groups of chamber works such a consistent formal template. His only authenticated trio for violin, viola and cello, K.563, was written about the same time. He called it a 'divertimento', and its origins in that tradition are clear from the number and types of movements (six, including two minuets). Yet this is chamber music of a status equivalent to that of the E major Piano Trio, not only in its broadly conceived outer movements and the ornamental Adagio, but also in the daring modifications of thematic structure in the fourth-movement set of variations.

Opera

Die Entführung aus dem Serail was composed between July 1781 and May 1782. The libretto, by Stephanie, after Bretzner, recalls that of *Zaide* and other Turkish operas of the time; Mozart told his father that it 'could hardly be better written for music'. Mozart's correspondence with Leopold shows the way in which he expected Stephanie to make significant changes to the original story: for instance, the part of Belmonte was expanded (three of his four arias were added by Stephanie, at least one as a result of Mozart's wishes), and Osmin, who at first had just one solo number, becomes the musical equal to the pairs of lovers. In reference to Osmin's new Act I aria, Mozart wrote 'I told Herr Stephanie just how the aria should go, and most of the music was finished before Stephanie had even done the text for it', revealing that he considered that the composer, not the librettist, had overall responsibility for the dramatic effect, and anticipating his famous comment in a letter from a few weeks later: 'In opera, the poetry must be altogether the obedient daughter of the music'.

Die Entführung blends traditional Singspiel elements – 'Turkish' music, spoken dialogue (even at crucial points in the plot) and comic scenes – with musical styles from other operatic genres: for example, *opera seria*, as in Konstanze's aria 'Martern aller Arten', and *buffa*, in the quartet finale to Act II. But Mozart moves beyond tradition in his dramatically effective, large-scale tonal planning.

The opera is organized round the 'Turkish' key of C major, with subsidiary emphasis on D major for moments of 'brassy brilliance' and B♭ major, to represent more sublime expression (see Bauman, 1988). The most famous example of his sharp delineation of mood and character within a single number is the turn from F major to A minor at the end of Osmin's Act I aria, which Mozart explained in a letter to his father as follows: 'a man who is in such a rage completely loses control and breaks all the rules, not being himself, and thus the music mustn't know what it's doing either'.

In a reflection of changing Viennese taste, Mozart's next operatic ventures were in connection with Italian libretti. Writing to his father on 7 May 1783, he said: 'I've examined at least a hundred libretti and more, but I've scarcely found a single one with which I am satisfied', and that 'I should dearly love to show what I can do in Italian opera'. In the same letter, he mentions that the librettist Da Ponte – recently employed by Joseph II – had promised to write something for him, but asked if in the meantime Varesco (the librettist of *Idomeneo*) might be persuaded to provide a libretto: 'the most important thing is that the whole story should be really *comic*; and if he can, he should introduce *two equally good female parts*, one of these to be *seria*, the other *mezzo carattere* [i.e. a character somewhere between comic and serious]. . . . The third female *character*, however, can be entirely *buffa*, and so can all the male ones, if necessary.'

In the summer of 1783, Mozart discussed with Varesco the plan of an opera, *L'oca del Cairo*, and about the same time he told his father of another libretto which interested him, probably *Lo sposo deluso* by Da Ponte. Both projects remained unfinished, possibly because neither was officially commissioned. During the next few years, he wrote single arias for insertion into other composers' operas or for specific singers. In early 1786, he composed the music for *Der Schauspieldirektor* (an overture, a trio, two arias and the 'Schlussgesang'), and a little later he put on a performance of *Idomeneo* in a revised version. His main production of 1786 was *Le nozze di Figaro*, with a libretto by Da Ponte.

Da Ponte based his libretto on Beaumarchais' notorious play, *La Folle Journée, ou Le Mariage de Figaro* (1778). Because of its strong political message, public performance of the play was censored in France until 1784, and Joseph II, in Vienna, forbade a performance in German translation in early 1785. In his memoirs, Da Ponte claimed to have persuaded Joseph to allow an adaptation of *Figaro* for operatic performance. Da Ponte changed the order of some sections, combined others, and added some numbers that are not in the play; overall, he transformed a political satire into a 'radiant' romantic comedy (for a recent interpretation of the central theme of *Figaro* as that of a pastorale, see Allanbrook, 1983).

The characters in *Figaro* correspond in general terms to those Mozart believed were essential to a truly comic libretto (letter of 1783, quoted above). The roles of the Countess and Susanna are of equal importance. The Countess comes closest to a female *seria* role, especially in her aria 'Dove sono'. Susanna is a *mezzo carattere*, her role incorporating the widest spectrum of emotional representation, from the comedy of her duet with Cherubino, to her intimate letter duet with the Countess, and her final, transcendent aria. *Buffo* elements are absorbed to varying degrees in the male roles, as in Figaro's tirade against women, Cherubino's lovesick 'Non so più', the Count's music at the beginning of the Act II finale, and the parody of *seria* style in Bartolo's vengeance aria.

The extended finales to Act II and IV also belong to the tradition of *opera buffa*. Mozart reflects Da Ponte's ingenious pacing of the dramatic action (underlined by changes in the poetic metre) in his masterly musical settings. Typically for a Viennese *opera buffa* of the 1780s (Platoff, 1984), the first finale (that is, to Act II) comprises the most complex point in the action, while the second (Act IV) resolves the drama, and is less vigorous in style. Each finale consists of a series of contrasting sections, delineated dramatically by the introduction of a new character or a new aspect of the plot, and musically by changes in tempo, metre, key or motivic construction. The finales are tonally self-contained (E♭ major for the second act, D major for the fourth), with internal sections in closely related keys. Da Ponte described the *buffa* finale as 'a kind of comedy or minor drama in itself. . . . This is the great occasion for showing off the genius of the composer and the ability of the singers in order to conduct the opera towards its climax.'

Soon after its Viennese premiere, *Figaro* was performed to great acclaim in Prague. By the time of Mozart's departure from Prague in February 1787, he had been invited to compose a new opera for the next season: *Don Giovanni*. Again the libretto was by Da Ponte, who gave it the subtitle 'dramma giocoso'. This term was first used by the Italian playwright Goldoni around 1750, to designate a new kind of comic opera including a variety of characters, ranging from comic to serious (Goldoni wrote a version of the Don Juan story in 1736 and Mozart set a revised version of one of Goldoni's libretti – *La finta semplice* – in 1768). Unlike the story of *Figaro*, based on a previously banned play of direct social relevance, that of Don Juan was familiar from diverse literary and popular sources (the first known dramatic setting, by Tirso de Molina, dates from the early 17th century): the libertine, Don Juan, proceeds relentlessly from one seduction to another until at last Heaven punishes him. The most direct model for the action and sometimes even the language for whole sections of Da Ponte's libretto was Giovanni Bertati's *Don Giovanni*, first performed with music by Giuseppe Gazzaniga in Venice early in 1787.

Since the story of Don Juan traditionally consisted of a loose succession of scenes, all designed to illustrate the depravity of Juan's character, it was up to the librettist to provide dramatic cohesion. Da Ponte gave the unfolding of the story a certain fatalistic logic by paralleling the action of Act I in Act II: both begin with exterior and end with interior sets, and the events of each act gradually bring together Giovanni's antagonists, culminating in the ball scene at the end of Act I and the banquet, Giovanni's descent to Hell and a moralistic chorus to conclude Act II. Episodes that correspond are not, however, always of the same significance, and there are some 'remainders', such as the graveyard scene, which have no counterpart. The parallel dramatic structure of the libretto of the two acts is underlined to a degree by Mozart's key scheme in the opening and closing sequences of the opera (though the progression from D minor to D major to D minor at the beginning is changed to D major, minor and then major at the end). The scheme is discussed in detail by Rushton (1981), who argues that Mozart provides clear 'collateral evidence' for tonal correspondences widely separated in real time, by marking these points with similar local harmonies, musical styles, melodies and instrumentation. The most famous case of this is the reappearance of a section of the D minor overture when Don Giovanni confronts the Commendatore for the last time.

In E.T.A. Hoffmann's highly influential short story, *Don Juan*, from the 19th century, Donna Anna is Don Giovanni's spiritual counterpart, a 'divine woman', doomed to die before the year is out, and forcing the 'cold, unmanly, ordinary Don Ottavio, whom she once thought she loved', to take revenge on her seducer, Don Giovanni. Donna Anna's ternary aria, no.10 (preceded by a dramatic accompanied recitative), is the opera's purest *seria*-style piece, with its wide-ranging melody unified by the stepwise relationship between the highest notes. In the 20th century, Donna Elvira is often interpreted as the central female character. Her personality is more complex than Donna Anna's, her music less conventional, even eccentric, as in her first aria (with malicious commentary by Don Giovanni and Leporello), where her first vocal entry appears to come a bar late, or in the leaping, 'hysterical' melodic contour in this and her other numbers.

The extent to which Don Giovanni is the true protagonist is open to question. Although he has the title role, and his exploits give the opera its substance, he never sings an aria about himself, and his only comment on the motivation for his activities ('women . . . don't you know that they are more necessary to me than the bread I eat?') is drawn from him by Leporello as his defence of his appalling behaviour. Despite his dark nature and his intimate contact with Donna Anna, the *seria* heroine, he sings most often in *buffa* style; if his style changes it is to ape those he preys on. As Rushton has put it: 'Giovanni needs Leporello as a shadow because he casts none of his own, so swiftly does he run. . . . Deliberately, Mozart allows him no depth.'

Don Giovanni, like *Figaro*, takes place during the span of a single day, with Don Giovanni's most outrageous behaviour taking place under cover of darkness: he attacks Donna Anna, then kills her father at the beginning, and he challenges the supernatural in the graveyard scene and is subsequently taken into Hell at the end. But while the characters of *Figaro* refine the morality of their time within conventional social structures, in *Don Giovanni*, Don Giovanni and Donna Elvira live wildly outside social conventions. And *Figaro* is based on human conflicts and reconciliations, while *Don Giovanni* invokes the supernatural.

1789–91: the path to a new style

FOLLOWING THE REMARKABLY FERTILE YEARS from 1781 to 1788, Mozart's production of large-scale works slowed down. Some commentators have suggested that this change of pace reflects his difficult personal circumstances during the late 1780s – especially his financial problems. By 1791, however, his situation had apparently improved. He had just received confirmation of his appointment as assistant Kapellmeister at St Stephen's Cathedral – an unpaid position, but in due course he would have taken up the prestigious job of Kapellmeister. He had also been offered concerts abroad and regular publication of his compositions. Others believe that the sketches for the later works indicate Mozart's increasing difficulty with the process of composition – though we can never know whether sketches for his earlier works are lost. A further explanation for Mozart's few large-scale works during these last years is that Viennese society was becoming less affluent, so subscription concerts and large orchestras were abandoned in favour of less expensive musical entertainment. Whatever the influence of external events, towards the end of his life Mozart's music became generally less lyrical, more concise, and sometimes explicitly experimental. Some scholars believe this development took place during the summer or autumn of 1788, at the time of the last symphonies; others see hints of change even earlier, in the two string quintets K.515 and K.516, the Piano and Violin Sonata K.526, and *Don Giovanni*, of 1787. By 1789, this tendency marked out such works as the last quartets and the opera *Così fan tutte*.

Instrumental works

The last three string quartets, K.575, K.589 and K.590, were completed in June 1789, and May and June 1790. Mozart's thematic catalogue records that the first was for 'seine Majestätt den König in Preussen'; and he told his fellow-mason, Puchberg (letter of July 1789), of his plan to dedicate a set of six quartets to the Prussian king. But in a letter of June 1790, Mozart confessed: 'Now I am forced to give away my quartets (this laborious work) for a trifling sum, just to get some money in hand'. The three works were finally published just after Mozart's death, with no dedication. Perhaps in homage to the cello-playing king, but equally possibly as a radical experiment with quartet texture, each of the four movements of K.575 has conspicuous cello passages, sometimes reaching up to more than an octave above middle C – the register (but not the timbre) of the first violin when it plays similar material. The cello is prominent also in the first movements of

K.589 and K.590 and the slow movement of K.589. In the minuet and trio movements and finales of the two last quartets, however, the soloistic cello writing disappears. The raw octaves after the double bar of the minuet of K.575, marked *forte* and then with a succession of *forte–pianos*, followed by a pointillistic exchange of spiky, *piano* crotchets between the three highest instruments, introduce a new 'effect' into Mozart's chamber music (not to be confused with the somewhat gauche unison passages in the early D minor quartet); and these octaves anticipate the bleak, unison octaves which open and return insistently during the first movement of K.589.

Mozart completed two further string quintets: K.593 in 1790 and K.614 in 1791. In K.593, in D major, the opening Larghetto and first eight bars of the following Allegro return, slightly varied, as the coda of the movement. Both initial and closing Larghettos include a progression from D major to E minor, a progression which also appears in the first four bars of the Allegro. The first Larghetto, however, does not include the dramatic tonic seventh chord which follows in bar 5 of the Allegro, while the coda's Larghetto contains this seventh chord, as well as some expressive melodic fragments which later form the basis of an internal section (bars 16 and following) of the next movement. The first movement of the E♮ major Quintet is uncharacteristically mosaic-like in its motivic construction. This movement reminded one commentator of 'a bad arrangement of a wind piece in mock-Haydn style'; another considers the whole work to be Mozart's last tribute to Haydn, with the finale indebted to Haydn's Quartet op. 64 no.6, the slow movement recalling the slow movement of Haydn's Symphony no.85, and the Trio probably influenced by the Trio of Haydn's Symphony no.88. Two other chamber works of the last years are the Clarinet Quintet, K.581 (1789), and the Adagio and Rondo, for glass armonica, flute, oboe, viola and cello, K.617 (1791). In the former, the rich tone of the clarinet is balanced against a string group; in the latter, the clear sound of Marianne Kirchgässner's instrument is surrounded by sinuous melodic wisps in the wind and strings in the minor-key Adagio, whilst the glass armonica is more equally balanced by the other instruments in the following, major-key section.

In the main keyboard works of his last years, the two sonatas K.570 and K.576 (both of 1789) and the Variations, K.613 (1791), Mozart conducts some of his most transparent experiments in musical form – transparent in the sense that he seems to work against a backdrop of 'expectations' set up in his earlier compositions. For instance, the theme of K.613 is based on an operatic number consisting originally of an instrumental introduction followed by a ternary-form song. In his variations, Mozart preserves the distinction between introduction and song by varying them in different ways (this is Mozart's only surviving independent set of variations in which the formal sections of each variation are not embellished similarly). It is not until the coda that motives from the introduction and song are contrapuntally combined. In the first movements of the piano sonatas, the 'expected', clear distinction between tonally stable first and second subjects and tonally unstable transitions and development is challenged at every turn. In K.570, the first apparently tonally stable area after the initial tonic is the subdominant; this passage in fact begins the transition; later, material derived from the transition appears within the second-subject area, while the opening of the second subject itself is a transposed version of the first subject. The development section begins with the tonally stable material from the exposition's first move to the subdominant, transposed to the flat mediant major. The finales of both K.570 and K.576 begin with a light, relaxed theme, yet go on to include intricate contrapuntal episodes laced with brilliant, organic, passage-work. The piano writing must have been a direct inspiration for Beethoven, especially in the third and fourth repeated sections of K.570, in relentless, fugal style, and bars 8 and following of K.576, with hammering left-hand triplets. Another late keyboard work is the contrapuntal Gigue, K.574, from 1789. It has been suggested that the eleven-note, minor-key theme in the Gigue's 'development' anticipates the twelve-note theme of the Gigue in Schoenberg's Suite, op. 29.

In 1791, Mozart wrote a short, ethereal piece for glass armonica, K.356 (617a). He also composed three pieces for mechanical organ: K.594 (1790), K.608 and K.616 (both from 1791). Mozart said he hated composing for mechanical organ because 'the little pipes are all high . . . and too childish for me', but nevertheless, in the piano duet or organ medium in which they are best known today, K.594 and K.608 are imposing works, block-like in construction, each consisting of two elaborate F minor sections framing a contrasting section in the major (the middle section of K.594 is an extrovert display piece in the tonic major, that of K.608 is a gentle Andante, in the relative major). In some early sources, K.608 is described as a fantasia, a title equally appropriate to K.594, since both pieces are idiosyncratic in terms of form, encompass a wide harmonic spectrum, and consist of three sections which must be performed without a break.

The two concertos of Mozart's last years are for piano and clarinet. He performed the Piano Concerto K.595 at his last public concert in 1791, but probably began it in 1788. All three movements are in the major, but invoke the minor mode. The piano's second subject in the first movement, for instance, begins in the dominant minor; an early section of the development introduces the distant region of flat supertonic minor; and the second movement's middle section turns to the tonic minor by way of the flat mediant major. A sonata rondo concludes the work, with fully-fledged development section, like so many of Beethoven's finales. Typical of Mozart's last works, yet prophetic, given 19th-century developments in cyclical form, is the tight thematic integration between movements: the main theme of the slow movement, for example, makes a radiant return as the second main theme of the finale (bar 65).

The Clarinet Concerto, K.622, is often described as valedictory in character, even though Mozart drafted the beginning of the first movement in a version for basset-horn, 584b (621b), perhaps as early as 1787. Mozart next wrote a version for basset-clarinet (a clarinet with extended downward compass): the music and the instrument do not survive, though modern reconstructions are available. The familiar version is an adaptation, probably by Mozart's publisher, of the basset-clarinet work. The orchestra is without oboes, and the clarinet is often set against the orchestral flutes and horns. The seamless melody of the first movement consists of flexible, overlapping phrases; the slow movement is chamber-music-like in its transparency of texture; and the finale is a bubbling, light rondo.

Vocal music
Between the completion of *Don Giovanni*, in October 1787, and his last operatic collaboration with Da Ponte, *Così fan tutte* (first performed in January 1790), Mozart fulfilled no operatic commissions, except for arias inserted into other composers' operas (some for singers who later performed in *Così*); he also, as in earlier periods, wrote some songs with piano accompaniment and concert arias, and he slightly revised *Don Giovanni* for its Viennese premiere. With the commission for *Così* Mozart began his last series of operatic masterpieces, in each of the main genres of the day: *Così* (*buffa*), *La clemenza di Tito* (*seria*), and *Die Zauberflöte* (Singspiel).

Così fan tutte is a story of deception, disguise and machination. The 19th century thought it immoral and implausible. For the 18th century, with its view of the underlying similarity of human nature (each sister falls for the other's lover in disguise and just as rapidly returns to her original partner), and for the 20th century, with its notions of dramatic alienation and circularity of plot, interest lies in 'the psychological steps by which characters move to an end known in advance' (Rosen, 1971).

The story is a tightly organized, symmetrically planned comedy. Unlike *Figaro* and *Don Giovanni*, there are no explicit *seria* roles. Instead, *Così*'s cast consists of three pairs of stylized characters: the two officers (Ferrando and Guglielmo), their fiancées (the sisters Dorabella and Fiordiligi), and the 'old philosopher' Don Alfonso, and his accomplice, the wily maid, Despina. Each character, except for Alfonso, who masterminds the action, has an aria in both acts. Alfonso sings in all the ensembles, except for the duets. His one aria (no.5) emerges from the preceding recitative and is dashed off in rapid syllabic style. The arias of Ferrando (and his additional cavatina, no.27) are lyrical and passionate, while Guglielmo is nearer to pure *buffo* style in his solo numbers. The first-act arias of the two sisters are in grand *seria* style, but verge on parody, since the emotions displayed are so excessive and inappropriate to the true dramatic situation. During the second act, the sisters' arias are more distinctly characterized: Dorabella's is simpler, Fiordiligi's seems to represent genuine conflict and repentance. In the duets, except for no.29 – the critical one for the symmetry of plot, where Fiordiligi gives in to Ferrando – the individual parts tend to be musically undifferentiated (just as the sisters' loyalties and officers' identities are interchangeable). In the larger ensembles the pairs (sisters and officers) sing in similar manners, which become more diversified when Alfonso and Despina are involved.

In place of precise musical characterization, *Così* offers variety and richness of orchestration: some of the most famous moments are the sensuous oboe line coinciding with the moment of Fiordiligi's capitulation; the leaping, mocking trumpet in Fiordiligi's first-act aria; and the combination of flutes, violins and bassoons which prefaces Guglielmo's Act II aria. The score also includes striking juxtapositions of different vocal types and groups. The opera opens, for example, with three duets for the same combination of male voices, a duet for two sopranos, a bass aria, a quintet for mixed, solo voices, a duet for baritone and tenor, and then – to fill out the registral range – a homophonic chorus. The exquisite sequence of instrumental and vocal sonorities is possibly *Così*'s most striking innovation, and was to be taken further in *Die Zauberflöte*.

Mozart composed three large-scale vocal works during his final year. *Die Zauberflöte* was virtually complete by July 1791 (the overture, the march of the priests and probably three second-act numbers were written later). He then went on to write the bulk of his last *opera seria*, *La clemenza di Tito* (to a libretto by Mazzolà, after Metastasio), for performance in Prague, on 6 September. Mozart's early biographers record that he wrote *La clemenza* in just eighteen days, with his pupil Süssmayr providing the *secco* recitatives. Recent research (discussed in Landon, 1988 and Tyson, 1987) suggests a more extended period of composition. About the same time as he was asked to write *La clemenza*, he received an anonymous commission (now known to be from the Austrian Count Walsegg) for a Requiem.

La clemenza has often been dismissed as frigid and conventional by comparison with the other late works. Yet there is no reason to suppose that it was primarily time constraints which led to the straightforward clarity of orchestration, homophonic choruses, and simple, effective instrumentation for the accompanied recitatives. If the arias are concise in form and the solo vocal writing relatively restrained, excepting the display arias for the *primo uomo*, Sesto, and *prima donna*, Vitellia, all these features are appropriate for the broad outlines of the opera's classical subject. Essentially, two patricians plot against their emperor, they are sentenced to death, but the humanitarian Tito – the Commendatore's alter ego, and of the same stock as Sarastro – forgives them. Franz Niemetschek, Mozart's early biographer, believed that *La clemenza* was Mozart's most 'polished' work of art: 'Mozart comprehended the simplicity, the quiet nobility of Titus and the whole plot, and conveyed this throughout his composition. Every part, even the smallest instrumental part, bears this stamp . . .'.

As with *Così fan tutte*, a remarkable feature of *Die Zauberflöte* is its variety of instrumental and vocal sonorities, ranging from the brilliance of the Trios of Boys and the Queen of Night's coloratura arias, the clarity of the Three Ladies' ensembles, Papageno's panpipes, the ring of bells (actually a glockenspiel), and Tamino's flute, to Sarastro's eloquent bass arias, and the dark sonority of the chorus of priests, accompanied by trombones and basset-horns. *Die Zauberflöte* was premiered at Schikaneder's Theater auf der Wieden, on 30 September 1791. Schikaneder's libretto follows many conventions of the popular plays and magic operas produced at his theatre during the preceding two years. In contrast, this was a project that was novel for Mozart. Previously, he had composed operas primarily to suit 'aristocratic' tastes, while *Die Zauberflöte* had to be a Singspiel in a style accessible to a much wider audience.

Among the many sources for *Die Zauberflöte* are Wranitzky's opera *Oberon* and also *Der Stein der Weisen* (with a text by Schikaneder and music by Schack, Mozart's first Tamino), which is in turn based on a fairy story by Liebeskind, *Lulu, oder Die Zauberflöte*, part of Wieland's collection, *Dschinnistan* (1786–9). The masonic aspect of *Die Zauberflöte* is influenced by the novel *Sethos*, by Terrasson (published in France in 1731). Mozart wrote other explicitly masonic works around this time, including the cantata *Laut verkünde unsre Freude*, K.623.

In the summer of 1791, a rival company in Vienna produced Müller's opera, *Kaspar der Fagottist*, also based on the *Dschinnistan* Lulu story. Some scholars believe that, in order to avoid direct comparison with *Kaspar*, Schikaneder changed the course of his plot for *Die Zauberflöte* after he had already written the first part. Thus *Die Zauberflöte* begins like a typical magic story, with the Queen of Night representing good, and Sarastro as the assumed villain (this follows the Kaspar story closely), but their roles are reversed during and after the Act I finale. Others believe that this change of perspective is only apparent and is in fact anticipated early in the opera.

A recent view is that the plot's apparent change of direction can be explained with reference to Hegelian dialectics and that the dialectical nature of the plot is underlined by the tonal organization of the music (Eckelmeyer, 1986). In Eckelmeyer's interpretation, the first act corresponds to a sonata-allegro exposition. The first-subject area, or Thesis, is framed by and contains music in, or closely related to, the masonic key of E♭: here the story seems like a conventional fairy tale. The second-subject area, or Antithesis, focuses on C major, and closely related keys: at this stage the 'reality' of the opera as presented earlier is reversed. The opening of Act II corresponds to a sonata-allegro development (the beginning of the Synthesis), with a less stable tonal scheme; and the finale of Act II is equivalent to the recapitulation of a sonata-allegro form, beginning and ending in E♭, but including C major and other keys from the 'second subject' area. In Act II, aspects of the Thesis and Antithesis sections are resolved: Tamino, Pamina and Papageno are tested and find their rightful places in the Temple society; and the uncertainties left at the end of the first act are clarified – the Queen's, Sarastro's and Monostatos' real characters, and the significance of the magic instruments. The opera ends with Tamino and Pamina united, representing a new Thesis.

Until recently it was thought that the motet *Ave, verum corpus* and the unfinished Requiem, K.626, were Mozart's first church works since the incomplete C minor Mass of 1783. But new research suggests that during his last years he also wrote some fragmentary church works and possibly the D minor Kyrie, K.341/368a (discussed above, p. 216). One reason for Mozart's return to sacred composition may have been his successful application for the position of assistant Kapellmeister at St Stephen's Church, in Vienna.

The only movement of the Requiem to be fully scored by Mozart is the Requiem aeternam. For the other sections up to and including the 'Hostias' (but excluding the 'Lacrymosa', of which he left the opening eight bars), he wrote the vocal parts, the bass line, with figuring, and indicated some of the orchestration. After Mozart's death, Constanze approached Eybler to complete the work, but when he failed to do so, she turned the project over to Süssmayr. Süssmayr claimed that the Sanctus, Benedictus and Agnus Dei were his own, original compositions, but he may have discussed the overall plan of the Requiem with Mozart and have had access to Mozart's sketches. Süssmayr reworked the Requiem aeternam and Kyrie to form the concluding 'Lux aeterna' and 'Cum sanctis tuis'. His completion has been criticized as stylistically inappropriate and other versions have been proposed, most recently by Maunder (1988) and Landon, whose recent edition incorporates all Eybler's work.

Of the ten movements containing Mozart's work, just two are mainly homophonic, the dramatic 'Dies irae', and the 'Lacrymosa' (as far as he wrote it); and only two movements begin and end in a major key, the 'Tuba mirum' and the 'Recordare'. The other movements include luxuriant, neo-Baroque-style counterpoint (for instance, the double fugue of the Kyrie, and the canonic writing of the 'Rex tremendae' and the 'Confutatis'). The generally dark and passionate character of the work is most simply accounted for by reference to the predominance of minor keys, the rich timbre of basset-horns and bassoons, the drama of trumpets and drums, and textural or thematic connections (such as the basset-horn counterpoint at the beginning of the Requiem aeternam anticipating the beginning of the 'Recordare', and the *forte*, leaping string chords just after the opening of the Requiem aeternam which are recalled in the 'Rex tremendae'). But Mozart's bold harmonic language is without doubt another, contributory factor. The D minor 'Dies irae', for instance, swings briefly towards

C minor at the second 'Quantus tremor est futurus'; and in the 'Tuba mirum', in B♮ major, the tenor soloist passes through F minor and G minor, and the alto through D minor and C minor; the homophonic ending to this movement contains strong G minor inflections, preparing for the G minor tonality of the next movement.

The work's most distant harmonic sequence – from A♭ minor, to G minor, to F major – occurs in the conclusion of the 'Confutatis' (beginning at 'Oro supplex'). Each of these three chords is approached by a progression from a diminished to a dominant seventh chord; essentially the same progression reappears in the 'Domine Jesu', at 'et de profundo lacu'; and the progression is only slightly modified in the 'Hostias', at the second statement of 'tu suscipe pro animabus illis'. Apart from such colouristic harmonic interrelationships, there is also evidence of Mozart's concern for overall harmonic planning. The six sections from the 'Dies irae' to the incomplete 'Lacrymosa' are in D minor, or closely related keys. Within this sequence, the 'Recordare', beginning and ending in F major, and the 'Confutatis', with A minor opening and an ending in F major, together form a complete tonal structure. Similarly, the 'Domine Jesu' and 'Hostias' of the Offertory form a unit: the prolonged E♮ major which opens the 'Hostias' must be interpreted as a neighbouring harmony to the D major chord with which the section ends; and D major is in turn the dominant chord for the G minor 'Domine Jesu'.

Had Mozart lived as long as his great contemporary, Haydn, the 'late' compositions might well have been regarded as transitional. As composer of the D minor and C minor piano concertos, the G minor Quintet, *Don Giovanni*, the G minor Symphony, K.550, and *Die Zauberflöte*, he became the symbolic torch-bearer for the new Romantic movement in German music. The formal variety of his Salzburg compositions and the compositional innovations – as opposed to the sheer dramatic force – of his very last works are, even two hundred years after the event, still little appreciated by comparison with his compositions from the period 1781–8.

ESTHER CAVETT-DUNSBY

The author wishes to thank Alec Hyatt King, Julian Rushton and Alan Tyson for their comments on this chapter.

Section 10

THE MUSIC

THE MUSIC

MANY OF MOZART'S WORKS can be dated with a degree of certainty, either through the existence of a dated autograph or on the basis of direct or circumstantial evidence regarding their composition. In the following lists of works, which are arranged genre by genre, and as ordered by *Köchel 6*, places and dates given without qualification may be considered reasonably definitive (though for the most part it is only the date that is taken direct from the autograph). Datings of works whose autographs survive with no indication of time or place of composition are in many cases suggested or supported by the evidence of handwriting and paper-studies. A date provided by Mozart's thematic catalogue (*Verzeichnüss*) should be understood generally, though not in all cases, as a guide to the time of *completion* of a work, and is often a pointer to a work's imminent performance. Square brackets for titles of works or movements indicate that these are not so given in the autograph. All places and dates are those of composition, rather than publication or first performance, unless otherwise stated.

The information appended to entries on individual works concerning fragments and sketch material has been supplied by John Arthur; it supplements his listing of independent material under 'Fragments and sketches' (pp. 340–51).

In the list of operas, each role is followed by its voice designation and by the name of the singer in the first performance.

Where only one Köchel number is given, it is identical in *Köchel 1* and *Köchel 6*. Two numbers indicates *Köchel 1* followed by *Köchel 6* (in parentheses). Where *Köchel 3* differs from *Köchel 6*, the order is *Köchel 1*, followed by *Köchel 3* and *6* (in parentheses). *Anh.* = *Anhang* (Appendix).

Libraries housing autograph manuscripts or first editions are identified by the system of RISM sigla adopted in *The New Grove* (see vol. 1, pp. xxxvi–lii).

AMA (Alte Mozart-Ausgabe): roman capital refers to series number (with any subdivisions indicated after an oblique), followed by the number of the work within that volume.

NMA (Neue Mozart-Ausgabe): roman capital refers to series number; arabic numeral refers to Werkgruppe number, and is followed by Abteilung (arabic) and Band (roman) numbers as appropriate.

(Where no reference is made, it is because the work in question is not to be found in AMA, or was not included in NMA at the time of preparation.)
Verzeichnüss = Mozart's *Verzeichnüss aller meiner Werke* (1784–91)
(For full details of Köchel, AMA, NMA and *Verzeichnüss*, see Select Bibliography.)

Abbreviations

A	alto, contralto
appx	appendix
attrib.	attributed
attribn	attribution
B	bass (voice)
b	bass (instrument)
bc	basso continuo
bn	bassoon
cl	clarinet
comp.	composed/composition
db	double bass
fl	flute
frag.	fragment
glock	glockenspiel
gui	guitar
hn	horn
hpd	harpsichord
kbd	keyboard
mand	mandolin
MS	manuscript
ob	oboe
obbl	obbligato
org	organ
perf.	performed/performance
pf	piano
pic	piccolo
qnt	quintet
qt	quartet
rec	recorder
rev.	revised/revision
S	soprano
str	string(s)
S,A,T,B	soprano, alto, tenor, bass (solo voices)
SATB	ditto (chorus voices)
T	tenor
timp	timpani
tpt	trumpet
trbn	trombone
v, vv	voice(s)
va	viola
vc·	cello
vn	violin

Operas

Mozart's contribution to the genre

The early operas

There are two senses in which it is possible to talk about an artist contributing to a genre. The less interesting would be in the sense of merely adding numerically to the works in that genre, the more interesting would be in the sense of adding to the scope of the genre, or indeed of transforming it. Mozart had added much to the genre in the first sense by the end of his teens: two large comic Italian operas, one small comic German opera, two large serious Italian operas, various settings of marginally theatrical texts by Metastasio. It is not an achievement entirely to be written off, but how should it be assessed?

At the end of the period, the scores of *La finta giardiniera* and *Il rè pastore* (1775) share much of the same thematic character as the violin concertos with which they are contemporaneous, but these are works which are lacking in dramatic resourcefulness either in terms of local effect or long-term planning – something which matters much more in the intricate extended *operà buffa* plot of the former than the bucolic simplicity of the latter. Perhaps the musical-dramatic high point of the early period had come in the catacombs scene at the end of Act I of *Lucio Silla* written when he was sixteen – an unbroken succession of numbers of not entirely sustained dramatic weight, or harmonic consequence, but with sepulchral anticipations of *Idomeneo* and even the statue's music in *Don Giovanni*. But this is exceptional. The great bulk of *Lucio Silla* still belongs to the rigid world of the singer's theatre, with a concentration of long bravura arias – that as yet possess a rather high proportion of passage-work to musical content.

Idomeneo

It is probable that the teenage Mozart saw the composition of opera as a rather limited technical problem, in which, if he followed the set text, and provided his singers with appropriate vehicles for display – no doubt with more felicity and dexterity than many of his elders – his task was largely fulfilled. By the time we reach *Idomeneo* (1780) we find him embattled with his librettist, with operatic convention and with the shortcomings of his singers. *Idomeneo* is a drama of almost unrelenting intensity which eschews traditional forms of theatrical pacing. Characteristic of the opera is the frequent suppression of a strong cadence at the conclusion of individual musical numbers, facilitating the uninterrupted course of the drama. Probably Mozart came to have doubts about the technique: the feeling of a natural, and accustomed, emphasis being repeatedly denied leads to a sense of breathlessness, and of a work almost bursting at the seams. In future, as in *Don Giovanni* (the overture and 'Or sai chi l'onore') he was to use such devices only sparingly, and the new numbers he supplied for the 1786 Viennese revival of *Idomeneo* represent a relaxation of this tendency. If Mozart never actually pursued such a continuum through the length of an operatic work again, the finales of the Da Ponte comedies and of *Die Zauberflöte* propose in their different ways more sophisticated solutions to the problems of extended operatic composition.

Die Entführung aus dem Serail

Die Entführung was never founded upon such dramatic ambitions. Mozart's intention was to court the Viennese public by playing with various popular operatic formulas. The result is a strange hybrid. Of the three main pivots of the plot – the confrontation between Konstanze and Pasha Selim, the interrupted escape, and the magnanimous act of Selim – only the first is given even partial musical articulation (and only in that Konstanze is permitted to react in musical terms whereas Selim is limited to speech). Complete with grand bravura arias – vastly richer in musical content than those of Mozart's adolescence – this side of the action which harks back to the world of *opera seria* is mostly separate from the comic action, which is provided with much fuller musical articulation, but which remains largely inconsequential in plot terms. Mozart at this stage seems to have had little conception of the serious comedy and he was unable easily to accommodate the two worlds (sentimental–heroic and broadly humorous) at the same time, and even avoids doing it – hence the absence of an escape ensemble. Thus it happens within the great quartet finale of Act II that their one important meeting gives rise in certain passages to an almost painful, if magnificent, intricacy of texture not to be found elsewhere in Mozart's music.

The Da Ponte operas

However beguiling the musical pyrotechnics of *Die Entführung* are, the gulf between it and the dramatic achievement of the three Da Ponte operas is profound. Mozart now took over the genre of the Italian comedy, the most characteristic feature of which was the extended finale of mounting confusion and tension, and without resisting its formulas vastly expanded its scope. These works possess a remarkable sureness of theatrical pacing. Each has its own sense of mercurial movement, crucial to which is the intentionally revolutionary multiplication of ensembles, and the general shortening (particularly in *Figaro* and *Don Giovanni*) of arias, although they remain bravura in character. The gulf between comic and serious worlds which existed in *Die Entführung* disappears. The lower orders in the Da Ponte comedies may not possess the solemnity of their aristocratic masters but they are not intrinsically less serious people, and all can be spaciously accommodated by Mozart within the same musical spans. Having said which, it would be quite wrong to elide the subtly different theatrical universes which each of the operas inhabits.

In *Figaro* we see a world which by exaggeration reminds us of the untidiness – along with the absurdity and sorrow – of everyday life: a world in which after all the frenetic energy of the day has subsided, very little has changed. In *Così fan tutte* on the other hand we see a morally realistic theorem concerning the fragility of human relations demonstrated in the most artificial manner. The musical presentation of this anecdote is not necessarily more structured than the other operas, but it is more conspicuously patterned – a patterning which is given emphasis by the opera's characteristic sudden shifts of tempo. And whereas in the overture to *Figaro* we find ourselves pitched forward from one subject to the next in a welter of thematic invention, while remaining entirely tonic–dominant bound and in a single tempo, in the overture to *Così fan tutte* the flighty repetitive thematic material of the main presto, rapidly modulated, can only be rescued tonally by the contrasting 'andante' gravity with which the motto theme of the introduction is reintroduced just before the end. The opera is constructed according to principles of self-reference and even within the overture Mozart has created a sense of axiomatic demonstration. By further contrast the use of material from later in the opera in the overture of *Don Giovanni* functions quite differently, atmospherically – with its great chords, halting tread and perilously towering chromatic scales – foreshadowing the doom of its protagonist.

Die Zauberflöte and La clemenza di Tito

Mozart worked on two operas during his last year – at length on *Die Zauberflöte* for the popular Viennese theatre and hurriedly, before bringing the latter to completion, on *La clemenza di Tito* to a commission from the Bohemian Estates for the coronation of Leopold II. Together they provide an enigmatic end to his theatrical career – *Tito* raising questions about an opera that might have been, and *Die Zauberflöte* about the ways in which Mozart's operatic style would have developed had he lived.

Probably *Tito*, with its subject dictated by the Bohemian Estates, would have lain outside Mozart's normal area of interest, but he expressed a level of satisfaction in his catalogue over Caterino Mazzolà's reworking of Metastasio's text, and the great beauty of much of the score suggests that he was not left entirely unmoved by this political drama. Nevertheless, Mozart's immense skills established by the end of his career in subsuming theatrical action into the musical structure are barely manifested – the single exception being, in a rather limited way, the first act finale. It is inconceivable, for instance, that given an adequate gestation period Mozart would have chosen to commence the opera's action with a simple recitative.

The text of *Die Zauberflöte* is an esoteric – partially an archaeological – object. For Mozart the ability of the spectator to divine meaning is a measure of his or her state of enlightenment. The drama catalyses, sublimates and realigns the elements or characters which were present at the outset: light banishes darkness, order chaos, and the allegorical process is celebrated in the final marriage of 'beauty and wisdom'. The hectic movement of the Italian comedies is replaced by something more measured. The vocal idiom is never really bravura because even when Mozart plays with the vocal heights and depths of the Queen of Night and Sarastro, texture is more at issue than display. Strange formal mutations occur as he explores the possibilities of action being more voice-based, and less sprung – as in the great ensembles of the Da Ponte comedies – from a choreographic motor: verse structure receives great emphasis, and declamatory passages of a new kind appear, strong in thematic quality and harmonic consequence.

JOHN STONE

List of works

K.38
Apollo et Hyacinthus seu Hyacinthi Metamorphosis
AMA V, no.2; NMA II:5/i
Intermedium. 3 acts (called Prologue, Chorus I and Chorus II), 9 numbers. Latin libretto by Rufinus (P.F.) Widl
Originally perf. before and between 5 acts of school play *Clementia Croesi*, also by Widl

First perf.: 13 May 1767, Great Hall, Salzburg University (constructed for student productions in 1661)
First UK perf.: 24 Jan 1955, Fortune Theatre, London
First US perf.: Apr 1976, Alice Tully Hall, New York

OEBALUS, King of Lacedaemonia
  Tenor Matthias Stadler (aged 22)
MELIA, daugher of Oebalus
  Treble Felix Fuchs (aged 15)
HYACINTHUS, son of Oebalus
  Treble Christian Enzinger (aged 12)
APOLLO, guest in Oebalus' house
  Alto Johann Ernst (aged 12)
ZEPHYRUS, friend of Hyacinthus
  Alto Joseph Vonterthon (aged 17)
TWO PRIESTS OF APOLLO
  Basses(?) Joseph Bründel (aged 18) Jacob Moser (aged 16)
CHORUS   2 ob, 2 hn, str, continuo

Zephyrus loves Melia, but she is to marry Apollo. In his jealousy Zephyrus secretly kills Hyacinthus and accuses Apollo of murder. Apollo summons winds to carry him away. The dying Hyacinthus reveals the truth and Apollo consoles the mourning family by changing their son into a flower.

The melody from the duet (no.8) reappears in the second movement of the Symphony in F, K.43 (autumn, 1767).

Mozart's first operatic venture was this charming school entertainment which was commissioned soon after the success of his music for the sacred Singspiel *Die Schuldigkeit des ersten Gebots*, K.35. The story is a version of the Greek myth, the first in which a god falls in love with one of his own sex and another is jealous. Widl avoided this potential embarrassment by inventing a sister for Hyacinthus. At the first performance all the parts were taken by students, including that of Oebalus, played by Stadler, the candidate in moral theology and law; the eleven-year-old composer added keyboard improvisations.

Autograph: D–B
Libretto: (first edition): Studienbibliothek, Salzburg (5607/I)
Recording: Mathis, Wulkopf, Augér, Schwarz, Salzburg Chamber Choir, Salzburg Mozarteum Orchestra, Hager. DG 2707 129 (2)

K.51 (46a)
La finta semplice (The Make-believe Simpleton)

AMA V, no.4; NMA II:5/ii
Opera buffa in 3 acts (9/13/4 scenes); sinfonia and 26 numbers. Libretto adapted by Marco Coltellini after Goldoni's, written for Salvatore Perillo in Venice 1764

First perf.: 1 May 1769(?), Archbishop's Palace, Salzburg
First UK perf.: 12 Mar 1956, Palace Theatre, London
First US perf.: 27 Jan 1961, Boston (in English, as *The Clever Flirt*)

ROSINA, a Baroness, (la Finta Semplice)
  Soprano Maria Magdalena Haydn (*née* Lipp)
DON CASSANDRO, a rich, foolish and miserly gentleman
  Bass Joseph Hornung
DON POLIDORO, a foolish gentleman, brother of Don Cassandro
  Tenor Franz Anton Spitzeder
GIACINTA, sister of Don Cassandro and Don Polidoro
  Soprano Maria Anna Braunhofer
FRACASSO, a Hungarian captain, brother of Rosina

  Tenor Joseph Nikolaus Meissner
NINETTA, a maid
  Soprano Maria Anna Fesemayer
SIMONE, lieutenant to Fracasso, in love with Ninetta
  Bass Felix Winter
Set on Cassandro's estate near Cremona, Italy
2 fl, 2 ob/eng hn, 2 bn, 2 hn/hn da caccia, str, continuo

The *commedia dell'arte*-style plot concerns two brothers, Polidoro and Cassandro, who are respectively too timid and too proud to woo a woman. Their sister and ward, Giacinta, is in love with Fracasso, who is billeted in their house, and his servant, Simone, is in love with her maid Ninetta. Since the brothers would never agree to their marriages Rosina decides to trick them. This she does successfully, and the opera ends happily with a triple betrothal, Rosina having agreed to marry Cassandro.

In 1768, Leopold Mozart took his son to Vienna and, anxious to promote his composing career there, persuaded the unscrupulous impresario, Giuseppe Afflisio, to commission an *opera buffa* on the unsupported grounds of the Emperor's enthusiasm for Wolfgang's music. Afflisio agreed to pay 100 ducats and the twelve-year-old speedily set the libretto. But, after a run-through at the house of Baron van Swieten, the premiere was repeatedly postponed and eventually abandoned altogether due to professional jealousy and Afflisio's loss of confidence in the project. The Mozarts returned to Salzburg and arranged the premiere there instead.

For the overture Mozart used his symphony K.45, written earlier in the year, omitting the third movement and altering the final chords to lead straight into the opening ensemble.

Autograph: Act I, D–B; Acts II, III, *PL–Kj*
Libretto: (Salzburg, 1769) 'per ordine Archibishop Sigismondo Schrattenbach', *F–Pn*, Yd 1316
Recording: Donath, Rolfe-Johnson, Berganza, Holl, Ihloff, Moser, Lloyd, Salzburg Mozarteum Orchestra, Hager. Orfeo Dig. SO 85844K (4)

K.50 (46b)
Bastien und Bastienne

AMA V, no.3; NMA II:5/iii
Singspiel in 1 act (7 scenes); intrada and 16 numbers. Libretto by Friedrich Wilhelm Weiskern and Johann Müller, with additions by Johann Andreas Schachtner, after the parody of Rousseau's *Le Devin du village, Les Amours de Bastien et Bastienne*, by Marie-Justine Benoîte Favart, Charles-Simon Favart and Harny de Guerville

First perf.: autumn 1768. Dr Anton Mesmer's house in Vienna(?)

First known modern perf.: Architektenhaus, Berlin, 2 Oct 1890
First UK perf.: 26 Dec 1894. Daly's Theatre, London (in English)
First US perf.: early 1905, Habelmann's Opera School, New York

BASTIEN, a shepherd
  Tenor
BASTIENNE, a shepherdess, in love with Bastien
  Soprano
COLAS, supposedly a magician
  Bass
SHEPHERDS and SHEPHERDESSES (*silent*)
2 ob/fl, 2 hn, str, continuo

Bastienne, distressed by the unfaithfulness of her lover Bastien, asks Colas, the local soothsayer, to help her. He suggests that when Bastien returns she must pretend to have lost interest in him. Colas tells Bastien that Bastienne has found another lover. Because the hero and heroine are fearful of losing one another, they are happily reunited.

Bastien und Bastienne was supposedly commissioned by Franz Anton Mesmer in Vienna in the summer of 1768 (before he became famous for his experiments with magnetism, which Mozart was to parody in *Così fan tutte*). On his return to Salzburg, Mozart may have composed recitatives to additional text by the court trumpeter Johann Andreas Schachtner to replace the spoken dialogue but there is no concrete evidence for this supposedly later version; possibly too, some of the music had been composed earlier in Salzburg, but half the paper used in this autograph was Viennese in origin (Tyson, 1987). Another setting of *Bastien und Bastienne*, with music by Johann Baptist Savio, was performed by Felix Berner's company of child actors in Vienna in 1764, and in Salzburg in 1766. They returned to Salzburg in the autumn of 1774 and performed it again. It is possible that Mozart's later version was used at this performance, but it is as likely to have been a revival of the Savio score, which has not survived. Of Mozart's early operas, this one was most often performed during his lifetime.

Autograph: PL–Kj
Libretto: Weiskern libretto (Vienna, 1764): *A–Wgm*
Recording: Mathis, Ahnsjo, Berry, Salzburg Mozarteum Orchestra, Hager. DG 2537 038 (cassette: 3306 038)

K.87 (74a)
Mitridate, rè di Ponto
AMA V, no.5; NMA II:5/iv (March (no.7) also NMA VII:17/2)
Opera seria in 3 acts (13/15/12 scenes); overture and 25 numbers. Libretto by Vittorio Amedeo

Cigna-Santi after Giuseppe Parini and Racine (also set by Quirino Gasparini in 1767 in Turin)

First perf.: 26 Dec 1770, Teatro Regio Ducal, Milan
First known modern perf.: 7 Aug 1971, Felsenreitschule, Salzburg
First UK perf.: 17 Mar 1979, Logan Hall, London (concert perf.)
First US perf.: 15 Aug 1985, Avery Fisher Hall, New York (concert perf.)

MITRIDATE, King of Pontus and other kingdoms, betrothed to Aspasia
  Tenor Guglielmo d'Ettore
ASPASIA, betrothed to Mitridate and already declared queen
  Soprano Antonia Bernasconi
SIFARE, son of Mitridate and Stratonica, in love with Aspasia
  *Soprano** Pietro Benedetti, known as Sartorino.
FARNACE, Mitridate's first son, also in love with Aspasia
  *Contralto** Giuseppe Cicognani
ISMENE, daughter of the King of Parthia, in love with Farnace
  Soprano Anna Francesca Varese
MARZIO, Roman tribune, Farnace's friend
  Tenor Gaspare Bassano
ARBATE, Governor of Nymphaium
  *Soprano** Pietro Muschietti
* = castrato
Sets for first production by the Galliari brothers
2 fl, 2 ob, 2 bn, 4 hn, 2 tpt, timp, str, continuo
According to Leopold, the Milan orchestra used forty-two string players, as well as two harpsichords. In no.7 (Act I scene 10,) Mozart reused a recently discovered (NMA 1970) March, K.62, written in Salzburg for the Serenade in D, K.100 (62a).

The story bears little historical relation to the Mithridates of *c.* 135–64 BC who fought courageously against Rome, but concerns rather a father and two sons who all love the same woman. When the death of the absent King is announced, his sons vie for the hand of Aspasia, who prefers Sifare. But the King returns, bringing Ismene with him. Farnace and Marzio plan to attack the King. Mitridate suggests to Ismene that Farnace will soon die and she can marry Sifare; he also confronts Aspasia with her unfaithfulness and Farnace with his designs. Farnace accuses Sifare, and all three are imprisoned. But the Romans attack, and Sifare and Farnace fight them successfully. Mitridate is fatally wounded, but before he dies he gives Aspasia to Sifare and forgives Farnace, who has conveniently fallen for Ismene.

On 7 February 1770, Leopold and Wolfgang attended the first of at least three musical parties given in Milan by Count Carl Joseph Firmian, the Governor General of Lombardy and a nephew of the former Salzburg Archbishop Firmian. It was thanks to him that Mozart, besides receiving a gift of the complete works of Metastasio, was invited to compose music for the wedding of Archduke Ferdinand of Austria (the serenata *Ascanio in Alba*), and was also commissioned to write an opera for the Christmas festival in Milan. According to the contract, Wolfgang was to receive 100 gold gulden (*gigliati*), plus free lodging. The recitatives were to be sent ahead in October, and the composer should arrive by 1 November to write the arias to suit the singers, as he would have expected. Wolfgang received the libretto on 27 July in Bologna, where he was studying counterpoint with Padre Martini.

The opening performance was Mozart's first great public and critical operatic success, and was greeted with shouts of 'Viva il Maestrino!' There were at least twenty performances. Leopold justifiably complained that the opera was given with three ballets (by Francesco Caselli) as intermezzos, making the performance six hours long.

Surviving autograph material: rejected original versions (complete) of nos. 1, 9, 16, 18 and 20; 4 drafts for cavata no.8 (F major, 83 bars, ? continuation lost; B♭ major, 106 bars, complete; F major, 53 bars, complete vocal part; G major, 58 bars, complete vocal part); 2 drafts for recitative 'Respira alfin' (Act I scene 13) (3 bars; 24 bars, ? continuation lost); original fragmentary attempts at aria no.13 (102 bars), aria no.14 (41 bars; ? continuation lost); unidentified fragmentary aria of Sifare (20 bars; ? continuation lost)

Dedication: The Duke of Modena
Autograph: Lost (see above). Three principal copies: 1) the most complete in *P–La*; 2) *F–Pn*; 3) *GB–Lbl*
Libretto: (Milan, 1770) *I–Bc*
Recording: Augér, Baltsa, Cotrubas, Gruberova, Hollweg, Salzburg Mozarteum Camerata Academica, Hager. DG 2740 180 (3)

K.111
Ascanio in Alba
AMA V, no.6; NMA II:5/v
Festa teatrale in 2 acts (5/6 scenes); overture and 33 numbers. Libretto by Abbate Giuseppe Parini

First perf.: 17 Oct 1771. Teatro Regio Ducal, Milan
First modern perf.: 25 Jan 1958. Landestheater, Salzburg (version by B. Paumgartner)

VENERE
  Seconda donna, Soprano   Geltrude Falchini
ASCANIO, her son
  Primo uomo, Mezzo-soprano*   Giovanni Manzuoli

SILVIA, a nymph of the family of Hercules
  Prima donna, Soprano   Antonia Maria Girelli-Aguilar
ACESTE, priest
  Tenor   Giuseppe Tibaldi
FAUNO
  Secondo uomo, Soprano*   Adamo Solzi
* = castrato
CHORUS of GENIES, SHEPHERDS and SHEPHERDESSES
Dancers, at the first production, were led by Charles le Picq, who choreographed the ballets, with Giovanni Favier, Anna Binetti (his wife) and Sig. Blache. Sets by the Galliari brothers
2 fl, 2 ob/eng hn, 2 bn, 2 hn, 2 tpt, timp, str, continuo

Venere (Venus) would like her son to be married to Silvia, but first her virtue must be proved. Cupid has arranged for Silvia to see Ascanio, and she has fallen in love with him without knowing his name. When they meet he pretends not to know who she is. Since she is promised to a stranger called Ascanio, she rejects his wooing. She thus passes the test and the pair are happily united.

Written for the wedding of Archduke Ferdinand of Austria and Maria Beatrice Ricciarda d'Este of Modena. Mozart began work on the score at the end of August 1771, when the libretto eventually arrived, after being approved by the Emperor in Vienna. He was also required to write the ballet music – one ballet, not two (Plath, 1965) – to be performed between the two acts. For discussion of the ballet music, see the piano arrangement K.Anh.207 (Anh.C27.06) in 'Dance and ballet music' work-list (p. 279). Some of the choruses were also danced. The score was complete by 23 September. The work was performed on the second day of the wedding festivities and was so well received (more so than the opera *Il Ruggiero*, by Hasse, which was performed on the first day) that three more performances were immediately scheduled for the following week. The fifteen-year-old composer had written the whole score in under a month. Ferdinand was so enthusiastic that he wrote to his mother, the Empress Maria Theresa, to ask if he might offer Mozart permanent employment at court, but she coldly disapproved of the idea.

At the end of October 1771 Mozart composed a 3/8 movement to add to the two-movement overture so that the work could be performed as a symphony, K.120 (111a).

Autograph: D–B
Libretto: (Milan, 1771) *I–Rsc*
Recording: Sukis, Baltsa, Mathis, Schreier, Augér, Salzburg Mozarteum Camerata Academica, Salzburg Mozarteum Orchestra, Hager. DG 2740 181 (3)

K.126
Il sogno di Scipione (Scipio's Dream)
AMA V, no.7; NMA II:5/vi
Serenata drammatica/Azione teatrale in 1 act; overture and 12 numbers. Libretto after Cicero by Pietro Metastasio, originally written in 1735 and set by Angelo Predieri, to celebrate birthday of Emperor Charles VI

First perf.: There are no documents to support the previously suggested date of 1 May 1772.
Archbishop's Palace, Salzburg

SCIPIONE
Tenor
COSTANZA
Soprano
FORTUNA
Soprano
PUBLIO, Scipione's stepfather
Tenor
EMILIO, Scipione's real father
Tenor
SOLOIST in licenza
Soprano
CHORUS of HEROES
SATB
Set in the kingdom of Massinissa, Africa, *c.* 149 BC.
2 fl, 2 ob, 2 bn, 2 hn, 2 tpt, timp, str, continuo

Scipione (Scipio) is asleep in his palace. He dreams that the goddesses Costanza and Fortuna ask him to choose one of them to protect him. Asking for time to decide, he is transported to heaven to visit his ancestors. Appearing among a chorus of heroes, Publio sings to him of the rewards of an honourable life, and Emilio tells him of the futility of life on earth. He asks to stay with them but is told that such a reward must first be won. He asks their advice on choosing a guardian goddess. They tell him he must make the choice himself. When he picks Costanza, Fortuna is enraged. But he remains steadfast, and returns to earth ready to follow Costanza.

The work was probably written between April and August 1771 (before *Ascanio in Alba*) for the celebration of the fiftieth anniversary on 10 January 1772 of the ordination of Archbishop von Schrattenbach. Mozart chose the libretto, which had been previously set six times, and left it unchanged except for the name Sigismondo, which replaced Carlo at the opening of the final licenza. Schrattenbach died at the end of the year (16 December), and the Mozarts hoped to see the work performed to celebrate the arrival of the, later notorious, Archbishop Hieronymus Colloredo in Salzburg. So the dedicatee's name was changed to Girolamo (the Italian form of Hieronymus), but there is no record of the work's performance. A second version of the aria of the licenza is reckoned to date from early 1772 and thus

to have originated specifically in connection with the election of the new Archbishop (NMA). Later in 1772 Mozart wrote a Presto which, with the two-section overture, became the Symphony K.161 + 163 (141a).

Autograph: D–B
Recording: Popp, Gruberova, Schreier, Ahnsjo, Moser, Salzburg Mozarteum Chamber Choir and Orchestra, Hager. DG 2740 218 (3)

K.135
Lucio Silla
AMA V, no.8; NMA II:5/vii
Dramma per musica in 3 acts (9/14/8 scenes); overture and 23 numbers. Libretto by Giovanni de Gamerra (who made first Italian translation of *Die Zauberflöte*)

First perf.: 26 Dec 1772, Teatro Regio Ducal, Milan
First known modern perf.: 14 Dec 1929, Prague
First UK perf.: 7 Mar 1967, Camden Town Hall, London (in English)
First US perf.: 19 Jan 1968, Peabody Concert Hall, Baltimore (in English)

LUCIO SILLA, dictator
Tenor Bassano Morgnoni
GIUNIA, intended wife of Cecilio
Prima donna, Soprano Anna de Amicis–Buonsollazzi
CECILIO, proscribed senator
Primo uomo, Soprano castrato Venanzio Rauzzini
LUCIO CINNA, Roman patrician friend of Cecilio and secret enemy of Lucio Silla
Soprano Felicità Suardi
CELIA, sister of Lucio Silla
Soprano Daniella Mienci
AUFIDIO, tribune of Lucio Silla
Tenor Giuseppe Onofrio
GUARDS, SENATORS, NOBLES, SOLDIERS, PEOPLE and MAIDENS
2 fl, 2 ob, 2 bn, 2 hn, 2 tpt, timp, str, continuo
Sets for the first production by the Galliari brothers (designs are in the Pinacoteca di Brera, Milan). Costumes by Francesco Motta and Giovanni Mazza
Set in Ancient Rome

The unpopular Lucio Silla, being rejected by Giunia, who loves the banished senator, Cecilio, decides to kill her. Cinna, Giunia and Cecilio (who has returned in secret) plan to kill Silla, but their plot fails. When Silla publicly proclaims his marriage to Giunia, she reveals his intention to kill Cecilio. Finally Silla forgives everyone, and Giunia and Cecilio are united, as are Celia and Cinna. Silla resigns his dictatorship.

Gamerra, an Italian poet who, thanks to Metastasio's support, held a position at the Viennese court, took the idea from Plutarch's account of the career of Lucius Cornelius Sulla (130–78 BC). After Mozart had started work, the Gamerra libretto was sent to Metastasio for approval, whereupon the older poet made several changes and cut out an entire scene, much to Leopold's, rather than Wolfgang's, consternation.

In March 1771 in Salzburg, Mozart had received a commission to write a new opera for Milan following the success of *Mitridate*. His career was progressing well; Milan was ruled by Austria and it was, therefore, an opportunity for further success in both Italy and Austria. He was offered 130 gold gulden (*gigliati*) for the work.

The rehearsal period was fraught with problems caused by recalcitrant singers, and the first performance started three hours after the audience arrived (due to the delayed arrival of the Archduke) and, since it was four hours long plus three ballets (choreographed by Charles le Picq and Giuseppe Salamoni), continued until two in the morning. But there were twenty-six performances of the opera to full houses, and the next production, of Paisiello's *Sismano nel Mongol*, had to be postponed. Despite this success, *Lucio Silla* was the last opera Mozart wrote for Italy.

The authorship of the 3 ballets (*La gelosìa del serraglio*, *La scuola di negromanzìa* and *La Giaccona*) is not stated in surviving copies of the printed libretto, and the Mozart family correspondence nowhere mentions Mozart as the composer of ballet music for the opera. Final chorus and closing ballet probably one and the same (NMA). Mozart's possible contribution to the first ballet, probably a pasticcio, is doubtful: sketches of an introduction and 32 numbers, entitled *Le gelosie del serraglio*. Primo ballo, K.Anh.109 (135a), 6 numbers of which can be traced to Starzer's ballet score *Les cinq sultanes* (1771), appear to be in the nature of a copy taken from the memory of performance (Senn, 1961b). Senn proposes date for K.Anh.109 (135a) of Jan–Feb 1773

Autograph: PL–Kj; A–Sm (K.Anh.109/135a)
Text: I–Mc, D–Bds
Recording: Schreier, Augér, Varady, Mathis, Donath, Krenn, Salzburg Radio and Mozarteum Choir and Orchestra, Hager. DG 2740 183

K.196
La finta giardiniera (The Make-believe Gardener)
AMA V, no.9; NMA II:5/viii
Opera buffa in 3 acts (15/16/8 scenes); overture and 28 numbers. Libretto (also set by Anfossi in Rome, 1773–4) by Giuseppe Petrosellini (previously attributed to Raniero de Calzabigi

and supposedly revised by Marco Coltellini, both attributions now believed wrong)

First perf.: 13 Jan 1775, Salvatortheater, Munich
First perf. as German Singspiel (*Die verstellte Gärtnerin*): 1(?) May 1780, Augsburg
First UK perf.: 7 Jan 1930, Scala Theatre, London (in English)
First US perf.: 18 Jan 1927, Mayfair Theater, New York (in English)

DON ANCHISE, Podestà of Lagonero, in love with Sandrina
   Tenor ?Signor Fiorini
MARCHESA VIOLANTE ONESTI, in love with Belfiore, disguised as a gardener, SANDRINA
   Soprano Rosa Manservisi
CONTINO BELFIORE, Formerly in love with Violante
   Tenor ?Johann Baptist Walleshauser
ARMINDA, Milanese noble woman, the Podestà's niece, formerly in love with Ramiro and now engaged to Belfiore
   Soprano
CAVALIER RAMIRO, in love with Arminda, but rejected by her
   Soprano* Tommaso Consoli
SERPETTA, servant of the Podestà and also in love with him
   Soprano Teresa Manservisi
ROBERTO, servant of Violante, pretending to be her cousin, in love with Serpetta, and also disguised as a gardener, NARDO
   Bass ?Giovanni Rossi (?Joseph Matthias Souter)
* = castrato
Set at the Podestà's residence in Lagonero
2 fl, 2 ob, 2 bn, 2 hn, 2 tpt, timp, str, continuo
Consoli and the Manservisi sisters certainly sang in the first performance. The others are unconfirmed.

In the opening *tutti* of the opera, Ramiro, Sandrina and the two servants reveal their unhappiness despite a cheerful exterior; only the Podestà is optimistic since he has fallen in love with Sandrina/Violante (much to Serpetta's fury). When Arminda and Belfiore arrive for their (arranged) wedding they both find themselves confronted by their former loves. Count Belfiore is particularly baffled because he thought he had killed Violante/Sandrina in a lovers' quarrel and she refuses to admit that she is in fact Violante. The furious Arminda has the heroine abducted and taken to a wild wood whence the other characters search for her and all (except the worthy and suspicious Ramiro) find themselves totally confused, so much so that Sandrina and the Count, who really do love one another, go completely mad.

Finally all misunderstandings are resolved by a triple wedding, Belfiore and Violante, Ramiro and Arminda, Nardo and Serpetta. The Podestà cryptically remarks that he will only marry when he finds another Sandrina.

On 6 December 1774, Mozart and his father travelled from Salzburg to Munich, whose Superintendant of Theatrical Entertainments had commissioned an *opera buffa* for the carnival season from Wolfgang. Its premiere was planned for 29 December but it was postponed so that there could be a longer rehearsal period. Though the premiere was a success for Mozart, the work was subsequently more successful as a Singspiel; Mozart copied the German version by Andreas Schachtner into the original score. He also slightly revised four numbers for the Augsburg premiere. Another contemporary German version is by the comic actor and bass F.J. Stierle.

Mozart composed a new finale to the overture, so that it could be performed as a symphony (K.121/207a).

Autograph: Act I lost during Mozart's lifetime. Acts II and III, *PL–Kj*. An 18th-century copy of the score, with Italian and German texts, is in *CS–Bm*.
Libretto: Italian version used by Anfossi: *I–Rsc*.
German text (Augsburg, 1780): *D–Mbs*
Recording: (In German) Unger, Hollweg, Donath, Norman, Cotrubas, Troyanos, Prey, North German Radio Chorus and Orchestra, Schmidt-Isserstedt. PHIL 6703 039 (3). (In Italian) Conwell, Sukis, Cesari, Moser, Fassbaender, Ihloff, McDaniel, Salzburg Mozarteum Orchestra, Hager. DG 2704 234 (4).

K.208
Il rè pastore. (The Shepherd King)
AMA V, no.10; NMA II:5/ix
Dramma per musica (also described by contemporary writers as 'Serenada' or 'Cantate') in 2 acts (8/13 scenes); overture and 14 numbers. Probably adapted by the Archbishop's chaplain Gianbattista Varesco from the 1751 libretto by Metastasio, which was based on *Aminta* by Torquato Tasso (1581) and set by many other composers

First perf.: 23 Apr 1775. Archbishop's Palace, Salzburg
First known modern perf.: 27 Jan 1906, Salzburg
First (staged) UK perf.: 8 Nov 1954, St Pancras Town Hall, London
First US perf.: 7 July 1971, Norfolk, Virginia

ALESSANDRO, King of Macedonia
   Tenor
AMINTA, shepherd, in love with Elisa, eventually discovered to be heir to the Kingdom of Sidon
   *Soprano**   Tommaso Consoli
ELISA, nymph of Phoenicia, in love with Aminta
   Soprano
TAMIRI, refugee princess, daughter of Stratone, disguised as a shepherdess and in love with Aegenore
   Soprano
AEGENORE, nobleman of Sidon, friend of Alessandro, in love with Tamiri
   Tenor
* = castrato
Set outside the Macedonian camp, near Sidon
Apart from the role of Aminta, the singers came from the Salzburg court and could have been those who sang in *La finta semplice*, like Consoli, and *Il sogno di Scipione*.
2 fl, 2 ob/eng hn, 2 bn, 4 hn, 2 tpt, str, continuo

Aminta and Elisa wonder who their new king will be, now that Alessandro (Alexander the Great) has liberated Sidon from the tyrannical Stratone. Aminta is told by Aegenore that he is the rightful heir to Sidon. Alessandro plans a marriage between Aminta and Tamiri. Elisa mistakenly believes that this is Aminta's wish, but in fact he would rather continue to be a shepherd and marry her. Tamiri accuses Aegenore of rejecting her. Finally Alessandro understands the confusion he has unwittingly caused and decrees that Aminta and Elisa should reign over Sidon, and Aegenore and Tamiri over the next kingdom he conquers.

Mozart was commissioned to write an opera to celebrate the visit to Salzburg of the Archduke Maximilian Franz, youngest son of Maria Theresa. Metastasio had based the libretto of *Il rè pastore* on the accounts by Justinian and Curtius of the gardener Abdalonymus being given the throne of Sidon by Alexander the Great (changing the name and profession of the hero); it had been set at least fourteen times before Mozart chose it. Varesco combined Metastasio's second and third acts into one and wrote a new finale. Very little is known about the first performance: it may even have been given as a concert performance, which would explain why contemporary accounts refer to it as 'Serenada' or 'Cantate'. To versions of overture and first aria, Mozart later added a Presto assai finale, K.102 (213c), to form a symphony.

Autograph: PL–Kj
Libretto: No copies of the printed libretto have been found
Recording: Schreier, Mathis, Augér, Ghazarian, Krenn, Salzburg, Mozarteum Orchestra, Hager. DG 2740 182 (3)

K.345 (336a)
Thamos, König in Ägypten
AMA V, no.12; NMA II:6/i
Play with music in 5 acts. Words by Tobias
Philipp, Baron von Gebler
First perf.: (part only) 4 Apr 1774, Kärnterthor
theatre, Vienna; (revised, with additions) 3 Jan
1776, Salzburg; (with further new material) 1779–
80, Salzburg

Bass soloist and chorus
2 fl, 2 ob, 2 bn, 2 hn, 2 tpt, 3 trbn, timp, str

Gebler, a freemason, based the play on an ancient
Egyptian tale, which bears some resemblance to that
of *Die Zauberflöte*. From a study of the autograph
material it would appear that the entr'actes and
choruses in the present form date, respectively, from
1776–7 and 1779–80. Two of the choruses (nos. 1
and 6) appear to be reworkings of ones composed in
1773 and performed in Vienna. A fourth entr'acte
was replaced by a third and final chorus (no.7b in
Köchel 6) to a text by Andreas Schachtner for
Salzburg performances by the Johann Böhm company, who visited Salzburg in 1776 and in April–
May 1779 and September 1779–March 1780. Böhm
used the *Thamos* music for a play entitled *Lanassa* by
Karl Martin Plümicke, to which was added an
overture in the form of Symphony K.184 (161a).
Böhm used this incidental music with *Lanassa* for
many years, especially in western Germany (for
example, during the Frankfurt coronation ceremonies in September 1790).

Fragment K.Anh.101 identified by Plath as belonging to the surviving autograph material of *Thamos*
(no.7a, bars 22–75)

Autograph: D–B
Libretto: (Prague and Dresden, 1773): A–Sm
Recording: Perry, Mühle, Altena, Thomaschke,
Van der Kamp, Netherlands Chamber Choir,
Collegium Vocale, Concertgebouw Orchestra of
Amsterdam, Harnoncourt. TELD A26.42702

K.344 (336b)
Zaide (Das Serail)
AMA V, no.11; NMA II:5/x
Singspiel in 2 acts (fragment). Libretto by Johann
Andreas Schachtner, after F.J. Sebastiani's *Das
Serail*

First known perf.: 27 Jan 1866, Frankfurt
First Vienna perf.: 4 Oct 1902
First UK perf.: 10 Jan 1953, Toynbee Hall,
London
First US perf.: 8 Aug 1955, Tanglewood

GOMATZ, a young man forced to serve the
Sultan
    Tenor
ZAIDE, a maiden of the harem
    Soprano
ALLAZIM, the Sultan's guardian
    Bass
THE SULTAN SOLIMAN
    Tenor
OSMIN, a slave trader
    Bass
FOUR SLAVES
    Tenors
GUARDS
    Tenor and Bass
ZARAM, head of the guards
    Speaking role
2 fl, 2 ob, 2 bn, 2 hn, 2 tpt, timp, str

Gomatz and Zaide are in love, and they persuade
Allazim to help them to escape from the harem. The
Sultan discovers this and has them brought back.
They plead for his forgiveness, which he grants on
discovering that Allazim had saved his life fifteen
years earlier.

Zaide was probably composed in Salzburg in 1779–
80, for a possible performance there and perhaps
with a view to one in Vienna at Joseph II's new
National Singspiel. Although Mozart did not
continue with work on the opera when he came to
Vienna, it was not long before he was engaged on
another 'Turkish' opera, one of similar but richer
design: *Die Entführung*. Only 15 complete numbers
exist; overture, final chorus (?and other closing
numbers) lacking. Sketch for aria no.6 (52 bars)
survives. The untitled and incomplete work was
found amongst Mozart's manuscripts after his death
and sold by his widow, Constanze, to J.A. André,
who published it in 1838 as *Zaide*.

Autograph: D–B
Recording: Blegen, Hollweg, Schöne, Moser, Holl,
Salzburg Mozarteum Orchestra, Hager. HM S
055832 H (2)

K.366
Idomeneo, rè di Creta
AMA V, no.13; NMA II:5/xi
Dramma per musica in 3 acts (10/6/11 scenes);
overture and 32 numbers, of which 2 are ballets.
Libretto by Gianbattista Varesco after Antoine
Danchet's *Idomenée*, set by Campra (Paris, 1712);
German version by Andreas Schachtner (1780)

First perfs.: 29 Jan 1781, Residenz Theater (now
the Cuvilliés), Munich. 13 Mar 1786, Auersperg
Palace, Vienna (with K.489 and 490)
First UK perfs.: 12 Mar 1934, Glasgow (amateur);
20 June 1951, Glyndebourne
First US perf.: 4 Aug 1947, Tanglewood (in
English)

IDOMENEO, King of Crete
Tenor Anton Raaff
IDAMANTE, his son
Soprano*/Tenor Vincenzo dal Prato
ILIA, a Trojan princess
Soprano Dorothea Wendling
ELETTRA, princess of Argos, daughter of
Agamemnon
Soprano Elisabeth Wendling
ARBACE, the King's confidant
Tenor Domenico de'Panzacchi
HIGH PRIEST OF NEPTUNE
Tenor Giovanni Valesi
VOICE OF NEPTUNE
Bass
* = castrato
CHORUSES of PRIESTS, TROJAN
PRISONERS, CRETANS, SAILORS
Set in Sidon, the capital of ancient Crete
Ballet (K.367) choreographed by Le Grand
Sets by Lorenzo Quaglio. Conducted by Christian
Cannabich
2 fl/pic, 2 ob, 2 cl, 2 bn, 4 hn, 2 tpt, 3 trbn, timp,
str, continuo

The part of Idamante is sung by either soprano or
tenor, Mozart having arranged the part for tenor
voice for an amateur performance in Vienna in
1786.

Ilia, captured by the Cretans, is in love with
Idamante, and needlessly fearful that he loves
Elettra who, in her turn, resents Ilia. Idomeneo
returns from the Trojan war, having vowed to
Neptune that, if he survives a terrible storm, he will
sacrifice the first person he meets on dry land.
Idamante greets him joyfully, but the King can only
turn away in remorse. Arbace, learning Idomeneo's
terrible secret, advises him to send Elettra home
with Idamante as escort. As Idamante and Elettra
prepare to leave, a fearful monster rises up from the
sea. Despite the love Ilia and Idamante have
declared, Idomeneo bids his son depart and never
return. Amidst the chaos wreaked by the monster
the King confesses his vow to the people, who advise
him to fulfil his promise. Idamante kills the monster
and is ready to accept his own death, but Ilia offers
herself instead. Neptune's voice intervenes, decree-
ing that Idomeneo should absolve himself by abdi-
cating in favour of Idamante.

Having completed nine operatic works, Mozart,
aged twenty-four, was commissioned to write an
opera by the Elector Karl Theodor of Bavaria,
formerly of Mannheim, who had moved to Munich
in January 1778. He began work in Salzburg in
October 1780 and moved to Munich in November
to complete the work with the singers, several of
whom he knew from Mannheim days. The opera
was successful but there were no further performances in other houses and the amateur perfor-

mance in Vienna took place five years later. The
Vienna performance included the following singers:
IDOMENEO Giuseppe Antonio Bridi
IDAMANTE Baron Pulini
ILIA Anna von Pufendorf
ELETTRA Maria Anna Hortensia, Countess von
Hatzfeld
Apart from the reworking of Idamante as a tenor,
Mozart rewrote the beginning of Act II, cutting the
recitative 10a, 'Tutto m'è noto', and substituting
10b, Scena con Rondo K.490, beginning 'Non più,
tutto ascoltai' (Ilia, Idamante), followed by the
Rondo 'Non temer, amato bene' (Idamante), with
obbligato solo violin. In Act III, the duet 20a, 'S' io
non moro', was cut and the duet K.489, 'Spiegarti
non poss'io' (Ilia, Idamante), substituted. The
performance material for the 1786 Vienna version
has not survived, so that there are few details except
for the two large substitutions (autographs: K.490
PL–Kj; K.489 *D–B*). Draft for aria no.30a, 'Torna la
pace' (127 bars), survives. Richard Strauss and
Lothar Wallerstein produced a famous version in
1931. Full score (Magdeburg, 1931), ed. R. Strauss,
copy in *GB–Lbm*, has expression marks, bowings and
additional wind parts to one aria, all in his
autograph

Autograph: K.366: Acts I, II, *PL–Kj*; Act III, *D–B*.
K.367: *D–B*
Libretto: D–Mmb. Two versions of the text (Italian
and German) were published in 1781

K.384
Die Entführung aus dem Serail (The Abduction from the Harem)
AMA V, no.15; NMA II:5/xii
Singspiel in 3 acts (10/9/9 scenes): overture and 22
numbers. Libretto by J. Gottlieb Stephanie Jnr
after Christoph Friedrich Bretzner's *Belmonte und
Constanze* (1780).

First perf.: 16 Jul 1782, Burgtheater, Vienna,
conducted by Mozart
First UK perf.: 24 Nov 1827, Covent Garden,
London (in English), with additions by Kramer
First US perf.: 16 Feb 1860, Brooklyn Athenaeum,
New York

KONSTANZE, a Spanish Lady
Soprano Catarina Cavalieri
BLONDE, her English maid
Soprano Therese Teyber
BELMONTE, a Spanish nobleman
Tenor Johann Valentin Adamberger
PEDRILLO, his servant
Tenor Johann Ernst Dauer
BASSA (PASHA) SELIM
Speaking role Dominik Jautz

OSMIN, overseer of his harem
Bass Johann Ignaz Ludwig Fischer
KLAAS, a sailor
Acting role
A mute servant
Acting role
TURKISH SOLDIERS, WOMEN and
GUARDS
Set on the Pasha's country estate in Turkey
2 fl/pic, 2 ob, 2 cl/basset-hn, 2 bn, 2 hn, 2 tpt,
timp, perc, str

Belmonte has arrived at the Pasha Selim's country house in search of his beloved Konstanze. Despite the efforts of the unfriendly Osmin to turn him away, he is reunited with Pedrillo, who has plans to help Konstanze and her maid Blonde to escape from the harem. He introduces Belmonte to the Pasha as a famous architect, thus securing him an entry to the house. Konstanze has steadfastly rejected the persuasive wooing of the Pasha. To assist their escape, Pedrillo gets the formidable Osmin well and truly drunk. But the elopement is discovered, and they are brought before the Pasha who, despite realizing that Belmonte is the son of his arch-enemy, graciously gives the four his blessing.

The composition of this opera coincided with Mozart's marriage to Constanze Weber and his permanent settling in Vienna as a freelance composer and performer. Despite the intrigues and complications which plagued the premiere, it proved to be Mozart's most popular opera in his lifetime, partly due to the fashion for plays and operas on oriental subjects. But it was of this piece that the Emperor, according to Niemetschek (1798), made his famous comment: 'Too beautiful for our ears, my dear Mozart, and vastly too many notes', to which Mozart replied 'Just as many as are necessary, your Majesty'.

Surviving frags and sketches: sketch for Lied and duet no.2, bars 176–235; fragmentary attempt at pf arrangement of aria no.12 (26 bars); fragmentary attempt at ensemble for abduction scene, 'Welch' ängstliches Beben' (text from original Bretzner libretto, Act I scenes 3–4), K.389 (384A) (151 bars; in draft score): dates probably from second half of 1781 (Tyson, personal communication); music breaks off after introduction of only 2 singers (Belmonte, Pedrillo); in Bretzner, this 'charming quintet or rather finale' (letter of Mozart to Leopold, 26 Sep 1781) began Act III: before decision to transform it into dialogue and closed numbers, Mozart had originally wished to place it at end of Act II; arranged and completed by Julius André (1853)

Autograph: Acts I, III, *PL–Kj*; Act II, *D–B*
Libretto: (Vienna, 1782): *A–Wn*

K.422
L'oca del Cairo (The Cairo Goose)
AMA XXIV, no.37; NMA II:5/xiii
Opera buffa/dramma giocoso in 2 acts (fragment); 6 numbers are scored. Libretto by Gianbattista Varesco

First perf.: 1860, Frankfurt (concert perf.); 6 Jun 1867, Paris (in arrangement by Victor Wilder including numbers from *Lo sposo deluso* and inserts Mozart wrote for Bianchi's *La villanella rapita*); 22 Aug 1936, Stadttheater, Salzburg
First UK perfs.: 12 May 1870, Drury Lane Theatre, London (Paris 1867 version); 30 May 1940, Sadler's Wells Theatre, London (reduced to 1 act and orchestrated by Hans Redlich)

DON PIPPO, Marquess of Ripasecca, in love with Lavina
Bass
DONNA PANTEA, his wife, thought dead, known as Sandra
?
CELIDORA, their daughter, in love with Biondello
Soprano
BIONDELLO, a wealthy gentleman
Tenor
CALANDRINO, Pantea's nephew, friend of Biondello
Tenor
LAVINA, Celidora's companion, lover of Calandrino
Soprano
CHICHIBIO, Pippo's servant in love with Auretta
Bass
AURETTA, Pantea's maid
Soprano
CHORUSES of TOWNSPEOPLE, SOLDIERS, SAILORS, SERVANTS
Set in the fictional sea port of Ripasecca
2 ob, 2 bn, 2 hn, 2 tpt, str

Don Pippo, determined to marry Lavina and to give Celidora to a certain Count Lionetto di Casavuota, has imprisoned both women in a fortress to prevent them seeing their lovers. He has told Biondello that he may marry Celidora in the unlikely event of his penetrating the castle. Calandrino decides to construct a huge mechanical goose and to arrange for Pantea/Sandra to smuggle Biondello into the prison inside it.

Despite his enthusiasm for the possibilities of a National Opera in German, Mozart agreed to write a new *opera buffa* for a group of Italian guest singers in 1783. Though keen to work with Da Ponte, whom he had recently met, and who had promised him a new libretto, he decided to ask Varesco, the Salzburg chaplain who had provided Mozart with the libretto for *Idomeneo*, to write him a new libretto, should the former's promises come to nothing. Mozart worked on the opera during his visit to Salzburg in 1783 and on his return to Vienna; however, by February 1784 he seems to have decided to set the opera aside temporarily, in favour of other work. The extant music concerns the marriage and escape preparations without mention of the *oca ex machina*. Libretto is unfinished: first act (some text revisions missing) extant. Vocal score published by Julius André (1855)

Surviving music: recitative preceding aria and trio no.4; duet no.1 (substance complete in draft score), aria no.2 (substance complete in draft score), aria no.3 (substance complete in draft score), quartet no.5 (substance complete in draft score), finale no.6 (substance complete in draft score), duet without no., 'Ho un pensiero' (substance complete in draft score); sketch for aria no.2 (20 bars); sketch for aria no.3 (58 bars); sketch for bars 99–116 of quartet no.5; sketch for bars 397–418 of finale no.6; sketch for whole of aria without no., 'Che parli, che dica' (92 bars). Complete score (copy by J.S. Mayr; ? originally complete), and frag. of score in copyist's hand of voice and bass parts, of aria and trio no.4 also survive

Autograph: D–B
Libretto: D–B

K.430 (424a)
Lo sposo deluso, ossia La Rivalità di tre donne per un solo amante (The Deluded Bridegroom, or the Rivalry of Three Women for the Same Lover)
AMA XXIV, no.38; NMA II:5/xiv
Opera buffa in 2 acts (fragment). Libretto by ?Lorenzo da Ponte

First UK perf.: 11 Feb 1956, City Opera Club (version by John Coombs using much the same music as Paris/London 1867/1870 (see previous entry))
First US perf.: 29 Jul 1969, Iowa University

19 numbers from *L'oca del Cairo* and *Lo sposo deluso* were used by Hans Erismann to form a work entitled *Don Pedros Heimkehr* to a text by Oscar Wälterlin and Werner Galusser. This was performed in Jan? 1953 in Zurich and again by Lemonade Opera at the Greenwich Playhouse, New York, on 1 Jun 1953

BOCCONIO PAPPARELLI, rich and stupid
  Bass
EUGENIA, a young and noble Roman lady who loves Asdrubale
  Soprano
DON ASDRUBALE, a Tuscan soldier who loves Eugenia

  Tenor
BETTINA, niece of Bocconio, in love with Asdrubale
  Soprano
PULCHERIO, friend of Bocconio
  Tenor
GERVASIO, Eugenia's tutor, in love with Metilde
  Bass
METILDE, singer and dancer, in love with Asdrubale
  Soprano
CHORUSES of EUGENIA'S and ASDRUBALE'S SERVANTS, etc.
Set on the Italian coast near Leghorn
2 fl, 2 ob, 2 bn, 2 hn, 2 tpt, timp, str

The plot has much in common with the classic *commedia dell'arte* situation of the old man wanting to marry a young girl who is in love with a dashing younger man. Naturally Bocconio is finally thwarted and the three couples are united.

It is supposed that Mozart, in his search for a good Italian libretto, abandoned *L'oca del Cairo* in favour of work on this, equally unsatisfactory, piece. (Regarding surviving music – Mozart seems to have attempted only the overture and 4 numbers – and dating, see concluding information.) The libretto is transmitted imperfectly in a manuscript copy and has its source in *Le donne rivali*, set by Cimarosa (Rome, 1780). The arrangement used by Mozart of this source includes a new role, that of Metilde.

The fine cast Mozart had in mind for the first performance included: Nancy Storace (Eugenia), Francesco Benucci (Bocconio), Catarina Cavalieri (Bettina), Sig. Pugnetti (Gervasio), Therese Teyber (Metilde), the bass Francesco Bussani (Pulcherio) and the baritone Stefano Mandini (Asdrubale), the last two mysteriously being cast for tenor roles. Vocal score published by Julius André (1855)

Surviving music: overture (substance complete in draft score; leads directly into no.1); quintet no.1 (substance complete in draft score); aria no.2 (substance complete in draft score); aria no.3 (substance complete in draft score); trio no.4 (complete); sketch for quartet no.1 (47 bars); sketch for aria no.2 (65 bars); sketch for trio no.4 (14 bars)
Dating: begun probably 1783 (?after Salzburg visit)

Autograph: PL–Kj
Libretto: D–B
Recording: Cotrubas, Rolfe-Johnson, Tear, Grant, London Symphony Orchestra, Davis. PHIL 6527 204

K.486
Der Schauspieldirektor (The Impresario)
AMA V, no.16; NMA II: 5/xv

Singspiel in 1 act (10 scenes); overture and 4 numbers. Libretto by Gottlieb Stephanie Jnr.

First perf.: 7 Feb 1786, the Orangery, Schönbrunn Palace, Vienna
First UK perfs.: 30 May 1857, St James' Theatre, London (in French); 14 Sep 1877, Crystal Palace, London (in English)
First US perfs: 9 Nov 1870, Stadttheatre, New York (in German, as *Mozart und Schikaneder*); 26 Oct 1916 New York (in English)

VOGELSANG, a singer
  Tenor Johann Valentin Adamberger
Mme HERZ, a singer
  Soprano Aloisia Lange
Mme SILBERKLANG, a singer
  Soprano Catarina Cavalieri
BUFF, an actor
  Bass Joseph Weidmann
the rest are speaking roles:
FRANK, an impresario
  Johann Gottlieb Stephanie Jnr
EILER, a banker
  Johann Franz Hieronymus Brockmann
HERZ, an actor
  Joseph Lange
Mme PFEIL, an actress
  Marie Anna Stephanie
Mme KRONE, an actress
  Johanna Sacco
Mme VOGELSANG, an actress
  Anna Marie Adamberger
2 fl, 2 ob, 2 cl, 2 bn, 2 hn, 2 tpt, timp, str

The libretto concerns an impresario's problems in assembling a group of actors and singers for a performance in Salzburg. Two sopranos quarrel over who is to be the prima donna, despite the tenor's attempts to pacify them. The morals pointed are that all artists should strive to perform their best, but that it is demeaning to presume superiority; in the end, the best judge of quality is the audience.

Der Schauspieldirektor was completed early in 1786 (the trio is dated 18 January, the finished Singspiel 3 February), at a time when Mozart was working on *Figaro*. It was commissioned by Emperor Joseph II, who wanted music for an entertainment at Schönbrunn in honour of his sister Marie Christine and her husband Duke Albrecht von Sachsen-Teschen, joint rulers of the Austrian Netherlands. It was performed as part of a double bill with Salieri's *Prima la musica e poi le parole*, and three public performances followed later in February at the Kärntnerthor theatre in Vienna. The Mozart work has continually been popular since, most often performed with updated dialogue.
Fragmentary attempt at arietta, in 4/4 (38 bars; in draft score; ? continuation lost), and sketch for trio, bars 100ff. (18 bars), survive

Autograph: US–NYpm
Libretto: (Vienna, 1786): *A–Wn*
Recording: Grist, Augér, Schreier, Moll, Dresden State Orchestra, Böhm (with *Die Entführung*). DG 2740 203 (3)

K.492
Le nozze di Figaro (The Marriage of Figaro)
AMA V, no.17; NMA II:5/xvi
Opera buffa in 4 acts (8/11/14/15 scenes); overture and 29 numbers. Libretto by Lorenzo da Ponte, after Beaumarchais

First perf.: 1 May 1786, Burgtheater, Vienna, conducted by Mozart, revived 29 Aug 1789 (with K.577 and 579)
First UK perf.: 2 May 1812, Pantheon, London
First US perf.: 10 May 1824, Park Theatre, New York (in English)

FIGARO, the Count's manservant
  Baritone Francesco Benucci
SUSANNA, the Countess's maid
  Soprano Nancy Storace
DR BARTOLO, physician in Seville
  Bass Francesco Bussani
MARCELLINA, the Countess's duenna
  Soprano Maria Mandini
CHERUBINO, the Count's page
  Soprano (trouser-role) Dorotea Sardi-Bussani
COUNT ALMAVIVA
  Baritone Stefano Mandini
DON BASILIO, a music master
  Tenor Michael Kelly
COUNTESS ALMAVIVA
  Soprano Luisa Laschi-Mombelli
ANTONIO, the chief gardener
  Bass Francesco Bussani
DON CURZIO, a lawyer
  Tenor Michael Kelly
BARBARINA, Antonio's daughter
  Soprano Anna 'Nannina' Gottlieb
CHORUS of VILLAGERS
Set on the Count's estate at Aguasfrescas outside Seville
2 fl, 2 ob, 2 cl, 2 bn, 2 hn, 2 tpt, timp, str, continuo

Figaro and Susanna are preparing for their wedding. Both are uneasy since the Count has designs on Susanna but Figaro is determined to outwit him. Bartolo and Marcellina enter: he is anxious to settle an old score with Figaro, she, furiously jealous of Susanna. The next arrival is Cherubino, boyishly in love with all women but especially the Countess. He hides in an armchair when the Count appears and overhears him trying to arrange an assignation with Susanna, but the

Count also has to hide as Don Basilio arrives too. His gossiping and insinuations bring the Count out, who then uncovers Cherubino. Figaro returns with a group of peasants, and asks the Count to perform his marriage to Susanna. The Count hesitates, but announces his intention to send Cherubino away on military service.

The unhappy Countess laments her husband's loss of interest in her. She and Susanna plan to trick him by sending Cherubino, disguised as Susanna, to a secret meeting with him. As they are dressing Cherubino the Count knocks on the door. Though Cherubino has locked himself in the next room the suspicious Count takes the Countess with him to fetch tools to break it down. In their absence Susanna locks herself in, having assisted Cherubino's escape through the window. Finding Susanna, the Count apologises, but Antonio arrives complaining that his flowers have been ruined by someone jumping out of the window. Figaro tries to save the situation by saying it was he, but the Count is not convinced, especially when Antonio produces the military commission Cherubino has dropped in his haste. Bartolo, Marcellina and Basilio join the Act II finale, insisting that Figaro is obliged to marry Marcellina in compensation for an old debt.

Figaro discovers that he is the son of Marcellina; to his even greater surprise Bartolo turns out to be his father. The Countess and Susanna concoct a letter to the Count suggesting that Susanna (the Countess in disguise) meet him in the garden later. The wedding celebrations take place, during which Susanna slips the Count the letter.

In the garden Barbarina searches for the pin that she has dropped. The Count told her to return it to Susanna in confirmation of their tryst. Figaro is furiously jealous when he overhears the reason for her search. He finds himself included in the confusing sequence of mistaken identity which unfolds, complicated by the arrival of the other main characters. When all is revealed, the Count has no option but to apologise.

Beaumarchais' play *Le Mariage de Figaro*, the sequel to his *Le Barbier de Séville*, was a *cause célèbre* thanks to its disrespectful portrayal of aristocratic *mores*. Thus, despite its great success in France, England and Ireland, the play was banned in Germany, although it was published there. Paisiello's opera *Il barbiere di Siviglia* had been successful in Vienna, and the play, *Figaro*, had aroused great interest. The moment had arrived for Mozart. After the disappointments of *Lo sposo deluso* and *L'oca del Cairo*, he had at last found the play and the librettist he had been searching for.

Mozart started work on the opera in October 1785 and completed it on 29 April 1786. Da Ponte persuaded the Emperor that he had taken out any passages which might offend, and the first performance was allowed to go ahead. For discussion of various aspects of composition of *Le nozze di Figaro*, see Tyson (1987)

Surviving frags and sketches: sketch for bars 59–64 of overture; frag. transmitting first version of bars 120–31 of cavatina no.3 (in draft score); fragmentary attempt at aria no.6 (82 bars: bars 16–43 lost; in draft score); fragmentary alternative version to duettino no.15 (5 bars); sketch for bars 803–49 of Act II finale no.16; sketch for bars 41–133 of aria no.18; group of 3 sketches for first part, and sketch for second part, of aria no.20; fragmentary attempt at duettino no.21 (64 bars; in draft score; sketchlike, bars 7ff.; preceded by 3 bars of recitative); sketch for bars 1–22 of Act III finale no.23; for recitative and aria no.28: fragmentary attempt at a recitative and rondò (34 bars; 36 bars; in draft score), sketch for rondò (30 bars), and sketch for final version of aria (37 bars; further 6 (?related) bars follow)

Autograph: Acts I, II, *D–Bds*; Acts III, IV, *PL–Kj*
Libretto: US–Wc

K.527
Il dissoluto punito, ossia Il Don Giovanni
AMA V, no.18; NMA II:5/xvii
Dramma giocoso (*Opera buffa* in Mozart's thematic catalogue), in 2 acts (20/14 scenes); overture and 24 numbers. Libretto by Lorenzo da Ponte

First perf.: 29 Oct 1787, National Theatre, Prague
First Vienna perf.: 7 May 1788, Burgtheater, Vienna (both premieres conducted by Mozart)
First UK perf.: 12 Apr 1817, King's Theatre, London (in English)
First US perf.: 7 Nov 1817, Park Theatre, New York

DON GIOVANNI, an extremely licentious young nobleman
   Baritone Luigi Bassi
THE COMMENDATORE, father of Donna Anna
   Bass Giuseppe Lolli
DONNA ANNA, betrothed to Don Ottavio
   Soprano Teresa Saporiti
DON OTTAVIO
   Tenor Antonio Baglioni
DONNA ELVIRA, a lady from Burgos, abandoned by Don Giovanni
   Soprano Caterina Micelli
LEPORELLO, Don Giovanni's servant
   Bass Felice Ponziani
MASETTO, a peasant
   Bass Giuseppe Lolli
ZERLINA, a peasant, betrothed to Masetto
   Soprano Caterina Bondini
CHORUSES of PEASANTS, SERVANTS and DEMONS
Set in 17th-century Seville

2 fl, 2 ob, 2 cl, 2 bn, 2 hn, 2 tpt, 3 trbn, timp, mand, str, continuo. Stage orchestras: Act 1 finale, (I) 2 ob, 2 hn, str (no vc), bn ad lib, (II) vns, db, (III) vns, db; Act 2 finale, 2 ob, 2 cl, 2 bn, 2 hn, vc

In the first act, Don Giovanni, after attempting to seduce Anna, is challenged to a duel by her father, whom he kills. Intent on proceeding as normal with his reckless amorous exploits, he meets Elvira, who has come to 'save' him, and Zerlina, who, although on her way to her wedding to Masetto, is fascinated but suspicious. At the end of the act he is openly accused, at the party to which he has invited them all, by the women who, with Ottavio and Masetto, are united by their determination to catch the villain. In the second act, he continues to foil them, and Leporello, ordered by Giovanni to assume his garb and seduce Elvira, also narrowly escapes their wrath. Master and servant meet in a graveyard where the statue of the Commendatore interrupts their conversation. Giovanni is unruffled, even when the statue accepts his invitation to dinner. In the finale, after Giovanni has rejected Elvira's final desperate offer of salvation, the statue arrives. Giovanni, unrepentant, is carried off to Hell by the spirits of the underworld. In the epilogue, the other characters prepare for the future in the light of recent events and, in a final ensemble, they point the moral of the tale.

Figaro had been withdrawn after nine performances in Vienna but, after its huge success in Prague, Da Ponte and Mozart started work on another opera for Bondini's company to perform there. Da Ponte was already busy with libretti for Martín y Soler and Salieri when Bondini suggested that Mozart might set the Bertati version of the Don Juan legend. The libretto combines elements of the original play by Tirso da Molina, Molière's *Le Festin de pierre* (1665), Goldoni's verse play, *Don Giovanni Tenorio* or *Il dissoluto* (1736), Righini's *Il convitato di pietra* and Bertati's libretto for Gazzaniga's successful one-act opera, *Don Giovanni Tenorio, or Il convitato da pietra* (February 1787).

For the first Vienna performance, Mozart and Da Ponte excluded Ottavio's aria 'Il mio tesoro' and substituted 'Dalla sua pace' (K.540a); in the second act, Elvira's 'In quali eccessi/Mi tradì' (K.540c) was also added, as well as the duet for Zerlina and Leporello, 'Restati qua/Per queste due manine' (K.540b), which is seldom included now. Mozart also made slight adjustments and additions to the second-act recitatives and the end of Leporello's aria 'Ah pietà'. The epilogue was omitted. For discussion of autograph of *Don Giovanni*, see Tyson (1990)

Sketch for combination of dances in Act I finale no.13 (16 bars) survives

Autograph: F–Pn
Libretto: Both 1787 versions, Prague and Vienna (incomplete, probably for the censor), *A–Wgm.* 1788 version, Vienna, *F–Pn, GB–Lbl*

K.588
Così fan tutte, ossia La scuola degli amanti (All Women Behave That Way, or The School for Lovers)
AMA V, no.19; NMA II:5/xviii
Opera buffa in 2 acts (16/18 scenes); overture and 31 numbers. Libretto by Lorenzo da Ponte

First perf.: 26 Jan 1790, Burgtheater, Vienna (conducted by Mozart)
First UK perf.: 9 May 1811, Haymarket Theatre, London (in Italian)
First US perf.: 24 Mar 1922, Metropolitan Opera House, New York

FERRANDO, an officer, in love with Dorabella
    Tenor   Vincenzo Calvesi
GUGLIELMO, an officer, in love with Fiordiligi
    Baritone   Francesco Benucci
DON ALFONSO, an old philosopher
    Baritone   Franceso Bussani
FIORDILIGI, a lady from Ferrara
    Soprano   Adriana Ferrarese del Bene
DORABELLA, her sister
    Soprano   Louise Villeneuve
DESPINA, the ladies' maid
    Soprano   Dorotea Sardi-Bussani
CHORUS
Set in 18th-century Naples
2 fl, 2 ob, 2 cl, 2 bn, 2 hn, 2 tpt, timp, str

The two soldiers make a bet with Don Alfonso that their sweethearts could not be unfaithful to them. He is sure that he can prove them wrong and they agree to do as he tells them. Their adoring ladies are horrified when Don Alfonso arrives to tell them their young men have been called up, and must leave immediately. After a tearful farewell they are furious when Despina suggests that it is no use moping and they should find some new lovers.

Alfonso lets Despina into the secret and they bring Ferrando and Guglielmo back to the house, dressed as Albanians. When the girls reject them they pretend to take poison. Despina, disguised as a doctor, brings them back to life with the help of a Mesmer magnet, insisting that the girls help her. The girls begin to find the attentions of the Albanians somewhat flattering. Dorabella is certainly game for a diversion and opts for the dark one . . . Guglielmo. Alone with him, she gives in, and accepts his gift of a locket. Fiordiligi, more conscience-stricken, rejects Ferrando. Ferrando is agonized by Guglielmo's account of Dorabella's capitulation and returns to Fiordiligi, who finally gives way. Don Alfonso wastes no time in arranging a double wedding, with Despina as lawyer.

No sooner is the contract signed than the soldiers' march is heard. The men vanish, only to reappear as soldiers once more. Don Alfonso is triumphant, and the four lovers have learned a salutary lesson.

It has been assumed that the Emperor Joseph II commissioned a new comic opera from Mozart and Da Ponte in the late summer of 1789. It may be that he suggested the subject, that of two men testing the faithfulness of their fiancées by each trying to seduce the other's girl, and succeeding. The idea was not new, but Da Ponte's libretto is wholly original. The opera was seldom performed after its initial performances in Vienna. Only over the last fifty years has it become part of the standard repertory, and it is at last appreciated as the perfect, serious and deeply personal comedy it is.

For discussion of comp. of *Così fan tutte*, see Tyson (1987)

Surviving frags and sketches: fragmentary first version, and a frag. relating to slightly later part, of aria no.26 (20 bars; 11 bars); sketches for A♭ major canon quartet, and sketches for bars 545–74, of Act II finale no.31

Autograph: Act I, *PL–Kj*; Act II, *D–B*
Libretto: *A–Wst*

K.620
Die Zauberflöte (The Magic Flute)
AMA V, no.20; NMA II:5/xix
Singspiel in 2 acts (19/30 scenes); overture and 21 numbers. Libretto by Emanuel Schikaneder.

First perf.: 30 Sep 1791, Theater auf der Wieden, Vienna
First UK perf.: 6 Jun 1811, His Majesty's Theatre, London (in Italian)
First US perf.: 17 Apr 1833, Park Theatre, New York (in English)

TAMINO, a foreign prince
  Tenor Benedikt Schack
PAPAGENO, a bird-catcher
  Baritone Emanuel Schikaneder
QUEEN OF NIGHT
  Soprano Josepha Weber-Hofer
PAMINA, her daughter
  Soprano Anna Gottlieb
SARASTRO, Priest of the Sun
  Bass Franz Xaver Gerl
THREE LADIES
  Sopranos Fräulein Klöpfer, Fräulein Hofmann, Elisabeth Weinhold-Schack
THREE BOYS
  Trebles *Nanette Schikaneder, *Matthias

Tuscher, *Master Handlgruber
SPEAKER
  Herr Winter
THREE PRIESTS
  Speaking role Urban Schikaneder
  Tenor Johann Michael Kistler
  Bass Christian Hieronymus Moll
MONOSTATOS
  Tenor Johann Joseph Nouseul
PAPAGENA
  Soprano Barbara Reisinger-Gerl
THREE SLAVES
  Speaking roles Karl Ludwig Gieseke, Wilhelm Frasel, Herr Starke
TWO MEN IN ARMOUR
  Tenor Johann Michael Kistler
  Bass Christian Hieronymus Moll
CHORUSES of PRIESTS, SLAVES and ATTENDANTS
*Mann, 1977
2 fl/pic, 2 ob, 2 cl/basset-hn, 2 bn, 2 hn, 2 tpt, 3 trbn, timp, glock, str
Set in Ancient Egypt
Scenery and costumes for first production by Joseph Gayl and Herr Nesslthaler

Tamino, rescued by three ladies from a fierce serpent, is enlisted by the Queen of Night to go with Papageno to rescue Pamina, imprisoned by Sarastro. They set off with a magic flute and a set of magic bells; three boys will guide them. Papageno finds Pamina, who escapes from the attentions of Monostatos, and persuades her to come with him to find Tamino. Tamino discovers that the queen is the villain, not Sarastro, who is the chief priest of the Temple of Wisdom. Sarastro agrees to accept Tamino, accompanied by Papageno, for initiation into the temple. Eventually, after passing the ordeals through darkness, silence and finally, with Pamina, fire and water, Tamino is united with Pamina, Papageno finds his dreamed-of Papagena, and the wicked queen is vanquished for ever by the forces of good.

In November 1790 Mozart agreed to collaborate with his old Salzburg friend Schikaneder on an opera for his theatre. He was keen to write a new German opera, and was unlikely to be commissioned to write an Italian opera by the new emperor. The plot combines elements of fairy story and pantomime with thinly disguised allusions to freemasonry. Schikaneder found the material for the story in Liebeskind's *Lulu*, an oriental fairy story published in 1786–9, but made substantial alterations to it, when, after completing several scenes, he transformed the wicked magician (Sarastro) into the high priest of Isis and Osiris.

Surviving frags and sketches: fragmentary attempt (K.Anh.102 (620a), 26 bars; in draft score) at, and sketch for bars 103ff. (?; 5 bars) of final version of, overture; sketches for bars 9–38, 39–85, 518–77 of Act I finale no.8; fragmentary attempt at march no.9 (12 bars); sketch for bars 18–21 of duet no.11; 2 sketches for cantus firmus, bars 206ff., sketch for march, bars 362–4, and fragmentary first version of bars 744–58 (in draft score; on reverse (lr) of first leaf of frag. are bars 736–8; in draft score) of Act II finale no.21

Autograph: D–Bds
Libretto (Vienna, 1791): *GB:Lbl*

K.621
La clemenza di Tito (The Clemency of Titus)
AMA V, no.21; NMA II:5/xx
Opera seria in 2 acts (14/17 scenes); overture and 26 numbers. Libretto by Caterino Mazzolà after Metastasio

First perf.: Sep 1791, National Theatre, Prague
First UK perf.: 27 Mar 1806, King's Theatre, London (in Italian). This was the first UK perf. of any Mozart opera
First US perf.: 4 Aug 1952, Tanglewood

VITELLIA, daughter of the deposed Emperor Vitellius, in love with Tito
  Soprano Maria Marchetti-Fantozzi
TITO, Emperor of Rome
  Tenor Antonio Baglioni
SESTO, Tito's friend, in love with Vitellia
  *Soprano** Domenico Bedini
ANNIO, Sesto's friend, in love with Servilia
  Soprano (trouser role) Carolina Perini
SERVILIA, Sesto's sister, in love with Annio
  Soprano Signora Antonini
PUBLIO, captain of the Pretorian guard
  Bass Gaetano Campi
* = castrato
CHORUS of SENATORS, AMBASSADORS, LICTORS, GUARDS and PUBLIC
Scene: Rome, 79–81 AD
Sets for first production by Pietro Travaglia and Sig. Preisig. Costumes by Cherubino Babbini
2 fl, 2 ob, 2 cl/basset-hn, 2 bn, 2 hn, 2 tpt, timp, str, continuo

Vitellia persuades Sesto to conspire with her against Tito, who does not return her love. Tito, hoping to marry Servilia, gives her up on discovering that she is in love with Annio. Publio sets off to tell Vitellia that Tito will marry her after all. But she has already sent Sesto to set fire to the capitol (which he does) and to kill Tito (which he does not). Tito discovers the plot. Annio urges Sesto to flee, but he is arrested by Publio and condemned to death. Tito tears up the death warrant. Although Vitellia finally confesses her part in the conspiracy, Tito pardons the conspirators and the opera ends happily.

In April 1789 Mozart had discussed plans for another Prague opera with Domenico Guardasoni, who had succeeded Bondini as impresario there. But the company left for Warsaw, and plans were laid aside until the summer of 1791, by which time Mozart was busy with *Die Zauberflöte*. A new *opera seria* was required to celebrate the coronation in Prague of Leopold II as King of Bohemia – not someone to whom Mozart owed a favour. However, despite his ill health, he agreed to do it and travelled to Prague at the end of August, taking Süssmayr along to write the recitatives. Twelve weeks after the first performance he was dead.

The Metastasio libretto *La clemenza di Tito* had been set by several others (including Caldara, Hasse and Gluck). It had already been adapted by Mazzolà (perhaps at Da Ponte's suggestion) according to Mozart's requirements, which would have been for something less formal and more realistic than the kind of thing Metastasio generally produced for a royal occasion. The 'lost' concert aria performed in Prague by Josepha Duschek on 26 April 1791 may well be Vitellia's aria 'Non più di fiori'.

After Mozart's death his widow arranged several concert performances of *La clemenza*. Six editions had been published by 1810.

For discussion of comp. of *La clemenza*, see Tyson (1987)

Surviving frags and sketches: fragmentary attempt (substance complete in draft score) at, and sketch for bars 46–74 of final version of, duet no.1; fragmentary attempt at duet no.3 (30 bars; in draft score); sketches for bars 1–9, 33–44 of trio no.10; sketches for bars 36–83, 88–91, 88–96 of trio no.14: on leaf, recto of which originally braced for an A major duet for Vitellia and Sesto; sketch for bars 28–34 of coro no.15; fragmentary attempt at rondò no.23 (45 bars [+ 18 'dal segno']; in draft score)

Autograph: D–B
Libretto: D–Dlb

AMANDA HOLDEN

Symphonies

MOZART'S OCCUPATION with the symphony spanned most of his compositional career: his earliest works in the genre date from 1764, the last from 1788. Their composition, however, was sporadic, not consistent, and the majority of them were written during well-defined, circumscribed periods.

Mozart's earliest symphonies, from K.16 to K.Anh.221 (45a), were composed between 1763 and 1766 and modelled in part on the symphonies of J.C. Bach, Karl Friedrich Abel and others that he encountered on the grand tour. All of them are in three movements, lacking a minuet and trio, and are scored for two oboes, two horns and strings. First movements are generally in expanded binary form and common time; second movements, also in binary form, have time signatures of 2/4, and tempo indications of Andante; concluding fast movements are usually in rondo form, with time signatures of 3/8. These generalities aside, however, Mozart's earliest symphonies sometimes depart from the norms of other works derived largely from the Italian opera house. The first movement of K.16, for example, is an expanded binary form of a type more common among Viennese symphonies (LaRue, 1980), K.19 incorporates into the second group a brief diversion based on the dominant minor, a procedure common among Salzburg symphonies of the 1750s (Eisen, 1988b), and K.22 includes an extended orchestral crescendo and a recurrence of *tutti* primary material at the middle and end of the movement, typical of Mannheim (LaRue, 1980). As a result, the early symphonies, and indeed the later ones as well, represent a mixture of Italianate and Austro-German traits.

The next group of symphonies, including K.43, 45 and 48, was composed in Vienna in 1767 and 1768 and again shows local influences, among them the inclusion of minuets and trios, the use of larger orchestral forces, and a greater variety of time signatures. First-movement form is variable and it is only with K.48 that a more fully developed sonata form, typical of several contemporary Viennese composers, is present. K.76 (42a) is sometimes claimed for this period as well, although the work lacks authentic sources (Eisen, 1989c).

There is no evidence that Mozart composed symphonies in Salzburg when he returned there in 1769. K.Anh.215, 217 and 218 (66c–e) are usually assigned to this period but sources for the works are unknown; their attribution to Mozart derives from the sometimes unreliable Breitkopf & Härtel manuscript catalogue (see 'Documents'). The only possible candidate for a symphony from this time is K.73; yet although it is written on Salzburg paper, the handwriting suggests a date of late 1769–early 1770, that is, after the beginning of the first Italian tour. Symphonies may have been redacted, as was common in Salzburg, from the orchestral cassations K.62/100 (62a), 63, 99 (63a) and a partly-lost work referred to in a letter of 18 August 1771 (K.deest). To the best of our knowledge, all of these compositions were written in the same year.

There is no doubt that Mozart was active as a symphonist during his time in Italy in 1770 and 1771. In a letter from Rome dated 25 April 1770 he wrote: 'When this letter is finished I shall finish my symphony which I've begun. . . . A[nother] symphony is being copied (the copyist is father), for we don't want to allow it to be copied, otherwise it would be stolen' and from Bologna on 4 August: 'Meanwhile I've composed four Italian sympho-

nies.' Traditionally these works are thought to be K.81 (73l), 84 (73q), 95 (73n) and 97 (73m). However, none of them is known in Mozart's autograph or other authentic copies, and there is no conclusive evidence that they are by him. K.95 (73n) and 97 (73m) are known only from the Breitkopf & Härtel manuscript catalogue and from editions published by Breitkopf & Härtel in 1881 as part of their complete works of Mozart. K.81 (73l) and 84 (73q) survive in non-authentic 18th-century manuscripts, but both have conflicting attributions: the former also survives in a copy attributed to Ditters, and the latter is listed in Breitkopf's 1775 thematic catalogue as a symphony by Leopold Mozart. It is consequently difficult to assess the claim that Mozart's symphonies of this period are heavily indebted to Italian models. The only surviving authentic 'Italian' symphonies are K.74, composed in Milan in 1770, and K.112, composed in Milan in November 1771. Although K.74 is typically Italian in its three-movement form, elision of first and second movements and truncated development amounting to little more than a transition, K.112 uncharacteristically includes a minuet and trio. While only one symphony, K.110 (75b), was composed in Salzburg between the first two Italian journeys, during the period December 1771 to about the middle of 1774, Mozart composed no less than seventeen such works, from K.114 to K.202 (186b). Stylistic and formal variety abounds early in this period, with many works representing unusual mixtures of Italian, Mannheim and local traits. K.133 and 134 are notable for reserving the restatement of the opening idea or first subject as a closing gesture at the end of a movement, a device also found in some of Michael Haydn's symphonies. Other works, including K.114 and the slow movement of K.128, are written in an intimate, quartet-like style. After about the middle of 1773, first movements are more regularly in a fully developed sonata form, possibly a legacy of Mozart's recent visit to Vienna, and thematic contrast, always characteristic of his style, becomes increasingly refined as a means of expression and as a structurally defining principle. Additionally, the symphonies display an increasing concern with counterpoint.

After 1775 Mozart composed increasingly fewer symphonies. In fact, there may be no independent Salzburg symphonies between K.200 (189k) of November 1774 (?1773) and K.318 of April 1779. A few opera overtures, including those to *La finta giardiniera* and *Il rè pastore*, were made into symphonies by the addition of finales, while others were derived from orchestral serenades by setting aside the concertante movements and one or two of the minuets and moderate-tempo movements. Authentic sources document this practice for K.204 (213a) and 250 (248b); probably symphonies were redacted from K.185 (167a) and 203 (189b) as well. The symphony version of K.250 (248b) shows several divergences from the original serenade version: a timpani part was added, and at the end of the first movement a fanfare for oboe, horn and trumpet; in one of the trios the accompaniment figure in the second violins was changed, in addition to having parts for oboes and bassoons added. Both serenades include new stylistic features: the rondo finale of K.204 (213a), composed in 1775, is unusual for alternating between a 2/4 Andantino grazioso and a 3/8 Allegro (a similar procedure occurs in the finale of the Violin Concerto K.218, also composed in 1775); and the slow movement of K.250 (248b) is an elaborate double theme and variations, uncommon for Mozart.

The limited output of the mid-1770s may reflect Mozart's growing dissatisfaction with Salzburg, which eventually led to his resignation from the Prince–Archbishop's service in 1777 and the subsequent trip to Munich, Augsburg, Mannheim and Paris. Mozart took numerous symphonies with him on this tour, but his newly composed symphonies amounted to a single work, the so-called *Paris* Symphony, K.297 (300a); Mozart's claim to have composed two symphonies in Paris is now discredited (Zaslaw, 1978). By his own admission, Mozart tailored K.297 (300a) to the Parisian audience. Like other popular symphonies of the time, he began the work with a *coup d'archet*, even if he thought the notion ridiculous: 'What a row the oxen here make of this business! – What the devil. I don't see any difference! They all begin together, just as in other places.' (letter of 12 June 1778) And in the last movement:

> . . . because I heard that here all last as well as first Allegros begin with all the instruments playing together and usually unisono, I began mine with two violins only, *piano* for the first eight bars – thereupon there was immediately a *forte*; the audience (as I expected) said 'Shh!' at the *piano* – then came the *forte*, and they began at once to clap their hands. (letter of 3 July 1778)

Nevertheless, Mozart must also have enjoyed writing for the large Parisian orchestra and he took advantage of the opportunity by including clarinets, an instrument not normally available to him in Salzburg.

Shortly after the first performance of the work, Mozart reported to his father the gist of a conversation he had had with Joseph Legros, director of the Concert Spirituel:

> – the symphony was a success with everyone – and Legros is so satisfied with it that he says it's his best symphony – but the Andante did not have the fortune to satisfy him – he says there are too many modulations in it – and too long – the reason is that the public forgot to applaud as long and as heartily as it did for the first and last movements – for the andante had the greatest success *with me*, and with all connoisseurs, amateurs and most of the public – it's just the opposite of what Legros says – it is quite natural – and short. – But in order to

please him (and as he maintains others as well) I did another movement – each is in its own way good – for each has its own different character – the last one pleases me better, however. (letter of 9 July 1778)

Although both Andantes – one in 6/8 and one in 3/4 – survive, it has been impossible to determine which of them is the earlier. According to the traditional view, the 6/8 movement is the original and the 3/4 the replacement; it has recently been argued, however, that the 3/4 movement was composed first (Tyson, 1987).

Returning to Salzburg in January 1779, Mozart was appointed court organist, replacing Anton Cajetan Adlgasser, who had died in 1777 during Mozart's absence. Although his obligations with regard to composition were non-specific – the appointment decree says only that 'he shall as far as possible serve the Court and the Church with new compositions made by him' – a significant number of works were written during this year and in 1780, including the symphonies K.318, 319 and 338. K.318 has a format similar to the French *opéra comique* overture: the first movement is complete to the recapitulation but is interrupted by an Andante leading to a brief transition before the return of the second group, and the main theme is reserved for the coda. K.319, unusual for its use of a central contrasting section as opposed to genuine development, was originally composed with three movements; Mozart added a minuet and trio, presumably for a Viennese performance of the work, in 1784 or 1785 (Tyson, 1987). The highly theatrical K.338, on the other hand, originally included a minuet and trio that Mozart later excised from the autograph. Although it has been suggested that the minuet K.409 (383f) is a later substitute for this movement, it is unlike K.338 with regard to its length, style and scoring. A further symphony from this period may be a redaction of the so-called *Posthorn* Serenade, K.320; however, authentic sources for a symphony version do not survive.

In Vienna Mozart composed only six symphonies. Not all of them, however, were written *for* Vienna. K.385, the *Haffner* Symphony, was composed in July 1782, at his father's request, for the ennoblement of the Mozarts' Salzburg friend Siegmund Haffner the younger. Some months later, in December, Mozart decided to perform the work at his forthcoming Lent concerts, and when he retrieved the score from his father in February 1783 he wrote: 'My new Haffner symphony has quite astonished me, for I had forgotten every single note of it. It must certainly make a good effect.' It was probably at this time that Mozart added flutes and clarinets to the first and last movements and set aside one of the two minuets mentioned in his letters of 27 July 1782 and 15 February 1783.

K.425, Mozart's first independent symphony, if not his first orchestral work, to include a slow introduction, was written at short notice in late

October and early November 1783 for a concert at Linz. Although it is the only late symphony for which there is no autograph, a reliable text of the work can be reconstructed from surviving authentic manuscript copies. Mozart probably performed the *Linz* in Vienna in 1784 or 1785 and it may have been for such a performance that he revised the symphony (Eisen, 1988a).

The third of Mozart's Viennese symphonies, K.504, dates from December 1786. Possibly, however, it was composed for his forthcoming trip to Prague, where it had its premiere on 19 January 1787. Unlike the *Haffner* and the *Linz*, the *Prague* lacks a minuet and trio and it has recently been shown that the last movement was composed first; possibly it was originally intended as a substitute finale for an early D major symphony, perhaps the *Paris* (Tyson, 1987).

Mozart's last three symphonies – the pinnacle of his symphonic achievement and among the most important and influential symphonies composed during the 18th century – were written in the space of six weeks or slightly longer during the summer of 1788 (the entries in Mozart's thematic catalogue are dated respectively 26 June, 25 July and 10 August). It is traditionally thought that Mozart never performed these symphonies but this is unlikely: not only does the idea run contrary to Mozart's normal practice, but the rapid dissemination and popularity of the works, especially K.550 and 551, as well as the fact that Mozart revised K.550, adding clarinets to the score, both suggest that he did. What is more, there were several opportunities to give the works in public: a remark in a letter of June 1788, about the time when he was working on K.543, suggests Mozart was planning a concert series in the immediate future; and concerts given at Leipzig in 1789, at Frankfurt in 1790, and in Vienna in 1791 all included symphonies.

Although it is tempting to dismiss the Romantic notion that the last symphonies represent a summation and culmination of Mozart's symphonic art – he can hardly have known these would be his last essays in the genre – they nevertheless typify some essential features of his symphonic style and development that are among his most enduring contributions to the symphony: a feeling of structural balance and proportion, a rich harmonic vocabulary, the delineation of function by distinctive and characteristic thematic material, and in particular a concern for orchestral textures which is manifested most clearly in the extensive and idiomatic wind writing.

K.16
E♭ major
AMA VIII/1 (Symphony no.1); NMA IV:11/i
London, [1764–5]
Molto allegro; Andante; Presto
2 ob, 2 hn, str

K.19
D major
AMA VIII/1 (Symphony no.4); NMA IV:11/i
London, 1765
Allegro; Andante; Presto
2 ob, 2hn, str
Possibly rev. later (see NMA IV:11/i, p. ix)

K.Anh.223 (19a)
F major
NMA IV:11/i
[London, 1765]
Allegro assai; Andante; Presto
2 ob, 2 hn, str

K.22
B♭ major
AMA VIII/1 (Symphony no.5); NMA IV:11/i
The Hague, Dec 1765
[Allegro]; Andante; Molto allegro
2 ob, 2 hn, str

K.76 (42a)
F major
AMA XXIV, no.3 (Symphony no.43); NMA IV:11/i
Presumed place and date of comp.: ?Vienna, autumn 1767
Allegro maestoso; Andante; Menuetto–Trio; Allegro
2 ob, 2 bn, 2 hn, str
Lacks authentic sources; attribn and dating uncertain (Eisen, 1989c). Earliest reference: Breitkopf & Härtel MS catalogue; earliest source: edition published by Breitkopf & Härtel, 1881. Dated Salzburg, summer of 1766 by Wyzewa and Saint-Foix (1936–46, I, 178)

K.43
F major
AMA VIII/1 (Symphony no.6); NMA IV:11/i
Vienna, autumn 1767
Allegro; Andante; Menuetto and Trio; Allegro
2 ob (fl), 2 hn, str
Possibly begun in Salzburg, summer 1767. Autograph includes crossed-out notation 'à Olmutz' where the Mozarts stayed from 26 Oct to 23 Dec 1767. Andante an arrangement of duet 'Natus cadit, atque Deus' from *Apollo et Hyacinthus*, K.38 (early 1767)

K.45
D major
AMA VIII/1 (Symphony no.45); NMA IV:11/i
[Vienna], 16 Jan 1768
[Molto allegro]; Andante; [Menuetto] and Trio; [Molto allegro]
2 ob, 2 hn, 2 tpt, timp, str
Rev. and reused (except Menuetto) as overture to *La finta semplice*, K.51 (46a)

K.Anh.221 (45a)
G major
NMA IV:11/i
The Hague, Mar 1766
Allegro maestoso; Andante; Presto
2 ob, 2 hn, str
Authentic copy (Lambach, Benediktinerstift,
probably copied 1767) transmits rev. version

K.Anh.214 (45b)
B♭ major
NMA IV:11/i
Presumed place and date of comp.: ?Vienna, early
1768
Allegro; Andante; Menuetto–Trio; Allegro
2 ob, 2 hn, str
Lacks authentic sources; attribn and dating
uncertain

K.48
D major
AMA VIII/1 (Symphony no.8); NMA IV: 11/i
Vienna, 13 Dec 1768
[Allegro]; Andante: Menuetto and [Trio]; [Molto
Allegro]
2 ob, 2 hn, 2 tpt, timp, str

K.73
C major
AMA VIII/1 (Symphony no.9); NMA IV:11/i
[Salzburg or Italy, late 1769–early 1770]
Allegro; Andante; Menuetto and Trio; [Molto
allegro]
2 ob (fl), 2 hn, 2 tpt, timp, str

K.81 (73l)
D major
AMA XXIV, no.4 (Symphony no.44); NMA
IV:11/ii
Presumed place and date of comp.: ?Rome, Apr
1770
Allegro; Andante; Allegro molto
2 ob, 2 hn, str
Lacks authentic sources; attribn and dating
uncertain. Non-authentic copy in Vienna,
Gesellschaft der Musikfreunde attributes work to
Mozart and give place and date of comp. as
Rome, Apr 1775 but also attrib. Leopold Mozart
in 1775 Breitkopf catalogue

K.97 (73m)
D major
AMA XXIV, no.7 (Symphony no.47); NMA
IV:11/ii
Presumed place and date of comp.: ?Rome, Apr
1770
Allegro; Andante; Menuetto–Trio; Presto
2 ob, 2 hn, 2 tpt, timp, str
Lacks authentic sources; attribn and dating
uncertain. Earliest reference: Breitkopf & Härtel

MS catalogue; earliest source: edition published
by Breitkopf & Härtel, 1881

K.95 (73n)
D major
AMA XXIV, no.5 (Symphony no.45); NMA
IV:11/ii
Presumed place and date of comp.: ?Rome, Apr
1770
Allegro; Andante; Menuetto–Trio; Allegro
2 ob, 2 tpt, str
Lacks authentic sources; attribn and dating
uncertain. Earliest reference: Breitkopf & Härtel
MS catalogue; earliest source: edition published
by Breitkopf & Härtel, 1881

K.84 (73q)
D major
AMA VIII/1 (Symphony no.11); NMA IV:11/ii
Presumed place and date of comp.: ?Milan and
Bologna, begun Jul 1770
Allegro; Andante; Allegro
2 ob, 2 hn, str
Lacks authentic sources; attribn and dating
uncertain. Non-authentic copies in Vienna,
Gesellschaft der Musikfreunde and Prague,
Národní Muzeum attrib. work to Mozart
(Vienna: W.A. Mozart; Prague: 'Mozart');
another copy, Prague, Národní Muzeum, attrib.
Ditters

K.74
G major
AMA VIII/1 (Symphony no.10); NMA IV:11/ii
[Milan, 1770]
[Allegro]–[Andante]; [Allegro]
2 ob, 2 hn, str

K.75
F major
AMA XXIV, no.2 (Symphony no.42); NMA IV:
11/ii
Presumed place and date of comp.: ?Salzburg,
early 1771
Allegro; Menuetto–Trio; Andantino; Allegro
2 ob, 2 hn, str
Lacks authentic sources; attribn and dating
uncertain. Earliest reference: Breitkopf & Härtel
MS catalogue; earliest source: edition published
by Breitkopf & Härtel, 1881

K.110 (75b)
G major
AMA VIII/1 (Symphony no.12); NMA IV:11/ii
Salzburg, Jul 1771
Allegro; [Andante]; Menuetto and Trio; Allegro
2 ob (fl), [2 bn,] 2 hn, str

K.Anh.216 (74g, Anh.C 11.03)
B♭ major

Presumed place and date of comp.: ?Salzburg, summer 1771
Allegro; Andante; Menuetto–Trio; Allegro molto
2 ob, 2 hn, str
Lacks authentic sources; attribn and dating uncertain (Allroggen, 1977). Earliest reference: Breitkopf & Härtel MS catalogue, where work described as including flutes, not oboes. MS copy, formerly Berlin, no longer extant

K.120 (111a)
D major
NMA IV:11/ii
[Milan, Oct–Nov 1771]
Presto
2 fl, 2 ob, 2 hn, str
Finale to form symphony with overture and first number of *Ascanio in Alba*, K.111 (Milan, 17 Oct 1771)

K.96 (111b)
C major
AMA XXIV, no.6 (Symphony no.46); NMA IV:11/ii
Presumed place and date of comp.: ?Milan, Oct–Nov 1771
Allegro; Andante; Menuetto–Trio; Molto allegro
2 ob, 2 hn, 2 tpt, timp, str
Lacks authentic sources; attribn and dating uncertain. Earliest reference: Breitkopf & Härtel MS catalogue; earliest source: edition published by Breitkopf & Härtel, 1881

K.112
F major
AMA VIII/1 (Symphony no.13); NMA IV:11/ii
Milan, 2 Nov 1771
Allegro; Andante; Menuetto and Trio; Molto allegro
2 ob, 2 hn, str
In autograph, Menuetto (not including Trio) entirely in Leopold Mozart's hand; originally an independent movement?

K.114
A major
AMA VIII/1 (Symphony no.14); NMA IV:11/ii
Salzburg, 30 Dec 1771
Allegro moderato; Andante; Menuetto and Trio; Molto allegro
2 fl (ob), 2 hn, str
Autograph includes rejected Menuetto

K.124
G major
AMA VIII/1 (Symphony no.15); NMA IV:11/ii
Salzburg, 21 Feb 1772
Allegro; Andante; Menuetto and Trio; Presto
2 ob, 2 hn, str

K.128
C major
AMA VIII/1 (Symphony no.16); NMA IV:11/iii
Salzburg, May 1772
Allegro maestoso; Andante grazioso; Allegro
2 ob, 2 hn, str

K.129
G major
AMA VIII/1 (Symphony no.17); NMA IV:11/iii
Salzburg, May 1772
Allegro; Andante; Allegro
2 ob, 2 hn, str
Probably begun earlier than May 1772 (Tyson, 1987)

K.130
F major
AMA VIII/1 (Symphony no.18); NMA IV:11/iii
Salzburg, May 1772
Allegro; Andantino grazioso; Menuetto and Trio; Molto allegro
2 fl, 4 hn, str
Rejected fragmentary attempt at slow movement (8 bars) survives in autograph score

K.132
E♭ major
AMA VIII/1 (Symphony no.19); NMA IV:11/iii
Salzburg, Jul 1772
Allegro; Andante; Menuetto and Trio; Allegro; [at end of manuscript:] Andantino grazioso
2 ob, 4 hn, str
?Alternative slow movements (Plath, 1974).
Andante based in part on Christmas song *Resonet in laudibus* (*Joseph, lieber Joseph mein*), also used by Mozart in *Gallimathias musicum*, K.32, no.2a (1766)

K.133
D major
AMA VIII/1 (Symphony no.20); NMA IV:11/iii
Salzburg, Jul 1772
Allegro; Andante; Menuetto and Trio; [Allegro]
[fl,] 2 ob, 2 hn, 2 tpt, str

K.134
A major
AMA VIII/1 (Symphony no.21); NMA IV:11/iii
Salzburg, Aug 1772
Allegro; Andante; Menuetto and Trio; Allegro
2 fl, 2 hn, str

K.161 + 163 (141a)
D major
AMA XXIV, no.10 (K.163 only) (Symphony no.50); NMA IV:11/iii
[Salzburg, 1773–4]
Allegro moderato; [Andante]; Presto
2 fl, 2 ob, 2 hn, 2 tpt, timp, str

Movements K.161 from overture to *Il sogno di Scipione* K.126 (1771); K.163 a newly composed finale to form symphony

K.184 (166a, 161a)
E♭ major
AMA VIII/2 (Symphony no.26); NMA IV:11/iv
[Salzburg, 30 Mar 1773]
Molto presto; Andante; Allegro
2 fl, 2 ob, 2 bn, 2 hn, 2 tpt, str
Date on autograph altered

K.199 (162a, 161b)
G major
AMA VIII/2 (Symphony no.27); NMA IV:11/iv
[Salzburg, 10 (?16) Apr 1773]
Allegro; Andantino grazioso; Presto
2 fl, 2 hn, str
Date on autograph altered

K.162
C major
AMA VIII/2 (Symphony no.22); NMA IV:11/iv
[Salzburg, 19 (?29) Apr 1773]
Allegro assai; Andantino grazioso; Presto assai
2 ob, 2 hn, 2 tpt, str
Date on autograph altered

K.181 (162b)
D major
AMA VIII/2 (Symphony no.23); NMA IV:11/iv
[Salzburg, 19 May 1773]
Allegro spiritoso; Andantino grazioso; Presto assai
2 ob, 2 hn, 2 tpt, str
Date on autograph altered

K.182 (166c, 173dA)
B♭ major
AMA VIII/2 (Symphony no.24); NMA IV:11/iv
[Salzburg, 3 Oct 1773]
Allegro spiritoso; Andantino grazioso; Allegro
2 ob (fl), 2 hn, str
Date on autograph altered

K.183 (173dB)
G minor
AMA VIII/2 (Symphony no.25); NMA IV:11/iv
[Salzburg, 5 Oct 1773]
Allegro con brio; Andante; Menuetto and Trio; Allegro
2 ob, 2 bn, 4 hn, str
Date on autograph altered. Rejected fragmentary attempt at slow movement (2 bars; only music for vn 1 notated) survives in autograph score

K.201 (186a)
A major
AMA VIII/2 (Symphony no.29); NMA IV:11/v
[Salzburg, 6 Apr 1774]
Allegro moderato; Andante; Menuetto and Trio;

Allegro con spirito
2 ob, 2 hn, str
Date on autograph altered

K.202 (186b)
D major
AMA VIII/2 (Symphony no.30); NMA IV:11/v
[Salzburg, 5 May 1774]
Molto allegro; Andantino con moto; Menuetto and Trio; Presto
2 ob, 2 hn, 2 tpt, str
Date on autograph altered

K.200 (173e, 189k)
C major
AMA VIII/2 (Symphony no.28); NMA IV:11/iv
[Salzburg, 17 (?12) Nov 1774]
Allegro spiritoso; Andante; Menuetto and Trio; Presto
2 ob, 2 hn, 2 tpt, timp, str
Date on autograph altered. Timp part, once extant in Mozart's autograph, now lost

K.121 (207a)
D major
AMA X; NMA IV:11/v
[Salzburg, late 1774–early 1775]
Allegro
2 ob, 2 hn, str
Finale to form symphony with overture to *La finta giardiniera* K.196 (1774–5)

K.204 (213a)
D major
NMA IV:12/iii
[Salzburg, after ?5 Aug 1775]
Allegro assai; Andante; Menuetto–Trio; Andantino grazioso–Allegro
2 ob, 2 bn, 2 hn, 2 tpt, str
Redacted from Serenade, K.204 (213a); date on autograph of Serenade altered

K.102 (213c)
C major
NMA IV:11/v
[Salzburg, *c*. Mar 1776]
Presto assai
2 ob (fl), 2 hn, 2 tpt, str
Finale to form symphony with versions of overture and first aria of *Il rè pastore*, K.208 (1775)

K.250 (248b)
D major
NMA IV:12/iv
[Salzburg, after ?Jun 1776]
Allegro maestoso–Allegro molto; Menuetto galante–Trio; Andante; Menuetto–Trio I–Trio II; Adagio–Allegro assai
2 ob, 2 bn, 2 hn, 2 tpt, timp, str
Redacted from Serenade, K.250 (248b) with new

timp part and other revs; date on autograph of Serenade altered

K.297 (300a)
D major
AMA VIII/2 (Symphony no.31); NMA IV:11/v
Paris, Jun 1778
Allegro assai; Andante; Allegro
2 fl, 2 ob, 2 cl, 2 bn, 2 hn, 2 tpt, timp, str
Paris Symphony. Two Andante movements, in 6/8 and 3/4, priority of comp. uncertain (NMA 6/8 movement comp. first; Tyson, 1987: 3/4 movement comp. first). Autograph first tpt part *c.* Dec 1786 transmits different version. Sketch for 3/4 Andante (complete vn part) and sketch for finale (bars 136–42) survive. Autograph of first movement and first autograph score of 6/8 slow movement contain numerous substantial cancellations

K.318
G major
AMA VIII/2 (Symphony no.32); NMA IV:11/vi
Salzburg, 26 Apr 1779
Allegro spiritoso–Andante–Primo tempo
2 fl, 2 ob, 2 bn, 4 hn, (2 tpt), str
Possibly intended as overture to *Zaide*, K.344 (366b). Tpt parts added 1782–3 (Tyson, 1987) Timp part in autograph by another hand

K.319
B♭ major
AMA VIII/2 (Symphony no.33); NMA IV:11/vi
Salzburg, 9 Jul 1779
Allegro assai; Andante moderato; Menuetto–Trio; Allegro assai
2 ob, 2 bn, 2 hn, str
Menuetto–Trio added 1784–5 (Tyson, 1987) Published Vienna, 1785 as op. 7 no.2

K.338
C major
AMA VIII/2 (Symphony no.34); NMA IV:11/vi
Salzburg, 29 Aug 1780
Allegro vivace; Andante di molto più tosto; Allegretto; Allegro vivace
2 ob, 2 bn, 2 hn, 2 tpt, timp, str
Cancelled Menuetto Allegretto (14 bars; ?originally complete) survives fragmentarily in autograph after first movement

K.385
D major
AMA VIII/3 (Symphony no.35); NMA IV:11/vi
Vienna, late Jul–early Aug 1782
Allegro con spirito; Andante; Menuetto–Trio; Presto
2 fl, (2 ob), (2 cl), 2 bn, 2 hn, 2 tpt, timp, str
Haffner Symphony. Originally comp. as serenade-like work for ennoblement of Siegmund Haffner in

Salzburg on 29 Jul 1782. Additional minuet mentioned by Mozart in letters of 27 Jul 1782 and 5 Feb 1783 apparently lost. Fls and cls added later, probably early 1783. Published Vienna, 1785 as op. 7 no. 1

K.425
C major
AMA VIII/3 (Symphony no.36); NMA IV:11/viii
Linz, late Oct–early Nov 1783
Adagio–Allegro spiritoso; Andante; Menuetto–Trio; Presto
2 ob, 2 bn, 2 hn, 2 tpt, timp, str
Linz Symphony. Possibly rev. Vienna, 1784–5 (Eisen, 1988a)

K.444 (425a)
G major
AMA VIII/3 (Symphony no.37)
[?Linz, Nov 1783 or later]
Adagio maestoso
2 ob, 2 hn, str
Introduction to Michael Haydn, Symphony Perger 16 (23 May 1783)

K.504
D major
AMA VIII/3 (Symphony no.38); NMA IV:11/viii
Vienna, 6 Dec 1786
Adagio–Allegro; Andante; Presto
2 fl, 2 ob, 2 bn, 2 hn, 2 tpt, timp, str
Prague Symphony. Presto possibly comp. first; intended as new finale to *Paris* Symphony, K.297 (300a) (Tyson, 1987)? Extensive sketch material for first movement and a fragmentary attempt at a slow movement (K.Anh.105/504a, 10 bars; in draft score) survive

K.543
E♭ major
AMA VIII/3 (Symphony no.39); NMA IV:11/ix
Vienna, 26 Jun 1788
Adagio–Allegro; Andante con moto; Menuetto–Trio; Allegro
fl, 2 cl, 2 bn, 2 hn, 2 tpt, timp, str

K.550
G minor
AMA VIII/3 (Symphony no.40); NMA IV:11/ix
Vienna, 25 Jul 1788
Molto allegro; Andante; Menuetto–Trio; Allegro assai
fl, 2 ob, (2 cl), 2 bn, 2 hn, str
2 versions, approximately contemporary, second with clarinets

K.551
C major
AMA VIII/3 (Symphony no.41); NMA IV:11/ix
Vienna, 10 Aug 1788

Allegro vivace; Andante cantabile; Menuetto
(Allegretto)–Trio; Molto allegro
fl, 2 ob, 2 bn, 2 hn, 2 tpt, timp, str
Jupiter Symphony. Origin of sobriquet obscure:
Vincent Novello was told by W.A. Mozart jr that
the title was coined by J.P. Salomon (1745–1815),
the London violinist and impresario (Novello,
1955)
Sketch material for finale survives

CLIFF EISEN

Concertos

THE ANTHROPOMORPHIC QUALITIES of Mozart's solo
concertos invite comparisons with his operatic and
concert arias. Both domains demonstrate Mozart's
genius in character portrayal while reconciling
virtuosity with the needs of dramatic expression;
both deploy prodigious melodic invention, a fluid
rhythmic language and a voluptuous orchestral
fabric.

The debt of Mozart's concertos to his solo vocal
music is revealed by many rhetorical details – for
example, the recitative-like passages in the slow
movements of many piano concertos (K.451, 466,
467, 537, 595). (Cf. also the vocal recitative in the
slow movement of K.271, perhaps inspired by
Joseph Haydn or Ignaz von Beecke.) The variety of
accompaniment patterns in the orchestra – as many
as three within a single phrase – and the vivacity
with which the ensemble responds to and provokes
the soloist, parallels the use of the orchestra in arias
and accompanied recitatives as alter ego of the
soloist.

Mozart is known to have tailored his writing to
the specific abilities of his singers and instrumentalists. Thus, the Concerto for Flute and Harp in C,
K.299 (297c), contains the low pitches $d\flat'$ and c' for
the flute, because the Comte de Guines had a tail-
piece on his instrument that enabled him to play
these pitches. The late works for clarinet (the
Quintet in A, K.581, the aria 'Non più di fiori' from
La clemenza di Tito, K.621, the Concerto in A, K.622,
and several fragments) were written for Anton
Stadler's special instrument, which extended four
semitones below the normal clarinet range to
notated c. The solo horn works for Joseph Leutgeb,
from the Quintet in E$\flat$, K.407 (386c) (?1782) to the
Concerto in D, K.412 (386b) + 514 (unfinished,
1791) document the gradual decline of Leutgeb's
technique: the high notes written b'' and c''' found in
the concertos K.417 (1783) and 495 (1786) are
omitted in K.447 (1787); by 1791, Leutgeb, who
was 59, evidently could no longer play notes below
written g'. (These were eliminated from the draft of
the work, whose corrected ambitus is limited to the
range g–a''; cf. work-list below.)

It is the concertos (and operas), not the sympho-
..ies, that reveal the evolution in Mozart's orchestral
writing in the Vienna years. The emancipation of
the winds, central to the development of his piano
concertos, reaches a turning-point with K.450
(1784), which opens with obbligato winds. From
this point on Mozart elevates the wind band to a
privileged entity within the orchestra: in the concertos K.482 and K.491 they occasionally push the
strings completely to the side. This transformation of
the orchestral texture does not manifest itself in the
symphonies until the *Prague*, K.504 (1786).

Writers such as Girdlestone (1948), Landon
(1956) and Forman (1971) have explored the
influence upon Mozart of concertos of the 1760s and
1770s, and much recent attention has been focused
by such writers as Jane Stevens upon 18th-century
descriptions of concerto form. Unfortunately, the
influence of Mozart's growth as an operatic composer upon the gestation of his concerto form has
been neglected, and this formal kinship between
Mozart's vocal and instrumental works deserves
attention.

Mozart created his first concertos by supplying
orchestral accompaniments to solo keyboard sonata
movements by composers such as Raupach,
Honauer, Schobert, Eckard and C.P.E. Bach, in
four pasticcio concertos transcribed in 1767 (K.37,
39, 40, 41). The piano part to each concerto
movement essentially reproduces the text of the
original solo work; only the orchestral ritornelli were
devised by Mozart. In the first movements the
binary sonata form of the original was transformed
by interpolating four such ritornelli: one precedes
the exposition with an introductory *tutti* in the tonic,
a second one underscores the arrival in the dominant
key at the midpoint, and a pair of ritornelli in the
tonic after the end of the recapitulation prepares and
follows the soloist's cadenza. The manner in which
Mozart constructed these ritornelli demonstrates his
ability, even as a youth, to abstract the proper
thematic and structural content of the ritornelli
from his source material. That he understood the
function of the orchestral ritornelli – i.e., to present
in capsule form the main thematic and cadential
gestures of the movement – is equally evident in his
early arias, for example, the licenza *Or che il dover* –
Tali e cotanti sono, K.36 (33i). In the A section of this
aria, the orchestral ritornelli display the same
hierarchical patterns and content as do those to the
pasticcio concertos, reflecting the formal relation
between sonata, concerto and aria forms. (Indeed,
sonata form rapidly extended its hegemony over all
other structures – first movement, slow movement,
minuet, rondo. . . .)

The formal archetype used by the arias in
Mozart's *opere serie* reflects his ability to use the
organization of the text as a basis for structural
design. The typical dramatic situation in such arias
is static, both forcing and enabling Mozart to derive

cumulative intensity through other means – in particular, through thematic and proportional syntax.

Static arias place intrinsic constraints on dramatic effectiveness. These seem to have led Mozart to seek a more dynamic dramaturgy from his libretti. The orderly patterns of thematic hierarchy he had developed for his *seria* arias are unsuited to continuously evolving dramatic situation; rigour of symmetry is inimical to free character development. However, these constraints do not exist in instrumental works, where consistent development of a hierarchy of ideas represents an ideal. Perhaps Mozart consciously concluded that the structure he was about to abandon in his dramatic music could be transferred with great effectiveness to the instrumental concerto. This would explain the temporal proximity between Mozart's first original works in the genre – the Violin Concerto in B♭, K.207, the Piano Concerto in D, K.175, the Concertone for two violins in C, K.190 (166b/186E) and the Bassoon Concerto in B♭, K.191 (186e), written from April 1773 to May 1774 – and his turning from *opera seria* towards *opera buffa* (*La finta giardiniera*, K.196 (1774–5)). The experiences of Mozart's second Italian journey may explain both this new direction in plot and aria structure and his awakened interest in instrumental concertos. In any case, Mozart seems to have written no instrumental concertos so long as he had opportunities to compose *opere serie*: from 1768 until 1773 his only essays in concerto form were further transcriptions, K.107, of three sonatas by Johann Christian Bach (*c.* late 1770).

By the time this happened, Mozart had devised a hierarchy of thematic structure and a consistency of proportions within his *opere serie* that were to serve him as a model for his instrumental concertos for the rest of his life. He seems to have perceived that greater complexity of thematic exposition in instrumental works could parallel the specific dramatic situation dictated by a text. The character and texture of Mozart's thematic motives, and the order of their presentation, reflect specific rhetorical purpose (e.g., expository, dynamic, cadential). This principle is revealed by Mozart's entire concerto *oeuvre* and is above all evident in the first movements, all of which observe so-called concerto first-movement form. (Contentions by Denis Forman that Mozart's concertos employ a variety of structural archetypes (Forman, 1971) are based upon distinctions of character rather than structure; neither the similarities nor the differences in content of individual concertos are adequately explained by his models.) From Mozart's first surviving original concerto – that for violin in B♭ major, K.207 – through to his last – the Clarinet Concerto in A major, K.622 – there is a common structure that distinguishes each of them from all other works of this type. (Regarding the dating of the B♭ major Violin Concerto (April 1773) before the D major Piano Concerto K.175 (December 1773), see the work-list.) Even Beethoven, who sought in many ways to emulate Mozart, did not choose to duplicate his concerto prototype – perhaps because of its great motivic complexity. As is generally acknowledged, Beethoven's motivic construction and usage reflect Haydn's practice; to Beethoven, Mozart's plethora of melodic ideas may have seemed profligate.

In the typical Mozartian opening ritornello no fewer than seven structural ideas, some of which may consist of similar motivic material, are discernible. Mozart's hierarchy thus enables him to construct movements of elaborate content without sacrificing cogency, thereby avoiding two pitfalls encountered in works by his contemporaries: mechanical formalism and lack of structural tautness. The concertos of his contemporaries commonly offer chains of musical ideas of similar character in loose, episodic discourse. Not even the finest concerto composers of Mozart's time (Viotti, Haydn) seem to have reached this symbiosis between rhetoric and form. While no two adjacent sections within the exposition or recapitulation of a Mozart concerto have the same structural or expressive function, a work such as Haydn's Cello Concerto in D (Hob. VIIb:2) (1783) contains several such repeated presentations of material (bars 41ff., 65ff.), during which the discourse loses focus; unlike Mozart's consistent concerto form, Haydn's and Viotti's individual concertos vary considerably in length, content and proportion.

Regarding the sources to the concertos, the review given by Blume (1956) is generally accurate, except that the manuscripts from the Prussian State Library that vanished after World War II are now in the Biblioteka Jagiellońska in Kraków. The autographs of the concertos for flute, oboe, bassoon, part of the Horn Concerto K.495, the violin Rondo K.373 and the Sinfonia Concertante for violin and viola, K.364 (320d), remain lost. Within the autographs themselves there exist certain textual problems. The piano concertos written for Mozart's personal use contain incompletely notated passages (e.g., K.482, 3rd movement, bars 164–72). Because Mozart sometimes notated solo and orchestral parts at different times, there are occasional solo/*tutti* harmonic clashes, inhibiting determination of a definitive version. Furthermore, scholars are gradually realizing that authentic performance parts (such as those at St Peter's in Salzburg) can offer us information concerning Mozart's performance practice that cannot be determined from autograph manuscripts. However, the autographs have enabled Wolfgang Plath and Alan Tyson to redraw the chronology of Mozart's legacy through studies of his handwriting and of the paper-types he used.

Piano Concertos

Solo instruments are not included in the listing of instruments.

K.37, 39–41 (nos 1–4)
See 'Arrangements, additions and transcriptions', and 'Concertos' (main text)

K.107/1–3
See 'Arrangements, additions and transcriptions', and 'Concertos' (main text)

K.175
D major
AMA XVI/1 (Piano Concerto no.5); NMA V:15/i
Salzburg, Dec 1773 (autograph)
Allegro; Andante ma un poco Adagio; Allegro
2 ob, [bn ad lib], 2 hn, 2 tpt, timp, str
Mozart's first original piano concerto; he perf. it in Mannheim (13 Feb 1778) and later, in Vienna. Range of solo instrument ($A'-d'''$) is narrower than that for the other concertos ($F'-f'''$). Flothuis considers that Mozart may have envisaged performance using organ (NMA V:15/i). Two different versions of the parts for obs and first hn exist. Possibility of using bn(s) to double bass line even when not called for in the score ('bn ad lib' above and elsewhere in this listing), reflects Classical period performance practice. Finale replaced in (?Feb) 1782 by the Rondo in D, K.382

K.238
B♭ major
AMA XVI/1 (Piano Concerto no.6); NMA V:15/i
Salzburg, Jan 1776 (autograph)
Allegro aperto; Andante un poco adagio; Rondeau (Allegro)
2 ob (= 2 fl in second movement), [bn ad lib], 2 hn, str
Later known perfs by Mozart: 4 Oct 1777 (Munich), 22 Oct 1777 (Augsburg)

K.242
F major
AMA XVI/1 (Piano Concerto no.7); NMA V:15/i
Salzburg, Feb 1776 (autograph)
Allegro; Adagio; Rondeau (Tempo di Minuetto)
2 ob, [bn ad lib], 2 hn, str
Lodron: 3 pf. Written for perf. by Countess Antonia Lodron and her 2 daughters, Aloisia and Josepha. Additional 3 pf perfs in Augsburg (22 Oct 1777) and Mannheim (12 Mar 1778), latter without Mozart's solo participation. A transcription for 2 pf also exists: from ?1779 (NMA). This version perf. by Mozart and Nannerl in Salzburg on 3 Sep 1780

K.246
C major
AMA XVI/1 (Piano Concerto no.8); NMA V:15/ii
Salzburg, Apr 1776 (autograph)
Allegro aperto; Andante; Rondeau (Tempo di Menuetto)
2 ob, [bn ad lib], 2 hn, str
Lützow; written for Countess Antonia Lützow. Mozart perf. it in Munich (4 Oct 1777) and used it as teaching piece. 3 sets of cadenzas survive. Surviving autograph 'continuo part' apparently designed for perf. with 2 pf and thus should not be used as a guideline for how Mozart played *col Basso* (see Ferguson, 1984/5)

K.271
E♭ major
AMA XVI/2 (Piano Concerto no.9) NMA V:15/ii
Salzburg, Jan 1777 (autograph)
Allegro; Andantino; Rondeau (Presto)
2 ob, [bn ad lib], 2 hn, str
Jeunehomme; written for Mlle Jeunehomme, a French virtuoso, during her visit to Salzburg. Third movement contains interpolated Menuetto (Cantabile). Mozart perf. it in Munich (4 Oct 1777) with K.238 and K.246, and perhaps in Vienna on 3 Apr 1781 and spring 1783. 2 sets of cadenzas exist, and 3 sets of lead-ins for the Finale

K.365 (316a)
E♭ major
AMA XVI/2 (Piano Concerto no.10); NMA V:15/ii
Salzburg, ?early 1779 (NMA)
Allegro; Andante; Rondeau (Allegro)
2 ob, 2 bn, 2 hn, str
2 pf. Dating from NMA. Presumably written for perf. with Nannerl, who probably played first part, it was also perf. by Mozart with Josepha Barbara Auernhammer in Vienna on 23 Nov 1781 and 26 May 1782. Authenticity of additional parts for 2 cl, 2 tpt, timp (allegedly added later, perhaps for Vienna perfs of 1781/2) not beyond doubt. Cl parts have been skilfully wound around existing wind voice-leading.

K.382
Rondo; D major
AMA XVI/4, no.28; NMA V:15/i
Vienna, ?Feb 1782
Allegretto grazioso
fl, 2 ob, [bn ad lib], 2 hn, 2 tpt, timp, str
Dating from NMA. Replacement finale for K.175; more properly termed a theme with variations. Mozart could have made substitution to avoid having both outer movements of K.175 use sonata form (a decision he also seems to have carried out for the Violin Concerto K.207, whose original sonata movement may have been replaced by Rondo K.269 (261a). In his own lifetime, one of Mozart's most popular works

K.414 (386a, 385p)
A major
AMA XVI/2 (Piano Concerto no.12); NMA

V:15/iii
Vienna, ?autumn 1782
Allegro; Andante; Rondeau (Allegretto)
2 ob, [bn ad lib], 2 hn, str
Mozart's letter to Leopold of 28 Dec 1782 relates how 2 works for a series of subscription concerts still remain to be finished: completed work generally assumed to have been K.414 (385p). Winds ad lib: can be played with str qt accompaniment. 2 sets of cadenzas survive, second dating from before Mar 1786. Second movement comp. to a theme of J.C. Bach, though not necessarily in his memory (he died 1 Jan 1782). Mozart perf. the work in Vienna and Salzburg. See Rondo, K.386. Sketch for first movement, bars 85ff. (K.385 0, 47 bars), survives

K.386
Rondo; A major
NMA V:15/viii
Vienna, 19 Oct 1782 (autograph)
Rondeaux (Allegretto)
2 ob, [bn ad lib], 2 hn, str (with obbligato vc)
Regarded by some as probable first version of, or replacement for, finale to K.414 (386a, 385p) (see Einstein, *Köchel 3*); by others as independent movement (see Tyson, 1987). Would be difficult to perform with str qt accompaniment; perhaps why Mozart replaced it. Original ending, discovered in 1980 by Tyson in British Library, misplaced shortly after Mozart's death and found its way into a miscellany of Süssmayr's manuscripts. Sterndale Bennett purchased remainder of autograph, cut it into pieces (some less than a full page), and dispersed it; several segments have disappeared. 19th-century transcription for solo pf by Cipriani Potter has been used as basis for reconstructions by Alfred Einstein and Paul Badura-Skoda/Charles Mackerras, but Potter did not have access to original ending. Earlier allegations that Mozart had not completed instrumentation appear to be unfounded. Recent edition by Tyson and Mackerras with cadenzas by Badura-Skoda uses Mozart's ending.

K.413 (387a)
F major
AMA XVI/2 (Piano Concerto no.11); NMA V:15/iii
Vienna, ?winter 1782–3 (before 28 Dec 1782)
Allegro; Larghetto; Tempo di Menuetto
2 ob, 2 bn, 2 hn, str
Dating from NMA. Winds ad lib: can be played with str qt accompaniment. Bns obbl only in second movement, where they were added later. First movement in 3/4 time, trait shared only with K.449 and K.491 amongst all concertos. Probably perf. by Mozart in Vienna on 11 Jan 1783; later perfs in Salzburg

K.415 (387b)
C major
AMA XVI/2 (Piano Concerto no.13); NMA V:15/iii
Vienna, ?winter 1782–3
Allegro; Andante; Rondeau (Allegro)
2 ob, 2 bn, 2 hn, 2 tpt, timp, str
Dating from NMA. Winds, brass, timp ad lib: can be played with str qt accompaniment. Sources show that work also perf. with winds and hns without tpts and timp. First perf. by Mozart on 23 Mar 1783, again on 30 Mar, and in Salzburg on 1 Oct 1783. Cancelled fragmentary attempt at a slow movement in C minor (17 bars; in draft score) survives in autograph

K.449
E♭ major
AMA XVI/2 (Piano Concerto no.14); NMA V:15/iv
Vienna, 9 Feb 1784 (autograph; *Verzeichnüss*)
Allegro vivace; Andantino; Allegro ma non troppo
2 ob, [bn ad lib], 2 hn, str
First Barbara Ployer concerto: can be played with str qt accompaniment. Perhaps begun 1782, completed spring 1784 (Tyson, 1987). Presumably perf. 17 Mar 1784. First movement in 3/4 time, a trait shared only with K.413 (387a) and K.491 amongst all concertos. In NMA, first movement one bar shorter than in all other editions

K.450
B♭ major
AMA XVI/2 (Piano Concerto no.15); NMA V:15/iv
Vienna, 15 Mar 1784 (*Verzeichnüss*)
Allegro; [Andante]; Allegro
fl (last movement only), 2 ob, 2 bn, 2 hn, str
Mozart's first concerto to begin with solo winds. Perhaps the most technically demanding of entire series. According to *Köchel 6*, perf. 24 Mar 1784. Second movement considerably revised. Sketch for main theme of finale (8 bars) survives

K.451
D major
AMA XVI/2 (Piano Concerto no.16); NMA V:15/iv
Vienna, 22 Mar 1784 (*Verzeichnüss*)
Allegro assai; Andante; Rondeau (Allegro di molto)
fl, 2 ob, 2 bn, 2 hn, 2 tpt, timp, str
An embellished version (Salzburg, St Peter) of the pf recitative in the second movement (bars 56–62) gives valuable evidence of authentic decoration of such passages, found in slow movements to K.466, 467, 537, and 595. According to *Köchel 6*, perf. 31 Mar 1784

K.453
G major
AMA XVI/3 (Piano Concerto no.17); NMA
V:15/v
Vienna, 10 Apr 1784 (letter); 12 Apr 1784
(*Verzeichnüss*)
Allegro; Andante; Allegretto
fl, 2 ob, 2 bn, 2 hn, str
Second Barbara Ployer concerto; perf. by her in
Döbling on 13 Jun 1784. Mozart's pet starling
learned finale theme (notated by Mozart 27 May
1784). 2 sets of cadenzas survive, one of dubious
authenticity. 2 fragmentary attempts at a slow
movement (K.Anh.59 (466a, 459a), 39 bars; in
draft score; K.Anh.65 (452c), 10 bars; in draft
score) survive

K.456
B♭ major
AMA XVI/3 (Piano Concerto no.18); NMA
V:15/v
Vienna, 30 Sep 1784 (*Verzeichnüss*)
Allegro vivace (*Verzeichnüss:* Allegro); Andante un
poco sostenuto; Allegro vivace
fl, 2 ob, 2 bn, 2 hn, str
Probably written for Maria Theresia Paradis
(1759–1824). Mozart's dating in his thematic
catalogue is suspect; work was probably finished
earlier, in order for blind Paradis to have learned
it in time for her Parisian perf(s), last of which
was on 2 Oct 1784 (see Leeson and Whitwell,
1973). 3 cadenzas for first movement and 2 for last
survive (none in autograph)

K.459
F major
AMA XVI/3 (Piano Concerto no.19); NMA
V:15/v
Vienna, 11 Dec 1784 (*Verzeichnüss*)
Allegro (*Verzeichnüss:* Allegro vivace); Allegretto;
Allegro assai
fl, 2 ob, 2 bn, 2 hn, (2 tpt, timp), str
Tpt and timp parts mentioned in Mozart's
thematic catalogue; these have not been found.
Could have been notated on subsequently lost
separate sheet (common procedure in some of
Mozart's concertos and many operas), though
there exists no other work in F by Mozart with
tpts and timp. Allegedly played along with K.537
in Frankfurt am Main on 15 Oct 1790 during
time of Leopold II's coronation; sometimes called
Second *Coronation* Concerto

K.466
D minor
AMA XVI/3 (Piano Concerto no.20); NMA
V:15/vi
Vienna, 10 Feb 1785 (*Verzeichnüss*)
Allegro; Romance; Rondo [Allegro assai]
fl, 2 ob, 2 bn, 2 hn, 2 tpt, timp, str

Premiered by Mozart 11 Feb 1785. No original
cadenzas survive, though they are mentioned in
the family correspondence. Fragmentary attempt
at a finale (39 bars; in draft score) survives in
autograph

K.467
C major
AMA XVI/3 (Piano Concerto no.21); NMA
V:15/vi
Vienna, Feb 1785 (autograph); 9 Mar 1785
(*Verzeichnüss*)
Allegro maestoso (*Verzeichnüss*); Andante; Allegro
vivace assai
fl, 2 ob, 2 bn, 2 hn, 2 tpt, timp, str
Premiered by Mozart 10 Mar 1785. No original
cadenzas survive. Sketched solo passages: first
movement, bar 380; perhaps second, bars 58–9; in
third movement, right-hand octaves at 302 and
304–6 should perhaps be broken; less certain for
143–4, 149–50, 394–5 and 400–01. Fragmentary
attempt at concerto first movement K.Anh.60
(502a) (19 bars; in draft score) to be connected
possibly with K.467

K.482
E♭ major
AMA XVI/4 (Piano Concerto no.22); NMA
V:15/vi
Vienna, 16 Dec 1785 (*Verzeichnüss*)
Allegro; Andante; [Rondo] Allegro
fl, 2 cl, 2 bn, 2 hn, 2 tpt, timp, str
Date of first perf. unknown (though likely to have
been perf. 23 Dec 1785). Mozart's first concerto to
include cls in original scoring. Third movement
contains interpolated minuet (Andantino
cantabile) whose solo part requires
ornamentation. No original cadenzas survive. In
NMA, first movement is 2 bars longer than in all
other editions. Sketched solo passages: second
movement, 181–2, third movement, 164–72, 346–
7, 353–6

K.488
A major
AMA XVI/4 (Piano Concerto no.23); NMA
V:15/vii
Vienna, 2 Mar 1786 (*Verzeichnüss*)
Allegro; Adagio; Allegro assai
fl, 2 cl, 2 bn, 2 hn, str
Begun in 1784 with obs (Tyson, 1987); replaced
by cls when work completed in 1786.
Exceptionally, first-movement cadenza notated in
score. (Apart from Concertone, K.190 (166b,
186E), in which cadenzas include orchestral
instruments, Mozart otherwise always notated
these on separate sheets.) Embellished version of
second movement, perhaps from Mozart's student
circle, reproduced in Kritischer Bericht of NMA.
Fragmentary attempt at a slow movement in D

(K.Anh.58 (488a), 10 bars; in draft score) and 3 fragmentary attempts at a finale (K.Anh.63 (488b), 23 bars; in draft score; K.Anh.64 (488c), 27 bars; in draft score; K.488d, 11 bars; in draft score) survive

K.491
C minor
AMA XVI/4 (Piano Concerto no.24); NMA V:15/vii
Vienna, 24 Mar 1786 (*Verzeichnüss*)
Allegro; [Larghetto]; [Allegretto]
fl, 2 ob, 2 cl, 2 bn, 2 hn, 2 tpt, timp, str
Allegedly premiered by Mozart on 7 Apr 1786. No original cadenzas survive. Solo part sketched and reworked later. Many spots notated in shorthand (first movement, bars 261–2, 467–70, third movement, bars 142–5, 155–6, 159–62); some passages (third movement, bars 45–8 and 61–4) lack a definitive version. Broken octaves may have been meant at third movement, bars 191 and 198, and broken thirds at 245–7 and 262–4. Portions of second movement (bars 67–73) may be ornamented. Conflicts between solo and orchestral harmonization in second and third movements and omissions in orchestral parts create particular textual problems not resolved in any published edition. First movement in 3/4 time, a trait shared only with K.413 (387a) and K.449 amongst all the concertos. Fragmentary attempt at slow movement (K.Anh.62 (491a), 3 bars) survives

K.503
C major
AMA XVI/4 (Piano Concerto no.25); NMA V:15/vii
Vienna, 4 Dec 1786 (*Verzeichnüss*)
Allegro maestoso; Andante; [Allegretto]
fl, 2 ob, 2 bn, 2 hn, 2 tpt, timp, str
Mozart's longest concerto (first movement: 432 bars; rondo, 382 bars); premiered by him on 5 Dec 1786. No original cadenzas survive. Probably begun winter 1784–5 (Tyson, 1987). Second movement sketched at bars 59–62 and otherwise requires ornamentation. Left-hand chord in third movement, bar 60, conflicts with orchestra and should be corrected, probably to $a+c'$. Sketches for bars 96–112, 134–8 [=312–16], 208–14 of first movement survive

K.537
D major
AMA XVI/4 (Piano Concerto no.26); NMA V:15/viii
Vienna, 24 Feb 1788 (*Verzeichnüss*)
Allegro; [Larghetto]; [Allegretto]
fl, 2 ob, 2 bn, 2 hn, 2 tpt, timp ad lib, str
Coronation Concerto. Probably begun by early 1787 (Tyson); played (apparent premiere) by

Mozart in Dresden on 14 Apr 1789. Owes popular subtitle to perf. by Mozart during time of Leopold II's coronation in Frankfurt am Main on 15 Oct 1790. No original cadenzas survive. Rehm (NMA) is surely correct that all winds and brass, not just tpts and timp, are ad lib; this is confirmed by texture of work. Decision to add tpts and timp made during comp. of first movement. Left hand of large portions of outer movements, and of entirety of second movement, missing from autograph; standard version, not without stylistic problems, originates with first edition (André) and may be Johann André's own work. Sketch for slow movement (entitled 'Romance', 16 bars) survives

K.595
B♭ major
AMA XVI/4 (Piano Concerto no.27); NMA V:15/viii
Vienna, 5 Jan 1791 (*Verzeichnüss*)
Allegro; Larghetto; Allegro
fl, 2 ob, 2 bn, 2 hn, str
Perhaps begun as early as 1788 (Tyson, 1987). Premiered by Mozart on 4 Mar 1791. Disputed third-movement lead-in, omitted from NMA, has been proven authentic with rediscovery of its autograph (Rehm, 1986b). In NMA, first movement is 7 bars longer than in all other editions

String concertos

K.190 (166b, 186E)
Concertone in C major for 2 violins, with oboe and cello
AMA XII/1, no.9; NMA V:14/ii
Salzburg, 31 May 1774 (autograph)
Allegro spiritoso; Andantino grazioso; Tempo di Menuetto (Vivace)
2 ob, [bn ad lib], 2 hn, 2 tpt, str
Obscured date on autograph earlier erroneously read as '3 May 1773'. Leopold Mozart uses unusual title 'Concertone' to refer to works by Mysliveček. Like the symphonie concertante, its form is indistinguishable from that of a concerto. In addition to 2 solo vns, occasional solo passages in K.190 (e.g. second movement cadenza) for ob and vc. Nothing known about comp. or perf. of work during Mozart's lifetime, though he is known to have taken work with him on Mannheim–Paris journey of 1777–8

K.207
Violin Concerto no.1 in B♭ major (AMA)
AMA XII/1; NMA V:14/i
Salzburg, 14 Apr 1773 (NMA; traditional dating: 14 Apr 1775 (autograph), altered)
[Allegro moderato]; Adagio; Presto
2 ob, [bn ad lib], 2 hn, str

With revised dating, K.207 antedates Piano Concerto in D, K.175, and therefore seems to be Mozart's first surviving original concerto. (First of orchestral serenades to include vn concerto movements – the *Antretter* Serenade in D, K.185 (167a) – dates from Aug 1773, i.e., after K.207.) Mozart's vn concertos probably written in first instance for perf. by Salzburg violinists (e.g. Antonio Brunetti), not himself, but are known to have been played by Mozart as well. Rondo K.269 (261a) may be a replacement finale for this work

K.211
Violin Concerto no.2 in D major (AMA)
AMA XII/1; NMA V:14/i
Salzburg, 14 Jun 1775 (autograph, altered to 1780 and back to 1775)
[Allegro moderato]; [Andante]; Rondeau (Allegro)
2 ob, [bn ad lib], 2 hn, str

K.216
Violin Concerto no.3 in G major (AMA)
AMA XII/1; NMA V:14/i
Salzburg, 12 Sep 1775 (autograph, altered to 1780 and back to 1775)
Allegro; Adagio; Rondeau (Allegro)
2 ob (= 2 fl in second movement), [bn ad lib], 2 hn, str
Alternative version of solo vn in third movement (bars 269–71, 276–80, 285–8) originates in autograph

K.218
Violin Concerto no.4 in D major (AMA)
AMA XII/1; NMA V:14/i
Salzburg, Oct 1775 (autograph, altered to 1780 and back to 1775)
Allegro; Andante cantabile; Rondeau (Andante grazioso – Allegro ma non troppo, alternating)
2 ob, [bn ad lib], 2 hn, str
Believed to be the 'Strasbourger Concerto' (Mozart's subtitle, from his letters), though some scholars think K.216 is meant. A perf. by Brunetti in Oct 1777 reported by Leopold in the correspondence

K.219
Violin Concerto no.5 in A major (AMA)
AMA XII/1; NMA V:14/i
Salzburg, 20 Dec 1775 (autograph, altered to 1780 and back to 1775)
Allegro aperto; Adagio; Rondeau (Tempo di Menuetto)
2 ob, [bn ad lib], 2 hn, str
Turkish Concerto; Adagio K.261 may be a replacement middle movement for this work

K.261
Adagio in E major for violin
AMA XII/1, no.6; NMA V:14/i
Salzburg, 1776 (autograph)
2 fl, [bn ad lib], 2 hn, str
Possibly a replacement middle movement for K.219 (for Antonio Brunetti?)

K.269 (261a)
Rondo (Allegro) in B♭ major for violin
AMA XII/1, no.7; NMA V:14/i
Salzburg, ?1775–7
Rondeaux (Allegro)
2 ob, [bn ad lib], 2 hn, str
Dating from NMA, after Plath. Perhaps a replacement finale for K.207 (for Brunetti?). Cf. K.382

K.364 (320d)
Sinfonia Concertante in E♭ major for violin and viola
AMA XII/1, no.10; NMA V:14/ii
Salzburg, ?summer or early autumn 1779
Allegro maestoso; Andante; Presto
2 ob, [bn ad lib], 2 hn, str
Dating from NMA. As is case for Concertone (but not for vn concertos or any other non-keyboard concertos), cadenzas survive. Va part is scordatura, i.e. player directed to tune a semitone higher and play in D. Work may owe origin to Mozart's abandonment of a sinfonia concertante for vn, va (also scordatura, to be tuned a whole tone higher), vc and orchestra in A, K.Anh.104 (320e), presumed to have been undertaken at about same time (see 'Fragments and sketches'). Identity of original soloists unknown: possibly Brunetti and violinist Joseph Hafeneder (NMA). Surviving autograph material includes (besides a fair copy of first- and second-movement cadenzas): a frag. transmitting first version of bars 349–57 of first movement (in draft score), a sketch-like version of first-movement cadenza and 2 sketches for slow-movement cadenza

K.373
Rondo (Allegretto grazioso) in C major for violin
AMA XII/1, no.8; NMA V:14/i
Vienna, 2 Apr 1781 (autograph)
2 ob, [bn ad lib], 2 hn, str
Written for Brunetti and first perf. in Vienna by him 8 Apr 1781 during concert at residence of Prince Rudolph Joseph Colloredo (1706–88), father of Archbishop

Wind concertos

K.313 (285c)
Flute Concerto no.1 in G major (AMA)
AMA XII/2, no.13; NMA V:14/iii

Mannheim, ?Jan or Feb 1778

Allegro maestoso; Adagio ma non troppo; Rondo (Tempo di Menuetto)

2 ob (= 2 fl in second movement), [bn ad lib], 2 hn, str

Dating from NMA. Commissioned by Dutch amateur, Ferdinand Dejean, as was K.314 (285d). Dejean paid Mozart on 14 Feb 1778. Andante K.315 (285e) may be a replacement middle movement for this work

K.314 (285d)
Flute Concerto no.2 in D major (AMA)
AMA XII/2, no.14; NMA V:14/iii

This version: Mannheim, ?Jan or Feb 1778

Allegro aperto; Adagio ma non troppo; Rondeau (Allegro)

2 ob, [bn ad lib], 2 hn, str

Dating from NMA. A transcription of Oboe Concerto in C, K.271k (q.v.) undertaken for Dejean

K.315 (285e)
Andante in C major for flute
AMA XII/2, no.15; NMA V:14/iii

Mannheim, ?Jan or Feb 1778

2 ob, [bn ad lib], 2 hn, str

Dating (NMA) supported by Plath (1978). ?An independent work; or possibly a replacement middle movement for K.313 (285c)

K.299 (297c)
Concerto in C major for flute and harp
AMA XII/2, no.12; NMA V:14/vi

Paris, ?Apr 1778

Allegro; Andantino; Rondeau (Allegro)

2 ob, [bn ad lib], 2 hn, str

Dating from NMA. Comp. for Adrien-Louis Bonnières de Souastre, Comte (not Duc) de Guines, flautist and former French envoy to England, and his harpist daughter, to whom Mozart also gave comp. lessons. De Guines' flute included a tail-joint enabling him to play d♭' and c' (cf. first and last movements) – pitches not used by Mozart in his other flute works

K.271k (=314)
Oboe Concerto in C major
NMA V:14/iii

?Salzburg, spring or summer (1 Apr–22 Sep) 1777

Allegro aperto; Adagio non troppo; Rondo (Allegretto)

2 ob, [bn ad lib], 2 hn, str

Dating from Paumgartner (1950), NMA. Comp. for Giuseppe Ferlendis. According to Mozart's letters, played by Friedrich Ramm in Mannheim 5 times in 1778; transcribed that year as Flute Concerto in D, K.314 (285d). Elements of ob version, discovered Salzburg 1920, not free of suspicion regarding their authenticity (cf. NMA).

Sketch for first movement, bars 51ff. (9 bars), survives

K.622
Clarinet Concerto in A major
AMA XII/2, no.20; NMA V:14/iv

Vienna, ?early Oct 1791

Allegro; Adagio; Rondo (Allegro)

2 fl, 2 bn, 2 hn, str

Entered in *Verzeichnüss* without date. Mozart mentions orchestrating the Rondo in the letter to Constanze of 7 Oct 1791. Opening Allegro is revision of fragmentary basset-hn concerto movement in G, K.584b (621b) (199 bars; in draft score; ? continuation lost), probably written year or two before, and possibly even as early as 1787 (Tyson, 1987). Written for Stadler's basset-cl, whose range extends down to written *c* (sounding *A*), may be connected with Süssmayr's attempt at basset-cl concerto for Stadler, begun by Süssmayr during journey made to Prague with Mozart in Sep 1791 for perf. of *La clemenza di Tito*. No evidence that Mozart had anything to do with adaptation of solo part for standard cl. NMA prints work in reconstructed version for basset-cl made by the late Ernst Hess, followed by standard version and facsimile of basset-hn fragment

K.191 (186e)
Bassoon Concerto in B♭ major
AMA XII/2, no.11; NMA V:14/iii

Salzburg, 4 Jun 1774 (autograph according to André)

Allegro; Andante ma adagio; Rondo (Tempo di Menuetto)

2 ob, [bn ad lib], 2 hn, str

Mozart allegedly comp. 3 bn concertos and a bn sonata for Thaddäus Baron von Dürnitz – for whom Mozart definitely wrote Piano Sonata in D, K.284 (205b). However, it is presently thought that K.191 does not belong to this set of 3, nor have Dürnitz's concertos surfaced

K.412 + 514 (386b)
Horn Concerto no.1 in D major (AMA)
AMA XII/2, no.16; NMA V:14/v

?Vienna, 1791

[Allegro]; Rondò (Allegro)

2 ob, 2 bn, str

Originally thought to be Mozart's first concerto for horn, it is his last. Like K.417, 447 and 495, written for Joseph Leutgeb. Both movements were drafted; notes in solo hn below written g' (sounding a) removed in first movement when draft completed. Draft of finale, in which hn marked Adagio and contains running commentary of insults in Italian, left unfinished (i.e. with scoring incomplete) at Mozart's death. Also contains notes below g' that are removed from standard finale version, allegedly dated Good Friday 6 Apr 1797 (read as

'1787' in *Köchel 1*, hence the number K.514), but which is actually a completion by Süssmayr dated 6 Apr 1792 (Tyson, 1987). Süssmayr's text differs from Mozart's, changing str accompaniment, cutting passages, deleting low notes, and notably introducing solo passage quoting Lamentations of Jeremiah, normally sung as part of Good Friday service. It is also longer by 6 bars. The parts for obs and bns for first movement notated on separate leaves. Süssmayr misunderstood Mozart's intentions and omitted the bns in his completion.

K.417
Horn Concerto no.2 in E♭ major (AMA)
AMA XII/2, no.17; NMA V:14/v
Vienna, 27 May 1783 (autograph)
[Allegro]; Andante; [Rondo (Allegro)]
2 ob, [bn ad lib], 2 hn, str
Mozart's first horn concerto for Joseph Leutgeb. First page of autograph bears inscription 'Wolfgang Amadé Mozart has taken pity on Leutgeb, ass, ox, and fool, in Vienna on 27 May 1783.'

K.447
Horn Concerto no.3 in E♭ major (AMA)
AMA XII/2, no.18; NMA V:14/v
Vienna, ?1787
[Allegro]; Romance (Larghetto); Allegro
2 cl, 2 bn, str
Dating from Tyson, Plath, NMA. Mozart's third concerto for Leutgeb (second being K.495). Not in *Verzeichnüss* (hence *Köchel 1*'s early dating of 1783). A Romance for hn and str qt by Michael Haydn (1795, publ. 1802) whose hn part, essentially identical to second movement of K.447, is given a different accompaniment, would appear to be Haydn's reconstruction of the movement from a solo hn part. See Rasmussen (1966–7) and Plath (1971/2)

K.495
Horn Concerto no.4 in E♭ major (AMA)
AMA XII/2, no.19; NMA V:14/v
Vienna, 26 Jun 1786 (*Verzeichnüss*)
Allegro maestoso (*Verzeichnüss*: Allegro); Romance (Andante cantabile); Rondo (Allegro vivace)
2 ob, [bn ad lib], 2 hn, str
Mozart's second concerto for Leutgeb. Autograph (partially lost) notated in 4 different colours of ink. According to Franz Giegling (NMA), this is not merely a joke but a code that depicts refinements of dynamics and colouristic inflection. There are in fact 3 different versions of K.495, whose first-movement lengths are all different: 218 bars (the standard version, Contore delle Arti e d'Industria edition published Vienna, 1803); 175 bars (edition published André, 1802); and 229 bars (Prague copy, ?early 19th century) (see NMA)

K.Anh.9 (297b, Anh.C 14.01)
Sinfonia Concertante for oboe, clarinet, bassoon and horn
See 'Doubtful and spurious'

ROBERT LEVIN

Miscellaneous instrumental

THE PRINCIPAL WORKS in this section are those carrying the titles serenade, cassation, divertimento and march, works that with a few exceptions were composed for performance in Salzburg.

Between 1769 and 1779 Mozart composed nine large-scale works for orchestra with the title cassation or serenade. All were composed for performance in Salzburg during the summer months, usually in the open air, and were designed to accompany and celebrate a particular social event. A recurring festivity in the Salzburg calendar was the end of the university year in early August, when students of logic and natural science would celebrate their progression from the preliminary part of their course to the second stage. In some years the musical celebrations of the logicians and natural scientists were organized separately; in other years they seemed to have joined forces. An orchestra was organized and a *Finalmusik*, as it was termed, was chosen. For instance, in 1776 it was a symphony by Joseph Haydn plus a march provided by an unknown local composer, and in 1777 a new work by the Salzburg composer Joseph Hafeneder was commissioned. But the most popular composer of *Finalmusiken* at this time was Mozart, whose music was played in 1769, possibly 1772, 1773, 1774, 1775, possibly 1777 and 1779. The performing routine was as follows: the musicians assembled at dusk, marched to the sound of music to the Archbishop's summer residence in the Mirabell Palace, played their serenade, returned across the Salzach bridge to the Kollegienplatz (now Universitätsplatz) and performed their serenade for a second time in front of the assembled professors and students. Two entries in Nannerl Mozart's diary in August 1775 record the rehearsal and performance of that year's *Finalmusik*, K.204 (213a). '8th: rehearsal of my brother's *Finalmusik* composed for the logicians ... 9th: was the *Finalmusik*, it started from here at 8.30, at the Mirabell it lasted until 9.45, from there to the college it lasted until after 11.00.'

Mozart's orchestral serenades consist of anything up to seven or eight movements built around the essential framework of an opening sonata form movement, at least two minuets and a brisk finale. On the autograph scores Mozart (sometimes his father) termed this part 'serenata', but each work had also an associated march which was played as the small orchestra moved from one place to another and to signal the end of the entertainment. Most of the marches have survived, but since they were usually composed separately by Mozart, they were treated as independent works by Köchel and AMA, and are so listed here.

As Nannerl's diary suggests, serenade performances were relaxed occasions, probably with long pauses between movements. An indication of their leisurely ambience is the inclusion of several concertante movements, usually for violin but in a couple of serenades for a small group of soloists.

Carl Bär (1960/61) was the first person to draw attention to an aspect of the performing practice of the serenades. As was the custom, Mozart labelled the lowest part in the score 'basso', meaning simply the lowest part and not the name of a specific instrument. In the case of these serenades, Bär has convincingly shown that the string section of the orchestra consisted of first and second violins, violas and double basses with no cellos. The absence of a string eight-foot pitch is partly compensated by bassoons and, occasionally, horns, but, more positively, its weakness increased the already bright sound of D major, the key of every serenade and cassation except two. It is this 'serenade quartet', as Bär calls it, that occurs as the solo group in the 'Serenata Notturna' (K.239).

Apart from concertante movements, marches and large, multi-movement structures, the orchestral serenades reveal some further features not found regularly in the composer's symphonies. Slow introductions, absent in Mozart's symphonies before the *Linz*, are the norm and those in K.250 (248b) and K.320 anticipate the content of the following first movements. (K.320 is especially interesting in that the Adagio maestoso is quoted verbatim in the Allegro con spirito, written out in longer note values at the beginning of the recapitulation.) As a probable consequence of their duration, three serenades have slow introductions to their finales too, something that is not encountered in the mainstream of orchestral literature until Beethoven. Again, as a possible consequence of scale, the key schemes of a few serenades are very adventurous; the D major Serenade, K.185 (167a), incorporates two movements in F major, and the first minuet movement of K.250 (248b) is not in the expected tonic of D, but in G minor! Movements like the last mentioned and the D minor Andante in K.320 are rare, if for students of Mozart's total *oeuvre* noteworthy, departures from the general atmosphere of sophisticated geniality and flamboyance. A few of the serenades were later converted into four-movement symphonies by Mozart (see pp.256–7); the most familiar example is the *Haffner* Symphony, which together with a march, K.408/2 (385a) is all that remains of a second *Haffner* serenade by Mozart. None of the serenades was published in Mozart's lifetime.

A second group of works composed in Salzburg in the 1770s was entitled 'divertimento'. These are chamber works usually for mixed ensembles of string and wind instruments, most commonly being string quartet plus two horns, used in three divertimentos. Leopold Mozart's letter of 13 April 1778 to his son provides direct evidence of the normal soloistic performance of these works and, moreover, indicates that the *basso* part was played on the violone at sixteen-foot pitch; the work referred to is the Divertimento in B flat, K.287 (271H). '[Herr Kolb played the first violin,] I was playing the second violin, Kolb's pupil the viola, Cassel the violone [*Bass*], and the two watchmen who had often played it at Kolb's, the French horns.'

Like the serenades, these divertimentos are leisurely works in up to six movements, plus, usually, a march. The medium of quartet plus horns was a common one in the period, found in the music of Joseph Haydn, Michael Haydn and others; the horns are normally rested in the slow movements. Given the largely subordinate role of the horns, Mozart's works for this medium, therefore, are virtually quartets and together with the divertimentos K.136–138 (125a–c), actually written for quartet, provided Mozart with his only opportunity to write string chamber music in Salzburg. Chroniclers of Mozart's chamber music (and players too) have often ignored this corner of the composer's output. The Notturno, K.286 (269a), written probably in 1776–7, employs four of these sextet ensembles, each group echoing in turn the phrases of the first group.

As in the case of the serenades, each work was associated with a specific occasion, usually a name-day. K.247, for instance, was composed in June 1776 to celebrate the name-day of Countess Antonia Lodron; since her house was a frequent venue for private concerts the divertimento was perhaps played indoors, the players marching to their positions.

In Vienna in the 1780s, Mozart did not compose a single orchestral serenade and provided only a couple of works in the Salzburg divertimento tradition, partly because Vienna did not have the equivalent *Finalmusik* tradition and partly because, for social occasions such as name-days, the medium of the wind band (*Harmoniemusik*) was favoured. Two works only from the Vienna period involve strings; neither was entitled divertimento or serenade by Mozart. *Ein musikalischer Spass* (*A Musical Joke*) is scored for the familiar ensemble of quartet plus two horns; when it was first printed by André (1802) the vignette on the title-page showed an ensemble of six players with a violone, not a cello player. *Eine kleine Nachtmusik* was scored explicitly for two violins, viola, cello and double bass, and was undoubtedly conceived as chamber music.

K.32
Gallimathias musicum
AMA XXIV, no.12; NMA IV:12/i

The Hague, Mar 1766
Molto Allegro; Andante; Allegro; Pastorella;
Allegro; Allegretto; Allegro; Molto adagio;
Allegro; Largo; Allegro; Andante; Menuet;
Adagio; Presto; Fuga
hpd, 2 ob, 2 hn, 2 bn, str
Leopold Mozart in his catalogue of Wolfgang's
music called the work 'A quodlibet with the title
Gallimathias musicum'. Quodlibet and
gallimathias both mean a musical *mélange* using
pre-existing tunes. Comp. to celebrate installation
of Prince William V of Orange as heir to Dutch
throne (11 Mar). Quotes folk tunes, some of which
cannot be identified, and music by Salzburg court
composer Eberlin

Only draft autograph material for 16 (out of
17) numbers, in a mixture of Wolfgang's and
Leopold's hands (Plath, 1960/61), survives; the
missing no.16 (Presto) is transmitted in a copy of
the missing original parts. Mozart's original
attempt (92 bars) at final fugue is cancelled from
bars 45–86: copy of parts follows Leopold's
lengthier reworking. 5 numbers in the MS (NMA
nos 2a, 6a, 11a–c) are omitted from the parts
copy; first attempts at nos 5 and 8 also survive

K.62
March in D major
NMA IV:12/i
Salzburg, probably summer 1769
Maestoso
2 ob, 2 hn, 2 tpt, str
Probably for Serenade K.100/62a; quoted by
Mozart in letter to his sister from Bologna, 4 Aug
1770; used (with added timp part) in *Mitridate*,
K.87 (74a)

K.100 (62a)
Serenade in D major
AMA IX/1, no.3; NMA IV:12/i
Salzburg, probably summer 1769
Allegro; Andante; Menuetto; Allegro; Menuetto;
Andante; Menuetto; Allegro
2 ob/fl, 2 hn, 2 tpt, str
Perf. unknown; perhaps as *Finalmusik* on 6 or 8
Aug (see K.63 and K.99); more likely on
unknown occasion. See also preceding entry

K.63
Cassation in G major
AMA IX/1, no.1; NMA IV:12/i
Salzburg, 1769
Marche; Allegro; Andante; Menuet; Adagio;
Menuet; Finale (Allegro assai)
2 ob, 2 hn, str
Probably perf. as *Finalmusik* on 6 or 8 Aug

K.99 (63a)
Cassation in B♭ major
AMA IX/1, no.2; NMA IV:12/i

Salzburg, 1769
Marche; Allegro molto; Andante; Menuet;
Andante; Menuet; Allegro; Marche da capo
2 ob, 2 hn, str
Probably perf. as *Finalmusik* on 6 or 8 Aug

K.113
Divertimento in E♭ major
AMA IX/2, no.15; NMA IV:12/ii
Milan, Nov 1771
Allegro; Andante; Menuetto; Allegro
2 cl, 2 hn (or 2 ob, ?2 cl, 2 eng hn, 2 bn, 2 hn), 2
vn, va, b [?db or vc and db]
Exists in 2 versions. Version I: described on
autograph as 'Concerto ò sia Divertimento a 8'
(first title added later?), possibly perf. in concert
on 22 or 23 Nov 1771 in Milan. Version II: rev.
wind parts but role of cls unclear; probably dates
from early 1773

K.136–138 (125a–c)
3 divertimentos
AMA XIV, nos 24–26; NMA IV:12/vi
Salzburg, [early] 1772 (autograph)
'No.I' in D major: Allegro; Andante; Presto
'No.II' in B♭ major: Andante; Allegro di molto;
Allegro assai
'No.III' in F major: [Allegro;] Andante; [Presto]
2 vn, va, b [?vc]
Comp. as set and best regarded as soloistic music
(with vc rather than db) of an informal nature;
title 'Divertimento' used almost exclusively in this
sense by Mozarts after K.131 (mid-1772)
(Webster, 1983). Possibly the works are the qts
unsuccessfully offered by Leopold Mozart to
Breitkopf for publication (letter of 7 Feb 1772)

K.131
Divertimento in D major
AMA IX/2, no.16; NMA IV:12/ii
Salzburg, Jun 1772
[Allegro;] Adagio; Menuetto; Allegretto;
Menuetto; Adagio – Allegro molto – Allegro assai
fl, ob, bn, 4 hn, 2 vn, va, b [?db or vc and db]
'Divertimento' on autograph in an unknown
hand; perhaps the work is an orchestral serenade
and the 1772 *Finalmusik* rather than a chamber
work. 4 horns found also in contemporary
Symphony in E♭ (K.132)

K.205 (173a, 167A)
Divertimento in D major
AMA IX/2, no.21; NMA VII:18
Salzburg, Jul 1773?
Largo – Allegro; Menuetto; Adagio; Menuetto;
Finale (Presto)
2 hn, bn, vn, va, b (solo)
Autograph undated and the title 'Divertimento'
written in unknown hand. Purpose of comp.
unknown; ?possibly to celebrate name-day of

Maria Anna Elisabeth von Antretter (26 Jul
1773). See also following entry

K.290 (173b, 167AB)
March in D major
AMA X, no.7; NMA VII:18
?Salzburg, summer 1772
2 hn, vn, va, b
Traditionally associated with Divertimento K.205
(167A); handwriting suggests the earlier comp.
date; original purpose unknown

K.185 (167a)
Serenade in D major
AMA IX/1, no.5; NMA IV:12/ii
Vienna, Jul–Aug 1773
Allegro assai; Andante; Allegro; Menuetto;
Andante grazioso; Menuetto; Adagio – Allegro
assai
2 ob/fl, 2 hn, 2 tpt, vn solo, str
Comp. Vienna, probably as *Finalmusik* for students
of Salzburg University, one of whom was
probably Judas Thaddäus von Antretter, whose
family was friendly with Mozarts. See also
following entry

K.189 (167b)
March in D major
AMA X, no.1; NMA IV:12/ii
Vienna, Jul–Aug 1773
Andante
2 fl, 2 hn, 2 tpt, 2 vn, b
For Serenade K.185 (167a); formerly bound up
with its autograph

K.203 (189b)
Serenade in D major
AMA IX/1, no.6; NMA IV:12/iii
Salzburg, Aug 1774
Andante maestoso – Allegro assai; [Andante;]
Menuetto; [Allegro;] Menuetto; [Andante;]
Menuetto; Prestissimo
2 ob/fl, bn, 2 hn, 2 tpt, vn solo, str
Probably written as 1774 *Finalmusik* and not as
earlier thought for name-day of Archbishop
Colloredo. See also following entry

K.237 (189c)
March in D major
AMA X, no.4; NMA IV:12/iii
Salzburg, summer 1774
2 ob, 2 bn, 2 hn, 2 tpt, 2 vn, b
Traditional association of this march with
Serenade K.203 (189b) not contradicted by
handwriting and paper studies

K.204 (213a)
Serenade in D major
AMA IX/1, no.7; NMA IV:12/iii
Salzburg, 5 Aug 1774 (autograph)

Allegro assai; Andante moderato; Allegro;
Menuetto; [Andante;] Menuetto; Andantino
[grazioso] – Allegro
2 ob/fl, bn, 2 hn, 2 tpt, vn solo, str
A *Finalmusik* first perf. according to Nannerl's
diary on 9 Aug. In 1783 Mozart converted work
into 4-movement symphony (see p. 256). See also
following entry

K.215 (213b)
March in D major
AMA X, no.3; NMA IV:12/iii
Salzburg, Aug 1775 (autograph)
2 ob, 2 hn, 2 tpt, str
For Serenade K.204 (213a)

K.214
March in C major
AMA X, no.2; NMA IV:13/2
Salzburg, 20 Aug 1775 (autograph)
2 ob, 2 hn, 2 tpt, str
Circumstances of comp. unknown. Perhaps to
precede a serenade by another composer

K.239
Serenata Notturna
AMA IX/1, no.8; NMA IV:12/iii
Salzburg, Jan 1776 (autograph)
Marcia (Maestoso); Menuetto; Rondeau
(Allegretto)
2 vn, va, db (solo), str, timp
Title written in Leopold Mozart's hand.
Circumstances of comp. unknown; time of year
suggests an indoor occasion

K.247
Divertimento in F major
AMA IX/2, no.24; NMA VII:18
Salzburg, Jun 1776 (autograph)
Allegro; Andante grazioso; Menuetto; Adagio;
Menuetto; Andante – Allegro assai
2 hn, 2 vn, va, b (solo)
Written for name-day of Countess Antonia
Lodron, 13 Jun; she was wife of Salzburg
hereditary marshal (Erbmarschall) and their
house was a centre for music making in the town.
See also following entry. Fragmentary attempt at
opening Allegro (K.288/246c, 77 bars;
?continuation lost) survives

K.248
March in F major
AMA X, no.5; NMA VII:18
Salzburg, Jun 1776 (autograph)
2 hn, 2 vn, va, b
For Divertimento K.247

K.250 (248b)
Serenade in D major (*Haffner*)
AMA IX/1, no.9; NMA IV:12/iv

Salzburg, Jul 1776 (autograph)
Allegro maestoso; Andante; Menuetto; Rondeau (Allegro); Menuetto galante; Andante; Menuetto; Adagio – Allegro assai
2 ob/fl, 2 bn, 2 hn, 2 tpt, vn solo, str
Commissioned by Siegmund Haffner jr, whose father had been a respected Salzburg businessman and public figure, to celebrate marriage of one of his sisters, Marie Elisabeth (1753–84) to Franz Xaver Späth (1750–1808). The wedding took place on 22 Jul; serenade played previous evening. Perf. on many occasions in subsequent years, also in shortened version as symphony (see p. 256). Not to be confused with second, partially lost *Haffner* Serenade that formed basis of *Haffner* Symphony, K.385. See also following entry

K.249
March in D major
AMA X, no.6; NMA IV:12/iv
Salzburg, 20 Jul 1776 (autograph)
Maestoso
2 ob, 2 bn, 2 hn, 2 tpt, str
For Serenade K.250 (248b)

K.251
Divertimento in D major
AMA IX/2, no.25; NMA VII:18
Salzburg, Jul 1776 (autograph)
Molto allegro; Menuetto; Andantino; Menuetto; Rondeau (Allegro assai); Marcia alla Francese
ob, 2 hn, 2 vn, va, b (solo)
Probably written to celebrate Nannerl Mozart's name-day, 26 Jul. Possibly perf. orchestrally as *Finalmusik* in 1777 but no direct evidence for this

K.286 (269a)
Notturno in D major
AMA IX/1, no.10; NMA IV:12/v
Salzburg, probably Dec 1776–Jan 1777
Andante; Allegretto grazioso; Menuetto
4 ensembles, each consisting of 2 hn, 2 vn, va, b
Circumstances of comp. unknown. Trio of minuet added later (Wyzewa and Saint-Foix, 1912). Webster (1983) regards as speculative and improbable the notion that Mozart intended adding a finale and that what survives is a frag., as many Austrian works from this time exhibit a similar 3-movement form.

K.287 (271b, 271H)
Divertimento in B♭ major
AMA IX/2, no.29; NMA VII:18
Salzburg, probably Jun 1777
Allegro; Andante grazioso con Variazioni; Menuetto; Adagio; Menuetto; Andante – Allegro molto
2 hn, 2 vn, va, b
A Salzburg masterpiece, written for name-day of

Countess Lodron (13 Jun); first perf. 16 Jun. No associated march has survived. Folk melodies employed in variation movement and finale. Perf. in Munich, with Mozart leading, 4 Oct 1777

K.320
Serenade in D major (*Posthorn*)
AMA IX/1, no.11; NMA IV:12/v
Salzburg, 3 Aug 1779 (autograph)
Adagio maestoso – Allegro con spirito; Menuetto (Allegretto); Concertante (Andante grazioso); Rondeau (Allegro ma non troppo); Andantino; Menuetto; Finale (Presto)
2 fl/pic, 2 ob, 2 bn, 2 hn, posthorn, 2 tpt, timp, str
Finalmusik for 1779. Posthorn calls provide appropriate farewell to year, though nickname is not contemporary. For 2 marches traditionally associated with K.320 see following entry. In 1783, Concertante and Rondeau played as 'Concertant-Simphonie' in Mozart's concert at Burgtheater on 23 Mar (letter of 29 Mar 1783)

K.335 (320a)
2 marches in D major
AMA X, no.8; NMA IV:13/2
Salzburg, probably beginning of Aug 1779
No.1: 2 ob, 2 hn, 2 tpt, str
No.2: 2 fl, 2 hn, 2 tpt, str
Maestoso assai (No.2)
Both to be connected with Serenade K.320? Probably only one march per perf. played. No.1 quotes beginning of J.C. Bach's aria 'Non sò d'onde viene' from *Alessandro nell' Indie*; no.2 quotes, apparently, a folksong with the words 'lustig sein die schwobemedle' (see Plath in NMA)

K.334 (320b)
Divertimento in D major
AMA IX/2, no.31; NMA VII:18
Salzburg, 1779–80
Allegro; Tema con Variazioni (Andante); Menuetto; Adagio; Menuetto; Rondo (Allegro)
2hn, 2 vn, va, b (solo)
Probably written for a member of the Robinig family in Salzburg, with whom Mozarts friendly. In Jul 1780 Sigismund von Robinig (1760–1823) completed his final examinations at the Faculty of Jurisprudence in University; perhaps work associated with a private celebration (Bär, 1960). See also following entry

K.445 (320c)
March in D major
AMA X, no.21; NMA VII:18
Salzburg, probably summer 1780
2 hn, 2 vn, b
Probably for Divertimento K.334 (320b). Dating from handwriting

K.408/1 (383e/1,383e)
March in C major
AMA X, no.9; NMA IV:13/2
Probably Vienna, 1782
2 ob, 2 hn, 2 tpt, str
Later arranged by Mozart for kbd for Constanze
to play. See also following entry

K.408/3 (383e/3,383F)
March in C major
AMA X, no.9; NMA IV:13/2
?Vienna, 1782
2 fl, 2 bn, 2 hn, 2 tpt, timp. str
This march and preceding one are Mozart's only
known surviving marches associated with Vienna:
possibly intended for use in his own concerts

K.409 (383f)
Minuet in C major
AMA X, no.11; NMA IV:11/x
?Vienna, 1782
2 fl, 2 ob, 2 bn, 2 hn, 2 tpt, timp, str
Regarded by Einstein (*Köchel 3*) as later addition
for Symphony K.338; in view of style and size
(being most extensive of Mozart's symphonic
minuets) probably intended for independent use,
perhaps in one of Sunday Augarten concerts, first
involving Mozart taking place on 26 May 1782

K.408/2 (385a)
March in D major
AMA X, no.9; NMA IV:13/2
Vienna, probably beginning of Aug 1782
2 ob, 2 bn, 2 hn, 2 tpt, timp, str
Together with a minuet (now lost) and the 4
movements of *Haffner* Symphony (K. 385),
originally formed serenade perf. in Salzburg in
Aug 1782 to celebrate ennobling of Siegmund
Haffner (1756–87). Autograph shows signs of
pressure under which Mozart comp. work: only
first 8 bars of timp part entered in score

K.477 (479a)
Maurerische Trauermusik
AMA X, no.12; NMA IV:11/x
Vienna, Nov 1785
2 ob, cl, 3 basset-hn, dbn, 2 hn, str
Written for a Lodge of Sorrows (memorial service)
for Count Franz Esterházy von Galantha and
Duke Georg August von Mecklenburg-Strelitz.
Some of the large wind band was added at the last
minute. Mozart incorporates the plainchant *tonus
peregrinus*, with its reference to the Lamentation
chants used in Passion Week and the Miserere of
the Requiem ceremony. However, Autexier
(1984/5) has advanced the hypothesis that the
work was composed in three successive versions.
1. A local version for the initiation of a new mason
to the lodge 'Zur wahren Eintracht', 12 Aug 1785.
2. An instrumental version perf. 17 Nov at a

Lodge of Sorrows. 3. A fuller instrumental version
(forces above), probably perf. 9 Dec 1785

K.522
Ein musikalischer Spass
AMA X, no.13; NMA VII:18
Vienna, 14 Jun 1787 (*Verzeichnüss*)
Allegro; Menuetto (Maestoso); Adagio cantabile;
Presto
2 hn, 2 vn, va, b (solo)
Satire on inept composition and performance.
Clumsy fugue in finale based on exercise by
Mozart's pupil Thomas Attwood (Heartz, 1973/
4). Tyson (1987) has shown that Mozart probably
began to write out parts for first movement before
end 1785, completing all parts for this movement,
presumably with perf. in view, at latest before end
1786; other movements completed 1787.
Fragmentary attempt at finale (K.Anh.108/522a
Allegretto, 24 bars; in draft score) survives

K.525
Eine kleine Nachtmusik
AMA XIII, no.9; NMA IV:12/vi
Vienna, 10 Aug 1787 (*Verzeichnüss*)
Allegro; Romance (Andante); Menuetto
(Allegretto); Rondo (Allegro)
2 vn, va, vc, db (solo)
Circumstances of comp. unknown. Mozart's
catalogue indicates that autograph originally had
5 movements; additional minuet and trio formed
second movement. Fragmentary attempt at slow
movement (K.Anh.69/525a, Larghetto, 16 bars; in
draft score) survives

K.546
Adagio and Fugue in C minor
AMA XIV, no.27; NMA IV:11/x
Vienna, 26 Jun 1788 (*Verzeichnüss*)
Adagio; [Fuga (Allegro)]
Fugue had been written for kbd duet in 1783 (see
K.426). For this version for str orchestra (purpose
of which unknown) Mozart added what he called
in his catalogue 'A short Adagio'. Work is part of
a broad Viennese tradition of church sonatas in 2
movements

DAVID WYN JONES

Dance and ballet

MOZART COMPOSED DANCE MUSIC throughout his life.
His first surviving dances, a set of minuets composed
in Salzburg, date from 1769; between that date and
1791 he composed over thirty sets of dances, as well
as a number of independent works, around 200
single dances in all, for Prague and Vienna, as well as
Salzburg. Mozart was an enthusiastic and accomplished dancer himself and there are several refer-

ences that affirm this. An entry in the diary of Johann Ferdinand von Schiedenhofen, a close friend of the Mozart family in Salzburg, reads '18 February [1776]. At 7 in the evening to the Marshal of the Household, where I supped. Then with company to the redout, driving there with the Chief Equerry as a lady, the Marshal as a cavalier . . . Baron Lilien's companion as a hairdresser, the elder Mozart as a porter and the son as the hairdresser's boy [*Friseurbub*], Count Überacker as a moor and myself as a lackey . . . apart from that there was a remarkable company of gods amongst the masqueraders. . . . About 420 persons were present today. I stayed until 4 a.m.' In the memoirs of the Irish tenor Michael Kelly, who had taken the roles of Don Basilio and Don Curzio in the first performance of *Le nozze di Figaro* in Vienna in 1786, there is a passage describing the presence of Kelly and Mozart at a supper party in Leopold Koželuch's house: 'After supper the young branches of our host had a dance, and Mozart joined them. Madame Mozart told me that great as his genius was, he was an enthusiast in dancing, and often said that his taste lay in that art rather than in music.'

In Vienna in the 1780s Mozart's enthusiasm for dancing coincided with a general upsurge in the popularity of the pastime, the beginning of the long association of that city with dancing. Dancing took place in inns, parks and dance halls but the highpoint of the year was the series of Carnival balls held under the auspices of the court in the Redoutensaal (actually two rooms, one large, one small) during Lent. Carnival lasted from Epiphany to the eve of Ash Wednesday (Fastnacht) and the masked ball formed a particular attraction in this concentrated period of revelry and entertainment. As a direct result of the liberal outlook of Joseph II, the dances were open to all ranks of society, who could mingle freely knowing that their identities and personalities were hidden by masks and sometimes very elaborate costumes. As *Kammermusicus* in the court from December 1787, Mozart's only duty was the composition of music for these Carnival dances. Until his death he spent most of December and January every year composing minuets, German dances and contredanses for the succeeding season. There is evidence of two distinct stages in the composition process. First, the dances were composed for string trio (and sometimes performed and even sold) and then orchestrated as needed. The result is some of the most infectiously joyous and charming dance music in the history of music; but Mozart's alleged remark on receiving payment for the task was a bitter one: 'Too much for what I do; too little for what I could do.' (This remark was first recorded in the *Allgemeine musikalische Zeitung* of 6 February 1799 in a collection of anecdotes about her husband supplied by Constanze Mozart.) In addition to his fee from the court, Mozart also received income from manuscript and printed sales of the dances. The publisher Artaria sold the dances in keyboard arrangement normally, while the full orchestral parts as well as arrangements for keyboard and for string trio could be purchased in manuscript form.

The string trio of two violins and a bass represented the basic dance band of the time and Mozart's earliest surviving dances, K.65a (61b), are scored for this combination. Later dances by Mozart are more fully scored with ample wind parts, but the string section remained a three-part one without violas, a tradition carried on by Beethoven when he wrote his Carnival dances in the 1790s. The dances that Mozart composed as imperial *Kammermusicus* are vividly scored, drawing from a full complement of piccolo, flutes, oboes, clarinets, bassoons, horns, trumpets, timpani and three-part strings. Within each group of dances each successive dance is differently scored, much of their charm being derived from this rich exploitation of differing tone colours. *Tutti* scoring with trumpets and timpani provide climactic moments within the sequence, while the piccolo provides a characteristic glint to many movements. (These piccolo parts were played by a flageolet and not the more modern, transverse piccolo.) Some of the trio sections feature more exotic instruments: the hurdy-gurdy in K.601, no.2 and K.602, no.3 and the two posthorns and five sleighbells in K.605, no.3 to evoke a sleighride. Occasionally, the dances include references to topical events, artistic and political. When Mozart was in Prague he attended one of the regular Thursday dances organized by the lawyer and university professor Johann Freiherr von Bretfeld, remarking that 'people flew about in sheer delight to the music of my *Figaro*, arranged for quadrilles and waltzes'. He himself wrote a contredanse based on Figaro's 'Non più andrai', one of a set of five contredanses, K.609, that probably dates from 1787–8. Two dances were associated with events in Austria's campaign against the Turks in 1788–91: *La bataille* (K.535) and *Der Sieg vom Helden Coburg* (K.587).

Mozart composed three main forms of dance: the minuet, the German dance and the contredanse. For nearly two hundred years the minuet had been the favourite dance of aristocratic society. In Mozart's time it was still a rather formal dance; the grace of the dancing couple weaving the characteristic S pattern was to be as much admired by onlookers as enjoyed by participants. Its social status as the traditional, polite dance of the aristocracy is clearly conveyed in the opera *Don Giovanni*, where it is danced in Act I by Don Ottavio and Donna Anna (both wearing masks). The durability of the minuet through the ages was due very much to its ability to incorporate steps from other dances and in Mozart's Viennese dances there is sometimes very little to distinguish a minuet from a German dance.

Essentially, the German dance was a much more vigorous dance for couples. Originally of folk origin it involved hopping, stamping, fast circular motion and much closer physical contact than the minuet. It was a comparatively new dance and Mozart's first examples were not composed until 1787, for Prague, but amongst the later dances for Vienna it is by far the most common, forty-nine examples as opposed to thirty-six minuets and many fewer contredanses. The appeal of the new dance in Vienna reflects the wider cross-section of society that attended the Imperial and Royal dances as a result of Joseph II's shrewd loosening of class structure in the 1780s. Once again, it is reflected in the party scene in *Don Giovanni*, where the German dance is danced by Don Giovanni, an aristocrat, and Zerlina, a peasant. A further indication of the informal nature of the German dance in comparison with the minuet is that it is the German dance that most readily features unusual instruments and extra-musical references.

Like the minuet, the contredanse is an old dance, the name being derived from the English 'country dance' which, when translated into 17th-century Franglais, emerged as contredanse. The dance was usually in duple time, notated variously as alla breve, 6/8 and 2/4; all three time signatures are found in Mozart's examples, but 2/4 is by far the most common and all the Viennese contredanses except one are so notated. The dance, for an ensemble rather than for a couple, had maintained its popularity with the lower classes while at the same time it allowed polite society to affect rusticity. In the Vienna of Mozart and Joseph II the meeting of classes in the contredanse was a more real one. As a dance in duple time it provided contrast with the triple time of the minuet and German dance.

Mozart's extensive contribution to dance music and his own enthusiasm for the pastime are a valuable reminder of the extent to which his music in general is permeated with the spirit of the dance; in particular, minuet movements in the composer's instrumental music make maximum impact when appreciated against this pervasive background. To take Mozart's last three symphonies, the minuet of the Symphony in E flat is clearly a German dance, that of the *Jupiter* a true minuet, while the finale of the E flat symphony is in the spirit of a contredanse. But what did audiences – and players too – make of the irregular phrases, syncopation, concentrated thematic material, counterpoint and unremitting minor key of the 'Menuetto' of the G minor symphony?

In comparison with dance music, ballet music forms only a minor part of Mozart's output, the most significant extant scores being *Les Petit Riens* and the ballet for the opera *Idomeneo*, the first of which is only partly by Mozart. Ballet in the middle of the 18th century was almost invariably associated with opera performances and particularly identified with French taste. Often it was a separate, additional entertainment during an operatic evening, featuring a series of danced movements that displayed individual and corporate skills, usually in a pastoral setting, but with little or no plot; it was exceptional for the composer of the ballet and the opera to be the same.

The ballet, *Les Petits Riens*, was all that eventuated from a plan by Mozart to compose an opera in the French language in Paris in 1778; the opera was to be called *Alexandre et Roxane* and the accompanying ballet was probably to be choreographed by the famous Jean-Georges Noverre. The opera never got beyond the planning stage and the only theatrical project to emerge from the Paris journey was the comparatively lowly one of composing some ballet music, again choreographed by Noverre, to follow performances of Piccinni's *Le finte gemelle*. Approximately one third of the ballet was by another composer (or perhaps composers), still unidentified.

Two years later, in December 1780, Mozart was in Munich preparing for the first performance in the following Carnival season of his opera *Idomeneo*. He was asked to compose the customary ballet as well, a task which he accepted readily, 'for now', as he wrote to his father on 30 December 1780, 'all the music will be by the same composer'. There is no plot in Mozart's completed movements and it is unclear at what point in the evening the *divertissement*, as the composer called it (an indication of the French influence), took place; it is likely to have varied in this respect, as well as in the number of movements, from one performance to the next.

(* = without trio)

K.65a (61b)
7 minuets
AMA XXIV, no.13; NMA IV:13/1/i
Salzburg, 26 Jan 1769
no.1 in G, no.2 in D, no.3 in A, no.4 in F, no.5 in C, no.6 in G, no.7 in D
2vn, b
Probably comp. for Carnival dances in Salzburg

K.103 (61d)
19 minuets
NMA IV:13/1/i
Salzburg, spring–summer 1772
No.1 in C, no.2 in G, no.3 in D, no.4 in F, no.5 in C, no.6 in A*, no.7 in D, no.8 in F, no.9 in C, no.10 in G, no.11 in F, no.12 in C, no.13 in G, no.14 in B♭, no.15 in E♭, no.16 in E*, no.17 in A*, no.18 in D, no.19 in G
2 ob/fl, 2 hn/tpt, 2 vn, b
Plath's study of Mozart's handwriting suggests given date rather than 1769 as previously thought. Originally 20 minuets (as indicated by NMA, which also has alternative key sequence); later recast as 12

K.104 (61e)
6 minuets
NMA IV:13/1/i
Probably autumn 1770
no.1 in C, no.2 in F, no.3 in C, no.4 in A, no.5 in G, no.6 in G
pic, 2 ob, 2 hn/tpt, 2 vn, b
Date from Plath's study of the handwriting. Nos 1 and 2 based on Michael Haydn's minuets P.79, nos 1, 3 (see Senn, 1964). During the summer Nannerl had sent many minuets of M. Haydn to Mozart in Italy so that he could prepare kbd arrangements

K.61g
2 minuets
NMA IV:13/1/i
Early 1770
no.1 in A*, no.2 in C
2 fl, str
No.1 is scored for 2 fl and str (including va) and is perhaps doubtful; the second survives in a kbd version only; it uses the same trio as K.104 (61e) no.3

K.123 (73g)
Contredanse in B♭
AMA XI, no.14; NMA IV:13/1/i
Rome, on or before 14 Apr 1770
2 ob, 2 hn, 2 vn, b
Sent from Rome to Salzburg by Leopold Mozart with an accompanying letter (14 Apr 1770) containing some suggestions from Mozart as to how it should be danced.

K.122 (73t)
Minuet in E♭*
AMA XXIV, no.13a; NMA IV:13/1/i
?Bologna, 24–27/28 Mar 1770
2 ob, 2 hn, 2 vn, b
Authenticity has been questioned and the suggestion made that it is based on music by Florian Johann Deller or Joseph Starzer (Senn, 1961a)

K.Anh.207 (Anh.C 27.06)
[Ballet music for *Ascanio in Alba*]
NMA IX: 27/ii
?Milan, late 1771
According to Plath (1965), K.Anh.207 (Anh.C 27.06) probably final version of ballet music, arranged (by Mozart?) for pf; 9 nos. Of probable first version, only bass part (copy) survives

K.Anh.109 (135a)
Le gelosie del serraglio
See *Lucio Silla*, K.135 ('Operas')

K.164 (130a)
6 minuets
AMA XXIV, nos 14a, 57; NMA IV:13/1/i
Salzburg, Jun 1772 (autograph)
nos 1–3 in D, nos 4–6 in G
fl, 2 ob, 2 hn/tpt, 2 vn, b
Autograph of nos 3 and 4 once owned by Clara Schumann, then Brahms

K.176
16 minuets
NMA IV/13/1/i
Salzburg, Dec 1773 (autograph)
no.1 in C, no.2 in G, no.3 in E♭*, no.4 in B♭*, no.5 in F, no.6 in D, no.7 in A*, no.8 in C, no.9 in G, no.10 in B♭*, no.11 in F, no.12 in D, no.13 in G, no.14 in C, no.15 in F, no.16 in D
2 ob/fl, bn, 2 hn/tpt, 2 vn, b
Probably for 1774 Carnival dances in Salzburg

K.101 (250a)
4 contredanses
AMA IX, no.4; NMA IV:13/1/i
Salzburg, ?1776
no.1 in F [Gavotte], no.2 in G (Andantino), no.3 in D [Presto], no.4 in F [Gavotte]
2 ob/fl, bn, 2 hn, 2 vn, b
Undated autograph carries also title *Ständchen* in Leopold Mozart's hand. Proposed date confirmed by handwriting and supported by watermark. In autograph score, first vn part, from third quarter of no.1 onwards, written out by Leopold

K.267 (271c)
4 contredanses
AMA XI, no.15; NMA IV:13/1/i
Salzburg, early 1777
no.1 in G, no.2 in E♭, no.3 in A, no.4 in D
2 ob/fl, bn, 2 hn, 2 vn, b
Probably for 1777 Carnival dances in Salzburg

K.Anh.10 (299b)
Ballet music: *Les Petits Riens*
AMA XXIV, no.10a; NMA II:6/ii
Paris, May–Jun 1778
Overture, no.1, no.2, no.3, no.4, no.5 (Agité), no.6 (Menuet), no.7 (Largo), no.8 (Vivo), no.9 (Andantino), no.10 (Allegro), no.11 (Larghetto), no.12 (Gavotte), no.13 (Adagio), no.14, no.15 (Gavotte gracieuse), no.16 (Pantomime), no.17 (Passepied), no.18 (Gavotte), no.19 (Andante), no.20 (Gigue)
2 fl, 2 ob, 2 cl, 2 bn, 2 hn, 2 tpt, timp, str
First perf. 11 Jun 1778, Opéra, Paris. 'New ballet' by Noverre for which Mozart was going to supply music (letter of 14 May 1778) was probably *Les Petits Riens*: originally given Vienna 1768 with music, according to Deutsch (1961b), probably by Franz Asplmayr. Mozart stated (letter of 9 Jul) that he composed 12 items, including overture.

Only copyist's score survives (discovered 1872); does not identify composers. Authorship of individual numbers can be ventured only on basis of style. Editor of NMA volume (Harald Heckmann) proposes following. Mozart: overture, nos 9–12, 15, 16, 18. Not Mozart: nos 1–3, 6, 19, 20. Not Mozart?: nos 4, 5, 7, 8, 13, 14, 17. *Köchel* 6, however, follows AMA in regarding only nos 1–6, 20 as unauthentic

K.300
Gavotte in B♭
NMA II:6/ii
Probably Paris, 1778
2 ob, 2 bn, 2 hn, str
Possibly a discarded movement from *Les Petits Riens*. See Chasse in A, K.Anh.103 (320f, 299d) ('Fragments and sketches')

K.363
3 minuets
AMA XXIV, no.14; NMA IV:13/1/ii
?Salzburg, summer 1783
no.1 in D*, no.2 in B♭*, no.3 in D*
2 ob, 2 bn, 2 hn, 2 tpt, timp, 2 vn, b
On evidence of handwriting Plath thinks traditional hypothetical date of summer 1780 too early. On basis of watermarks Tyson (1987) suggests time of Mozart's 1783 Salzburg visit (end July–end Oct)

K.367
Ballet music for *Idomeneo*
AMA V, no.14; NMA II:6/ii
Jan 1781
Chaconne [Allegro] – Larghetto – [Allegro]; Pas seul de Mr Le Grand (Largo – Allegretto – Più Allegro); Passepied pour Mad. selle Redwen; Gavotte; Passacaille
2 fl, 2 ob, 2 cl, 2 bn, 2 hn, 2 tpt, timp, str
Which numbers were originally employed, and in what order and position, cannot now with certainty be ascertained. Daniel Heartz, editor for NMA of opera, suggests that last 3 dances probably deleted before premiere (revision of Passacaille incomplete); Chaconne and Pas seul no doubt perf. at end of opera. Choreographer was Le Grand, ballet master at Munich court. Numerous deleted passages in autograph

K.409 (383f)
Minuet in C
See 'Miscellaneous instrumental'

K.446 (416d)
[Music for a pantomime]
AMA XXIV, no.18; NMA II:6/ii
Vienna, Feb 1783
str
Perf. Vienna, Hofburg, 3 Mar 1783. Only

incomplete first-vn part (in 2 versions) for 15 nos survives; other str parts, as well as introduction and rest of music today unknown. Mentioned by Mozart in letters of 15 Feb and 12 Mar 1783

K.461 (448a)
6 minuets
AMA XI, no.16; NMA IV:13/1/ii
Vienna, 1784 (autograph)
no.1 in C, no.2 in E♭, no.3 in G, no.4 in B♭, no.5 in F, no.6 in D*
2 ob/fl, 2 bn, 2 hn, 2 vn, b
Not entered in *Verzeichnüss*; therefore probably before 9 Feb 1784? No.6 survives incomplete. For unknown Carnival dances in Vienna? Sketch for no.6 (8 bars) survives

K.462 (448b)
6 contredanses
AMA XI, no.17; NMA IV:13/1/ii
?Salzburg, summer 1783
no.1 in C, no.2 in E♭, no.3 in B♭, no.4 in D, no.5 in B♭, no.6 in F
2 ob, 2 hn, 2 vn, b
Autograph is dated 1784 in unknown hand, but since that of K.463 (448c) contains citation of melody of K.462 (448b), no.5, both sets probably closely linked in time (Tyson, 1987). Wind parts added later. No.3 published with K.534, K.535, K.535a in kbd version by Artaria (Vienna, 1789)

K.463 (448c)
2 minuets
AMA XI, no.18; NMA IV:13/1/ii
?Salzburg, summer 1783
no.1 in F*, no.2 in B♭*
2 ob, bn, 2 hn, 2 vn, b
Tyson (1987) suggests possible that work at least begun on this set in Salzburg: Minuet 2 and Contredanse 2 written on Salzburg paper; Minuet 1 and its Contredanse on a Viennese paper. Trio section of each minuet is a contredanse and longer than enclosing minuet

K.509
6 German dances
AMA XI, no.6; NMA IV:13/1/ii
Prague, 6 Feb 1787 (*Verzeichnüss*)
no.1 in D, no.2 in G, no.3 in E♭, no.4 in F, no.5 in A, no.6 in C
pic, 2 fl, 2 ob, 2 cl, 2 bn, 2 hn, 2 tpt, timp, 2 vn, b
Written in Prague for a Carnival dance, probably at the palace of Count Johann Pachta. Every dance followed by a linking passage to next. Mozart wrote on autograph: 'Each German dance has its Trio, or rather Alternativo; after the Alternativo the German dance is to be repeated, then the Alternativo again, then the lead in [Eingang] to the following German dance'. Autograph kbd version thought to be slightly earlier

K.534
Contredanse in D
AMA XXIV, no.27; NMA IV:13/1/ii
Vienna, 14 Jan 1788 (*Verzeichnüss*)
pic, 2 ob, 2 hn, side drum, 2 vn, b
Instrumentation from *Verzeichnüss*. Orchestral
version printed for first time in NMA, but minus
pic and side drum parts, which seem to be missing
from new source. This source entitles dance *La
Tempesta*; *Verzeichnüss* has the German *Das
Donnerwetter*; one of two surviving kbd versions,
published by Artaria in 1789, calls it *La Tempeté*

K.535
Contredanse in C
AMA XI, no.20; NMA IV:13/1/ii
Vienna, 23 Jan 1788 (*Verzeichnüss*)
pic, 2 cl, bn, tpt, side drum, 2 vn, b
For Redoutensaal. Called *La Bataille* in autograph
and *die Batallie* in *Verzeichnüss*, where
instrumentation is different. A kbd version
advertised in *Wiener Zeitung* on 19 Mar 1788,
entitled *Die Belagerung Belgrads*, a reference to siege
of Belgrade by Austrian troops following official
declaration of war against Turks on 9 Feb; siege
not to end until 8 Oct 1789. See K.462 (448b)

K.535a
3 contredanses
Vienna, ?early 1788
no.1 in C, no.2 in G, no.3 in G
Survive in kbd version only. Not entered in
Verzeichnüss, so orchestration not known. See
K.462 (448b). Considered doubtful on grounds of
source and style (NMA)

K.536
6 German dances
AMA XI, no.7; NMA IV:13/1/ii
Vienna, 27 Jan 1788 (*Verzeichnüss*)
no.1 in C, no.2 in G, no.3 in B♭, no.4 in D, no.5
in F, no.6 in F
pic, 2 fl, 2 ob/cl, 2 bn, 2 hn/tpt, timp, 2 vn, b
For Redoutensaal. Mozart's first German dances
as *Kammermusicus*. Published together with K.567
by Artaria (Vienna, 1789). This publication,
together with an annotation on the surviving
autograph frag. of K.536, no.6 and all secondary
sources, suggests that K.536 and K.567 originally
formed a cycle of 12 dances: K.536 nos 1–5, K.567
nos 1–5, K.536 no.6, K.567 no.6

K.567
6 German dances
AMA XI, no.8; NMA IV:13/1/ii
Vienna, 6 Dec 1788 (*Verzeichnüss*)
no.1 in B♭, no.2 in E♭, no.3 in G, no.4 in D, no.5
in A, no.6 in C
pic, 2 fl, 2 ob/cl, 2 bn, 2 hn, 2 tpt, timp, 2 vn, b
For Redoutensaal. See K.536

K.568
12 minuets
AMA XI, no.1; NMA IV:13/1/ii
Vienna, 24 Dec 1788 (*Verzeichnüss*)
no.1 in C, no.2 in F, no.3 in B♭, no.4 in E♭, no.5
in G, no.6 in D, no.7 in A, no.8 in F, no.9 in B♭,
no.10 in D, no.11 in G, no.12 in C
2 fl/pic, 2 ob/cl, 2 bn, 2 hn, 2 tpt, timp, 2 vn, b
Mozart's first minuets as *Kammermusicus*. Published
by Artaria (Vienna, 1789)

K.571
6 German dances
AMA XI, no.9; NMA IV:13/1/ii
Vienna, 21 Feb 1789 (*Verzeichnüss*)
no.1 in D, no.2 in A, no.3 in C, no.4 in G, no.5 in
B♭, no.6 in D
2 fl/pic, 2 ob/cl, 2 bn, 2 hn/tpt, timp, perc, 2 vn, b
For Redoutensaal. Comp. in str trio format
perhaps as early as 1787 (Tyson, 1987). 'Turkish
music' (characterized by percussion and pic) adds
piquancy in Trio of no.6 and in coda. Austria's
campaign against Turks lasted from 1788 to 1791

K.585
12 minuets
AMA XI, no.2; NMA IV:13/1/ii
Vienna, Dec 1789 (*Verzeichnüss*)
no.1 in D, no.2 in F, no.3 in B♭, no.4 in E♭, no.5
in G, no.6 in C, no.7 in A, no.8 in F, no.9 in B♭,
no.10 in E♭, no.11 in G, no.12 in D
2 fl/pic, 2 ob/cl, 2 bn, 2 hn, 2 tpt, timp, 2 vn, b
For Redoutensaal. Paper-studies suggest that
minuets 1–4 in str trio format probably comp.
earlier, in *c.* 1788 (Tyson, 1987). Published in kbd
version by Artaria (Vienna, 1791)

K.586
12 German dances
AMA XI, no.10; NMA IV:13/1/ii
Vienna, Dec 1789 (*Verzeichnüss*)
no.1 in C, no.2 in G, no.3 in B♭, no.4 in F, no.5 in
A, no.6 in D, no.7 in G, no.8 in E♭, no.9 in B♭,
no.10 in F, no.11 in A, no.12 in C
pic, 2 fl, 2 ob/cl, 2 bn, 2 hn, 2 tpt, timp, perc, 2
vn, b
For Redoutensaal. Published in kbd version by
Artaria (Vienna, 1791)

K.587
Contredanse in C
AMA XI, no.21; NMA IV:13/1/ii
Vienna, Dec 1789 (*Verzeichnüss*)
fl, ob, bn, tpt, 2 vn, b
For Redoutensaal. Called *Der Sieg vom Helden
Coburg* in *Verzeichnüss*. Quotes warsong about
triumphs of General Friedrich Josias von Coburg-
Saalfeld (1737–1815). Under his leadership
Austrian troops had won a succession of victories
over Turks in summer and autumn of 1789,
culminating in occupation of Bucharest

K.106 (588a)
3 contredanses
AMA XXIV, no.15
?Jan 1790
No.1 in D, no.2 in A, no.3 in B♭
2 ob, 2 bn, 2 hn, 2 vn, b
Not in *Verzeichnüss*. Preceded by an *Ouverture* of 34
bars. Perhaps not comp. for Redoutensaal.
Speculative dating is that of *Köchel 6*. Considered
doubtful on grounds of source and style (NMA)

K.599
6 minuets
AMA XI, no.3; NMA IV:13/1/ii
Vienna, 23 Jan 1791 (*Verzeichnüss*)
no.1 in C, no.2 in G, no.3 in E♭, no.4 in B♭, no.5
in F, no.6 in D
2 fl/pic, 2 ob/cl, 2 bn, 2 hn, 2 tpt, timp, 2 vn, b
For Redoutensaal. Together with K.601 and
K.604 gathered together to form a cycle of 12
dances. Published in kbd and str trio versions with
K.601 and K.604 by Artaria (Vienna, 1791)

K.600
6 German dances
AMA XI, no.11; NMA IV:13/1/ii
Vienna, 29 Jan 1791 (*Verzeichnüss*)
no.1 in C, no.2 in F, no.3 in B♭, no.4 in E♭, no.5
in G, no.6 in D
pic, 2 fl, 2 ob/cl, 2 bn, 2 hn, 2 tpt, timp, 2 vn, b
For Redoutensaal. Trio of no.5 called *Der
Kanarienvogel* (*The Canary*), a popular Viennese pet
– Mozart owned one – and perhaps too a
reference to a Carnival costume. Published in kbd
and str trio versions by Artaria (Vienna, 1791).
Also transmitted as a cycle of 13 dances with
K.602 and K.605

K.601
4 minuets
AMA XI, no.4; NMA IV:13/1/ii
Vienna, 5 Feb 1791 (*Verzeichnüss*)
no.1 in A, no.2 in C, no.3 in G, no.4 in D
2 fl/pic, hurdy-gurdy, 2 ob/cl, 2 bn, 2 hn, 2 tpt, 2
vn, b
For Redoutensaal. See K.599

K.602
4 German dances
AMA XI, no.12; NMA:13/1/ii
Vienna, 5 Feb 1791 (*Verzeichnüss*)
no.1 in B♭, no.2 in F, no.3 in C, no.4 in A
2 fl/pic, 2 ob/cl, 2 bn, 2 hn, 2 tpt, timp, hurdy-
gurdy, 2 vn, b
For Redoutensaal. No.3 called *Die Leyerer* in
Verzeichnüss. For no.3, see also K.611. See K.600

K.603
2 contredanses
AMA XI, no.22; NMA IV:13/1/ii

Vienna, 5 Feb 1791 (*Verzeichnüss*)
no.1 in D, no.2 in B♭
pic, 2 ob, 2 bn, 2 hn, 2 tpt, timp, 2 vn, b
For Redoutensaal

K.604
2 minuets
AMA XI, no.5; NMA IV:13/1/ii
Vienna, 12 Feb 1791 (*Verzeichnüss*)
no.1 in B♭, no.2 in E♭
2 fl, 2 cl, 2 bn, 2 tpt, timp, 2 vn, b
For Redoutensaal. See K.599

K.605
3 German dances
AMA XI, no.13; NMA IV:13/1/ii
Vienna, 12 Feb 1791 (*Verzeichnüss*)
no.1 in D, no.2 in G, no.3 in C
2 fl/pic, 2 ob, 2 bn, 2 hn/tpt, 2 posthorns, timp, 5
sleighbells, 2 vn, b
For Redoutensaal. Trio of no.3 called *Die
Schlittenfahrt* (*The Sleighride*). Only nos 1 and 2 in
Verzeichnüss; perhaps no.3 and coda completed to
end cycle of 13 dances. See K.600

K.607 (605a)
Contredanse in E♭
AMA XXIV, no.17; NMA IV:13/1/ii
Vienna, 28 Feb (*Verzeichnüss*)
fl, ob, bn, 2 hn, 2 vn, b
For Redoutensaal. In *Verzeichnüss* Mozart called
the dance *Il Trionfo delle Donne*; quotes theme from
Anfossi's opera of that name which had received
10 perfs at Burgtheater between May 1786 and
Jan 1787. Currently lost autograph breaks off
after 53 fully-scored bars: ? continuation lost

K.606
6 German dances
AMA XXIV, no.16; NMA IV:13/1/ii
Vienna, 28 Feb 1791 (*Verzeichnüss*)
nos 1–6 in B♭
2vn, b
In *Verzeichnüss* Mozart called them *Landlerische*
[*sic*]. Wind parts of fl, ob, bn, and 2 hn (as in
K.607) not extant

K.609
5 contredanses
AMA XI, no.23; NMA IV:13/1/ii
Vienna, probably 1787–8
no.1 in C, no.2 in E♭, no.3 in D, no.4 in C, no.5
in G
fl, side drum, 2 vn, b
Not in *Verzeichnüss*. No.5 is a rescored version of
K.610. On basis of watermark Tyson (1987)
suggests given date rather than traditional 1791.
Perhaps Mozart's first contredanse as
Kammermusicus

K.610
Contredanse in G
AMA XI, no.24; NMA IV:13/1/ii
?Salzburg, summer 1783
2 fl, 2 hn, 2 vn, b
Called *Les filles malicieuses* on autograph;
significance not known. Entered by Mozart in
Verzeichnüss only on 6 Mar 1791, but Tyson's
paper-studies (1987) point to work's comp. at
time of Mozart's Salzburg visit, or perhaps very
soon after

K.611
German dance in C
AMA XI, no.12; NMA IV: 13/1/ii
Vienna, 6 Mar 1791 (*Verzeichnüss*)
2 fl, 2 ob, 2 bn, 2 tpt, timp, hurdy-gurdy, 2 vn, b
Equals K.602 no.3, *Die Leyerer*

Arrangements of dance and ballet music

K.103 (61d)
12 minuets
NMA IX:27/2
Orchestral version, probably Salzburg,
early–mid-1772

K.176
11 minuets
NMA IX:27/2
Orchestral version (of 16 minuets), dated
Salzburg, Dec 1773

K.269b
4 contredanses
NMA IX:27/2
Salzburg, probably Jan 1777
?Doubtful. For Count Johann Rudolf Czernin.
Originally 12 numbers

K.Anh.207/Anh.C 27.06
9 piano pieces
NMA IX:27/2
Probably Milan, Sep 1771
Arrangement doubtful. Pf arrangement of ballet
music to *Ascanio in Alba* (Plath, 1965)

DAVID WYN JONES

Chamber music

Harmoniemusik and other works for multiple wind instruments

No combination of wind instruments possesses the
perfectly balanced ensemble qualities of the string
quartet. Many options have been tried, from groups
of all the same to groups of entirely dissimilar
instruments. The one offers superb blend, but little
contrast, the other contrast, but very limited blend.
The nearest the Classical composer found to his ideal
was in *Harmoniemusik*, with its nucleus of a pair of
horns, with bassoons beneath to provide the bass,
and one or more pairs of treble instruments above.
Such groups proved effective in the open air, and for
many years were regularly employed as military
bands. The aristocracy, with its large palaces and
gardens, also found these ensembles ideally suited to
its needs.

The Milan and Salzburg *Harmoniemusik*
Mozart's *Harmoniemusik* divides naturally into three
phases of his life. The earliest pieces, the divertimentos K.186 (159b) and K.166 (159d) seem to have
been the result of a commission that Mozart gained
while in Milan in 1773. Musically these pieces are
very slight: what is remarkable about them is their
instrumental combination which exceptionally
involved no fewer than three pairs of treble instruments above the horns and bassoons at a time when
Harmoniemusik was almost always limited to a single
pair. But in fact little of the music is in more than
three real parts: most of the thematic writing is
melodic thirds played by the oboes and English
horns, and the clarinets perform the sort of binding
note role more commonly associated with horns.
The bassoons normally play together on a single bass
line. The development in Mozart's style between
these pieces and the series of five sextet divertimentos
he wrote for his Archbishop in Salzburg in the mid-
1770s is quite remarkable. These more traditionally
scored works show a superiority beyond contemporary practice that one has come to associate with
Mozart. He has liberated his pairs of instruments
from the generally conceived parallel writing, and
has in particular transformed the first bassoon part
from contributing to the bass line as a first priority to
performing its more natural role as a tenor instrument. This became essentially a new voice to the
ensemble.

The Vienna *Harmoniemusik*
Before 1782, *Harmoniemusik* had played a surprisingly limited role in Vienna's musical life. It was the
music of the tavern and of the military, but only one
member of the court, Prince Schwarzenberg, had
taken any interest in it at all. Towards the end of
1781 Mozart seems to have heard rumours that the
Emperor was thinking of following Schwarzenberg's
lead. In October he wrote the Serenade in E♭ major,
K.375, scored for the traditional sextet *Harmonie*,
with clarinets as the treble instruments. He related
to his father on 3 November 1781 how he had
written it with considerable care in the hope of
influencing court opinion. But using a sextet combination proved fruitless because he found his new
composition already out of date when in April 1782

the Emperor established his *Harmonie* as an octet, with a second pair of treble instruments. His ensemble of two oboes, two clarinets, two horns and two bassoons became the standard that others were only too anxious to follow. Mozart, apparently eager for employment by providing repertory for this new ensemble, reacted quickly, and spent part of the summer of 1782 composing the C minor Serenade, K.388 (384a), and adding oboe parts to his sextet E♭ Serenade to make it suitable for the new combination. But this course of action also proved worthless, because a further element in the Emperor's revolutionary scheme for his *Harmonie* was to enjoy a repertory of transcriptions of operas and ballets, and in the main eschew original compositions. Mozart briefly attempted to compete here also. He worked on a transcription of *Die Entführung aus dem Serail*, but even this failed to impress the Emperor, probably because Johann Went, once oboist to Prince Schwarzenberg but now with the Emperor, was able to complete his transcription of the opera before the composer. So far as is known, none of Mozart's *Harmoniemusik* ever found a place in the imperial library.

That the serenades have survived to become much the best known works of their genre is thanks partly to the fine editions that André published of them in 1811, but even so they cannot be said to be typical octets. The E♭ Serenade, in spite of some structural imperfections of its sextet form, is a work ideally suited to that combination, and it is a tragedy that it should have been so generally ignored as such, principally because both André and Breitkopf published only the octet form in their critical editions. Mozart seems to have arranged the octet version with furious speed, as the handwriting in the autograph reveals. Nevertheless he went to considerable lengths to integrate the oboe parts fully into the texture, except that in the two minuet movements he simply added oboe parts into the earlier sextet autograph.

The reference he made on 27 July 1782 to writing a 'Nacht Musique' (he had used the same expression regarding the sextet on 3 November 1781) in great haste indeed probably refers to this and not, as traditionally suggested, the C minor Serenade, which shows no signs of haste, either in the music, or on the page. This work is imbued with the emotional tensions so typical of Mozart's music in that key, and this, together with its four-movement format, makes it more symphonic in concept than a serenade. It is intensely, almost unremittingly, serious, and really highly inappropriate material for the relaxed background music that was the normal role of *Harmoniemusik*. Perhaps Mozart wrote it for a special occasion now long forgotten. Even its last two movements, where matters normally become less formal, are if anything more so as Mozart interpolates canonic devices into both minuet and trio, and, but for the relief of an interlude in the relative major coloured

by the warmer tones of clarinets and horns, remorselessly maintains the strict régime of minor mode and double reed timbre until the closing bars of the superb set of variations that form the finale.

Another original feature of the Emperor's *Harmonie* was that he took into its ranks only first-class instrumentalists, whom he simultaneously employed in the Burgtheater. In this way he was able to tempt the Stadler brothers to remain in Vienna, and become the first full-time professional clarinettists in the imperial city. Mozart's friendship with the elder Stadler, Anton, is quite evident, and one consequence of their relationship occurred on 23 March 1784 in Stadler's benefit concert in the Burgtheater. This was the first, albeit partial, known performance of the Serenade in B♭ major, K.361 (370a), in the opinion of many the finest piece of *Harmoniemusik* ever written. Its proportions are stupendous. It is in seven large-scale movements, with a slow introduction to the first, second trios added to both minuets, and with two extra movements between the second minuet and the finale. And unprecedentedly Mozart used no fewer than thirteen instruments. He chose two pairs of horns, in different keys, to allow himself their fuller support in foreign tonalities. He again used three pairs of treble instruments, here oboes, clarinets and basset-horns. He kept the normal two bassoons, and most sensibly added weight to the bass by writing also for an instrument of sixteen-foot pitch, choosing the double bass probably because it was the only possibility that he had available to him at the time. Had he been writing in 1785, Theodor Lotz's arrival in Vienna with his rudimentary contrabassoon might have persuaded the composer otherwise. In fact the Serenade's date has never been conclusively established, and though possibly written for the 1784 performance, paper-type analysis makes a 1781–2 date more probable, and perhaps there is truth in the hypothesis (stemming from a doubtful passage in Nissen's *Biographie*) that the composer wrote it for performance at his wedding celebrations.

Basset-horn music, and wind duets

The simple formality of the canonic Adagio for two basset-horns and bassoon, K.410 (440d, 484d), and the Adagio in B♭ for two clarinets and three basset-horns, K.411 (440a, 484a), would suggest that Mozart conceived these short pieces with some ceremonial use in mind, while the basset-horn trios, K.Anh.229 (K.439b), were more probably intended for the social pleasure of their participants. It is highly likely that two of these would have been the Stadler brothers, possibly supplemented as necessary by one or more of three men, presumably related, named Griessbacher, assuming they were still in Vienna. Anton and Raymond Griessbacher were employed by Prince Nikolaus Esterházy in 1776–8 as clarinettists, while the Stadler brothers themselves attested in November 1781 to playing basset-horn trios (no composer mentioned) with Jakob, coincidentally also a bassoonist.

Also deserving of a mention here are Mozart's excursions into a type of wind music that was particularly popular in his day, the duet for a pair of identical instruments. The Sonata in B♮ major, K.292 (196c), is probably of this type, and written for two bassoons, though nowadays it is known only in its published form, for bassoon accompanied by cello. Mozart probably composed the work for the Munich amateur bassoonist Thaddäus von Dürnitz. The instrumentation of Mozart's twelve duos, K.487 (496a), has long been in doubt, but the fact that all twelve were written in C major must militate against their composition for any but a brass instrument. The reluctance to accept these pieces as being for the horn is natural, in view of their exceptional range, and use of chromatic notes rarely if ever seen in other examples of Mozart's horn writing. But in fact this very writing offers positive evidence that Mozart wrote them for horn. The chromatic notes used are all available to a highly skilled hand horn player, and Mozart avoided other notes simply because they are virtually unobtainable on the valveless horn, especially *a* and *d'*, which would form part of the obvious vocabulary of any stringed or woodwind instrument. As to the excessively high top notes – up to *g''* – Mozart invariably adopted the only approach to them open to a brass player, via an ascending scale passage. These were not pieces for public performance, but as with most similar duets or larger ensembles more commonly written by instrumentalists, for the private enjoyment of the players – in this case probably Joseph Leutgeb, Mozart's intimate since his Salzburg childhood and probably the dedicatee of all his solo horn works.

Finally a short reference must be made to the quite remarkably scored Divertimento in C major, K.188 (240b), for two flutes, five trumpets and four timpani. This has obvious parallels of scoring with the ten Pieces that used to constitute K.187 before E.F. Schmid was able to show in 1937 that these were arrangements of movements by Starzer and Gluck. Mozart's purpose in writing this work remains an enigma, and even dating it has caused controversy, Köchel's notion being retarded by some to 1777 before Plath's analysis of the composer's handwriting, suggesting the probability of mid-1773, and with it the possibility of an Italian commission.

K.186 (159b)
Divertimento in B♮ major
AMA IX/2, no.18; NMA VII:17/i
Milan and/or Salzburg, probably Mar 1773
Allegro assai; Menuetto; Andante; Adagio; Allegro
2 ob, 2 cl, 2 eng hn, 2 hn, 2 bn
Not published before AMA. For fifth movement, Mozart used theme of *Le gelosie del serraglio*,

K.Anh.109 (K.135a), no.31. Dating from handwriting. Trio rescored with 2 eng hn. Other side of tipped-in leaf containing final version of Trio contains 16 cancelled bars of music in G♯ minor (3/8) for 2 ob, 2 hn, str, dating from *c.* 1764–5. (Plath in NMA, Kritischer Bericht)

K.166 (159d)
Divertimento in E♮ major
AMA IX/2, no.17; NMA VII:17/i
Salzburg, 24 Mar 1773 (autograph)
Allegro; Menuetto; Andante grazioso; Adagio; Allegro
2 ob, 2 cl, 2 eng hn, 2 hn, 2 bn
Not published before AMA. Third movement derives from slow movement of a Symphony in D by Paisiello (1772), fourth movement from *Le gelosie del serraglio*, K.Anh.109 (K.135a), no.30. Minuet, bars 12ff., rewritten; trio rewritten

K.188 (240b)
Divertimento in C major
AMA IX/2, no.20; NMA VII:17/i
Salzburg, ?mid-1773
Andante; Allegro; Menuetto; Andante; Menuetto; (Gavotte)
2 fl, 3 tpt in C, 2 tpt in D, 4 timp
Not published before AMA. Dating from handwriting

K.292 (196c)
Sonata in B♮ major
AMA X, no.14; NMA VIII:21
Munich, probably early 1775
Allegro; Andante; Rondo (Allegro)
2bn? (bn, vc)
Dietrich Berke, NMA editor, suggests 2 bn the more likely instrumentation. First published for bn and vc by J.J. Hummel, Berlin (plate no.1299 – Berke suggests before 1800, though it is not in 1802 catalogue). Uri Toeplitz (1978) considers work to be spurious

K.213
Divertimento in F major
AMA IX/2, no.22; NMA VII:17/i
Salzburg, Jul 1775 (autograph)
Allegro spiritoso; Andante; Menuetto; Contredanse en Rondeau (Molto allegro)
2 ob, 2 hn, 2 bn
Written, probably as dinner music, for Archbishop Colloredo

K.240
Divertimento in B♮ major
AMA IX/2, no.23; NMA VII:17/i
Salzburg, Jan 1776 (autograph)
Allegro; Andante grazioso; Menuetto; Allegro
2 ob, 2 hn, 2 bn
See K.213. Original 32 bars after bar 66 of finale cancelled and rewritten

K.252 (240a)
Divertimento in E♭ major
AMA IX/2, no.26; NMA VII:17/i
Salzburg, probably between Jan and Aug 1776
Andante; Menuetto; Polonaise (Andante); Presto
assai
2 ob, 2 hn, 2 bn
See K.213

K.253
Divertimento in F major
AMA IX/2, no.27; NMA VII:17/i
Salzburg, Aug 1776 (autograph)
Theme and Variations (Andante); Menuetto;
Allegro assai
2 ob, 2 hn, 2 bn
See K.213

K.270
Divertimento in B♭ major
AMA IX/2, no.28; NMA VII:17/i
Salzburg, Jan 1777 (autograph)
Allegro molto; Andantino; Menuetto (Moderato);
Presto
2 ob, 2 hn, 2 bn
See K.213

K.361 (370a)
Serenade in B♭ major [gran Partitta]
AMA IX/1, no.12; NMA VII:17/ii
Vienna, probably 1781–2
Largo – Molto allegro; Menuetto; Adagio;
Menuetto (Allegretto); Romance (Adagio –
Allegretto – Adagio); [Theme and variations
(Andante)]; Finale (Molto allegro)
2 ob, 2 cl, 2 basset-hn, 2 hn in F, 2 hn in B♭, 2 bn,
db
Tyson's paper-type analysis (1987) makes above
date the most probable, though earliest known
perf. was in Anton Stadler's benefit concert in the
Burgtheater on 23 Mar 1784. No printed score
until B&H 1861. Until NMA 1979, all imprints
except over-edited B&H 1861 publication used as
primary source the corrupt first edition of the
parts of 1803. Most early editions divided work
and arranged it for other instrumental
combinations. Sixth movement also appears, in
slightly altered form, in the Flute Quartet,
K.Anh.171 (285b). Frag. K. deest (8 bars),
preserved on fol. 6r of first movement of Serenade
K.375, version 1, possibly part of the original
attempt at variation movement for K.361?

K.375
Serenade in E♭ major
AMA IX/1, no.13 – version 2 only; NMA
VII:17/ii
1: Vienna, before 15 Oct 1781; 2: Vienna,
probably Jul 1782
Allegro maestoso; Menuetto; Adagio; Menuetto;

Finale (Allegro)
1: 2 cl, 2 hn, 2 bn
2: 2 ob, 2 cl, 2 hn, 2 bn
First version first performed at house of court
painter Joseph von Hickel; second was a hastily
revised version presumably to accord with the
newly formed octet *Harmonie* of the Emperor.
Possibly the 'Nacht Musique' to which Mozart
made reference in his letter of 27 Jul 1782. All
editions of version 1 used defective source material
until OUP 1979. Fragmentary attempt at first
movement, version 2 (5 bars), survives

K.388 (384a)
Parthia (Serenade) in C minor
AMA IX/1, no.14; NMA VIII:17/ii
Vienna, 1782 (autograph)
Allegro; Andante; Menuetto in canone; Allegro
2 ob, 2 cl, 2 hn, 2 bn
Arranged later as a str qnt K.406 (516b). Frag. (2
bars) preserved on fol. 8v of autograph score
possibly original attempt at finale?

K.410 (440d, 484d)
Adagio in F major
AMA X, no.15; NMA VIII:21
Vienna, probably 1782
2 basset-hn, bn
Written for no known purpose. Date given is
supported by Tyson's paper-type analysis (1987)

K.411 (440a, 484a)
Adagio in B♭ major
AMA X, no.16; NMA VII:17/ii
Vienna, probably 1782–3
2 cl, 3 basset-hn
Written for no known purpose. Date given is
supported by Tyson's paper-type analysis (1987)

K.Anh.229 (439b)
25 Pieces (all but last in B♭ major) – they divide
naturally into 5 divertimentos
AMA XXIV, no.62; NMA VIII:21
Vienna, ?1781–2, or *c.* 1785
No.1: Allegro; Menuetto (Allegretto); Adagio;
Menuetto; Rondo (Allegro)
No.2: Allegro; Menuetto; Larghetto; Menuetto;
Rondo (Allegro)
No.3: Allegro; Menuetto; Adagio; Menuetto;
Rondo (Allegro assai)
No.4: Allegro; Larghetto; Menuetto; Adagio;
Allegretto
No.5: Adagio; Menuetto; Adagio; Romance
(Andante); Polonaise
3 basset-hn
Autograph MS lost, and accurate dating
impossible. Presumably written for Stadler
brothers (Constanze mentioned Anton's possession
of some basset-hn trios in letter to André dated 31
May 1800), with perhaps Jakob Griessbacher in

1781–2, or Anton David or Vincent Springer in about 1785. (NMA suggests 1788 as possible upper limit on stylistic grounds.) Early printed versions are for combinations such as 2 cl, bn; 2 cl, 2 hn, bn; or 2 basset-hn, bn. There is an alternative and possibly authentic last movement to Divertimento no.2. For first demonstration of likelihood that written for 3 basset-hns, see Whewell (1962)

K.deest
Harmonie transcription of *Die Entführung aus dem Serail*, K.384
Vienna, in progress 20 Jul 1782
Probably for 2 ob, 2 cl, 2 hn, 2 bn
Possibility that transcription in Donaueschingen (D–DO Mus Ms 1392) in 16 movements may be Mozart's own has been recently proposed by Bastiaan Blomhert (1987)

K.487 (496a)
12 Duos
AMA XV, no.3; NMA VIII:21
Vienna, 27 Jul 1786 (autograph)
Allegro; Menuetto (Allegretto); Andante; Polonaise; Larghetto; Menuetto; Adagio; Allegro; Menuetto; Andante; Menuetto; Allegro
2 hn
Autograph MS of nos 1, 3 and 6 survives dated as above. On these pages Mozart made no mention of instrumentation, but notwithstanding extraordinarily high tessitura of some movements and liberal use of chromatic notes, expert opinion now favours 2 hn

ROGER HELLYER

Wind instruments with strings and piano
Quartets for wind and strings It was in Breitkopf's 1782–4 catalogue that the prototype wind quintet was advertised, which in course of time developed into the standard instrumental combination in wind chamber music. Even if Mozart was aware of it, he disregarded the combination absolutely, and indeed trios or quartets in similar vein. His conviction was firm that when using wind instruments in chamber music individually rather than in pairs, he could only guarantee the homogeneity he considered essential to his ensemble by finding it within his accompanying instruments, be it a keyboard instrument or a group of strings. Accompanying a chosen wind instrument with strings was in no sense new, and by far the most common practice was to replace the first violinist of a string quartet with a wind soloist. Mozart's four quartets for flute and his one for oboe are in this mould. The first two flute Quartets probably belong to a commission the composer won while in Mannheim in 1777–8, and while the first quartet, K.285, was quickly finished,

the second (K.285a) fails to meet its high standards, suggesting that Mozart was quickly bored by his task. The third quartet, K.Anh.171 (K.285b), seems to be a product of the composer's first year in Vienna, and also established as Viennese is the Quartet K.298, probably written in 1786 as *Hausmusik* for the Jacquin family. The thematic ideas of all its three movements are taken from the music of his contemporaries, and, as Alfred Einstein (1945) suggests, is a parody of the insipidity and perfunctoriness of style so commonly found in their writing.

Finer by far than these was the Quartet for Oboe and Strings, K.370 (386b), that Mozart wrote in Munich early in 1781 for Friedrich Ramm, the principal oboist in the orchestra of the Elector of Bavaria. Mozart had first met Ramm in Mannheim late in 1777 and had immediately been overwhelmed by the quality of his tone, which he found delightfully pure. In this work Mozart discovered the intimacy of chamber music: he avoided concertante tendencies by finding many subtle ways to integrate the voices, especially by dovetailing melody and countermelody. The second movement is an emotionally potent aria in D minor, remarkably a mere thirty-eight bars long. The finale Rondeau includes one extraordinary episode in which the oboist plays in 4/4 time while the strings, apparently unaware, continue with their 6/8 accompaniment. This section begins very threateningly in the minor mode, and the tension is relieved only as major key and compound rhythm return simultaneously, even in mid-phrase. The return of the rondo theme demonstrates Mozart's sheer delight in the high register of the oboe, which at such moments is quite as apparent as his well-known love for the lowest notes on the clarinet.

Quintets for wind and strings To accompany the horn in the Quintet K.407 (386c), Mozart in effect chose a string quintet with the first violin displaced by the wind soloist. In all probability this use of two violas was unprecedented, but the more sombre quality of Mozart's accompaniment seems to have found at least one imitator in Franz Krommer, who employed similar string combinations in accompanying works for bassoon, clarinet and even flute. With the autograph of this quintet missing since its sale in a London auction in March 1847, it remains uncertain when and for whom Mozart wrote the work, but the likelihood is that it was a work of his early years in Vienna, and in all probability either for Joseph Leutgeb or for Jakob Eisen, the Emperor's second horn player. A letter from Constanze Mozart to the Offenbach music publisher André on 31 May 1800 suggests that both men may have possessed copies of the work.

The most expansive of all Mozart's wind chamber music was his Clarinet Quintet, K.581, wherein he wedded the solo instrument to the complete string quartet. This magnificent composition possesses the grandeur and stature proper to one of Mozart's last pieces of chamber music – indeed it is truly a full member of that genre with no trace of the concertante style so prevalent generally in works for wind soloist and strings. Mozart conferred upon it the full Classical four-movement form, the extra movement being a minuet, remarkably with two trios, one of which the composer sensibly scored for strings alone in order to allow the wind player some necessary respite. The work was one of Mozart's finest inspirations, sadly known to us now only in a corrupt version since the dedicatee, Anton Stadler, ever short of funds, is thought to have pawned or sold Mozart's autograph while on his European tour between 1791 and 1796. Thus modern editions have had to rely on the first printed edition by André in 1802, which was intended for a clarinet of standard dimensions rather than the instrument for which Mozart wrote, especially built for Stadler with a footjoint elongated to permit notes down to a written *c*. Mozart's inventiveness and artistry were always ready to encompass such new challenges, and modern reconstructions of the Quintet and the later Clarinet Concerto have demonstrated what fluid use Mozart made of this new extension to a tessitura already very wide by woodwind standards.

Wind chamber music with piano By far the most difficult task Mozart set himself, and wherein lay his most dazzling achievement, was the composition of the Quintet for piano and four wind instruments, K.452. He was especially conscious of the added difficulties involved in writing for single as opposed to pairs of wind instruments, and made the point in particular when he wrote to his father on 10 April 1784: 'I composed . . . a quintet, which called forth the very greatest applause. . . . It is written for 1 oboe, 1 clarinet, 1 horn, 1 bassoon and the pianoforte.' The lack of blend between four different wind instruments meant to Mozart that chord passages unsupported by the piano would have to be brief. The instruments would therefore have to be contrasted in various permutations against the piano, with none of them being allowed to be disproportionately prominent. Mozart adopted a patchwork method in order to build up themes of any length, by stitching together an array of short motifs, supported by constantly varying instrumental combinations. This method risked a superficial instability but ultimately provided its fundamental unity. The result impressed even the composer himself, who called it the best work he had ever composed. So far as is known, this was the first piano and wind quintet ever written, which makes Mozart's achievement the more remarkable.

He overcame different ensemble problems in the Trio in E♭ major, K.498, written for one member each of the string, woodwind and keyboard families. In choosing the viola rather than the cello Mozart refused the simple expedient of adding weight to the bass, and coupled it to the clarinet, a wind instrument with similar range and similarly mellow if more potent solo characteristics. His choice of movements is also unusual – none of them slow, but a notable lack of pace or virtuosity about either of the outer movements. The first was in addition essentially monothematic. All the more remarkable, then, was his achievement, a perfectly integrated composition containing some of his most delicious melodies, and an interplay between the instruments full of subtle blends and contrasts. The whole was unified by one of the most innovative formal frameworks he ever devised. The work becomes ever more inspired as it reaches its conclusion, and it prompted Einstein (1945) to comment:

> How well Mozart now understands not only how to end a work but how to close it, with a distillation of melodic and contrapuntal beauty that does not merely satisfy the listener but leaves him enchanted! The last word music can utter as an expression of the feeling of form is here spoken.

K.285
Quartet in D major
AMA XIV, no.28; NMA VIII:20/2
Mannheim, 25 Dec 1777 (autograph)
Allegro; Adagio; Rondeau
fl, vn, va, vc
Written for Ferdinand Dejean (1731–97), surgeon in Dutch East India Company, who also commissioned Flute Concerto in G, K.313 (285c). Original 38 bars after bar 56 of finale rewritten

K.285a
Quartet in G major
NMA VIII:20/2
Mannheim, between 25 Dec 1777 and 14 Feb 1778
Andante; Tempo di Menuetto
fl, vn, va, vc
Probably part of the Dejean commission (see K.285). Survives only in Artaria edition of 1792 which conflates it with Allegro of K.285 to produce a single, hybrid 3-movement work

K.370 (368b)
Quartet in F major
AMA XIV, no.30; NMA VIII:20/2
Munich, early 1781
Allegro; Adagio; Rondeau (Allegro)
ob, vn, va, vc
Written for Friedrich Ramm, principal oboist to Elector of Bavaria

K.Anh.171 (285b)
Quartet in C major
NMA VIII:20/2
Vienna, 1781–2
Allegro; [Theme and Variations (Andantino)]
fl, vn, va, vc

First movement has been authenticated thanks to autograph sketch for bars 149–58 of the Allegro, on same leaf used to sketch no.2 from Act I of *Die Entführung aus dem Serail*. Tyson's paper-type analysis (1987) reveals that it is of a type used by Mozart in works written in 1781, also Serenade in B♭, K.361 (370a), sixth movement of which is essentially same as second one here (arranged, ?not by Mozart)

K.407 (386c)
Quintet in E♭ major
AMA XIII, no.3; NMA VIII:19/2
Vienna, possibly late 1782
Allegro; Andante; Rondo (Allegro)
hn, vn, 2 va, vc
Probably written for Joseph Leutgeb

K.452
Quintet in E♭ major
AMA XVII/1; NMA VIII:22/1
Vienna, before 21 Mar 1784 [*Verzeichnüss*, 30 Mar]
Largo – Allegro moderato; Larghetto; Allegretto
pf, ob, cl, hn, bn
Written for perf. in Mozart's benefit concert in the Burgtheater on 21 Mar 1784, but concert postponed until 1 Apr because of opera performance in Liechtenstein Palace on that night. Sketch for first movement, bars 71ff. (20 bars), survives

K.498
Trio in E♭ major
AMA XVII/2, no.7; NMA VIII:22/2
Vienna, 5 Aug 1786 (*Verzeichnüss*)
Andante; Menuetto; Rondeaux (Allegretto)
pf, cl, va
Known as *Kegelstatt* Trio. According to Karoline von Pichler, written for Franziska von Jacquin. Probably first performed privately by her with Mozart on viola and Stadler on clarinet

K.298
Quartet in A major
AMA XIV, no.29; NMA VIII:20/2
Vienna, probably late 1786 or 1787
[Theme and Variations (Andante)]; [Menuetto]; Rondieaoux (Allegretto grazioso, mà non troppo presto, però non troppo adagio. Così – così – con molto garbo, ed Espressione)
fl, vn, va, vc
Finale theme, based on an arietta from Paisiello's *Le gare generose* (first perf. Vienna, autumn 1786), provides earliest possible comp. date of work. Mozart is known to have heard Paisiello's opera in Prague in Jan 1787
A parody composition probably written for Jacquin family – autograph once in possession of Baron (Gottfried?) Jacquin

K.581
Quintet in A major
AMA XIII, no.6; NMA VIII:19/2
Vienna, 29 Sep 1789
Allegro; Larghetto; Menuetto; Allegretto con Variazioni
cl, 2 vn, va, vc
Written for Anton Stadler, and given first performance by him on 22 Dec 1789 in Burgtheater in one of Christmas concerts of Vienna Society of Musicians

ROGER HELLYER

Piano and strings

Background
The early works in this category belong firmly in the tradition of the keyboard sonata for harpsichord or piano with the accompaniment of (ad lib) violin or flute and, occasionally, cello. The genre's formal outline, content and technical demands were conditioned for most of the century by the lucrative amateur domestic market at which it was directly aimed. The content was typical of the Rococo period which nurtured it: simple, melodic, major-mode and unrelentingly diatonic and homophonic – conversation in the truly *galant* sense of having little to talk about, but doing it above all politely and charmingly. The keyboard part had to be self-sufficient, lest no 'accompaniment' was available, and the music was intended less for the detached listener than for the players themselves.

The early works
Written when Mozart was between six and eight years of age, the two sets of violin sonatas, K.6–7, 8–9, constituted his first publications (op.1 and op.2, Paris, 1764). The movements that survive in manuscript are in Leopold's handwriting and for keyboard only, causing speculation as to their authenticity. Visits to London (1764–5) and Holland (1765–6) produced two further sets of sonatas, K.10–15 and K.26–31, published as op.3 (with optional cello) and op.4 respectively. All these juvenilia share common features of style and technique with popular contemporaries such as Eckard, Schobert, Honauer and J.C. Bach: melody and accompaniment are clearly separated, the violin plays in thirds, sixths or octaves with the melody, and the cello, when present, doubles the essential bass note, the onlooking servant to an animated *tête-à-tête* (see K.15. second movement). Phrasing is foursquare, mostly restricted to root-position primary triads. In the later works, harmony is more adventurous, with the occasional chromatic chord, and one senses its increasing use as a determinant of structure, however rudimentary: phrasing and texture also figure more prominently.

The mature violin sonatas

After a twelve-year gap resulting in several master-pieces in larger forms (the Piano Concerto in E♭ major K.271, the symphonies in G minor K.183 (173dB) and A major K.201 (186a)), these works were written in the first half of 1778 in Mannheim, and Paris (see list for details), where they were published – confusingly, as op.1 – later that year. If we expect to find the quality of the larger master-pieces in these sonatas, we will be disappointed; Mozart continued to accept the prevailing view that these were amateur domestic fare. However, a greater maturity is evident in K.301 (293a), in the details of thematic presentation, the setting up of tensions to be resolved over longer time-spans and the closer alliance of figuration and structuring; furthermore, Mozart has discovered how to use texture as a component in the developmental process. In the E minor Sonata, K.304 (300c) we are close to the world of early Romanticism with the presentation of melodic/thematic material in different colouristic guises, and the tighter integration of the sonata-form sections, as witness the codetta, bar 59ff., incorporating material from all areas. K.305's first movement (293d) shows the most satisfying handling of sonata form and the central movement of K.306 (300l) becomes an operatic scena in the finale – akin to the conspiracy music in *Figaro* – with a written-out cadenza involving both instruments.

Mozart's second set of mature sonatas was pub-lished in 1781, shortly after he had moved to Vienna. One, however (K.296 in C), was composed in Mannheim at the time of the previous set; its slow movement, with its strong subdominant leaning and veiled pentatonicism, suggests the Celtic aura of some of Field's slow movements.

In spite of their superiority to the previous set and their enthusiastic review in Cramer's *Magazin der Musik* shortly after publication, they do not compare very well with the contemporary 'Haydn' quartets, for example, although on occasion they may breathe the same air. The subtlety of the phrasing in the opening movement of K.376 (374d) in F and its exploration of themes outside the development section proper are cases in point, although the structure is weakened by the harmonic indecisive-ness of the transition. However, the finale, in Haydnesque popular vein, is hard to resist.

Texture plays a vital role in K.377 (374e) (also in F), in the Beethovenian development and the reprise into which it imperceptibly blends. What gives this work pride of place in the set is the central theme and variations in the relative minor, with a similar feeling of brooding introspection to that of the finale of the D minor Quartet K.421 (417b); indeed the last Siciliana variation may well have inspired the quartet finale's theme. The sonata's last movement, in spite of a livelier middle section, never completely loses its sense of quiet, measured rhetoric, a quality also in evidence in the B♮ Sonata K.378 (317d),

where it is allied to an expansiveness which brings to mind the piano concertos of Mozart's early Vienna years. So intertwined are material and instruments in the Romantically inclined middle movement of K.380 (374f) in E♭, that it is difficult to separate main and subsidiary formal areas. The 'op.II' set ends with a Rondeau in which neither the theme's jaunty nor its lyrical aspects prepare us for the tensions which Mozart will generate in the two episodes.

The variations for violin and piano

Only six of the twenty-six violin sonatas contain variation movements, each with six variations or the equivalent. Of the two independent sets, written around the same time as the sonatas just discussed, that in G minor on the French song 'Au bord d'une fontaine' (also called 'Hélas, j'ai perdu mon amant'), K.360 (374b), similarly has six variations of almost unrelieved gloom. K.359 (374a), based on another French song 'La Bergère Célimène', in G major, has twelve variations and is more interesting, allowing the composer to explore different sonorities (Var. XI) and textures (IV and VIII).

The late sonatas

In these four works, any apologies for medium or market become redundant: all are equally worthy to take their places beside the last three symphonies and the string quintets.

K.454, in B♭ major, has a Largo introduction with the piano revelling in its cantabile rendering of the melody, and a finale which is one of the easy, long-limbed rondos which B♭ seems to call forth with Mozart, whereas the development of K.481's first movement (E♭) deals with the combined essences of the subjects and synthesizes the principal theme from the finale of the *Jupiter* Symphony in the process; this reappears in the coda, which is also developmental. The predominantly antiphonal character of the Adagio becomes a contrasting top-and-bottom interplay in the variations which con-clude the work. Subtler contrasts are built into the opening of K.526 in A, with a 6/8–3/4 hint of hemiola and a blurring of the anacrusis associated with the initial V–I cadence, which is later deve-loped. There is a Brahmsian leanness in the octave doublings of the deeply-felt Andante, and the same kind of elliptical harmonic shifts familiar from the late quintets. The Presto finale, with the cut and characteristics of a fast gavotte, draws together the first-movement melodic material (including the anacrucial ambiguities) and the octave-writing and harmonic shifts of the Andante.

The last sonata, K.547 in F, ('Eine kleine Klavier Sonate für Anfänger mit einer Violine') is indeed a pleasant duo for beginners which, nevertheless, like the contemporary beginners' keyboard Sonata in C, K.545, contains a wealth of characteristic late Mozartian detail.

The mature piano trios

These comprise six works, the earliest being the 'Divertimento à 3' in B♭, K.254, composed in August 1776. Like the K.10–15 set, the cello doubles the keyboard part almost continually, though the violin fares better. There is nothing 'diverting' about the serious central Adagio, even if keyboard and violin engage in successive monologues rather than dialogue.

In K.496 in G major of ten years later, all three instruments discuss more or less equally in the first movement's development section and the Andante, while the cello's contribution to the *minore* variation of the finale is lugubriously telling. Its greater emancipation is celebrated at the outset of K.502 (B♭) with a bubbling arpeggio and gently insistent cross-melodies; the keyboard writing reminds one of the high profile of the piano concerto in Mozart's *oeuvre* at this time, particularly in the Larghetto.

For all the quality which it shares with its predecessor, K.542 in E major is curiously restrained. The piano's seamless first subject seems more clothed harmony than Mozartian melody, a fact confirmed in its decorated repetition. A Schubertian serenity imbues the Andante grazioso, and his chromaticism tinges the later harmonies. The Allegro is in the best tradition of Mozart's chamber finale writing – fluid and uncluttered with a perfect balancing of disparate elements and textures. Belonging as it does to the astonishing summer of the last three symphonies (1788), it stands, with the B♭, K.502, at the apex of the piano trios.

Completed three weeks later, the C major Trio, K.548, is more than a chip from the *Jupiter* torso, as is occasionally implied. The slightly formulaic first-movement exposition is less a display of musical good manners than a foil to the varied development. In the Andante cantabile, one is conscious of the approaching world of early 19th-century chamber slow movements and this persists in the well-put-together finale in which the glint seems at times a trifle metallic. Mozart's farewell to the medium is the rather tentative K.564 in G, although the childlike, quasi-folkish ingenuousness of the material, from the musette opening through the carefully threaded theme of the variations to the skipping humour of the finale, always gives pause in the case of such a composer at such a stage.

The piano quartets

Mozart had few models to match up to in these two masterpieces, and the fact that he eschewed the conventional piano-with-accompaniment format explains, according to Nissen, the publisher Hoffmeister's cancellation – with the composer's agreement – of his contract for the projected three works. Certainly the epigrammatic austerity of the G minor (K.478) was too much for the Viennese amateurs. From the very beginning the feel of early Romantic chamber music with piano, of Hummel, Moscheles

and Mendelssohn, pervades. The quartets seem to combine public and private with ease, and the juxtaposition of concerto-like piano writing and string chamber intimacy is never incongruous. Revelling in the instrumental colours at his disposal, Mozart targets the first movement's development section to show the use of timbre as anything but a surface phenomenon, allying it to motivic working-out, dynamics, texture and dissonance, to produce a powerful exploration of the movement's material. The tempering of tragedy with lyricism (a feature of all Mozart's G minor works) does not result in comfortable music and this feeling hovers over the beautiful central Andante; the finale, similarly, is far from the frothy confections of many lesser composers.

The weighting of strings towards the tenor and bass registers, darkly powerful in K.478, imparts mellowness to K.493 in E♭, and this is heard at the outset, although the piano is soon preoccupied with its own figurations, often in decorative answer to the strings' plainer fare. The second of the three movements, Larghetto, features, at times, rapt dialogue between piano and strings, the rests being as eloquent as the sounds. Exchange of material between piano and strings is also prominent in the finale and accounts for much of its pace and high spirits in spite of the Allegretto marking.

Piano and violin

K.6
Violin Sonata in C major
AMA XVII/1, no.1; NMA VIII:23/i
Salzburg, Brussels, Paris, 1762–4
Allegro; Andante; Menuet I and II; Allegro molto
Published with K.7 as op.1 (Paris, 1764). First 3 movements survive separately (in kbd version in Leopold Mozart's hand) in so-called 'Nannerl Notenbuch': Allegro dated Brussels, 14 Oct 1763; Minuet II dated [Salzburg] 16 Jul 1762

K.7
Violin Sonata in D major
AMA XVIII/1, no.2; NMA VIII:23/i
Paris, 1763–4
Allegro molto; Adagio; Menuet I and II
Published with K.6 as op.1 (Paris, 1764). Menuet I survives (in kbd version in Leopold Mozart's hand) in so-called 'Nannerl Notenbuch', dated Paris, 30 Nov 1763

K.8
Violin Sonata in B♭ major
AMA XVIII/1, no.3; NMA VIII:23/i
K.8 and K.9 comp. Paris, 1763–4, and published there, 1764, as op.2
Allegro; Andante grazioso; Menuet I and II
Allegro survives (in kbd version in Leopold

Mozart's hand) in so-called 'Nannerl Notenbuch', dated Paris, 21 Nov 1763

K.9
Violin Sonata in G major
AMA XVIII/1, no.4; NMA VIII:23/i
See K.8
Allegro spiritoso; Andante; Menuet I and II

K.10–15
6 Sonatas for hpd, vn (fl), vc
See 'Piano Trios' below

K.26
Violin Sonata in E♭ major
AMA XVIII/1, no.11; NMA VIII:23/i
K.26–31 comp. The Hague, Feb 1766, and published there and in Amsterdam as op.4. Dedicated to Princess of Nassau-Weilburg
Allegro molto; Adagio poco andante; Rondeaux (Allegro)
No extant manuscripts for this set

K.27
Violin Sonata in G major
AMA XVIII/1, no.12; NMA VIII:23/i
See K.26
Andante poco adagio; Allegro

K.28
Violin Sonata in C major
AMA XVIII/1, no.13; NMA VIII:23/i
See K.26
Allegro maestoso; Allegro grazioso

K.29
Violin Sonata in D major
AMA XVIII/1, no.14; NMA VIII:23/i
See K.26
Allegro molto; Menuetto and Trio

K.30
Violin Sonata in F major
AMA XVIII/1, no.15; NMA VIII:23/i
See K.26
Adagio; Rondeaux (Tempo di Menuetto)

K.31
Violin Sonata in B♭ major
AMA XVIII/1, no.16; NMA VIII:23/i
See K.26
Allegro; Tempo di Menuetto (Moderato)
Last movement is a set of 6 variations

K.301 (293a)
Violin Sonata in G major
AMA XVIII/2, no.25; NMA VIII:23/i
Mannheim, early 1778
Allegro con spirito; Allegro
K.301 originally intended for kbd with fl

accompaniment
6 sonatas of 'op.1' set dedicated to Maria Elisabeth, Electress of the Palatinate. Published, together with K.302–306 (K.293a, b, c, 300c, 293d, and 300l) in Paris, 1778, as op.1 nos 1–6

K.302 (293b)
Violin Sonata in E♭ major
AMA XVIII/2, no.26; NMA VIII:23/i
Mannheim, early 1778
Allegro; Rondeau (Andante grazioso)
See K.301 (293a)

K.303 (293c)
Violin Sonata in C major
AMA XVIII/2, no.27; NMA VIII:23/i
Mannheim, early 1778
Adagio–Molto allegro; Tempo di Menuetto
See K.301 (293a)

K.305 (293d)
Violin Sonata in A major
AMA XVIII/2, no.29; NMA VIII:23/i
Paris, summer 1778
Allegro di molto; Thema (Andante grazioso)
See K.301 (293a). For dating see Plath 1976/77. Paper purchased in Mannheim (Tyson, 1987). Thema followed by 6 variations

K.296
Violin Sonata in C major
AMA XVIII/2, no.24; NMA VIII:23/i
Mannheim, 11 Mar 1778 (autograph). Published in Vienna by Artaria, 1781 as no.2 of set of 6 sonatas, op. 2, prepared (rather badly) for publication by set's dedicatee, Mozart's piano-pupil Josepha Auernhammer
Allegro vivace; Andante sostenuto; Rondeau (Allegro)
Carefully written autograph informs us that Mozart wrote sonata for 'Mademoiselle Therese' [Pierron], his pupil and stepdaughter of Privy Court Councillor Serrarius, in whose house he stayed during months before leaving Mannheim on 14 Mar 1778

K.304 (300c)
Violin Sonata in E minor
AMA XVIII/2, no.28; NMA VIII:23/i
Mannheim–Paris, 1778
Allegro; Tempo di Menuetto
See K.301 (293a). First movement comp. Mannheim (Plath, 1976/7), where paper was purchased (Tyson, 1987). With exception of Piano Quartet in G minor, K.478, Mozart's only completed work in minor key for pf with str

K.306 (300l)
Violin Sonata in D major
AMA XVIII/2, no.30; NMA VIII:23/i

Paris, summer 1778
Allegro con spirito; Andantino cantabile;
Allegretto
See K.301 (293a)
Fragmentary first versions of first movement (68
bars) and finale (Andante grazioso con moto, 77
bars; part in draft score) survive

K.378 (317d)
Violin Sonata in B♭ major
AMA XVIII/2, no.34; NMA VIII:23/i
Probably Salzburg, 1779–80, or early 1781 before
Mozart's arrival in Vienna. Published (see K.296)
as op. 2 no.4
Allegro moderato; Andantino sostenuto e
cantabile; Rondeau (Allegro)

K.379 (373a)
Violin Sonata in G major
AMA XVIII/2, no.35; NMA VIII:23/ii
Vienna, probably Apr 1781 and published (see
K.296) as op.2 no.5
Adagio; Allegro; Thema (Andantino cantabile)
Thema has 5 variations followed by its repeat and
a coda. Thought to be work comp. (according to
letter to father, 8 Apr 1781) between 11 and 12
o'clock one night for perf. next day at concert for
Archbishop Colloredo. Confesses to having played
kbd part entirely from memory, since he had no
time to write it out

K.376 (374d)
Violin Sonata in F major
AMA XVIII/2, no.32; NMA VIII:23/ii
Vienna, summer 1781; published (see K.296) as
op. 2 no.1
Allegro; Andante; Rondeau (Allegretto grazioso)

K.377 (374e)
Violin Sonata in F major
AMA XVIII/2, no.33; NMA VIII:23/ii
Vienna, summer 1781; published (see K.296) as
op. 2 no.3
Allegro; [Thema (Andante)]; Tempo di Menuetto
In cancelled attempt at slow movement (16 bars),
surviving in autograph score, theme played by
kbd alone

K.380 (374f)
Violin Sonata in E♭ major
AMA XVIII/2, no.36; NMA VIII:23/ii
Vienna, summer 1781; published (see K.296) as
op. 2 no.6
Allegro; Andante con moto; Rondeau (Allegro)

K.359 (374a)
12 Variations in G major on the French song *La bergère Célimène*
AMA XVIII/2, no.44; NMA VIII:23/ii
Vienna, Jun 1781; published there by Artaria in

1786
Thema (Allegretto)
Köchel 6 maintains view that K.359 (374a) and
K.360 (374b) probably to be associated with
variations for Countess Thiennes de Rumbeke
(1755–1812), mentioned by Mozart in letter to his
father of 20 Jun 1781. Possible, however, that
Mozart referring to variations for piano only, such
as K.265 (300e)

K.360 (374b)
6 Variations in G minor on the French song *Hélas! j'ai perdu mon amant*
AMA XVIII/2, no.45; NMA VIII:23/ii
Vienna, probably early summer 1781; published
there by Artaria in 1786
Thema (Andantino)
Song also known as *Au bord d'une fontaine*. See
K.359 (374a)

K.454
Violin Sonata in B♭ major
AMA XVII/2, no.40; NMA VIII:23/ii
Dated Vienna, 21 Apr 1784 (*Verzeichnüss*);
published there same year by Torricella (with 2 pf
sonatas, K.284 (205b) and K.333 (315c)) as op. 7
no.3
Largo–Allegro; Andante [originally Adagio];
Allegretto [originally Allegro]
First perf. of this work (by Mozart and Italian
violinist Regina Strinasacchi) at concert on 29
Apr 1784 in Vienna's Kärntnerthor theatre in
presence of Joseph II, has given rise to story
similar to Mozart's description of that of K.379
(373a). This time, Emperor asked to see empty pf
part. In fact, autograph with squeezed writing
and different-coloured inks, bears story out to
some extent. *Verzeichnüss* dating one of a number
of slightly inaccurate, retrospective datings to be
found on first couple of pages of Mozart's
catalogue (Leeson and Whitwell, 1973). Cancelled
fragmentary attempt at a vn sonata in C major (2
bars) precedes, in autograph score, first movement
of K.454

K.481
Violin Sonata in E♭ major
AMA XVIII/2, no.41; NMA VIII:23/ii
Completed Vienna, 12 Dec 1785 (*Verzeichnüss*);
published there by Hoffmeister following year
Molto allegro; Adagio; [Thema] (Allegretto)
Finale has 6 variations, last an Allegro, extended

K.526
Violin Sonata in A major
AMA XVIII/2, no.42; NMA VIII:23/ii
Dated Vienna, 24 Aug 1787 (*Verzeichnüss*);
published there by Hoffmeister same year
Molto allegro; Andante; Presto
Rondo finale modelled on finale of sonata for kbd,

v, vc, op.V no.5 by K.F. Abel, who had died on 20 Jan 1787. Fragmentary attempt at apparently vn sonata first movement K.Anh.50/526a (16 bars), probably to be linked with K.526

K.547
Violin Sonata in F major
AMA XVIII/2, no.43; NMA VIII:23/ii
Vienna, 10 Jul 1788 (*Verzeichnüss*)
Andantino cantabile; Allegro; [Thema] Andante
Only an incomplete autograph of what appears to be kbd part of 6 variations survives (K.54 (138a, 547a, 547b)). Modified version of second movement used for first movement of doubtful kbd sonata K.Anh.135 (547a)

Piano Trios

K.10
Sonata in B♭ major
AMA XVIII/1, no.5; NMA VIII:22/2
London, 1764; published there following year together with K.11–15 as op.3
Allegro; Andante; Menuetto I and II
hpd with vn (or fl) and vc (ad lib) accompaniment
For dedication of set to Queen Charlotte, Wolfgang received 50 guineas. Advertised on 20 Mar 1765 in *Public Advertiser* ('This Day are published . . .'). Engraved at Leopold Mozart's expense; copy of op.III (and the op.I and II sonatas) presented to British Museum before Mozarts' departure from England in Aug 1765 (King, 1984 [1985])

K.11
Sonata in G major
AMA XVII/1, no.6; NMA VIII:22/2
See K.10
Andante; Allegro; Menuetto (da capo Allegro)
hpd with vn (or fl) and vc (ad lib) accompaniment

K.12
Sonata in A major
AMA XVIII/1, no.7; NMA VIII:22/2
See K.10
Andante; Allegro
hpd with vn (or fl) and vc (ad lib) accompaniment

K.13
Sonata in F major
AMA XVIII/1, no.8; NMA VIII:22/2
See K.10
Allegro; Andante; Menuetto I and II
hpd with vn (or fl) and vc (ad lib) accompaniment

K.14
Sonata in C major
AMA XVIII/1, no.9; NMA VIII:22/2
See K.10
Allegro; Allegro; Menuetto I and Menuetto II en Carillon
hpd with vn (or fl) and vc (ad lib) accompaniment

K.15
Sonata in B♭ major
AMA XVIII/1, no.10; NMA VIII:22/2
See K.10
Andante maestoso; Allegro grazioso
hpd with vn (or fl) and vc (ad lib) accompaniment

K.254
Divertimento à 3 in B♭ major
AMA XVII, no.4; NMA VIII:22/2
Salzburg, Aug 1776 (autograph); published by Heina in Paris, ?1782 as op.3
Allegro assai; Adagio; Rondeau (Tempo di Menuetto)
pf, vn, vc
Advertised on 15 Jan 1783 in Cramer's *Magazin der Musik*, Hamburg

K.496
Trio in G major
AMA XVII, no.6; NMA VIII:22/2
Vienna, 8 Jul 1786 (*Verzeichnüss*); published there by Hoffmeister later that year
Allegro; Andante; [Thema] Allegretto
pf, vn, vc
'Thema' followed by 6 variations, last of which a double variation with coda. First page of autograph has superscription 'Sonata'. See second of Three Trio movements, K.442 ('Fragments and sketches')

K.502
Trio in B♭ major
AMA XVII, no.8; NMA VIII:22/2
Vienna, 18 Nov 1786 (*Verzeichnüss*); published there by Artaria in 1788, together with K.542 and K.548, as op.15 no.1
Allegro; Larghetto; Allegretto
pf, vn, vc

K.542
Trio in E major
AMA XVII, no.9; NMA VIII:22/2
Vienna, 22 Jun 1788 (*Verzeichnüss*); published there later that year as op.15 no.2 (see K.502)
Allegro; Andante grazioso; Allegro
pf, vn, vc
No doubt new trio mentioned by Mozart in letter to Michael Puchberg before 17 Jun 1788. See

K.563. Fragmentary attempt at finale in 6/8 (65 bars) survives in autograph score

K.548
Trio in C major
AMA XVII, no.10; NMA VIII:22/2
Vienna, 14 Jul 1788 (*Verzeichnüss*); published there later that year as op.15 no.3 (see K.502)
Allegro; Andante cantabile; Allegro
pf, vn, vc

K.564
Trio in G major
AMA XVII, no.11; NMA VIII:22/2
Vienna, 27 Oct 1788 (*Verzeichnüss*); published in *Storace's Collection of Original Harpsichord Music*, issued by Birchall and Andrews (London, 1789)
Allegro; [Thema] (Andante); Allegretto
pf, vn, vc
Thema has 6 variations and short coda. Stephen Storace and his sister Nancy, who had known Mozart well in the 1780s, left for England with their friend, and pupil of Mozart, Thomas Attwood, in 1787. Apart from publishing first edition of K.564, Storace had included in his anthology, earlier in 1787, first English edition of Mozart's Eb Piano Quartet, K.493, a few months after Viennese first edition. Printed from different source, possibly an early MS copy obtained with Mozart's help (King, 1984)

Piano Quartets

K.478
Piano Quartet in G minor
AMA XVII, no.2; NMA VIII:22/1
Vienna, 16 Oct 1785 (*Verzeichnüss*); published there by Hoffmeister in 1785–6
Allegro; Andante; [Rondo]
pf, vn, va, vc
According to Nissen, K.478 to be first of 3 such works to be published by Hoffmeister, but full project abandoned when Hoffmeister realized that public not buying work, finding it too difficult. Apparently Mozart was made present of advance payment on condition that he should not write remaining 2 qts contracted for

K.493
Piano Quartet in Eb major
AMA XVII, no.3; NMA VIII:22/1
Vienna, 3 Jun 1786 (*Verzeichnüss*); published there by Artaria in 1787 as op.13
Allegro; Larghetto; Allegretto
pf, vn, va, vc
See K.478 and K.564. Fragmentary attempt at finale (K.Anh.53/493a, 11 bars) and sketch for final version of finale (47 bars) survive

DEREK CAREW

Strings alone

MOZART PRODUCED thirty-five works of this kind (including one arrangement) from the age of twelve onwards, right up to the summer of 1791. With one exception, he was not an innovator, but rather built both on the music of a few other composers and on the inspiration of his own genius, often combining wonderful mastery of form and technique with the expression of deep, intimate feeling. He began with two simple little duos, K.46d in C major and K.46e in F major, both completed on 1 September 1768, and both for a melody instrument (presumably violin) and bass. Each comprises a charming Allegro, followed by two minuets. Mozart's first quartet, K.80 (73f), in G major, followed on 15 March 1770. Composed at Lodi, on his way to Milan, this is a brisk, cheerful piece modelled perhaps on G.B. Sammartini.

Italianate also were the influences on the six quartets which followed between the autumn of 1772 and the early part of 1773: K.155 (134a) in D major, K.156 (134b) in G major, K.157 in C major, K.158 in F major, K.159 in Bb major and K.160 (159a) in Eb major. The first was written in Bolzano or Verona, and all the others in Milan: all are in three movements. Mozart numbered the works 1 to 6 himself, and the succession of keys in this set, being at intervals of a fourth, seems to suggest a cyclical purpose. Here and there is some striking music, such as the passionate Allegro in C minor in K.159, and the canonic writing in the first movement of K.155. Another set of six quartets followed very soon, composed in August and September 1773, and all written in Vienna: K.168 in F major, K.169 in A major, K.170 in C major, K.171 in Eb major, K.172 in Bb major and K.173 in D minor. (Here too the succeeding tonalities, at intervals of – roughly speaking – a third, indicate a cyclical purpose.) Haydn's quartets op.17 and op.20 were composed in 1771 and 1772 respectively and it is likely that Mozart heard them. This is not merely a matter of melodic and stylistic resemblances, but is also suggested by the fact that each of Mozart's six works, like each of Haydn's, is in four movements. There are other formal links. Like Haydn, Mozart used a theme and variations for a first movement, in K.170, and in K.173 wrote a remarkable fugue for the finale, a device favoured by his older, and still probably unmet, contemporary. Immediately after K.173, Mozart composed his first string quintet, K.174 in Bb major, which he dated December 1773. This Salzburg work may have been inspired, at successive stages of its evolution, by the quintets in C major and G major which Michael Haydn wrote at about this time, each with the title 'Notturno'. Mozart's is clearly an experimental work, full of abundant melodic invention, but with distinctly limited use of the second viola and an unimaginative treatment of the cello.

In the next three years, preoccupation with the larger instrumental forms seems to have kept Mozart away from chamber music with strings, and it was probably not until early in 1777, at Salzburg, that he returned to this medium. Then again came an experimental work, the Divertimento in B♭, K.266 (271f), for two violins and a bass. But falling, as it seems to, so near the forward-looking Piano Concerto in E♭ major, K.271, this trio is strangely old-fashioned as well. Comprising just an Adagio and a Minuet, it is an unadventurous work, redolent of the kind of sonata that Leopold Mozart had composed, and engraved himself, in 1740.

At this point in Mozart's life came a series of prolonged distractions: his great journeys to France and Germany (the latter reaching its peak in the seminal splendour of *Idomeneo*), removal to Vienna, courtship and marriage. All this meant that nearly five years were to elapse before he returned to chamber music with strings. When he did so, towards the end of 1782, there were probably two principal factors at work. One was the publication in 1781 of Haydn's op.33 quartets, and the other was Mozart's friendship with him, which must date from this period. It seems unlikely, however that when Mozart completed his Quartet in G major, K.387, on 31 December 1782, he intended it as the first of a set of six to be dedicated to Haydn. Such intentions probably did not take shape for at least another year. By that time Mozart had grasped even more fully the stylistic implications of his friend's op.33 – the art of musical discourse among four equal partners, the new way of generating thematic momentum and the like. These sterling qualities Mozart developed and enhanced as he gradually composed five more quartets: K.421 (417b) in D minor (June 1783); K.428 (421b) in E♭ major (June–July 1783); K.458 in B♭ major (9 November 1784); K.464 in A major (10 January 1785) and K.465 in C major (14 January 1785). His famous and touching dedication speaks of them as 'the fruit of long and laborious effort', and this is borne out by the overall chronology and possibly by some evidence of paper-types. Despite his seemingly effortless mastery of the instrumental forms, Mozart was never to find quartet composition easy.

However, he left another instance of his genius for string chamber music in the two wonderful duets for violin and viola, K.423 in G major, and K.424 in B♭ major, which he probably wrote in October 1783. It is said that they were occasioned by an illness of his friend Michael Haydn which prevented him from composing more than four of a set of six such duets commissioned by the Archbishop of Salzburg. Mozart's two supplements are masterpieces of bold harmony, contrapuntal ingenuity and rhythmical variety, all enriched by double-stopping which sometimes creates the illusion of more players than just two. The influence of the experience gained in composing K.387 is quite clear. The isolated Quar-tet in D major, K.499, completed on 19 August 1786 to a commission by the publisher Franz Anton Hoffmeister may lack some of the intimacy and charm of the 'Haydn' six, but is a powerful, disturbing masterpiece in its own right.

The same disturbing quality is found much more in the two string quintets which followed in 1787: K.515, in C major, on 19 April, and K.516, in G minor, on 16 May. Both works benefit from the freedom that Mozart had now won for the cello and from the imaginative use of the second viola. The passionate, melancholy character of K.516 is famous, but no less remarkable is the prevalence of strongly contrasting minor keys in K.515 and the violence of some of its rhythms. When Mozart wanted to make these masterpieces better known, in 1788, he advertised copies for sale together with his own arrangement for string quintet (known now as K.406/516b) of the sombre Wind Serenade in C minor, K.388.

The wonderful String Trio in E♭ major, K.563, completed on 27 September 1788 was described by Mozart himself as 'Divertimento a sei Pezzi'. Its unfailing excellence shows that he had no difficulty in mastering this awkward medium, and that despite the great exertions of his two last symphonies, his power of invention was still unflagging. For this there is indeed continuing evidence in such diverse masterpieces as the Clarinet Quintet and *Così fan tutte*. Thus, any difficulty that Mozart may have had in starting the Quartet K.575, intended to be the first of six for the cello-loving King of Prussia, may well be largely due to that patron's passion. When in June 1790 Mozart himself said the task was still 'troublesome', he was surely alluding partly to the imbalance that had been caused by the need to give some prominence to the cello, and to his own innovations of texture and emphasis, much weight being given to the finales. The three quartets which he completed are the D major, K.575, entered in his catalogue in June 1789; the B♭ major, K.589, entered in May 1790; and the F major, K.590, entered in June 1790.

That Mozart's innovations were not just transient is shown by several features of his last chamber music for strings, the two superb quintets: K.593 in D major, completed December 1790, and K.614 in E♭ major, completed 12 April 1791. The formal novelty of K.593's first movement ('Larghetto – allegro – larghetto – allegro') is unique in all Mozart's instrumental music, and the astonishing finale with its contrapuntal brilliance continues the style of the finale of K.590. So too does the finale of K.614, which includes some extraordinary fugal virtuosity. The very opening of K.614, with the violas playing unaccompanied in thirds, surely extends the idea of the royal cello, by giving prominence to the generally less favoured instruments. From such points of style and form, these splendid last quintets can be seen as the crown of a continuum unique in Mozart's music of any type. It should be remembered that, however great the best of the quartets, it is the quintets in which Mozart towers above all others as a profound innovator in this kind of chamber music.

ALEC HYATT KING

String Sonatas, Duos, Trios

K.46d
Sonata in C major
NMA VIII:21
Vienna, 1 Sep 1768 (autograph)
Allegro; Menuetto I, II
vn, b
In autograph, tempo indication of first movement in Leopold Mozart's hand

K.46e
Sonata in F major
NMA VIII:21
Vienna, 1 Sep 1768 (autograph)
Allegro; Menuetto I, II
vn, b
In autograph, headings of both movements in Leopold Mozart's hand

K.266 (271f)
Trio in B♭ major
AMA XXIV, no.23a; NMA VIII:21
Supposedly Salzburg, early 1777
Adagio, Menuetto (Allegretto)
2 vn, b

K.423
Duo in G major
AMA XV, no.1; NMA VIII:21
? Salzburg, Jul–Oct 1783
Allegro; Adagio; Rondeau (Allegro)
vn, va

K.424
Duo in B♭ major
AMA XV, no.2; NMA VIII:21
? Salzburg, Jul–Oct 1783
Adagio – Allegro; Andante cantabile; Thema [con Variazioni] (Andante grazioso)
vn, va

K.563
Trio in E♭ major
AMA XV, no.4; NMA VIII:21
Vienna, 27 Sep 1788 (*Verzeichnüss*)
Allegro; Adagio; Menuetto (Allegretto); Andante; Menuetto (Allegretto); Allegro
vn, va, vc
Entered in *Verzeichnüss* as '*Ein Divertimento . . . di sei Pezzi*'. Berke (1982) suggests that not enough evidence exists to establish for certain the identity

of so-called 'Puchberg' Trio (K.563 or Piano Trio in E, K.542?), the work mentioned in Mozart's letters of 16 Apr 1789 and on or before 8 Apr 1790

String Quartets

K.80 (73f)
G major
AMA XIV, no.1; NMA VIII:20/1/i
Lodi, 15 Mar ('alle 7. di sera') 1770 (autograph)
Adagio; Allegro; Minuetto; Rondeau
Quartet originally consisted of 3 movements; Rondeau added later: [?] Vienna, 1773, or Salzburg, early 1774 (*Köchel 6*). (Paper-analysis of Rondeau suggests date of composition within period 1773–5 (Tyson, 1987).) Trio deleted and written out in revised form by Leopold Mozart (*Köchel 6*)

K.136–138 (125a–c)
Three Divertimentos
See 'Miscellaneous instrumental'

K.155 (134a)
D major
AMA XIV, no.2; NMA VIII:20/1/i
Supposedly Bolzano, Verona, end Oct–early Nov 1772
[Allegro]; Andante; Molto Allegro
In autograph, tempo indication of last movement in Leopold Mozart's hand. K.155–160 form qt cycle

K.156 (134b)
G major
AMA XIV, no.3; NMA VIII:20/1/i
Supposedly Milan, end 1772
Presto; Adagio; Tempo di Menuetto
In autograph, headings of last 2 movements in Leopold Mozart's hand. Original slow movement (Adagio, 24 bars) discarded; replacement movement is rhythmically and texturally more elaborate

K.157
C major
AMA XIV, no.4; NMA VIII:20/1/i
Supposedly Milan, end 1772 or early 1773
[Allegro]; Andante; Presto
In autograph, tempo indication of second movement in Leopold Mozart's hand

K.158
F major
AMA XIV, no.5; NMA VIII:20/1/i
Supposedly Milan, end 1772 or early 1773
Allegro; Andante un poco Allegretto; Tempo di Minuetto
In autograph, tempo indications of first 2 movements in Leopold Mozart's hand

K.159
Bb major
AMA XIV, no.6; NMA VIII:20/1/i
Supposedly Milan, early 1773
Andante; Allegro ('assai' deleted); Rondo (Allegro grazioso)
In autograph, tempo indications of outer movements, and possibly second movement, in Leopold Mozart's hand

K.160 (159a)
Eb major
AMA XIV, no.7; NMA VIII:20/1/i
Supposedly Milan, Salzburg, early 1773
Allegro; Un poco Adagio; Presto
In autograph, tempo indications of first 2 movements in Leopold Mozart's hand

K.168
F major
AMA XIV, no.8; NMA VIII:20/1/i
Vienna, Aug 1773 (autograph)
Allegro; Andante; Menuetto; Allegro
In autograph, date and tempo indications of first and (?) last movements in Leopold Mozart's hand. K.168–173 form qt cycle

K.168a
Minuet in F major
NMA VIII:20/1/i
? early 1775
Without trio. Dating from Plath (1976/7)

K.169
A major
AMA XIV, no.9; NMA VIII:20/1/i
Vienna, Aug 1773 (autograph)
Molto Allegro; Andante; Menuetto; Rondeaux (Allegro)
In autograph, date in Leopold Mozart's hand

K.170
C major
AMA XIV, no.10; NMA VIII:20/1/i
Vienna, Aug 1773 (autograph)
[Thema] Andante; Menuetto; Un poco Adagio; Rondeaux (Allegro)
In autograph, date and tempo indications of first, third, and last movements in Leopold Mozart's hand

K.171
Eb major
AMA XIV, no.11; NMA VIII:20/1/i
Vienna, Aug 1773 (autograph)
Adagio – Allegro assai – Adagio; Menuetto; Andante; Allegro assai
In autograph, date in Leopold Mozart's hand

K.172
Bb major
AMA XIV, no.12; NMA VIII:20/1/i
Vienna, ?Sep 1773
[Allegro spiritoso]; Adagio; Menuetto; Allegro assai

K.173
D minor
AMA XIV, no.13; NMA VIII:20/1/i
Vienna, [?Sep] 1773 (autograph)
Allegro ma molto moderato; Andantino grazioso; Menuetto; Allegro
In autograph, date and tempo indication of first movement in Leopold Mozart's hand. An earlier version of fugal finale (83 bars) survives

K.387
G major
AMA XIV, no.14; NMA VIII:20/1/ii
Vienna, 31 Dec 1782 (autograph)
Allegro vivace assai; Menuetto (Allegretto (first edition; Allegro: autograph)); Andante cantabile; Molto Allegro
Bars 125–42 of finale revised. First qt of celebrated set of 6 dedicated to Joseph Haydn. Set published by Artaria as op.X (Vienna, 1785). (Mozart's heartfelt Italian dedication is dated 'il p.^{mo} Settembre 1785'.)
K.387 appeared as no.1; for other qts of set, see below: K.421 (417b), 428 (421b), 458, 464 and 465. At private performance of last 3, on 12 Feb 1785, Haydn declared to Leopold Mozart (then in Vienna visiting Wolfgang): 'Before God and as an honest man I tell you that your son is the greatest composer known to me either in person or by name. He has taste and, what is more, the most profound knowledge of composition.'

K.421 (417b)
D minor
AMA XIV, no.15; NMA VIII:20/1/ii
? Vienna, Jun 1783
Allegro moderato ('moderato' cancelled in autograph, but present in first edition); Andante; Menuetto (Allegretto); Allegretto ma non troppo (originally Allegretto, then Andante)
According to Constanze (see Rochlitz; 1798–9), K.421 (417b) was being written during her first confinement (the baby, Raimund Leopold, was born 17 Jun 1783). Fragmentary attempt at slow movement (1 bar; only music for vn I written down) survives in autograph. Published by Artaria (Vienna, 1785) as op.X, no.2. See String Quartet in G, K.387

K.428 (421b)
Eb major
AMA XIV, no.16; NMA VIII:20/1/ii
? Vienna, Jun–Jul 1783

Allegro non troppo; Andante con moto; Menuetto
(Allegretto (first edition; Allegro: autograph));
Allegro vivace
Published by Artaria (Vienna, 1785) as op.X,
no.4. See String Quartet in G, K.387

K.458
B♭ major ('Hunt')
AMA XIV, no.17; NMA VIII:20/1/ii
Vienna, 9 Nov 1784 (*Verzeichnüss*)
Allegro vivace assai; Menuetto (Moderato);
Adagio; Allegro assai
Nickname from hunting-call character of first
movement's opening. Mozart apparently began
first movement in Vienna, spring or summer 1783
(Tyson, 1987), writing (to judge from ink) up to
bar 106; movement probably completed
somewhat later, possibly in latter half of 1784,
from which time apparently also date the slow
movement and finale (Tyson, 1987). Minuet and
Trio, fragmentary earlier version of Minuet (10
bars), and a fragmentary attempt at a finale in
polonaise rhythm (K.Anh.68 (589a), 65 bars; in
draft score from bar 9), can be assigned also to
1784 (Tyson, 1987). Another fragmentary attempt
at finale, a Prestissimo in ¢ time (13 bars; deleted),
survives in autograph on fol.29v; revised, final
version begins on fol.30r. Published by Artaria
(Vienna, 1785) as op.X, no.3. See String Quartet
in G, K.387

K.464
A major
AMA XIV, no.18; NMA VIII:20/1/ii
Vienna, 10 Jan 1785 (*Verzeichnüss*)
Allegro; Menuetto; Andante ('cantabile' deleted)
Allegro non troppo (first edition; Allegro:
autograph)
Judging from surviving autograph material for
'Haydn' quartets, it appears that composition of
K.464 may have given Mozart the most difficulty:
see in autograph, for instance, changes in
construction of Andante (set of variations), and
alterations in bars 9–17 of Minuet. Frag. in A
major K.Anh.72 (464a) (170 bars) – rondo in 6/8
time – should probably be regarded as rejected
attempt at finale. Published by Artaria (Vienna,
1785) as op.X, no.5. See String Quartet in G,
K.387

K.465
C major ('Dissonance')
AMA XIV, no.19; NMA VIII:20/1/ii
Vienna, 14 Jan 1785 (*Verzeichnüss*)
Adagio – Allegro; Andante cantabile (originally
Adagio); Menuetto (Allegretto: first edition;
Allegro: autograph); Allegro molto (first edition;
Allegro: autograph)
Nickname from controversial harmonic audacities
of opening slow introduction. Published by

Artaria (Vienna, 1785) as op.X, no.6. See String
Quartet in G, K.387

K.499
D major ('Hoffmeister')
AMA XIV, no.20; NMA VIII:20/1/iii
Vienna, 19 Aug 1786 (*Verzeichnüss*)
Allegretto; Menuetto (Allegretto); Adagio; Molto
Allegro (the 'Molto' a later addition in autograph:
also found in first edition)
Published by Hoffmeister (Vienna, 1786)

K.546
Adagio and Fugue in C minor
See 'Miscellaneous instrumental'

K.575
D major ('Prussian')
AMA XIV, no.21; NMA VIII:20/1/iii
Vienna, Jun 1789 (*Verzeichnüss*)
Allegretto (Allegro: *Verzeichnüss*); Andante;
Menuetto (Allegretto); Allegretto
Deleted fragmentary attempt at finale
('Rondeaux', 8 bars; only music for vn I notated)
survives in autograph score. *Verzeichnüss* entry:
'. . . for His Majesty the King of Prussia' (on
commission?): Mozart had visited the cello-
playing Friedrich Wilhelm II in spring 1789. 3
quartets (K.575, 589 and 590), now known as the
'Prussian' qts, were eventually comp. (published
by Artaria, without dedication, just after Mozart's
death). For probable comp. sequence of
movements of K.575, 589 and 590, see Tyson
(1987). See String Quartet in E minor, K.417d
('Fragments and sketches')

K.589
B♭ major ('Prussian')
AMA XIV, no.22; NMA VIII:20/1/iii
Vienna, May 1790 (*Verzeichnüss*)
Allegro; Larghetto; Menuetto (Moderato);
Allegro assai
Fragmentary attempt at minuet (K.Anh.75
(458a), 9 bars) and 2 fragmentary attempts at
finale (K.Anh.71 (458b), 10 bars; 'Allegretto', 18
bars; in autograph score; deleted; only music for
vn I notated) survive. See String Quartet in D,
K.575

K.590
F major ('Prussian')
AMA XIV, no.23; NMA VIII:20/1/iii
Vienna, Jun 1790 (*Verzeichnüss*)
Allegro moderato; Andante (autograph;
Allegretto: first edition); Menuetto (Allegretto);
Allegro
Sketch for minuet (42 bars; in short-score form)
and fragmentary attempt at finale (K.Anh.73
(589b), 16 bars; only some music for vn I and vc
notated) survive. See String Quartet in D, K.575

String Quintets (2 vn, 2 va, vc)

K.174
B♭ major
AMA XIII, no.1; NMA VIII:19/1
Salzburg, Dec 1773 (autograph)
Allegro moderato; Adagio; Menuetto ma
allegretto (autograph); Allegro
Supposedly written early in 1773 under influence
of Michael Haydn's Notturno in C, Perger 108
(dated 17 Feb 1773), and later revised (provided
with new trio and finale) in light of Notturno in
G, Perger 109 (dated 1 Dec 1773)

K.515
C major
AMA XIII, no.4; NMA VIII:19/1
Vienna, 19 Apr 1787 (*Verzeichnüss*)
Allegro; Menuetto (Allegretto); Andante
(originally Larghetto); [Allegro]
Above order of inner movements follows first
edition of Artaria (Vienna, 1789); sequence of
movements transmitted by present state of
autograph (adopted by NMA) reverses this order.
MS copies of qnts K.515, 516 and 406 (516b)
offered on subscription by Mozart in *Wiener
Zeitung* on 2, 5 and 9 Apr 1788; on account of
poor response, Mozart extended offer, on 25 Jun,
to 1 Jan 1789. Autograph score preserves
cancelled passage in finale (following bar 212; in
draft score)

K.516
G minor
AMA XIII, no.5; NMA VIII:19/1
Vienna, 16 May 1787 (autograph; *Verzeichnüss*)
Allegro; Menuetto (Allegretto); Adagio ma non
troppo; Adagio – Allegro
Frag. K.Anh.86 (516a) (G minor, 6/8, 8 bars; in
draft score) represents attempt at gypsy-style
finale; 2 melodic sketches for finale also survive:
[a] G minor, 6/8, 6 bars; resembles opening theme
of G minor Symphony K.550; [b] G major, 6/8, 8
bars. Fragmentary pf arrangement of slow
movement (6 bars) also exists: followed on same
leaf, of a paper-type found in K.516 (Tyson,
personal communication), by *Musikalisches
Würfelspiel* K.516f. Published by Artaria (Vienna,
1790). See String Quintet in C, K.515

K.406 (516b)
C minor
AMA XIII, no.2; NMA VIII:19/1
Vienna, probably 1788
Allegro; Andante; Menuetto in canone; [Allegro]
Arrangement of Wind Serenade in C minor,
K.388 (384a). 10 of score's 13 leaves (fols. 3–11,
and 13) of paper-type apparently used by Mozart
first in Dec 1787 and for most 1788 scores (Tyson,
1989); although first 2 leaves are of paper-type

used elsewhere by Mozart only in Act I of *Don
Giovanni* (Tyson, 1990), apparent consistency of
ink used in both opening Allegro and Andante
(fols. 1–7r) suggests that these 2 movements may
have been written down at same time (probably
in 1788). (Different inks of following movements
might suggest, but not necessarily, somewhat more
extended period for completion.) See String
Quintet in C, K.515

K.593
D major
AMA XIII, no.7; NMA VIII:19/1
Vienna, Dec 1790 (*Verzeichnüss*)
Larghetto (autograph; Adagio: *Verzeichnüss*) –
Allegro; Adagio; Menuetto (Allegretto); Allegro
Probably much of first, second and fourth
movements written before Mozart's trip to
Frankfurt in Sep 1790 (Tyson, 1987). Original vc
arpeggios in Trio (bars 14–28) rewritten (scored
lower). Initial chromatic, scalic figure of finale
altered in autograph by another hand: the zigzag
variants, which simplify performance but distort
movement's character and structure, probably
originated in Artaria's publishing house (Hess,
1961). See fragmentary Quintet movement in D,
K.Anh.83 (592b) ('Fragments and sketches')

K.614
E♭ major
AMA XIII, no.8; NMA VIII:19/1
Vienna, 12 Apr 1791 (*Verzeichnüss*)
Allegro di molto; Andante; Menuetto (Allegretto);
Allegro
See fragmentary Quintet movements in E♭,
K.Anh.81 (613a) and K.Anh.82 (613b)
('Fragments and sketches')

JOHN ARTHUR

Piano: sonatas and other works

Sonatas
Eighteen sonatas (including the composite K.533/
K.494), seventeen sets of variations and approximately sixty-five other pieces survive of Mozart's
output for solo piano, along with a set of variations
and six sonatas for two pianists. Of these, it cannot
be presumed that the average concertgoer would
know much more than the rondo *alla Turca* from
K.331 (300i), the theme that opens the same sonata,
the C minor and D minor Fantasias (K.475 and
K.397 (385g)) and conceivably the delightful D
major Sonata for piano duet, K.448. The more
knowledgeable might be familiar with, though
unable accurately to name, the pieces and sonata
movements they had been allowed to mangle in
their youth. Much of Mozart's solo piano music is all

too tempting to piano teachers: there is always a clear and satisfying melodic line and uncomplicated accompaniment within the reach of an infantile span; pleasing enough results may be achieved without too depressing a labour; and, as Joseph II might have said, there are not too many notes.

Teachers are still apt to ignore the evidence that the youthful composer was blessed with a prodigious humanity, evidence that shines through when a mature talent deigns to play one of these 'easy' works. Tainted as much by schoolroom association as by the unjust platitude that Mozart was not Beethoven, the best of this rich corpus is too often passed over in favour of works by later pianist–composers with hearts and techniques flaunted on sleeves. From even the most casual study of the sonatas it is evident that their 'simplicity' is actually restraint: the observation of the decorum of a musical form. The flare-ups of passion and overt virtuosity in the concertos and, indeed, some of the fantasias and later variations, were clearly thought unsuitable to the air of the more intimate (perhaps more academic) sonata.

Variations and other pieces
'I would rather neglect the piano than composition,' Mozart wrote to his father on 7 February 1778, 'for with me the piano is only a sideline, though, thank God, a very good one', and his corpus of variations and short pieces exemplifies this ambivalent attitude. For at least the first half of his brief career, keyboard performance as much as composition represented a livelihood, and the seventeen sets of variations, ingenious workings out of often highly popular or diplomatically chosen themes, were ideal recital pieces. Some, such as the thinly charming Fischer set, became the young performer's 'signature tunes' and were consequently much in demand. It is significant that variations were among the few of his keyboard works published in his lifetime. Parry's condemnation in *Grove* (1889) that, not being 'a man of deep feeling or intellectuality', Mozart's 'variation-building is neither impressive nor genuinely interesting', is too sweeping, ignoring the strengths of K.455, K.460 and the sets in sonatas K.284 and K.331.

The first series of short pieces (the London Sketchbook, K.Anh.109b (151a–ss)) was set down on paper during a visit to England in 1764–5. There may have been many more than the simple ones he had the time or inclination to copy down. They fall into two groups, written April–December 1764 and January–July 1765, the first group being of particular interest since it was set down during Leopold's bout of quinsy, when there was no piano to hand.

Although he did not need a keyboard to help him compose, Mozart used the piano for private experiments with counterpoint, as witnessed by a number of incomplete works from the early 1780s. Quite possibly he simply could not be bothered to write

them all down. One must remember his childish love of maths: the fun lay in the execution.

Duets
Music for two pianists was most unusual when Mozart's K.19d Duet Sonata in C was composed in 1765. Indeed, Leopold is said to have claimed that it was the first sonata to have been written for the medium. (That may have been the showman in him.) A letter of Nannerl to Breitkopf & Härtel in 1800 claimed that her brother had written down other such, still in her possession. Alas they are now lost, but they may have numbered a duet still earlier than K.19d. Two more duet sonatas, K.381 (123a) and K.358 (186c) were composed before Charles Burney's four sonatas were published in 1777, and two duets by J.C. Bach the following year. W.F. Bach wrote duets and Johann Christian wrote successors to his op.15, but none of these works was published.

The duet has never thrown off its air of a variety turn – strangely, since it is no less difficult and certainly no more amusing for two pianists to join forces than four string players. Its appeal for Mozart was limited, of course, by the lack of variety in the tone (there is nothing like four hands loudly busy at one keyboard to remind one that the piano is percussive), but by K.448 and 497 he had sufficient experience in orchestral and vocal writing to make the most of its quasi-conversational potential. Undoubtedly he was happiest writing for two pianos, where the 'vocal' jokes are apt to be less and the mechanical range is so much greater. There is a *galant* finesse to the two-piano Sonata in D, K.448 (375a), and the sombre two-piano Fugue K.426 is unparalleled. It is significant, however, that he arranged the latter for strings; as if the duet form were for him essentially sociable, humorous, anti-academic indeed. One cannot sit through, much less play, K.448 or the Double Piano Concerto K.365 without smiling.

Pianos
Mozart was working at a time when Burney's 'scratch with a note at the end of it' was developing, at a bewildering rate, into what we think of as a piano, and in his professional travels must have been called upon to perform on several varieties of keyboard instrument. Salzburg's Mozart Museum contains a piano by Anton Walter of Vienna. This has two octaves less than the modern keyboard, a damper pedal operated by the player's knee and a knob on the frontpiece to control the damper between hammer and string for an *una corda* effect. The Beethoven piano in Vienna has five pedals: to elevate the dampers, place a felt between hammer and string, place parchment over the strings for a 'harpsichord' effect, create a total sostenuto effect in the lower register and an *una corda* pedal. There is also a stop on the right-hand side of the keyboard

giving one a choice of *una* or *due corde* effects. Within ten years of Mozart's death, Erard was to make a piano for Napoleon I, with 'sourdine', 'janissary', 'bassoon' and 'celeste' among its effects.

Anyone lucky enough to have played Mozart on a fortepiano of the Longman and Broderip or early Viennese type will vouch for the immediate impression of clarity, particularly in the lower octaves. Where a passage of low-lying, rapid 'Alberti' (broken-chord) bass is apt to produce, within the great metal frame of a modern grand, a kind of sonic mud, on the fortepiano each note stands as clear of its neighbour as on a harpsichord. Smooth speed is easily attainable on an instrument whose notes take only an ounce of pressure to sound and whose keys have a quarter-inch touch. Another startling discovery is the eerie sound of *una corda* playing: thin and bloodless, never muffled. The Mozart household possessed an instrument from the workshop of Franz Jakob Spaeth, but we know from a letter to Leopold of 17 October 1777 that Mozart's favourite piano was that made by the Augsburger, Johann Andreas Stein. The appropriate passage needs full quotation:

> This time I shall begin at once with Stein's pianofortes. Before I had seen any of this make, Späth's claviers had always been my favourites. But now I much prefer Stein's, for they damp ever so much better than the Regensburg instruments. When I strike hard, I can keep my finger on the note or raise it, but the sound ceases the moment I have produced it; in whatever way I touch the keys, the tone is always even. It never jars, it is never stronger or weaker or entirely absent; in a word, it is always even. It is true that he does not sell a pianoforte of this kind for less than 300 gulden, but the trouble and the labour that Stein puts into the making of it cannot be paid for. His instruments have this splendid advantage over others, that they are made with escape action. Only one maker in a hundred bothers about this. But without an escapement it is impossible to avoid jangling and vibration after the note is struck. When you touch the keys, the hammers fall back again the moment after they have struck the strings, whether you hold down the keys or release them.

Mozart's ideas on keyboard technique

The technical demands in the sonatas vary little from the first group to the last, suggesting that Mozart's prodigious, early technique remained little altered. His letters give frequent insights into his strong views on the subject. That to Nannerl of 7 June 1783 recommends quiet hands and flexible wrists and deplores inaccurate speed. 'Supposing that you do play sixths and octaves with the utmost velocity (which no one can accomplish, not even Clementi) you only produce an atrocious chopping effect and nothing else whatever.' Elsewhere he insists on precise attention to dynamics and on the strict tempo that should be observed by the left hand when the right is playing tempo rubato in an adagio.

His criticism of Clementi's mechanical panache, of Vogler's rushed performance of one of the concertos, and a cruelly funny letter of 23 October 1777 depicting the gross affectations of Maria Stein's playing build up a picture of a pianist happier with a display of 'taste' (24 April 1784), 'feeling' (28 April 1784) and 'proper precision' (13 November 1777) than with technical ostentation. He writes to Leopold on 22 November 1777, 'You know that I am no great lover of difficulties'. It was doubtless because he mastered pianistic 'difficulty' at such a tender age that his respect (and arguably his most challenging work for piano solo) were reserved for the slow movement. 'It is much easier to play a thing quickly than slowly: in difficult passages you can leave out a few notes without anyone noticing it. But is that beautiful music?'

Influences and keyboard inheritance

J.C. Bach Arguably the closest to Mozart's pianistic ideal in his marriage of Italian and German styles was Johann Christian Bach. Mozart's admiration is evident in quotations, from Bach's Quintet in D, op.11 no.6, in the Rondo K.485 and from the fourth sonata of a set of six, op.17, in the Allegro of K.333. 'I love him (as you know) and respect him with all my heart', he writes. 'And as for him, there is no doubt but that he has praised me warmly, not only to my face, but to others also, and in all seriousness – not in the exaggerated manner which some affect.' (letter of 27 August 1778)

J.S. Bach Though the piano and organ masterpieces of Bach *père* were still largely unknown in Vienna at the time, Mozart was introduced to them in 1781 through his involvement, as performer and arranger, in Baron van Swieten's Sunday morning private concerts. This encounter bore substantial fruit not only in Mozart's church music, but also in the extraordinary Prelude and Fugue in C, K.394 (383a), and in the contrapuntal flavour of the later sonatas.

Haydn Joseph Haydn is singled out by Einstein as the second influence after J.C. Bach, but his greatest legacy to Mozart was his demonstration of the potential of the string quartet. Although he stands at the head of the piano sonata tradition, it could be argued that the tradition came down to Beethoven through Clementi, and passed Mozart by. In their discreet way, Haydn's piano sonatas are revolutionary where Mozart's seek perfection within a respected structure. Haydn's six sonatas of 1773 may be reflected in the irregularity of K.282 (189g) and, were it not for the purely Mozartian tone of its rondo, K.281 (189f) could be read as a homage. If the work of Haydn's younger brother Michael affected Mozart in his keyboard music, it was only in the realm of the meditative slow movement: 'a kind of reverie that often attained the summit of his artistic creation' (Saint-Foix, 1932).

Leopold Mozart Leopold's influence on the development of his son's piano playing and composition cannot be overstated. Himself a distinctly Salzburger composer, he supplied Mozart's earliest keyboard models: Telemann, C.P.E. Bach, Hasse and Kirchoff.

Eckard In Brussels Mozart came across the sonatas of Johann Eckard, pianist, composer and pupil of C.P.E. Bach. Having inherited the then innovatory sonata form from Bach, Eckard developed it into a three-movement format. A devotee of the broken-chord 'Alberti' accompaniment, prevalent in the earlier of Mozart's piano works.

Schobert Sonata form was also developed by Johann Schobert, a Paris-based harpsichordist and composer with a greater popular following than the dusty Eckard. Despite Leopold's ever-protective fears of a tasteless influence ('Low and not at all what he should be', he called him), Schobert's use of minor keys and tempo rubato to pathetic effect left a beneficial mark on K.310 (300d).

Clementi In standing for so much that Mozart claimed to abhor, Clementi unwittingly helped define Mozart's piano aesthetic. Although the Clementi sonatas before 1780 lack grace or subtlety, being little more than vehicles for his virtuoso talents, and although he produced nothing of maturity before 1791, he was yet a professional presence to be reckoned with. As popular trifles, Clementi's early sonatas represent public renown and easy money; Mozart's attack on them in a letter addressed to Nannerl is conceivably charged with envious irritation as much as fraternal concern:

> Everyone who either hears them or plays them must feel that as compositions they are worthless. They contain no remarkable or striking passages except those in sixths or octaves. And I implore my sister not to practise these passages too much, so that she may not spoil her quiet, even touch and that her hand may not lose its natural lightness, flexibility and smooth rapidity. (7 June 1783)

After a degrading 'contest' of their talents on Christmas Eve 1781, Mozart grew increasingly venomous on the subject of his rival's skill as either pianist ('a Mechanicus') or composer ('ciarlatano'). Even a year and a half later he was to write, 'Apart from this, he can do nothing, absolutely nothing, for he has not the slightest expression or taste, still less, feeling.'

If Clementi cannot be said to have been an influence, Mozart pandered to similar tastes for mechanical display in certain of his sets of variations and works for four hands.

Tonality

Mozart's keyboard writing is notable for the restraint of its tonal progressions in comparison with Haydn's. In the Haydn sonatas, tonality wanders for the sake of variety and surprise, and his enharmonic devices can even result in changes of key signature within a movement. Mozart's modulations, on the other hand, are always demanded by the logic of sonata structure: he employs simple, even neutral tonal bases such as C, D, F, B♭ and E♭, and any surprise effects are the more surprising for their infrequency. The blandness of his chosen keys means that departures that sound startling can be less than revolutionary, such as the diminished seventh chord in bars 15–16 of the Andante K.283 (189h).

There are exceptions. The shorter fantasias are, by their nature, quasi-improvisatory and surprising. The Sonata K.310 (300d) employs the 'tragic' key of A minor and its dark mood and overtly dramatic feel have tempted observers to form unwise connections with the darkness of 1778 in Mozart's life. In its use of A major, K.331 (300i) explores the opposite pole with a tonality that suits the sonata's hybrid, showy nature. The C minor of the Sonata K.457 and Fantasia K.475 is the most obvious exception example of an expressive tonality, yet even K.457 is anchored by an E♭ major Adagio at its centre.

Solo piano: Sonatas

K.279 (189d)
C major
AMA XX, no.1; NMA IX:25/i
Munich, early 1775
Allegro; Andante; Allegro
K.279–283 comp. when Mozart was in Munich for premiere of *La finta giardiniera*, probably as travelling repertoire that might also be readily copied for would-be patrons

K.280 (189e)
F major
AMA XX, no.2; NMA IX:25/i
Munich, early 1775
Allegro assai; Adagio; Presto

K.281 (189f)
B♭ major
AMA XX, no.3; NMA IX:25/i
Munich, early 1775
Allegro; Andante amoroso; Rondeau: Allegro
Haydn influence noticeable (perhaps homage?) In Rondo, claimed as Mozart's first departure from J.C. Bach's influence, good humour vies with virtuosity

K.282 (189g)
E♭ major
AMA XX, no.4; NMA IX:25/i
Munich, early 1775
Adagio; Menuetto I and II; Allegro
This and K.331 are only pf sonatas with first movements not in sonata form

K.283 (189h)
G major
AMA XX, no.5; NMA IX:25/
Munich, early 1775
Allegro; Andante; Presto

K.284 (205b)
D major
AMA XX, no.6; NMA IX:24/i
Munich, early 1775
Allegro; Rondeau en polonaise: Andante; Thema:
Andante (and 12 variations)
Comp. for Baron Thaddäus von Dürnitz (1756–
1807). First sonata for which Wyzewa and Saint-
Foix find no model. Mozart's first use of variations
within a sonata (only other is to open K.331) and
his first set of them to have depth as well as
variety. Fragmentary attempt at first movement
(71 bars) survives at head of autograph score

K.309 (284b)
C major
AMA XX, no.7; NMA IX:25/i
Mannheim, Oct–Nov 1777
Allegro con spirito; Andante un poco adagio;
Rondeau: Allegretto grazioso
Written for Rosina [Rosa] (b. 1764), daughter of
the Mannheim court musician and composer
Christian Cannabich. Mozart comp. Andante as a
musical portrait of Rosa (letter of 6 Dec 1777).
Also signs of impression made by Mannheim
orchestral devices

K.311 (284c)
D major
AMA XX, no.9; NMA IX:25/i
Mannheim, Oct–Nov 1777
Allegro con spirito; Andante con espressione;
Rondo: Allegro

K.310 (300d)
A minor
AMA XX, no.8; NMA IX:25/i
Paris, summer 1778
Allegro maestoso; Andante cantabile con
espressione; Presto
Displays, like K.309, understanding of new
piano's enhanced dynamic and sostenuto capacity

K.330 (300h)
C major
AMA XX, no.10; NMA IX:25/ii
?Salzburg, 1783
Allegro moderato; Andante cantabile; Allegretto
K.330–333 probably to be regarded as teaching
and perf. material prepared before Mozart's
return to Vienna from Salzburg. For first edition
of K.330, among other alterations, Mozart added
4-bar coda to Andante

K.331 (300i)
A major
AMA XX, no.11; NMA IX:25/ii
?Salzburg, 1783
Andante grazioso; Menuetto & Trio; Alla Turca:
Allegretto
Showpiece sonata with fashionable 'Turkish'
flavour. Makes no use of sonata form

K.332 (300k)
F major
AMA XX, no.12; NMA IX:25/ii
?Salzburg, 1783
Allegro; Adagio; Allegro assai
In Adagio, first edition presents highly
embellished decoration of reprise

K.333 (315c)
B♭ major
AMA XX, no.13; NMA IX:25/ii
?Linz, 1783
Allegro; Andante cantabile; Allegretto grazioso
No doubt a concert vehicle for Mozart's own use

K.457
C minor
AMA XX, no.14; NMA IX:25/ii
Vienna, 14 Oct 1784 (*Verzeichnüss*)
Molto Allegro; Adagio; Allegro assai (in first
edition; [Allegro] agitato in copy)
Published and usually perf. with Fantasia in C
minor, K.475 (see separate entry). Dedicated to
pupil Therese von Trattner, wife of Johann
Thomas von Trattner, publisher and printer

K.533 (with K.494)
F major
AMA XXII, no.8 and XXII, no.14; NMA
IX:25/ii
Rondo: Vienna, 10 Jun 1786 (autograph). Allegro
and Andante: Vienna, 3 Jan 1788 (*Verzeichnüss*)
Allegro; Andante; Rondo: Allegretto (autograph:
Andante)
Rondo, K.494, in expanded form (with a new 27-
bar cadenza), later joined by Mozart to Allegro
and Andante to form sonata, published by
Hoffmeister (Vienna, 1788). Allegro's seemingly
effortless contrapuntal passages are reminder that
Mozart had been arranging Bach fugues for
Swieten's str ensembles. Comparatively narrow
range of K.494 led Einstein to suggest that it was
comp. for older piano than K.533

K.545
C major
AMA XX, no.15; NMA IX:25/ii
Vienna, 26 Jun 1788 (*Verzeichnüss*)
Allegro; Andante; Rondo: Allegretto grazioso
Entered in Mozart's thematic catalogue with
description 'for beginners'. Unpublished during
Mozart's lifetime

K.570
B♭ major
AMA XX, no.6; NMA IX:25/ii
Vienna, Feb 1789 (*Verzeichnüss*)
Allegro; Adagio; Allegretto
Possibly teaching material? First edition (Vienna, 1796) with vn accompaniment probably spurious. Fragmentary attempt at a sonata first movement (K.Anh.31/569a, 19 bars) probably to be linked to K.570 (Tyson, 1987)

K.576
D major
AMA XX, no.17; NMA IX:25/ii
Vienna, Jul 1789 (*Verzeichnüss*)
Allegro; Adagio; Allegretto
Traditionally associated with Mozart's supposed commission to write 'six easy sonatas for Princess Friederike' of Prussia (letter to Puchberg, 12–14 Jul 1789). However, this commission is unproven and musical character of K.576 would seem to resist such a connection

Solo piano: Variations

K.Anh.208 (24)
8 Variations in G major
on *Laat ons Juichen* by C.E. Graaf (1723)
AMA XXI, no.1; NMA IX:26
The Hague, Jan 1766
Based on a Dutch song and published in The Hague, 1766

K.25
7 Variations in D major
on *Willem van Nassau*
AMA XXI, no.2; NMA IX:26
Amsterdam, Feb 1766
Based on a Dutch national song, possibly early 17th century

K.180 (173c)
6 Variations in G major
on 'Mio caro Adone' from Salieri's *La Fiera di Venezia* (Vienna, 1772)
AMA XXI, no. 4; NMA IX:26

K.179 (189a)
12 Variations in C major
on Minuet (finale of Oboe Concerto no.1 by J.C. Fischer)
AMA XXI, no.3; NMA IX:26
Salzburg, summer 1774
This set was Mozart's showpiece in Munich in 1774 and Paris 1778 and is good example of contemporary taste, given Leopold's reference to its popularity

K.354 (299a)
12 Variations in E♭ major
on 'Je suis Lindor' from A.L. Baudron's incidental music to *Le Barbier de Séville* by Beaumarchais
AMA XXI, no.9; NMA IX:26
Paris, spring/summer 1778
One of Mozart's most highly valued concert pieces, played frequently by him later in Vienna

K.265 (300e)
12 Variations in C major
on *Ah vous dirai-je Maman* (French song)
AMA XXI, no.6; NMA IX:26
Vienna, 1781–2
Traditional dating of 1778 (during period of mother's illness and death in Paris) now considered to be erroneous. Revised date supported by Plath's handwriting studies

K.353 (300f)
12 Variations in E♭ major
on *La Belle Françoise*
AMA XXI, no.8; NMA IX:26
Vienna, 1781–2

K.264 (315d)
9 Variations in C major
on 'Lison dormait' from N. Dezède's *Julie* (Paris, 1772)
AMA XXI, no.5; NMA IX:26
Paris, late summer/autumn 1778

K.352 (374c)
8 Variations in F major
on 'Dieu d'amour' (March), chorus from *Les Mariages samnites* by Grétry (Paris, 1776)
AMA XXI, no.7; NMA IX:26
Vienna, Jun 1781

K.398 (416e)
6 Variations in F major
on 'Salve tu, Domine' from *I filosofi immaginarii* by Paisiello (Vienna, 1781)
AMA XXI, no.10; NMA IX:26
Vienna, Mar 1783
Showy concert vehicle with 3 cadenzas

K.460 (454a)
8 Variations in A major
on 'Come un agnello' from *Fra i due litiganti* by Sarti (Milan, 1782)
AMA XXI, no.12
See 'Fragments and sketches'

K.455
10 Variations in G major
on 'Les Hommes pieusement' ('Unser dummer Pöbel meint') from *La Rencontre imprévue* by Gluck (Vienna, 1764)
AMA XXI, no.11; NMA IX:26
Vienna, 25 Aug 1784 (*Verzeichnüss*)
Mozart improvised variations on this air, probably in Gluck's presence, at a concert on 23

Mar 1783; fragment of nearly 5 complete variations (in which variations V and VIII of the final version follow variation III) probably from this time

K.500
12 Variations in B♭ major
on anonymous Allegretto (by Mozart?)
AMA XXI, no.13; NMA IX:26
Vienna, 12 Sep 1786 (*Verzeichnüss*)

K.54 (547a, 547b)
5 Variations in F major
NMA IX:26
Vienna, Jul 1788
Theme probably original. Hoffmeister's first edition (Vienna, 1793) has spurious 4th variation and coda (the latter missing in autograph). Reworked from vn sonata, K.547

K.573
9 Variations in D major
on Minuet from vc sonata op.4 no.6 by J.P. Duport
AMA XXI, no.14; NMA IX:26
Potsdam, 29 Apr 1789 (*Verzeichnüss*)
Possibly written in honour of Duport, chamber music director of Friedrich Wilhelm II, to whom Mozart presented at this time. Mozart's thematic catalogue lists only 6 variations

K.613
8 Variations in F major
on 'Ein Weib ist das herrlichste Ding' by B. Schack or F. Gerl, from Schikaneder's play *Der dumme Gärtner* (Vienna, 1789)
AMA XXI, no.15; NMA IX:26
Vienna, Mar 1791

Miscellaneous

K.1a
Andante in C major
NMA IX:27/i
Salzburg, early 1761

K.1b
Allegro in C major
NMA IX:27/i
Salzburg, early 1761

K.1c
Allegro in F major
NMA IX:27/i
Salzburg, 11 Dec 1761

K.1d
Minuet in F major
NMA IX:27/i
Salzburg, 16 Dec 1761

K.1 (1e)
Minuet in G major
AMA XXII/1, no.1; NMA IX:27/i
Salzburg, Dec/Jan 1761/2

K.1f
Minuet in C major
NMA IX:27/i
Salzburg, Dec/Jan 1761/2

K.2
Minuet in F major
AMA XXII, no.2; NMA IX:27/i
Salzburg, Jan 1762

K.3
Allegro in B♭ major
AMA XXII, no.12; NMA IX:27/i
Salzburg, 4 Mar 1762

K.4
Minuet in F major
AMA XXII, no.3; NMA IX:27/i
Salzburg, 11 May 1762

K.5
Minuet in F major
AMA XXII, no.4; NMA IX:27/i
Salzburg, 5 Jul 1762

K.9a (5a)
Allegro in C major
NMA IX:27/i
Summer 1763

K.33B
Piano piece (untitled) in F major
NMA IX:27/ii
Zurich, beginning Oct 1766

K.61gII
Minuet in C major
NMA IX:27/ii
1770

K.94 (73h)
Minuet in D major
AMA XXII, no.5; NMA IX:27/ii
Salzburg, 1769

K.284a
Prelude in C major
AMA XXIV, no.24; NMA IX:27/ii
Munich, beginning Oct 1777
Known as Capriccio, K.395 (300g). This 4-section praeambulum is work arising from Nannerl's commission in postscript to her father's letter of 28–9 Sep 1777

K.315a (315g)
8 minuets
NMA IX:27/ii
Salzburg, end 1773
Orchestral version has not survived. Trio of no.8 has nothing to do with this set, being written later, around 1779–80 (Plath, 1976/7)

K.394 (383a)
Prelude and fugue in C major
AMA XX, no.18; NMA IX:27/ii
Vienna, Apr 1782
Comp. to satisfy Constanze's desire for fugue. In letter to Nannerl (20 Apr 1782) Mozart describes its origins and how prelude comp. while fugue being written down

K.408/1 (383e)
March in C major
NMA IX:27/ii
Vienna, probably 1782
Arranged from one of Marches for orchestra, K.408

K.396 (385f)
Fantasia in C minor
AMA XX, no.19; NMA IX:27/ii
See Sonata movement in C minor for pf and vn, K.396 (385f) ('Fragments and sketches')

K.397 (385g)
Fantasia in D minor
AMA XX, no.20; NMA IX:27/ii
Vienna, ?early 1782 or later
Originally a frag? Last 10 bars missing in first edition (Vienna, 1804); supplied probably by A.E. Müller for the later Breitkopf & Härtel edition (Hirsch, 1944)

K.399 (385i)
Suite in C major
AMA XXII, no.10; NMA IX:27/ii
Vienna, probably 1782
Ouverture; Allemande; Courante
Frag. Sarabande incomplete (6 bars). Style of Handel

K.453a
Marche funebre del Sig.r Maestro Contrapunto
NMA IX:27/ii
Vienna, 1784
Comic death march in spirit of Act I of Così

K.475
Fantasia in C minor
AMA XX, no.21; NMA IX:25/ii
Vienna, 20 May 1785 (*Verzeichnüss*)

Adagio; Allegro; Andantino; Più allegro; Tempo primo
Published with Sonata in C minor K.457 (Vienna, 1785) as op.11, though with its wealth of fully developed ideas can stand alone

K.485
Rondo in D major
AMA XXII, no.7; NMA IX:27/ii
Vienna, 10 Jan 1786 (autograph)
Not entered in Mozart's thematic catalogue. Dedication (to Charlotte von Würben?) on autograph has been erased

K.509
6 German dances
NMA IX:27/ii
Prague, 6 Feb 1787
Contrary to his usual practice, Mozart seems to have written the pf arrangement before orchestral version (Flothuis, 1980a)

K.511
Rondo in A minor
AMA XXII, no.9; NMA IX:27/ii
Vienna, 11 Mar 1787 (autograph and *Verzeichnüss*)

K.540
Adagio in B minor
AMA XXII, no.16; NMA IX:27/ii
Vienna, 19 Mar 1788 (*Verzeichnüss*)
Described by Hutchings as finest single work for pf. Only known independent piece in B minor. Fragmentary attempt (K.deest, 6 bars) survives in copy by Aloys Fuchs

K.574
Eine kleine Gigue in G major
AMA XXII, no.7; NMA IX:27/ii
Leipzig, 16 May 1789 (autograph)
Modelled on gigue from Handel's 8th Suite in F minor. Written extempore in notebook of K.I. Engel, court organist at Leipzig

K.355 (576b)
Minuet in D major
AMA XXII, no.6; NMA IX:27/ii
Vienna, ?c. 1789–91
Autograph unknown; published by Mollo (Vienna, 1801) with a trio in B minor by the Abbé Stadler

K.236 (588b)
Andantino in E♭ major
AMA XXII, no.15
Vienna, ?c. 1790
Theme by Gluck; intended for variations?

Piano duet (one keyboard): Sonatas

K.19d
Sonata in C major
NMA IX:24/ii
London, summer 1765
Salzburg family portrait of 1780–81 may show
Nannerl and Wolfgang playing this, given that
her left and his right hand are crossed as at one
moment in Rondo

K.381 (123a)
Sonata in D major
AMA XIX, no.3; NMA IX:24/ii
Salzburg, mid-1772
Allegro; Andante; Allegro molto
Performed with Nannerl in Paris and Vienna.
'Best described as a reduction of an Italian
symphony' (Einstein)

K.358 (186c)
Sonata in B♭ major
AMA XIX, no.2; NMA IX:24/ii
Salzburg, 1773–4
[Allegro]; [Adagio]; Molto presto
Performed with Nannerl in Paris and Vienna.
Notable for a brilliant finale

K.497
Sonata in F major
AMA XIX, no.4; NMA IX:24/ii
Vienna, 1 Aug 1786 (*Verzeichnüss*)
Adagio; Allegro di molto; Andante; [Allegro]

K.521
Sonata in C major
AMA XIX, no.5; NMA IX:24/ii
Vienna, 29 May 1787 (*Verzeichnüss*)
Written for Franziska von Jacquin

Variations

K.501
Andante with 5 variations in G
AMA XIX, no.6; NMA IX:24/ii
Vienna, 4 Nov 1786 (*Verzeichnüss*)
Theme of unknown provenance (probably
Mozart's own). Originally intended for 2 pf but
published as conventional duet for 1 pf, 4 hands

Piano duet (two keyboards)

K.426
Fugue in C minor
AMA XIX, no.7; NMA IX:24/i
Arranged in 1788 for str qt or str band with
Adagio introduction as K.546 (which has in turn
been arranged for 2 pf)

K.448 (375a)
Sonata in D major
AMA XIX, no.8; NMA IX:24/i
Vienna, Nov 1781
Possibly work played by Mozart and his pupil
Josepha Auernhammer, at private concert on 23
Nov 1781. Described by Einstein as high point of
development of *concertante* style

PATRICK GALE

Mechanical organ and armonica

Mechanical organ
Compositions for a mechanical instrument have the
peculiar virtue of sounding exactly as the composer
intended, so long as said instrument survives; for
once in a creator's life, personal interpretation,
human error and editorial whim cannot interfere. In
an age before wax or electrical recording, and where
publication and reputation were at best erratic, the
exact and relatively long-lived account of one's
creation promised by a machine must have wielded
a certain attraction, however puny or undignified
the machine in question. Two of the Mozart organ
barrels survived (or were duplicated) long enough to
be in the possession of Haydn's clockmaker, Pater
Primitivus Niemecz in 1801.

In this instrument, cursed by the reluctant
composer, a clock set a pinned barrel in motion at
regular intervals which in turn dictated the sounding of pipes. The flue pipes were tucked away behind
the clockwork, or boxed in beneath it. The clockwork motor driving the organ was usually separate
from that driving the accompanying timepiece,
doubtless because the instrument needed rewinding
far more often and thus could be allowed to fall
conveniently silent without one's losing track of the
time. Stopped pipes were introduced so as to lower
the instrument's pitch, but to judge by Mozart's
complaints, Count Deym's instrument had none.
Ever since Elizabeth I gave one to the Sultan of
Turkey in 1599, clockwork organs had been popular
diplomatic gifts among the German aristocracy and
merchant classes, not least for the ruinous expense
they represented. Fashionable demand was fed by
such diverse patrons as Frederick the Great, Marie
Antoinette, Cardinal Richelieu and Napoleon. The
Flötenuhr industry flourished in Breslau, Dresden,
Vienna and Augsburg, but especially in Berlin,
where Frederick had Swiss clockmakers brought
under Abram-Louis Hugue in the 1760s. Vienna's
best organ builders included the brothers Johann
Nepomuk and Leonard Maelzel, friends of Beethoven, and the mechanical builders Joseph Hain,
Johann Adolf Heyer and Johann Georg Strasser.
Strasser's giant barrel organ – effectively a mechanical orchestra – had barrels of two of Mozart's piano
concertos and one of his string quartets.

Count Deym's waxworks

The *Wiener Zeitung* of 26 March 1791 tells of Herr Müller (alias Joseph Count Deym von Stržitéž – he changed his name to Müller after a duel), the art collector, opening his Mausoleum on the ground floor of number 1355 of the Himmelpfortgasse in memory of Field-Marshal Baron von Loudon (*recte* Laudon). It was advertised as:

> splendidly illuminated till ten o'clock at night . . . the sight of it will not fail to surprise everyone who visits this Mausoleum and thereby renews the memory of this great and meritorious man. . . . The seats are arranged in the best possible way and each person pays 1 fl. for a first place and 30 kr. for a second; upon the stroke of each hour a Funeral Musique will be heard, and will be different every week. This week the composition is by Herr Kapellmeister Mozart.

An account of the gallery, published six years later, indicates that Mozart's composition, which it says 'surpasses, in precision and clarity, everything which was ever attempted or designed for this kind of artistic product', was still in public use.

Under the name Müller Deym ran the *Kunstkabinett* on Stock-im-Eisen-Platz, moved his collection (and, presumably, the instrument with Mozart's music) to the Kohlmarkt, then again to Rotenturmstrasse on the Danube Canal in 1798. After the composer's death, a wax mask of Mozart joined that of Joseph II in the collection. The din in the collection must have been insufferable, unless performances were very carefully staggered, since among the items on display were a musical bracket clock, an automatic piano, a 'mechanical pan', a musical pyramid, two flute-playing Spanish youths (mechanical, one assumes), The Bedroom of the Graces and a mechanical canary.

The music

Laudon died on 14 July 1790 and tradition associates K.594 with the work commissioned by 'Müller' later that year. It should further be noted that there is no evidence beyond conjecture that Deym also commissioned K.608 and K.616; this is inferred because the music is mechanical and Deym's was Vienna's only performance place for such works. A letter to Constanze of 3 October 1790 shows Mozart far from keen to proceed with his commission:

> I compose a bit of it every day but I have to break off now and then as I get bored. If it were for a large instrument, the work would sound like an organ piece, then I might get some fun out of it. But as it is the works consist solely of little pipes, which sound too high-pitched and too childish for my taste.

Evidently by this stage in his career, Mozart could achieve a substantial work with even a minimum level of interest. There is a solemn complexity to K.594 and K.608 above and beyond the terms of Deym's bombastic memorial description of the former. The extraordinary enhanced recapitulation of the K.594 Adagio material drives King (1955) to the claim: 'There are few passages in all his music that surpass the power and pathos of these thirty-seven bars. Their sustained chromaticism, to which no parallel can be found in his own works, is remarkably advanced for 1790.' Given that this is music for little more than a glorified waxworks show, the severely cerebral fugue in K.608 (which held such appeal for Beethoven that he copied it out) is positively subversive.

It is tempting to believe Deutsch's conjecture that the enchanting bell-like clarity of the Andante, K.616, was intended for Deym's automaton. This small confection would not be out of place in a scene of *Die Zauberflöte* and would be admirably suited to such sinister mechanical trickery.

Surviving instruments

Deym's instruments with Mozart barrels are assumed destroyed, but the K.616 Andante is played in a shortened version by a fine instrument once in the Heyer Museum and now in the Musikwissenschaftliches Institut und Musikinstrumentensammlung der Karl Marx Universität in Leipzig. For an illustration see Ord-Hume, 1982. Ord-Hume also tells of a mechanical barrel organ in the Nationaal Museum van Speelklok tot Pierement in Utrecht found to play an arrangement by 'Mozart' of a Tyrolean song.

Glass armonica

The earliest record of musical glasses played in Europe is to be found in the *Theorica musicae* of Gaffurius (Milan, 1492). A 1596 inventory of the Ambras collection, presently housed in the Kunsthistorisches Museum, Vienna, lists 'Ain Instrument von Glaswerck' with a scale of three and a third octaves. It was not until the 18th century, however, that the glasses began to be used for serious musical performance. By the mid-century an Irishman, Richard Pockrich, had developed a technique of stroking a glass's rim – a subtle improvement upon striking the glass with a stick. Gluck performed a concerto for twenty-six glasses in the Haymarket Theatre in London in April 1746 and repeated the performance in Copenhagen in 1749. In 1761 one Ann Ford published a manual recommending dampening of the fingertips. In the same year, Benjamin Franklin was inspired by a performance in Cambridge by Edmund Delaval to improve the existing method. He fastened a 'scale' of the bowls of glasses on a single horizontal rod spun by a crank and pedal action, and proposed calling his new instrument the armonica (no relation to the mouth organ); his design was executed by Charles James.

Later innovations included automatic moistening of the glasses by a shallow reservoir through which they spun, a keyboard and a sounding-board. Goethe claimed that in the sound of the armonica he could detect 'Das Herzblut der Welt' ('the heart's-blood of the world'), while in the same era the instrument was banned in some towns by the German police, on the grounds that it had a dangerous deranging effect.

The Adagio in C, K.356 (617a), was composed for the celebrated blind armonica player Marianne Kirchgässner, but she was not the first executant of the instrument whom Mozart encountered: the English player Marianne Davies embarked on a European tour with her sister Cecilia in 1768 and met the Mozarts in Vienna in 1773.

Thanks to The *Morning Chronicle*'s review of Marianne Kirchgässner's performance (probably of K.617) at a Haydn–Salomon concert at the Hanover Square Rooms, on 17 March 1794, we have some idea of the instrument's charm and limitations:

> Her taste is chastened, and the dulcet notes of the instrument would be delightful indeed, were they more powerful and articulate; but that we believe the most perfect execution cannot make them. In a smaller room, and an audience less numerous, the effect must be enchanting. Though the accompaniments were kept very much under, they were still occasionally too loud.

Mechanical organ and armonica

K.594
Adagio and Allegro in F minor
for mechanical organ
AMA XXIV, no.27a; NMA IX:27/ii
Vienna and elsewhere, Oct–Dec 1790
Adagio; Allegro; Adagio
Entered in Mozart's catalogue as *Ein Stück für ein Orgelwerk in einer Uhr* ('a piece for an organ in a clock'). Survives, like K.608, in form of transcriptions on 4 staves made early in 19th century

K.608
Fantasia in F
for mechanical organ
AMA X, no.19; NMA IX:27/ii
Vienna, 3 Mar 1791
Allegro; Andante; Tempo primo
Entered in Mozart's catalogue as *Ein Orgel Stück für eine Uhr* ('an organ piece for a clock')

K.616
Andante in F major
for mechanical organ
AMA X, no.20; NMA IX:27/ii
Vienna, 4 May 1791 (*Verzeichnüss*)
Entered in Mozart's catalogue as *Ein Andante für eine Walze in einer kleine Orgel* ('an andante for a cylinder in a small organ'). For possibly related frag. see K.615a ('Fragments and sketches')

K.617
Adagio and Rondo
for glass armonica, fl, ob, va, vc
AMA X, no.18; NMA VIII:22/1
Vienna, 23 May 1791 (*Verzeichnüss*)
Composed for blind armonica virtuoso Marianne Kirchgässner (1769–1808), who perf. it in Kärntnerthor theatre on 19 Aug. Fragmentary Fantasia (Adagio) in C major K.Anh.92/616a (13 bars; part in draft score) probably first attempt at K.617

K.356 (617a)
Adagio in C major
for glass armonica
AMA X, no.17; NMA IX:27/ii
Vienna, 1791
No doubt a companion piece for K.617

PATRICK GALE

Sacred music

Masses

At present sixteen complete Mass Ordinary settings by Mozart are accepted as authentic, in addition to two incomplete masterpieces, the C minor Mass K.427 (417a) and the Requiem K.626. Two isolated Kyrie settings also survive complete, an early work for SATB and strings, K.33, and a much finer one for chorus and orchestra in D minor K.341 (368a). There are also a number of fragmentary movements, most of them very short.

Naturally, many of Mozart's early Mass Ordinary settings were the product of his duties as a member of the Salzburg court establishment, though others, as we know from his letters and those of his family, were written for occasional use on his early travels as a child prodigy. The early Kyrie mentioned above was composed in Paris and is dated 12 June 1766. A more important work, and Mozart's earliest known complete Mass setting, is the C minor Mass K.139 (47a), which is now identified with the work which he directed before the imperial court in Vienna on 7 December 1768. The occasion was the dedication of the new Orphanage Church (Waisenhauskirche) and the setting is therefore appropriately in the tradition of the *missa solemnis*, with the standard fugal sections to end the Gloria and Credo. Of the other three Mass settings which date from this period, two, K.49 (47d) in G major and K.65 (61a) in D minor, are musically unpretentious works in the *missa brevis* tradition. A third, K.66 in C major (known as the *Dominicus* Mass), is one of the best-known of Mozart's juvenile settings. A more ambitious work of the *solemnis* type, it was first performed on 15 October 1769 at St

Peter's, Salzburg, at the first Mass celebrated by Mozart's childhood friend Cajetan Hagenauer. In the autumn of 1773 the work was revived under the direction of Leopold Mozart in a performance in the Jesuit Church 'Am Hof' in Vienna.

The three Italian journeys undertaken by the Mozarts between December 1769 and March 1773 allowed Wolfgang to observe Italian liturgical practice during this period. In the meantime, the death of Mozart's tolerant former employer, Siegmund, Count von Schrattenbach, in 1771 had set in motion a new attitude to church music in Salzburg which was to affect Mozart until his final departure for Vienna in 1781. Although his successor, Hieronymus Colloredo, scarcely deserves some of the adjectives hurled at him over the years by pious Mozartians, he was undoubtedly far more influenced than Schrattenbach by Enlightenment views on church music and sought after a rational and functional approach which stressed concision and subordinated musical considerations to the audibility of the text. A famous letter written by Mozart to Padre Martini on 4 September 1776 explains that 'a Mass, with the whole Kyrie, the Gloria, the Credo, the epistle sonata, the Offertory, the Motet, the Sanctus and the Agnus, must . . . last no longer than three-quarters of an hour'. Colloredo also showed interest in introducing German hymns into the Salzburg liturgy, but the so-called 'ban on fugues' repeatedly mentioned in the Mozart literature is now known to be a fiction. It has also been pointed out that masses by Salzburg predecessors of Mozart such as Eberlin are frequently no longer than the limits in force under Colloredo.

However, the fact remains that most of the settings dating from the next Salzburg period (1773–7, interrupted by extended visits to Vienna and Munich) are concise and make much use of uncomplicated choral declamation with little repetition of phrases. The first of these is the Missa Brevis in G major, K.140 (235d, Anh.C 1.12), which was regarded as dubious by the editors of the sixth edition of Köchel (1964) but has now been reclassified as authentic. A more ambitious setting from the same year (1773) is the *Missa Sanctissimae Trinitatis*, K.167, whose scoring with four trumpets in the orchestra suggests performance on a solemn occasion. Mozart returned to the *missa brevis* form for works written in the following year: K.192 (186f) in F major and K.194 (186h) in D major. They are unassuming, somewhat functional works with much choral declamation, little text repetition and no final fugues for Gloria or Credo. K.192 has a Credo based on the four-note motto later used for the finale of the *Jupiter* Symphony; this was not an innovation but a traditional figure. If some of this music has a quality of routine, the restrictions and petty frustrations of life in Salzburg can partly be held to blame.

Six further Mass Ordinary settings date from the two-year period between Mozart's return from Munich on 7 March 1775 and his departure with his mother for Paris on 23 September 1777. The most elaborate of them is K.262 (246a), which was probably composed in Salzburg in June or July 1775 for an as yet unidentified occasion (see Tyson, 1987). The others, of the *missa brevis* type, all have their points of interest. The C major Missa Brevis K.220 (196b), known as the *Spatzenmesse* (*Sparrow* Mass) from the chirping violin figures in its Sanctus, is a good example of the recapitulation convention in which the music of the Kyrie returns for the 'Dona nobis pacem' of the Agnus Dei. Three further settings, K.257 (dated November 1776), K.258 (December 1775) and K.259 (December 1775 or 1776) (Tyson, 1987) are all of the *brevis* type and all (like K.262) in C major. The reason for the choice of this key for so many of the Salzburg Mass settings was apparently the need to use trumpets in D with the organ tuned to high choir pitch, confirmed in a few cases by the existence of added woodwind parts written in D major, a tone above the strings and organ. Noteworthy features of this group of works include the reappearance of the traditional four-note motto (also used in K.192) in the Credo of K.257 (hence known as the *Credo* Mass) and the organ obbligato part in K.259 (the *Organ* Mass). The final setting from this period is K.275 (272b) in B♭ major, which was performed in St Peter's on 21 December 1777. It is a *missa brevis* scored without trumpets, which are excluded by the choice of key (though Michael Haydn used B♭ trumpets in Salzburg church music).

Mozart's final years in Salzburg (1779–81), following the unhappy Paris–Mannheim period, were marked by a further increase in tension with his employer, culminating in his resignation and decision to settle in Vienna. Although Mozart's dissatisfaction with life at Salzburg was deep-seated and long-lasting, it has been suggested that Colloredo's reformist attitude to church music may have played a part in bringing matters to a head. An archiepiscopal letter of 29 June 1780 (on which Mozart gave his views in characteristically colourful language) demanded less elaborate church music and the introduction of German hymns. Certainly Mozart's last two Salzburg masses, K.317 and 337 (both in C major) suggest that he would have found the consequent restriction of his artistic freedom unacceptable. The former work, which is the most celebrated of all his Salzburg settings, is known as the *Coronation* Mass, not, as often stated, because it was sung at the ceremonial coronation of a statue of the Virgin Mary but because Salieri directed a performance at the coronation of Leopold II in 1791 in Prague, where it became known in court circles as the *Krönungsmesse*. It essentially follows the *missa brevis* convention, but with recurring material and more freedom than usual. The lovely Agnus Dei, a florid soprano solo in aria style, is particularly well-known today.

Mozart was not professionally involved with church music in Vienna, and would indeed probably not have found the climate for its composition more sympathetic than in Salzburg. Joseph II shared Colloredo's aspirations for a rationally ordered church music with musical elaboration firmly held in check, and seems to have been in sympathy with the Koblenz *Gravanima* (1769) and the Munich *Nuntiatur* (1785) which sought to establish a national order for church music in spite of any papal opposition. It is noteworthy that Haydn composed no masses between 1782 and 1796, by which time the restrictions imposed by Josephianism were gradually being lifted. Not surprisingly, therefore, Mozart produced only two further Mass settings during the last ten years of his life: the C minor Mass and the Requiem, both of which can be regarded as occasional works. Both are unfinished.

The C minor Mass, K.427 (417a) was apparently intended as a thanks offering for his marriage to Constanze Weber, as Mozart intimates in a letter of 4 January 1783, which describes the work as lying half-finished on his desk. The Kyrie and Gloria are complete, but the Credo breaks off after the 'Et incarnatus', which itself has missing string parts requiring editorial reconstruction. Mozart seems to have completed the Sanctus and Benedictus, but the surviving copy is in a corrupt state which obscures his intentions. H.C. Robbins Landon has demonstrated that the Sanctus was originally written for double chorus, not for the four-part and five-part choruses of the surviving version. There is no Agnus Dei. Despite its unfinished state a version of the work was performed in St Peter's, Salzburg, on 26 October 1783 under Mozart's direction and with Constanze, for whom the florid soprano arias may have been intended, taking part. The work, a *missa solemnis* on a far larger scale than most of the Salzburg masses, belongs to the tradition of the cantata mass, in which successive portions of text are laid out as separate movements rather than set continuously. Although an incomparably greater work than the early Salzburg masses, it has sometimes been criticized for a lack of stylistic cohesion. Mozart's interest in the antique or 'learned' style, which was fostered by the gatherings in the household of Baron Gottfried van Swieten in which he participated, is evidenced by his use of archaic continuo textures in some of the solo movements, as well as the double chorus writing and the pseudo-Handelian scoring at the beginning of the Credo. However, there is nothing in the *stile antico* fugal writing which goes beyond the strict contrapuntal discipline he had already mastered in Salzburg. The Mass includes a number of florid arias which suggest Italian influence. One of them is the well-known 'Et incarnatus', in which a soprano part of almost Baroque expansiveness unfolds a sinuous dialogue with the wind instruments. In 1785, Mozart salvaged eight numbers from the unfinished work for the cantata *Davidde penitente*, K.469 (libretto attributed to Lorenzo da Ponte), which was first performed in the Burgtheater on 13 March.

One mystery of Mozart scholarship is the provenance of the magnificent, isolated D minor Kyrie, K.341 (368a). Traditionally, the work has been tentatively assigned to the period in 1780–81 that Mozart spent in Munich, mainly because the orchestra includes clarinets, which were not available in Salzburg. Unfortunately, the autograph is lost and there is no concrete evidence to support this dating: it is even possible that the work remained a fragment, completed after Mozart's death. The suggestion, however (Tyson, 1987), that K.341 may have been composed around 1788 as part of a studious attempt to master the kind of music expected from a Kapellmeister at St Stephen's (by analogy with the numerous church fragments and copies from this time), or that it originated in connection with Mozart's duties as unpaid assistant Kapellmeister to Leopold Hofmann from 9 May 1791 onwards (Landon, 1988) should probably be resisted on stylistic grounds (John Arthur, personal communication).

K.33
Kyrie; F major
AMA III/1, no.1
Paris, 12 Jun 1766 (autograph)
SATB, str

K.139 (47a)
Missa Solemnis; C minor
(***Waisenhausmesse***)
AMA III/1, no.4; NMA I:1/1/i
?Vienna, autumn 1768
S, A, T, B, SATB, 2 ob, 4 tpt, 3 trbn, timp, str, org
Perf. at opening of Orphanage Church in Rennweg, Vienna, 7 Dec 1768

K.49 (47d)
Missa Brevis; G major
AMA I/1, no.1; NMA I:1/1/i
Vienna, 1768 (autograph)
S, A, T. B, SATB, [3 trbn], str, org
Draft for Gloria (S, SATB, b, org; 18 bars) and alternative version of Credo, bars 182–95 (K.Anh.20a (626b/25), 15 bars) survive

K.65 (61a)
Missa Brevis; D minor
AMA I/1, no.2; NMA I:1/1/i
Salzburg, 14 Jan 1769 (autograph)
S, A, T, B, SATB, str, org
Perf. at Salzburg collegiate church, 5 Feb 1769
Sketch for Kyrie (4 bars) and 3 rejected versions of Benedictus in autograph score (9 bars; 8 bars; 13 bars) survive

K.66
Missa; C major (*Dominicus* Mass)
AMA I/1, no.3; NMA I:1/1/i
S, A, T, B, SATB, 2 ob, 2 hn, 2 [+2] tpt, [3 trbn], timp, str, org
Salzburg, Oct 1769 (autograph)
Comp. for first Mass celebrated by Cajetan Hagenauer (Father Dominicus), first perf. St Peter's, Salzburg, 15 Oct 1769; later revived, under Leopold's direction in the Jesuit Church 'Am Hof', Vienna, autumn 1773
Draft for Gloria, bars 310–43 (SATB; 34 bars), and beginning and end of rejected original version of Credo, bars 134ff. (8 bars; 6 bars), survive in autograph score

K.140 (235d, Anh.C 1.12)
Missa Brevis; G major
NMA I:1/1/i
?Salzburg, 1773
S, A, T, B, SATB, 2 vn, b
Considered dubious by editors of *Köchel 6* but now considered authentic: see Senn, NMA I:1/1/i, xiii ff. Parts have autograph corrections

K.167
Missa; C major ('in honorem Sanctissimae Trinitatis')
AMA I/1, no.5; NMA I:1/1/ii
Salzburg, Jun 1773 (autograph)
SATB, 2 ob, 4 tpt, [3 trbn], timp, 2 vn, b, org

K.192 (186f)
Missa Brevis; F major
AMA I/1, no.6; NMA I:1/1/ii
Salzburg, 24 Jun 1774 (autograph)
S, A, T, B, SATB, 2 tpt (added later by Mozart). [3 trbn], 2 vn, b, org

K.194 (186h)
Missa Brevis; D major
AMA I/1, no.7; NMA I:1/1/ii
Salzburg, 8 Aug 1774 (autograph)
S, A, T, B, SATB, [3 trbn], 2 vn, b, org

K.220 (196b)
Missa Brevis; G major (*Spatzenmesse*)
AMA I/1, no.8; NMA I:1/1/ii
1775–6
S, A, T, B, SATB, 2 tpt, [3 trbn], timp, 2 vn, b, org

K.262 (246a)
Missa Longa; C major
AMA I/2, no.12; NMA I:1/1/ii
Salzburg, 1775 (Jun or Jul: see Tyson, 1987)
S, A, T, B, SATB, 2 ob, 2 hn, 2 tpt, [3 trbn, timp], 2 vn, b, org

K.257
Missa; C major (*Credo*)
AMA I/1, no.9; NMA I:1/1/iii
Salzburg, Nov 1776 (autograph)
S, A, T, B, SATB, 2 ob, 2 tpt, [3 trbn], timp, 2 vn, b, org
Sketch possibly for a Gloria (30 bars; ? to be associated with K.257) and various sketches for Credo survive on a single sketchleaf

K.258
Missa Brevis; C major (*Spaur* or *Piccolominimesse*)
AMA I/2, no.10; NMA I:1/1/iii
Salzburg, Dec 1775 (see Tyson, 1987) (autograph)
S, A, T, B, SATB, 2 ob, 2 tpt, timp, 2 vn, b, org

K.259
Missa Brevis; C major (*Organ Solo*)
AMA I/2, no.11; NMA I:1/1/iii
Salzburg, Dec 1775 or 1776 (Tyson, 1987) (autograph)
S, A, T, B, SATB, 2 ob, 2 tpt, timp, 2 vn, b, org
Cancelled fragmentary attempt at Sanctus (21 bars) survives in autograph score

K.275 (272b)
Missa Brevis; B♭ major
AMA I/2, no.13; NMA I:1/1/iv [not yet pubd]
Salzburg, late 1777
S, A, T, B, SATB, 2 vn, b, org
Perf. St Peter's, Salzburg, 21 Dec 1777, and probably the B♭ Mass referred to by Mozart in letter of 12 Jul 1791 to Baden choirmaster, Anton Stoll

K.317
Missa; C major (*Coronation*)
AMA I/2, no.14; NMA I:1/1/iv [not yet pubd]
Salzburg, 23 Mar 1779 (autograph)
S, A, T, B, SATB, 2 ob, 2 hn, 2 tpt, 3 trbn, timp, 2 vn, b, org

K.337
Missa Solemnis; C major
AMA I/2, no.15; NMA I:1/1/iv [not yet pubd]
Salzburg, Mar 1780 (autograph)
S, A, T, B, SATB, 2 ob, 2 bn, 2 tpt, 3 trbn, timp, 2 vn, b, org
Fragmentary attempt at Credo (Tempo di Ciaccoña, 136 bars) survives in autograph score

K.341 (368a)
Kyrie; D minor
AMA III/1, no.5
?Munich, Nov 1780–Mar 1781
SATB, 2 fl, 2 ob, 2 cl, 2 bn, 4 hn, 2 tpt, timp, str, org
Origins unknown: Otto Jahn's suggested dating followed by all editions of Köchel. See above text

K.427 (417a)
Missa; C minor
AMA XXIV, no.29; NMA I:1/1/v
Vienna, *c.* end 1782–*c.* Oct 1783, Salzburg
2S, T, B, SSAATTBB, fl, 2 ob, 2 bn, 2 hn, 2 tpt, 3
trbn, timp, str. org
Fragment. Kyrie and Gloria complete; Credo
incomplete: only 'Credo in unum Deum' and 'Et
incarnatus est' written (substance complete in
draft score). Reconstruction of Sanctus (only wind
and timp. parts survive in Mozart's hand) and
Benedictus (nothing extant in autograph) can be
attempted on basis of secondary source material.
Agnus Dei not composed. Fragmentary attempt at
'Gratias' (?; 1 bar; in draft score) survives in
autograph score; 2 sketches for a 'Dona nobis
pacem' (3 bars; 8 bars; ? represent post-Salzburg
attempt at completion) also survive. Perf. St
Peter's, Salzburg, 26 Oct 1783. For comp. dates,
see Tyson (1987)

Requiem

The most celebrated of all Mozart's sacred works is
the Requiem, K.626, composed late in 1791 and left
unfinished at his death. The composition history of
the work is surrounded by a mass of anecdotal
evidence of variable quality. It is certain that
Mozart received a commission in the summer of
1791 from Count Walsegg-Stuppach (1763–1827, a
fellow-freemason) for a Requiem in memory of his
wife, who had died on 14 February at the age of
twenty. Walsegg, who is now regarded as a harmless
crank rather than the villainous plagiarist depicted
by 19th-century biographers of Mozart, was a
passionate music-lover who held private concerts in
his castle at Stuppach at which works by various
composers were played. Walsegg recopied the parts
himself and invited the listeners to guess the identity
of the composer (report by Anton Herzog, discovered by O.E. Deutsch and reprinted in translation
in Landon, 1988). There is no reason to believe that
he seriously intended to pass off Mozart's Requiem
as his own composition.

A number of early biographers (including Rochlitz, 1798, Niemetschek, 1798 and the anonymous
author of an article in the *Salzburger Intelligenzblatt*
for 7 January 1792) give details of the financial
transactions which took place and relate that
Mozart, by now increasingly ill and depressed, took
the Count's grey-clad emissary as a messenger of
death and worked feverishly on the Requiem in the
conviction that he was writing it for himself.
However naive and unacceptable the view of
Mozart's character many of these stories present,
their Hoffmannesque aspects appealed hugely to the
Romantic imagination and still retain a hold on the
public mind today. Although Mozart had financial
problems and was not in the best of health, his letters

of the period give no reason to believe that he was
haunted by thoughts of mortality. Furthermore, it
has been pointed out that the handwriting of the
autograph is fluent and robust, not at all suggesting
the work of a sick man (Hildesheimer, 1977).

Work on the Requiem was delayed by two major
projects – the operas *La clemenza di Tito* and *Die
Zauberflöte*, the former involving the visit to Prague of
August–September 1791 – and again by the Clarinet Concerto, K.622, and *Eine kleine Freimaurerkantate*, K.623. About 20 November 1791 Mozart's final
illness set in, and on 5 December he died, with the
score still incomplete. The famous account of
Mozart's death written by his sister-in-law Sophie
Haibel in 1825 describes him as supervising a read-
through of the score on his death-bed and discussing
the completion of the work with his pupil Franz
Xaver Süssmayr, who is generally believed to have
composed the *secco* recitatives for *La clemenza di Tito*.
Other writers confirm that Mozart had discussed the
score with Süssmayr. However, after Mozart's death
Constanze initially gave the score to another former
pupil, Joseph Eybler, for completion. When asked at
a later stage to explain her failure to turn to
Süssmayr immediately she replied that she had been
'annoyed' with him for reasons which she had since
forgotten. Eybler added some instrumentation to
Mozart's autograph, but was unable to complete the
task. According to one account it was only after
approaching several other composers that Constanze turned to Süssmayr, who produced the
completion which became standard, though its
validity is increasingly challenged today. For some
reason Süssmayr also forged Mozart's signature and
the date 1792 on the autograph score, though it was
common knowledge that Mozart was already dead
by then. Landon, 1988, gives a facsimile of Süssmayr's forged signature together with authentic
Mozart signatures for comparison.

The controversy about the extent of Süssmayr's
contribution to the score has continued unabated to
the present day, and no more than a summary of the
issues involved is possible here. Many of the statements advanced at the time were the work of
interested parties. Süssmayr claimed to have
'prepared' the Sanctus, Benedictus and Agnus Dei,
which are not found in Mozart's autograph. This
was widely (though perhaps wrongly) interpreted as
a claim to sole authorship of these sections. As such,
it was disputed by Constanze and her supporters,
who generally took the view that his work was
minimal and purely routine. Investigation of the
paper-types found in the autograph score (Tyson,
1987) indicates that none of the work was written
down before Mozart's return to Vienna from Prague
in September. The autograph reveals that Mozart
composed the introit and the essential material of
the Kyrie; the instrumentation of the latter was
completed by Süssmayr and F.J. Freystädtler.
Mozart also composed, in outline, the six sections of

the sequence (though the final 'Lacrimosa' breaks off after eight bars) and the two sections of the offertory ('Domine Jesu Christe' and 'Hostias et preces'). The incomplete draft for these eight movements contains all the vocal parts, a meticulously figured basso continuo and some important indications as to the accompanying instrumentation. Much of Süssmayr's work on these sections can legitimately be described as routine filling-in of accompanying parts. He added some touches of his own, including the trombone entry which occurs halfway through the 'Tuba mirum', though the more thematically important trombone melody at the beginning of the movement is by Mozart. For the closing sections (Sanctus, Benedictus, Agnus Dei, communion) nothing survives in Mozart's hand, but much of the music is on a high enough level to arouse strong suspicions in the minds of most commentators that they contain at least some authentic material. Despite Süssmayr's claim to be the sole author of the Sanctus, Benedictus and Agnus Dei, this view derives some support from an interesting statement by Constanze to Maximilian Stadler (1826) that Süssmayr removed some small pieces of paper (Zettelchen), from Mozart's desk after his death. The final communion simply repeats music from Mozart's introit and Kyrie, in accordance with conventional practice in the Viennese concerted Mass, and according to at least one early biographer at Mozart's request. A surviving sketchleaf discovered by Wolfgang Plath (Plath, 1963) shows that Mozart intended to complete the 'Dies irae' with an 'Amen' fugue, not the simple plagal cadence in Süssmayr's version. This sketch has been completed in the edition by Richard Maunder.

Much recent work on the Requiem has concentrated on the problems of disentangling Süssmayr's material from Mozart's and devising versions which approach Mozart's intentions more closely. The version by Franz Beyer (1971), which has been chosen in preference to Süssmayr's for several recent recordings, emends much of Süssmayr's added instrumentation and makes a number of other changes, including the addition of a brief orchestral coda to the 'Osanna' fugue. Beyer also criticized Süssmayr's part-writing, especially his tendency to soften Mozart's archaic cadence formulae by adding dominant sevenths and supplying thirds to chords which Mozart had intended as open fifths. A more radical solution has been proposed by Richard Maunder (and recorded in 1983 by Christopher Hogwood and the Academy of Ancient Music on the L'oiseau-lyre label). Maunder rejects the Sanctus, the Benedictus and the continuation of the 'Lacrimosa' as spurious additions by Süssmayr, basing his arguments on their alleged ineptitude and faulty musical grammar, and also makes a brave attempt to complete Mozart's projected 'Amen' fugue. In general, however, the tendency of 20th-century scholarship is to conclude that Süssmayr's role in the completion of the work was less than was commonly supposed a century ago. To many, the fine quality of the Agnus Dei seems difficult to reconcile with the mediocrity of Süssmayr's own church music, and certain features of the Sanctus and Benedictus strongly suggest that they too are based on authentic material. In 1989, Landon prepared a new edition, using all the extant material by Eybler but retaining all the remaining additions by Süssmayr unchanged. This new version has been recorded and was first performed at the Cheltenham Festival 1990.

Stylistic studies of the Requiem have also illuminated the extent to which Mozart relied on conventional models. The work as a whole shows a fusion of learned, operatic and masonic elements, this time more successfully integrated than in the C minor Mass. Commonly cited models are the Requiem by Mozart's Salzburg colleague Michael Haydn (1771) and a setting by Florian Gassmann which seems to have influenced Mozart's introit. The quoted psalm tone (in this case the tonus peregrinus) in the verse of the introit ('Te decet hymnus') was a conventional feature, found in introit settings by Georg Reutter the younger. The same device occurs in Michael Haydn's Requiem and in Mozart's own Masonic Funeral Music, K.477 (479a), which resembles a Mass introit in form. The famous trombone solo in the 'Tuba mirum' was also a conventional feature in Mass settings from the Hofkapelle tradition, employed in works by Fux and Georg Reutter the younger. Other movements are in the 'learned' church style of which Mozart had, as he often claimed, a complete mastery. The Kyrie is set as a double fugue on a subject of a conventional minor-key type also found in Bach, Handel and Haydn. The other two fugal movements are the 'Osanna' (a conventional feature of the Viennese Mass) and the projected unrealized final 'Amen' fugue probably intended for the sequence. The frequent canonic passages ('Recordare', 'Confutatis maledictis' and especially the opening of the introit) and the recurring neo-Baroque cadence formulae are also part of the more archaic stratum of the Requiem. The masonic elements include the prominent basset-horns, which featured in the wind bands or 'columns of harmony' normally heard at masonic gatherings of the period. Mozart's sensitivity to their unearthly solemnity is heard unforgettably at the opening of the whole work. The 'Hostias et preces' is another of the masonic movements, set in the manner of a hymn in the 'wisdom' key of E♭ major. The priestly tone of the bass solo in the 'Tuba mirum', with its calm rising and falling tenths, is in the manner of Sarastro's music in Die Zauberflöte, and the movement ends with a sententious chorus in Mozart's masonic manner. The opening of the 'Dies irae', which recalls the Queen of Night's aria 'Der Hölle Rache kocht in meinem Herzen' in Die Zauberflöte, reinforces an association of the key of D minor in Mozart's music with concepts of doom or divine vengeance, a flat plane against which the E♭ major of the 'Hostias' stands out as one of the emotional climaxes of the work. From an analytical point of view, the Requiem is exceptionally strongly integrated, with the opening five-note figure D–C♯–D–E–F recurring in various forms in most of the movements (including the disputed Agnus Dei). The opening melody of the 'Dies irae', transformed into the major, forms the basis of the Sanctus, and its ending is reused as the fugue subject of the 'Osanna'.

K.626
Requiem; D minor
AMA XXIV, no.1; NMA I:1/2/i–ii
Vienna, late 1791
S, A, T, B, SATB, 2 basset-hn, 2 bn, 2 tpt, 3 trbn, timp, str, org
Fragment. Surviving autograph music: Introit: 'Requiem aeternam'; (complete); Kyrie (substance complete in draft score); Sequence: 'Dies irae' (substance complete in draft score), 'Tuba mirum' (substance complete in draft score), 'Rex tremendae' (substance complete in draft score), 'Recordare' (substance complete in draft score), 'Confutatis' (substance complete in draft score), 'Lacrimosa' (breaks off after 8 bars; in draft score); Offertory: 'Domine Jesu' (substance complete in draft score), 'Hostias' (substance complete in draft score). No autograph material for Sanctus, Benedictus, Agnus Dei extant. Sketch for bars 7ff. of 'Rex tremendae' (5 bars), and sketch for an 'Amen' fugue (16 bars), probably for close of Sequence, survive. Completed by F.X. Süssmayr

Miscellaneous sacred music

A high proportion of Mozart's ecclesiastical works in forms other than the Mass Ordinary cycle also date from the Salzburg period, though some are the product of his travels round Europe as a child prodigy. The most substantial works apart from the mass settings are the Vespers and Litanies, all composed in conjunction with Mozart's duties as a church musician for the Salzburg court musical establishment. Of the three known sets of Vespers the first, K.193 (186g) (completed July 1774), comprises only a single psalm (*Dixit Dominus*), and a Magnificat. With its bustling string writing, choral declamation interspersed with short 'learned' passages and 'church' scoring without upper woodwind or violas, the music recalls many of Mozart's Mass movements of the same period.

Two further settings (K.321 and 339), both dating from 1779–80, are more substantial, each including a full set of five psalms (the same ones in both works) and Magnificat. The fact that both sets follow the Roman liturgy proves that the Cathedral was the intended location, since St Peter's followed the Benedictine order, with only four Vesper psalms. It has been pointed out (NMA critical commentary) that the liturgical description *Vesperae de Dominica* applied to K.321 is strictly speaking incorrect, since Sunday Vespers include Psalm 113 (*In exitu Israel*) rather than Psalm 116 (*Laudate Dominum*) as set by Mozart. As mentioned above, both K.321 and K.339 in fact include the same set of psalms. However, it is possible that lax 18th-century practice allowed a deviation from the strict requirements of the liturgy. The better-known set, which ranks among Mozart's most enduring church compositions, is K.339, the *Vesperae solennes de confessore* of 1780. Here the full complement of psalms gives Mozart the opportunity to use a more varied range of styles, ranging from an austere fugal setting of *Laudate pueri* to the justly famous *Laudate Dominum*, a radiant soprano aria with alternating choral sections and an optional obbligato bassoon part (the corresponding text in K.321 is also set as an aria, this time with obbligato organ). Mozart continued to take an interest in both works after his departure from Salzburg, for he wrote to his father (letter of 12 March 1783) asking for copies with a view to performances at the Van Swieten private concerts.

Mozart's four known litanies were all apparently composed for ceremonial and processional use in accordance with local custom. Litanies are processional chants in responsorial form addressed in most cases to the Virgin and the saints (who may include saints venerated by local custom) or to the Sacrament. They have an alternating responsorial form in sections punctuated by the response 'Ora pro nobis' and 'Miserere nobis'. The Kyrie and Agnus Dei from the Mass Ordinary are also included. Two of the litanies are settings of the Litany of Loreto, the use of which had been officially approved by Pope Sixtus V in 1557, while the other two set the Litany of the Sacrament. All four litany settings fall within Salzburg church usage, as exemplified by a long line of Salzburg church musicians (Biechteler, H.I.F. and C.H. Biber, Eberlin, Adlgasser and Leopold Mozart) as well as by works by better-known figures from the mainstream Viennese tradition (Fux, Caldara, Georg Reutter the younger and Bonno). The Salzburg church calendar for 1772 prescribes performances of litanies with concerted music for the 'forty-hour prayer' in Holy Week (beginning on Palm Sunday at about 6.30 in the main choir of the cathedral) as well as for the feasts of St Nepomuk, St Roche and St Michael and within their octaves. Mozart's settings, the last three of which are on a large scale, are in the multi-movement cantata form evolved by Neapolitan composers of the end of the 17th century. The Mass-derived texts (Kyrie, Agnus Dei) are often set in a manner which closely recalls his own settings as part of the Mass Ordinary cycles, with much homorhythmic choral declamation, busy accompanying string figuration and a minimum of text repetition. Other portions of the text are set as arias, often of some elaboration (an example is the florid tenor setting of *Panis vivus* from K.125 or the soprano aria setting of the Agnus Dei in K.243). The long texts, with their constantly recurring refrains, pose compositional problems which Mozart has to overcome by exercising concision, though K.243 does find room for a freely executed quasi-fugue in the final section.

The early setting of the Litany of Loreto, K.109 (74e), an unpretentious five-movement work dating from May 1771, is modelled on Leopold Mozart's Marian litany in F major. A second, more expansive setting of the Litany of Loreto K.195 (186d) was added in 1774. Mozart's two sacramental litanies (*Litaniae de venerabili altaris sacramento*) stand in a similar relationship to each other. The setting in B♭ major of March 1772 (K.125) is closely based on a setting in C major by Leopold, though it surpasses its model. It was followed four years later by a finer setting in E♭ major, K.243. On 20 November 1777 Mozart asked his father to send the performing material for this work to him in Mannheim for a projected performance in Augsburg, one of several reports of early performances of these works we have from Mozart and his father and sister.

The miscellaneous shorter church works, which number about two dozen, fall into various different categories. Our overall view of them has changed somewhat in recent years because some have been rejected as spurious. Two psalm settings in Mozart's hand, *De profundis clamavi*, K.93 (Anh.A 22), *Memento Domine David*, K.Anh.22 (93a, Anh.A 23) and another in Leopold's hand, *Justum deduxit Dominus*, K.326 (93d, Ahn. A 4), are now known to be copies of settings by Georg Reutter the younger and Johann Ernst Eberlin (see Pfannhauser, 1954), and two further works, *Cibavit eos*, K.44 (73u) and the fragment *In te Domine speravi*, K.Anh.23 (166h), long accepted as authentic, are now considered dubious. Two substantial compositions have apparently been lost: an early *Stabat Mater* of 1766, K.33c, and a *Miserere* K.Anh.1 (297a), which Mozart claimed to have written during his Paris period (letter to Leopold of 5 April 1778). About half of the known shorter works were composed in Salzburg, the rest at various points in his adolescent travels. Seven of the surviving pieces are for the Proper of the Mass (six offertories and one gradual) and there are early settings of *Veni Sancte Spiritus*, K.47, and of the Te Deum, K.141 (66b).

The cantus firmus motet *Quaerite primum*, K.86 (73v), is an academic exercise in *stile antico* counterpoint, composed as part of Mozart's candidature for admission to the Accademia Filarmonica of Bologna on 9 October 1770. An improved version of the work by Padre Martini, to whom Mozart submitted the motet for comment, also survives. Among the more substantial works special mention should go to the celebrated motet *Exsultate, jubilate*, K.165 (158a), composed in Milan in January 1773 for the castrato Venanzio Rauzzini, who had also taken a leading role in *Lucio Silla*. It is in the form of a three-movement cantata in a sinfonia-like form, with *secco* recitative linking the first two movements, the second of which is a warmly expressive aria in A major, standing in an unusual mediant relationship with the main tonic, F major. The final movement is the well-known 'Alleluia'. Not surprisingly a number of obvious influences, most notably those of the Salzburg musicians Leopold Mozart, Michael Haydn and Johann Ernst Eberlin, have been detected in the earlier adolescent works. The three-movement *Benedictus sit Deus*, K.117 (66a), quotes the plainsong Tone VIII four times in the voice-order STBA, a procedure which Mozart may have derived from the use of the same device in his father's *Convertentur sedentes*, while the above-mentioned Te Deum has been shown to be modelled on an earlier setting by Michael Haydn. The fine, but little-known double-choir motet *Venite populi*, K.260 (248a), of 1776 was justly admired by Brahms, who conducted a performance of it in Vienna on 8 December 1872. The most celebrated of all Mozart's small-scale ecclesiastical works, the tiny jewel-like motet *Ave, verum corpus*, K.618, for SATB with strings and organ was composed in Baden, where Constanze was taking the waters, on 17 June 1791. The recipient was probably the Baden church musician and schoolmaster Anton Stoll, who presumably performed it on Corpus Christi. Some writers have suspected masonic influence in the style of the work, which is somewhat redolent of the great pantheistic choruses and ceremonial music of *Die Zauberflöte*.

The seventeen epistle sonatas are also the product of Mozart's duties as a church musician in Salzburg, and were designed to be played between the reading of the Epistle and Gospel at High Mass. The relatively small scale of these concise single movements is explained by the requirements of the Salzburg liturgy, in which, as Mozart explained in a famous letter to Padre Martini of 4 September 1776, 'a Mass with all the Kyrie, Gloria, Credo, epistle sonata, offertory or motet, Sanctus and Agnus Dei (even the most solemn, when the Prince [Bishop] himself says Mass) must not last longer than three-quarters of an hour at the most'. Mozart's first occasion to compose such works would have come on his appointment as Konzertmeister of Salzburg Cathedral on 9 August 1772. The epistle sonatas have sometimes been miscalled 'organ sonatas', but in most cases the organ is no more than a continuo part, the notation varying from work to work. The majority are scored for two violins and bass (designated 'Organo e Basso'), with the organ playing a continuo role usually indicated by a figured bass (no figuring is provided for the earliest group, K.67, 68 and 69). Most of these early sonatas are short, bright, effective sonata allegro movements (an exception is the slower moving K.67 (41h). There are occasional concessions to the learned style, notably in the snatches of canonic writing in K.68 (41i), bars 14ff., and K.225 (241b), bars 51ff., but elsewhere the tone is unblushingly *galant*, with the momentum maintained by tremolando writing for violins and pounding basses. Three slightly later sonatas (K.244, 245, 263) all boast written-out organ parts, and although these parts rarely depart from the role of harmonic filling-in, they sometimes add discreet touches of interest, notably by the use of holding notes. A low pedal A requiring the use of the pedalboard appears at one point (K.245, bars 44–8). K.274 (271d) and 278 (271e) revert to figuring for the organ, but the latter expands the orchestra by the addition of oboes, trumpets and timpani. The five further sonatas composed during the final Salzburg period (up to Mozart's final departure for Vienna in 1781) include some of the most ambitious and distinguished works of the series. One sonata from this group, K.329 (317a) again adds wind parts and timpani to the three-part string band and features independent interest for the organ at some points (the pedalboard is required in bars 50–58). K.336 (336d) actually has two organ parts (marked *solo* and *ripieno*) and takes on the character of a miniature concerto movement with an elaborate solo part for the organist.

Short sacred works

K.20
God is our Refuge ('Chorus')
See 'Songs, vocal ensembles and canons'

K.34
Scande coeli limina (offertory); C major
AMA III/2, no.17; NMA I:3
Kloster Seeon, Bavaria, possibly end 1766/early 1767 (for feast of St Benedict)
S, SATB, 2 tpt, timp, 2 vn, b, org

K.47
Veni Sancte Spiritus; C major
AMA III/1, no.7; NMA I:3
Vienna, (?autumn) 1768
S, A, T, B, SATB, 2 ob, 2 hn, 2 tpt, timp, str, org

K.117 (66a)
Benedictus sit Deus (offertory); C major
AMA III/2, no.20; NMA I:3
?Vienna, Oct–Nov 1768
Possibly same work as 'grand offertory', K.47b (designated lost in *Köchel 6*: perf. at Orphanage Church, Vienna, 7 Dec 1768
S, SATB, 2 fl, 2 hn, 2 tpt, timp, str, org

K.141 (66b)
Te Deum; C major
AMA III/1, no.13; NMA I:3

Salzburg, probably end 1769
SATB, 4 tpt, [timp], 2 vn, b, org

K.143 (73a)
Ergo interest (motet); G major
AMA III/2, no.21; NMA I:3
Salzburg, late 1773
S, str, org

K.85 (73s)
Miserere; A minor
AMA III/1, no.8; NMA I:3
Bologna, Jul–Aug 1770
ATB, figured org bass

K.86 (73v)
Quaerite primum (antiphon); D minor
AMA III/1, no.9; NMA I:3
Bologna, 9 Oct 1770
SATB
Exercise for Accademia Filarmonica, Bologna

K.108 (74d)
Regina coeli (votive antiphon BVM); C major
AMA III/1, no.10; NMA I:3
Salzburg, May 1771
S, SATB, 2 ob/fl, 2 hn, 2 tpt, timp, str, org

K.72 (74f)
Inter natos mulierum (offertory); G major
AMA III/2, no.18; NMA I:3
Salzburg, May–Jun 1771, or end 1770s (for later dating see under 'Manuscript copies' (pp. 180–81)
SATB, 2 vn, b, org
For St John the Baptist's Day, 24 Jun

K.127
Regina coeli (votive antiphon BVM); B♭ major
AMA III/1, no.11; NMA I:3
Salzburg, May 1772
S, SATB, 2 ob/fl, 2 hn, str, org

K.165 (158a)
Exsultate, jubilate (motet); F major
AMA III/2, no.22; NMA I:3
Milan, Jan 1773
S, 2 ob, 2 hn, str, org
For Rauzzini, perf. Milan, 17 Jan 1773; later rev. (with fl) in Salzburg (?1779)

K.197 (Anh.C3.05)
Tantum ergo; D major
AMA III/1, no.15; NMA I:3
?Salzburg, 1772
SATB, 2 tr, str, org
Doubtful (Münster, 1963)

K.198 (158b, Anh.C3.08)
Sub tuum praesidium (offertory); F major
AMA III/2, no.24; NMA I:3

?Salzburg, 1774
S, S, str, org
Doubtful; autograph missing – survives in a late
18th-century copy and in other later diverging
copies. See Federhofer, NMA, p.x

K.222 (205a)
Misericordias Domini (offertory); D minor
AMA III/2, no.25; NMA I:3
SATB, 2 vn, [va], b, org
Munich, early 1775

K.260 (248a)
Venite populi (offertory *de venerabili*
***sacramento*); D major**
AMA III/2, no.26; NMA I:3
SSAATTBB, 2 vn ad lib, b, org
Salzburg, 1776

K.277 (272a)
Alma Dei creatoris (offertory); F major
AMA III/2, no.28; NMA I:3
Salzburg, 1777
S, A, T, SATB, 2 vn, b, org

K.273
Sancta Maria, mater Dei (gradual); F major
AMA III/2, no.27; NMA I:3
Salzburg, 9 Sep 1777 (autograph)
SATB, str, org
For feast of BVM, 12 Sep

K.146 (317b)
Kommet her, ihr frechen Sünder (aria); B♭
major
AMA VI/1, no.10; NMA I:4/iv
Salzburg, ?Mar–Apr 1779
S, str, org

K.276 (321b)
Regina coeli (votive antiphon BVM); C major
AMA III/1, no.12; NMA I:3
Salzburg, ?1779
S, A, T, B, SATB, 2 ob, 2 tpt, timp, 2 vn, b, org

K.343 (336c)
O Gottes Lamm; F major
Als aus Ägypten; C major (German sacred
songs)
AMA III/1, no.16; NMA III:8
S, b
Prague or Vienna, ?early 1787. For dating see
Ballin, NMA, Kritischer Bericht, pp. 116–17

K.618
Ave, verum corpus (motet); D major
AMA III/2, no.31; NMA I:3
Baden, 17 Jun 1791 (autograph)
SATB, str, org

Epistle sonatas

K.67 (41h)
E♭ major
AMA XXIII, no.1; NMA VI:16
Salzburg, ?1772
2 vn, b, org

K.68 (41i)
B♭ major
AMA XXIII, no.2; NMA VI:16
Salzburg, ?1772
2 vn, b, org

K.69 (41k)
D major
AMA XXIII, no.3; NMA VI:16
Salzburg, ?1772
2 vn, b, org

K.144 (124a)
D major
AMA XXIII, no.4; NMA VI:16
Salzburg, 1774
2 vn, b, org

K.145 (124b)
F major
AMA XXIII, no.5; NMA VI:16
Salzburg, 1774
2 vn, b, org

K.212
B♭ major
AMA XXIII, no.6; NMA VI:16
Salzburg, Jul 1775 (autograph)
2 vn, b, org

K.241
G major
NMA VI:16
Salzburg, Jan 1776 (autograph)
2 vn, b, org

K.224 (241a)
F major
AMA XXIII, no.7; NMA VI:16
Salzburg, early 1780
2 vn, b, org

K.225 (241b)
A major
AMA XXIII, no.8; NMA VI:16
Salzburg, early 1780
2 vn, b, org

K.244
F major
AMA XXIII, no.9; NMA VI:16
Salzburg, Apr 1776 (autograph)
2 vn, b, org (solo)

K.245
D major
AMA XXIII, no.10, NMA VI:16
Salzburg, Apr 1776 (autograph)
2 vn, b, org (solo)

K.263
C major
NMA VI:16
Salzburg, ?Dec 1776
2 tpt, 2 vn, b, org (solo)
Possibly for Mozart's Mass in C, K.259

K.274 (271d)
G major
AMA XXIII, no.11; NMA VI:16
Salzburg, 1777 (autograph)
2 vn, b, org

K.278 (271e)
C major
AMA XXIII, no.12; NMA VI:16
Salzburg, probably Lent 1777
2 ob, 2 tpt, timp, 2 vn, vc, b, org
On autograph: 'Sonata pro festis Palii'

K.329 (317a)
C major
AMA XXIII, no.14; NMA VI:16
Salzburg, ?Mar 1779
2 ob, 2 hn, 2 tpt, timp, 2 vn, vc, b, org (solo)
Possibly for Mozart's Mass in C, K.317

K.328 (317c)
C major
AMA XXIII, no.13; NMA VI:16
Salzburg, ?early 1779
2 vn, b, org (solo)

K.336 (336d)
C major
AMA XXIII, no.15; NMA VI:16
Salzburg, Mar 1780 (autograph)
2 vn, b, org (solo)
Probably for Mozart's Mass in C, K.337 (Mar 1780, autograph)

Litanies, Vespers, Vesper Psalms

K.109 (74e)
Litaniae Lauretanae BVM; B♭ major
AMA II, no.1; NMA I:2/i
Salzburg, May 1771 (autograph)
S, A, T, B, SATB, [3 trbn], 2 vn, b, org

K.125
Litaniae de venerabili altaris sacramento; B♭ major
AMA II, no.2; NMA I:2/i
Salzburg, Mar 1772 (autograph)

S, A, T, B, SATB, 2 ob/fl, 2 hn, 2 tpt, [3 trbn], str, org
Cancelled first version of Viaticum (9 bars) survives in autograph score; Pignus shortened for a later perf. (NMA)

K.195 (186d)
Litaniae Lauretanae BVM; D major
AMA II, no.3; NMA I:2/i
Salzburg, [?by May] 1774 (autograph)
S, A, T, B, SATB, 2 ob, 2 hn, [3 trbn], str, org

K.193 (186g)
Dixit Dominus, Magnificat; C major
AMA II, no.5; NMA I:2/ii
Salzburg, Jul 1774 (autograph)
S, A, T, B, SATB, 2 tpt, 3 trbn, timp, 2 vn, b, org

K.243
Litaniae de venerabili altaris sacramento; E♭ major
AMA II, no.4; NMA I:2/i
Salzburg, Mar 1776 (autograph)
S, A, T, B, SATB, 2 ob/fl, 2 bn, 2 hn, 3 trbn, str, org
Kyrie begun end 1774/early 1775; rest a year later? (Tyson, 1987)

K.321
Vesperae de Dominica; C major
AMA II, no.6; NMA I:2/ii
Salzburg, 1779
S, A, T, B, SATB, [bn], 2 tpt, [3 trbn], timp, 2 vn, b, org
See fragmentary Magnificat in C, K.321a ('Fragments and sketches')

K.339
Vesperae solennes de confessore; C major
AMA II, no.7; NMA I:2/ii
Salzburg, 1780 (autograph)
S, A, T, B, SATB, [bn], 2 tpt, [3 trbn], timp, 2 vn, b, org

DAVID HUMPHREYS

Oratorios, sacred dramas and cantatas

A SMALL GROUP OF WORKS in dramatic forms dates from Mozart's early years. One curiosity from his apprentice period is his contribution to the allegorical drama *Die Schuldigkeit des ersten Gebots*, K.35, which was first performed in the Rittersaal in the Archbishop's residence on 12 March 1767, when the composer was eleven. Mozart composed the first part (probably with some help from his father, whose hand appears in the surviving autograph);

the second and third parts, by Michael Haydn and Anton Cajetan Adlgasser, have been lost. The work is an offshoot of the 17th-century tradition of Jesuit school drama, conforming to a long-standing Salzburg practice, whereby the students of the Gymnasium performed an annual play either in the archbishop's residence or in the cathedral. The libretto, whose author is now known to have been the Salzburg cloth merchant and councillor Ignaz Anton Weiser, is a religious drama peopled by allegorical figures (Christian, Spirit of the World, Spirit of Christ, Mercy, Justice) and cast in operatic form. Not surprisingly this mixture was less than stimulating to the young composer, and the result was one of the less promising of Mozart's early scores. None of the arias, which are separated by operatic *secco* recitative, has any real character, and the vocal writing is often angular and graceless.

Almost immediately afterwards Mozart produced the *Grabmusik*, K.42 (35a), a cantata following a convention of medieval origin, in which devotions were performed during Holy Week before an image or relief of the tomb of Christ (the *Heilige Grab*, located in a side chapel or at the side of the main altar of the church). Originally it had the form of a mystery play, but by Mozart's time it had been transformed in the light of the Baroque *rappresentazione sacra*. The libretto given to the eleven-year-old Mozart, which has been tentatively attributed to either J.A. Wimmer or J.A. Schachtner, is a dialogue in cantata form between a soul which has passed beyond the grave and an angel, with a closing chorus of praise. Both singers are given a recitative and aria, with an extended duet preceding the closing chorus. The music, while not untouched by the influence of Mozart's Salzburg colleagues, shows a certain advance on *Die Schuldigkeit des ersten Gebots*, featuring an expressive G minor aria with divided violas 'Betracht dies Herz', and a solemn E♭ major duet. Some years later (the exact date is uncertain) Mozart composed a simple strophic soprano aria, 'Kommet her', K.146 (317b), which may have been intended for insertion in another German oratorio or cantata (listed above under 'Short sacred works').

Two more large-scale sacred works were for concert rather than church use. The first was the Italian oratorio *La Betulia liberata*, K.118 (74c), composed in the summer of 1771. It has been identified with the work referred to in two letters from Leopold Mozart (14 March and 19 July 1771) which mention an oratorio to a libretto by Metastasio commissioned from Wolfgang by Don Giuseppe Ximenes, Prince of Aragon, an émigré member of a noble Spanish family living in Padua. He was a music-lover who held concerts in his private residence and corresponded with Padre Martini (twenty-one letters from him to Martini survive from the period 1770–81). The absence of any further mention of the work in the Mozart family correspondence of this period probably implies that

the performance never took place; it has been suggested that Ximenes may have substituted a setting of the same libretto by the Paduan composer Giuseppe Calegari (Callegari), a word-book for which was published in 1771. Nevertheless, Mozart continued to take an interest in the work. In a letter of 21 July 1784 he asked his father for a copy with a view to using some of the music for an oratorio for the Tonkünstler-Societät, though this performance too seems not to have taken place. *La Betulia liberata*, which gives ample testimony to the enormous advance which Mozart had made in four years, owes much to his early experiences with opera (especially with *Mitridate*) and contains some remarkably prophetic features. The conventional aria types can be discerned in the rage aria for Achior ('Terribile d'aspetto') and the bravura type ('D'ogni colpa la colpa maggiore') worked with an assurance far beyond the earlier scores. There are also some powerful choruses and a remarkable C minor aria with choral interjections ('Pietà, se irato sei'), with a sensitively scored accompaniment featuring pizzicato strings which almost recalls Gluck. The work is preceded by a stormy D minor overture with no major-key contrast, and including four horns and two trumpets.

For two charity concerts for the benefit of musicians' widows on 13 and 15 March 1785 Mozart produced the cantata *Davidde penitente* by salvaging music from the unfinished C minor Mass, K.427 (417a), for eight of its ten movements. Although the performances were poorly attended and this music is now usually heard in its original setting, the fine quality of Mozart's two new arias (nos 6 and 8) should justify an occasional hearing for the cantata.

Among the occasional works which Mozart was asked to produce in connection with freemasonry are three complete cantatas (a fourth remained unfinished), of which two were written to be played at Viennese lodge meetings. The cantata *Die Maurerfreude*, K.471, to a libretto by Franz Petran, was performed in the presence of Leopold Mozart in the lodge 'Zur gekrönten Hoffnung' ('Crowned Hope') on 24 April 1785, with the tenor solo sung by Johann Valentin Adamberger. It was performed in honour of Ignaz von Born, Grand Master of the lodge 'Zur wahren Eintracht' ('True Concord'), to a text praising Joseph II for the protection which he had afforded the masons. The music, appropriately set in the masonic 'wisdom' key of E♭ major, is of ceremonial character and includes two broadly conceived tenor arias, the second of which closes with a male-voice chorus for TTB reiterating the praise of Joseph. It is known that Mozart was greeted with a later performance of this work on a visit to the Prague lodge 'Zur Wahrheit und Einigkeit' ('Truth and Unity') when he visited the city in August 1791. A second masonic cantata, *Laut verkünde unsre Freude*, K.623, was his last completed work, entered in his thematic catalogue on 15 November 1791 three days before its first performance at the reconstituted lodge 'Zur neugekrönten Hoffnung' ('New Crowned Hope'). In 1792, after Mozart's death, an edition of this work was published for the benefit of his widow. The forces include the usual three-part male chorus with a tenor solo and a less prominent solo part for a bass. In view of its proximity to *Die Zauberflöte* it is not surprising to find echoes of the latter work in the character of the march-like opening chorus (repeated at the end of the work) and a gentle F major duet in 3/8 which is redolent of the homely piety of 'Bei Männern, welche Liebe fühlen'. The tenor aria, which again was probably sung by Adamberger, also evokes memories of *Die Zauberflöte*. The cantata for voice and piano, *Die ihr des unermesslichen Weltalls Schöpfer ehrt*, K.619, was apparently commissioned by the poet, a Hamburg merchant named F.H. Ziegenhagen, who was a member of the masonic lodge in Regensburg. Despite the scoring with piano, Mozart approached Ziegenhagen's text in the spirit of a cantata with alternating aria, recitative and arioso sections and a piano part which is conspicuously orchestral in character.

K.35
Die Schuldigkeit des ersten Gebots
AMA V, no.1; NMA I:4/i
Early 1767 (perf. Salzburg, 12 Mar 1767)
Part I of sacred drama to libretto by I.A. Weiser. Part II by M. Haydn, Part III by A.C. Adlgasser
3 S, 2 T, 2 ob/fl, 2 bn, 2 hn, trbn, str
Abandoned attempt at recitative (bars 1–3) after aria no.7 survives

K.42 (35a)
Grabmusik (cantata)
AMA IV, no.1; NMA I:4/iv
Salzburg, 1767 (?perf. Salzburg Cathedral, 7 Apr 1767, final recitative and chorus added *c.* 1772) (see Rehm, 1986a)
S, B, SATB, [2 ob], 2 hn, str

K.118 (74c)
La Betulia liberata (oratorio)
AMA IV, no.4; NMA I:4/ii
Text by Metastasio
Completed Salzburg, summer 1771.
Commissioned, Mar, in Padua, but apparently not perf.
3 S, A, T, B, SATB, 2 ob/fl, 2 bn, 4 hn, 2 tpt, str

K.429 (468a)
Dir, Seele des Weltalls (cantata)
AMA XXIV, no.36a–b; NMA I:4/iv
Text by L.L. Haschka
Vienna, *c.* 1785–91?
T, TTB, fl, 2 ob, cl, 2 hn, bn, str

Fragment. First 2 movements completed in draft score; third, also in draft score, breaks off after 17 bars. First 2 movements completed and arranged M. Stadler. For account of dating, see Zeileis (1985)

K.469
Davidde penitente (oratorio)
AMA IV, no.5; NMA I:4/iii
Text attrib. L. da Ponte
Vienna, Mar 1785. Perf. Burgtheater, 13 and 15 Mar 1785
Music borrowed from Mass in C minor K.427 (417a) except for 2 arias (nos 6 and 8), dated 6 and 11 Mar (*Verzeichnüss*)
2 S, T, SATB, 2 fl, 2 ob, cl, 2 bn, 2 hn, 3 trbn, str

K.471
Die Maurerfreude (cantata)
AMA IV, no.2; NMA I:IV/iv
Text by F. Petran
Vienna, 20 Apr 1785 (*Verzeichnüss*). Perf. at lodge 'Zur gekrönten Hoffnung', Vienna, 24 Apr 1785
T, TTB, 2 ob, cl, 2 hn, str

K.619
Die ihr des unermesslichen Weltalls Schöpfer ehrt (cantata)
AMA VII/1, no.40; NMA I:4/iv
Text by F.H. Ziegenhagen
Vienna, Jul 1791 (*Verzeichnüss*)
S, pf
Sketch for bars 151ff. (?) and rejected first version of bars 128ff. (31 bars) survive

K.623
Laut verkünde unsre Freude (cantata)
AMA IV, no.3; NMA I:4/iv
Text by ? (probably Johann Georg Karl Ludwig Giesecke, 1761–1833)
Vienna, 15 Nov 1791 (*Verzeichnüss*). Perf. at lodge 'Zur neugekrönten Hoffnung', Vienna, 18 Nov 1791
2 T, B, fl, 2 ob, 2 hn, str

K.623 (623a)
Lasst uns mit geschlungnen Händen
See 'Doubtful and spurious'

DAVID HUMPHREYS

Voice and orchestra

THE BULK OF MOZART'S OUTPUT for voice and orchestra is formed by nearly fifty arias which he composed intermittently from his childhood until the last year of his life (the surviving examples span a period of twenty-six years from 1765 to 1791). They were designed to fulfil various functions. Many were intended for insertion into operas by other composers, generally in cases where the original was found to be unsuitable for one reason or another. These works, fitted into comic operas by a dozen lesser masters including Anfossi, Paisiello, Bianchi, and Martín y Soler (see list) but never heard today in their original context, enable us to see Mozart's operatic activities in a fascinating new light. Others, more justifiably referred to today as 'concert arias', were written for concert work by professional singers, most commonly sopranos or castrati, or (especially in his adolescent years) as demonstrations of the young composer's powers to represent the standard *Affekte* of love, rage, or jealousy in music (see below). Since the original performers of these isolated arias (e.g. the soprano Nancy Storace, the tenor Johann Valentin Adamberger and the basses Ludwig Fischer and Franz Gerl) created major roles in Mozart's mature operas, these works also afford insight into their technique and expressive capabilities as singers.

As the composition of these arias spans a quarter of a century, they give a valuable opportunity to observe changing taste in vocal music during this period. The adolescent arias solidly adhere to the convention of Metastasian *opera seria* in its mid-18th-century form, exemplified by Johann Adolf Hasse and Nicolò Jommelli, prolific composers with reputations which extended almost throughout Western Europe. These formal, heroic bravura arias gradually give place to the production of inserted items for *opere buffe* for performance in the Viennese theatre of the 1780s. Despite a gradual change from the conservative da capo aria to the rondo forms or bipartite slow–fast type of the Viennese period, the predominance of the formal, large-scale aria forms a constant thread running through the whole series. Most of the earlier arias are for soprano (either females or castrati), but the inserted arias of the 1780s are scored for a wider variety of voices, including some ensembles. Although only a few of the arias have retained real popularity today, many of the Viennese examples in particular show Mozart at the height of his powers, including works of searching depth which would not be out of place in any of his mature operas. Inevitably, however, the span of the single aria deprived him of the capacity to develop characterization on a large scale, which is one of the most highly prized features of his mature operas. Apart from the distinction between *seria* and *buffa* styles, a useful distinction can be drawn between items written for professional singers such as Aloisia Lange (*née* Weber) (for whom Mozart composed a whole series of arias from 1778 onwards) and those composed for amateur singers such as the Countess Paumgarten (K.369) or the aristocratic dilletanti who took part in a concert revival of

Idomeneo in 1786. The latter group are generally less technically demanding. Mozart's well-known claim to be able to fit an aria to a singer like 'a well-made suit of clothes' is amply borne out by the consideration he showed for the sexagenarian tenor Anton Raaff (K.295) or the limited range of the castrato Francesco Ceccarelli (K.374). Mozart's letters contain a wealth of information about the genesis of the arias which were commissioned as repertoire pieces by the singers, who sometimes also chose the text.

Many of Mozart's adolescent arias were the product of his travels round the European musical centres as a child prodigy. The earliest known aria, *Va dal furor portata*, K.21 (19c), dates from the London visit of 1764–5 and illustrates many common features of the earlier examples. Like many of them, it has a text extracted from the classic libretti of Metastasio, whose *Demofoonte*, *Artaserse* and *Ezio* provided a constant source of love or rage arias on which the developing prodigy could cut his teeth. A letter written by Leopold Mozart from Vienna on 30 July 1768 to Lorenz Hagenauer in Salzburg shows that Wolfgang's facility at composing arias accommodated to the stock *Affekte* of the Metastasian stage was consciously used as a demonstration of the boy's powers:

> I asked someone to take any portion of the works of Metastasio, open the book and put before little Wolfgang the first aria which he should hit upon. Wolfgang took the pen and with the most amazing rapidity wrote, without hesitation and in the presence of several eminent persons, the music for this aria for several instruments. He did this in the house of Capellmeister Bonno, Abbate Metastasio, Hasse and the Duke de Braganza and the Prince von Kaunitz.

The same impression is given by the famous report by the lawyer Daines Barrington submitted to the Royal Society on 28 September 1769, which records an episode in which Mozart improvised a 'jargon recitative' and a sinfonia for a love aria to the word 'affetto', followed by another recitative and sinfonia for a 'Song of Rage' to the word 'perfido'. Despite some angularities and occasional incoherencies in K.21 (19c), the music itself is a good demonstration of a 'rage' aria in mid-century style. Among the other childhood arias are two, K.36 (33i) and K.70 (61c), of the type known as licenze, additional arias with or without closing chorus inserted at the end or in the middle of an operatic performance, the text being unconnected with the plot and composed especially in praise of a person of rank in the audience. Both K.36 (33i) and K.70 (61c) are addressed to Archbishop von Schrattenbach.

The arias Mozart composed during the Italian journey of 1770 include a series of settings of texts from *Demofoonte*. Again, the letters of Mozart's family help to place these works in the context of Italian musical life of the time. Leopold Mozart writes home from Milan on 13 March 1770: 'Last

Sunday I could not possibly write, because Wolfgang had to compose three arias and a recitative with violins [i.e. *accompagnato*] for the concert which took place yesterday at Count Firmian's house, and I was forced to copy out the violin parts myself and then have duplicates made so that they would not be stolen.' The aria with recitative (*Misero me*) referred to by Leopold is K.77 (73e) which is designated 'scena', the usual description of an aria with introductory recitative; in the Metastasian convention the end of a major aria was followed by the exit of the singer and thus defined a scene (the 'exit convention'). The *accompagnato* section of K.77 is a remarkable document in which the hero laments his fate to the accompaniment of extreme modulations, abrupt tempo changes and the stock assortment of nervous or dramatic string figurations. As so often in the earlier examples, the following aria, *Misero pargoletto*, which is somewhat conventional by comparison, keeps to the da capo form which had already been partially abandoned in the reform operas of Gluck. The work as a whole nevertheless stands out sharply as one of the most distinguished of the arias of Mozart's adolescence.

Three further arias, K.209, 210, 217, were almost certainly composed for *buffa* operas performed at the Salzburg court during the following years (1772–7), which Mozart spent mainly at home. While *Con ossequio, con rispetto*, K.210, a tenor aria for Piccinni's *L'astratto, ovvero Il giocator fortunato*, is recognizably a *buffa* aria, with its scudding violin triplets and patter-writing for the singer, the beautiful *Voi avete un cor fedele*, K.217 (probably for a version of Galuppi's *Le nozze di Dorina*), is in serious style, contrasting a warmly expressive opening melody with dramatic changes of tempo as the moods alternate. One indication that the music of J.C. Bach may have played a part in reawakening Mozart's interest in the form is the *Rondeau* section of the recitative and aria *Ombra felice . . . Io ti lascio*, K.255, composed for the castrato Francesco Fortini, which is partly modelled on a setting by Bach of the same text.

The arias of the following period show Mozart's renewed contact with the grand tradition of *opera seria* which was to culminate in the composition of *Idomeneo* in 1780. In particular, Mozart's experience with the Mannheim orchestra, about which he speaks with enthusiasm in his letters, and later, with the musical tradition at Munich in 1780–81, stimulated him to new heights of inventive power. This period saw the production both of genuine concert arias, apparently written to order by singers, and others written as insertions or replacements in earlier operas by other composers. *Ah, lo previdi*, K.272, of August 1777 was composed, before Mozart left Salzburg on his ill-fated Mannheim–Paris visit, for the singer Josepha Duschek, for whom he was later to compose *Bella mia fiamma*, K.528. The high esteem in which K.272 was held by Mozart is witnessed by several references in the family correspondence, and is amply justified by its bold harmonic excursions and rapidly changing tempi.

Most of the subsequent arias have their points of interest, and many scale remarkable heights of virtuosity. *Alcandro lo confesso*, K.294 (Mannheim, 24 February 1778), came into being in close proximity with K.295. As Mozart explains in a letter to his father (28 February 1778), he originally intended to write the aria for the tenor Anton Raaff, but after a while changed his mind and rescored it for soprano, the singer being Aloisia Weber, whom he at one time intended to marry. It is repeatedly referred to in his letters of 1778, which record his delight with her interpretation. The music features expressive woodwind scoring with clarinets (unavailable in Salzburg, as Mozart ruefully observed) and shows off Aloisia's prodigious range by ascending to high *e'''*. This text had also previously been set by J.C. Bach, as Mozart himself pointed out. An ornamented version of the soprano part survives (mentioned in a letter of 12 April 1783) and we also learn of a later performance by Aloisia in Vienna on 11 March of the same year. The aria which Mozart eventually substituted for Raaff was K.295, also mentioned in the letter of 28 February 1778, which records Raaff's enthusiastic reception of the work and also Mozart's considerate compliance with his request that certain difficult passages be shortened and simplified: the tenor part generally reflects Mozart's anxiety not to overstretch the vocal resources of the sixty-three-year-old singer. The aria is in the two-section form with *prima* and *seconda parte* which Mozart was rapidly coming to prefer to the old-fashioned da capo form.

Another recitative and aria, K.486a (295a) was composed for Dorothea Wendling, wife of the Mannheim court flautist. A gently expressive work in E♭ major, it again suggests a response to a singer of limited powers. Mozart reports that Frau Wendling herself chose the text, and that 'she and her daughter are quite mad about the aria'. A sharp contrast is afforded by *Popoli di Tessaglia*, K.316 (300b), a bravura aria of extraordinary virtuosity with a soprano part rising to *g'''*. Mozart's delight with the piece (expressed in a letter of 30 July 1778 when the aria was still unfinished) has not been altogether endorsed by later critics, some of whom have found it overblown and vapid. Two arias fall approximately within the Munich period of *Idomeneo*. *Ma che vi fece*, K.368, is another multi-sectional soprano aria with introductory recitative, constructed on a broad scale and of great virtuosity. The recipient is unknown, but the name of Elisabeth Wendling (daughter of Dorothea), the creator of the role of Elettra in *Idomeneo*, has been suggested. *Misera, dove son!*, K.369, set to another Metastasio text, was intended for Countess Paumgarten, favourite of Elector Karl Theodor.

Mozart's solo arias and ensembles from the Viennese period are more varied in character, with new items for Italian *opere buffe* now predominating over commissioned arias for concert work. Although many of the arias are on a large scale and marked by a serious intensity of tone, the writing has the new warmth and intimacy of Mozart's Viennese manner and there are few pieces in the old heroic style. Only three of the Viennese arias, K.432 (421a), K.512 and K.538, have texts by Metastasio, and the second of these is a resetting of a text Mozart had used before (K.294). Among the arias of this period are a number of groups of pieces written for single productions. Three were composed for Anfossi's *Il curioso indiscreto* (K.418, 419, 420), an opera in which Mozart's participation gave rise to theatrical intrigue (letter, 2 July 1783). The opera was a failure except for Mozart's two arias, 'the second of which, a bravura, had to be repeated'. Other opera productions of works by Cimarosa, Anfossi, Paisiello and Bianchi are also featured (see list) together with two for *Il burbero di buon cuore* by his rival Martín y Soler. The second of these Soler insertions, *Vado, ma dove?* (K.583), is justly one of Mozart's most celebrated single arias, a slow movement featuring prominent lower woodwind in a style which often recalls the writing for Elvira in *Don Giovanni*.

Other arias are associated with Mozart's own operas, including the Viennese production of *Don Giovanni* (1788), the revival of *Figaro* in 1789, and a remarkable concert performance of *Idomeneo* which took place on 13 March 1786 in the palace of Prince Johann Adam Auersperg. A special feature of some of the Viennese arias is the use of obbligato instruments. The well-known *Ch'io mi scordi di te*, K.505 (entitled 'Scena con Rondo'), has an elaborate piano obbligato part composed (as the entry in Mozart's catalogue mentions) for Mozart himself. The singer was Nancy Storace, who created the role of Susanna in *Figaro*. More unusual still is *Per questa bella mano*, K.612, with an elaborate obbligato part for double bass, composed for Franz Gerl (the original Sarastro in *Die Zauberflöte* and the bassist Friedrich Pischelberger, who played in the orchestra at the Freihaustheater in the employment of Emanuel Schikaneder. In general, the Viennese arias are marked by a turning away from the sometimes extravagant virtuosity of the Mannheim and Munich periods, but exceptions can be found, such as *No, che non sei capace*, K.419, from the Anfossi revival cited above. The old-fashioned bravura style of *Ah, se in ciel*, K.538, with a text by Metastasio, might indeed seem surprising in so apparently late a work; however, the recent redating of the aria from 1788 to 1778 (see work-list) makes sense of the palpably older manner evident here, which reflects the brilliant and somewhat aloof style and technique of Aloisia Weber. Two works which lie outside the genuine aria tradition are *Ich möchte wohl der Kaiser sein*, K.539, a comic song to a German text for bass, and *Nehmt meinen Dank*, K.383, supposedly written for a benefit concert of Aloisia Lange in 1782.

Arias and scenes

K.21 (19c)
Va, dal furor portata
AMA VI/I, no.1; NMA II:7/i
Text from Metastasio's *Ezio*
London, 1765
T, 2 ob, 2 bn, 2 hn, str
Survives in 2 copies by Leopold Mozart; one represents, no doubt, a paternal, rev. version

K.23
Conservati fedele
AMA VI/I, no.2, and XXIV, no.54; NMA II:7/i
Text from Metastasio's *Artaserse*
The Hague, Oct 1765
S, str
?rev. Jan 1766; ?published The Hague, 1766

K.36 (33i)
Or che il dover . . . Tali e cotanti sono
AMA VI/1, no.3; NMA II:7/i
Salzburg, Dec 1766
T, 2 ob, 2 bn, 2 hn, 2 tpt, timp, str
Licenza: perf. on anniversary of coronation of Siegmund von Schrattenbach, Archbishop of Salzburg, on 21 Dec 1766

K.70 (61c)
A Berenice . . . Sol nascente
AMA VI/1, no.4; NMA II:7/i
Salzburg, ?Dec 1766
S, 2 ob, 2 hn, str
Licenza in praise of Siegmund von Schrattenbach, Archbishop of Salzburg, perhaps for insertion in production of Sarti's *Vologeso* on 28 Feb 1767, or for perf. in 1769

K.71
Ah più tremar non voglio
AMA XXIV, no.39; NMA II:7/iv
Text from Metastasio's *Demofoonte*
Probably Italy, spring 1770
T, 2 ob, 2 hn, str
Only 48 bars (fully scored) extant; ? continuation lost

K.78 (73b)
Per pietà, bell'idol mio
AMA VI/1, no.6; NMA II:7/i
Text from Metastasio's *Artaserse*
c. 1766
S, 2 ob, 2 hn, str

K.deest
Cara, se le mie pene
NMA II:7/i
Salzburg, *c.* 1769
S, 2 hn, vn, va, b

K.88 (73c)
Fra cento affanni
AMA VI/I, no.9; NMA II:7/i
Text from Metastasio's *Artaserse*
Milan, 1770
S, 2 ob, 2 hn, 2 tpt, str

K.79 (73d)
O temerario Arbace . . . Per quel paterno amplesso
AMA VI/1, no.7; NMA II:7/i
Text from Metastasio's *Artaserse*
c. 1766
S, 2 ob, 2 bn, 2 hn, str
Fragmentary attempt at scena (K.73D, 3 bars) survives

K.77 (73e)
Misero me . . . Misero pargoletto
AMA VI/1, no.5; NMA II:7/i
Text from Metastasio's *Demofoonte*
Milan, Mar 1770
S, 2 ob, 2 bn, 2 hn, str

K.82 (73o)
Se ardire, e speranza
AMA XXIV, no.48a; NMA II:7/i
Text from Metastasio's *Demofoonte*
Rome, 25 Apr 1770 (autograph)
S, 2 fl, 2 hn, str

K.83 (73p)
Se tutti i mali miei
AMA VI;/1, no.8; NMA II:7/i
Text from Metastasio's *Demofoonte*
Rome, Apr–May 1770
S, 2 ob, 2 hn, str
MS bears evidence of extensive cuts; ?made at request of singer

K.74b
Non curo l'affetto
NMA II:7/i
Text from Metastasio's *Demofoonte*
Probably Milan or Pavia, early 1771
S, 2 ob, 2 hn, str

K.209
Si mostra la sorte
AMA VI/1, no.11; NMA II:7/i
Salzburg, 19 May 1775 (autograph)
T, 2 fl, 2 hn, str
Probably for insertion in production of unidentified *opera buffa*

K.210
Con ossequio, con rispetto
AMA VI/1, no.12; NMA II:7/i
Salzburg, May 1775 (autograph)
T, 2 ob, 2 hn, str
Probably for insertion in production of Piccinni's *L'astratto, ovvero Il giocatore fortunato* (see K.256)

K.217
Voi avete un cor fedele
AMA VI/1, no.13; NMA II:7/i
Text after Goldoni's *Le nozze di Dorina*
Salzburg, 26 Oct 1775 (autograph)
S, 2 ob, 2 hn, str
Perhaps for insertion in Galuppi's *Le nozze di Dorina*

K.256
Clarice cara mia sposa
AMA VI/1, no.15; NMA II:7/ii
Salzburg, Sep 1776 (autograph)
T, 2 ob, 2 hn, str
For Antonio Palmini; probably for insertion in production of Piccinni's *L'astrato, ovvero Il giocatore fortunato* (see K.210). Sketch in G major, 6/8 (K.626b/35, 72 bars), survives

K.255
Ombra felice . . . Io ti lascio
AMA VI/1, no.14; NMA II:7/ii
Text from *Arsace* attrib. G. de Gamerra (opera by M. Mortellari)
Salzburg, Sep 1776 (autograph)
A, 2 ob, 2 hn, str
For Francesco Fortini

K.272
Ah, lo previdi . . . Ah, t'invola agl'occhi miei
AMA VI/1, no.16; NMA II:7/ii
Text from V.A. Cigna-Santi's *Andromeda* (opera by Giovanni Paisiello)
Salzburg, Aug 1777 (autograph)
S, 2 ob, 2 hn, str
For Josepha Duschek

K.294
Alcandro, lo confesso . . . Non sò d'onde viene
AMA VI/1, no.17; NMA II:7/ii
Text from Metastasio's *L'Olimpiade*
Mannheim, 24 Feb 1778 (autograph)
S, 2 fl, 2 cl, 2 bn, 2 hn, str
For Aloisia Weber (see text). Sketch for bars 72ff. survives. NMA reconstructs a second, variant form of the aria on the basis of a diverging vocal part for the third section of the aria

K.295
Se al labbro mio non credi
AMA VI/1, no.18; NMA II:7/ii
Text from *Artaserse* (opera by Hasse). Text for this aria not in Metastasio's libretto, but attrib. A. Salvi
Mannheim, 27 Feb 1778 (autograph)
T, 2 fl, 2 ob, 2 bn, 2 hn, str
MS bears evidence of extensive cuts and alterations made at the singer Anton Raaff's request

K.486a (295a)
Basta vincesti ... Ah, non lasciarmi
AMA XXIV, no.61; NMA II:7/ii
Text from Metastasio's *Didone abbandonata*
Mannheim, 27 Feb 1778
S, 2 fl, 2 bn, 2 hn, str
For Dorothea Wendling; date from Mozart's letter
to his father, 28 Feb 1778. Inspired by a Galuppi
setting (see Plath, 1975)

K.316 (300b)
Popoli di Tessaglia ... Io non chiedo
AMA VI/1, no.19; NMA II:7/ii
Text from Calzabigi's *Alceste*
Probably begun Jul 1778; Munich, 8 Jan 1779
(autograph)
S, ob, bn, 2 hn, str
For Aloisia Weber; in a letter to her from Paris,
dated 30 Jul 1778, Mozart related how the aria
was already half finished

K.368
Ma che vi fece ... Sperai vicino
AMA VI/1, no.20; NMA II:7/ii
Text from Metastasio's *Demofoonte*
Salzburg, 1779–80
S, 2 fl, 2 bn, 2 hn, str
Dating from Plath (1976/7)

K.369
Misera, dove son! ... Ah! non son io
AMA VI/1, no.21; NMA II:7/ii
Text from Metastasio's *Ezio*
Munich, 8 Mar 1781 (autograph)
S, 2 fl, 2 hn, str
for the Countess Josepha Paumgarten

K.374
A questo seno ... Or che il cielo
AMA VI/1, no.22; NMA II:7/ii
Text from G. de Gamerra's *Sismano nel Mogol*
Vienna, Apr 1781
S, 2 ob, 2 hn, str
Perf. (according to Mozart's letter to Leopold of
the same date), Vienna, 8 Apr 1781; for Francesco
Ceccarelli

K.119 (382h)
Der Liebe himmlisches Gefühl
AMA XXIV, no.40; NMA II:7/iii
?Vienna, 1782
S, [2 ob, 2 hn, str]
Accompaniment exists only in kbd reduction

K.383
Nehmt meinen Dank
AMA VI/1, no.23; NMA II:7/iii
Vienna, 10 Apr 1782 (autograph)
S, fl, ob, bn, str
For a benefit concert for Aloisia Lange (*née*
Weber)

K.416
**Mia speranza adorata ... Ah, non sai, qual
pena**
AMA VI/ii, no.24; NMA II:7/iii
Text from G. Sertor's *Zemira*
Vienna, 8 Jan 1783 (autograph)
S, 2 ob, 2 bn, 2 hn, str
For Aloisia Lange; perf. at a concert in the
Mehlgrube on 11 Jan and later at Mozart's
Burgtheater concert on 23 Mar

K.178 (417e)
Ah, spiegarti, oh Dio
AMA XXIV, no.41; NMA II:7/iii
?Vienna, Jun 1783
S
Accompaniment exists only in kbd reduction;
?version of K.418

K.418
Vorrei spiegarvi, oh Dio
AMA VI/2, no.25; NMA II:7/iii
Vienna, 20 Jun 1783 (autograph)
S, 2 ob, 2 bn, 2 hn, str
For Aloisia Lange; comp. for insertion in
production of Anfossi's *Il curioso indiscreto* at the
Burgtheater, 30 Jun 1783. Sketch (77 bars)
survives in copy

K.419
No, che non sei capace
AMA VI/2, no.26; NMA II:7/iii
Vienna, Jun 1783
S, 2 ob, 2 hn, 2 tpt, timp, str
As K.418. Sketch material (for bars 1–29 and for
bars 93–7) survives

K.420
Per pietà, non ricercate
AMA VI/2, no.27; NMA II:7/iii
Vienna, 21 Jun 1783 (autograph)
T, 2 cl, 2 bn, 2 hn, str
For Johann Valentin Adamberger. Comp. for
production of Anfossi's *Il curioso indiscreto*, but not
perf. Two diverging melody sketches for beginning
of aria (14 bars; 33 bars) survive

K.432 (421a)
**Così dunque tradisci ... Aspri rimorsi
atroci**
AMA VI/2, no.29; NMA II:7/iii
Text from Metastasio's *Temistocle*
?Vienna, 1783
B, 2 fl, 2 ob, 2 bn, 2 hn, str
?For Ludwig Fischer

K.431 (425b)
Misero! o sogno ... Aura, che intorno spiri
AMA VI/2, no.28; NMA II:7/iii
?Vienna, Dec 1783

T, 2 fl, 2 bn, 2 hn, str
For Johann Valentin Adamberger. ?Perf. at the Vienna Tonkünstler-Societät concerts of 22 and 23 Dec 1783; Mozart refers to the work sung by Adamberger at those concerts, however, as a 'Rondeaux' (letter to Leopold of 24 Dec 1783)

K.490
Non più tutto ascoltai ... Non temer, amato bene
AMA V/13, appx 13; NMA II: 5/xi
Vienna, 10 Mar 1786 (*Verzeichnüss*)
S, 2 cl, 2 bn, 2 hn, vn solo, str
For concert perf. of *Idomeneo*, on 13 Mar 1786 at the Auersperg palace; intended for perf. by tenor voice

K.505
Ch'io mi scordi di te ... Non temer, amato bene
AMA VI/2, no.34; NMA II: 7/iii
Text from 1786 addition to *Idomeneo* (K.490 above)
Vienna, 26 Dec 1786 (autograph; *Verzeichnüss*: 27 Dec)
S, 2 cl, 2 bn, 2 hn, pf, str
For Nancy Storace, pf part for Mozart himself

K.512
Alcandro, lo confesso ... Non sò, d'onde viene
AMA VI/2, no.35; NMA II:7/iv
Text from Metastasio's *L'Olimpiade*
Vienna, 19 Mar 1787 (autograph; *Verzeichnüss*: 18 Mar)
B, fl, 2 ob, 2 bn, 2 hn, str
For Ludwig Fischer

K.513
Mentre ti lascio
AMA VI/2, no.36; NMA II:7/iv
Text from Duca Sant'Angioli-Morbilli's *La disfatta di Dario*
Vienna, 23 Mar 1787 (*Verzeichnüss*)
B, fl, 2 cl, 2 bn, 2 hn, str
For Gottfried von Jacquin

K.528
Bella mia fiamma ... Resta, o cara
AMA VI/2, no.37; NMA II:7/iv
Text from D.M. Sarcone's *Cerere placata*
Prague, 3 Nov 1787 (autograph; *Verzeichnüss*)
S, fl, 2 ob, 2 bn, 2 hn, str
for Josepha Duschek

K.538
Ah se in ciel, benigne stelle
AMA VI/2, no.38; NMA II:7/iv
Text from Metastasio's *L'eroe cinese*
Vienna, 4 Mar 1788 (autograph; *Verzeichnüss*)

S, 2 ob, 2 bn, 2 hn, str
For Aloisia Lange. The 1786 score is a rev. version of a 1778 composition (Tyson, 1987); a voice-part and bass-line particella, which can be assigned on the evidence of paper and handwriting to the earlier date, transmits bars 24–193 (first beat) of the 1788 version: the remaining voice-part (to bar 207) appears to be a 1788 addition. Possibly perf. as entr'acte in C.P.E. Bach's *Auferstehung*, conducted by Mozart (Landon, 1989) on 4 Mar 1788

K.539
Ich möchte wohl der Kaiser sein
AMA VI/2, no.39; NMA II: 7/iv
Text by J.W.L. Gleim
Vienna, 5 Mar 1788 (autograph; *Verzeichnüss*)
B, pic, 2 ob, 2 bn, 2 hn, cymbals, bass drum, str
German warsong, for Friedrich Baumann (perf. in Leopoldstädter Theater, 7 Mar 1788)

K.540a
Dalla sua pace
AMA V/18; NMA II:5/xvii
Text attributed to Lorenzo da Ponte
Vienna, 24 Apr 1788 (autograph; *Verzeichnüss*)
T, fl, 2 ob, 2 bn, 2 hn, str
Comp. for Viennese production of *Don Giovanni*; for Francesco Morella

K.540c
In quali eccessi ... Mi tradì
AMA V/18, NMA II:5/xvii
Text by Lorenzo da Ponte
Vienna, 30 Apr 1788 (autograph; *Verzeichnüss*)
S, fl, 2 cl, 2 bn, 2 hn, str
Additional item for Viennese production of *Don Giovanni*; for Catarina Cavalieri

K.541
Un bacio di mano
AMA VI/2, no.40; NMA II:7/iv
Text attributed to Lorenzo da Ponte
Vienna, May 1788 (*Verzeichnüss*)
B, fl, 2 ob, 2 bn, 2 hn, str
Comp. for production of Anfossi's *Le gelosie fortunate* in the Burgtheater, 2 Jun 1788; for Francesco Albertarelli. Mozart used the main theme of this arietta again in the first movement of the *Jupiter* Symphony, K.551

K.577
Al desio, di chi t'adora
AMA V/17, appx 3; NMA II:5/xvi
Text attributed to Lorenzo da Ponte
Vienna, Jul 1789 (*Verzeichnüss*)
S, 2 basset-hn, 2 bn, 2 hn, str
Later addition to *Le nozze di Figaro*, replacing Susanna's 'Deh vieni'; for Adriana Gabrieli ('la Ferrarese')

K.578
Alma grande e nobil core
AMA VI/2, no.42; NMA II:7/iv
Text by G. Palomba
Vienna, Aug 1789 (*Verzeichnüss*)
S, 2 ob, 2 bn, 2 hn, str
Comp. for insertion into production of Cimarosa's
I due baroni at the Burgtheater, Sep 1789; for
Louise Villeneuve

K.579
Un moto di gioia
AMA V/17, appx 2, and VII/1, no.36; NMA
II:5/xvi
Text attributed to Lorenzo da Ponte
Vienna, Aug 1789
S, fl, ob, bn, 2 hn, str
Later addition to *Le nozze di Figaro*, replacing
Susanna's 'Venite inginocchiatevi'; for Adriana
Gabrieli ('la Ferrarese'). Not in *Verzeichnüss*. Pf
arrangement also survives in autograph

K.582
Chi sà qual sia
AMA VI/2, no.43; NMA II:7/iv
Text attributed to Lorenzo da Ponte
Vienna, Oct 1789 (*Verzeichnüss*)
S, 2 cl, 2 bn, 2 hn, str
For production of Martín y Soler's *Il burbero di
buon cuore* at the Burgtheater, 9 Nov 1789; for
Louise Villeneuve

K.583
Vado, ma dove?
AMA VI/2, no.44; NMA II:7/iv
Text attributed to Lorenzo da Ponte
Vienna, Oct 1789
S, 2 cl, 2 bn, 2 hn, str
As K.582 above

K.584
Rivolgete a lui lo sguardo
AMA VI/2, no.45
Text attributed to Lorenzo da Ponte
Vienna, Dec 1789 (*Verzeichnüss*)
B, 2 ob, 2 bn, 2 tpt, timp, str
Comp. for *Così fan tutte*; replaced by 'Non siate
ritrosi'. For Francesco Benucci

K. deest
No caro fà corragio
Vienna, for perf. in *La quacquera spiritosa* by Pietro
Guglielmi (1728–1804), Burgtheater, 13 Aug
1790. Mozart's accompanied recitative introduces
an inserted aria by Domenico Cimarosa (1749–
1801). (Biba, 1980, p.659 (item 1563))

K.612
Per questa bella mano
AMA VI/2, no.46; NMA II:7/iv

Vienna, 8 Mar 1791 (*Verzeichnüss*)
B, fl, 2 ob, 2 bn, 2 hn, db solo, str
For Franz Gerl (the first Sarastro) and Friedrich
Pischelberger (double bassist at the
Freihaustheater)

K.Anh.245 (621a)
Io ti lascio
NMA II:7/iv
?Vienna, *c.* 1788
B, str
Traditional assignment to Prague, Sep 1791
would appear to be incorrect: only surviving leaf
(containing the last 17 bars) is on a Viennese
paper used by Mozart almost entirely in 1788
(Tyson, 1987). Constanze's claim (letter to
Breitkopf & Härtel, 25 May 1799) that only the
vn parts were by Mozart, the rest by Jacquin,
cannot be proven or necessarily disproven from
the MS fragment alone; the existence of a copy of
a G major version with added wind parts ascribed
to Jacquin, would seem, however, to leave the
possible nature of a contribution by Jacquin still
open to debate

Duets and ensembles

K.479
Dite almeno in che mancai
AMA VI/2, no.32; NMA II:7/iii
Text by G. Bertati
Vienna, 5 Nov 1785 (autograph; *Verzeichnüss*)
S, T, B, B, 2 ob, 2 cl, 2 bn, 2 hn, str
For insertion in F. Bianchi's *La villanella rapita*,
perf. in Burgtheater, 28 Nov 1785

K.480
Mandina amabile
AMA VI/2, no.33; NMA II:7/iii
Text by G. Bertati
Vienna, 21 Nov 1785 (autograph; *Verzeichnüss*)
S, T, B, 2 fl, 2 ob, 2 cl, 2 bn, 2 hn, str
As K.479 above. Published by Sieber, Paris 1789

K.489
Spiegarti non poss'io
AMA V/13, appx 7; NMA II:5/xi
Vienna, 10 Mar 1786 (*Verzeichnüss*)
S, T, 2 ob, 2 bn, 2 hn, str
For concert perf. of *Idomeneo* on 13 Mar 1786 at
Auersperg palace

K.540b
Per queste due manine
AMA V/18; NMA II:5/xvii
Text attributed to Lorenzo da Ponte
Vienna, 28 Apr 1788 (*Verzeichnüss*)
S, B, 2 fl, 2 ob, 2 bn, 2 tpt, str
Additional item for Viennese production of *Don
Giovanni*

K.625 (592a)
Nun liebes Weibchen
S, B
See 'Arrangements and additions'

DAVID HUMPHREYS

Songs, vocal ensembles and canons

MOZART'S SOLO SONGS WITH PIANO, which number about thirty, date from a period before the great flowering of the German Lied in the early 19th century, conforming instead to the simpler stylistic ideal of 18th-century song. In general, Mozart himself probably attached little importance to them, but in the mature songs he was able to extract the maximum potential even from the limited form of the strophic parlour song, while often in the tiniest examples too his musical personality shows through unmistakably. The handful of more ambitious through-composed songs, mostly dating from the period 1785–7, include works of real distinction and scope which transcend the sphere of the miniature and strikingly prophesy the development of the Lied into a higher art-form in the hands of Schubert.

The three surviving adolescent songs are of little artistic merit. The earliest, a setting of Johann Peter Uz's *An die Freude*, K.53 (43b, 47e), composed in Vienna in the autumn of 1768, is a strophic piece in aria style with only the voice part and unfigured bass indicated. Two other teenage songs, *Wie unglücklich bin ich nit*, K.147 (125g), and *O heiliges Band*, K.148 (125h), are even simpler. The first has a written-out keyboard part in the manner of a continuo filling-in, but the second, a setting of a nineteen-stanza hymn by Ludwig Friedrich Lenz in honour of the Salzburg lodge of St John, reverts to the melody-and-bass method. The melody ends with a brief refrain for a unison chorus. (For dating of K.147 and 148, see work-list.)

Two French *ariettes*, *Oiseaux, si tous les ans*, K.307 (284d), and *Dans un bois solitaire*, K.308 (295b), composed in Mannheim in late 1777 or early 1778 are more substantial and characteristic works. Despite their unambitious designation, the second in particular is a work of some scope which shows operatic habits of thought clearly in the dramatic, declamatory treatment of the vocal line and the quasi-orchestral accompanying figures in the piano part. There are changes of tempo, a short break into recitative and dramatic pauses, though little of the vocal virtuosity which would be expected in a genuine stage or concert aria. The French texts, by respectively Ferrand and De la Motte, are handled with assurance.

The solo songs from the remainder of Mozart's career vary widely in character and elaboration. Two of the works usually categorized as songs are in reality German hymns with figured-bass organ accompaniment, written under the influence of Enlightenment pressures for simpler and more 'rational' forms in church music (*O Gottes Lamm* and *Als aus Ägypten*, K.343 (336c)) (see under 'Short sacred works'). Two other songs, *Die Zufriedenheit*, K.349 (367a) and *Komm, liebe Zither*, K.351 (367b), are for voice and mandolin, though the first of these also exists in an alternative version with piano; and another, *Lied zur Gesellenreise* (K.468), has an accompaniment marked for organ in Mozart's autograph. Many of the songs from the main body of solo songs with piano are strophic. The simplest of them (e.g. *Sei du mein Trost*, K.391 (340b), and *Verdankt sei es dem Glanz der Grossen*, K.392 (340a)) are no more than a dozen bars in length. In general, the character of the piano part gives a good indication of the level of elaboration of the setting. A few of the simplest examples have no piano introduction or coda (*Lied der Freiheit*, K.506), but more often the piano closes with a short concluding phrase or a repetition of the end of the vocal melody (*Die Verschweigung*, K.518). Occasionally a short piano cadence punctuates the halfway point in the verse (*Das Traumbild*, K.530). Elsewhere the piano plays a discreet, but appropriate accompanying role, employing characteristic keyboard figuration. An archaic feature which looks back to composers of an older generation such as Johann Adam Hiller is the doubling of the voice by the piano's right hand (*Sehnsucht nach dem Frühlinge*, K.596, well known for the resemblance of its melody to the main theme of the finale of the Piano Concerto in B♭, K.595).

However unpretentious, these miniatures are mature examples of Mozart's art. His experience with opera constantly stood him in good stead, enabling him to characterize a poem unerringly within the limits of a simple strophic setting. In *Die Alte*, K.517 (piano part only sketchily indicated), Mozart uses a parodistic neo-Baroque idiom to depict the grumbling nostalgia of the old woman of Hagedorn's poem, marking the voice part 'a little through the nose'. *Das Traumbild*, K.530, is set in the masonic 'wisdom' key of E♭ major to a melody which strikingly recalls 'Bei Männern, welche Liebe fühlen' from *Die Zauberflöte*, memories of which are also evoked by the broad, hymn-like melody of the aforementioned masonic song *Lied zur Gesellenreise*. Also worthy of mention are the charming *Das Kinderspiel*, K.598, and the patriotic song *Lied beim Auszug in das Feld*, K.552.

The best known of Mozart's songs are the handful of through-composed examples from the Viennese period in which he took the song beyond the bounds of the miniature. The most celebrated of all is his setting of Goethe's *Das Veilchen* (K.476), which again shows his mastery of characterization on an economical scale. The shrinking violet and the haughty shepherdess of Goethe's poem are clearly articulated in Mozart's first two paragraphs, and the song also features an unexpectedly intense middle section in the minor with a reversion to recitative texture at the climactic point (bars 44–51). In the final bars the voice declaims the words 'Das arme Veilchen' (an addition by Mozart) over a held piano chord. Also on a larger scale is *Das Lied der Trennung*, K.519, a warm, sensitive setting of a poem by K.E.K. Schmidt, which compromises with the strophic principle by repeating the first stanza in varied form after a middle section which, once again, leads to a declamatory climax. The style and F minor tonality of the song evoke memories of Barbarina's cavatina in Act IV of *Figaro*. Another through-composed song, headed *Als Luise die Briefe ihres ungetreuen Liebhabers verbrannte*, K.520, shows undisguised operatic influence, especially in the violinistic accompanying figures and expressive chromatic octaves of the piano part. One of Mozart's finest songs is *Abendempfindung an Laura*, K.523, a more extended piece setting a poem by J.H. Campe(?) in which a disappointed lover meditates on mutability and the inevitability of death. Mozart's through-composed setting employs a wide-ranging tonal scheme, using a short piano phrase first heard in bars 11–12 to impart a sense of unity. The song, which is imbued with gentle melancholy, owes little to a borrowed operatic tradition and is perhaps Mozart's most prophetic. *An Chloe* (K.524), which has also achieved some popularity, is a more extrovert piece with a somewhat clearer debt to the aria, though virtuoso writing for the voice is avoided.

Mozart's canons, though inevitably of minor importance in his output, are accomplished and often highly entertaining. Broadly, they fall into two categories, both of them hallowed by tradition: pedagogic exercises in counterpoint, and rounds for recreational singing in company.

The writing of canons, in the ecclesiastical and scholarly tradition, was associated with the craft of imitative counterpoint in the supposed 'golden age' style which 18th-century pedagogues attributed to Palestrina and his school. The scholastic study of counterpoint in the learned tradition was centred in Italy, and strongly influenced the musical tradition in the Viennese Hofkapelle where one of its greatest exponents, Johann Josef Fux, spent most of his career. The handful of surviving early canons by Mozart are partly the fruits of his studies in counterpoint with Padre Martini. They include a five-part canonic Kyrie, K.89 (73k), which is written out in full, and a further group in the more usual form of a single line with the successive entries indicated by the *signum congruentiae*, or in enigmatic form by an inscription. Highly ingenious are the four texted puzzle canons, K.89aII (73r) of which the first (marked with the inscription *Sit trium series una*) is closely modelled on a canon from Martini's *Storia della musica* (Bologna, 1770). The second, *Cantate Domino omnis terra*, is a nine-part round also indicated

by an inscription: *Ter ternis canite vocibus*. The third and fourth (also texted puzzle canons, are respectively *a 3* (canon at the twelfth with a *pars ad placitum* and *a 6* (a six-in-three perpetual canon). Also associated with the didactic tradition of canon as a contrapuntal discipline are a series of later canons produced under Mozart's guidance by the young English composer Thomas Attwood, who came to him for a course of lessons in the summer of 1785. His surviving workbook, which is a fascinating record of Mozart's teaching technique, includes three-part and four-part canons by Mozart (K.508a nos 1 and 2 and K.deest), as well as K.507 and 508, in what is believed to be Attwood's copy of Mozart's versions with variants. Fourteen two-part canons from the workbook apparently composed by Attwood with Mozart's guidance (K.508a nos 3–8 and K.deest) were traditional exercises designed to improve Attwood's imitative technique. An example of a dedication canon copied by Attwood is the double canon K.228 (515b), which Mozart also included in the album of Joseph Franz von Jacquin. Like some of the other canons, it was subsequently printed with the addition of a text (*Ach, zu kurz ist unsers Lebens Lauf*).

Like his Salzburg colleague Michael Haydn, Mozart was also an active composer of rounds for recreational singing in company. The exclusive use of the round form is in fact the most useful musical distinction between this category and those just discussed, which also include other types. Naturally, they are also all texted. The words vary in character from sacred texts (*Alleluia*, K.553, *Ave Maria*, K.554) to comic, dialect or obscene texts, some of which were bowdlerized in the early editions. A special case is *V'amo di core*, K.348 (382g), an echo canon for three four-part choirs, allegedly modelled on a canon by Martini. Even the rounds are sometimes indebted to the *stile antico*, which can form a deliberately incongruous contrast with the words. *Leck mich im Arsch*, K.231 (382c), is based on a traditional cantus firmus formula in semibreves, humorously elaborated with repeated-note patter figures producing rapid-fire antiphony between the voices. Mozart's canons are tellingly placed in social context by a work such as *Caro bell'idol mio* (K.562) of 1788, which shares the key and the characteristics of the wedding canon in *Così fan tutte*, composed a year later.

One fascinating curiosity is the non-liturgical secular piece for SATB, *God is our Refuge*, K.20, written in London in June 1765, and presented by Leopold to the British Museum, where it now forms part of the British Library collections. Following a then current English fashion for a sacred text in a secular composition, it is not only Mozart's only known setting of an English text, but also his earliest surviving vocal piece. (See King, 1984a and b)

The few remaining works for voices and ensemble are slight, and also mainly domestic in character.

They include the six Notturni for three voices and three instruments (either three basset-horns or two clarinets and basset-horn), slight but charming love-songs to Italian texts. A key figure in their dissemination was Gottfried von Jacquin, a fact which (together with other musicological evidence) has led scholars to suspect that he may have had a hand in the composition of some of them (Plath, 1971).

Songs
(For v and pf accompaniment unless otherwise stated)

K.53 (47e)
Freude, Königin der Weisen (An die Freude); F major
AMA VII/1, no.2; NMA III:8
Text by Johann Peter Uz (1720–96)
Vienna, autumn 1768
kbd notated as unfigured bass

K.147 (125g)
Wie unglücklich bin ich nit; F major
AMA VII/1, no.5; NMA III:8
Text of unknown authorship
Salzburg, ?1772, or ?1775–6, or Vienna, ?c. 1784.
The dating of this song and K.148 (125h) is disputed. Plath's study of the handwriting (1976/7) appears to exclude the later date; on the other hand, it is very unlikely that Mozart would have composed a strictly masonic song (such as K.148 (125h)) before becoming a mason in Dec 1784
kbd marked 'Cembalo' in autograph

K.148 (125h)
O heiliges Band (Lobgesang auf die feierliche Johannisloge); D major
AMA VII/1, no.4; NMA III:8
Text by Ludwig Friedrich Lenz (1717–80)
Salzburg, ?1772, or ?1775–6, or Vienna, ?c. 1784.
See previous entry
v solo with refrain for unison chorus; kbd notated as unfigured bass

K.307 (284d)
Oiseaux, si tous les ans (Ariette); C major
AMA VII/1, no.9; NMA III:8
Text by Antoine Ferrand (1678–1719)
Mannheim, between 30 Oct 1777 and 13–14 Mar 1778
Written for Augusta Wendling, daughter of Mannheim flautist J.B. Wendling

K.308 (295b)
Dans un bois solitaire (Ariette); A♭ major
AMA VII/1, no.10; NMA III:8
Text by Antoine Houdart de la Motte (1672–1731)

Mannheim, between 30 Oct 1777 and 13–14 Mar 1778
Written for Augusta Wendling; see previous entry

K.349 (367a)
Was frag' ich viel nach Geld und Gut (Die Zufriedenheit); G major
AMA VII/1, no.11a; NMA III:8
Text by Johann Martin Miller (1750–1814)
?Munich, winter 1780–81
v, mand (alternative version with pf)
Possibly intended for same dedication as following song, K.351 (367b)

K.351 (367b)
Komm, liebe Zither; C major
AMA VII/1, no.13; NMA III:8
Text of unknown authorship
?Munich, winter 1780–81
v, mand
Autograph lost; an old copy states that it was comp. in 1780 for a certain Herr Lang, a Munich horn player. E.A. Ballin in NMA questions authenticity

K.392 (340a)
Verdankt sei es dem Glanz der Grossen; F major
AMA VII/1, no.16; NMA III:8
Text by Johann Timotheus Hermes (1738–1821)
Vienna, late 1781 or early 1782 (or Salzburg, c. 1780?)

K.391 (340b)
Sei du mein Trost (*An die Einsamkeit*); B♭ major
AMA VII/1, no.15; NMA III:8
Text by Johann Timotheus Hermes (1738–1821)
Vienna, late 1781 or early 1782 (or Salzburg, c. 1780?)

K.390 (340c)
Ich würd' auf meinem Pfad mit Tränen; (An die Hoffnung); D minor
AMA VII/1, no.14; NMA III:8
Text by Johann Timotheus Hermes (1738–1821)
Vienna, late 1781 or early 1782 (or Salzburg, c. 1780?)

K.468
Die ihr einem neuen Grad (Lied zur Gesellenreise); B♭ major
AMA VII/1, no.18; NMA III:8
Text by Joseph Franz von Ratschky (1757–1810)
Vienna, 26 Mar 1785 (*Verzeichnüss*)
Accompaniment marked for org in autograph, pf in *Verzeichnüss*
?Perf. in lodge 'Zur wahren Eintracht' on 16 Apr during ceremony which saw Leopold Mozart's promotion to Second Degree ('Geselle': 'journeyman')

K.472
Ihr Mädchen, flieht Damöten ja! (Der Zauberer); G minor
AMA VII/1, no.19; NMA III:8
Text by Christian Felix Weisse (1726–1804)
Vienna, 7 May 1785 (*Verzeichnüss*)

K.473
Wie sanft, wie ruhig fühl' ich hier (Die Zufriedenheit); B♭ major
AMA VII/1, no.20; NMA III:8
Text by Christian Felix Weisse (1726–1804)
Vienna, 7 May 1785 (*Verzeichnüss*)

K.474
Der reiche Tor, mit Gold geschmükke (Die betrogene Welt); G major
AMA VII/1, no.21; NMA III:8
Text by Christian Felix Weisse (1726–1804)
Vienna, 7 May 1785 (*Verzeichnüss*)

K.476
Ein Veilchen auf der Wiese stand (Das Veilchen); G major
AMA VII/1, no.22; NMA III:8
Text by Johann Wolfgang von Goethe (1749–1832)
Vienna, 8 Jun 1785 (*Verzeichnüss*)
Published with K.519 by Artaria (Vienna, 1789)

K.506
Wer unter eines Mädchens Hand (Lied der Freiheit); F major
AMA VII/1, no.25; NMA III:8
Text by Johannes Aloys Blumenauer (1755–98)
Vienna, ?late 1785

K.517
Zu meiner Zeit (Die Alte); E minor
AMA VII/1, no.26; NMA III:8
Text by Friedrich von Hagedorn (1708–54)
Vienna, 18 May 1787 (*Verzeichnüss*)
Mozart indicates that song is to be sung 'ein bischen [*sic*] durch die Nase' (*Verzeichnüss*)

K.518
Sobald Damötas Chloen sieht (Die Verschweigung); F major
AMA VII/1, no.27; NMA III:8
Text by Christian Felix Weisse (1726–1804)
Vienna, 20 May 1787 (*Verzeichnüss*)

K.519
Die Engel Gottes weinen (Das Lied der Trennung); F minor
AMA VII/1, no.28; NMA III:8
Text by Klamer Eberhard Karl Schmidt (1746–1824)
Vienna, 23 May 1787 (*Verzeichnüss*)

K.520
Erzeugt von heisser Phantasie (Als Luise die Briefe ihres ungetreuen Liebhabers verbrannte); C minor
AMA VII/1, no.29; NMA III:8
Text by Gabriele von Baumberg (1766–1839)
Vienna, 26 May 1787 (autograph; *Verzeichnüss*)

K.523
Abend ist's, die Sonne ist verschwunden (Abendempfindung an Laura); F major
AMA VII/1, no.30; NMA III:8
Text by (?) Joachim Heinrich Campe (1746–1818)
Vienna, 24 Jun 1787 (*Verzeichnüss*)
Published with K.524 by Artaria (Vienna, 1789)

K.524
Wenn die Lieb' (An Chloe); E♭ major
AMA VII/1, no.31; NMA III:8
Text by Johann Georg Jacobi (1740–1814)
Vienna, 24 Jun 1787 (*Verzeichnüss*)

K.529
Es war einmal, ihr Leutchen (Des kleinen Friedrichs Geburtstag); F major
AMA VII/1, no.32; NMA III:8
Text by Johann Eberhard Friedrich Schall (1742–90)
Prague, 6 Nov 1787 (*Verzeichnüss*)
Final stanza by Joachim Heinrich Campe (1746–1818)
The title refers to Crown Prince Friedrich of Anhalt-Dessau, whose ninth birthday on 27 Dec 1778 is celebrated by poem

K.530
Wo bist du, Bild (Das Traumbild); E♭ major
AMA VII/1, no.33; NMA III:8
Text by Ludwig Heinrich Christoph Hölty (1748–76)
Prague, 6 Nov 1787 (*Verzeichnüss*)
Published under Gottfried von Jacquin's name

K.531
Was spinnst du? (Die kleine Spinnerin); C major
AMA VII/1, no.34; NMA III:8
Text: first strophe of unknown authorship; two last strophes by Daniel Jäger (Breitkopf edition)
Vienna, 11 Dec 1787 (*Verzeichnüss*)
Children's song

K.552
Dem hohen Kaiser-Worte treu (Lied beim Auszug in das Feld); A major
NMA III:8
Text of unknown authorship
Vienna, 11 Aug 1788 (*Verzeichnüss*)

K.596
Komm, lieber Mai (Sehnsucht nach dem Frühling); F major
AMA VII/1, no.37; NMA III:8
Text by Christian Adolf Overbeck (1755–1821)
Vienna, 14 Jan 1791 (*Verzeichnüss*)
Published with following 2 songs, K.597–8, by
Alberti (Vienna, 1791)

K.597
Erwacht zum neuen Leben (Im Frühlingsanfang); E♭ major
AMA VII/1, no.38; NMA VII:8
Text by Christian Christoph Sturm (1740–86)
Vienna, 14 Jan 1791 (*Verzeichnüss*)
See K.596

K.598
Wir Kinder, wir schmecken der Freuden recht viel (Das Kinderspiel); A major
AMA VII/1, no.39; NMA III:8
Text by Christian Adolf Overbeck (1755–1821)
Vienna, 14 Jan 1791 (*Verzeichnüss*)
See K.596

Vocal ensembles

K.20
God is our Refuge ('Chorus'); G minor
AMA III/1, no.6; NMA III:9
Text: psalm 46, v.1
London, Jun 1765
SATB
Autograph partly in hand of Leopold Mozart;
presented by him to British Museum, Jun 1765

K.436
Ecco quel fiero istante (notturno)
AMA VI/2, no.30; NMA III:9
Text by Metastasio (*Canzonette*)
Vienna, ?1787, or probably later
S, S, B, 3 basset-hn
Dating from Tyson (1987). NMA editor C.-G.
Stellan Mörner proposes following order for 6
Notturni as authentic: K.439, 438, 436, 437, 346
(439a), 549. ?Part of series by G. von Jacquin
(Plath, 1971/2). Fragmentary attempt at vocal
parts (2 bars) survives in autograph score

K.437
Mi lagnerò tacendo (notturno)
AMA VI/2, no.31; NMA III:9
Text by Metastasio (*Siroe*)
Vienna, ?1787, or probably later
S, S, B, 2 cl, basset-hn
See K.436. Cancelled attempt at the
accompaniment, scored for 2 cl in C and basset-hn
in G (12 bars: only music for cl I (12 bars) and cl
II (3 bars) written), survives in autograph score of
instrumental parts

K.438
Se lontan, ben mio (notturno)
AMA XXIV, no.46; NMA III:9
Text by Metastasio (*Strofe per musica*)
Vienna, ?1787, or probably later
S, S, B, 2 cl, basset-hn
See K.436

K.439
Due pupille amabili (notturno)
NMA III:9
Vienna, ?1787, or probably later
S, S, B, 3 basset-hn
See K.436

K.346 (439a)
Luci care, luci belle (notturno)
NMA III:9
Vienna, ?1787, or probably later
S, S, B, 3 basset-hn
See K.436

K.441
Liebes Mandel, wo ist's Bandel?
AMA VII/1, no.17; NMA III:9
?Text (in Viennese dialect) by Mozart
Vienna, ?1786
S, T, B, str
Dating from Tyson (1987). Comic trio for
Constanze, Mozart and Jacquin, documenting loss
and retrieval of one of Constanze's ribbons. A
complete score for S, T, B, b (without
introduction) and a partially scored frag. (18 bars;
? continuation lost) of a full score are all that
survive in Mozart's hand

K.549
Più non si trovano (notturno) (*Verzeichnüss: Eine kleine Canzonette*)
AMA VI/2, no.41; NMA III:9
Text by Metastasio (*L'Olympiade*)
Vienna, 16 Jul 1788 (*Verzeichnüss*)
S, S, B, 3 basset-hn (accompaniment not
mentioned in *Verzeichnüss* and of questionable
authorship)

Canons

K.89aI (73i)
Canon a 4; A major
AMA XXIV, no.53; NMA III:10
1772
Dating from Plath (1976/7)

K.89 (73k)
Kyrie a cinque con diversi canoni (a 5); G major
1772
Dating from Plath (1976/7). Autograph sketch
also survives

K.89aII (73r)
4 puzzle canons
1. Sit trium series una (*a* 3); F major
2. Ter ternis canite vocibus (*a* 9); G major
3. Clama ne cesses (*a* 2 with *tertia pars si placet*);
C major
4. Ter voce ciemus/Voce ter insonuit (*a* 6); B♭
major
NMA III:10
1772
Dating from Plath (1976/7). Sketch material also
survives

K.Anh.109d (73x)
14 canonic studies
1772
Dating from Plath (1976/7). Sketch material also
survives

K.Anh.A 33
Cantemus Domino *a* 3
1772
Fair copy; earlier attempts at solution survive

K.deest
Canon *a* 8; A minor
?1774
Dating from Plath (1976/7). On a leaf which
contains other contrapuntal material, as well as
contredanse melody sketch K.626b/44 (16 bars)
(Zaslaw, 1971/2)

K.229 (382a)
Canon *a* 3; C minor
AMA VII/2, no.42; NMA III:10
?Vienna, *c.* 1782
Added text (Hölty) beginning 'Sie ist dahin'
(Breitkopf)

K.230 (382b)
Canon *a* 2; C minor
AMA VII/2, no.43; NMA III:10
?Vienna, 1782
Added text (Hölty) beginning 'Selig, selig'
(Breitkopf)

K.231 (382c)
**Leck mich im Arsch (Mozart) (*a* 6); B♭
major**
AMA VII/2, no.44; NMA III:10
?Vienna, *c.* 1782
Substitute text beginning 'Lasst froh uns sein'
(Breitkopf)

K.233 (382d)
**Leck mir den Arsch fein recht schön sauber
(Mozart); B♭ major**
AMA VII/2, no.46; NMA III:10
?Vienna, *c.* 1782
Substitute text beginning 'Nichts labt mich mehr
als Wein' (Breitkopf)

K.234 (382e)
**Bei der Hitz' im Sommer ess ich (Mozart); G
major (*a* 3)**
AMA VII/2, no.47; NMA III:10
?Vienna, *c.* 1782
Substitute text beginning 'Essen, Trinken'
(Breitkopf)

K.347 (382f)
Canon *a* 6; D major
AMA VII/2, no.48; NMA III:10
?Vienna, *c.*1782
Added texts beginning 'Wo der perlende Wein'
(Breitkopf): 'Lasst uns ziehn' (Köchel)

K.348 (382g)
V'amo di core (*a* 12); G major
AMA VII/2, no.49; NMA III:10
?Vienna, *c.* 1782
A 16-v. solution is also technically possible

K.507
Canon *a* 3; F major
AMA VII/2, no.50; NMA III:10
Vienna, after 3 Jun 1786
Added text beginning 'Heiterkeit und leichtes
Blut' (Härtel)

K.508
Canon *a* 3; F major
AMA VII/2, no.51; NMA III:10
Vienna, after 3 Jun 1786
Added text beginning 'Auf das Wohl aller
Freunde' (Härtel)

K.508A
Canon *a* 3; C major
NMA III:10
Vienna, after 3 Jun 1786
Transmitted in 3 sketches

K.508a 1–2
2 canons
NMA III:10
1. Canon *a* 3 (*Canone a tre soprani*); F major
2. Canon *a* 3; F major
Vienna, after 3 Jun 1786

K.508a 3–8 and K.desunt
14 canons *a* 2
Vienna, after 3 Jun 1786
Used as part of Attwood's course of study with
Mozart in Vienna. 2 canons at each interval from
unison to seventh

K.deest
Canon *a* 4; F major
NMA III:10
Summer 1786?
From Attwood Sketchbook

K.232 (509a)
Lieber Freistädtler, lieber Gaulimauli
(Mozart) (*a* 4); G major
AMA VII/2, no.45; NMA III:10
Vienna, after 4 Jul 1787
Substitute text beginning 'Wer nicht liebt Wein'
(Härtel)

K.228 (515b)
Canon *a* 4; F major
AMA VII/2, no.41; NMA III:10
Vienna, 24 Apr 1787 (autograph)
Entered by Mozart in a commonplace book
belonging to Joseph Franz von Jacquin, with the
remark (in English) 'dont never forget your true
and faithfull [*sic*] friend'. Also a surviving sketch,
as well as a variant form in Attwood Sketchbook.
Added text beginning 'Ach! zu kurz' (Härtel)

K.553
Alleluia (*a* 4); C major
AMA VII/2, no.52; NMA III:10
Vienna, 2 Sep 1788 (*Verzeichnüss*)
Sketches also survive

K.554
Ave Maria (*a* 4); F major
AMA VII/2, no.53; NMA III:10
Vienna, 2 Sep 1788 (*Verzeichnüss*)

K.555
Lacrimoso son'io (*a* 4); A minor
AMA VII/2, no.54; NMA III:10
Vienna, 2 Sep 1788 (*Verzeichnüss*)
Substitute text beginning 'Ach zum Jammer'
(Breitkopf)

K.556
Grechtelt's enk (Mozart) (*a* 4); G major
AMA VII/2, no.55; NMA III:10
Vienna, 2 Sep 1788 (*Verzeichnüss*)
Substitute text beginning 'Alles Fleisch'
(Breitkopf)

K.557
Nascoso e il mio sol (*a* 4); F minor
AMA VII/2, no.56; NMA III:10
Vienna, 2 Sep 1788 (*Verzeichnüss*)
Sketches also survive

K.558
Gehn wir im Prater (Mozart) (*a* 4); B♭ major
AMA VII/2, no.57; NMA III:10
Vienna, 2 Sep 1788 (*Verzeichnüss*)
Substitute text beginning 'Alles ist eitel hier'
(Breitkopf). Sketches also survive

K.559
**Difficile lectu mihi mars (Mozart) (*a* 3); F
major**

AMA VII/2, no.58; NMA III:10
Vienna, 2 Sep 1788 (*Verzeichnüss*)
Substitute text beginning 'Nimm, ist's gleich
warm' (Breitkopf). Sketch also survives

K.560a (559a)
O du eselhafter Peierl (*a* 4); F major
AMA VII/2; NMA III:10
1785–7

K.560b
**O du eselhafter Martin (Jakob) (*a* 4); G
major**
Vienna, 2 Sep 1788
The music is virtually identical to K.560a, though
a tone higher. Substitute text beginning 'Gähnst
du' (Breitkopf)

K.561
Bona nox! bist a rechta Ox (*a* 4); A major
AMA VII/2, no.60; NMA III:10
Vienna, 2 Sep 1788 (*Verzeichnüss*)
Substitute text beginning 'Gute Nacht'
(Breitkopf). Sketch also survives

K.562
Caro bell'idol mio (*a* 3); A major
AMA VII/2, no.61; NMA III:10
2 Sep 1788 (*Verzeichnüss*)
Substitute text beginning 'Ach süsses teures
Leben' (Breitkopf)

K.562a
Canon *a* 4; B♭ major
NMA III:10
?Vienna
Untexted

K.Anh.191
**Canon *a* 4 (Canone a due Violini, Viola e
Basso); C major**
AMA XXIV, no.51; NMA III:10
?Vienna, date uncertain
Another (?earlier) version (21 bars), notated fifth
lower, also survives

DAVID HUMPHREYS

Arrangements and additions; transcriptions of works by other composers

MOZART'S TRANSCRIPTIONS were made with various
ends in view. In addition to a number of miscellaneous pieces, two main groups of works can be
distinguished, one the product of his career as a
keyboard player and the other associated with his

activities in Viennese private music circles and concert life. The first of these groups, the so-called 'pasticcio concertos', comprise seven early piano concertos transcribed from keyboard sonata movements by a number of Mozart's contemporaries. They are connected with Mozart's early career as a child prodigy. Four of the concertos, written in 1767 when he was eleven years old, are composite transcriptions compiled from sonata movements by Raupach, Honauer, Schobert, Eckard, C.P.E. Bach and one unidentified composer. Three more, this time derived from complete sonatas by J.C. Bach, followed in 1772. The fact that the autographs of both groups are partly in the hand of Leopold Mozart raises the possibility that the transcriptions may contain an element of his own work. Although of little more than curiosity value today, the pasticcio concertos have a musicological interest in demonstrating the models and influences which led to the formation of Mozart's piano style, and as lessons in technique they must have stood him in good stead when he came to compose the Salzburg concertos of the 1770s and the Viennese masterpieces of the 1780s. The original sonata movements are elaborated with discreet orchestral accompaniments and added ritornelli which are apparently Mozart's own work, though perhaps composed with help from Leopold. Mozart's cadenzas for two of the concertos (K.40 and K.107, 1) also survive.

Two other examples from the Salzburg years require only brief mention. Mozart made various alterations to his father's setting of the Litany of the Sacrament, as Leopold's recently discovered autograph shows (Senn, 1971/2), and subsequently used this work as the model for his own setting (K.125). A transcription of a gavotte from Gluck's *Paride ed Elena* for two flutes, five trumpets and timpani almost certainly belonged to a suite of ten transcriptions of music by Joseph Starzer and Gluck for these instruments which survives in Leopold's hand (K.187/Anh.C 17.12).

The second main group of transcriptions was the product of Mozart's famous relationship with Baron van Swieten, whose eager cultivation of the music of Bach and Handel reflects an enthusiasm for the 'learned' styles of the past. Mozart was a regular visitor to Van Swieten's house, as we learn initially from a letter to Leopold Mozart (10 April 1782): 'I go to the house of Baron Van Swieten every Sunday at 12 o'clock – and nothing is played there but Handel and Bach. I am making a collection of Bach's fugues, those of Sebastian as well as Emanuel and Friedemann.' A year later he was still attending Van Swieten's house 'every Sunday from 12 to 2 o'clock' (letter to Leopold, 4 January 1783) and eleven months later still (6 December 1783) he begged his father to send him some Bach fugues from Salzburg. It was undoubtedly for the Van Swieten circle that Mozart prepared a set of five transcriptions for string quartet of four-part keyboard fugues

by J.S. Bach (K.405). Mozart has also been credited with the authorship of a set of six transcriptions of fugues by J.S. and W.F. Bach for string trio (K.404a) with newly composed introductions replacing the original preludes, but these are now regarded as dubious (Kirkendale, 1964). Still more Bach transcriptions for string quartet and string quintet (also with new introductions) are even less likely to be his, though they too almost certainly emanated from Van Swieten's group.

During his years in England, Van Swieten had become familiar with the Handel oratorios, and on his return to Vienna he founded the Gesellschaft der Associierten Cavaliers, a concert society dedicated to the performance of oratorio. On the death of the previous director, Joseph Starzer, on 22 April 1787, Mozart took over the direction of these oratorio concerts, which were sometimes private and sometimes public. His first engagement with the society was a performance of C.P.E. Bach's *Auferstehung und Himmelfahrt Jesu* on 26 February 1788. It was repeated on 4 March, in public in the Burgtheater on 7 March and again in private four days later. C.P.E. Bach's score necessitated few alterations, but Mozart provided additional instrumentation for one item, the aria *Ich folge dir, verklärter Held* (K.Anh.109g no.19/537d).

Other commissions from Van Swieten resulted in Mozart's so-called 'additional accompaniments' for Handel's *Acis and Galatea, Messiah, Ode for St Cecilia's Day* and *Alexander's Feast*, entered in his thematic catalogue between November 1788 and July 1790 and repeated at various Van Swieten concerts in the last years of Mozart's life. German translations of Handel's English texts were used. We are particularly well informed about the first performance of the *Messiah* transcription, which took place on 6 March 1789 in the rooms of Count Johann Esterházy, with Mozart directing the orchestra and Ignaz Umlauf the singers (a choir of twelve and four soloists). By Mozart's time the decline of the continuo principle had made Handel's orchestration seem sparse and incomplete to musicians, and Mozart therefore supplied additional wind parts to give a result more acceptable to contemporary audiences. The wind parts include clarinets, which were not regular members of Handel's orchestra. For the most part the wind instruments double or underscore the string parts and reinforce the tuttis, but occasionally Mozart gives them some independent melodic interest. The accompaniment to 'The people that walked in darkness' (translated into German as 'Das Volk, das im Dunkeln wandelt') is enriched with chromatic woodwind writing in Mozart's Viennese manner, betraying a misunderstanding of the expressive function of Handel's spare string octaves. The solo in 'The trumpet shall sound' ('Sie schallt, die Posaun') is given to a horn (alterations and cancellations in the score for this movement show that it gave him considerable trouble). Mozart's Handel adaptations enjoyed considerable prestige during the 19th century, and elements of his 'additional accompaniments' for *Messiah* are familiar to British audiences from their incorporation into the edition by Ebenezer Prout (1902), but with the emergence of a more scholarly attitude to the performance of Handel's works in the 20th century they are only occasionally heard today. However, before we condemn them as tasteless period pieces we should remember the contribution Van Swieten's society made to the re-emergence of German oratorio; this process led to Haydn's *Die Schöpfung* (*The Creation*) and *Die Jahreszeiten* (*The Seasons*), for both of which Van Swieten wrote the libretti.

K.37
Clavier concerto; F major
AMA XVI/1, no.1; NMA X:28/2
Salzburg, Apr 1767
kbd, 2 ob, 2 hn, str
Source:
I   H.F. Raupach op.1 no.5
II   ?
III L. Honauer op.2 no.3

K.39
Clavier concerto; B♭ major
AMA XVI/1, no.2; NMA X:28/2
Salzburg, Jun 1767
kbd, 2 ob, 2 hn, str
Source:
I   H.F. Raupach op.1 no.1
II   J. Schobert op.17 no.2
III H.F. Raupach op.1 no.1

K.40
Clavier concerto; D major
AMA XVI/1, no.3; NMA X:28/2
Salzburg, Jul 1767
kbd, 2 ob, 2 hn, str
Source:
I   J. Honauer op.2 no.1
II   G. Eckard op.1 no.4
III C.P.E. Bach W.117
Also cadenza K.624 (626aII, C)

K.41
Clavier concerto; G major
AMA XVI/1, no.4; NMA X:28/2
Salzburg, Jul 1767
kbd, 2 ob, 2 hn, str
Source:
I   J. Honauer op.1 no.1
II   H.F. Raupach op.1 no.1
III J. Honauer op.1 no.1

K.107, 1
Clavier concerto; D major
NMA X:28/2
1772
kbd, 2 vn, b
Source: J.C. Bach op.5 no.2
Dating from Plath (1976/7)
Also cadenzas K.624 (626aII, A–B)

K.107, 2
Clavier concerto; G major
NMA X:28/2
1772
kbd, 2 vn, b
Source: J.C. Bach op.5 no.3

K.107, 3
Clavier concerto, E♭ major
NMA: 28/2
1772
kbd, 2 vn, b
Source: J.C. Bach op.5 no.4

K.284e
J.B. Wendling, Flute Concerto (?additional wind parts)
Mannheim, Nov 1777,
Lost; mentioned in letter of 21 Nov 1777

K.deest
Keyboard arrangements of ballet music by Christian Cannabich
Mannheim, Dec 1777
Mentioned in *Köchel 6* under K.284e. Referred to in Mozart's letter to his father of 6 Dec 1777. Of 6 known collections of Cannabich ballet arrangements published by J.M. Götz only nos 1, 3, 4, 6 have so far been found. 4th of these (containing 6 arrangements of numbers from ballet *Ulisse et Orphée*), arranged for pf, vn, va, vc, possibly by Mozart. Collection nos 2 and 5, for pf, vn, va, vc, and pf, vn, respectively, also possibly by Mozart (Münster, 1975)

K.404a
Six preludes and fugues; D minor/G minor/F major/F major/E flat major/F minor
Vienna, 1782
vn, va, vc
Sources:
1   prelude ?original, fugue J.S. Bach BWV 853
2   prelude ?original, fugue J.S. Bach BWV 883
3   prelude ?original, fugue J.S. Bach BWV 882
4   prelude J.S. Bach BWV 527/ii, fugue J.S. Bach BWV 1080 no.8
5   prelude and fugue, J.S. Bach BWV 526/ii and iii
6   prelude ?original, fugue W.F. Bach Fugue no.8
dubious (Kirkendale 1964, Holschneider 1964, Kirkendale 1965)

K.405
5 fugues; C minor/E♭ major/E minor/D minor/D major
Vienna, 1782
2 vn, va, vc
Sources: J.S. Bach BWV 871/876/878/877/874
Transcribed in Kirkendale (1962/3). For a sixth fugue, in C minor (after BWV 891), see K.deest ('Fragments and sketches')

K.293e
Cadenzas to arias by J.C. Bach
For discussion of the various autographs (in the hands of Leopold, Wolfgang and Nannerl) listed under K.293e, see Plath, 1960/61, 1971/2 and 1976/7

K.592
G.F. Handel, *Ode for St Cecilia's Day*
NMA X:28/1/iv
Vienna, Jul 1790
Original scoring: S, T, SATB, fl, 2 ob, 2 tpt, timp, lute, str (additional fl, 2 cl, 2 bn, 2 hn, rev. tpt parts)

K.625 (592a)
?B. Schack, 'Nun, liebes Weibchen' (duet from E. Schikaneder's *Der Stein der Weisen*)
AMA VI/ii, nos 6, 7
Vienna, Aug 1790
Original scoring: S, B, ?pf (accompaniment rescored for fl, 2 ob, 2 bn, 2 hn, str)

K.624 (626aII, D–O, see below)
Cadenzas for keyboard concertos by other composers
NMA X:28/2
H, D (Anh.61a), F–G, for J.S. Schroeter's op.3 nos 1, 4, 6, respectively
K for concerto in D major by I. von Beecke
N, O for unidentified concerto
L lost
E (Anh. C 15.10) unauthentic
I (Anh. C 15.11) fragmentarily surviving prelude; *c.* 1777 (NMA IX:27/ii)

K.626b/28
C.W. von Gluck, Gavotte from *Paride ed Elena* (1769)
c. 1773
2 fl, 5 tpt, timp
Original scoring for orchestra. Dating from *Köchel* 6. Part of Divertimento K.187 (Anh. C 17.12). Autograph, like that of K.187 (Anh. C 17.12), is in the hand of Leopold Mozart (Tyson, 1987)

K.deest
L. Mozart, *Litaniae de venerabili altaris sacramento* (1762)
NMA X:28/3–5/i

Original scoring: S,A,T,B, SATB, 2 hn, str (various changes)

K.deest
J. Haydn, *Armida* (1783)
Vienna, ?
Adaptation of, and revised ending for, Act 1 duet (finale), 'Cara, sarò fedele'. See Landon, 1989

K.470a
G.B. Viotti, Violin Concerto in E minor, no.16 (additional tpt and timp parts)
Vienna, Apr 1785
The Andante for violin and orchestra, K.470 (lost), may have been intended for this work (disputed in *Köchel* 6). Speculative dating is that of *Köchel* 6

K.Anh.109g no.19 (537d)
C.P.E. Bach, 'Ich folge dir', from *Auferstehung und Himmelfahrt Jesu* (1787)
Vienna, Feb 1788
Original scoring: T, tpt, str (additional fl, ob, tpt)

K.566
G.F. Handel, *Acis and Galatea* (1718)
NMA X:28/1/i
Vienna, Nov 1788
Original scoring: S, T, T, B, SATTB, rec, 2 ob, bn, 2 vn, va, bc (additional 2 fl, 2 cl, bn, 2 hn)

K.572
G.F. Handel, *Messiah* (1742)
Vienna, Mar 1789
Original scoring: S, A, T, B, SATB, 2 ob, 2 tpt, timp, str (additional 2 fl, 2 cl, 2 bn, 2 hn, 3 trbn, rev. tpt parts)

K.591
G.F. Handel, *Alexander's Feast* (1736)
Vienna, Jul 1790
Original scoring: S, T, B, SATB, 2 rec, 2 ob, 3 bn, 2 hn, 2 tpt, timp, str (additional 2 fl, 2 cl, rev. tpt parts)

DAVID HUMPHREYS

Miscellaneous

K.Anh.109b, 15a–ss (15a–ss)
London Sketchbook
London, 1765
Short pieces on 2 staves for kbd or sketches for orchestra. Several nos from collection have appearance of kbd versions of orchestral or chamber music. Fragmentary nos: 38 (15nn, 3 bars); 42 (K.15rr, 12 bars); 43 (15ss, 23 bars)

K.393 (385b)
Solfeggios for voice
AMA XXIV, no.49
Vienna, ?Aug 1782
Dating from *Köchel 6*; no.1 ('per la mia cara Costanza') breaks off after 62 bars; no.5: no music entered on b stave

K.453b
Exercise book for Barbara Ployer
Facsimile in Lach, *Mozart als Theoretiker* (Vienna, 1918)

K.485a (506a)
Attwood Studies
NMA X:30/i
Vienna, 1785–6

K.Anh.294d (516f)
Musikalisches Würfelspiel
Vienna, 1787

Fragments and sketches

In the following list, detailed entries are provided only for independent fragments and sketches. Information concerning fragments and sketches relating to completed works has been prepared by John Arthur and appended to entries on individual 'parent' works in the main work-lists: such related fragments and sketches are cross-referenced here by the Köchel numbers of the works to which they are related. Some substantial independent fragments (e.g., the *Requiem* and the C minor Mass) receive full entries not here but in the main work-lists; these are cross-referenced below. Apart from the few instances designated as sketches, the works listed below are fragments – pieces left incomplete by Mozart, for whatever reason, or pieces which perhaps, occasionally, were finished by Mozart but come down to us incomplete. Omitted are study material and a number of items whose intentions are not clear.

Operas

See under main work-list: K.87 (74a); K.344 (336b); K.366; K.384; K.422; K.430 (424a); K.486; K.492; K.527; K.588; K.620; K.621

Symphonies

K.Anh.100 (383g)
First movement of a Symphony in E♭ major
? Vienna, May 1782
fl, 2 ob, bn, 2 hn, str
Adagio – Allegro
97 bars. Lost; mentioned in Nissen (1828). Speculative dating from *Köchel 3*, *Köchel 6*

K.467a (383i)
Sketch; C major
?1782
G2 clef
22 bars; unilinear. Possibly for pf concerto, symphony or, stylistically most likely, for overture (?*Die Entführung*); followed on same leaf by sketch for Piano Concerto in A K.414 (385p), probably completed last months of 1782 (Tyson, 1987)

See under main work-list: K.130; K.183 (173dB); K.297 (300a); K.338; K.504; K.551

Concertos

Piano concertos

K.Anh.57 (537a)
Piano Concerto movement in D major
NMA V:15/viii
? possibly summer 1786
pf, str [? +: other instruments not indicated]
21 bars; only music for pf written out. Dating from Tyson (1987)

K.Anh.61 (537b)
Piano Concerto slow movement (?) in D minor
NMA V:15/viii
? end 1786
pf, fl, 2 ob, 2 basset-hn, 2 bn, 2 hn, str
6 bars; in draft score. Dating from Tyson (1987)

See under main work-list: K.414 (385p); K.415 (387b); K.450; K.453; K.466; K.467; K.488; K.491; K.503; K.537

String concertos

K.Anh.56 (315f)
First movement of a Concerto in D major for violin and piano
AMA XXIV, no.21a; NMA V:14/ii
Mannheim, [begun Nov] 1778 (autograph)
Allegro
vn, pf, 2 fl, 2 ob, 2 hn, 2 tpt, timp, str
120 bars; in draft score from soloists' entry. Intended for an 'accademie des amateurs' led by Ignaz Franzl (see letter of Mozart to Leopold, 12 Nov 1778)

K.Anh.104 (320e)
First movement of a Sinfonia Concertante in A major for violin, viola and cello
NMA V:14/ii
1779–80
Allegro
vn, va, vc, 2 ob, 2 hn, str
134 bars; fully scored to soloists' entry: in draft score thereafter. Dating from Tyson (1987). Plath

(1976/7) accepts dating in *Köchel 6*: 'Summer or autumn 1779'

See under main work-list: K.364 (320d)

Wind concertos

K.293 (416f)
First movement of an Oboe Concerto in F major
AMA XXIV, no.20; NMA V:14/iii
Mannheim, Nov 1778
ob, 2 cl, 2 bn, 2 hn, str
70 bars; fully scored to entry of soloist: in draft score thereafter. Dating from NMA

K.370b
First movement of a Horn Concerto in E♭ major
NMA V:14/v
?1781
hn, 2 ob, 2 hn, str
Surviving portions of disrupted autograph transmit 127 bars; in draft score. According to Tyson (1989a) (after H. Jeurissen's discussion in Pizka, 1980), possibly some leaves missing between fol.4 and present fol.5 (i.e., between bar 71 and present bar 72: bar nos according to NMA reconstruction, which, accepting Jeurissen's version in Pizka, is silent over possible missing music after bar 71); further music missing between present bars 95 and 96 (c. 9 bars), and 122 and 123 (c. 8 bars); ? continuation lost. Dating from Tyson (1987). ? For Leutgeb; [?] or possibly for Viennese Hofkapelle hornplayer Jacob Eisen (NMA). ? Possibly connected with fragmentary Rondo for horn K.371 (q.v.).

K.371
Rondo in E♮ major for horn
AMA XXIV, no.21; NMA V:14/v
Vienna, 21 Mar 1781 (autograph)
Rondeau (Allegro)
hn, 2 ob, 2 hn, str
279 bars; substance complete in draft score. AMA and NMA transcriptions contain 219 bars: further 60 bars, the true bars 27–86, preserved on previously unknown bifolium (Tyson, 1989a)
? Connected with fragmentary Horn Concerto movement K.370b; ? possibly independent work. ? For Leutgeb; [?] or possibly for Viennese Hofkapelle hornplayer Jacob Eisen (NMA)

K.494a
First movement of a Horn Concerto in E major
NMA V:14/v
? mid–end 1785, or possibly later
hn, 2 ob, 2 hn, str
91 bars; some passages incompletely scored:

? continuation lost. Dating from Tyson (1987). NMA suggests date of summer 1786 on basis of handwriting. ? For Leutgeb; [?] or possibly for Viennese Hofkapelle hornplayer Jacob Eisen (NMA)

See under main work-list: K.271k; K.622; K.412 + 514 (386b)

Miscellaneous instrumental

K.246b (320B)
Divertimento movement in D major
NMA VII:18
?1773
2 hn, str
41 bars. Paper-type suggests date from c. Mar 1773 to c. May 1775 (Tyson, 1987); handwriting suggests end 1772 to early 1773 (Plath, 1976/7). Frag. transmits last 27 bars of an exposition section and 14 bars after double bar

See under main work-list: K.247; K.522; K.525

Dance and ballet

K.299c
Sketches for a ballet
NMA II:6/ii
? Paris, 1778
Unilinear. Sketches for only 16 nos extant (numbered 12–27)

K.Anh.103 (299d)
Chasse in A major
NMA II:6/ii
? Paris, 1778
2 fl, 2 ob, 2 bn, 2 hn, str
32 bars; Mineur section in draft score. Dating from Tyson (1987)

K.Anh.107 (535b)
Contredanse in B♭ major
NMA IV:13/1/ii
?1790–91
fl, ob, bn, hn, 2 vn, b
24 bars; only music for vn I written out. Dating from Tyson (1987). ? Related to other late contredanses, such as K.603, no.2

See under main work-lists: K.367; K.446 (416d); K.461 (448a); K.607 (605a); also 'Operas', K.135

Chamber music
Harmoniemusik and other works for multiple wind instruments

K.384B
Slow movement in E♮ major
NMA VII:17/ii

?1782

2 ob, 2 cl, 2 bn, 2 hn

19 bars (not 18, as given in *Köchel 6*). For dating see NMA. [?] Attempt at slow movement for a projected serenade in B♮ (Flothuis, 1969), or, perhaps connected with composition of slow movement for Serenade in C minor K.388 (384a). See wind frags K.384b, K.Anh.96 (196g, 384c)

K.384b
March in B♭ major
NMA VII:17/ii
?1782
2 ob, 2 cl, 2 bn, 2 hn
4 bars. [?] Part of a projected serenade in B♮ (Flothuis, 1969). See wind frags K.384B, K.Anh.96 (196g, 384c)

K.Anh.96 (196g, 384c)
Movement in B♭ major
NMA VII:17/ii
?1781–3
2 ob, 2 cl, 2 bn, 2 hn
16 bars. ? An opening Allegro. Dating from Tyson (1987). [?] Part of a projected serenade in B♮ (Flothuis, 1969). See wind frags K.384B, K.384b

K.Anh.95 (440b, 484b)
Allegro assai in B♭ major
NMA VII:17/ii
? Vienna, end 1785
2 cl, 3 basset-hn
22 bars. Speculative dating from NMA; however, first 6 bars of cl I part noted down on fol.3 of Adagio in B♮, K.411 (440a, 484a) (also for 2 cl, 3 basset-hn), paper-type of which suggests dating of 1782–3 (Tyson, 1987)

K.Anh.93 (440c, 484c)
Adagio in F major
NMA VII:17/ii
?1787–9
cl, 3 basset-hn
6 bars. Dating from Tyson (1987). See fragmentary Adagio in F, K.Anh.94 (580a)

K.484e
Allegro in F major
NMA VII:17/ii
? Vienna, end 1785
32 bars. Of this work (? originally completed) only fragmentary basset-hn I part known. Speculative dating from NMA

K.Anh.94 (580a)
Adagio in F major
NMA VII:17/ii
?1788
Probably cl, 3 basset-hn
73 bars; melodic line complete; from bar 29 in

draft score. As combination of cl, 3 basset-hn, probably employed in K.Anh.94 (580a), can be found in fragmentary Adagio in F, K.Anh.93 (440c, 484c), Tyson (1987) suggests given possible dating on basis of dating of latter frag.

See under main work-list: K.361 (370a); K.375; K.388 (384a)

Wind instruments with strings

K.Anh.91 (516c)
First movement of a Quintet in B♭ major
AMA XXIV, no.22a; NMA VIII:19/2
1790–91
Allegro
cl, 2 vn, va, vc
93 bars: lost continuation presumed; ? originally complete. Dating from Tyson (1987). See following Rondò in E♭ major, K.516d

K.516d
Rondò in E♭ major
NMA VIII:19/2
cl, 2 vn, va, vc
8 bars. Einstein (*Köchel 3*) considered Allegro in B♮, K.Anh.91 (516c), and Rondò in E♭, K.516d, to be attempts, respectively, at opening movement and slow movement of a projected B♭ major quintet. Yet, position of K.516d on verso of a sketch-leaf (containing some entries from 1787) would seem to reduce likelihood of its being part of another work, and even, perhaps, of its being a serious attempt at an independent movement: ? possibly teaching material

K.Anh.90 (580b)
First movement of a Quintet in F major
NMA VIII:19/2
Probably 1787
Allegro
cl, basset-hn, vn, va, vc
102 bars; part in draft score. Breaks off at double bar. Dating from Tyson (personal communication)

K.Anh.88 (581a)
Quintet movement in A major
NMA VIII:19/2
?1790
cl, 2 vn, va, vc
110 bars; in draft score: last 21 bars unknown to NMA and *Köchel 6*. Main melody nearly identical to that in Ferrando's aria 'Ah! lo veggio' from *Così*: ? frag. written after opera as piece of domestic amusement for Anton Stadler (Tyson, 1987)

See under main work-list ('Wind instruments with strings and piano'): K.Anh.171 (285b)

Piano and strings

Piano and violin

K.372
First movement of a Sonata in B♭ major
AMA XVIII/ii, no.31; NMA VIII:23/ii
Vienna, 24 Mar 1781 (autograph);
'Sonata I'
Allegro
65 bars; completed by M. Stadler (total 198 bars)

K.403 (385c)
Sonata in C major
AMA XVIII/ii, no.38; NMA VIII:23/ii
?1784; 'Sonate Premiere. Par moi W:A: Mozart
pour ma très chère Epouse'
Allegro moderato; Andante – Allegretto
Allegretto unfinished (20 bars); completed by M.
Stadler (total 144 bars). Dating from Tyson
(1987). See fragmentary Violin Sonata movement
in A, K.Anh.48 (480a, 385E)

K.404 (385d)
Andante and Allegretto in C major
[Two probably independent movements published
together after Mozart's death; *Köchel 1* considered
both movements to be part of fragmentary sonata
from 1782: not disputed by *Köchel 6*]
AMA XVIII/ii, no.39; NMA VIII:23/ii
[a] Andante in C major
? end 1780s
?Frag.: ? complete 18-bar piece
Autograph lost. Dating suggested on stylistic
grounds
[b] Allegretto in C major
? Dec 1785 – Dec 1786
?Frag.: ? complete 24-bar piece
Suggested dating from Tyson (personal
communication)

K.Anh.48 (480a, 385E)
First movement of a Sonata in A major
NMA VIII:23/ii
?1784
Allegro
34 bars. Written probably around time of Sonata
in B♭, K.454 (dated 21 Apr 1784) (Tyson, 1987):
K.454 is on same paper-type as frag. (Tyson,
personal communication); the fragmentary Violin
Sonata in C, K.403 (385c) is also on same paper-
type (Tyson, 1987)

K.402 (385e)
Sonata in A
AMA XVIII/ii, no.37; NMA VIII:23/ii
? Aug or Sep 1782; 'Sonata II ᵈᵃ'
Andante, ma un poco adagio – [Fuga] Allegro
moderato
Fugue unfinished; completed by M. Stadler

(autograph lost; Kirkendale (1979) suggests, for
stylistic reasons, completion may begin after F
major entry in bars 51–5). Speculative dating
from *Köchel 3*, *Köchel 6*

K.396 (385f)
Sonata movement in C minor
NMA VIII:23/ii
? Aug or Sep 1782
27 bars; vn part notated in bars 23–27. Completed
for kbd alone by M. Stadler (total 72 bars).
Speculative dating from *Köchel 3*, *Köchel 6*

K.Anh.47 (546a)
First movement of a Sonata in G major
NMA VIII:23/ii
?1790–91
31 bars; part in draft score. Dating from Tyson
(1987)

See under main work-list: K.306 (300l); K.377
(374e); K.454; K.526

Piano and cello

K.Anh.46 (374g)
Andantino in B♭ major
?1782–3
Andantino sostenuto e cantabile
33 bars; part in draft score. Dating from Tyson
(1987). ? Intended for musician who played
obbligato vc part in Piano Rondo in A, K.386

Piano and two or more instruments

K.442
Three Trio movements
[Three separate movements published together
after Mozart's death]
AMA XVII/2, no.5; NMA VIII:22/2
pf, vn, vc
[a] Trio movement in D minor
?1786–7
[Allegro]
55 bars; completed by M. Stadler (total 230 bars).
Dating from Tyson (personal communication)
[b] Trio movement in G major
?1786–7
Tempo di Menuetto
151 bars; ? continuation lost; completed by M.
Stadler (total 248 bars). Dating from Tyson
(personal communication). ? Possibly attempt at
finale for Piano Trio in G, K.496
[c] Trio movement in D major
?1790–91
Allegro
133 bars; completed by M. Stadler (total 228
bars). Dating from Tyson (personal
communication)

K.Anh.54 (452a)
Quintet movement in B♭ major
? early 1784
pf, ob, cl, basset-hn, bn
35 bars. Lost; mentioned in Nissen (1828). Dating from *Köchel 6*. Plath (1965/6) considers Romanze in A♭ for keyboard, K.Anh.205 (Anh.C 27.04) (first edition: Mollo, Vienna, 1802) to transmit frag. in transposed, arranged, and completed form (total 67 bars)

K.Anh.55 (387c, 452b)
Movement in D major
?1784–6
pf, 2 hn, 2 vn, b
29 bars; part in draft score. Dating from Tyson (1987). ?Orchestral

K.Anh.52 (495a)
Trio movement in G major
NMA VIII:22/2
?1787–8
pf, vn, vc
19 bars; part in draft score. Presumably first movement. Dating from Tyson (1987)

K.Anh.51 (501a)
First movement of a Trio in B♭ major
NMA VIII:22/2
?1784–5
pf, vn, vc
25 bars. Dating from Tyson (1987)

See under main work-lists: ('Wind instruments with strings and piano') K.452; ('Piano Quartets') K.493; ('Piano Trios') K.542; ('Mechanical organ and armonica') K.617

Strings alone

String Trios

***Köchel 6*, p. 281 (under K.266 (271f))**
Trio movement in C major
NMA VIII:21
?1784–5
2 vn, vc
12 bars; only music for vn I written out. Frag. appears to be slow movement. Dating above (from Tyson, personal communication) reflects dated instances of paper-type of frag. in Mozart's autographs. Not to be connected with Trio in B♭, K.266 (271f); ? to be connected with following frag. (q.v.) K.deest

K.deest
Trio movement in C major
? possibly end 1785 to end 1786
2 vn, vc

16 bars. Frag. has character of finale. Dating from Tyson (personal communication). Vn melody similar to main theme of finale of String Quartet in C, K.465. Autograph auctioned Sotheby's, New York, 7 Jun 1988. ? To be connected with preceding frag. (q.v.)

K.Anh.66 (562e)
First movement of a Trio in G major
NMA VIII:21
?1790–91
Allegro
vn, va, vc
100 bars; from bar 98 in draft score; frag. breaks off 9 bars into development section; ? 'work in progress'. Dating from Tyson (1987)

String Quartets

K.deest
First movement of a Quartet in E major
NMA VIII:20/1/iii (Kritischer Bericht)
? second half 1782
10 bars. Dating from Tyson (see Mozart, 1985, under 'Editions'). Modelled on J. Haydn's op.17 no.1. ? Serious attempt to write quartet, or perhaps to be regarded as study

K.deest
Fugue in G minor
NMA VIII:20/1/iii
? end 1783 to early 1784, or later
12 bars; music sketch-like in appearance. On fol.15r of so-called Barbara Ployer Exercise Book K.453b. This leaf is a Steyr paper, probably obtained on Mozart's journey to Vienna from Salzburg in 1783 (Tyson, 1987). Fugue follows, on same leaf, unidentified vocal sketch and sketch for Minuet in D, K.461 (448a), no.6

K.deest
Fugue in C minor
NMA VIII:20/1/iii
? Vienna, 1782–4
10 bars. Survives in copy by Fuchs. Speculative dating from NMA. ? Study or teaching material

K.Anh.77 (385m, 405a)
Fugue in C major
NMA VIII:20/1/iii
?1790–91
12 bars. Dating from Tyson (1987). ? Study or teaching material

K.Anh.76 (417c)
Fugue in D minor
NMA VIII:20/1/iii
?1786–9
11 bars. Dating from Tyson (1987). ? Study or teaching material

K.417d
First movement of a Quartet in E minor
NMA VIII:20/1/iii
?c. 1790
Allegro
50 bars; part in draft score. [?] Probably
represents attempt at minor-key quartet for
'Prussian' set (Tyson, 1987)

K.Anh.74 (587a)
First movement of a Quartet in G minor
NMA VIII:20/1/iii
?1786–7
25 bars. Dating from Tyson (1987). Frag. will
have been abandoned at latest by around end
1789 since verso of leaf containing frag. transmits
sketches for Act II finale of *Così*. Plath suggests
dating of 1782–3 (see Wolf, 1980)

See under main work-list: K.421 (417b); K.458;
K.464; K.575; K.589; K590

String Quintets: 2 vn, 2 va, vc

K.Anh.80 (514a)
First movement of a Quintet in B♭ major
AMA XXIV, no.55; NMA VIII:19/1
Probably 1787
122 bars; part in draft score; breaks off at double
bar. Dating from Tyson (personal
communication). ? Abandoned on musical
grounds

K.Anh.87 (515a)
Quintet movement in F major
NMA VIII:19/1
?1791
Andante
10 bars; part in draft score; ? 'work in progress'.
Dating from Tyson (1987). Following fragmentary
Quintet movement in A minor, K.Anh.79 (515c)
(q.v.) and this frag. possibly attempts,
respectively, at opening movement and slow
movement of a projected A minor quintet (Tyson,
1987)

K.Anh.79 (515c)
First movement of a Quintet in A minor
NMA VIII:19/1
?1791
Allegro moderato
72 bars; part in draft score; ? 'work in progress'.
Dating from Tyson (1987). One of most
significant of Mozart's frags, providing interesting
glimpse into Mozart's late instrumental style: n.b.
recitatve-like opening, II♭ inflection (bars 10ff.),
and pizzicato passage for vc (bars 17ff.).
See preceding fragmentary Quintet movement in
F, K.Anh.87 (515a)

K.Anh.83 (592b)
First movement of a Quintet in D major
NMA VIII:19/1
?1787–9
19 bars. Dating from Tyson (1987). ? Not to be
connected with String Quintet in D K.593

K.Anh.81 (613a)
First movement of a Quintet in E♭ major
NMA VIII:19/1
?1785–8
71 bars; part in draft score. Dating from Tyson
(1987). ? Not to be connected with String Quintet
in E♭, K.614. ? Abandoned on musical grounds.
See following frag. K.Anh.82 (613b)

K.Anh.82 (613b)
First movement of a Quintet in E♭ major
NMA VIII:19/1
1786–91
19 bars; part in draft score. Dating from Tyson
(1987). ? Connected with String Quintet in E♭
K.614. See above frag. K.Anh.81 (613a)

See under main work-list: K.516

Piano: Sonatas and other works

Solo Piano Sonatas

K.deest
Sonata movement in C major
NMA IX:25/ii
? Salzburg, 1771
25 bars. Dating from Plath (see Rehm, 1986)

K.400 (372a)
Sonata movement in B♭ major
AMA XXIV, no.26; NMA IX:25/ii
?1782–3
Allegro
91 bars; completed by M. Stadler (total 148 bars).
Dating from Tyson (personal communication).
Names 'Costanza' and 'Sophie' cited above mock-
pathetic music in development section

K.Anh.29 (590a)
First movement of a Sonata in F major
NMA IX:25/ii
?1787–9
8 bars. Dating from Tyson (1987): on same paper-
type found in kbd frags K.Anh.30 (590b),
K.Anh.37 (590c) (? all for same work), and
K.Anh.33 and 40 (383b) (q.v.) ? Not to be
connected with Mozart's claim, in letter to
Michael Puchberg of 12–14 Jul 1789, to be
writing 6 'easy sonatas' for Princess Friederike.
See fragmentary Sonata movement in G minor,
K.312 (189i, 590d)

K.Anh.30 (590b)
Sonata movement in F major
NMA IX: 25/ii
?1787–9
Allegro [originally Presto]
15 bars. ? Finale movement. Dating from Tyson (1987). See above kbd frag. K.Anh.29 (590a)

K.Anh.37 (590c)
Rondo in F major
NMA IX:25/ii
?1787–9
33 bars. Dating from Tyson (1987). See above kbd frag. K.Anh.29 (590a)

K.312 (189i, 590d)
First movement of a Sonata in G minor
AMA XXII, no.13; NMA IX:25/ii
?1790–91
Allegro
106 bars; further music entered in autograph by unknown hand (total 145 bars); 178 bars (completed version) in 1st edition (Vienna, 1805). Dating from Tyson (1987). ? Sonata for Princess Friederike (see above kbd frag. K.Anh.29 (590a)), or work intended to bring in some ready cash (see letter to Puchberg of 12 Jun 1790)

See under main work-list: K.284 (205b); K.570

Variations

K.Anh.38 (383c)
Theme in C major
NMA IX:26
?1783; 'Thema Man[ualiter]'
?org
?Frag.: complete 16-bar theme. Dating from Tyson (1987). Followed on same leaf by fragmentary Fugue in C minor, K.Anh.39 (383d); both hastily written: ? teaching material

K.460 (454a)
Variations in A on 'Come un agnello' from *Fra i due litiganti* by Sarti (Milan, 1782)
NMA IX:26
? Vienna, Jun 1784
56 bars: autograph contains theme and 2 variations only: ? fragmentary record of work fully realized in perf. by Mozart (see letter of 9–12 Jun 1784). Version with 8 variations doubtful (Fischer, 1958, 1959); authenticity defended by Paul and Eva Badura-Skoda (1959); possibly by Sarti, based on performance of Mozart's (Fischer, 1978/9)

See under main work-list: K.455

Miscellaneous

K.9b (5b)
[Without title]; B♮ major
NMA IX:27/i
?1764
43 bars. Dating from Plath (NMA IX:27/i)

K.72a
Molto allegro in G major
NMA IX:27/ii
Verona, before 6 Jan 1770
35 bars. ? By Mozart; only source is S. dalla Rosa portrait

K.73w
Fugue in D major
NMA IX:27/ii
? early 1773; 'Fuga septimi toni'
7 bars. Dating from Plath (NMA IX:27/ii)

K.401 (375e)
Fugue in G minor
AMA XXII, no.11; NMA IX:27/ii
? Salzburg, 1773
org
95 bars; completed by M. Stadler (total 103 bars). Dating from Plath (NMA IX:27/ii)

K.deest
Fugue in E minor
NMA IX:27/ii
?1782
6 frags (sketch-like in appearance) survive: 15; 11; 4; 4; 3; 20 bars. Dating from Tyson (personal communication). Bachian

K.153 (375f)
Fugue in E♭ major
AMA XXIV, no.25/1; NMA IX:27/ii
? Salzburg, 1783
27 bars: completed by S. Sechter (total 66 bars). Dating from Tyson (1987). A related 6-bar frag. of music also survives

K.Anh.41 (375g)
Fugue in G major
NMA IX:27/ii
? Salzburg, *c.* 1776–7
27 bars. Dating from Plath (1976/7). Study 'in modo plagali' (ibid.)

K.375h
Fugue in F major
NMA IX:27/ii
? Salzburg, 1783
13 bars. Dating from Tyson (1987)

K.Anh.33 and 40 (383b)
Fugue in F major
NMA IX:27/ii
?1787–9
17 bars. Dating from Tyson (1987)
? Related to kbd sonata frags K.Anh.29, 30, 37
(590a–c) (q.v.)

K.Anh.32 (383C)
Fantasia in F minor
NMA IX:27/ii
?1789
Adagio
14 bars. Dating from NMA IX:27/ii

K.Anh.39 (383d)
Fugue in C minor
NMA IX:27/ii
?1783
8 bars. Dating from Tyson (1987). See above
Theme in C, K.Anh.38 (383c) ('Variations').
? Teaching material

K.Anh.34 (385h)
Adagio in D minor
NMA IX:27/ii
?1786–91
4 bars. Dating from Tyson (1987). NMA
transcription incomplete: the crotchet d' on beat 4
of bar 3 is tied, in autograph, over bar-line; bar 4
of autograph contains crotchet f'' (tied over from
beat 4 of bar 3)

K.154 (385k)
Fugue in G minor
AMA XXIV, no.25/2; NMA IX:27/ii
?1782
30 bars; completed by S. Sechter (total 54 bars).
Dating from Tyson (personal communication)

K.Anh.34 (385h/II, 576a)
Minuet in D major
NMA IX:27/ii
?1786–91
8 bars. Dating from Tyson (1987)

Köchel 6, p. 738 (under K.Anh.20a (626b/25))
[Without title]; E♭ major
NMA IX:27/i
18 bars

K.Anh.39a (626b/27)
Fugue in C minor
NMA IX:27/ii
? end 1780s
27 bars. Dating from Plath (NMA IX:27/ii)

K.Anh.C 27.10
Fugue in E major
NMA IX:27/ii

?10 bars; completed by A.A. Klengel (total 48
bars). ? By Mozart

K.deest
Fugue in D minor
NMA IX:27/ii
31 bars. ? By Mozart

See under main work-list: K.397 (385g); K.399
(385i); K.540

Piano duet (one keyboard)

K.357 (497a)
Allegro in G major
AMA XIX, no.1; NMA IX:24/2
?1788
98 bars. Dating from Tyson (personal
communication). K.357 (497a) and fragmentary
Movement ('Andante') in G for piano duet,
K.357 (500a) (q.v.), published as Sonata, in
completion by Julius André, in 1853

K.357 (500a)
Movement in G major
AMA XIX, no.1; NMA IX:24/2
?1791
[Andante]
160 bars (not 158, as given in *Köchel 6*). Dating
from Tyson (personal communication).
? Domestic, humorous composition. Not to be
connected with fragmentary Allegro in G for
piano duet K.357 (497a) (q.v.); description of
frag. as 'Variation and Coda', and supposed
connection with Variations in G for piano duet,
K.501 (*Köchel 6*), mistaken

Piano duet (two keyboards)

K.Anh.42 (375b)
First movement of a Sonata in B♭ major
AMA XXIV, no.60; NMA IX:24/1
?1782–3
Grave – Presto

K.Anh.43 (375c)
First movement of a Sonata in B♭ major
NMA IX:24/1
?1782–3; 'per la sig:ra Costanze Weber – ah –'
16 bars. Dating from Tyson (1987)

K.deest
Larghetto and Allegro in E♭ major
NMA IX:24/1, supplement
?1782–3
108 bars; part in draft score; completed by M.
Stadler (total 226 bars). In addition to score,
fragmentary primo part (70 bars) also survives.
Dating from Tyson (1987)

K.Anh.45 (375d)
Fugue in G major
NMA IX:24/1
? Dec 1785 – Dec 1786
23 bars. Dating from Tyson (1987)

K.Anh.44 (426a)
Allegro in C minor
NMA IX:24/1
? Dec 1785 – Dec 1786
22 bars. Dating from Tyson (1987)

Mechanical organ

K.Anh.35 (593a)
Adagio in D minor
NMA IX:27/ii
?1790–91
9 bars. Dating from Tyson (1987). ? To be
connected with completed mechanical org works
of 1790–91 (K.594 or K.608)

K.615a
[Without title]; F major
1791
? mechanical org
4 bars. Associated by *Köchel 3* (supplement), *Köchel
6* with Andante for mechanical org, K.616. Frag.
survives at head of recto of a leaf containing
sketches for *Die Zauberflöte*; this leaf is of same
paper-type as K.616 (Tyson, personal
communication). Plath regards frag. as possible
wind piece (see NMA VII:17/ii, p.xiv)

Sacred Music

Masses

K.Anh.18 (166f)
Kyrie in C major
Probably first half 1772
Adagio – Allegro
SATB, 2 ob, 2 hn, 2 tpt, timp, str
49 bars. Dating from Plath (1976/7)

K.Anh.19 (166g)
Kyrie in D major
Probably Salzburg, first half 1772
SATB, 2 ob, 2 hn, str, org
12 bars; ?copy. Dating from Plath (1976/7)

K.Anh.16 (196a)
Kyrie in G major
?1788 or later
Adagio – Andante
SATB, 2 tpt, timp, str, org
13 bars; further 21 bars by M. Stadler. Paper-type

of frag. found in dated scores between Dec 1787
and Feb 1789 (Tyson, 1987). This paper-type also
that of 3 fragmentary copies made by Mozart of
church works by Georg Reutter the younger:
Kyrie in D, K.91 (186i); De profundis clamavi
(psalm), K.93 (Anh.A 22); Memento Domine
David (psalm), K.Anh.22 (93a, Anh.A 23). Other
late fragmentary church works (see below): Kyrie
in C, K.Anh.13 (258a); Kyrie in C, K.Anh.15
(323); Gloria in C, K.Anh.20 (323a); Kyrie in D,
K.Anh.14 (422a)

K.Anh.13 (258a)
Kyrie in C major
?1787–91
SATB, 2 tpt, timp, 2 vn, b, org
9 bars. Paper-type of frag. found, with one
apparent exception from 1787, only in scores from
1790–91 (Tyson, 1987)

K.322 (296a)
Kyrie in Eb major
AMA III/i, no.3
? early 1779
Largo
S, A, SATB, 2 ob, 2 bn, 2 hn, 2 tpt, timp, str, org
24 bars (some instrumentation by M. Stadler);
completed by Stadler (total 34 bars). Dating from
Plath 1976/7). Paper-type of frag. found elsewhere
only in fragmentary Concerto for vn and pf,
K.Anh.56 (315f), begun Nov 1778 (Tyson,
personal communication). Supposed Kyrie frag.
K.Anh.12 (296b) and K.322 (296a) are one and
the same

K.296c
Sketch for Sanctus (?) in Eb major
?1777–9
? SATB, ob, vn, b
18 bars. Dating from Tyson (1987)

K.Anh.15 (323)
Kyrie in C major
AMA III/i, no.4
?1788 or later
Allegro moderato
SATB, 2 ob, 2 hn, 2 tpt, timp, str, org
37 bars; ? continuation lost; completed by M.
Stadler (total 53 bars). Fols. 1 and 2 are of paper-
type found in dated scores between Dec 1787 and
Feb 1789 (Tyson, personal communication; see
also Tyson, 1987)

K.Anh.20 (323a)
Gloria in C major
? 1788 or later
SATB, ? 2 ob, ? 2 bn, 2 tpt, timp, str, org
26 bars; instrumentation partial. Paper-type of
frag. found in dated scores between Dec 1787 and
Feb 1789 (Tyson, 1987)

K.Anh.14 (422a)
Kyrie in D major
?1788 or later
SATB, 2 ob, bn, str, org
11 bars. Paper-type of frag. found in dated scores
between Dec 1787 and Feb 1789 (Tyson, 1987)
See under main work-list: K.49 (47d); K.65 (61a);
K.66; K.257; K.259; K.337; K.427 (417a)

Requiem
See under main work-list: K.626

Miscellaneous sacred music

Short sacred works

K.Anh.23 (166h)
In te Domine speravi (vocal fugue)
?1774
SATB
34 bars. Dating from Plath (1976/7).
Doubtful: ? study copy (Federhofer, 1958)

Vespers

K.321a
Magnificat in C major
NMA I:2/ii
? Salzburg, 1779
Allegro con spirito
S, T, SATB, [bn], 2 tpt, [3 trbn], timp, 2 vn, b,
org
7 bars; autograph lost. Dating from *Köchel 6*.
? Fragmentary attempt at Magnificat from
Vesperae de Dominica K.321

See under main work-list ('Litanies, Vespers,
Vesper Psalms'): K.125

Oratorios, sacred dramas and cantatas
See under main work-list: K.35; K.429 (468a);
K.619

Voice and orchestra

Arias

K.209a
Un dente guasto e gelato
NMA II:7/iv
? Salzburg, summer 1772
B, hn, vn, b
16 bars; ? continuation lost. Dating from Plath
(1976/7)

K.440 (383h)
In te spero, o sposo amato
Text from Metastasio's *Demofoonte*

AMA XXIV, no.47; NMA II:7/iv
?1782
S, b
81 bars; set out on 2 staves. On paper of a type
first used by Mozart in 1781 (Tyson, personal
communication). For Constanze, according to her
letter of 25 Feb 1799 to Breitkopf & Härtel. No
doubt Mozart identified with Metastasio's Prince
Timanthes, secretly married to Dirce
(= Constanze), the 'wrong' girl, as his father
Demophoon (= Leopold) would consider her. In
aria Dirce expresses her faith in Timanthes

K.435 (416b)
Müsst' ich auch durch tausend Drachen
AMA XXIV, no.45; NMA II:7/iv
? early 1783
T, fl, ob, cl, 2 bn, 2 hn, 2 tpt, timp, str
143 bars; substance complete in draft score.
Dating from Tyson (1987). A sketch for vocal line,
over 60 bars, also survives

K.433 (416c)
Männer suchen stets zu naschen
AMA XXIV, no.43; NMA II:7/iv
?1783
B, 2 ob, 2 hn, str
76 bars; substance complete in draft score

K.580
Schon lacht der holde Frühling
AMA XXIV, no.48; NMA II:7/iv
Vienna, 17 Sep 1789 (*Verzeichnüss*)
S, 2 cl, 2 bn, 2 hn, str
195 bars; in draft score; final ritornello not written
down in autograph. For Josepha Hofer; insertion
aria in German version of Paisiello's *Il barbiere di
Siviglia*, which was not, however, given in Vienna
in Mozart's lifetime (*Köchel 6*)

See under main work-list ('Arias and scenes'):
K.71; K.79 (73d); K.256; K.294; K.418; K.419;
K.420

Ensembles

K.434 (424b, 480b)
Del gran regno delle amazoni
Text from G. Petrosellini's *Il regno del amazoni*
AMA XXIV, no.44; NMA II:7/iv
? second half 1786
T, B, B, 2 ob, 2 bn, 2 tpt, str
106 bars; in draft score. Dating from Tyson
(1987). 2 sketches (K.626b/33) also survive: [a] T,
B, B, ob, bn, vn; for bars 31–97; [b] S, S, T, B, ob,
?vn; 24 bars; ? ideas for middle section (not
realized in frag.)

See under main work-list ('Operas'): K.384

Songs, vocal ensembles and canons

Songs

K.Anh.25 (386d)
'Bardengesang auf Gibraltar'
Text by J.N.C.M. Denis
NMA III:8
Vienna, end 1782
S, [? and chorus,] pf [orchestral reduction]
58 bars; ? continuation lost. Surviving frag. of this short-score sketch preserves only 3 complete stanzas of ode's total of 11. Commissioned by Hungarian lady to honour the poet; ? abandoned on account of pomposity of verse: see letter of Mozart to Leopold, 28 Dec 1782

K.441a
Ja! grüss dich Gott
? Vienna, 1783
B
20 bars: voice part only. Survives in copies by Fuchs. Speculative dating from *Köchel 3*, *Köchel 6*. Authenticity questioned by Ballin (1964)

K.Anh.26 (475a)
Einsam bin ich meine Liebe
NMA III:8
?1785
S, pf [? orchestral reduction]
8 bars; music appears hastily written. Speculative dating from *Köchel 3*, *Köchel 6*

K.deest
[Vocal composition]
?1780s
S, pf
8 bars; S and pf staves braced with blank upper stave (? for another vocal part). Frag. transmits following text: 'Freude! O welche Freude! Naide! Sprich, was fehlet mir?' Autograph auctioned J.A. Stargardt, Marburg, Jun 1980

Vocal ensembles

K.Anh.24a (43a)
Ach, was müssen wir erfahren
NMA III:9
? Vienna, after 15 Oct 1767
S, S
31 bars; vocal parts for 1 stanza. Regarded as fragmentary by NMA on account of lack of accompaniment. Written on the death, from smallpox, of the Archduchess Maria Josepha

K.532
[Grazie agl'inganni tuoi]
Text by Metastasio (*La libertà di Nice*)
AMA VII/1, no.35; NMA III:9

? Vienna, 1787
S, T, B, fl, 2 cl, 2 bn, 2 hn, b
26 bars; vocal parts complete; partially instrumented (bars 1–10 only). Based on setting by M. Kelly of same canzonetta, published as duet (? its original form) for 2 S with pf in his *Reminiscences* (1826). Kelly mentions here variations by Mozart on his melody: lost, if ever written down

K.Anh.5 (571a)
Caro mio Druck und Schluck
Text by Mozart
AMA XXIV, no.50; NMA III:9
?1789
S, T, T, B [, ?pf]
54 bars. Survives fragmentarily: ? originally complete; now lost copy formed basis of AMA edition. Vocal parts of this comic quartet labelled for Constanze ('C'), Mozart ('M'), and for 2 unidentified singers ('F' and 'H'). ? Written before journey in spring 1789 to Prussian court: phrase 'schluck und druck' appears in Mozart's letter from Dresden of 13 Apr 1789

See under main work-list: K.436; K.437

Canons
See under main work-list: K.89 (73k); K.89aII (73r); K.Anh.109d (73x); K.Anh.A 33; K.508A; K.228 (515b); K.553; K.557; K.558; K.559; K.561; K.Anh.191 (562c)

Arrangements etc.

K.deest
J.S. Bach, Fugue in B♭ minor, BWV 891, from *Das wohltemperirte Clavier*, ii; C minor
? second half 1782
Original scoring: kbd
Mozart's scoring: 2 vn, va, vc
39 bars; completed by M. Stadler

K.deest
G.F. Handel, Fugue from Keyboard Suite no.2 in F major (1720)
?1782–3; 'Fuga i:ᵐᵃ del sig: Handel'
Original scoring: kbd
Mozart's scoring: 2 vn, va, vc
20 bars. Dating from Tyson (personal communication). Autograph auctioned Sotheby's, New York, 27 Jun 1989

Miscellaneous

K.385n
Fugue *a* 4 in A
?1782
12 bars. Dating from *Köchel 6*

K.443 (404b)
Fugue (Trio sonata movement) in G major
?1782
37 bars; completed by M. Stadler (total 122 bars).
Paper-type used by Mozart mainly in first Vienna
years (up to end 1783), and occasionally in later
years (Tyson, personal communication)

K.Anh.78 (620b)
[Contrapuntal study]; B minor
NMA II:5/xix
?c. 1783
18 bars. Evidence of ink and paper suggests
probably no direct connection with *Die Zauberflöte*,
K.620

See under main work-list: K.15a–ss; K.393 (385b).

JOHN ARTHUR

Doubtful and spurious

While, on the whole, Mozart scholarship is less
plagued by the problems of attribution than many
other composers of the second part of the 18th
century – the Haydn brothers are among the worst
in this respect – nevertheless there are some interesting problems among this group of works. Since the
publication of the sixth edition of Köchel in 1964,
the number of these doubtful and spurious works has
increased greatly, especially since the sources in
Prague (and Czechoslovakia in general) were catalo-
gued only in the 1960s.

Every famous composer who lived between 1750
and 1800 was, during his life, subjected to this kind
of thievery. There was no copyright in those days
(although in England authors had certain, if
limited, rights in respect of reprinting), and composers such as Dittersdorf, Reutter the younger,
Johann Christian Bach, Vanhal and many others
suffered at the hands of unscrupulous publishers and
copyists who were ready to substitute a well-known
name for a less well-known one. The case of Pater
Roman Hoffstetter and 'Haydn's op.3' string quartets is now famous: the Parisian publisher Huberty
simply erased Hoffstetter's name from the engraved
plates of what would later become known as
Haydn's op.3 and caused Haydn's name to be
substituted. Copyists did the same. Sometimes the
mistaken identity arose for another reason, such as
the copyist's inability to read the name of the
composer: in Lambach Abbey (Upper Austria) we
read 'Joesky' for 'Toeschi'. Sometimes a manuscript
was circulated anonymously. In Lambach there is a
manuscript on which the composer is listed as 'woas
neamt recht' (dialect for 'no one knows'); others
there are listed as 'Autore: Italico' or 'Autore:

Signore Dilettante'. There is a certain symphony in
E♭ major variously attributed to Anton Filtz, Ignaz
Franzl, J.C. Bach, Wenzel Pichl and Joseph Haydn
(Hob. I: Es 13). A Mass in C is found under
the names of Joseph Haydn (Hob. XXII: C43),
Michael Haydn, Aumann, Krottendorfer, Reid-
inger and Schneider. It will prove very difficult, if
not impossible, ever to unravel the tangled skein
of fact and fiction in such cases of multiple attribution.

Musicians of those days were fully aware of the
problems of authenticity. In the 'Afterword' to the
thematic catalogue of music published in 1762 by
Breitkopf & Härtel, Leipzig, we read:

> ... What conflicts would have to be solved, what secret
> struggles won, if one were to attempt to give every
> author his due and if one were to find the right author
> for pieces which appear under *various names*! And if in
> such doubtful cases, of which there were all too many,
> one could not settle anything through enquiries, how
> easily one would be led away from one's better
> judgment into error instead of following the correct
> path!

And twelve years later, in the ninth supplement of
the Breitkopf Catalogue, there is the following
'Nachricht':

> The publication of this IXth Supplement was against
> all expectations largely delayed: it was wished to avoid
> the charge that old music was mixed with new, or pieces
> listed under wrong names; and for those reasons it was
> necessary to proceed with redoubled caution. This
> accusation has always been levelled at the *manuscript
> music*; but whether the amateur is always better off if he
> adheres for that reason to *printed and engraved music* may
> be seen if he examines pages 11, 16, 24 and 35 of this
> Supplement: for Herr Cammerm[usicus] Eichner in
> Berlin assures us that the 2 piano concertos listed on the
> latter page are not by him. We assure ... the public that
> such irregularities are not placed there by us on
> purpose, and that on the contrary, we shall try to
> discover them rather than profiting by them.

In the course of the next twenty-five years the
situation if anything worsened. Instead of manuscript copies distributed by professional copyists –
which was the custom in central Europe – printed
editions gradually took over. In Paris the publishers
continued to print series (*opera*) of works by unknown composers, substituting the names of popular
favourites such as Haydn, Pleyel, Vanhal, Carl
Stamitz or Rosetti. Mozart's name spread outside
Vienna slowly, so that at his death there were very
few spurious editions of his music, but within a few
years his fame increased with lightning rapidity so
that it became lucrative for publishers to issue works
by lesser-known names under Mozart's. As early as
Niemetschek's biography of 1798, we read the
following, revealing words, which were later used by
Köchel as the motto for his 'Spurious Compositions':

With his [Mozart's] works the dealers and music establishments made mischief to such an extent that the public was misled and the name of the great master generally misused. His name was attached to many a pot-boiler quite unworthy of it . . .

It seemed to the editor and publisher of this *Compendium* that it would serve little purpose to list here all the doubtful and spurious works wrongly attributed to Mozart, especially since many dozens are not even listed in the sixth edition of Köchel and this would have taken up an inordinate amount of space which the material hardly warrants (e.g. four dozen songs and 40 masses and requiems just in *Köchel 6* alone, 60 smaller church works missing in *Köchel 6*, etc.) We have adopted a different solution. There are a number of really interesting doubtful and spurious works attributed to Mozart which the public knows and loves but which still remain shrouded in textual mystery: the famous Sinfonia Concertante for four winds, K.Anh.9; the Missa K.140; the 'Paris' Overture K.Anh.8; the 'Twelfth Mass' so beloved in England and America, of which the editor has discovered the name of the real composer (see below). These works and others like them seemed worth including and in more detail than just a mere listing.

The material has been so organized that it follows the arrangement in Köchel (i.e. Masses first, etc.) Omitted from this list are all works definitely by 'foreign' composers that were simply copied by Mozart.

A. Vocal music

I. *Masses*

K.115 (166d)
Missa Brevis in C – probably an incomplete copy of a 'foreign' work
K.116 (90a)
Missa Brevis in F – probably Leopold Mozart's incomplete copy of a 'foreign' work
K.140 (234d; C1.12)
Missa Brevis in G – the most famous of the doubtful masses; recently Walter Senn (1959) and in the NMA (I:1/1/i, 1968) has tried to show its authenticity by means of the manuscript parts from Leopold Mozart's library in Heilig-Kreuz-Kirche (now Stadtarchiv, Augsburg) which contain corrections in Mozart's hand but for which the title-page (cover), which would have contained the composer's name, is now wanting. Nevertheless, there is a certain doubt of the work's authenticity.
K.Anh.232 (C1.04) in G and (from Gloria) C
– particularly famous through Novello's edition as No.12, and especially the Gloria ('from the celebrated Twelfth Mass'), in Anglo-Saxon

countries. According to the inventory at Litomyšl (Czechoslovakia), the work is by Wenzel Müller (1767–1835), the celebrated composer of German light opera. There is another source as well (Pfannhauser 1971/2).
K.Anh.233 (C1.06 in B♭)
– Constanze thought the work to be by Süssmayr, but in Göttweig Abbey it is listed as by Pichler.
K.233a (C1.07) in D
– probably by Johann Michael Demmler (d. 1784), cathedral organist at Augsburg
K.235c (C1.11) in C
– by Franz Novotny, Haydn's organist at Eisenstadt
K. C1.20 in C
– also known under Leopold Mozart: the Benedictus is identical with the Salve Regina K.92 (q.v.)
K. C1.21 in C
– also under J. Haydn (Prague): is by Martin Heimerich, Graz 1795 (op.II) (Pfannhauser, 1971/2)
K. C1.24 in B♭
– probably by F.X. Süssmayr (Kremsmünster Abbey)
K. C1.29 in E♭
– attributed to J. Haydn (Hob. XXII: Es 11) as well as Mozart (Prague, Harburg) – doubtful
K. C1.34 Missa Solemnis in C
– by Johann Neubauer (Pfannhauser, 1971/2)

II. *Smaller Church Music*

Salve Regina in F, K.92 (Anh.186c, C3.01)
– doubtful; identical with the Benedictus of Mass in C (C1.20) (q.v.)
Antiphon (Introitus) in D minor: 'Cibavit eos';
Chorus 'Ex adipe', K.44 (73u)
– probably Wolfgang's autograph copy of a work by a polyphonic master
Tantum Ergo in B♭, K.142 (Anh.196d, C3.04)
– doubtful; although in NMA this and the following may be by Johann Zach (1699–1773) (Münster, 1965)
Offertorium sub expositio venerabili
'Convertentur sedentes' in D, K.177 & 342 (final chorus 'Benedicite angeli') (Anh.240a–b, C3.09)
– by Leopold Mozart
Tantum Ergo in D, K.197 (Anh.186e, C3.05)
–as above, K.142
Offertorium 'Sub tuum praesidium', K.198 (158b, C3.08)
– doubtful in its present state, perhaps a contrafactum
Offertorium in G 'Exaudi Domine', K.Anh.186g (C3.07)
– doubtful
Offertorium in C 'O supremum coeli numen' (K.deest) MS Stadtpfarrkirche Wels (Upper

Austria), first perf. 15 Nov 1771
 – doubtful
Miserere in C minor, 11 movements, K.Anh.241
(C3.10)
 – doubtful

III. *Oratorios*

Abramo ed Isacco, K.Anh.241a
 – by Joseph Mysliveček, comp. 1776, perf.
 Munich, 1777. Also attrib. J. Haydn (Hob.
 XXI:A)

IV. *Cantatas, etc.*

Cantata for Prince Alois Liechtenstein in A♭
'Durchlauchtigster', K.Anh.242 (C4.01)
 – doubtful
Two Choruses from *Thamos*, 'Schon weichet' and
'Gottheit', K.Anh.243
 – different settings from those written by
 Mozart, perhaps part of the original music by
 J.T. Sattler which Mozart's music replaced
Final chorus for *Eine kleine Freymaurer-Kantate*,
K.623 (623a) 'Lasst uns mit geschlungnen
Händen'
 – this chorus marks the closing of the lodge,
 when the Brothers join hands in circle. It is
 included in the first edition printed for
 Constanze's benefit, but is not in Mozart's
 autograph, is in a different key (F), and does
 not use the orchestra but only an organ. It was
 no doubt used at the end of the first
 performance of the cantata which Mozart
 conducted in November 1791, but it was
 probably composed by one of the other Brother
 musicians in Mozart's lodge.

V. *Italian Arias, Duets and Terzettos with Orchestra*

Terzetto for soprano, tenor and bass and orchestra
in G minor 'Tremer mi sento in petto',
K.Anh.243a (C7.03)
 – doubtful; the characters (Circe, Anassandro,
 Ulisse) suggest an opera on the subject of *Circe*,
 but the libretto has not yet been identified.
Recitative 'Perche t'arresti?' and Aria in E♭ 'Per
te nel carcer nero' for soprano and orchestra,
K.Anh.187 (C7.01)
 – doubtful

VI. *Lieder (see Introduction)*

Wiegenlied 'Schlafe, mein Prinzchen', K.350
 – by Bernard Flies

B. Instrumental Music
VII. *Symphonies (in their presumed chronological order)*

A minor, K.Anh.220 (16a)

– discovered in Denmark in the 1970s but very
 doubtful
C, K.Anh.291d (16b, C11.01)
 – by Leopold Mozart (Breitkopf Cat. 1766)
B♭, K.17 (Anh.223a, C11.02)
 – doubtful
E♭, K.18 (Anh.109[1], Anh.A51)
 – by K.F. Abel (Mozart has substituted
 clarinets for the printed oboe parts in Abel's
 English edition, but Abel may have used
 clarinets when performing the work)
B♭, K.Anh.216 (74g, A51)
 – doubtful
F, K.98 (223b, C11.04)
 – doubtful, also attrib. J. Haydn
G, K.deest 'Neue Lambacher Sinfonie'
 – by Leopold Mozart
D, K.Anh.219 (291b)
 – by Leopold Mozart
G, K.Anh.293 (C11.09)
 – by Leopold Mozart
F, K.Anh.293c (C11.10)
 – pastiche: I.Pleyel; II.Gyrowetz; III.Gyrowetz

VIII. *Sinfonie concertante*

E♭, Anh.9 (297b, C14.01) for oboe, clarinet, horn,
bassoon and orchestra
 – doubtful. The work survives in one 19th-
 century copy. In its present state the work can
 hardly have been composed by Mozart.
 Recently it has been proposed that the
 orchestral sections are genuine and the solo
 sections adapted (Leeson–Levin, 1978; Levin,
 1986 and 1988). There is no proof whatever
 that this version has anything to do with the
 Sinfonia Concertante for flute, oboe, horn and
 bassoon which Mozart composed for his friends
 in Mannheim.

IX. *Overtures*

B♭, K.Anh.8 (311a, C11.05)
 – doubtful. This extraordinary overture, scored
 for a large orchestra (2 fl, 2 ob, 2 cl, 2 bn, 2 hn,
 2 tpt, timp, str), is written with a knowledge of
 late Mozart (e.g. *La clemenza di Tito* overture)
 and has a certain dramatic flair, but appears to
 have been first published in Paris about 1802. A
 performance by students of the Conservatoire
 there is recorded on the first edition as having
 taken place on 16 fructidor, an X (3 Sep 1803).

X. *Concertos*

Violin conc. D, K.271a (271i)
 – doubtful
Violin conc. E♭, K.268 (365b, C14.04)
 – doubtful

Violin conc. D, K.Anh.294a (C14.05) 'Adelaide'
 – spurious: by Henri Casadesus, 1930
Bassoon conc. B♭, K.Anh.230a (C14.03)
 – spurious: strong inner evidence that François
 Devienne was the composer (Hess, 1957)

XI. *Divertimentos, etc.*

C for 2 fl, 5 tpt, 4 timp, K.187 (159c, C17.12)
 – spurious: by Leopold Mozart, his
 arrangement of dances by Starzer and Gluck,
 but one number (Gluck: Gavotte from *Paride ed
 Helena*, 1769) may have been adapted by
 Wolfgang
E♭ for wind sextet, K.289 (271g)
 – doubtful
E♮ for wind octet, K.Anh.224 (C17.04)
 – doubtful
F for wind octet, K.Anh.225 (C17.05)
 – doubtful
B♭ for wind octet, K.Anh.182 (C17.01)
 – dubious arrangement of movements from
 Serenade K.361 (370a) and Divertimento
 K.Anh.226 (second movement)
B♭ for wind sextet, K.Anh.227 (C17.02)
 – doubtful
E♭ for wind octet, K.Anh.228 (C17.03)
 – doubtful
E♮ for wind octet, K.Anh.225 (C17.07)
 – doubtful
Many other doubtful wind band divertimentos in
Prague and other libraries in Czechoslovakia.

XII. *String Quartets*

4 quartets (B♭, C, A, E♭), K.Anh.210–13
(C20.01–4)
 – spurious: by Joseph Schuster (1748–1812),
 autograph Padua
6 quartets (C, G, E♭, F minor, D, B♭), K.Anh
291a (C20.05)
 – doubtful

XIII. *Sonatas*

6 violin sonatas (F, C, F, E♭, C minor, E minor)
K.55–60 (Anh.209c–209h, C 23.01–6)
 – doubtful

XIV. *Dance Music*

A. Minuets

6 (D, D, D, G, G, G) for orch., K.105 (61f)
 – dubious; although in NMA, they are now
 considered to be by Michael Haydn (Plath
 1971/2, 33).

6 (C, F, C, A, G, G) for orch., K.104 (61e)
 – dubious: first two are arrangements of
 minuets by Michael Haydn, perhaps the others
 too
6 (C, A, D, B♭, G, C) for orchestra, K.61h
 – doubtful; possibly also by Michael Haydn

B. German Dances

9 contredanses or Quadrilles for large orch. (D, D,
D, B♭, D, D, F, B♭, C), K.510 (K.Anh.293b,
C13.02)
 – probably not authentic
Overture in D and 3 contredanses (C, A, B♭),
K.106 (588a)
 – doubtful
3 contredanses (C, G, G), K.535a (for orchestra?
for piano?)
 – doubtful
For other doubtful dances, many K.deest, see
NMA IV:13/1/ii (Flothuis, 1988)

H.C. ROBBINS LANDON

Lost

I. Vocal

Sacred

K.33c Stabat Mater. Leopold Mozart's
 Catalogue, 1768
K.47b (=117/66a) Offertorium for the
 Waisenhaus, Vienna, 1768. *Not* identical with
 K.117 (66a); K.47b is lost
K.Anh.1 (297a) Miserere for Paris, 1778. Eight
 movts
K.Anh.11 (315e) Semiramis. Never started?
K.416a German opera. Probably never started
K.615 'Viviamo felice', final chorus for G. Sarti's
 opera *Le gelosie villane*, Vienna, 20 Apr 1791
K.deest 'Quel destrier'. One of the '15 Italian
 arias', 1765–6, listed by Leopold in his
 catalogue. See Zaslaw (1983), pp. 334–5
Leopold Mozart's Catalogue, *c.* 10 other arias
 (not necessarily for S), 1764–5
K.deest Aria, Olmütz, 1767, for daughter of
 Olmütz physician Dr Joseph Wolf (letter of
 Leopold Mozart, 28 May 1779): not to be
 associated with the song 'An die Freude' K.53
 (47e) (Pfannhauser, 1954b)
K.deest 5 Metastasio settings, Vienna, before 30
 July 1768. Written by Wolfgang in the houses
 of Bonno, Metastasio, Hasse, Duke of Braganza
 and Prince Kaunitz, as demonstrations of his
 musical ability (Leopold's letter of 30 July
 1768). K.45 c–g, Kunze, NMA II:7/i
K.Anh. 2 (72b, 73A) Aria 'Misero tu non sei',
 Milan, 26 Jan 1770

Secular vocal

K.Anh.3 (315b) Scena, St Germain, Aug 1778, for S, 2 ob, 2 cl, 3 hn, pf, str. For Tenducci; see Oldman (1961) for the work's possible relationship to J.C. Bach. The circumstances of the scena's composition are described in Mozart's letter to Leopold of 27 Aug 1778, in which the work is described as being scored for pf, ob, hn, bn. A more detailed description of its orchestration is provided in a short report by Burney, quoted by Daines Barrington in his *Miscellanies* of 1781 (Deutsch, 1961)

K.Anh.11a (365a) Recitative and Aria 'Warum, O Liebe' . . . 'Zittre, töricht Herz', Munich, Nov 1780

K.569 Aria 'Ohne Zwang, aus eignem Triebe', with orch

K.deest 'Ein kleines Liedchen', NMA III: 8(K.13), p.40

K.Anh.11a (477a) Per la ricuperata salute di Ophelia'. See King (1955), p. 224

K.deest Two masonic Lieder: 'Des Todes Werk'; 'Vollbracht ist die Arbeit der Meister'. See Autexier (1984), pp. 36ff

K.Anh.255a (Anh.C B.16) Lied 'Meine weise Mutter spricht'

K.deest Lied, Vienna *c.*1785. According to an anecdote contained in the autobiography of Mozart's contemporary Adalbert Gyrowetz, a song written in a tavern for a party at the house of Franz Bernard von Kees, privy councillor and patron of music. *Biographie des Adalbert Gyrowetz*, (Vienna, 1848), p. 10

K.Anh.4(572a) Double Canon 'Lebet wohl, wir sehen uns wieder' and 'Heult noch gar, wie alte Weiber'. See Rochlitz, *AMZ*, iii (1800–01), cols 450ff

II. Instrumental

K.Anh.222 (19b) Symphony in C major: doubtful
K.Anh.215 (66c) Symphony in D major: doubtful
K.Anh.217 (66d) Symphony in Bb: doubtful
K.Anh.218 (66e) Symphony in Bb: doubtful
K.Anh.8 (311A) Second *Paris* Symphony: never written. See Zaslaw (1978)

Miscellaneous instrumental

K.41a 6 Divertimentos
K.41c Marches
K.deest Cassation in C major
K.544 March in D
K.33a Solos for various instruments
K.33h Piece for wind band
K.41b Many pieces for wind band
K.41d Many minuets
K.565 Contredanses

Concertos

K.206a Concerto for vc

K.470 Andante in A for a concerto for vn

K.47c Tpt Concerto, 1768, for the Waisenhaus, Vienna. Leopold Mozart's letter of 23 Nov 1768

K.Anh.9 (297B): see 'Doubtful and spurious' (original work in its first state is in any case lost)

K.deest Concertos for bn in C, Bb, Bb: see *Köchel 3*, p. 254

K.deest Various solos for the vn. Probably K.46d and 46e

K.33b Solos for vc, comp. for Prince Joseph Wenzeslaus zu Fürstenberg

K.deest Solo for viola da gamba and b, for Prince Joseph Wenzeslaus zu Fürstenberg, see *Köchel 3*, p.51 (under K.33b)

K.41g Nachtmusik for 2 vn and b. Maria Anna Mozart's letter of 8 Feb 1800 to Breitkopf & Härtel

K.deest 6 trios for 2 vn and vc. Leopold Mozart's Catalogue; see *Köchel 3*, p.xxiv

K.Anh.199–202 (33d–g) Sonatas for pf in G, Bb, C, F

K.Anh.206 (21a) Variations for pf in A (London, 1765)

K.41e Fugue for pf. Leopold Mozart's Catalogue

K.284f Rondo for pf, for Elector Karl Theodor's daughter. Mozart's letter of 29 Nov 1777

K.32a Capricci for pf. Constanze Mozart's letter to Breitkopf & Härtel of 2 Mar 1799

K.41f Fugue *a* 4. Leopold Mozart's Catalogue

K.284e Additional accompaniments for fl concertos by J.B. Wendling

H.C. ROBBINS LANDON

Section 11

MOZART AND THE THEATRE OF HIS TIME

MOZART AND THE THEATRE OF HIS TIME

ON MONDAY 15 JULY 1782 the placards outside Vienna's Burg-theater announced the fifth performance (out of twenty-six in Mozart's lifetime) of *Die Lästerschule*, a comedy adapted by Friedrich Ludwig Schröder. A seemingly trivial detail, perhaps, but it is an appropriate starting-point for a consideration of the unusually close relationship between the spoken theatre and opera in Vienna in the last quarter of the 18th century. The significance of the date will not have escaped those who recall that the first of Mozart's Vienna operas, *Die Entführung aus dem Serail*, was to receive its belated premiere performance the next day, 16 July. The particular link between the play given on the Monday and the new Singspiel on the Tuesday is that Johann Ernst Dauer, the actor who played Karl Denholm in *Die Lästerschule* – the reckless but warm-hearted Charles Surface of Sheridan's *The School for Scandal* – was to create the role of Pedrillo for Mozart. Nor was Dauer the only actor in the Sheridan play who also had an important career as a singer: Johann Joseph Nouseul, the Werling in *Die Lästerschule*, was to create the role of Monostatos in *Die Zauberflöte* nine years later.

Other information can be gleaned from this juxtaposition of Engish comedy and German opera. There was no chance of the Pedrillo having a quiet evening before the new opera; the stage hands cannot have been able to work undisturbed on the sets for the opera; and indeed, its final dress rehearsal had to be fitted in so as not to interrupt the theatre's lengthy unbroken sequence of evening performances. A more general point is that the delightful central scene of *The School for Scandal* might almost be a blueprint for two scenes in a later Mozart opera. This is not to suggest that Mozart's librettist was copying Sheridan, but rather to point out that the lingua franca of contemporary *opera buffa* and spoken comedy blurs the distinction between genres. Charles Surface's scoundrelly brother Joseph is trying to seduce Lady Teazle; her husband's arrival sends her scuttling behind a screen, where she overhears some home truths. The arrival of Charles in turn obliges Sir Peter Teazle to hide, and from what he overhears he realizes that he has misjudged Charles. Joseph leaves the room, and Sir Peter and Charles look behind the screen; it is not the 'little French milliner' Joseph had claimed, of course, but Lady Teazle. There is a general resemblance here to *Figaro*, with Cherubino and then the Count concealing themselves in and behind the chair in Act I, and Susanna taking the place of Cherubino in the closet in Act II. For all the similarity, these are stock comic situations, equally familiar on the operatic and the dramatic stage, and in many European centres.

In the Vienna of Mozart's day plays could be turned into operas, operas into plays. Sometimes, as with Beaumarchais' *Le Barbier de Séville*, the two genres co-existed. G.F.W. Grossmann's adaptation, *Der Barbier von Sevilla*, was given ten times between 1781 and 2 August 1783 (its predecessor, Joseph Raditschnigg's translation, had been given twenty times in the previous five years). Then, from 13 August 1783 until October 1788, there were no fewer than sixty-one performances of Paisiello's *Il barbiere di Siviglia*. The play re-entered the repertory in 1791, to be joined by the opera in 1793; in one form or the other the work was seldom absent for long until well into the new century.

Mozart and his family as theatre-goers

'We arrived here yesterday evening, and an hour later, namely at 6 o'clock, went to the opera.' Thus, before news of their health, acquaintances, or travelling problems, Leopold Mozart begins a letter to his wife from Mantua on 11 January 1770. The enthusiasm of both father and son for the theatre in general, and opera in particular, is attested in innumerable comments in the family correspondence. During their first visit to Vienna between September 1762 and January 1763 Leopold mentions having been to the opera by himself (Gluck's *Orfeo*, on 10 October), and later visits of the whole family to a comedy and to the opera are recorded in the letter of 24 November. It is not certain that the Mozarts went to the theatre in London, but the tone of Leopold's letter of 8 February 1765, with its report on operas performed, implies that he was speaking from first-hand experience. Even at Olmütz (Olomouc), whither the Mozarts repaired in 1767 in a vain attempt to escape the smallpox outbreak in Vienna, Leopold went to the theatre despite his worries about the illness of his children.

As Mozart grew older, so his theatre attendance grew more frequent – the letters written home from the three Italian journeys contain not only the evidence of their numerous visits to the opera houses but also shrewd, often witty observations by the young composer on the works they heard – by the most famous composers of the day, like Hasse and Piccinni, and by unfamiliar ones like Michelangelo Valentini.

Naturally, there is less in the family correspondence about the spoken theatre than opera, but Mozart's desire to be kept informed about the performances of Schikaneder's company during its seasons in Salzburg is clear from the letters between Leopold and Nannerl in Salzburg, and Mozart in Munich, from November 1780 until January 1781; and again between Leopold and Nannerl in May 1786, when Schikaneder was in Salzburg with his opera troupe.

Salzburg had little to offer. – 'If only there were a theatre there that deserved the name – for that is the sole source of my entertainment here...' wrote Mozart to his father on 26 May 1781, in the first months of his independent life in the capital. A few weeks later he made the same point to his sister (4 July 1781), continuing:

'I wish you could see a tragedy here! I don't know a theatre anywhere where every kind of play is *excellently* performed; but here that's true of each role – the smallest, most insignificant role is well cast, and understudied.' Again, nine years later, during the unfortunate visit to Frankfurt for the coronation of Leopold II, he used almost the same words in a letter to his wife: 'My sole entertainment is the theatre'. (3 October 1790)

Even if we often do not know what plays Mozart went to, his taste was catholic enough to cover every genre from classical tragedy and opera through high comedy, ballet and pantomime down to the coarser products and antics of the suburban theatres – he not only enjoyed going to farces, whether in Italy, Munich or Vienna, he began to write two Hanswurst comedies himself. Despite the fact that most of his operatic commissions were for settings of Italian texts, he preferred to think of himself as a German composer (letter of 5 February 1783). He had been disappointed in November 1777 to discover how wretched the singers were at the famous German National Theatre at Mannheim (letter of 14 November). Yet within a few weeks we find him beginning to pin his hopes on another patriotic endeavour, the German National-Singspiel that Joseph II was intending to establish in Vienna. In a postscript to his mother's letter from Mannheim of 10/11 January 1778 he asks his father to enlist the services of his friends in Vienna to try and secure him the post of Kapellmeister to the proposed new company. Though no official appointment was forthcoming, the rest of Mozart's life was largely marked by his desire to find employment with the German company in Vienna, even if the only practical proceeds were to be the commissions (and the fees) for *Die Entführung* in 1782, and for *Der Schauspieldirektor* in 1786.

The principal reason for the failure of the National-Singspiel lies in the absence of more than a handful of estimable works written for it. Despite the temporary success achieved by some of the Singspiels of Umlauf, Ulbrich, and later Dittersdorf, the only outstanding successes were Mozart's *Die Entführung*, and works translated and adapted from French originals (one of them Gluck's *La Rencontre imprévue*).

Vienna's theatres in the 1780s

Until 1776 the theatrical life of Vienna was exceedingly complex – and from the court's angle, exceedingly expensive to run. Four kinds of activity jostled for court approval, public acclaim, and financial subsidy: French spoken theatre (abandoned in 1772), ballet under the direction of Noverre (active in Vienna from 1767 until 1774, and again, briefly, in 1776), Italian opera – occasionally briefly abandoned for financial reasons, but invariably restored – and German spoken theatre. The bankruptcy of a series of aristocratic lessees finally decided Joseph II in March 1776 to place the German theatre under direct control of the court; it would play in the Imperial and Royal Theatre by the Hofburg (Burgtheater), opposite the Michaelerkirche, and be named the German National

Theatre. At the same time the Emperor decreed that three months' notice was to be served on the orchestra, Italian singers, and surviving ballet-dancers (the orchestra and singers were reprieved). Henceforth the other court theatre, the Imperial and Royal Theatre by the Carinthian Gate (Kärntnerthor theatre), situated at the back of the present Staatsoper, on the site of Sacher's Hotel, was to be leased to any director who was prepared to offer a programme of operas and Singspiels. The Burgtheater was normally used by its company only on Sunday, Tuesday, Thursday and Saturday, in a repertory of Italian operas and German plays, and lessees of the Kärntnerthor theatre (which returned to full court control in 1785) were permitted to use the Burgtheater without additional charge on Monday and Wednesday (the theatre was closed on Friday).

In January 1778 the Emperor realized a personal ambition with the foundation of the German National-Singspiel. However, it soon became clear that its organizers would have to rely to a considerable extent on translations of French and Italian operas; even Gluck's *Die unvermutete Zusammenkunft, oder Die Pilgrime von Mekka*, which with a total of fifty-one performances came second in the total performance-list to Grétry's *Zemire und Azor* (56), was itself a translation of the work originally staged at court in 1764 as *La Rencontre imprévue*. The National-Singspiel remained active until February 1787, with a gap from March 1783 until October 1785. Of the seventy-odd works given, only Umlauf's *Die Bergknappen* and *Die pücefarbenen Schuhe*, Mozart's *Die Entführung aus dem Serail*, and Dittersdorf's *Der Apotheker und der Doctor*, deserve attention as local products that were also successful.

After the abandonment of the Singspiel venture, performances of its most successful works did not immediately dry up, though they were mainly given in the Kärntnerthor theatre. From this time, Viennese keen to hear opera in their own language were mainly obliged to go out to the suburban theatres.

Until the relaxing of theatre licensing laws in 1776 (the so-called Spektakel-Freiheit) there were no theatres apart from those owned by the court. In 1781 a talented theatre director, Karl Marinelli (he was later ennobled), opened a theatre in the Leopoldstadt suburb, beyond the Danube Canal. With Wenzel Müller, soon joined by Ferdinand Kauer, to run the musical side of the performances, Marinelli was in a strong position in spring 1787 to fill the gap left by the final closure of the National-Singspiel. His repertory soon included several operas (two by Martín, three by Dittersdorf, and the ones by Schenk and Gassmann named at the end of Table 1), though it was mainly filled by farces that employed the talents of a skilful troupe headed by Johann La Roche as Kasperl. The other suburban theatre of major importance was opened in the Wieden suburb in 1787, beyond the Karlsplatz to the south of the city. It became important from spring 1790, when Emanuel Schikaneder became director of the Freihaustheater auf der Wieden, as it was called. It was he who in spring 1791 gave

Mozart the opportunity for what might have been a new start to his career when he invited him to set *Die Zauberflöte*.

Other theatres – in the Josephstadt and Landstrasse suburbs – were of later or ephemeral importance, and the court staged private performances at its palaces of Schönbrunn and Laxenburg. There was also a large number of often highly competent private theatres, including that of Prince Auersperg, for whom Gluck directed his *Alceste* in February 1786 and Mozart revised and directed *Idomeneo* in March 1786. A normally reliable commentator estimated in the 1790s that there were around ninety amateur theatres as well as the five professional companies in Vienna, which according to the census of 1790 had a population of 207,014 persons.

The spoken theatre in Vienna in the 1780s

The repertory of plays in the court theatres during Mozart's years in Vienna was dominated by the second-rate, and relied heavily on imports. Of the major German dramatists, Lessing was represented by four plays. *Minna von Barnhelm* had been performed since 1767, at first with the famous old Hanswurst, Gottfried Prehauser, playing a servant. But in the 1780s only the domestic tragedy *Emilia Galotti* reached double figures, with fourteen performances. Goethe was even less in evidence, with just a handful of performances of three minor plays (*Clavigo* was given five times in 1786) during Mozart's years in Vienna. Schiller, by three years Mozart's junior, appears in the repertory list only with *Fiesco*, mutilated to satisfy the censor, and given eleven times between 1787 and Mozart's death.

This was a transitional period for the German stage: the great classical dramatists were not to become established in Vienna until much later, and even those vastly productive and popular second-raters, Iffland (born 1759) and Kotzebue (born 1761), had hardly begun to rule the roost when Mozart died. All the same, three of Iffland's early domestic dramas, *Das Verbrechen aus Ehrsucht*, *Die Jäger* and *Die Mündel*, had notched up nearly fifty performances between them by the end of 1791; and Kotzebue's first three major successes in Vienna, *Menschenhass und Reue*, *Die Indianer in England* and *Die Sonnenjungfrau*, achieved a half-century of repetitions even more rapidly. The principal purveyor of plays to the Viennese theatre during the 1780s was Friedrich Ludwig Schröder (born 1744). A native of Schwerin, he was director of the Hamburg theatre from 1771 to 1780, and again from 1785 to 1800. From 1780 he was in Vienna for five seasons, working as actor and playwright. Few of his plays are original – he translated and adapted with great facility and skill from the Italian, French, and especially the English, theatres. The best measure of his contemporary success, in Vienna as elsewhere, lies in the performance figures – whereas hardly any of his rivals wrote more than two or three plays that at this time topped twenty performances, there is no difficulty in listing twenty by Schröder that exceeded this number, and eight, including his adaptation of *Hamlet*, were in the years ahead to total a remarkable 830 performances between them. We shall return to Schröder shortly as adaptor of English plays, but he also demands consideration for his memoirs (*Friedrich Ludwig Schröder. Beitrag zur Kunde des Menschen und des Künstlers*, edited by F.L.W. Mayer, 2 vols, Hamburg, 1819), which include a lively account of the state of the Viennese theatres in the early summer of 1791, with detailed comments on some of the singers of Schikaneder's company who were a few months later to create roles in *Die Zauberflöte*.

Native Austrian dramatists of any distinction were few and far between. Even Schikaneder and his principal colleagues and rivals in the Volkstheater were largely Germans who settled in Vienna. Gottlieb Stephanie ('the Younger') too was a German – from Breslau – but after his capture in the Seven Years' War he became a mainstay of the national stage in Vienna, writing a series of comedies (of which *Der Deserteur aus Kindesliebe* of 1773 was the most often performed; in Mozart's Vienna years his four most popular pieces topped sixty repetitions), and attaining wider fame as librettist for Singspiels by Umlauf and Dittersdorf – and immortality as librettist of Mozart's *Die Entführung* and *Der Schauspieldirektor*. Among authors who enjoyed considerable success with one or two dramas each are the brothers Weidmann: Joseph, with *Der Dorfbarbier* – a moderately successful play from 1785, an immensely popular Singspiel from 1796, when it was turned into a libretto for Johann Schenk; and Paul, who with plays like *Der Bettelstudent* and *Die schöne Wienerinn* enjoyed modest popularity for many years. The German aristocrat Graf Törring, with the eagerly parodied *Agnes Bernauerin*, and the Austrian Graf Brühl, with the comedies *Das Findelkind* and *Der Bürgermeister*, upheld the honour of the amateur dramatist, and C.H. von Ayrenhoff wrote two very successful short comedies, *Der Postzug* and *Die Batterie*. Other dramatists who had extensive successes with one or two titles are Engel, Spiess, Schletter, the poet and parodist Alois Blumauer (the tragedy *Erwine von Steinheim*), Möller with the military play *Der Graf von Walltron*, Rautenstrauch with the comedy *Der Jurist und der Bauer*, Brandes with the tragedy *Olivie*, and Ziegler with two plays, one each in the comic and tragic veins, both first played in Vienna in 1790: *Liebhaber und Nebenbuhler in einer Person*, and *Mathilde, Gräfin von Giesbach*.

Thus far we have considered plays that with more or less justification were claimed to be German original plays. Even the offering of quite generous prize-money had however failed to unearth much genuine local talent. The bulk of the repertory, in the 1780s as well as in earlier and later periods, consisted of plays translated and adapted for the Viennese stage. Translations from the French were numerous. Marivaux's *Les Fausses Confidences* (translated by Gotter as *Die falschen Vertraulichkeiten*) was quite frequently given; Lemierre's *La Veuve du Malabar*, adapted by Plümicke under the title *Lanassa*, was often given; elsewhere it was performed with Mozart's Symphony in E flat, K.184 (161a), and parts of the *König Thamos* score. Diderot's *Le Père de Famille*, in

Lessing's translation as *Der Hausvater*, was both a popular success and also the starting-point for Baron Gemmingen's sequel, *Die Familie*, which from 1781 in Schröder's arrangement was even more popular than Diderot's play; in it one of the characters appeared as a bird-man – we do not need to look back to the Baroque age for carnival masks and intermezzo clowns to find an immediate predecessor for Papageno, especially as these plays were in the repertory when Schikaneder was a member of the court theatre in the mid-1780s. Apart from the double existence of *Le Barbier de Séville*, already noted, Beaumarchais was also regularly represented by *Eugénie*, not to mention *Le Mariage de Figaro* in its operatic form.

Italian plays were also common in the repertory. Two adaptations of Gozzi shared around twenty-five performances, and in the 1780s Goldoni was still represented by about a dozen works, roughly equally divided between opera libretti and straight comedies; his four most popular plays ran up over sixty performances.

Easily the most prolific source of successful plays on the Viennese stage at this period was England. No fewer than seven of Shakespeare's plays were staged in the court theatres at this time, in addition to Stephen Storace's operatic adaptation of *The Comedy of Errors*, *Gli equivoci*. Of the Shakespeare titles, *Coriolanus*, *Henry IV* and *Othello* enjoyed only eleven performances between them; *Romeo and Juliet*, in a dreadful free adaptation by Weisse, was given ten times, *Cymbeline* (under the name *Imogen*) eighteen times, *King Lear* twenty-two times, and *Hamlet*, that perennial success, had run up thirty-six repetitions by the time of Mozart's death. The Bard would have had some difficulty in recognizing his tragedies in these Viennese performances which, in German perversions based on the adaptations of David Garrick, with happy endings, can have been anything but authentic. Far more popular were the products of a dozen and more British dramatists, from Beaumont and Fletcher's *Rule a Wife and Have a Wife* (adapted by Schröder as *Stille Wasser sind betrüglich*), Wycherley's *The Country Wife* (*Das Landmädchen*, shown twenty-three times between 1776 and 1791), John Crowne's *Sir Courtly Nice* (*Die unmögliche Sache*) and John Banks's *The Unhappy Favourite* (*Die Gunst der Fürsten, oder Elisabeth und Essex*) from the 17th century on via Farquhar's *The Beaux' Stratagem* (*Die Glücksritter*, twenty performances 1783–91), *The Recruiting Officer* (*Die Werber*), and especially *The Constant Couple* (*Der Ring*, twenty-four performances between 1783 and 1789, in which year Schröder brought out a continuation, *Die unglückliche Ehe durch Delicatesse*; both parts remained in the repertory until the mid-19th century, totalling nearly two hundred performances in the Burgtheater alone) on to more or less contemporary English-language authors: Richard Cumberland's *The West Indian* (*Der Westindier*) and *The Brothers* (*Das Blatt hat sich gewendet*), the elder George Colman's *The Jealous Wife* (*Die eifersüchtige Ehefrau*) and *The Clandestine Marriage* (*Die heimliche Heyrath*, 21 performances 1781–91), Goldsmith's *She Stoops* to Conquer (*Irrthum auf allen Ecken*, 22 performances 1784–91) and *The Good-natur'd Man* (*Zu gut, ist nicht gut*), Sheridan's *The Rivals* (*Die Nebenbuhler*) and, as we have seen, *The School for Scandal*; also Sophia Lee's *The Chapter of Accidents* (*Glück bessert Thorheit*), Colley Cibber's *The Careless Husband* (*Der flatterhafte Ehemann*) and *The Double Gallant* (*Der doppelte Liebhaber*), and – a particular favourite with the Viennese – Arthur Murphy's *All in the Wrong* (*Alle irren sich*), though it only reentered the repertory at the end of 1791. More difficult to trace, but now firmly identified, are Frederick Pilon's *The Deaf Lover* (*Der taube Liebhaber*, which came into the repertory in November 1782, two years after its London premiere, and rapidly attained thirty-six performances), and Hannah Cowley's *Who's the Dupe?* (*Der Schulgelehrte*). Schröder even dramatized Fanny Burney's novel *Evelina* as *Viktorine* (1784), and with it scored one of his typical successes. With Muzzarelli's comic ballet *Il Capitaneo Cook alli Ottaiti* proving highly popular at the end of 1791 and beginning of 1792, the English influence on the Viennese repertory may be seen to extend to every genre.

Opera in Vienna in the 1780s

The court musical establishment in the 1780s can be swiftly outlined. Joseph II was emperor from 1780 until his death on 20 February 1790. He was succeeded by his brother Leopold, Grand Duke of Tuscany. The High Chamberlain and Supreme Director of the Court Theatres (Hofmusikgraf) from April 1776 until January 1791 was Franz Xaver, Count (from September 1791 Prince) Orsini-Rosenberg; his successor (until 1796) was Johann Wenzel, Count Ugarte. (Rosenberg, both in name and office, is a curious omission from the otherwise invaluable list in Köchel.)

The Hofkapellmeister from 1774 until 1 March 1788 (when he was officially pensioned, a mere six weeks before his death) was Giuseppe Bonno. He was succeeded by Antonio Salieri (in office until 1 June 1824). From 1789 Salieri's deputy was Ignaz Umlauf. The officially appointed court composers were Gluck (1774–87), Salieri (until his elevation following Bonno's retirement) and, from 7 December 1787, Mozart ('Kammermusicus').

The years from 1778 were marked by the establishment in the Burgtheater of the German Singspiel company; from 1776 Italian opera had been largely confined to the Kärntnerthor theatre, and operated on a fairly modest scale. From Lent 1783, when the activities of the National-Singspiel were interrupted, a fine ensemble was appointed which, with already established stars like Catarina Cavalieri, Therese Teyber, Aloisia Lange and Johann Valentin Adamberger (until the mid '80s he was mainly employed in the German repertory), was to be responsible for the baptism of Mozart's three operas to texts by Da Ponte. Among the acquisitions of 1783 were Nancy Storace, Rosa Manservisi, Michael Kelly, Francesco Bussani, Francesco Benucci, and Maria and Stefano Mandini, with the then almost totally inexperienced Lorenzo da Ponte as librettist.

As can most clearly be seen from the performance figures of Table 1, the repertory of the Court Opera during the 1780s was dominated by composers born in Italy. Paisiello comes an easy first, both in terms of the number of works performed, and the popularity of four of them in particular; yet of the fifteen operas by him given in the 1780s, only *Il rè Teodoro in Venezia* was commissioned for, and first given in, Vienna. Salieri doubtless owes his comfortable second place partly to his influential position in the musical establishment, especially from 1788 on (in fact he hardly added to his reputation with most of the works of his later years), but it would be misguided as well as ungenerous to deny the pleasing qualities of many of his operas. However, only *Axur, rè d'Ormus*, the revised Italian version of his successful French setting of Beaumarchais' *Tarare* (Paris, Opéra, 8 June 1787), enjoyed prolonged popularity (100 performances until 1805). Third place is taken by the Spaniard Martín y Soler, who following six successful years in Italy came to Vienna in 1785 as a thirty-one-year-old and proceeded to write three very popular operas for the Burgtheater, of which *Una cosa rara* especially enjoyed a renown that makes Mozart's quotation from it in the Act II finale of *Don Giovanni* natural as well as ironic. Cimarosa, though his one opera written for Vienna, the immensely successful *Il matrimonio segreto*, dates from two months after Mozart's death, was the fourth most often played opera composer in the Vienna of Mozart's time owing to the number as much as the quality of his works that were staged at the Burgtheater (as at most of the leading European houses). Pietro Alessandro Guglielmi, another prolific and widely valued opera-composer in his day, was represented in Vienna by seven operas in the 1780s and early '90s, all but one of them in the comic vein, and though he was of the generation before that of Mozart, his works remained in the repertory in Vienna until just into the new century. Sarti's sixth place is due almost entirely to his one great international success, *Fra i due litiganti il terzo gode*, which following its first rendition in the Burgtheater in May 1783 was given a further sixty-two times in six years, which makes Mozart's apt quotation from it in *Don Giovanni* hardly surprising.

We may think that Mozart's seventh place in the performance-lists (see Table 2) during his lifetime is modest in the extreme, yet he was the most-often performed non-Italian composer, and one can easily argue that his relative success is unexpectedly marked in a city as notoriously fickle and conservative in its taste as Vienna. Grétry owes his high position in the table, far ahead of other French composers, to *Zémire et Azor*, one of the most successful of the works staged by the National-Singspiel company, though others of his *opéras comiques* enjoyed briefer popularity.

Of the rest of the opera composers on the Viennese scene between 1781 and 1791 Dittersdorf and Umlauf deserve honourable mention as natives who made good, and the young Joseph Weigl (born 1766) had already achieved his first success with *Il pazzo per forza* (twenty-four performances between 1788 and 1791). The other major figure, Gluck, at the end of his life, and in the years following his death in 1787, was unfashionable; his comparatively strong position in the list is due almost entirely to the great popularity during the National-Singspiel years of his French opera of 1764, *La Rencontre imprévue*, in a German version. Otherwise worthy of mention are the Englishman Stephen Storace's success in 1785 and succeeding seasons with *Gli sposi malcontenti*, and the enduring if hardly spectacular esteem for the melodramas of Georg Benda, the only Bohemian/north German composer to enjoy any popularity in Vienna.

The changes at the Court Opera that were introduced by the new Emperor in 1791 were not destined to have much effect on Mozart, though it is possible that the preference of Empress Maria Louisa for *opera seria* may have had some bearing on the decision of the Bohemian Estates to commission *La clemenza di Tito*. Be that as it may, a castrato – Angelo Testori – was among the newly engaged singers for Vienna. His début was in Nasolini's *Teseo a Stige* on 24 November 1791, the Empress's birthday, and he sang in two further serious works later that season. Leopold II also installed a ballet ensemble under the direction of Antonio Muzzarelli (whose comic ballet about Captain Cook in Tahiti has already been mentioned as one of the theatrical events of Mozart's last weeks). Further, a new opera house was planned, which was to be built on the site of the Stallburg. These innovations, however, had hardly begun to be realized by the time of Mozart's death.

Table 1

Composers of operas performed at the Court
Theatres, 1781–91, in descending order of
popularity (measured by number of
performances)

LTh = Theater in der Leopoldstadt
adW = Theater auf der Wieden
1 = first staged before 1781
2 = remained in repertory after 1791
* = written for Vienna

Most frequently performed works:

Composer: Paisiello
Total number of performances: 294
Il barbiere di Siviglia (13.8.1783–10.10.1788)[2]
61 performances
Il rè Teodoro in Venezia
(23.8.1784–19.2.1791)*
59 performances
Gli astrologi immaginari (as **Die
eingebildeten Philosophen**, apart from 4
performances in Italian in 1783
(22.5.1781–10.11.1786)
40 performances
La molinara (13.11.1790–10.12.1791)[2]
31 performances
La contadina di spirito (6.4.1785–10.2.1786)[2]
21 performances
11 further operas by Paisiello, none of them
written for Vienna, received a total of 82
performances. In addition, **Das Mädchen von
Frascati** (= **La frascatana**) was given 9 times in
LTh, 1787–8, and **Die eingebildeten
Philosophen** was staged adW on 24.1.1789.

Composer: Salieri
Total number of performances: 185
Axur, rè d'Ormus (8.1.1788–3.12.1790)[2]*
50 performances
La scuola de' gelosi (22.4.1783–13.12.1786)
27 performances
La grotta di Trofonio (12.10.1785–4.1.1788)*
26 performances
Il talismano (10.9.1788–22.5.1791)
21 performances
7 further operas by Salieri, all of them written for
Vienna, received a total of 61 performances. In
addition, **Der Rauchfangkehrer** was given 7
times, 1786–87, **Die Zauberhöhle des
Trofonius** 8 times, 1789, and **Der Jahrmarkt
von Venedig** (= **La fiera di Venezia**) 9 times,
1791, all in LTh.

Composer: Martín y Soler
Total number of performances: 141
L'arbore di Diana (1.10.1787–3.3.1791)[2]*
(revived in German in 1802)
66 performances

Una cosa rara (17.11.1786–25.2.1791)[2]*
55 performances
Il burbero di buon cuore
(4.1.1786–20.1.1790)*
20 performances
In addition, **Cosa rara, der seltne Fall** was
given 87 times in 1787–91 (121 in all), **Der Baum
der Diana** 47 times, 1788–91 (78 in all) in LTh,
and a sequel, **Der Fall ist noch weit seltner**
(Schikaneder/Schack), was given adW on
10.5.1790.

Composer: Cimarosa
Total number of performances: 124
Il falegname (25.7.1783–6.1.1790)
23 performances
Le trame deluse (7.5.1787–1.9.1791)
20 performances
7 further operas by Cimarosa, none of them
written for Vienna, received a total of 81
performances.

Composer: Guglielmi
Total number of performances: 112
La pastorella nobile (24.5.1790–13.12.1791)[2]
36 performances
La bella pescatrice (26.4.1791–29.12.1791)[2]
27 performances
Le vicende d'amore (16.6.1784–31.5.1786)
21 performances
4 further operas by Guglielmi, none of them
written for Vienna, received a total of 28
performances. In addition, **Robert und Kalliste**
(= **La sposa fedele**) was staged adW on
2.9.1790.

Composer: Sarti
Total number of performances: 108
Fra i due litiganti il terzo gode (28.5.1783–
30.5.1789)[2] (from 14.9.1787 in German as **Im
Trüben ist gut fischen**)
63 performances
Le gelosie villane (17.9.1783–17.1.1785)[1,2]
25 performances
3 further operas by Sarti, none of them written for
Vienna, received a total of 20 performances.

Composer: Mozart
Total number of performances: 105
Die Entführung aus dem Serail
(16.7.1782–4.2.1788)[2]*
38 performances
Le nozze di Figaro (1.5.1786–9.2.1791)[2]*
38 performances
3 further operas by Mozart, all of them written for
Vienna, received a total of 29 performances; see
table 2.

Composer: Grétry
Total number of performances: 100

Zemire und Azor (19.7.1781–30.12.1787)[1]

38 performances

7 further operas by Grétry, none of them written for Vienna, received a total of 62 performances. In addition, **Zemire und Azor** was given 31 times in 1790–91 (54 in all) in LTh, and a sequel, **Der Ring der Liebe** (Weidmann/Umlauf), received 3 performances in 1786–7 in the Kärntnerthor theatre.

Composer: Dittersdorf
Total number of performances: 72
Der Apotheker und der Doctor
(11.7.1786–9.9.1787)[2]*
(on 5 evenings only one of the two acts was performed)

33 performances

3 further operas by Dittersdorf, all of them written for Vienna, received a total of 39 performances. In addition, **Der gefoppte Bräutigam** was given 9 times in 1786–7, **Der Apotheker und der Doctor** 17 times in 1788–9 and **Hieronymus Knicker** 12 times in 1789, all in LTh; and **Im Dunkeln ist nicht gut munkeln** was staged in February 1789, and **Der Gutsherr oder Hannchen und Gürge** on 2(?).3.1791, both adW.

Composer: Gluck
Total number of performances: 70
Die unvermuthete Zusammenkunft (= La Rencontre imprévue)
(12.2.1781–19.10.1787)[1,2,]*

42 performances

3 further operas by Gluck, 2 of them written for Vienna, received a total of 28 performances. In addition, **Die unvermuthete Zusammenkunft**, under the title **Die Pilgrime von Mekka**, was given 23 times in LTh in 1789–91.

Composer: Umlauf
Total number of performances: 70
Das Irrlicht (17.1.1782–6.8.1787)[2]*

32 performances

5 further operas by Umlauf, all of them written for Vienna, received a total of 38 performances.

Composer: Anfossi
Total number of performances: 56
6 operas by Anfossi, none of them written for Vienna; the most successful, with 16 performances in 1788–9, was **Le gelosie fortunate**. In addition, **Die Eifersucht auf der Probe** (= Il geloso in cimento) was given 12 times in LTh in 1787–9.

Composer: Storace
Total number of performances: 40
Gli sposi malcontenti (1.6.1785–27.7.1788)*

29 performances

Gli equivoci* received 11 performances between 1786 and 1791

Composer: Benda
Total number of performances: 37
Medea (20.2.1781–5.12.1791)[1,2]

20 performances

Ariadne auf Naxos received 17 performances between 1781 and 1791. **Ariadne auf Naxos** was also staged adW in May 1790.

Composer: Joseph Weigl
Total number of performances: 33
Il pazzo per forza (14.11.1788–4.11.1791)*

24 performances

3 further operas by Weigl, all of them written for Vienna, received a total of 9 performances.

Composer: Monsigny
Total number of performances: 33
4 operas by Monsigny, none of them written for Vienna; the most successful, with 17 performances between 1782 and 1786, was **Röschen und Colas**.

Composer: [Philidor]
Total number of performances: 21
2 operas attributed to Philidor, neither written for Vienna; the more successful, **Der Fassbinder** (16 performances, 1781–8), an adaptation of Audinot's **Le Tonnelier**, is probably not by Philidor; the other, **Das Rosenfest zu Salenci** (**La Rosière de Salenci**), was a collaborative venture.

Composer: Gazzaniga
Total number of performances: 20
2 operas, of which the one written for Vienna, **Il finto cieco** (20.2.1786, 3 performances) was a failure; **La dama incognita**, a revised version of **La vendemmia** (Florence, 1778), received 17 performances in 1784–5.

In the period under review, no other composer had more than 16 performances (Ruprecht and Tritto) in the Court Theatres.
Schenk, represented there only by **Im Finstern ist nicht gut tappen** (1787: 11 performances), was at this time more in demand in the suburban theatres: LTh **Die Weinlese** 61 performances, 1785–91 and **Die Weihnacht auf dem Lande** 39 performances, 1786–91; adW **Das unvermutete Seefest** (9.12.1789) and **Der Erntekranz** (9(?).7.1791).

Similarly, two of Gassmann's operas totalled 11 performances in the Court Theatres at this time, whereas in LTh **Die Gräfinn** (= La contessina) had 16 performances in 1786–8, and **Die Liebe unter den Handwerksleuten** (= L'amore artigiano) 5 in 1790.

Table 2
Performances of Mozart operas in Vienna, 1782–91

opera	year	Jan	Feb	Mar	Apr	May	June	July	Aug	Sept	Oct	Nov	Dec
Die Entführung aus dem Serail	1782							4	4	2	1		1
	1783	1	1	*									
	1784												
	1785											3	
	1786	2	1	**		2		1	1			2	2
Der Schauspieldirektor			4										
Le nozze di Figaro						4		1	1	1		1	1
Die Entführung	1787	1	1				1	2	1			2	1
	1788		1										
Il dissoluto punito, ossia Il Don Giovanni						6	2	3	1		1	1	1
Figaro	1789								2	3	3	3	
	1790	1	1			5	2	2	1	2	1		
Così fan tutte		3	2				2	2	1				
Figaro	1791	2	1										
Die Zauberflöte										1	c.20?	***	

* On 3 March 1783 Mozart and some friends performed a pantomime of Mozart's composition (K. 416d) during the interval of the Carnival Ball at the Redoutensaal.

** On 13 March 1786 Mozart directed a private performance of his revised score of *Idomeneo, rè di Creta* in the Palais Auersperg.

*** On 6 November the 24th performance of *Die Zauberflöte* was announced; by the time of Mozart's death the number had perhaps risen to about 45 performances.

PETER BRANSCOMBE

Section 12
PERFORMANCE PRACTICE

BESIDES DETAILED STUDY of Mozart's music, performers require a thorough knowledge of the social history, organology, iconography and theoretical writings (especially instrumental treatises) of his times to achieve substantial 'authenticity'. Comprehension of late 18th-century playing techniques and expressive ideals is essential to this cause, especially those relating to short-necked, predominantly gut-strung stringed instruments with pre-Tourte bows, valveless brass instruments, woodwind instruments without Boehm's bores and keywork (including the Stadler 'clarinet' with the extended lower compass for which Mozart wrote K.622), and 'Viennese' pianos, particularly those of Stein with their characteristic touch, tone and articulation. Vital, too, is foreknowledge of instances where Mozart's notation fails to convey precisely his intentions, e.g. the arpeggiation of chords, the addition of ornamentation and continuo realizations, and the register of horn or cello/bass parts (e.g. in the slow movement of K.482, Mozart's indications suggest an interpretation other than the intended unison cello/bass rendering).

Expression

Traditionally, the performer's role consists in conveying faithfully, yet personally, the composer's intentions according to the music's mood(s), character(s) and style(s). The 18th century witnessed the culmination of the 'doctrine of the affections', the ultimate aim of which was the musical expression of specific human emotions, characterized by certain musical devices which are to some extent standardized and identifiable. Descriptive words at the beginning of a piece, movement or section suggested broadly its mood and approximate tempo – from Grave, Leopold Mozart (1756) infers 'sadly and earnestly, hence very slow indeed', whilst Allegro suggests 'a gay, but not hurried tempo'; and tempo, metre, rhythm, the choice of accompaniment, dynamic variations, harmony, melody and tonality – broadly speaking, certain keys appear to have held particular emotional meanings in Mozart's music (see Steblin, 1983) – were composers' principal means for the creation of such a language of the emotions (Sulzer, 1771–4).

Tempo

Most of Mozart's compositions incorporate simple tempo directions such as Andante, Adagio, Allegretto or Allegro, without additional terms qualifying the prevailing moods and expressions, and only rarely include such extreme markings as Largo or

Prestissimo. Nevertheless, Mozart was meticulous in his annotation of tempi (see his numerous amendments to his six 'Haydn' quartets), especially in distinguishing between *alla breve* and 4/4 for purposes of accentuation. Badura-Skoda (1957) points out that the AMA incorporates several examples (notably the slow movements of K.466 and K.595) where the original *alla breve* sign is omitted from Andante and Larghetto movements, thereby implying a somewhat slower tempo than Mozart doubtless intended and falsifying the melodic shape and accentuation of his text.

Unlike Quantz (1752) and Türk (1789), Mozart appears not to have based his tempi on the human pulse; but, judging from his letters, he favoured tempi which allowed clarity of articulation, and he criticized performers who adopted over-fast speeds. The note-content (in particular the shortest note-value) or a particular phrase of a movement invariably governed its ideal tempo within the sphere of the Italian term designed to characterize it (see L. Mozart, 1756; Türk, 1789). Individual movements (variations apart) were generally performed uniformly as regards tempo, although some flexibility, whether or not indicated, was necessary in order to capture the character and mood of certain phrases, sentences or paragraphs of the structure.

Tempo rubato

Four types of tempo rubato were applied in Mozart's time, the most common involving a natural flexibility of the prescribed melodic rhythm within a constant tempo, chiefly in slow movements (see Türk, 1789). Mozart was acclaimed for his exploitation of this technique (see Anderson, 1938). Other types of rubato commonly practised included the modification of dynamics, the written-out displacement of natural accents, and the flexibility of actual tempo by introducing arbitrary, unwritten accelerandos or ritardandos to clarify phrase structure.

Rhythmic alteration

A flexible approach to rhythm, especially to dotted rhythms, was a notable characteristic of 18th-century style, a dotted note invariably being lengthened and its complementary note shortened and played in 'lifted' style (see L. Mozart, 1756). Although Mozart was comparatively precise in notating rhythms, there remain examples of dotted rhythms which should ideally be brought into conformity with double-dotted rhythms, as well as instances where the length of a quaver or the rhythm of a dotted figure require alteration to accommodate triplet quaver movement in other parts.

Dynamics

Mozart indicated dynamic markings only sparingly in his early works. Only rarely were the extreme dynamics *pianissimo* and *fortissimo* and such gradations as *mezzo-forte* or *mezzo-piano* included; however, his basic markings (*forte* and *piano*) call not for sudden, 'terraced' changes from dynamic extremes, but for a more graduated and expansive approach to dynamics. Parallels between instrumental performance and the human voice (either in speech or vocal performance) were commonly cited by theorists with regard to shaping and colouring phrases. As dynamic inflection was inherent in vocal performance, such fundamental dynamic indications were regarded as a framework around which to build an expressive interpretation. Nuances were thus generally applied (whether notated or not) to establish the 'peaks' and general contours of phrases, as well as their expressive content, and were also freely employed to highlight dissonances, cadences (especially interrupted cadences), ornaments, chromatic notes, and such like.

Broadly speaking, Mozart's later works incorporate dynamics more freely (e.g. Rondo, K.511), but the performer still has to provide nuances where appropriate – pianists might introduce a *forte* dynamic (if not so indicated) in octave passages and full chords; passages in broken chords over several octaves; cadential trills in allegros, and virtuoso scales in developments; tremolo and quasi-tremolo figures such as broken octaves; and invariably in runs for the left hand – although these examples are not without exception (Badura-Skoda, 1957).

Badura-Skoda also notes the frequent occurrence of *calando* in Mozart's autographs and suggests that 'becoming softer' was intended, not (as later) also 'becoming slower'.

In string playing, the so-called divisions of the bow, four types of nuanced bowings (Division 1 = < >; Division 2 = >; Division 3 = <; Division 4 = < > < >), helped players to 'apply strength and weakness in all parts of the bow' (L. Mozart, 1756). They were so much accepted practice that sustained strokes (without nuance) were exceptions rather than the rule. Most pre-Tourte bows were unsuited to the production of accents in the modern sense. Mozart's use of 'sf', 'fp', and 'mfp', as substitutes for >, requires careful differentiation in the strength of the initial accent, and a distinction should doubtless be drawn between 'fp' and his common indication 'for : pia', which suggests that the *forte* should be sustained at rather greater length.

Articulation

The art of articulation embraces myriad aspects of vocal/ instrumental technique that determine how notes succeed one another, notably fingering for most instruments, tonguing patterns for winds, categories of touch for keyboards, breathing and enunciation for the voice, and bow-management for the violin family.

In string playing, the fundamental stroke of pre-Tourte bows was non-legato. Staccato bowing involved even greater articulation and was invariably conveyed by lifting the bow from the string after each stroke, tempo permitting. True legato bowing was achieved only by slurring, which was increasingly exploited during the period, especially in slow movements, as a means of emulating the qualities of the human voice.

Three types of piano touch were distinguished by late 18th-century theorists – staccato, legato and the 'ordinary' manner. C.P.E. Bach (1753/62), Marpurg (1755) and Türk (1789) recommend that when playing with ordinary touch the finger must be lifted before the next note is played (for legato, the finger remains on the key for the full note-value), but opinions differ regarding the degree of articulation. The oft-quoted view that legato touch was employed only when indicated (by an appropriate Italian term or slurs) was not universally endorsed. It had effectively become the norm well before 1800 (see Milchmeyer, 1797), Türk (1789) making a distinction between articulation and legato slurs and warning that the annotation of slurs in the opening bars of a movement implied a legato interpretation until otherwise indicated (by dashes or rests). Traditionally, the first note under a slur was emphasized slightly and the convention of slurring appoggiaturas and other such dissonances to their 'resolutions' (except possibly when the resolution is delayed) was tacitly understood.

Mozart employed slurs inconsistently, adding them as either articulation guidelines or as indications of legato (rarely as phrasing marks) and usually writing them by the bar with no break intended between each. However, although legato style was in the ascendancy in the late 18th century, Mozart's own piano playing was described as 'subtle but broken-up; no legato' (Beethoven), and Czerny claimed that Mozart's school was characterized by 'briliant playing, more with an eye to staccato than legato' (Badura-Skoda, 1957). Furthermore, although he enthused about the pedal mechanism of Stein's pianos, Mozart added no pedal indications, doubtless leaving pedalling to the performer's taste according both to context and the capability of the instrument available.

Mozart annotated articulation slurs somewhat sparingly. Such indications often required supplementation from the performer (see L. Mozart, 1756) and were invariably accompanied by staccato dots or strokes (in print, usually wedges), between which it is impossible to make any consistent distinction throughout his *oeuvre*. Türk was one of the first theorists to draw such a distinction, dots tending to imply a less pronounced staccato than strokes. This is doubtless the case in late Mozart, when he used dots more freely, the stroke retaining its dual purpose of staccato and accent, generally (but not exclusively) in *forte* contexts.

Phrasing

Phrasing was generally considered analogous to punctuation marks in language or breathing in singing. Mozart's music tended to be articulated into a series of events – motives and phrases (*Einschnitte*) on the smaller, and sections on the larger level. Although his balanced, complementary phrasing was rarely indicated, it was occasionally implied in the notation (by breaking of the beams). It was carefully articulated in performance, by pausing briefly on the last note of one phrase and starting anew on the first note of its successor, reducing slightly the tonal volume of the last note and re-establishing it with the first of the next phrase (Sulzer, 1771–4), or by shortening the last note of one phrase when necessary to separate it from the first note of the next (Türk, 1789).

Accentuation

Intelligent accentuation and, in some cases, prolongation of important notes were vital for comprehension of the performer's, and hence the composer's, intentions. 18th-century musicians observed the three categories of accent used in everyday speech – 'grammatic', 'rhetorical' and 'pathetic' – in their performances (see Rousseau, 1768; Sulzer, 1771–4). The notes of rhythmic stress (*note buone*), the first note of a phrase, a note that is longer or markedly higher or lower than its predecessors, and dissonant notes are common instances when prolongation invariably provided a flexible, musicianly solution. These 'grammatic accents' were not all given equal emphasis. The first accent in the bar was traditionally the strongest (Sulzer, 1771–4) and was accommodated in string playing by the traditional rule of down bow; this long-standing principle required such notes to be played with the stronger down bow and the unaccented beats with the weaker up stroke (see L. Mozart, 1756). Such 'uneven' playing was never indicated in music, despite the attempts of some theorists. Sulzer (1771–4) indicates accentuation by a short line (–) and the degree of emphasis by the number of such lines, while Türk (1789) explains his approach in tabular form, using dynamics to indicate the appropriate degree of emphasis.

Performers required a sound harmonic knowledge and appreciation of timbre in order to implement 18th-century theories of accentuation and phrasing. In string playing, uniformity of tone colour within the phrase was widely encouraged, and the higher left-hand positions were increasingly exploited for expressive purposes. Furthermore, sequences were played wherever possible with matching fingerings, bowings and string changes, and open strings were invariably avoided when stopped notes were technically viable – in descending scale passages involving more than one string (especially slurred), in trills (except in double trills where there was no alternative), appoggiaturas and other such ornaments, and in most melodic or expressive contexts. Evidence is conflicting regarding the incidence of portamenti. However, the fact that some theorists rejected them outright suggests that they were employed by some string and vocal performers, especially in solo contexts.

Vibrato

Vibrato was employed sparingly as an expressive ornament in Mozart's time, although Leopold Mozart's reference (1756) to violinists, who 'tremble consistently on each note as if they had the palsy', suggests that Geminiani's recommendation (1751) of, essentially, a continuous vibrato in the approved modern fashion, had some disciples. It was generally added to long sustained or final notes in a phrase, and at a speed appropriate to the music's dynamic, tempo and character (Leopold Mozart distinguishes three vibrato speeds – slow, accelerating and fast). The use of vibrato by performers other than string players is sparsely documented, but judging from Mozart's letters about Meisner and Ramm, it was doubtless part of contemporary vocal and wind technique.

Ornamentation

Although ornamentation in the Classical period was heavily indebted to the theories of C.P.E. Bach (1753–62), who regarded ornaments as 'indispensable', and Türk (1789), Mozart was also influenced by the south German tradition (L. Mozart, 1756), the ornaments most commonly encountered in his music being the trill, mordent, turn, appoggiatura, *gruppetti* and the arpeggio. Trills were generally begun on the beat with the upper auxiliary, except where, for example, chains of trills or the need to preserve a melodic line dictated otherwise. They were invariably modified by the addition of preparations or terminations and by varying the number, rhythm, speed and nuances of the notes comprising the ornament. When the trill was preceded by one or more small notes, these latter were generally played on the beat and included as part of the ornament. Terminations were sometimes incorporated in the text, either as an integral part of the rhythmic scheme or extra-rhythmically as small notes, but might be supplied at will (determined by taste and context) by the performer. The speed of the trill repercussion was to conform with the music's tempo and character – L. Mozart (1756) gives four speeds: slow, medium, rapid and accelerating – and was normally regular throughout (L. Mozart, 1756), except, of course, with the more expressive accelerating (with crescendo) trill (when the terminating turn adopted the speed and dynamic reached at the peak of the acceleration), normally reserved for cadenza usage, and when articulation was required between the trill and its ensuing note. Many theorists required the main trill-note to be impressed well on the ear and thus prescribed that it should be dwelt upon immediately before the termination (L. Mozart, 1756), especially in the case of anticipatory terminations.

Mordents were normally played on the beat and comprised a rapid alternation of the main note with a lower auxiliary a tone or semitone below, the number of repercussions depending on musical context. However, some writers imply a pre-beat interpretation (L. Mozart, 1756), and L. Mozart extends the mordent category by adding two similar 'biting' ornaments, which on his own admission (3/1787), resemble respectively a disjunct double appoggiatura and a slide.

Turns were variously interpreted but were generally played either on the note (on the beat) or after the note indicated;

sometimes, however, an anticipation was rhythmically more appropriate. The turn-rhythm was generally regular but both accented and unaccented types also occurred in a variety of unequal rhythms according to musical context.

The appoggiatura, written as a small note, was played on the beat and slurred to the 'main' note it preceded (even if not so indicated), subtracting its value (not necessarily, but in most cases with Mozart, the one written) from that note. There were three main types – long (or variable), short and 'vocal'. The long variety provided an expressive accent (Türk, 1789) and usually (but not invariably) took half the value of the main note (a third or two-thirds as long when the main note was dotted). The short appoggiatura, played quickly, lightly and unaccented, was usually employed when the main note was itself a passing-note or had a staccato marking, and in almost all rising appoggiaturas. Opinion varied as to whether it should be played on or before the beat. The so-called 'vocal' appoggiatura was added by the performer, notably to stress strong syllables in the text of recitatives and arias (it was, however, also relevant to instrumental music) when a musical phrase concluded with two notes of the same pitch after, most commonly (but not exclusively), a downward leap of the interval of a third. The first of the two notes was invariably taken as a 'vocal' appoggiatura, thereby 'filling out' that interval.

Most groups of small notes were played before the beat, subtracting their value from the preceding note (see Milchmeyer, 1797), but Türk's opposition to this (2/1802), citing examples from Mozart's *oeuvre*, and Leopold Mozart's (1756) compromise on-beat, unaccented suggestion prove that no definitive rule should be formulated. Indeed, many such *gruppetti* resemble specific ornaments and may be best interpreted as their lookalikes.

Mozart indicated *arpeggiando* (generally an upward spreading of a chord from its bass note) by an oblique line drawn through the chord, but this sign is rarely reproduced nowadays. Türk advocates that such arpeggios should normally begin on the beat, but Milchmeyer recommends playing them as anticipations quickly or slowly according to context, a solution favoured by Neumann (1986).

Improvisation
Although some passages of Mozart's written texts were doubtless filled out in performance with accompaniments, arpeggiated chords or more elaborate embellishments (e.g. the slow movement of K.466, K.595 bars 218–53 or the finale of K.482, bars 164–72), these were fragmentary not by intent but on account of shortage of time. Improvisation in Mozart's music was otherwise confined (continuo realizations excepted) largely to solo contexts or passages of ensemble music in which a solo texture prevailed (L. Mozart, 1756), and was most common in concertos (cadenzas, fermatas and *Eingänge*) and arias (most notably at fermatas and in melodic variation of da capos pre-*c*. 1780) (see Neumann, 1986).

Although the trend was certainly to decorate a theme if it recurred unembellished by the composer, Mozart invariably wrote out his ornamentations fully himself (e.g. Rondo, K.511); inclusion of any further embellishment (e.g. the recapitulations of sonata-form movements) proved superfluous, not least on structural grounds (see Rosen, 1971). Although one of the principal objects of extempore embellishment was to demonstrate the performer's skill, it was also supposed to serve an expressive role and be kept within the bounds of moderation and discretion (see Hiller, 1780; Türk, 1789), as in Mozart's own embellished version of 'Ah se a morir me chiama' (*Lucio Silla*, K.293c). However, Mozart left little opportunity for melodic embellishment in his mature operas, his only concessions to such decoration being at cadential points, in the execution of 'vocal' appoggiaturas, or between sections of a rondo, where a short *Eingang*-like link passage was invariably required – e.g. 'Dove sono' (*Le nozze di Figaro*).

The interpretation of fermatas ranged from a straightforward prolongation of the note, chord or rest to improvised embellishment of that note or chord, an *Eingang* ('lead-in') or even an extended cadenza. Cadenzas, of variable length and indefinite form, were normally extemporized by the performer and were generally introduced towards the end of a composition or movement on a pause either on the dominant of the key or, in the case of concertos, on the tonic six-four chord. Ending with a trill on the dominant (seventh) chord, they served as vehicles for technical display – even the conservative Leopold Mozart (1756) admitted the use of special effects such as the trill in sixths and the accelerating trill in cadenzas – although musicianship and tasteful expression were prime considerations of most 18th-century theorists.

The cadenza also fulfilled an architectural function, its climactic passage for the soloist balancing the orchestral exposition in the concerto structure, as well as a dramatic one of allowing the soloist free rein for unfettered display. Contrary to tradition, Mozart wrote down many cadenzas and lead-ins. Most of his extant piano concerto cadenzas (after *c.* 1777), though varied in content, adopt a tripartite design (with the exception of some second and third movement examples) bound together, as it were, in one harmonic progression, the first (and largest) subdivision commencing either with a principal theme of the movement or with an energetic flourish (possibly with thematic affinities) emanating naturally from the six-four chord. A more reflective section, invariably sequential, of fluctuating tonality follows, based on material from the main body of the movement. A descent to a sustained chord or long note in the lower register eventually serves as a point of departure for further technical display, incorporating scalic runs, arpeggios and suchlike, prior to the brief, normally non-thematic closing transition to the final cadential trill.

Eingänge normally occurred on fermatas over an imperfect cadence on the dominant of the succeeding section. Although of varied length, they were generally non-thematic and were shorter than cadenzas, comprising chiefly scalic passages, leaps, ornaments, etc. (see Türk, 1789), by way of an appropriate link to the next part of the movement (commonly a rondo).

Continuo

Throughout most of the 18th century a continuo keyboard instrument – normally a harpsichord in concert, a harpsichord or fortepiano in opera and an organ in church – customarily provided harmonic support to the orchestra (see Koch, 1802). There is persuasive evidence to suggest, too, that the soloist was normally expected to play a continuo role in the *tuttis* of Mozart's piano concertos. Mozart's indication *col basso* (or his duplication of the bass) in the piano part in his manuscripts in non-solo passages, the provision of a figured bass for the piano during *tuttis* in all 18th-century editions of the concertos, a realization in Mozart's hand of a continuo part for K.238, and the incorporation of continuo figures, in Leopold Mozart's hand, in some of the manuscripts of the early, lightly scored concertos all add weight to this theory (see Badura-Skoda, 1957). And the Artaria edition (1785) of, for example, K.415 (387b), one of the few printed before Mozart's death, includes a figured bass (added by the publisher) for the *tuttis* which 'carefully distinguishes sections of mere doubling of the bass from full chordal accompaniment'. (Rosen, 1971) However, a more recent theory, advanced by Rosen amongst others, suggests that the piano soloist fulfilled a continuo role only in the absence of wind instruments.

Orchestral size and proportions

Orchestral size and instrumental proportions varied considerably according to local custom, availability of resources, musical genre and the performing venue, but the standard large late 18th-century orchestra comprised 2 flutes, 2 oboes, 2 clarinets, 2 bassoons, 2 or 4 horns, 2 trumpets, timpani and strings. The preferred number of each stringed instrument varied, Koch (1802) and Petri (2/1782) favouring a 'modern', fairly equal-voiced arrangement and Quantz (1752), Galeazzi (1791–6) and Petri (1767) preferring a string section with the violins predominant (see Stowell, 1988). Furthermore, Galeazzi's recommendation that, with in excess of 16 violins, it was necessary to double the winds is endorsed by an exceptional performance of one of Mozart's symphonies (probably K.297/300a) at the Vienna Tonkünstler-Societät (April, 1781) by an orchestra of 40 violins, 10 violas, 8 cellos, 10 double basses and doubled wind (with 6 bassoons).

The composition of orchestras in Mozart's sphere thus varied widely from season to season and occasion to occasion. Relevant data can easily confuse, as orchestras were invariably enlarged by the introduction of dilettantes, apprentices or town waits, who played when larger forces were required, or diminished through leave of absence, illness etc.; and some musicians were versatile enough to play more than one instrument. Zaslaw (1977) claims that no systematic pattern of growth in orchestra sizes can be detected 1774–96. But classification of orchestras according to the types of organizations which supported them reveals a clear statistical trend: 'private orchestras averaged 7 violinists, church orchestras 12, opera and theatre orchestras 14, while concert orchestras averaged 19'. This is supported by Koch's statement (1802) that 4–5 first violins, 4–5 seconds, 2–3 violas, 2–3 cellos and 2 double basses would suffice for church and theatre music, but that for symphonies (where there are more wind instruments) a string section of 6.6.4.4.3 represents the smallest number permitting satisfactory balance.

A flexible approach to instrumentation was both customary and inevitable. Some orchestral passages, for example, were performed by solo strings as appropriate, even if not so indicated, thus providing for variety of texture and timbre and, perhaps, more satisfactory balance. And Mahling (NMA) claims that, in addition to delineating the beginning or the end of a soloistic passage, the indications 'Tutti' and 'Solo' in some of Mozart's concertos relate to the composition of the ensemble, 'Solo' designating a reduction of the orchestra to the first desks of the strings (but only 1 cello and 1 double bass) and a simple one-player-per-part wind setting. Mozart himself remarked that his concertos K.413 (387a), 414 (385p) and 415 (387b) 'can be performed with full orchestra, or with [just] oboes and horns, or merely *a quattro*' and that K.449, too, may be performed '*a quattro*' (meaning most probably as a piano quintet, but possibly without the wind parts). Although not specifically indicated, it was tacitly understood that bassoons should augment the cellos and double basses on the bass line, and that timpani should be added whenever trumpets were present (notably in K.318, but not in cases, like K.184 (161u), where chromaticism renders their use less idiomatic).

Orchestral direction

Methods of orchestral direction in Mozart's time varied according to local custom, musical genre and the performing venue. C.P.E. Bach recommended (1753–62) that opera and instrumental music be controlled from the keyboard and that only for choral performances was time-beating necessary. Mozart himself is known to have directed some of his operas from the keyboard, but when the composer was not directly involved as a performer/director, the direction was shared, a keyboard player normally assuming particular responsibilities towards the singers and the concertmaster towards the orchestra. Shared direction was also the rule in performances of instrumental music, the concertmaster normally assuming the more important role, especially when, later in the century, the basso continuo became texturally less significant. The logistics of the venue (e.g. the position of the organ) invariably affected the direction of church performances. However, shared responsibility was again the rule, the concertmaster normally directing the orchestra in instrumental and solo vocal items and the overall director managing the choruses, either from the organ or, especially in large buildings, beating time visually with his hands, a roll of paper or parchment, or with a stick.

Orchestral placement

Although there were no standard concert orchestra placements, there were widely adopted general principles in Mozart's time, notably forward placement of the principal melodic instruments/voices (and invariably the weaker instruments such as the flutes), central location of the section principals and the bass/continuo group for easy observation and communication, and wide separation of the loudest and softest instruments. Other placements were dependent on visual or acoustical problems peculiar to the venue, but it was common practice to position first and second violins opposite each other; and, according to contemporary pictorial evidence, the violas were placed, at least for some of Mozart's symphonies, behind the woodwind, endorsing Meude-Monpas' view (1787) that the wind instruments were invariably positioned *en bloc*, while, in the interests of placing the bass instruments near the violins, the violas were accommodated wherever space allowed. Evidence also confirms that the most important features of the amphitheatrical arrangement, introduced to London by Haydn in 1791, were commonly employed abroad well before that date.

Orchestral placement in churches posed greater hazards, the position of the main organ (when required) and problems of distance invariably causing ensemble difficulties, even with someone beating time. A forward position of the singers was generally advised, with the principal violinist and bass players in close contact with the organist (Koch, 1802). Some theorists advocated an orchestral arrangement in tiered staging, invariably in amphitheatre fashion, on account of the tonal advantages and less strained performances that generally resulted (see Stowell, 1988).

Orchestral placements for opera aimed at optimum blend and ensemble, in particular good sightlines for everyone to the concertmaster and continuo group, these latter also requiring close contact with the singers on stage. Quantz (1752), like the Italians and English, recommends using two harpsichords, but by the last quarter of the century, most German orchestras included only one harpsichord, placed centrally between the strings on one side and the winds on the other (see Koch, 1802).

Pitch, tuning and temperament

A confusing variety of pitches coexisted internationally, nationally and even in the same locality in the 18th century (see Mendel, 1968 and 1978). Quantz (1752), like Praetorius before him, was one of the first 18th-century theorists to disapprove of such pitch discrepancies and to recommend the adoption of a uniform pitch standard. Although his stance encouraged a trend towards reasonable local uniformity in instrument pitches, there is no question of an extant mean pitch in Europe during the 18th century. But it is reasonable to presume, on the evidence of many contemporary woodwind instruments, theoretical sources and numerous English and German organs, that pitches approximately a semitone below $a' = 440$Hz were most common in Mozart's time.

A variety of tuning systems also coexisted during the period, many theorists recognizing that a good, unequal temperament could realize the particular qualities of different keys (see Steblin, 1983), while others (notably Marpurg, 1776) favoured the greater unity of character offered by equal temperament. Interestingly, most string players adopted a modifed type of mean-tone temperament, in which a sharpened note was considered a 'comma' (i.e. about 22 cents) lower in pitch than the flattened form of the note a tone higher. L. Mozart (1756) provides two scales, leading through the flats and sharps respectively, as an intonation exercise in distinguishing between the large diatonic 'semitones' and the small chromatic 'semitones'.

Orchestral tuning methods were somewhat haphazard during Mozart's time. Some theorists (e.g. Quantz, 1752) suggested that the concertmaster should tune his violin to the keyboard and then direct each instrumentalist to tune to him, whereas others recommended that a trumpet (or horn) or a group of wind instruments should first tune to an appropriate note from the keyboard and then play it for their colleagues to tune to.

Perhaps Mozart's most important requirement of his interpreters was a restrained, expressive and vocal style. Details regarding the specific technical problems (shifting, fingering, breathing etc.) related to this goal are beyond the scope of this article. But Mozart performers nowadays, while acknowledging the different playing characteristics and techniques of period instruments, should always be guided by Leopold Mozart's dictum (1756), echoed by Türk (1789): 'The human voice glides quite easily from one note to another; and a sensible singer will never make a break unless some special kind of expression, or the divisions or rests of the phrase demand one. And who is not aware that singing is at all times the aim of every instrumentalist; because one must always approximate to nature as nearly as possible.'

ROBIN STOWELL

Section 13

RECEPTION

RECEPTION

Contemporary assessments

I tell you before God, as an honest man, your son is the greatest composer known to me in person and by name: he has taste, but above this he has the greatest knowledge of composition. (letter from Leopold Mozart to his daughter Nannerl, 16 February 1785)

Haydn's famous declaration at a quartet party in February 1785 to Leopold Mozart is the link which closes the circle between Mozart's time and the present day. Our contemporary assessment which places Mozart and Haydn far ahead of their contemporaries is confirmed by their assessment of each other, and specifically – in this instance – by Haydn's testimony concerning Mozart. His response is unconditional – what is obviously true for us was true for him. There were many – and the rapid progress of Mozart's music in Prague is an example – who had equally few reservations. Perhaps of equally great interest, however, are the instances in which Mozart's music proved difficult to assimilate.

At the opposite pole to Haydn's enthusiasm were the criticisms levelled against the 'Haydn' string quartets K.421 (417b) and 465 by the composer Giuseppe Sarti, surviving only in paraphrase in 19th-century issues of the *Allgemeine musikalische Zeitung*, but said to have been known to Mozart. Sarti's criticisms are entirely unusual in their vehemence – positing rules of composition to which the quartets do not conform, and which derive from a Pythagorean theory of natural harmony (he gives as his source a 'mathematical-physicist' called Gottlob) that could have little relevance in an age when the compromise of equal temperament had opened up so many chromatic possibilities. Sarti argues not merely that Mozart has offended his aural sensibilities, but also – implausibly – that he was theoretically ignorant. Perhaps, however, the most significant thing about these views is the apparent isolation of them. Sarti's position is undoubtedly anachronistic, and he is the only critic who comes near to assaulting Mozart on the grounds of outrageous modernism.

Much more typical are the views of Ernst Ludwig Gerber in his *Historisch-Biographisches Lexicon der Tonkünstler* (1790):

This great master had from his early acquaintance with harmony become so deeply and inwardly intimate with it, that it is hard for an unskilled ear to follow his works. Even the skilled must hear his things several times.

There are certain threads – not always mutually consistent – running through the criticism. The complexity of the works can be admired and deplored simultaneously. The difficulty of performing a work, or the difficulty in comprehending it – or indeed the difficulty that the popular audience as opposed to the critic might have – may be regarded as deficiencies.

Dittersdorf, in his autobiography (1799), recalled making such a point in an interview (*c.* 1786) with Joseph II:

> He is indisputably a great original genius, and I have never yet found anyone who possessed such an astonishing wealth of ideas. I wish he were not so lavish with them. He leaves his hearer out of breath: for scarcely has one thought through one idea, than stands there already in its place another, which drives out the first, and this goes on continuously without cease, so that in the end none of these real beauties can be preserved in the memory.

Later on in the conversation Mozart and Haydn are likened respectively to the poets Klopstock and Gellert:

> one must read Klopstock's poetry more than once to reveal all its beauties – Gellert's beauties already lie wholly unveiled at a single glance.

The problem of following Mozart's works, then, is not only said to be greater than the generality, but also than Haydn's which are of comparable sophistication. Given the closeness of Gerber's and Dittersdorf's opinions it might be hard to know how much is ready-made opinion and how much experience – certainly Gerber also agrees with Dittersdorf about the accessibility of Haydn's music. Perhaps the best insight into the difficulty lies in the problems attendant upon performance of Mozart's music.

These are raised by Adolph von Knigge in his *Dramaturgische Blätter* (Hanover, 1788) in coming to terms with *Die Entführung aus dem Serail*, where he writes in much the same vein as Gerber and Dittersdorf: 'One beautiful thought', he remarks, 'drives out another, and removes it from the admiration of the hearer.' Knigge's bewilderment had led him to discuss the work's difficulties with the Hanover company's musical director Bernard Anselm Weber (not related to Mozart's in-laws). Almost all the score's most distinctive features are exposed and questioned. The wind instruments are too 'talkative', 'obscuring' the melody and 'tangling' the harmony:

> The knowledgeable feel the worth of these passages, but for popular utterance they are of no use. The same occurs with the pile of modulations and numerous enharmonic movements, which, beautiful though they sound on the keyboard, make no effect in the orchestra, partly because they are never delivered with sufficient purity, whether by the singer or by the players, partly because the resolutions alternate too fast with the discords, so that only a skilled ear can pursue the harmonic process.

But Knigge, having expressed his disquiet, can only retrace his steps. 'Yet O!' he writes, 'all composers should be in a position to commit such faults!'

The argument that exact performance and repeated hearings might be necessary for comprehension is given a further dimension by Goethe's first experience of hearing *Die Entführung*. He writes to the composer Philipp Christoph Kayser, with whom he collaborated on several operatic projects:

> Recently die Entführung aus dem Serail, composed by Mozart was given. Everyone professed themselves for the music. The first time they played it quite moderately, the text itself is very bad and I also was not at one with the music. The second time it was very badly played and I even left. Yet the piece maintained itself and everyone praised the music. When they gave it for the fifth time, I went to it again. They acted and sang better than before, I separated out the text and understand now the difference between my judgment and the impression on the public and know where I am.

Certainly Mozart's music was becoming sufficiently fashionable – at least in some quarters – by the late eighties for the enthusiasm to be regarded with a degree of suspicion. A Viennese correspondent of the *Journal des Luxus und der Moden* (Weimar, June 1788) – guilty of a degree of posturing himself – describes how the previous winter he had been entertained at numerous parties at which a piano quartet of Mozart's – presumably the more recently published E♭ K.493 – was indifferently performed. He writes of his irritation at what he felt to be the insincere pleasure that the company had taken in a work which seemed to him noisy and tedious. Finally, however, the greatness of the work is revealed to him at an intimate gathering:

> What a difference, when this much talked about art-work is performed with the greatest precision by four capable musicians who have studied it well, in a quiet room, in which as well the suspension of every note does not escape the listening ear, in the presence of only two or three attentive people.

It is perhaps an inevitable part of the powerful impression of Mozart's music that by the end of his life some of the rhetoric was becoming questionable. It is understandable how the tone of one correspondent in the *Chronik von Berlin* (2 October 1790) might arouse indignation:

> Mozart belongs among those extraordinary men, whose glory will endure for centuries. His great genius embraces as it were the entire compass of musical art; it is rich in ideas; his works are a torrent, in full flood, which carries forth all in its wake. None before has surpassed him, and deep reverence and admiration will posterity not deny him. One must be still more than connoisseur to be able to form an opinion of him. What a masterpiece, this music of today! For the connoisseur how interesting? how great, how overwhelming, how enchanting the harmony! For the great masses too? That is another question.

Description breaks down – does the torrent carry all before, or only people of the most refined taste? A few months later another correspondent of the same paper poured scorn on such talk, if anything expressing himself even more picturesquely:

Nor was there any lack, variously from Mozart's warm friends, of declaring that, 'Since Mozart wrote his *Don Juan*, *Hippocrene* and *Aganippe* are so dried up, that for all composers yet to come not a single drop more of inspiration is to be scooped from Helicon'. If one chatters away superficially thus, whether one is a connoisseur, an intelligent fellow or a numskull is easily decided, and there then the numskull stands.

Quite evidently we have entered the realms of journalistic hyperbole and invective, and while little intelligent is going to be said, the existence of such material suggests the extent to which Mozart had become celebrated within the German-speaking world by the last years of his life. Years later Goethe, in *Die italienische Reise* (1816), recalled that period and his contemporaneous collaboration with Kayser on the opera *Scherz, List und Rache*, in which they had cultivated a musical style of deliberate economy:

> All our pains therefore to confine ourselves to the plain and narrow, went for nothing, as Mozart stepped forth. Die Entführung aus dem Serail knocked everything down, and in the theatre our own so carefully manufactured piece is never mentioned.

Posthumous assessments

Dear Beethoven,

You journey now to Vienna to fulfil your long contested wishes. Mozart's genius mourns still and weeps over the death of its pupil. With the inexhaustible Hayden he found refuge, but no exercise; through him he wishes once more to become allied with someone. Through unceasing diligence receive it: *Mozart's spirit from Hayden's hands*.

The imagery of Count Waldstein's famous inscription in Beethoven's album of 29 October 1792, if somewhat confused, nevertheless testifies to Mozart's reputation in Germany in the period immediately following his death. He had become proverbial. Allusions to Apollo and Orpheus had sufficed for the inscriptions in Mozart's album; now Mozart's spirit stood in their place in the young Beethoven's. The beginnings of a modern canon are in view, within which Mozart was always to occupy a key position, and his contribution was to be frequently defined in relation to the great successor first wished on him by Waldstein.

How did Beethoven view this apostolic succession? It is known that he had temperamental reservations about certain works (the Italian operatic comedies, as he told the poet Rellstab) and that he had particular favourites. Carl Czerny recalled an almost impenetrably enigmatic remark of Beethoven's:

> Once with me Beethoven saw the score of the six Mozart quartets. He rapped the 5th in A and said: That is a work! There Mozart said to the world: see what I could do, if the time had come for you!

Much here depends, of course, on accurate reporting and even then the meaning is elusive. It is possible that Beethoven was arguing that Mozart had a compositional potential that could only be partially, or intermittently, fulfilled within the confines of the age in which he lived, or simply that he (Beethoven) found himself more profoundly convinced by some of Mozart's compositions than others. And perhaps he saw himself – or at least Czerny did – as the fulfilment of Mozart's promise.

The need in retrospect to see Mozart's and Beethoven's music as atemporally interdependent is found in an article by Schumann written in 1833:

> Clarity, repose, grace, the distinguishing mark of the artworks of antiquity, are also those of the Mozartian school. . . . Should this brilliant manner of thinking and composing perhaps one day be supplanted by a formless mystic one, as it will in time, which even casts its shadow upon art, so may that other ancient art not become forgotten, in which Mozart reigned, and that above all Beethoven shook at the joints till it quaked, not perhaps without the agreement of his princely predecessor Wolfgang Amadeus.

This all-inclusive characterization of style was of course fraught with danger. Schumann was famously drawn into denying an impassioned aspect to the G minor Symphony, K.550, preferring to describe it as of 'hovering Grecian grace', as if Mozart's music could possess no other quality (although *pace* some interpreters a certain grace and buoyancy may be a requirement of performance).

Fifteen years later, in his essay *The Artwork of the Future*, Wagner developed a superficially similar thesis:

> From Haydn and Mozart it was possible and necessary for a Beethoven to arrive: the genius of music urgently demanded it, and without delay he was there . . .

Within Wagner's historical scheme – which ultimately requires the unification of all the arts in music drama – Haydn evolved the symphony from the dance, Mozart invested it with 'rich and joyous songfulness', and Beethoven developed instrumental ('absolute') music bequeathed him by Haydn and Mozart to such a level of intensity that it could only erupt into the fully-fledged poetic expression of the finale of the Ninth Symphony. From this point the way forward could – as he saw it in 1849 – only be through music drama, and further exploration of the instrumental genres was rendered redundant. The operas of Gluck and Mozart are regarded as historically aberrant pointers to this glorious future.

It is perhaps specifically against the background of the constructions of Schumann and Wagner that Mahler could utter the commonplace observation to Natalie Bauer-Lechner: 'Only when we understand the difference there is between Mozart's G minor Symphony and the Ninth can we properly evaluate Beethoven's achievement'. But of course it was not with the compact forms of Mozart's symphonic writing that Mahler should have made his comparison, so much as with the structurally resourceful finales of the operas.

At his most acute the painter Delacroix might have recognized the inadequacy of such views. He writes in his Journal on 19 February 1847, ten days after attending a performance of *Don Giovanni*:

> Saw two acts of the *Huguenots*: where is Mozart? Where is the grace, the expression, the unifying energy, the inspiration and the knowledge, the comedy and the terror?

This is not entirely typical of Delacroix, who is inclined to sentimentalize Mozart by characterizing him as a representative of a 'well-ordered age'. There is here a special ambivalence: the aspect of symmetry which Delacroix attributes to Mozart's music can give rise to a sense of impatience which he cannot entirely justify, and he sometimes finds it to be less exciting than the music of Beethoven or Weber, the forms of which he regards as less hackneyed or predictable, but which he also thinks to be less perfect or complete. At the same time, Mozart's famous remark, made at the time of *Die Entführung*, that 'the passions, violent or not, must never be pressed to the extent of exciting disgust', is more than once invoked. In one instance it is quoted at a time of great political upheaval (1849), against the barbarities of Meyerbeer, Berlioz, Hugo and the contemporary world, as if Mozart would have understood his age to possess the orderliness of his music, and as if the subject matter of *Figaro* and *Don Giovanni* reflected any such complacency. On another occasion he uses it to attribute to Mozart the belief (not justified from the actual passage) that 'music is able to express all passions, all sorrow, all suffering' without paining the ear. Evidently the intention is to extrapolate a basic principle for all the arts using Mozart as authority.

Rather characteristically for the 19th century, Delacroix's knowledge of Mozart's music, beyond two or three operas which he knows extremely well, is somewhat inexact, and he is inclined to rank Cimarosa's *Il matrimonio segreto* – today somewhat relegated – as their peer, or even prefer it. In this he is not alone – Goethe despite all his grand pronouncements concerning Mozart's operas prefers the Cimarosa, and Nissen's biography of Mozart also mentions the widespread estimation of *Il matrimonio segreto* alongside Mozart's comedies. Berlioz too, in his Memoirs, links the two composers in a self-parodic dismissal which suggests that any pleasure he ever took in Mozart's operas lay in something other than proportion or decorousness of expression, referring to:

> Mozart, whose operas are all alike in their chill beauty, so trying to the patience! . . . As for Cimarosa, to the devil with his eternal and unique Secret Marriage which is even more tedious than the Marriage of Figaro, without being anywhere near as musical . . .

At the end of the 19th century we find an opinion which is far removed from all the preceding in its detached musical and historical judgment. Brahms can take cognizance of the shift in expressive climate between Mozart and Beethoven but this has no bearing in his view on actual musical worth:

I understand very well that the new personality of Beethoven, the new outlook, that people accorded his work, let it appear to them greater, more important. But surely fifty years afterwards one must be able to rectify this judgment. I grant you that the Beethoven concerto [he is comparing the C minor Piano Concerto with that of Mozart] is more modern, but not as important! I see as well that Beethoven's first symphony made such a colossal impression on people. That is just the new outlook! But the three last Mozart symphonies are still much more important! People, here and there, already today sense this!

If for his contemporaries Mozart's music above all presented a problem of assimilation, their acknowledgment of the fact – even if somewhat stereotyped – at least suggested a concern with substance. In the 19th century, on the other hand, and even latterly, when comprehension seems to be assumed by all, the response to Mozart's achievement is at times very superficial. Something like Delacroix's formulation 'unifying energy' (l'énergie réunie) is rare, and inevitably, as his juxtaposition of 'comedy' and 'terror' makes clear, it was *Don Giovanni* – which of all Mozart's works held a special place in the 19th-century imagination – that he had in mind. Perhaps in the contemporary world the kind of historical placement and significance given to Mozart in the 19th century has some small hold. Notions of '18th-century elegance', of 'decorousness' or of 'perfection' have a certain currency, and while continuing to contain their grain of truth also possess an almost infinite capacity for vulgarization (see 'Myths and legends', below). Indeed, the bland nature of these characterizations is inevitably much less reflective of people's experience of the music than, say, the popular images of Beethoven's heroism, or Berlioz's Romantic sensibility.

Perhaps more significant is simply the factor of availability. Much more of the music is generally known than in the 19th or early 20th century. Hundreds of works which previously seemed marginal are continually being performed and recorded – and heard by many millions of people across six continents. The phenomenon is not, of course, a specifically Mozartian one but a symptom of the growth of the music industry, and of a communications explosion. Against this sea of individual response across so many cultural frontiers, to attempt to discern particular tendencies in the appreciation of Mozart's oeuvre is today inevitably to approach the impossible.

Myths and legends

THERE ARE ALWAYS TWO ASPECTS to myths: the basic narrative ingredients, and the meanings and significances that different people read into them. In the case of Mozart a list of popular ingredients is easy to assemble: the infant prodigy, the prodigal adult, the early death in macabre circumstances – including the mysterious commission of a Requiem Mass and the belief that he had been poisoned (prototypically by a jealous musical rival, Salieri, although the list of candidates has been much added to by a band of conspiracy theorists, whose paranoid ramblings constitute a flourishing industry).

The infant prodigy

There can be no doubt about the brilliance of Mozart's early career and it is probable that outside the German world it took a considerable time after his death for his adult achievement to begin to eclipse the image of the precocious infant. Indeed it is probably still a popular misconception that many of the great works date from early youth – but while it is true that there are flashes of inspiration in many of the early works, probably the first which has a firm footing in the modern repertoire is the 'little' G minor Symphony, K.183 (173dB), written when he was seventeen. Nevertheless, the shade of 'the prodigy of Salzburg' has come to haunt two centuries of musically talented children and the lids of chocolate boxes.

The prodigal adult

The myth in its most extreme form – the contemporaneously popular myth created by Peter Shaffer in his play *Amadeus* and the film of the play – is that of an entirely trivial man who in the words of Bernard Levin testifies to 'the terrible truth' that 'any channel, even an unworthy one, will serve as an aqueduct through which the pure water of art can flow from Heaven to earth, and not be tainted by the corrupt vessel that serves it'. A nearer truth would be that Mozart's art is a distillation of experience (of previous works of art, of the world) by a great and sensitive intelligence – an intelligence, moreover, which Mozart had as much right to claim his own as Mr Levin presumably does his. Once this has been recognized it may be allowed that Mozart did not always behave seriously or respectfully (though he often did), that he enjoyed indulging in coarse, scatological humour (which corresponded to a social norm even indulged in by his severe father), and that his finances were seldom under control (although on the mend at the time of his death).

Perhaps the greatest single piece of damage done to Mozart's personal reputation by one of his contemporaries is to be located in the icy pronouncement of the aristocratic novelist Karoline Pichler:

> Mozart and Haydn, whom I knew well, were men who displayed in their personal intercourse no other outstanding mental ability and almost no sort of intellectual cultivation of a learned or higher direction. Everyday characters, flat humour, and with the first a scantly sensible life-style, was all that they publicly manifested, and what depths, what worlds of fantasy, harmony, melody and feeling yet lay concealed within these unbrilliant exteriors! Through what inner revelation came to them this understanding, how must they have seized it, to bring forth such powerful effects, and express in tones, feelings, thoughts, passions, that every hearer must feel with them, and be spoken to as well from the greatest depth?

There is an aspect of classical *topos* in this idea of the foolish exterior which conceals divine attributes. Perhaps even Alcibiades' eulogy of Socrates in the *Symposium* is recalled, and at least she allows that Haydn and Mozart might have 'seized' inspiration rather than being innocent victims of it. Nevertheless, there is an unpleasant element of social disdain involved. There is no more paradox in Haydn's and Mozart's achievement than in the fact that Karoline Pichler's evident gentility has failed to save the ninety volumes of her collected works from almost complete posthumous obscurity.

It is such details as a description by her of Mozart jumping over tables and chairs and miaowing like a cat that are fastened on by Wolfgang Hildesheimer in his popular biography of the composer. Hildesheimer finds such things more credible than accounts of Mozart behaving with decorum and dignity, but even his favourite description of Mozart – that by Joseph Lange – tells a slightly different story from the one he claims:

> Never was Mozart less to be apprehended in his speech and action as a great man than when he was busy with an important work. Then he spoke not only with haphazard confusion, but sometimes made jokes of a kind which with him one was not used to; indeed he even deliberately neglected his behaviour . . .

It is implicit in this passage – despite Hildesheimer – that the aspect of crazed eccentricity which may have overcome Mozart at times of hardest concentration did not constitute a single standard of behaviour for his entire existence.

Following tradition, both Shaffer and Hildesheimer, in the process of patronizing Mozart, also insist on the low character of his wife Constanze. Constanze came from a poor but well-educated musical and theatrical family. She spoke fluent French and Italian and was a sufficiently able singer to take solo parts at public performances. After Mozart's death she also proved a resourceful provider for her family.

The legend of the poisoning

As Mozart's health declined in the latter part of 1791, he became prey to paranoid fantasies – that he had been poisoned by acqua toffana (a slow poison of Italian invention), and that the same enemy who had poisoned him had also been the author of the mysterious commission of the Requiem on which he continued to work (the commission in fact was from a nobleman of refined narcissism, Count Walsegg, who wished to pay tribute to his recently deceased wife and at the same time pass the composition off as his own). Evidently Mozart was also the originator of the accusation that Salieri was the poisoner, as Mary Novello notes from an interview with Mozart's younger surviving son in 1829: 'The son denies he [Salieri] poisoned him [Mozart] although his father [Mozart] thought so . . .'.

It is possible to hazard a guess as to how this came about. Mozart had believed – probably with some justification – that Salieri had been intriguing against him since the former's arrival in Vienna. The subject was raised in letters to his father (31 August 1782, 7 May 1783 and 2 July 1783) and to Michael Puchberg (end of December 1789), as well as from Leopold Mozart to his daughter (28 April 1786). But in his very last surviving letter of 14 October 1791, written to his wife, who was taking the waters at Vienna's nearby spa town Baden, he was surprised by Salieri's effusive reception of him the previous evening. He had collected Salieri and the singer Catarina Cavalieri (Salieri's protégée) in his carriage and taken them to his box for a performance of *Die Zauberflöte*:

> You cannot believe how kind they both were, – how very pleased they were not only with my music, but the libretto and everything else. – They both said it was an *operone*. – Worthy to be performed at the greatest festivity and before the greatest monarchs, – and they would certainly often go to see it, for they had never seen as beautiful or agreeable a spectacle. – He listened and watched with total attention, and from the overture to the last chorus, there was not a single piece which did not elicit from him a bravo or a bello, and they could scarcely leave off from thanking me for this kindness . . .

What had occasioned this comic *rapprochement* between Mozart and Salieri remains obscure, but it would not be surprising, given Mozart's declining state, if such fulsomeness began to play upon his imagination. The melodrama of Mozart's death was thus perhaps a mixture of unfortunate coincidence and his own creation, though one which ultimately tends more to the commonplace than the sublime.

The Mozartian topic in literature

CLOSELY RELATED to both the critical assessment of Mozart and the stock of myths surrounding him, is a body of material – concerning Mozart's life and death and the special status accorded to *Don Giovanni* in the 19th century – which justifies particular examination on the grounds of continued literary interest. These texts, in the way they manipulate certain traditions, have much in common.

E.T.A. Hoffmann
The first influential text to reflect these involvements is a short story by E.T.A. Hoffmann. Hoffmann's imagination had been so taken over by Mozart's music that in his attempt to identify with the great composer he changed his third name from Wilhelm to Amadeus. But Hoffmann's studied eccentric brilliance as a writer was never reflected in his musical career, his musical compositions being marked more by a dull competence. Only through his prose and various fictional *alter egos* – the most famous of which was Kapellmeister Johannes Kreisler – was he able to imagine himself into musical greatness. Questions of identity and identification figure conspicuously in his tale *Don Juan* (1814). The tale is a clear ancestor of the psychoanalytic school of operatic interpretation.

The narrator, a composer, visiting a strange town, finds himself in a private box attending a performance of *Don Giovanni*. Sitting there alone during the performances he meets, as if in a hallucination, the singer of the part of Donna Anna, whose passionate identification with the role causes disquiet among the audience. Calling upon the narrator's sympathy – for she has recognized him – she tells him: 'I have sung you, and am your melodies'. The narrator, inspired by the performance and this apparition, is suddenly able to reveal the true significance of the opera – the text of which he regards as superficially trivial. Don Juan was by birth a figure of superior nature who used his endowments to seek the divine through female love. No woman that he found satisfied his yearning, but he became at length, through carnal satiety and disillusion, a fallen spirit. Donna Anna, another figure of superior nature, would have been the woman in whom he found salvation, but she came upon the scene too late – Giovanni is beyond redemption and she herself becomes damned through her desire for him. She prevaricates with what are regarded as the unworthy solicitations of Don Ottavio (described as 'cold, unmanly and ordinary' – thus starting a malign and discreditable tradition of his representation), knowing full well that she will be dead long before a year's mourning has elapsed. The narrator learns, the morning after the performance, of the death of the singer of the part of Donna Anna during the night.

Pushkin

Pushkin's two 'little tragedies' *Mozart and Salieri* and *The Stone Guest* were worked on concurrently during the period 1826–30, and have strong thematic links. But while Pushkin draws inspiration from Mozart and his works, the plays are certainly not in essence an attempt to interpret them.

In *Mozart and Salieri* we see the confrontation between the spontaneity of the life and the creativity of Mozart, and the dry industry of Salieri who jealously poisons him. Mozart, open-hearted and guileless, fails to perceive the difference which troubles Salieri. Dismissing a legend that Beaumarchais had once poisoned somebody, he remarks to Salieri:

> He was a genius,
> Like you and me. And villainy and genius
> Are incompatibles. Am I not right?

and it is this thought – referring to a legend that Michelangelo had stabbed a model to recreate Christ's death agony – that plagues Salieri at the end:

> Could it be he's right
> And I no genius? Villainy and Genius
> Are incompatibles. It cannot be.
> And Buonarroti? Was he calumniated
> By foolish rumour? Did the man who built
> The Vatican in fact commit no murder?

In *The Stone Guest* Don Juan is seen not as a cold-blooded seducer and murderer but as a figure comparable to Pushkin's fictionalized Mozart. A poet of recklessly passionate, insouciant character, he cannot see how greatly he is at odds with the rest of the world. His lyrical nature is explained when one of the characters responds to some of his verses sung by the actress Laura:

> Of all life's pleasures,
> Music yields pride of place to love alone,
> And even love's – a melody

(Translations by Avril Pyman, from *Alexander Pushkin: Selected Works*, Moscow, 1974)

The play most closely parallels the course of *Don Giovanni* in its graveyard scene (its text is in fact prefaced with Leporello's address to the statue from Da Ponte's libretto), but the parallel is introduced to make an important contrast. Don Juan is shocked to the core that the statue should respond, and when in the last scene it comes for him, his end is an abrupt and brutal act – he falls the simple victim of uncomprehending dislike, and petty vengeance.

Kierkegaard

In Kierkegaard's *Either/or* (1843) – a philosophical discussion within a fictionalized format between the characters A and B arguing between, respectively, aesthetic and moral modes of existence – we meet a clear attempt to interpret Mozart and his work. The essay 'The Immediate Stages of the Erotic' forms the first part of A's disquisition. Near the outset we are confronted with the following proposition: 'if ever Mozart became wholly comprehensible to me, he would then become fully incomprehensible to me'. The point of this paradox is that the experience of music is in essence of fleeting sensuousness, and if it were possible to imagine it fixed and containable it would lose its meaning. The aesthetic notion of this uncontainability is perhaps the most interesting aspect of the essay, but at least as formulated it implies the not very satisfactory corollary that the musically expert understands less than the beginner: the seduced knows more than the seducer and indeed, in relation to Mozart, Kierkegaard regards himself as a 'young girl', no doubt the 'giovin principiante' of the catalogue aria in *Don Giovanni*.

Kierkegaard presents the argument that the medium of music through its essential character finds its ultimate subject matter in the story of Don Juan. Into the character of Don Juan he reads 'sensuous genius' – desire and its fulfilment without reflection – a quality he regards as being historically defined by the Christian era's exclusion of physical pleasure from its notion of the spiritual. The developed art of music is, Kierkegaard argues, another product of the same process of exclusion and definition. Mozart in bringing the two together thus creates a classic work – indeed *the* classic work – beside which even his own *Le nozze di Figaro* and *Die Zauberflöte* are to be regarded as ill-focused and unsatisfactory.

Kierkegaard's reading of the opera fails in several ways. While favouring certain images of Don Juan which do not derive from the text of the opera, he deplores in the Molière character the petty acts of violence and deception which are also the stock-in-trade of the Mozartian one, but which he somehow manages to ignore. Nor ultimately does he explain how it is possible for the Commendatore – who within his system stands in opposition to Don Giovanni as pure spirit – to find proper musical expression.

Mörike

The novella *Mozart auf der Reise nach Prag* (*Mozart's Journey to Prague*, 1855) pictures Mozart on the way to the premiere of *Don Giovanni*. Ostensibly drawn from a hidden source and strongly based upon mid-19th-century traditions about Mozart's life, the tale possesses an elegiac tone. Mozart and his wife's journey to Prague in mid-September 1787 (just over a fortnight before their historical journey) is broken when they are generously entertained by an aristocratic family from whose garden Mozart has absent-mindedly stolen an orange. Mozart tells the small party of how when conceiving the final scene of *Don Giovanni* he had been suddenly struck by the horror that he might not live to complete it. The most sensitive of the company, Eugenie, is seized with a premonition 'that this man would quickly and irresistibly be consumed in his own ardour', thus linking his short existence with that of his most celebrated character.

Shaw

Bernard Shaw wrote two fictional texts on the Don Juan theme, the short story *Don Giovanni Explains* (1887) and the play *Man and Superman* (1903). In the first a young woman is met on a train by the shade of Don Giovanni after a performance of the opera. In the second, a modern comedy, there is a lengthy dream sequence in which the characters are transmogrified into legendary prototypes. Both are conceived as attacks on social institutions and marriage in particular – hell is the place where social illusion and hypocrisy are endlessly perpetuated. The fact of sexual attraction, Shaw argues, does not make marriage natural, and *Man and Superman* culminates in a parody of the final scene of *Don Giovanni* in which the hero Jack Tanner is browbeaten into marriage by Ann Whitefield as she screams 'yes' and he screams 'no'.

Neither of these texts is primarily intended as commentary on Mozart or his opera, but in so far as they both use fantastic means to provide a secret history of the events in the opera, it is difficult to expunge a sense that this is a secondary purpose. That Shaw ultimately sees Mozart as an unconscious forerunner of his own brand of moral realism is implicit in the Devil's remark in *Man and Superman* that Mozart had been a former occupant of hell who 'moped and went to heaven'.

'FROM BRAHMS [I learned] . . . much of what I had unconsciously absorbed from Mozart' (Schoenberg, 1975). The notion of influence is a problematic one. Nevertheless, in his article 'National Music (2)' (1932, posthumously published), Schoenberg, writing at the other end of the Austro-German musical history and listing the composers from whom he has learnt (primarily Bach and Mozart, secondarily Beethoven, Wagner and Brahms), has some crisp answers:

> From *Mozart:*
> 1. Inequality of phrase-length.
> 2. Co-ordination of heterogeneous characters to form a thematic unity.
> 3. Deviation from even-number construction in the theme and its component parts.
> 4. The art of forming subsidiary ideas.
> 5. The art of introduction and transition.   (Schoenberg, 1975)

Interestingly, Schoenberg in making his selection goes straight to the heart of those aspects of Mozart's music – the multiplicity of ideas and the dexterity of their deployment and transformation – which had left Mozart's contemporaries in a state of slightly confused admiration (see 'Contemporary assessments', above). He also indicates how potent Mozart's example was even beyond those composers (Haydn and Beethoven) who, like him, exploited the formal possibilities of the Classical sonata.

Such is the primacy of the experience of Mozart's music to Schoenberg that its entry into his compositional process is more subliminal ('unconscious') than that of Brahms – although with reflection it is not difficult for him to pinpoint the relation. As Schoenberg acknowledged in his famous essay 'Brahms the Progressive', for Brahms – at the beginning of his career (when much of the music was less widely known) – the example of Mozart was not so pervasive and indeed Brahms had to go to special lengths to revive interest in the instrumental music (see Fellinger, 1983), particularly the piano concertos. Thus Brahms's position in regard to Mozart is rather similar to Schoenberg's in regard to Brahms: there is present an active need to assimilate the example. He returns to Mozart in response to compositional demands which he has formulated for himself.

Brahms's music virtually never recalls the sonority or thematic cast of Mozart's music – as it does that of Beethoven, Schubert or Schumann – nor does it possess its overlying structural symmetries. To this extent the influence is entirely unsuperficial – in contradistinction to the music, say, of Hummel, which Schumann a generation earlier could recognize as being 'school of Mozart' – and even Beethoven could come in for criticism by Brahms for only superficially realizing the compositional significance of Mozart's C minor Piano Concerto in his own C minor Piano Concerto, which had invited an obvious comparison (see 'Posthumous assessments', above). Schoenberg's argument, on the other hand, links Mozart with the compositional pursuits of the late 19th and early 20th century, and not only with Brahms and himself – he also cites examples of the emancipation of phrase structure and motivic invention in the works of Bruckner, Strauss, Mahler and Reger. Indeed the last three – all of Schoenberg's generation and personally known to him – chose to recognize Mozart as a particular progenitor.

Wagner Schoenberg places somewhat out of the Mozartian line of development, commenting (not altogether accurately), in relation to ensembles from *Figaro*, on the comparatively symmetrical movement ('two by two measure construction') generally present in Wagner's scores. Wagner himself is normally reticent about any direct link between Mozart's music and his own – his official conception of musical history is too linear (see 'Posthumous assessments', above). Nevertheless, on 30 May 1870 we find him proclaiming in regard to *Die Zauberflöte*:

> Mozart is the founder of German declamation – what fine humanity resounds in the Priest's replies to Tamino! Think how stiff such high priests are in Gluck. (Cosima Wagner, *Diaries*)

No formal analysis is provided, but the singling out of this scene from the first act finale is interesting. This is declamatory writing which Wagner himself barely equalled before *Das Rheingold*. Here we have realized 'the possibility of regarding themes and motives as if they were complex ornaments, so that they can be used against harmonies in a dissonant way.' This formulation in fact again comes from Schoenberg, in his itemization of things he learnt from Wagner. Admittedly Mozart was not the first person to evolve such a technique, but he almost certainly evolved it independently of 17th-century examples (notably Monteverdi), and it was this example with which Wagner was familiar. The possibility that Wagner sees is the dissolution of 18th-century musical forms. This particular discussion of Mozart, as reported by Cosima Wagner, ends with the reflection: 'He did not complete his work, which is why one cannot really compare him to Raphael, for there is still too much convention in him.' That Mozart might have wished to explore such a technique further had he lived is extremely plausible (see 'Mozart's Opinions and Outlook: Opera', pp. 154–7). Wagner's apparent recognition of this creates a link not only between Mozart and himself, but also, as a consequence, between Mozart and a great deal of operatic practice of the post-Wagnerian era.

This single example is not the only way in which Mozart in his operas anticipates the expansion of musical structures by later composers. Schoenberg tends to ignore this (in 'Brahms the Progressive' he discusses the tonal inconsequentiality of traditional passages of recitative, and arioso, to which might be added spoken dialogue); nevertheless, it would be hard to ignore the unprecedented levels of long-term tonal and motivic planning which are a feature of the operas, and which become more marked as Mozart's career developed, culminating in *Così fan tutte* and *Die Zauberflöte*. In the first act of *Così fan tutte* we find a proto-serial piece of organization: there are, not including the overture, sixteen substantial musical numbers, with eight major keys utilized twice and no key recurring until each has been used once. There are various small anomalies within this pattern, but the overall purpose would seem to be the prevention of any key coming to supplant the C major tonic of the overture, while avoiding any restriction to C major. At the beginning of Act II Mozart introduces an elaborate triadic system for suppressing the tonic until the ninth number (since it is to dominate at the end):

E♭ triad	19.	G	(Una donna a quindici anni)
	20.	B♮	(Prenderò quel brunettino)
	21.	E♭	(Secondate, aurette amiche)
B♭ triad	22.	D	(La mano a me date)
	23.	F	(Il core vi dono)
	24.	B♮	(Ah lo veggio)
C triad	25.	E	(Per pietà)
	26.	G	(Donne mie, le fate a tanti)
	27.	C minor/major	(Tradito, schernito)

Before the C major of the motto and the finale (nos 30 and 31) there are only two intervening numbers. The A major duet (no.29) 'Fra gli amplessi' has a symmetrical relation with 'Ah guarda, sorella' (no.4), also in A major, and also lying on the inside of a C major structure (that of the overture and opening scene: C–G–E–C). Perhaps only the key of 'È amore un ladroncello' (no.28 in B♭) is not dictated by the grand tonal scheme.

Così fan tutte is also full of motivic cross-references which link the different parts of its span, but the irony is that while this in the Schoenbergian sense – at least in terms of large-scale tonal planning – is the most progressive of Mozart's operatic scores, it remained very little regarded for nearly a century after its composition. Wagner's irritation at the subject matter prevented him from seeing any merit in the music, and the score remained to be re-evaluated by Mahler and Strauss.

The example which might have been suggestive apparently fell on deaf ears. Perhaps the lessons were to be learned from other Mozart scores. *Die Zauberflöte* and *Don Giovanni* – the motivic weave of the one, the tonal gravity of the other – were more congenial. But even here the relation is not always direct, or directly considered. Mahler, in writing the huge spans of his symphonies, if he thought of historical precedent, tended to think of earlier symphonies rather than those Mozart operas which he had spent a life time polishing in performance.

Analogous compositional processes form themselves in response to analogous requirements. What is certain is that for generations of composers the sense of both process and requirement was formed with knowledge and experience of Mozartian example.

JOHN STONE

Section 14

MOZART LITERATURE

MOZART LITERATURE

Biography and biographers

Ancestry and genealogy

Much of the information about these fascinating topics is scattered. For both sides of Mozart's family, a useful (and probably the most easily accessible) summary is to be found in the early chapters of Schenk (1975). It is interesting that musicality emerged in Mozart's mother's family – the Pertls – one generation earlier than it did in his father's. Regarding the latter's side, there are several pertinent chapters in Schmid (1948), who did much research into Suabian origins. Of particular value is Plate 2 in this book: a map of a small area to the south and south-west of Augsburg showing a score or so of little towns or villages, each marked with the date at which the Mozart name is first recorded. A clear chronological pattern of convergence towards the city emerges.

Deininger (1942/3) includes an article by Erich Valentin on Maria Anna Viktoria Mozart (1793–1857), a descendant of Leopold Mozart's younger brother Josef Ignaz. Attached to it is a fine genealogy of ten generations of the direct line of the Mozart family from David Mozart (c. 1620–1685). This is of interest because, since Mozart's own line died out with his sons, it reveals Maria Anna Viktoria's younger brother, Aloys Josef Anton, as the ancestor of all the Mozarts of the 19th and 20th century, and mentions the occupations of many in the male line. A note in *Acta Mozartiana* of November 1983 states that the last member of the direct Mozart line, Caroline Jacobine, died at Augsburg in 1965.

The talents of the early Mozarts, as architects, master masons and sculptors, are set out in a well illustrated monograph by Adolf Layer (1971). As a possible example of another aspect of the family's artistic affinities, there is a study by Ludwig Wegele (1969) of Anton Mozart, a gifted painter of the late 16th century, whose relation to the above-mentioned David has so far eluded the genealogists. No comprehensive study of Leopold Mozart by a single author has yet been published, but he is the subject of a fine chapter in Schmid (1948) and his youth up to 1737 is described by Layer (1975). The most recent book on Leopold is by Erich Valentin (1987), which though not comprehensive is the longest by a single author. There is also a useful collection of essays about him edited by Wegele (1969).

General

The first significant, separate biography of Mozart was written by Franz Xaver Niemetschek (1798), a Czech teacher and music critic who was able to use numerous papers sent to him by Mozart's widow. Although adulatory in tone, his book is valuable as reflecting the general attitude to Mozart of that decade, and it is a primary source. He also reveals how highly regarded Mozart's music was in Bohemia and shows early appreciation of some then little-known masterpieces. No other biography of substance appeared until 1828, when Constanze Mozart saw into print the immense work compiled by her second husband Georg Nikolaus Nissen, a Danish diplomat whom she married in 1809. After his death in 1826 the book was completed by J.H. Feuerstein, a Dresden physician. Including an appendix, also of 1828, the book runs to well over nine hundred pages, many of them devoted to the transcription of important original documents and other sources then still in Constanze's possession. Although the whole is rather shapeless and lacks an index, it is still a useful source of information sometimes overlooked by later writers.

The first biography in English (1845) was written by Edward Holmes, an intimate of the literary and musical circle formed by Vincent Novello and his wife Mary Sabilla. Novello had himself intended to write a Mozart biography and in 1829 travelled for this purpose to Salzburg and Vienna, where he collected a good deal of information from surviving relatives and friends of the composer. The travel diaries which he and his wife kept were edited by Rosemary Hughes and Nerina Medici di Marignano (1956). Ultimately Novello gave all his material to Holmes, who made good use of it, being a stylish and perceptive writer with an instinctive appreciation of Mozart's genius. He praised some then little-known music, including, for instance, *Idomeneo* long before its true worth began to be appreciated even by scholars.

It fell to Otto Jahn, spurred by the anticipation of the first centenary of Mozart's birth, to undertake the first definitive study of his life and music. Jahn, distinguished as a classical scholar, apparently began planning his huge task in 1847 and the first volume of his four-volume biography appeared in 1856 (the last in 1859). He seems to have had little training in music, yet he handled his huge accumulation of source material with consummate skill and lucidity. Although he laboured under the difficulty that many works were still unpublished, he gave a remarkably balanced account of his subject and his judgments fairly reflect the standards of his time. Unavoidably perhaps, he idealized his subject, but his was a great achievement. When preparing his second edition (1867), he had the advantage of using Köchel's catalogue. Jahn's work was more or less kept up to date in a third edition (1889–91), and in a fourth (1905–7), both by Hermann Deiters. The fifth edition, prepared by Hermann Abert (1919–21), amounted in large parts to an almost new book. Although retaining much of Jahn's biographical account, Abert included a good deal of redating and some lengthy chapters of his own, such as those on Mozart's personality, on the piano concertos and on *Don Giovanni*. Anna Abert, his daughter, made some minor revisions in the 1955 edition: it is a tribute to the quality of the book that it is still worth reading, although it now seems to be beyond the possibility of any future revision. It is a multi-layered monument originating in the great Romantic tradition of 19th-century musical biography. The sole English translation (1882) was of the second edition.

In 1912 there appeared the first two volumes of the 'vie musicale' by Wyzewa and Saint-Foix, one of the most extraordinary ventures in critical biography undertaken for Mozart or indeed for any other composer. The authors divided his life into thirty-four periods, each of which was prefaced by a fairly detailed biography, while the following critical section discussed each work in remarkable detail. After Wyzewa's death in 1917, Saint-Foix completed the task at intervals with three volumes of his own. Both authors were totally in love with their subject and their style is one of adoring affection, combining some sensitive, acute judgments with others that were idiosyncratic. This was generally because, when redating many of Mozart's undated compositions, they relied on a combination of instinctive judgment, stylistic criteria and external influences. Though much of the chronology is now obsolete, their great work is still worth reading because of its remarkable insight into Mozart's mind.

Wyzewa's and Saint-Foix's numbering was quoted in both the third and the sixth edition of Köchel, but when Einstein came to write his own book (1945), he seems to have owed little to these predecessors, despite a tribute to them in his preface. Einstein's study is a classic, in five parts, 'The Man', 'The Musician', 'The Instrumental Works', 'The Vocal Works', 'Opera'. Many of his critical assessments and historical judgments are of the highest quality. He treats Mozart's life not in the usual biographical sequence but under such headings as 'Catholicism and Free-masonry', 'Patriotism and Education' and so on. Perhaps the only weakness of the book is an over-Romantic approach – rather surprising in a scholar of such an otherwise rigorous cast of mind. Consequently some of his conjectures need to be read with caution. Schenk (1955) offers, in over 750 pages, the most comprehensive one-volume biography of recent years: the 1975 revision includes the results of recent research. Though lacking in style, and somewhat noncommittal in judgments, it is crammed with facts and has the merit of being exceptionally detailed.

Another example of the separation of life and works is found in an extremely readable book by Jean and Brigitte Massin (1959). While conveying some traditional judgments, their text is shrewd, penetrating, and often shows a nice sense of irony. They discuss the music work by work in chronological order, with thoroughness and perception. Massin includes tables of the keys that Mozart used and of the types of music composed at all periods of his life. A broadly comparable English book is the two-section tome ('Man'– 'Musician') by Arthur Hutchings (1976). Lavishly illustrated (though not always relevantly to subject or period), it is written with real insight and has many pertinent appreciations of unfamiliar masterpieces, most notably perhaps in the church music. Of English 'Life and Works' on a smaller scale there is a good example by Ivor Keys (1980), and Stanley Sadie's critical biography (1982) of some 25,000 words, reprinted with corrections from his article in the *New Grove* provides a sound, lucid introduction. A long biography, and with an entirely radical approach, is the study by Hildesheimer (1977), well known as a novelist and playwright. Written with provocative realism, it seeks to create a new image of Mozart. But some of the arguments appear confused, and it would have been a better book if the author's quasi-psychological attitude were matched by musical under-standing. Shaffer's notorious, irrelevant film *Amadeus* leans heavily on Hildesheimer. Landon's study (1988) devoted solely to the year 1791 is believed to be the sole long account of any comparably short period in Mozart's life. Written with great zest, it corrects many old, tenacious errors, and is enlivened by many documents, some familiar, others little known to English readers. The book takes full account of the social and historical background to the growth and completion of all the familiar masterpieces of the final year.

Landon (1989) is the sole book in English (and probably in any other language) devoted entirely to the last decade of Mozart's life. This is a detailed, biographical study, written with panache and insight to provide another vivid account of the historical, personal and social circumstances in which Mozart's creativity reached such astonishing peaks. Landon also says a good deal about some elements in his innovatory style of composition and throws fresh light on familiar ground – for instance the musical and personal relations of Mozart and Haydn. The book is fully documented, with some new, and much little known, information.

By far the best of the pictorial biographies is that based on a collection formed by Maximilian Zenger, completed by O.E. Deutsch (1961). In this sumptuous production the text, captions and commentary are in both German and English, and although now in need of some revision, it is a triumph of scholarly selection and presentation. One of its great strengths is the clear distinction made between the relatively few genuine portraits of Mozart and the large number of those which are unauthenticated or forged.

One particular aspect of Mozart biography which has elicited an enormous literature comprises his last illness, death and burial. Because of the difficulty of interpreting the symptoms of his numerous illnesses, whether given by himself or by others (notably Leopold), there will probably never be complete agreement among the experts. Probably the most balanced summary is that by Carl Bär (2/1972). Although his conclusion that Mozart's fatal illness reflected many symptoms of uraemia has now been questioned, the value of his book lies in its objective description and the lucid detachment with which he records the historical facts of Mozart's funeral and the legal requirements which governed both it and his burial. This topic is further discussed in a most interesting book by Peter J. Davies (1989), an Australian doctor who has studied Mozart's health record in great detail, and has attempted a fresh diagnosis of his recurrent symptoms in the light of modern medical knowledge. Davies also examines Mozart's complex character and behavioural pattern in psychoanalytical terms, and with the aid of a glossary, explains and rationalizes much that has hitherto been regarded as eccentric or obscure.

The fact that Mozart was a freemason and an active member of several lodges in Vienna is fairly well known. Full historical details were given by Deutsch (1932), in an objective and still indispensable monograph. The relation of Mozart's freemasonry to his music, although exemplified in a number of specially composed works and, of course, in *Die Zauberflöte*, has sometimes led to rather adventurous speculations. One interesting book of this kind is by Katharine Thomson (1977), its extent being indicated by its title, *The Masonic Thread in Mozart*. Her thesis is summed up in her view that 'the life story of Mozart illustrates the struggle of a great artist to break the bonds of feudalism and to liberate himself from all feudal ideas, including those expressed in music'. Given that freemasonry was fundamental to his 'struggle', she detects musical allusions with a wealth of appropriate rhythms and melodies, in upwards of ninety compositions of every type. This curious book is interesting as a clever piece of special pleading. There is a similar tendency to speculative writing, although much better founded in newly discovered documents, in P.A. Autexier's rather arcane essay (1984). Landon (1982) discusses in great detail an anonymous painting, now in Vienna, which he identifies as a meeting of the lodge 'Crowned Hope' perhaps in 1790. He makes out a good case for identifying Mozart and others among those present, but an imperfect understanding of the nature of artistic patronage has led him into some rather dubious chronological assumptions.

Local
This type of book seems to be peculiar to Mozart and originates in his continuous wide-ranging travels. The earliest of consequence is by Pohl (1867) and offers much detail relevant to the Mozart family's fifteen-month stay in London. More recent books cover Mozart's visits to towns in central Europe. They have a number of features in common – they are generally well illustrated, with some reproductions of local documents, pictures of buildings associated with Mozart, stage settings and singers, little-known concert notices, and occasionally a description of an instrument, generally an organ, on which he played. Such are: Nettl (1938), Bohemia; Kipp (1941), Alsace; Mohr (1968), Frankfurt-am-Main; Gottron (1951), Mainz; Würtz (1977), Mannheim; Thies (1941?), Munich; Caflisch and Fehr (1952), Zurich; Staehelin (1968), Switzerland.

Analytical and critical studies

General
The book edited by Landon and Mitchell (1956) was first published to mark the bicentenary of Mozart's birth. Some of the essays in it are as valuable today as when they were written, for

instance Blume's analysis of the sources of the concertos and Landon's lengthy study of their musical origin and development. Paul Hamburger's full-length examination of the concert arias said much that was new at the time and is still worth reading. Another most valuable contribution from Blume was 'Mozart's style and influence'. A little later (1963) came *The Creative World of Mozart* edited by Paul Henry Lang, a significant title which comprises some longish articles originally contributed to the *Musical Quarterly*. The essay on Mozart and Haydn by Ernst Fritz Schmid is exemplary and highly informative, while Blume's 'Requiem but no Peace' is a remarkable essay in lucid detective work. Lang's own short introduction on the spirit of Mozart is a masterly summary of the quasi-metaphysical essence of the music.

A conference report edited by André Verchaly (1958) is more concentrated than most and comprises just over a dozen contributions on foreign influences on Mozart's compositions. Particularly good are those by Schmid on Mozart's Suabian heritage, a similar one by V. Dobias on Mozart and Czech music, and Landon on the Romantic predecessors of Mozart's G minor Symphony, K.183. Another book of similar origin, edited by Friedrich Lippmann (1978), covers many aspects of Mozart and Italy. The editor's own analysis of the subtleties of Mozart's word-setting is noteworthy, while Finscher contributed a long investigation of Mozart's first string quartet, K.80. The volume as a whole is a solid contribution to scholarship.

An individual view of rare quality is given in the fourth and fifth chapters of Charles Rosen's *The Classical Style: Haydn, Mozart, Beethoven* (1971). The plan of this superlative work of criticism sets Mozart firmly in the context of his great contemporary and his successor. Chapter four, 'Serious Opera', sees Mozart, though working in an obsolescent form, as much indebted to Gluck. Rosen fails, rather curiously, to appreciate the dramatic excellence of much of *La clemenza di Tito*. Chapter five is devoted entirely to Mozart and exemplifies his genius in concerto, string quintet and comic opera – all written with revelatory authority and incisiveness.

Vocal music
Sacred
The most recent and comprehensive study of Mozart's entire church music is by K.G. Fellerer (1985). It offers a well documented summary of the liturgical basis of Mozart's numerous and very varied sacred compositions, followed by a work by work discussion of all the main types – masses, litanies, German and Latin church music and the like. Though rather sparing of critical judgment, this is a very useful book and is rounded off by a long discussion of Mozart's church music as it was regarded in the 19th century and the part it played in liturgical reforms of that period. Ever since Mozart's death, his Requiem has been almost universally performed in the version completed by his pupil Süssmayr.

Richard Maunder has prepared an edition of the music from which all Süssmayr's contributions have been removed, and has written a book (1988) to explain and justify his procedures. Maunder examines the nature of Mozart's counterpoint, his models for the Requiem, and many other problematical aspects of the expurgated torso. Some of his arguments seem rather naive in musical terms.

Secular

Operas – general studies   Dent's classic study (1913) was written for a time when neither the operagoing public nor even the musical world had much understanding of Mozart's true stature as a dramatic composer. Apart from *Die Zauberflöte* and *Don Giovanni* (generally given in mangled versions), the earlier masterpieces were very little known. Besides rehabilitating Mozart, Dent sought to give as much of the historical background to his operas as possible. When the second edition (1947) appeared Dent wrote as follows in the preface: 'I have cut out large quantities of dead wood. . . . I have done my best to bring the book up to date in accordance with modern historical research, but I have rewritten for the general reader rather than for the musicologist.' Comparison between the two editions shows that a good deal of what Dent first wrote is still very important. Understandably perhaps for his time, Dent had very little to say about any of the operas before *Idomeneo*. The balance was handsomely redressed by William Mann (1977), who provides a thorough discussion of every single number in all Mozart's stage works from *Die Schuldigkeit des ersten Gebots* right through to the finale of *La clemenza di Tito*. Mann writes with great affection and deep understanding of Mozart's dramatic skill, of his endlessly subtle use of key changes to highlight shifting emotional situations and above all does full justice to the grandeur and symphonic subtlety of the great ensembles of the masterpieces from *Idomeneo* onwards. Some readers, however, may find his obtrusively casual style of writing distinctly irritating. Issued in anticipation of the bicentenary of Mozart's birth, the handsomely illustrated 1955–6 issue of the *Opera Annual*, edited by Harold Rosenthal and devoted almost entirely to Mozart, is something of a period piece. Among famous names contributing short but significant essays were Dent, 'The Modern Cult of Mozart'; Pritchard, 'Conducting Mozart'; and Böhm, 'Problems in Mozart'. There is also a section headed 'Singing in Mozart's operas. Personal recollections by some of the great Mozart singers of our time'. Those contributing include Brownlee, Novotna, Helletsgruber, Steuart Wilson, and Patzak. A very useful monograph on the early operas is provided by Carolyn Gianturco (1976). She writes especially well of the court life and the social and historical occasions from which quite a number of them originated. Despite some weaknesses of linguistic understanding, she sheds much light on such early indications of genius as the best numbers in *La finta semplice* and on the path of the boy's dramatic development towards the charm of *La finta giardiniera*.

There are several useful books which deal with smaller groups of operas. One such is that by Christopher Benn (1946). It is still valuable for the practical and realistic solutions that it suggests to the problems of staging in the last four operas. It is valuable also for the long introduction by Richard Capell who gives a brilliant account of the way in which Mozart's stature as a dramatist in England changed gradually in the pre-first-war period. The book also includes reproductions in colour of ten of the very stylish costume designs made by Kenneth Green for productions at Glyndebourne, and for Sadlers Wells – three designs for *Così fan tutte* immediately after the war. There is a similar practical approach in R.B. Moberley's (1967) detailed account of *Figaro*, *Don Giovanni* and *Die Zauberflöte*. In a class by itself there is Brigid Brophy's 'new view of Mozart, his operas and his age', (1964). A book of enormous enthusiasm, it is rich in irrelevant psychological overtones and is written in almost blissful ignorance of the music, enhanced by a wealth of literary exuberance.

More soundly based is the work of an American philosopher, Irving Singer (1977), who has devoted an entire book to 'the concept of love' in the operas of Mozart and Beethoven. (As four-fifths of it concern the former, it is in place here.) The author commands a fine style, free from jargon and writes with great erudition and total sincerity. But the reader may feel that his learning sometimes transcends the bounds of reality and common sense. Mozart's librettists, particularly Da Ponte, would probably have been bewildered by the psychological nuance and subtlety which this author reads into their texts. They were, after all, hastily written, with little or no time for serious, consistent portrayal of character and profound feelings.

There may also be recommended a book by Janos Liebner (1972) which is of particular interest as giving the views of an experienced continental critic and artistic director (of the Berlin Opera, 1964–9). His chapter on *Idomeneo* is exceptionally perceptive. The most recent book on a group of Mozart's operas is that by Andrew Steptoe (1988), which is valuable for its concentration on the three with libretti by Da Ponte. Steptoe, a psychologist by profession, gives a generous, penetrating account of the historical background to *Figaro*, *Don Giovanni* and *Così fan tutte*, and places this sequence and their composer in the social and musical context of 1785–9. The chapter on '*Così fan tutte* and contemporary morality' opens new, important perspectives on this intriguing topic.

Individual Operas The two-hundredth anniversary of the first production of *Idomeneo* was marked by a splendid volume of essays edited by Rudolph Angermüller and Robert Münster (1981). Besides the catalogue of a large commemorative exhibition, there are a score of essays on the opera, its stage history and its text. Angermüller contributes a study of the staging up till the 19th century and Münster a penetrating essay on the Munich orchestra of 1781. S. Köhler writes about the 1931 revival by Wallerstein and

Richard Strauss, and Helmut Hell on the Wolf-Ferrari arrangement of the same year. Sumptuously illustrated, this book is indispensable.

Somewhat similar in approach, and likewise marking a bicentenary, is Angermüller's *Figaro* (1986). Lavishly illustrated with colour reproductions of designs made for German opera houses, the book describes in detail the relation of Da Ponte's text to Beaumarchais' *Le Barbier de Séville* and *Le Marriage de Figaro*, and provides a summary of the growth of Mozart's opera. Angermüller also lists the original libretto and subsequent adaptations, following this by a description of the original manuscript and printed sources of the music. Wolfgang Pütz adds a chapter on the reception of the opera during the last two centuries. There is a thirteen-page list of books and articles.

There are probably more books about *Don Giovanni* than any other Mozart opera. Abert's very penetrating study, extracted from his revision of Jahn (1976), is a classic of its kind. The bicentenary of the first production in Prague was marked by an important collection of essays by Czech scholars edited by Jan Kristek (1987). Perhaps the most original is 'The Theatre of Mozart's Don Giovanni' by Jiří Hilmera, which traces in detail the architecture and history of the 'Nostitz Theatre', while Vera Ptáčková contributes a seminal essay about the sets used in the original production.

Another book on *Don Giovanni*, edited by Rushton (1981), is in the valuable series of Cambridge Opera Handbooks (each well illustrated and on a broadly similar plan – creation, antecedents, dramatic qualities and some historical aspects). Rushton includes a sound account of 'Don Juan before Da Ponte' by Edward Forman and a speculative, stimulating essay 'Don Giovanni as an idea' by Bernard Williams. Rushton himself provides a sensible examination of the problems of the libretto and a good summary of the various methods of staging the opera from its earliest decades up to the present time. Two other handbooks are *Le nozze di Figaro* by Carter (1987) and *Die Entführung aus dem Serail* by Bauman (1987). In Carter's book a specialist author, Michael Robinson, contributes a good pre-history 'Mozart and the opera buffa tradition'. Carter describes the transition of the text from Beaumarchais to Da Ponte and adds a penetrating account of the metrical subtleties of the latter's verse. Carter rounds off his study with admirable essays on Mozart's brilliant diversification of character by musical means, and the history of the opera in performance during two centuries. Bauman, an American scholar, writing without collaboration, covers all the ramifications of *Die Entführung* and besides offering the same coverage as Carter's last two chapters includes an excellent account of the nature of 'oriental' opera as seen by Western musicians before and during Mozart's time. This is the first book in English on *Die Entführung* and a good one too. Two more handbooks, *Idomeneo*, edited by Julian Rushton and *Die Zauberflöte*, edited by Peter Branscombe, are in preparation (1990).

Of other books on *Die Zauberflöte* the study of it as a masonic opera by Jacques Chailley (1968) is extraordinarily elaborate. Although his pursuit of symbolism may seem rather exaggerated, he has much that is persuasive and original to say about the unity of the libretto. The important illustrations include many unfamiliar objects used in the masonic ceremonies. This is an absorbing book but should be used with caution. Nettl's general survey (1932) of this opera deserves brief mention because it contains a detailed analysis of Goethe's project for a continuation of *Die Zauberflöte*.

Songs

Apart from a few acknowledged masterpieces, dating from Mozart's last years, his thirty songs have not been very highly rated. A recent book (1984) by E.A. Ballin (the editor of the songs for the *Neue Mozart-Ausgabe* – Ser.III, Werkgruppe 8) does much to redress the balance. He shows that Mozart responded very strongly to the emotions expressed in the poems that attracted him. (Their quality, as poetry, is mostly of as little significance as in many of those that attracted Schubert.) Ballin also analyses the unsuspected range of Mozart's harmonic and rhythmical resource deployed in these slender pieces which he compares in style and approach both to Haydn's essays in the Lied and to the productions of such lesser contemporaries as J.A. Steffan, J.C. Hackel and others.

Comparative

There are a number of books, mostly small, which compare Mozart with another creative artist, or present him as seen through another's eyes. Such are: Nagel (1904), Goethe; P. Nettl (1949), Goethe; Haas (1951), J.S. Bach; German (1971), Mickiewicz; Valentin (1960/66), Hermann Hesse.

A recent book which approximates to this category is *pro AMADEUS contra* (1988), comprising four essays severally by Rudolph Angermüller and Otto Biba. It originated in an exhibition mounted in Tokyo in 1987 and planned to demonstrate the contrasts and affinities in the life-style and character of Mozart and Salieri during their Viennese years. It also assesses their personal relationship and is strongly to be recommended for its sane, scholarly discussion of topics too often clouded by emotion and fantasy.

Instrumental music

The popularity of the two broad categories of Mozart's music – vocal and instrumental – is fairly reflected in the chronology of the growth of their respective literature. Before roughly the late 1930s, the quantity of books and articles about the operas and the church music was already considerable (though much is now outdated), whereas the literature about any type of the instrumental music was relatively sparse. With one exception, it was not until after 1945 – when such groups as the piano concertos and the string quintets slowly won greater popularity – that the balance was slowly redressed and comprehensive studies began to appear.

Symphonies

The first really comprehensive study in any language is by Neal Zaslaw (1989). It treats the growth of Mozart's mastery of the symphonic style chronologically, taking full account of all the influences he felt during his boyhood and throughout all his travels. Zaslaw analyses the music of every symphony in minute detail, and describes the varying background to orchestral performances in Vienna and other cities. He offers an excellent chapter on 'performance practice', and another – more challenging – on 'Meanings for Mozart's symphonies'. In one of the appendices he summarizes 'the status of 97 symphonies', as to their authenticity or otherwise. This is a magisterial book, in the grand manner, perhaps a little overloaded with detail, but of exceptional thoroughness.

Far more modest in scale but still eminently readable is the stylish book by Saint-Foix (1932) and well deserving its English translation fifteen years later. Written with insight and affection, very much in the spirit of Saint-Foix's own continuation of the 'Vie Musicale' mentioned above (p. 406), this study is still fresh and stimulating. More up to date is Stanley Sadie's shorter book (1986). It was fortunately able to incorporate a lot of recent research into problems of the chronology and authenticity which affect quite a number of the early symphonies. It is a crisp, stylish guide to the growth of Mozart's symphonic style, and opens fresh windows on the reader's view of even such familiar marvels as the finale of the *Jupiter* Symphony.

As an instance of multifaceted modern musicology, there may be cited the published symposium, edited by Larsen and Wedin (1987), on the Symphony in A minor, K.16a, 'del Sigr Mozart'. The speakers examined minutely textual and bibliographical origins, paper types, form, harmony, melodic types, symphonies by other composers active in the early 1760s, and other topics. They concluded that K.16a is on the whole unlikely to be by W.A. Mozart.

Serenades, etc.

The term 'serenade' covers a varying number of Mozart's works, according to interpretation. Hausswald (1951) includes divertimentos and cassations as well as those generally so called, and among the divertimentos mentions the String Trio K.563. Though rather unexciting to read, this is a very thorough study of the evolution of Mozart's entertainment music, in all its great variety of structure, melodic and rhythmical patterns. Erik Smith (1982) addresses a more general public, and – rather oddly but usefully – includes dances, ballet music and marches. He 'places' each type or group in its biographical or social context, and points up his stylishly written criticism with many instances of Mozart's inventive brilliance, even in ephemeral forms. Throughout the great variety of his orchestral music, Mozart was continually experimenting with new combinations of instruments. The growth of his feeling for timbre is examined in a systematic study by Carl Thieme (1936).

Concertos

Pianoforte It is one of the most remarkable facts in the whole of Mozart literature that the first comprehensive study of the concertos, in any language, was the work of a bilingual English scholar writing in French. Girdlestone's distinguished book (1939) was the fruit of some two decades' intensive work. (Because of the War his own English version did not appear until 1948.) Although the style may bear a superficial resemblance to the manner of Wyzewa and Saint-Foix, the treatment is in fact more rigorous and better focused. While sometimes apparently bewildered by the lack of any conformity in Mozart's first-movement forms, Girdlestone wrote with a wide-ranging knowledge of Mozart's music as a whole and of the relation of his concertos to the tonal and formal diversity of his other masterpieces from the same periods. The title 'Companion' used by Hutchings (1948) is a fair indication of his delightful style. For although successfully expanded from a thesis, his book is quite devoid of the dryness often found in such work. He writes with zest and enthusiasm and includes an excellent introductory chapter entitled 'The Mozartian conception', where he reveals an instinctive understanding of the almost inexhaustible richness of the composer's imagination.

Forman's unique book (1971) is confined to the first movements. Written with exceptional discernment and an admiration that is always tempered by articulate coolness, it seeks with considerable success to determine formal patterns within the protean diversity of Mozart's imagination; the analyses and arguments are clarified by a brilliant series of 'musical references and construction tables'. The only full-scale study by an American scholar is the work of Hans Tischler (1966). It is a structural analysis in the sense of the phrase developed by the inter-war German tradition of scientific investigation. It is not easy reading but is highly rewarding.

For the less specialized reader, there is Radcliffe's genial, lucid exposition (1978), which discusses the concertos in fairly conventional terms and has much of interest to say about the richness of Mozart's tonal language. He does not, however, make the reader fully aware of the significance of the concertos as one of the continuing peaks of Mozart's creativity.

Other concertos Some two dozen of these compositions are examined by King (1968) in what is inevitably rather a discontinuous booklet, the reason being that apart from the sequences of concertos for violin and for horn, all the others were composed either as singletons or at the most in pairs. Within these constraints, the text places the works in the circumstances and personal circle which produced them and indicates the unfailing resourcefulness of Mozart's formal and harmonic invention.

It is unfortunate that one of the most popular and frequently recorded of Mozart's wind concertos, the Symphonie Concertante for oboe, clarinet, horn and bassoon, K.Anh.9 (297b, Anh. C 14.01), has very little to do with him. (For a discussion of its authenticity and the sole extant source – a manuscript of the mid-19th century – see 'Doubtful and spurious' (p. 353).) The history of this piece, its form, harmony, instrumentation and much else about it are discussed in comprehensive detail by Levin (1988). He concludes that only the solo parts may derive from the Sinfonie Concertante for flute, oboe, horn and bassoon, K.Anh.9 (297B), which Mozart composed in Paris in 1778.

Interpretation The earliest significant book to discuss the sound world of Mozart's keyboard music was that by Brunner (1933), which attempted to relate, however slightly, performance technique to the construction and tonal qualities of the fortepiano of Mozart's own time. To a lesser extent this question is addressed in a much more comprehensive book by Eva and Paul Badura-Skoda (1957). The authors, the wife well known as scholar and editor and the husband as a pianist, cover not only the concertos but a good many of the most important sonatas and variations and other chamber works with keyboard as well. Although some of the matter – e.g. 'the Urtext problem' – has become a little dated, this is still the best and most rational general discussion of a large number of some possibly insoluble problems. The long recent study (1986) by Frederick Neumann can perhaps be most conveniently mentioned here because the greater part of it deals with Mozart's instrumental compositions. (His vocal chapters include discussion of appoggiaturas, recitative and arias.) Neumann is concerned that the problem of ornamentation and improvisation be considered primarily in terms of musicianship, which often leads him into rather subjective arguments. Although this is a provocative book, it is written from a wide knowledge of 18th-century sources, and a deep affection for the music.

Chamber music
In some 25,000 words King (1968, rev. edn. 1986) assesses the sixty-odd compositions in this category, almost half of them being the string quartets. He traces Mozart's gradual mastery of this medium, which he always found difficult. The book likewise attempts to show how, while reaching peaks in other chamber works (notably the string quintets) equal to the best of the quartets, Mozart also maintained an astonishingly high level within a remarkable variety of media, some of which, such as the quintet for piano and wind instruments, he seems virtually to have invented.

Pianoforte works
Dennerlein (1951) is apparently the only comprehensive chronological study written since that attempted by Lorenz in 1866. It deals with every category of Mozart's copious output, much of which is

still relatively little known. It covers all his music for two hands, for four hands at one piano, and for two pianos, and includes the works for mechanical organ and armonica. Dennerlein analyses not only the complete compositions but substantial fragmentary pieces, small introductory preludes (such as those Mozart wrote for fugues by J.S. Bach) and a number of partially doubtful works as well. Despite some of the dating now having been inevitably superseded, this is a very thorough handbook to the growth of style and form in all that Mozart composed for his own favourite instrument.

Other Mozart literature

DURING THE LAST CENTURY there have been a number of journals devoted entirely to Mozart. The earliest of significance was the *Mitteilungen für die Mozartgemeinde in Berlin* (1895–1925). It established what was a regular pattern for such productions, blending the transactions of the society with a number of important scholarly articles. The 'Mitteilungen' of the Mozarteum in Salzburg first appeared in 1918 but ceased in 1921. They resumed, however, in 1952 as *Mitteilungen der Internationalen Stiftung Mozarteum*, and are still current. At first, it was mainly devoted to one of the chief functions of the Mozarteum – to co-ordinate details of performance of Mozart's works from every country in the world where they are played – and over the years has maintained a remarkably high degree of success. Such information is still given, in summary. For some time, the *Mitteilungen* have included the annual report of the Mozarteum (first published separately in 1881) and reports from numerous branches. Of recent years it has included an increasing number of significant scholarly articles and its purpose as a record is rounded off by valuable obituary notices and birthday tributes to its senior members.

The first *Mozart-Jahrbuch* appeared in 1923, but this series came to an end, presumably through lack of support, with the third volume in 1929. A continuation ultimately appeared as the *Neues Mozart-Jahrbuch* in 1941, in obviously difficult circumstances, and this too only lasted for three issues. Finally, in 1950 the concept of a yearbook recommenced with the original title *Mozart-Jahrbuch*, under the auspices of the Mozarteum, and has continued more or less annually ever since. All three sequences are a rich repository of Mozart research, with many contributions by outstanding scholars, though it must be said that in recent years the quality of the articles has been rather variable. Some of the most valuable volumes have been those comprising the papers read at formal meetings of members of the Mozarteum with a summary of discussions held at them. Of such meetings, the most fruitful were those devoted to a particular aspect or period of Mozart's life and music. In recent years the *Jahrbuch* has expanded to include full-length reviews of notable books on Mozart and his times.

Acta Mozartiana was first issued in 1954 as the 'Mitteilungen der Deutschen Mozart-Gesellschaft' and has achieved some international circulation. While serving primarily as a record of the remarkable work of this society and its widespread meetings, the journal also includes some scholarly articles, but rather more given to the expression of views and ideas. One of its most valuable features is reviews of local publications which might otherwise be little known outside Germany.

The first comprehensive study of Mozart's use of keys was written by Lüthy (1931). Although somewhat dated in its approach, it is useful for the comprehensive way in which it discusses the theories of key usage in general during and just after Mozart's time, and analyses his use of all the major and minor keys throughout his music. Mozart as a teacher has long been a topic of interest to scholars: the first systematic attempt, by the Austrian musicologist and composer, Robert Lach (1918), to analyse his methods is still valuable.

The distinguished French critic, Jean Chantavoine, made an intensive examination of Mozart's reuse of his own melodies (1948). Dividing his material into chapters according to the major operas, and with the aid of 565 music examples, he distinguishes five distinct categories of reuse which shed some new light on the workings of Mozart's musical imagination and creativity. Partly similar in purpose is Flothuis's investigation (1969) of Mozart's reuse of his own compositions and his arrangements of works by others.

Bibliography

Köchel-Verzeichnis

Ludwig Ritter von Köchel (1800–77) trained in law, became a famous mineralogist and was a life-long devotee of Mozart. He began collecting material for his great catalogue about 1851, and when it appeared in 1862 it was the first chronological, thematic presentation of all the music of any great composer. For each work, Köchel gave the musical incipit (with incipits of each movement where appropriate), the location of the autograph when known, the first edition whenever possible, all this being followed by references to the then standard editions of the music and to the most important scholarly discussion of it. Köchel also devised and included a classification of Mozart's entire output in twenty-three groups which later served as the basis for the *Alte Mozart-Ausgabe* (to whose financial support he made a substantial contribution).

This simple plan was largely maintained in subsequent editions, though much expanded to take account of continually growing publication and research. (See King, 1955, for a detailed account.) The second edition, by Paul Count Waldersee (1905), made few alterations to Köchel's chronology but added references to the *Alte Mozart-Ausgabe*. But the third edition, prepared by Alfred Einstein (1937), made far-reaching, radical changes and redated many compositions, especially those prior to 1784, the year when Mozart began his own dated, thematic catalogue (first issued in facsimile 1938; another facsimile, with commentary by Alan Tyson, 1989). Einstein also listed a large quantity of late 18th-century and early

19th-century editions (from information mostly supplied to him by O.E. Deutsch and C.B. Oldman), the majority of which were of significance solely as some evidence of popularity. Einstein made a thorough revision of Köchel's appendices of doubtful and supposit-ious works. He decided that some of them were genuine and included them in the main order together with numerous autograph fragments, previously listed in an appendix.

The editors of the sixth edition (1964) were faced with a colossal task. They had to take account of twenty-seven years of Mozart research (carried on assiduously all over Europe even during World War II and in the USA) and all the extra knowledge gained during the preparation of the *Neue Mozart-Ausgabe* which began to appear from 1955 onwards. Thus new chronological problems arose because the editors found it necessary to revise yet again the dates of a good many works which Einstein had already redated. The task facing the compilers of the seventh edition is truly formidable and radical rethinking of some principles of the inclusion and exclusion of Mozart literature is clearly essential.

An interesting by-product of the 1937 Köchel appeared in 1951, *Der kleine Köchel*, which comprises a summary of Mozart's entire output, with short conventional titles. It is presented first in Köchel number order and then in the twenty-three original groups of the *Alte Mozart-Ausgabe* with a twenty-fourth section for 'Ver-schiedenes'.

The Autographs
The only specialized study is the magisterial collection of essays by Tyson (1987), which brings together the results of his exhaustive scrutiny of the paper-types of a very large number of the autographs of complete and fragmentary compositions. Full details of the chronological implications of Tyson's work are given under 'Autographs' (pp. 173–6) and 'Manuscript copies' (p. 180); it should, perhaps, be mentioned that some of his research is speculative.

Musical literature
The first attempt to compile a systematic list of books and articles about Mozart was that by Otto Keller (1927). He drew on various earlier efforts such as those of Constantin von Wurzbach (1869) and of Henri de Curzon (1906). But a great deal of Keller's work was original, for he included articles in over five hundred newspapers and periodicals and drew on an extensive collection of press notices recording little-known performances of Mozart's operas and various instrumental works. Keller's compilation exceeded 4,520 entries. It was arranged by subjects, with a special section on iconography. The index comprised people, places and subjects.

Over forty years later came another, even larger, compilation by Rudolph Angermüller and Otto Schneider (1976). By no means all of Keller was subsumed into this bibliography, which exceeded

6,400 entries arranged alphabetically, with two indexes, the first similar to Keller's and the second comprising references from Köchel numbers. This immense labour included nothing published after 1970 and though some of its principles (for example the listing of anonymous works) are rather idiosyncratic, it is an essential work of reference. The same two compilers were responsible for two continuations, the first covering the years 1971 to 1975 (1978), and the second, 1976 to 1980 (1982).

Music

The catalogues of Mozart's music issued by innumerable firms are mostly ephemeral and of little more than commercial interest. The first editions, however, are of great historical and often textual importance. The first systematic and indeed exhaustive listing of them is that by Gertraut Haberkamp (1986). The result of some ten years' intensive research, it comprehends the holdings of 108 libraries worldwide, 101 institutional, seven private. Published in two volumes, one of text, the other of title-pages (which regrettably are not transcribed in the text volume), this magisterial work of reference covers all first editions issued up to 1805. It establishes new criteria for describing the points by which a first edition and reprints from the original plates can be identified.

The sole attempt to describe the Mozart holdings of any major national library seems to be by King (1984). This book lists all the autographs and important copies in the British Library, gives some account of their provenance, textual or personal interest, and, with the help of fifty-seven varied illustrations, attempts to describe the general character of the collections, including printed music, some musical literature, and visual material.

The *Mozart-Handbuch*

This distinctive, multi-purpose compilation deserves a paragraph to itself, for it comprises a very detailed chronology with a special regrouping of the Köchel catalogue and a very useful bibliography. The chronology includes the lives of both Mozart's father and mother and his own, the last running to some seventy pages, with invaluable, comprehensive references to general sources and to relevant numbers in the bibliography. The compilers, Otto Schneider and Anton Algatzy (1962) have regrouped Mozart's entire output in twenty-one sections. Each work is identified by Köchel number and a conventional title and there is a wealth of information about the music given in the form of references to articles in periodicals, Festschriften and the like. There is also a section devoted to the chronology of the life of Mozart's wife, her children and Mozart's cousin, Maria Anna, the 'Bäsle'. A large genealogical tree of both Mozart's parents, back to the early seventeenth century, rounds off this section. The bibliography runs to some 3,900 items and is selected with scholarly judgment.

ALEC HYATT KING

Section 15
COLLECTED EDITIONS

COLLECTED EDITIONS

Early printed editions

The earliest printed sources of Mozart's works date from 1764. In this year, in the middle of the grand tour which took the Mozart family across Europe, Marie Charlotte Vendôme in Paris issued Mozart's sonatas for keyboard and violin, K.6–9; a little later, in London, Leopold Mozart issued the same works again privately. The publication of printed sources of Mozart's works then continued until the composer's death in 1791 and ultimately extended to the first complete collected edition (*Alte Mozart-Ausgabe* = AMA), whose initial instalments began appearing in January 1877.

With their collective publication 'Mozart-Drucke' at the beginning of the 1930s, Otto Erich Deutsch (1883–1967) and Cecil B. Oldman (1894–1969) laid the scholarly foundation for investigation of a field until then little researched. The subsequent new editions of the Köchel Catalogue (3/1937, with Supplement: 1947; 6/1964) drew upon their findings, as did the *Neue Mozart-Ausgabe* in its infancy, taking them as the point of departure for the task of collecting the printed sources for the new Mozart edition. Nevertheless, until well into the second half of the 20th century there was lacking, 'as usual, a detailed categorization and characterization of the individual editions and their issues'. Not until the two-volume publication of Gertraut Haberkamp in 1986 (from whose Foreword the above is quoted: I, 7), which treated the first editions of Mozart's works, was this painful gap tardily, if not belatedly, closed. A work of enormous scope (see 'Mozart Literature', p. 420), it has once and for all placed research into the printed Mozart sources on a firm foundation. In the future no publication or individual investigation will be able to ignore the contribution of Gertraut Haberkamp (the present article itself, particularly in the opening pages, is likewise indebted to her research).

This now standard work of 1986 (to say nothing of the continuous striving on the part of the NMA to provide information on the early printed sources) was preceded by the internationally compiled catalogue of first and early printed editions of Mozart's music up to *c.* 1800, first published in 1975 in volume 6 of Series A/I of the *Répertoire International des Sources Musicales*, and again in 1978 as an offprint. The RISM catalogue includes almost 3,500 entries (individual editions and collections), following the system of ordering of the NMA; it cites the original

titles in usual short form, and records the whereabouts of the editions insofar as the owners themselves have reported their holdings to the cataloguers of this music-bibliographical directory. 'For each work cited, the first edition is listed first; subsequent editions follow as nearly as possible in chronological order or according to publisher [. . .] The termination date of 1800 has been exceeded here more frequently than usual; in such cases, however, the whereabouts of the sources should not be regarded as complete. – The task (and one made all the more demanding by publishing practices around 1800) of systematically ordering and locating the numerous early Mozart editions (of works both in original and in arrangement), whether single editions, collections or partial or complete editions, can be carried on only with the patient and attentive co-operation of all users of this catalogue' (Karlheinz Schlager, from the 'Vorbemerkung'). A new volume now in preparation as supplement to RISM A/I of 1975 will include approximately 4,000 additional entries: not only corrigenda and supplemental information concerning whereabouts of the sources, but also editions and impressions missing from the catalogue of 1975.

In her catalogue of the first printed editions of Mozart's works, Gertraut Haberkamp describes 228 first editions issued during the period 1764 to 1805. These include some '374 works either known to be by Mozart or attributed to him but as yet to no other composer' (accordingly, then, also compositions from Köchel, Anh. C: 'Doubtful and spurious works'). For a handful of pieces, she gives special treatment to other types of editions, such as piano reductions, parts and transcriptions, so that the corpus of works embraces another ten numbers. Her descriptions in the text volume of the catalogue give an exhaustive picture of Mozart editions during the years 1764 to 1805, touching on everything from format to technique of printing (type, engraved plate, lithography), kind of edition (score, piano reduction or parts), pagination and layout, content, watermark, year of publication (confirmed by advertisements) and, finally, place of printing of the individual editions as well as their subsequent impressions over an extended period of time. While the facsimile volume reproduces only the title page of each of the first impressions, the sections 'Kriterien' and 'Anmerkungen' in the text volume give detailed information both about the edition proper and the distinguishing traits and characteristics of its various impressions. This phenomenon, previously scarcely recognized and long in need of explication and systematic investigation, was taken in hand by Haberkamp, a fact which underlines once more the importance of her catalogue to future research. A single example serves for many: the Fantasy and Sonata in C minor, K.475 and 457, was first issued in 1785 by Artaria in Vienna. Already for the second impression twelve pages were newly engraved; for the third, an additional nine pages. For the fourth impression still another page was removed and replaced. The fifth and sixth impressions differ from the preceding by the inclusion of an opus number on page two. The seventh 'impression' was engraved afresh and thus bore the notice 'Nouvelle Edition' (Haberkamp's catalogue always cites at least one owner for each of these seven 'impressions', but more usually several). The fact that a first edition is transmitted in various impressions differing from one to the next in greater or lesser detail necessarily influences the present-day shaping of the musical text, at least in those instances where the autograph is lacking (as in the case of K.475 and 457).

Of the 228 first editions published by 1805, 78 editions including 131 works were issued during Mozart's lifetime (i.e., from 1764 until early December 1791). Their publishers include: Ignaz Alberti, Vienna; Johann André, Offenbach a. M.; Artaria & Co., Vienna; Birchall & Andrews, London; Heinrich Philipp Bossler, Speyer; Boyer/Le Menu, Paris; Jean Pierre De Roullède, Paris; Rudolph Gräffer, Vienna; Heina, Paris – Godefroy, Brussels; Hoffmeister & Co., Vienna (later also Leipzig); Burchard Hummel, The Hague, and Johann Julius Hummel, Amsterdam (later also Berlin), the two latter both independently and jointly; Leopold and Anton Koželuch/Musikalisches Magazin, Vienna; Normalschul-Buchdruckerei, Prague; Bernhard Schott, Mainz; Franz Anton Schrämbel (Institute for the Deaf and Dumb), Vienna; Jean Georges Sieber, Paris; Christoph Torricella, Vienna; Marie Charlotte Vendôme (*Aux adresses ordinaires de Musique*), Paris; Georg Philipp Wucherer, Vienna: and Leopold Mozart (private press).

By far the leader among these was Artaria in Vienna, with over 60 editions, followed by Hoffmeister, likewise in Vienna, with some 13. All other publishers issued just below a total of 10 editions, although a single edition is not rare. More than half of the editions were devoted to keyboard and chamber music, the rest to the remaining genres of Mozart's output. Thus during Mozart's lifetime perhaps only two of the eighteen completed musico-dramatic works were published in full, namely *Die Entführung aus dem Serail* and *Don Giovanni* (both in vocal score, by Schott, Mainz). Appearing side by side with these and also in vocal score were individual issues of pieces from *Die Zauberflöte*, a few of which were distributed in Mozart's lifetime, the remainder of the 38 issues by 1793 (Koželuch, Vienna). Of the 49 authentic symphonies, only 3 appeared in Mozart's lifetime (K.319, 297/300a, 385); of the 23 piano concertos, only 6 (K.175 and 382, 413/387a, 414/385p, 415/387b, 453, 595). Certain types of works – for instance, all other instrumental concertos – were neglected entirely.

In contrast to his father Leopold, who in earlier years devoted himself with energy and success to the publication of his son's works (in later years, too, but with less success), Mozart did not take an active interest in these matters. Yet he was always ready to push the publication of works if he thought it would directly help to spread his fame, improve his reputation or, as later in Vienna, ameliorate his economic situation. For the rest, however, the modest number of publications during Mozart's lifetime resulted from a certain restraint on the part of composer and publisher alike. Works such as the piano concertos, which (particularly during the Vienna years) Mozart composed expressly for himself and for his 'academies' (concerts), he chose to withhold for the time being. He writes, for instance, to his father concerning the piano concertos K.449–51 and 453: 'I find, though, that it works more to my advantage if I hold them back for myself a couple of years and only let them become known through print.' On the other hand, Viennese publishers in particular were confronted with such a wide dissemination of Mozart's compositions through copyists' workshops that their own publishing activities necessarily had to be curtailed.

Although, or rather perhaps because Mozart knew his publishers in Paris (and later in Vienna) more or less personally, not one letter to them survives. That he scarcely took a hand in supervising publications of his works is furthermore verified by the faulty musical texts of most of the first editions up to 1791. In the earlier years it was Leopold Mozart who played a role in the production process, despite the fact that the family's many travels left little time for proof-reading. Later it was the publishing houses themselves, with their readers and correctors, who supervised the editions, and it appears that Mozart only occasionally intervened (either directly, or through his pupil Josepha Auernhammer). This direct or indirect control may in fact account for the striking textual disparities between autograph and edition, although this is a point which can as yet hardly be proved. Instances of such disparities are the Artaria editions of the six string quartets dedicated to Joseph Haydn, K.387, 421 (417b), 428 (421b), 458, 464 and 465, and the Fantasy and Sonata in C minor for piano, K.475 and 457. For the latter two Köchel numbers, the situation is rather more complicated, as the autographs are lost; but at least in the case of the Sonata a substitute primary source is preserved – a dedication copy with autograph entries. Both of the above-named Artaria editions appeared in the year 1785.

In addition to Artaria, Hoffmeister and Koželuch in Vienna, Bossler in Speyer, Schott in Mainz and Sieber in Paris, who throughout this period published such editions only sporadically, the following houses or individuals brought out a number of first editions posthumously (with a termination date of 1805): Johann and Johann Anton André, Offenbach; Friedrich Gotthelf Baumgärtner, Leipzig; Johann August Böhme, Hamburg (only two works from K.Anh.C); Breitkopf (from 1796 on, Breitkopf & Härtel), Leipzig; Bureau des arts et d'industrie, Vienna; Johann Cappi, Vienna (one authentic work and two works from K.Anh.C); Joseph Eder, Vienna (only one work from K.Anh.C); Gombart & Co., Augsburg; Günther & Böhme, Hamburg; Hoffmeister & Kühnel, Leipzig; Joseph Hraschanzky, Vienna; L'Imprimerie du Conservatoire, Paris (only one work from K.Anh.C); Pierre Le Duc, Paris; J. Hieronymus Löschenkohl, Vienna (only works from K.Anh.C); Johann Jakob Lotter, Augsburg; Mollo & Co., Vienna; Musikalisches Magazin auf der Höhe, Brunswick; Mutzenbecher, Hamburg; Johann Karl Friedrich Rellstab, Berlin (exclusively works from K.Anh.C); Schmidt (Schmied) & Rau, Leipzig; Nikolaus Simrock, Bonn; Søren Sønnichsen, Copenhagen; J.P. Thonus, Leipzig (on commission of Breitkopf & Härtel); Johann Traeg, Vienna; Johann Wenzl, Prague; Franz Heinrich Ziegenhagen, Hamburg; and Constanze Mozart (private press).

Finally, from 1805 until the beginning of the AMA (January 1877) another 65 authentic works by Mozart (including transcriptions) were printed for the first time, mainly by (but excluding André and Breitkopf & Härtel): Joseph Aibl, Munich; Artaria, Vienna; Samuel Chappell, London; August Cranz, Hamburg; Anton Diabelli, Vienna; Jacques Léopold Heugel, Paris; Julius Kistner, Leipzig; Ambrosius Kühnel, Leipzig; Christopher Lonsdale, London; Carl Friedrich Peters, Leipzig; Nikolaus Simrock, Bonn; Carl Anton Spina, Vienna; and Johann Traeg, Vienna.

In the successive periods 1791 to 1805, and 1805 to the early 1870s, André in Offenbach and Breitkopf & Härtel in Leipzig clearly led the way as publishers of Mozart's music, even though they had issued little by him during his lifetime. Only towards the end of 1787 did André bring out an edition of the Piano Trio, K.496 (actually nothing more than a reprinting of an edition issued the previous summer by Hoffmeister in Vienna); in 1790 he published the first vocal score of the Rondo for soprano, K.577, composed for inclusion in Le nozze di Figaro. As for Breitkopf & Härtel, Leopold Mozart had troubled himself in vain. In the years after Mozart's death, both publishers surfaced only occasionally, but with the turn of the century entered into a bitter rivalry. Until well into the 19th century the Offenbach firm held the lead: in 1799–1800 Johann Anton André (1775–1842) had acquired from Constanze Mozart the greater part of Mozart's musical estate (chiefly autographs). This not only laid the foundation for the publisher's ensuing editorial policy but also placed him in the distinctly advantageous position of being able, after 1800, to preface his editions with the remark 'Edition faite d'après la partition en manuscrit', or (more frequently and more correctly) 'Edition faite d'après le manuscrit original de l'auteur'.

Breitkopf & Härtel held second place in the earlier decades of the 19th century, but with the *Oeuvres complettes* took the bold step as early as 1798 (to 1806) of attempting to produce a complete edition. There followed numerous first and early editions, and in 1868, with stepped-up production, the full score editions of the eight large (completed) operas, beginning with *Idomeneo*, K.366. The editorial work on this last project was carried out by Julius Rietz (1812–77). With the subsequent publication of the AMA and the many editions derived from it, the Leipzig house would eclipse André once and for all. The significance of the role played by the Offenbach house in issuing early editions of Mozart's works nevertheless remains supreme.

The number of early printed editions (including both original editions and arrangements of every kind) reached monumental, and as yet still barely comprehensible, proportions in the first half of the 19th century (a first, albeit incomplete overview of the editions and their publishers is given in K.Anh.E, pp. 941ff.); yet there remained at the inception of the AMA some two hundred works, or rather, approximately one third of Mozart's total production, unprinted. The first 'complete edition' was actually, then, the very first edition of this portion of his works.

Preliminary to the discussion of the complete editions, specifically the AMA and the NMA, a few brief but important facts concerning terminology are worth reviewing, for they will assist us in assessing the qualitative relationship between 'first' and 'early' edition. With respect to the Mozart sources, 'first edition' (*Erstdruck*) means the earliest printing of a work; 'early edition' (*Frühdruck*), on the other hand, normally indicates a new edition, be it from the same publishing firm as the first edition, or from another. 'Early edition' can also mean, however, a revised edition either by the same publisher or by another publisher. The terminological concepts 'first edition'/'early edition' thus designate nothing more than the chronological positions of the editions; they indicate nothing about the quality of the sources. And if ordinarily the two concepts (especially the latter) are reserved for that period of the production of early printed editions confined to the years 1764–*c*. 1805, in principle there is nothing to prevent their usage to cover later periods, as long as first editions of Mozart's works continue to appear: for instance, as recently as 1981, the Symphony in F major, K.Anh.223 (19a).

The value of an edition from the early years of print production is obviously determined by the quality of the source itself, which in turn depends to a large extent upon the sources from which it is derived (e.g. autograph, authorized copy), or upon the control exercised either in the publishing house during the actual printing or by the composer himself. Inasmuch as Mozart rarely supervised editions of his own works, as already observed, it necessarily follows that the early editions brought out after 1791 by a conscientious publisher, such as André, might be of substantially greater value as source material than a great many of the first editions brought out during Mozart's lifetime.

The old Breitkopf & Härtel Collected Edition (AMA)

Attempts to lay hold of Mozart's musical heritage and to make it accessible to the public in the form of a 'complete edition' of all of his works or of the individual genres – such as the piano works – began shortly after the composer's death. Of these early editions, the above-mentioned *Oeuvres complettes* of Breitkopf & Härtel (1798–1806) first and foremost laid claim, at least in its title, to being a 'complete edition' of the composer's creative production. Immediately preceding this undertaking, however, for the Easter Fair of 1798, the Brunswick publisher Johann Peter Spehr (*Musikalisches Magazin der Musik*) advertised a 'complete collection and edition of Mozart's works': subsequently, six instalments of five pieces each appeared in 1798–9 (for the most part keyboard music, chamber music with keyboard instrument, and songs). Gottfried Christoph Härtel (1763–1827), from 1796 the sole proprietor of the Leipzig publishing house and from the beginning of his publishing activity interested in a complete edition of the works of Mozart, took advantage of the announcement of the Brunswick publisher, the impending doom of whose project he prophesied, and now gave notice to the musical public of a 'correct and complete collection' of the 'authentic compositions of Mozart'. He thereupon (on 15 May 1798) turned to Constanze Mozart in Vienna and solicited her support for this project, excusing himself first for writing to her about the undertaking only after having announced it. Constanze answered with reticence on 26 May 1798. She was cautious in her assistance with regard to information and the handing over of 'unprinted authentic compositions' of Mozart. Nevertheless, there began during this period the negotiations which Constanze (cleverly counselled by Georg Nikolaus Nissen) carried on with both André and Breitkopf & Härtel and at the end of which Johann Anton André emerged the clear victor (see above, 'Early printed editions'). The *Oeuvres complettes* of Breitkopf & Härtel was organized and designed to appear in three parts: *I. Klaviersachen* (in seventeen volumes, 1798–1806), *II. Partituren grösserer Werke als*

Opern, Cantaten, Kirchenstücke etc. and *III. Musik für mehrere Instrumente in Stimmen, als: Sinfonien, Concerte, Quintetten, Quartetten etc*. The latter two groups were never completed, although several of the works did see publication, among them: two masses (K.257 and 317), the Requiem, *Don Giovanni* and twenty of the piano concertos (from K.238 on).

Neither the *Oeuvres complettes* nor any other edition indebted to it or issued independently of it (see the listing in K.Anh.D, pp. 915–24) is in truth a complete edition of Mozart's works. This claim was first fulfilled by the AMA, or more precisely: *Wolfgang Amadeus Mozart's Werke. Kritisch durchgesehene Gesammtausgabe*, published by Breitkopf & Härtel in Leipzig. Systematically arranged in twenty-four series and ultimately bound together in linen, the individual volumes were issued in instalments from January 1877 to December 1883, with addenda to 1910 (in Series XXIV: Supplement). The critical commentaries, a great many of which were never completed, were issued separately from the musical volumes under the title *W. A. Mozart's Werke. Kritisch durchgesehene Gesammtausgabe*.

The initiator of this first complete edition of Mozart's works (today called the 'Alte Mozart-Ausgabe') and the driving force behind it was Ludwig Ritter von Köchel. His celebrated catalogue, the *Chronologisch-thematisches Verzeichnis sämtlicher Tonwerke Wolfgang Amadé Mozarts*, was begun in 1851 and published in 1862 by Breitkopf & Härtel. Today it is simply called the 'Köchel-Verzeichnis'. (For more on Köchel and his catalogue, see 'Mozart Literature: Köchel-Verzeichnis', pp. 418–19.) Only a few years earlier, in 1856–9, Breitkopf & Härtel had issued a four-volume Mozart biography by the classical scholar Otto Jahn (1813–69). This second work, likewise by an 'outsider', together with Köchel's monumental index of autographs, copies and editions, laid the foundation on which to build the first complete Mozart edition.

In a hand-written codicil to his will on 12 April 1874, Köchel explains that for many years he had occupied himself with 'realizing a complete edition of Mozart's work'; he sketches his negotiations in the first place with Breitkopf & Härtel (at that time not yet beyond the planning stage) and stipulates that one-third of the total costs of the Leipzig publisher would be paid from an anonymous donation guaranteed by Köchel himself. Köchel, who in the codicil reveals himself as the anonymous donor, goes on to enumerate in four points in what form and towards what purpose the anonymously guaranteed subvention should be paid out after his death. In a 'postscript' to the codicil he reports that in April 1876 Breitkopf had solicited subscribers for the complete edition and writes: 'on 4 September 1876 I assured them in writing of this guaranteed subscription: through Dr L.R. v. Köchel, an admirer of Mozart in Vienna would send to Leipzig 15,000 Gulden Austrian currency (= 10,000 Reichsthaler) in ten six-month instalments of 1,500 Gulden Austrian currency at the beginning of September and March of each year'. Annotations referring to the transfer of the first two instalments (4 September 1876 and 3 March 1877) end the postscript to the codicil.

The Proceedings of the Internationale Stiftung Mozarteum in Salzburg record that on 26 February 1875 'preliminary steps had been successfully taken towards the publication of the complete edition of the works of W.A. Mozart'. On 10 March, the President of the Stiftung, Karl Freiherr von Sterneck-Daublebsky, arranged for a meeting the following day in the Chiemsee-Hof, seat of the state government of Salzburg. Constituting the first order of business was the 'Question of the publication of Mozart's works'. The reason for this most decisive meeting was a letter of 3 March 1875 from Köchel in Vienna to the Internationale Mozartstiftung, sent in response to a written request from Salzburg a week earlier (27 February) seeking Köchel's 'Opinion on a complete critical edition of Mozart's works'. The scholar begins his letter with the familiar, and still thoroughly applicable, words: 'It has long been my unshakable belief that one can do no higher honour to a man of great genius than through an accurate edition of his complete works.' After reporting in his letter the steps he had already taken towards this complete edition, not only with respect to content but also financially (whereupon he enters into the details of his negotiations with Breitkopf), he concludes: 'I can but reiterate, I can think of no finer or worthier mission of the Internationale Mozartstiftung than that of vigorously supporting the undertaking of the publication of Mozart's works, such as that already auspiciously begun by the firm of Breitkopf & Härtel, which promises the utmost success in its future development. [Here Köchel is probably referring to the publication mentioned earlier in his letter, and also earlier in this essay, of the eight-volume, full-score edition of the more substantial operas, beginning with *Idomeneo*.] Nor would it be any less gratifying to me to think that by this representation of the facts I have to the best of my ability furthered this honourable undertaking.' Undoubtedly on the strength of this statement from Köchel the Mozartstiftung decided on 11 March 1875 to patronize and to support the AMA. Although the project was additionally sponsored by, among others, the imperial houses in Vienna and Berlin, the first volume (Series I: Masses, volume 1) was to be dedicated to the 'magnanimous patroness' in Salzburg.

As mentioned above, the publisher Breitkopf & Härtel had issued a prospectus in April 1876 soliciting subscriptions to 'Mozart's Works', the director of the firm, Dr. Jur. Hermann Härtel (b. 1803), having decided shortly before his death on 4 August 1875 in favour of proceeding with the edition. Although the official term of publication

and first delivery was 'January 1877', the first instalment had already been printed by December 1876 (this is deduced from a letter of 15 December from Breitkopf to the Mozartstiftung in Salzburg). Among the works delivered were the masses K.49/47d and K.65/61a (Series I/1, edited by Franz Espagne) and the songs (Series III, edited by Gustav Nottebohm).

Ludwig Ritter von Köchel in every respect played the role of energetic and successful initiator of the AMA, but with the deliberate intention of remaining behind the scenes. Lending materials from his own collection, he placed at the disposal of the publisher and the individual editors over 150 valuable score copies of Mozart's works, which were in turn used for the emendation of the musical texts laid before the engraver. He likewise co-operated, in the brief period remaining to him, as 'Inspector' of the edition, as the active editors affectionately named him. Among these editors were: Johannes Brahms, Franz Espagne, Joseph Joachim, Gustav Nottebohm, Carl Reinecke, Julius Rietz, Ernst Rudorff, Philipp Spitta, Paul Graf von Waldersee and Franz Wüllner.

The main corpus of the edition was completed in a brief seven years (Köchel himself had projected a completion period of only five years!), a scholarly, organizational and technical achievement of the first order, and one scarcely conceivable today. Yet what is lacking above all in the AMA is a unified editorial principle. And although one must classify the edition as a scholarly–critical edition, it is nevertheless not always quite clear in individual instances what is actually the original in the way of musical text and what is editorial emendation. The critical reports (*Revisionsberichte*) likewise do not always help to clarify the situation, for what one editor thought worth reporting in the way of emendation, another editor took for granted, entering without comment his revision of the musical text. Especially lamentable is the fact that the critical reports to Series VIII (symphonies) and XIII to XXII (chamber music and keyboard music, including the keyboard concertos) offer only an 'Index of the original manuscripts consulted', and this in list form, thus making impossible a critical verification of the musical text.

The Neue Mozart-Ausgabe (NMA)
Aside from these frustrating shortcomings (at least by modern standards), the AMA lags behind the present state of knowledge of Mozart's music inasmuch as research has not stood still since the termination of this first complete edition. The *oeuvre* has remained essentially the same, but in a few cases has altered quite substantially: unknown works have come to light; others have proved to be spurious or doubtful. The status of the sources has altered, in some cases for the worse, for instance where an autograph is no longer accessible, but in some cases

also for the better: autographs once believed to be lost have again come to light (partly in connection with the ongoing researches of the NMA). Looking beyond the autographs, critical source studies have cast a completely new light on the transmission of Mozart's works in copies and early editions. New knowledge has also been gained with regard to the chronology of the works, not only as a result of the successive editions of the *Köchel-Verzeichnis* (up to the sixth edition of 1964), but also, more recently, from the pioneering researches of Wolfgang Plath (handwriting analysis) and Alan Tyson (paper and watermark studies). A new scholarly–critical edition of the collected works of Mozart has been the inevitable result.

The first steps in this direction were taken as early as 1940–41 by the Internationale Stiftung Mozarteum in Salzburg, but its plans were to be thwarted by the Second World War as it spread throughout Europe. At the end of the war, in 1945, the Stiftung revived its discussions and after long deliberation finally announced in the *Mozart-Jahrbuch 1953* (issued 1954) the beginning of the 'New Mozart-Edition'. The title in full was to read: *Wolfgang Amadeus Mozart. Neue Ausgabe sämtlicher Werke, in Verbindung mit den Mozartstädten Augsburg, Salzburg und Wien herausgegeben von der Internationalen Stiftung Mozarteum Salzburg*. Together with the slightly older *Neue Bach-Ausgabe*, the NMA stands at the head of what has now come to be known as the 'hour of the complete edition' (Karl Vötterle, 1956). Its first volumes began appearing in 1955; its first Editor-in-Chief, until his premature death at the beginning of 1960, was the Haydn and Mozart scholar Ernst Fritz Schmid.

The scholarly and editorial work of the edition is carried out largely in the two Mozart cities Augsburg and Salzburg. At Bärenreiter-Verlag in Kassel, to which the publication of the edition is entrusted, this south German–Austrian element remains manifest. The founder of the publishing house was Karl Vötterle (1903–75), who set up its original headquarters in Augsburg, the city of his and Leopold Mozart's birth. In 1927 he transferred the venture to Kassel and there led the firm to international fame. Working with such people as Friedrich Gehmacher (1900–76) and Richard Spängler of the Internationale Stiftung Mozarteum Salzburg, Vötterle was likewise to found and to guide with great effect the activities of the *Neue Mozart-Ausgabe*. Through the ensuing co-operative effort of Bärenreiter-Verlag and the Stiftung Mozarteum, the productive capacity of the NMA was placed on a firm footing. In 1960 the editorial direction was handed over to Wolfgang Plath and Wolfgang Rehm, joined in 1973 by Rudolph Angermüller (until 1980) and Dietrich Berke. The financial backing of the edition has been guaranteed by the *Pro Mozart* campaign initiated by the Stiftung Mozarteum. Past and active contributors to this campaign include private individuals and foundations (until the middle of the 1970s, first and foremost the Volkswagen Foundation) and public enterprises in Austria and the German Democratic Republic. The German Federal Republic plays an even more special role: through an academic programme, the federal government and the free state of Bavaria share in equal measure the financial burden of furthering the musicological work of the NMA.

The NMA aims to be an historical–critical edition and to offer as such the latest state of philological–musicological procedure as well as practical knowledge (particularly with regard to performance) of Mozart's creative production. From the beginning, the new edition set itself the goal of serving in equal measure both theory and practice. Contrary to its predecessor, the AMA, which was virtually exclusively oriented toward the scholarly, the NMA has gained a new and vital voice. It caters for the requirements arising out of the new attitude developed towards performance in the course of the present century, to which the term 'faithful to the work' might be applied. As a performance ideal, faithfulness to the work is realizable only when editions reproducing the unadulterated wishes of the composer are made available.

With 130 projected volumes divided into 10 series representing 34 categories of compositions, the greatest portion of the NMA is already complete (by 1989, 114 volumes, including 12 volumes from the Supplement, Series X, and 54 critical reports, issued separately, had been published). By 1991, the bicentenary of Mozart's death, the main corpus should be completed: this includes 105 volumes in Series I–IX and 15 of the projected volumes in the Supplement. This will be followed in the ensuing decade by the remaining outstanding volumes of the Supplement, as well as by the remaining critical reports to the volumes already published.

The editing and realization of the NMA (and the same holds true for all editions of similar scope), call for a planning schedule consisting of the following stages:

– The content of the individual volumes is fixed.
– With respect to the actual editing, detailed guidelines are formulated. At the present time, these include some thirty pages of close-set type, which serve the individual editors as guiding principles and aim to ensure the highest degree of uniformity within the edition itself.
– For each work, all accessible sources, that is, autographs, copies, first editions, early editions and printed libretti, are entered in a card file and reproductions are ordered from the libraries, archives or private collectors. When the NMA is eventually complete, there will exist for future Mozart researchers a virtually lacuna-free source archive in the form of microfilms and photocopies.
– For each volume an elaborate source index is drawn up from the card file (whose information is perpetually updated and expanded). This, together with the relevant microfilms or photocopies, is then placed at

the disposal of the assigned editor. As far as possible, this source catalogue conveys information about the quality of the sources and their relationship to one another.

– Before printing of the manuscript, the editorial direction examines and, if necessary, corrects the text on the basis of the relevant source materials.

– Before final publication, the assigned editor and editorial direction alike must undertake the burdensome responsibility of once more proof-reading the whole.

Among the additional tasks of the NMA is the clarification of encroaching scholarly problems, such as the question of authenticity, or of chronology as related to analyses of Mozart's handwriting and musical notation from various phases of his creative career. Other peripheral aspects of the edition include the recognition and sorting of the numerous sketches, fragments and drafts which Mozart, contrary to what is usually assumed about his creative activity, left behind.

Just how far-reaching the problem of authenticity is can be demonstrated by the fact that in addition to the more than six hundred unequivocally authentic works by Mozart, there are approximately a further four hundred which are spurious or only loosely attributed to Mozart and handed down only in peripheral sources. In the NMA itself this almost unmanageably large complex of questions can be dealt with only in a few chosen, but significant, instances, in the Supplement volumes, reserved expressly for 'Works of doubtful authenticity'. Sheltered in this expansive Supplement are areas of research long hidden from view, such as the topic of 'Mozart as arranger of works by other composers' or 'Mozart as teacher'. The supplementary volumes that have already appeared have forced these topics into the theoretical and practical consciousness just as the two documentary NMA volumes of pictures and text have shed light on some of the more obscure aspects of Mozart's life. These and the seven-volume edition of the Mozart family correspondence, a sort of 'literary companion' to the *Neue Mozart-Ausgabe*, have well laid the foundation for a new biographical treatment of Mozart. Of the still outstanding supplementary volumes, three comprehensive studies falling under the general heading 'Documentation of the autograph tradition' deserve special mention, namely: a facsimile edition, with commentary, of Mozart's own handwritten thematic catalogue of his works (1784–91); a catalogue of watermarks found in the papers of Mozart's autographs; and an analysis of Mozart's handwriting, arranged according to chronological criteria.

Like every scholarly undertaking, work on the NMA requires stamina, diligence, insight, imagination, a sense of responsibility and, most especially, the courage to take a stand, not only in the matter of textual interpretation but also in that of musical taste. At the same time, of course, one runs the risk of coming face to face with one's own deficiencies. In his 'Betrachtungen im Sinne der Wanderer', the first collection of aphorisms at the conclusion of Book II of *Wilhelm Meisters Wanderjahre*, Goethe describes the pursuit of the philologist, and in the process gently works his way round to this question of inner struggle. With Goethe's familiar but forever enduring 'philological maxim', the present contribution to the printed tradition of Mozart's works draws to a close:

The philologist is dependent on the congruity of the written tradition. He takes as his point of departure a manuscript; within are substantial lacunae, scribal errors which obscure the meaning, and all the other usual complaints characteristic of a manuscript. Now he finds a second copy, a third; by comparing them, he approaches ever closer the intelligence and sense of the thing handed down. Now he goes even further and demands of his intuitive faculty that, independent of secondary resources, it be ever more capable of grasping and disclosing the congruity of the subject treated. Because this, moreover, requires an especial tact, an especial absorption in his departed author, and a certain degree of ingenuity, one can scarcely blame the philologist when in matters of taste he ventures a judgment which nevertheless will sometimes fail him.

WOLFGANG REHM
(Translated by Faye Ferguson)

Select Bibliography

Bibliographies and catalogues

Angermüller, R. and Schneider, O., *Mozart-Bibliographie (bis 1970)*. (*Mozart-Jahrbuch*), Kassel, 1976. *Mozart-Bibliographie 1971–1975, mit Nachträgen zur Mozart-Bibliographie bis 1970*. Kassel, 1978. *Mozart-Bibliographie 1976–1980, mit Nachträgen zur Mozart-Bibliographie bis 1975*. Kassel, 1982

Keller, O., *Wolfgang Amadeus Mozart: Bibliographie und Ikonographie*. Berlin, 1927

Köchel, L. Ritter von, *Chronologisch-thematisches Verzeichnis sämtlicher Tonwerke Wolfgang Amadé Mozarts*. Leipzig, 1862; 1937 ed. A. Einstein, with suppl. 3/1947; 6/1964 ed. F. Giegling, A. Weinmann and G. Sievers, rev. 1984

——, *Der kleine Köchel*. Ed. H. von Hase. Wiesbaden, 1951

Mozart, W.A., *Verzeichnüss aller meiner Werke*. Facsimile ed. O.E. Deutsch. Vienna, 1938; Eng. edn, 1956. Also ed. E. Müller von Asow, Vienna, 1943, 2/1956

Neue Mozart-Ausgabe, 'Verzeichnis der verschollenen Mozart-Autographe der ehemaligen Preussischen Staatsbibliothek Berlin (BB)', in *Bericht über die Mitarbeitertagung in Kassel 29.–30 Mai 1981* (private printing, 1984)

Periodicals

Acta Mozartiana. Ed. E. Valentin, Augsburg, 1954–

Allgemeine musikalische Zeitung. Leipzig, 1798–1849

Mitteilungen der Internationalen Stiftung Mozarteum. Ed. G. Rech and R. Angermüller, Salzburg, 1952–

Mitteilungen für die Mozartgemeinde in Berlin. Berlin, 1895, 1900–12, 1925–

Mozart-Jahrbuch. Ed. H. Abert, Munich, 1923–4, 1929

Mozart-Jahrbuch des Zentralinstituts für Mozartforschung der Internationalen Stiftung Mozarteum. Ed. G. Rech, 1951–; ed. R. Angermüller and others, 1976– . Salzburg, 1951–

Mozarteums Mitteilungen. Ed. R. Lewicki, Salzburg, 1918/19–1920/21

Neues Mozart-Jahrbuch. Ed. E. Valentin, Regensburg, 1941–3

Letters

Anderson, E., ed., *The Letters of Mozart and his Family*. London, 1938; rev. 2nd edn by A.H. King and M. Carolan. London, 1966; rev. 3rd edn by S. Sadie and F. Smart, London, 1985

Bauer, W.A., Deutsch, O.E., and Eibl, J.H., eds, *Mozart. Briefe und Aufzeichnungen*. Gesamtausgabe. 7 vols, Kassel etc., 1962–75

Müller von Asow, E., ed., *Gesamtausgabe der Briefe und Aufzeichnungen der Familie Mozart*. Berlin, 1942

Schiedermair, L., ed., *Die Briefe W.A. Mozarts und seiner Familie*. Erste kritische Ausgabe. 5 vols, Munich and Leipzig, 1914

Editions

W.A. Mozart: Neue Ausgabe sämtlicher Werke. Ed. Schmid, E.F., Plath, W. and Rehm, W. Internationale Stiftung Mozarteum Salzburg. Kassel, 1955–

W.A. Mozart: Neue Ausgabe sämtlicher Werke. Editionsrichtlinien musikalischer Denkmäler- und Gesamtausgaben. Kassel, 1967, pp.99–132 (commissioned by the Gesellschaft für Musikforschung, ed. G. von Dadelsen)

Neue Mozart-Ausgabe editions of the concertos: forewords by Flothuis, M. (V:15/1 and 4); Wolff, C. (V:15/2–3); Badura-Skoda, P. and E. (V:15/7); Rehm, W. (V:15/8); Mahling, C.H. (V:14/1–2); Giegling, F. (V:14/3–6)

Wolfgang Amadeus Mozart, The Six 'Haydn' Quartets: Facsimile of the Autograph Manuscripts in the British Library, Add. MS 37763. Introduction by Alan Tyson. British Library Music Facsimiles, 4 (London, 1985), pp.v–xv

Books and articles

Abert, A.A., 'Methoden der Mozartforschung', *Mozart-Jahrbuch 1964*, Salzburg, 1965, pp.22–7

Abert, H., *W.A. Mozart*. Neu bearbeitete und erweiterte Ausgabe von O. Jahns 'Mozart'. Leipzig, 1919. 3rd edn with index by E. Kaps. Leipzig, 1966

——, *Mozart's 'Don Giovanni'* (Eng. trans. extracted from above title). London, 1976

Albrecht, H., *Die Bedeutung der Zeichen Keil, Strich und Punkt bei Mozart (Fünf Lösungen einer Preisfrage) = Musikwissenschaftliche Arbeiten*, no.10, 1957

Algarotti, F., *Opere*. Livorno, 1763

Allanbrook, W.J., *Rhythmic Gesture in Mozart: Le nozze di Figaro and Don Giovanni*. Chicago, 1983

Allroggen, G., 'Zur Frage der Echtheit der Sinfonie KV Anh.216 = 74g', in *Wolfgang Amadeus Mozart*, ed. G. Croll. Darmstadt, 1977, pp.462–73

Alth, M. von and Obzyna, G., *Burgtheater 1776–1976: Aufführungen und Besetzungen von zweihundert Jahren*, 2 vols. Vienna, n.d.

Angermüller, R., 'Mozart und Metastasio', *Mitteilungen der Internationalen Stiftung Mozarteum*, 26 (1978), p.12

——, 'Ein grosser Genius kann nicht würdiger geehrt werden . . .': Die Neue Mozart-Ausgabe der Internationalen Stiftung Mozarteum: Eine Edition des Mainzer Akademien-Programms*. Mainz, 1984 (private printing)

——, *Figaro: Mit einem Beitrag von Wolfgang Pütz: 'Le Nozze di Figaro' auf dem Theater*. Salzburg, 1986

——, and Biba, O., *pro AMADEUS contra: Weiner Musikleben zur Zeit Mozarts und Salieris*. Munich, 1988

——, and Münster, R., eds, *Bayerische Staatsbibliothek, Wolfgang Amadeus Mozart: Idomeneo 1781–1981. Essays. Forschungsberichte*. Katalog. Munich, 1981

Arthur, J., and Schachter, C., '*Das Veilchen*: a commentary on the autograph and an analysis of the music', *Musical Times*, 130 (1989), 149–55

Autexier, Ph.A., *Mozart & Liszt sub Rosa*. Poitiers, 1984

——, 'Wann wurde die Maurerische Trauermusik uraufgeführt', *Mozart-Jahrbuch 1984/5*, Salzburg, 1985, pp.6–8

——, 'Les Quatuors de Mozart dédiés à Joseph Haydn', *L'Education musicale*, 327 (April) 1986

——, *Mozart, chronologie, l'oeuvre, dictionnaire*. Paris, 1987a

——, 'La Musique maçonnique', *Dix-huitième siècle*, 19 (1987b), pp.97–104

Babitz, S., 'Modern Errors in Mozart Performance', *Mozart-Jahrbuch 1967*, Salzburg, 1968, pp.62–89

Bach, C.P.E., *Versuch über die wahre Art das Clavier zu spielen* (Berlin, i, 1753; ii, 1762; i and ii repr. 1957). Eng. trans. W.J. Mitchell as *Essay on the True Art of Playing Keyboard Instruments*, New York, 1949; repr. London, 1974

Badura-Skoda, Eva and Paul, 'Zur Echtheit von Mozarts Sarti-Variationen KV.460', *Mozart-Jahrbuch 1959*, Salzburg, 1960, pp.127–39

——, *Mozart-Interpretation*. Vienna, 1957. Eng. trans. L. Black as *Interpreting Mozart on the Keyboard*, London, 1962; repr. 1970

Ballin, E.A., *Der Dichter von Mozarts Freimaurerlied 'O heiliges Band' und das erste erhaltene deutsche Freimaurerliederbuch*. Tutzing, 1960

——, ed., *Wolfgang Amadeus Mozart: Neue Ausgabe sämtlicher Werke*, Serie III. Werkgruppe 8: Lieder. Kassel, etc., 1963; Kritischer Bericht, 1964

——, *Das Wort-Ton-Verhältnis in den klavierbegleiteten Liedern W.A. Mozarts*. Kassel, 1984

Bär, C., 'Die "Musique vom Robinig"', *Mitteilungen der Internationalen Stiftung Mozarteum*, 9 (1960), pp.6–11

——, 'Zum Begriff des "Basso" in Mozarts Serenaden', *Mozart-Jahrbuch 1960/61*, Salzburg, 1961, pp.133–55

——, *Mozart: Krankheit-Tod-Begräbnis*. 2nd edn, Salzburg, 1972

——, 'Er war . . . kein guter Wirth', *Acta Mozartiana*, 25 (1978), Heft 2, pp.30–53

Bauer-Lechner, N., *Recollections of Gustav Mahler*. Eng. trans. D. Newlin. Cambridge, 1980

Bauman, T., *North German Opera in the Age of Goethe*. Cambridge, 1985

——, *Die Entführung aus dem Serail*. Cambridge, 1987

Beales, D., *Joseph II: i. In the Shadow of Maria Theresia, 1741–1780*. Cambridge, 1987

Benn, C., *Mozart on the Stage*. With an introduction by Richard Capell. London, 1946

Berke, D., 'Nochmals zum Fragment eines Streichtrio-Satzes in G-dur KV Anh.66 (562e)', *Acta Mozartiana*, 29 (1982), pp.42–7

Berlioz, H., *The Memoirs of Berlioz*. Translated and edited by D. Cairns. London, 1969

Beyer, F., 'Mozarts Komposition zum Requiem. Zur Frage der Ergänzung', *Acta Mozartiana* 18 (1971), Heft 2, pp.27–33

Biba, O., '(W.A.M.) Accompagnato-Rezitativ zu einer Arie von Domenico Cimarosa . . . als Einlage für die Oper "La quacquera spiritosa" von Pietro Guglielmi (1728–1804) "No caro fà corraggio"', Item 1563 Cat. *Österreich zur Zeit Kaiser Josephs II*. Melk, 1980

——, 'Par Monsieur François Comte de Walsegg', *Mitteilungen der Internationalen Stiftung Mozarteum*, 29 (1981), pp.34–40

Bilson, M., 'Some General Thoughts on Ornamentation in Mozart's Keyboard Works', *Piano Quarterly*, 95 (1976), p.26

Blom, E., *Mozart*. London, 1955

Blomhert, B., *The Harmoniemusik of 'Die Entführung aus dem Serail' by Wolfgang Amadeus Mozart: study about its authenticity and critical edition*. Diss., Utrecht, 1987

Blume, F., 'The Concertos (1): Their Sources', in *The Mozart Companion*, ed. H.C.R. Landon and D. Mitchell. London, 1956, pp.200–33

Branscombe, P., ed., *Die Zauberflöte*. Cambridge, forthcoming

Brook, B.S., general ed., *The Symphony, 1720–1840*, Series B, Vol. VII: Franz Asplmayr, Three symphonies, ed. D.C. Monk; Leopold Hofmann, Four symphonies, ed. G. Cook Kimball; Wenzel Pichl, Three symphonies, ed. A. Zakin. Salzburg Part I,

Leopold Mozart, Three symphonies, ed. C. Eisen. New York, 1984

Brophy, B., *Mozart the Dramatist*. London, 1964; rev. edn 1988

Brown, M., 'Mozart's Songs for Voice and Piano', *Music Review*, 17 (1956), pp.19ff

Bruford, W.H., *Germany in the Eighteenth Century*. Cambridge, 1959

Brunner, F., *Das Klavierklangideal Mozarts und die Klaviere seiner Zeit*. Augsburg, 1933

Caflisch, L., and Fehr, M., *Der junge Mozart in Zürich. Ein Beitrag zur Mozart-Biographie auf Grund bisher unbekannter Dokumente* (140. Neujahrsblatt der allg. Musikgesellschaft Zürich auf das Jahr 1952). Zurich, 1952

Caldwell, J., *Editing Early Music*. London, 1985

Carse, A., *The Orchestra in the 18th Century*. Cambridge, 1940

Carter, T., ed., *Le nozze di Figaro*. Cambridge, 1987

Chailley, J., *Musique et ésotérisme: 'La Flûte enchantée', opéra maçonnique*. Paris, 1968; rev. edn 1975. Eng. trans. H. Weinstock, New York, 1971

Chantavoine, J., *Mozart dans Mozart*. Paris, 1948

Chesnut, J.H., 'Mozart's teaching of intonation', *Journal of the American Musicological Society*, 30 (1977), no.2, pp.254–71

Curzon, H. de, *Essai de bibliographie mozartienne*. Revue critique des ouvrages relatifs à W.A. Mozart et ses oeuvres. Paris, 1906

Da Ponte, L., *An extract from the life of Lorenzo Da Ponte, with the history of several dramas written by him, and among others 'Il Figaro', 'Il Don Giovanni' and 'La scuola degli amanti' set to music by Mozart*. New York, 1819.

——, *Memoirs of Lorenzo Da Ponte*. Eng. trans. E. Abbott, New York, 1967

Davies, P.J., 'Mozart's illness and death', *Journal of the Royal Society of Medicine*, 76 (1983), pp.776–85, and *Musical Times*, 125 (1984), pp. 437–42, 554–61

——, 'Mozart's Manic-Depressive Tendencies', *Musical Times*, 128 (1987), pp.123–6 and 191–6

——, *Mozart in Person: his character and his health*, Westport, Conn., and London, 1989

Deininger, H.F., *Die Deutsche Schauspielergesellschaft unter der Direktion von Johann Heinrich Böhm, einem Freunde der Familie Mozart, in Augsburg in den Jahren 1779 und 1780 = Augsburger Mozartbuch: Zeitschrift des historischen Vereins für Schwaben*, 55/56 (1942/3)

Delacroix, E., *Journal 1822–1863*. Paris, 1981

Dennerlein, H., *Der unbekannte Mozart. Die Welt seiner Klavierwerke*. Leipzig, 1951

Dent, E.J., *Mozart's Operas: a Critical Study*. London, 1913; rev. edn 1947; 3rd edn 1955

Deutsch, O.E., *Mozart und die Wiener Logen. Zur Geschichte seiner Freimaurer-Kompositionen*. Vienna, 1932

——, *Mozart und seine Welt in zeitgenössischen Bildern*. Originated by M. Zenger. Kassel etc., 1961a

——, *W.A. Mozart. Neue Ausgabe sämtlicher Werke. Serie X: Supplement, Werkgruppe 34. Mozart. Die Dokumente seines Lebens*. Ed. O.E. Deutsch. Kassel etc., 1961b. Eng. trans. *Mozart. A Documentary Biography* by E. Blom, P. Branscombe and J. Noble, London, 2nd edn 1966

——, *W.A. Mozart. Neue Ausgabe sämtlicher Werke. Serie X: Supplement, Werkgruppe 31: Nachträge Bd.1 Addenda und Corrigenda zu Mozart. Die Dokumente seines Lebens*. Ed. J.H. Eibl. Kassel etc., 1978

Dickson, P.G.M., *Finance and Government under Maria Theresia 1740–1780*. Oxford, 1987

Dies, A.C., *Biographische Nachrichten von Joseph Haydn*. Vienna, 1810; rev. edn H. Seeger, Berlin, 1959

Dunning, A., 'Mozart's Kanons', *Mozart-Jahrbuch 1971/2*, Salzburg, 1973, pp.227–40

Eckelmeyer, J., 'Structure as a hermeneutic guide to The Magic Flute', *Musical Quarterly*, 72 (1986), pp.51–73

Eibl, J.H., 'Süssmayr und Constanze', *Mozart-Jahrbuch 1976/7*, Kassel etc., 1978, pp.277–80

——, 'Kirchenmusik in den Mozartschen Familienbriefen', *Mozart-Jahrbuch 1978/9*, Kassel etc., 1979, pp.18–21

Einstein, A., *Mozart: His Character, his Work*. Eng. trans. A Mendel and N. Broder, New York, 1945; London, 1946

Eisen, C., 'Some Lost Mozart Editions of the 1780s', *Mitteilungen der Internationalen Stiftung Mozarteum*, 32 (1984), pp.64–70

——, 'Contributions to a New Mozart Documentary Biography', *Journal of the American Musicological Society*, 39 (1986), pp.615–32

——, 'New Light on Mozart's "Linz" Symphony, K.425', *Journal of the Royal Musical Association*, 113 (1988a), pp.81–96

——, 'The Symphonies of Leopold Mozart: their Chronology, Style and Importance for the Study of Mozart's Earliest Symphonies', *Mozart-Jahrbuch 1987/8*, Salzburg, 1988b, pp.181–93

——, Review of Alan Tyson, *Mozart: Studies of the Autograph Scores* (Cambridge, Mass., and London, 1987), *Music & Letters*, 70 (1989a), pp. 101–4

——, 'Salzburg 1750–1803', in *The Classical Era*, ed. N. Zaslaw (vol.5 of *Man and Music*, general ed. S. Sadie). London, and Englewood Cliffs, 1989b, pp.166–87

——, 'Problems of Authenticity Among Mozart's Early Symphonies: the examples of K.Anh.220 (16a) and 76 (42a)', *Music & Letters*, 70 (1989c), pp.505–16

Federhofer, H., 'Probleme der Echtheitsbestimmung der kleineren kirchenmusikalischen Werke W.A. Mozarts', *Mozart-Jahrbuch 1958*, Salzburg, 1959, pp.97ff, and [for continuation] *Mozart-Jahrbuch 1960/61*, Salzburg, 1961, pp.43ff

Federhofer-Königs, R., 'Mozarts Lauretanische Litaneien KV 109 (74e) und 195 (186d)', *Mozart-Jahrbuch 1967*, Salzburg, 1968, pp.111–20

——, 'Mozartiana im Musikaliennachlass von Ferdinand Bischoff', *Mozart-Jahrbuch 1965/6*, Salzburg, 1967, pp.15–38

Fehr, M., *Die Familie Mozart in Zürich*. Zurich, 1942

Feicht, H., 'Die Kenntnis Mozarts in Polen', in *Bericht über den Internationalen Musikwissenschaftlichen Kongress Wien Mozartjahr 1956*, ed. E. Schenk. Graz, 1958, pp.191–4

Fellerer, K.G., 'Mozarts Kirchenmusik und ihre liturgischen Voraussetzungen', *Mozart-Jahrbuch 1978/9*, Kassel etc., 1979, pp.22–6

——, *Die Kirchenmusik W.A. Mozarts*. Laaber, 1985

Fellinger, I., 'Brahms' View of Mozart', in *Brahms*, ed. R. Pascall. Cambridge, 1983, pp.41–57

Ferguson, F., 'Mozart's Keyboard Concertos: Tutti Notations and Performance Models', *Mozart-Jahrbuch 1984/5*, Kassel etc., 1986, pp.32–9

Ferguson, H., *Keyboard Interpretation from the 14th to the 19th Century, an introduction*. London, 1975

Finscher, L., 'Aspects of Mozart's Compositional Process in the Quartet Autographs: I. The Early Quartets; II. The Genesis of K.387', in *The String Quartets of Haydn, Mozart and Beethoven: Studies of the Autograph Manuscripts*, ed. C. Wolff. Cambridge, Mass., 1980, pp.121–53

Fischer, K. von, 'Sind die Klaviervariationen über Sartis "Come un'agnello" von Mozart?', *Mozart-Jahrbuch 1958*, Salzburg, 1959, pp.18–29

——, 'Sind die Klaviervariationen KV.460 von Mozart?', *Mozart-Jahrbuch 1959*, Salzburg, 1960, pp.140–45

——, '"COME UN'AGNELLO – Aria del SIGr SARTI con Variazioni"', *Mozart-Jahrbuch 1978/9*, Salzburg, 1979, pp.112–21

Flothuis, M., 'Mozarts Bearbeitung eigener und fremder Werke', *Mitteilungen der Internationalen Stiftung Mozarteum*, 2 (1969)

——, 'Neue Erkenntnisse in Bezug auf Mozarts Tanzmusik', *Mitteilungen der Internationalen Stiftung Mozarteum*, 28 (1980a), Doppelheft 3/4, pp.12–15

——, 'A Close Reading of the Autographs of Mozart's Ten Late Quartets', in *The String Quartets of Haydn, Mozart and Beethoven: Studies of the Autograph Manuscripts*, ed. C. Wolff, Cambridge, Mass., 1980b, pp.154–73

Forman, D., *Mozart's Concerto Form: The First Movements of the Piano Concertos*. London and New York, 1971

Galeazzi, F., *Elementi teorico-pratici di musica*. 2 vols. Rome, 1791–6

Geminiani, F., *The Art of Playing on the Violin*. London, 1751; facs. edn D. Boyden, Oxford, 1952

Gerbert, M., *De Cantu et Musica Sacra a prima ecclesiae aetate usque ad praesens tempus*. Monasterium Sancti Blasii, 1774

German, F., *Mickiewicz i Mozart*. Katowice, 1971

Gianturco, C., *Le opere del giovane Mozart*. Pisa, 1976; 2nd edn rev. 1978. Eng. trans. as *Mozart's Early Operas*, London, 1981

Girdlestone, C.M. *Mozart et ses concertos pour piano*. Paris, 1939. Eng. trans. by the author as *Mozart's Piano Concertos*, London, 1948; rev. edn New York, 1964

Goethe, J.W. von, *Italienische Reise*. Stuttgart and Tübingen, 1816; Weimar, 1886. Eng. trans. by W.H. Auden and E. Mayer, 1963

Gottron, A., *Mozart und Mainz*. Mainz, 1951

——, 'Wie spielte Mozart die Adagios seiner Klavierkonzerte?', *Musikforschung*, 13 (1960), p.334

Grimm, F.M. von, *Correspondance littéraire* etc. Paris, 1877–82; Munich, 1977

Haas, R., *Bach und Mozart in Wien*. Vienna, 1951

Haberkamp, G., *Die Erstdrucke der Werke von Wolfgang Amadeus Mozart. Musikbibliographische Arbeiten Bd.10/I*. Tutzing, 1986. Vol.I; Textband, Vol.II: Bildband

Hadamowsky, F., *Die Wiener Hoftheater (Staatstheater) 1776–1966: i, 1776–1810*. Vienna, 1966

Harmon, R., 'The Performance of Mozart's Church Sonatas', *Music & Letters*, 34 (1970), p.51

Hausswald, G., *Mozarts Serenaden: Ein Beitrag zur Stilkritik des 18. Jahrhunderts*. Leipzig, 1951. Nachdruck mit einem Vorwort und einer neuen Bibliographie von E. Kroher, Wilhelmshaven, 1975

Heartz, D., 'The Genesis of Mozart's "Idomeneo"', *Mozart-Jahrbuch 1967*, Salzburg, 1968, pp.150–64. Repr. in *Musical*

Quarterly, 55/1 (1969), pp.1–19

——, 'Thomas Attwood's Lessons in Composition with Mozart', *Proceedings of the Royal Musical Association*, 100 (1973/4), pp.175–83

——, 'Mozart and his Italian Contemporaries: La Clemenza di Tito', *Mozart-Jahrbuch 1978/9*, Kassel etc., 1978, pp.275–93

——, 'Goldoni, Don Giovanni and the dramma giocoso', *Musical Times*, 120 (1979), pp.993–8

——, 'La Clemenza di Sarastro', *Musical Times*, 124 (1983), pp.152–7

Hess, E., 'Ist das Fagottkonzert KV Anhang 230a von Mozart?', *Mozart-Jahrbuch 1957*, Salzburg, 1958, pp.223–32

——, 'Die "Varianten" im Finale des Streichquintettes KV 593', *Mozart-Jahrbuch 1960/61*, Salzburg, 1961, pp.68–77

Heuberger, R., *Erinnerungen an Johannes Brahms*, ed. K. Hofmann. Tutzing, 1971

Hildesheimer, W., *Mozart*. Frankfurt a.M., 1977. Eng. trans. M. Faber, New York, 1982; London, 1983

Hiller, J.A., *Anweisung zum musikalisch-zierlichen Gesange*. Leipzig, 1780. Facs. edn, Leipzig, 1976

Hirsch, P., 'A Mozart Problem', *Music & Letters*, 25 (1944), p.209

Holmes, E., *The Life of Mozart, Including his Correspondence*. London, 1845; repr. 1932

Holschneider, A., 'C.Ph.E. Bachs Kantate "Auferstehung und Himmelfahrt Jesu" und Mozarts Aufführung des Jahres 1788', *Mozart-Jahrbuch 1968/70*, Salzburg, 1971, pp.264–80

Hutchings, A., *A Companion to the Mozart Piano Concertos*. London, 1948; 2nd edn 1950, repr.1989

——, *Mozart: The Man, The Musician*. London, 1976

Jahn, O., *W.A. Mozart*. Leipzig, 1856; 2nd edn 1867; 3rd edn by H. Deiters, 1889–91; 4th edn by H. Deiters 1905–7. Eng. trans. P. Townsend, London, 1882 and 1891

John, N., ed., *Opera Guide 22: Così fan tutte*. London, 1983

Keller, H., *Phrasierung und Artikulation*, Kassel, 1955

Kelly, M., *Reminiscences of Michael Kelly*, London, 1826; new edn, R. Fiske, London, 1975

Keys, I., *Mozart: His Music in his Life*. London, 1980

King, A.H., *Mozart in Retrospect*. London, 1955; rev. edn 1970, repr. 1976

——, *Mozart Chamber Music*. London, 1968; rev. edn 1986

——, *Mozart Wind and String Concertos*. London, 1978; 2nd edn 1986

——, *A Mozart Legacy: Aspects of the British Library Collections*. London, 1984a

——, 'The Mozarts at the British Museum', *Festschrift Albi Rosenthal*, ed. R. Elvers (Tutzing, 1984b [1985]), pp.157–79

——, Review of Alan Tyson, *Mozart: Studies of the Autograph Scores*, in *The Journal of Musicological Research*, 8/3–4 (1989), pp.386–95

Kipp, W., *Mozart und das Elsass*. Colmar, 1941

Kirkendale, W., 'KV405: Ein unveröffentlichtes Mozart-Autograph', *Mozart-Jahrbuch 1962/3*, Salzburg, 1964, pp.140–55

——, 'More Slow Introductions to Fugues of J.S. Bach', *Journal of the American Musicological Society*, 17 (1964), pp.43–65

——, *Fuge und Fugato in der Kammermusik des Rokoko und der Klassik*. Tutzing, 1966; Eng. trans. (enlarged) 1979

Klafsky, A.M., 'Michael Haydn als Kirchenkomponist', *Studien zur Musikwissenschaft*, 3 (1915), p.5

Koch, H.C., *Musikalisches Lexikon*, Frankfurt a.M., 1802; facs. edn Hildesheim, 1969

Köchel, L. Ritter von, *Die Kaiserliche Hof-Musikkapelle in Wien von 1543 bis 1867*. Vienna, 1869; repr. 1976

Köhler, K-H., 'Die Erwerbung der Mozart-Autographe der Berliner Staatsbibliothek – ein Beitrag zur Geschichte des Nachlasses' *Mozart-Jahrbuch 1962/63*, Salzburg, 1964, pp.55–67

Kristek, J., ed., *Mozart's 'Don Giovanni' in Prague*. Prague, 1987

Kunze, S., 'Die Vertonungen der Arie "Non so d'onde viene" von J.Chr. Bach und von W.A. Mozart', *Analecta musicologica*, 2 (1965), p.85

——, 'Die Arie KV 621a von W.A. Mozart und Emilian Gottfried von Jacquin', *Mozart-Jahrbuch 1967*, Salzburg, 1968, pp.205–28

Kurth-Voigt, L.E., *Perspectives and Points of View: the early works of Wieland and their background*. Baltimore, 1974

Lach, R., *Mozart als Theoretiker*, Vienna, 1918

Landon, H.C.R., 'The Concertos (2): Their Musical Origin and Development', in *The Mozart Companion*, ed. H.C.R. Landon and D. Mitchell. London, 1956, pp.234–82

——, *Beethoven*. Zurich, 1970. Eng. edn London, 1970

——, *Haydn: Chronicle and Works*. 5 vols. London, 1976–80

——, *Mozart and the Masons: New Light on the Lodge 'Crowned Hope'*. London, 1982

——, *1791: Mozart's Last Year*. London, 1988

——, *Mozart: the Golden Years*. London and New York, 1989

——, and Mitchell, D., eds, *The Mozart Companion*. London, 1956; 2nd edn 1965

Lang, P.H., ed., *The Creative World of Mozart: studies by eminent scholars*. New York, 1963

Langegger, F., *Mozart: Vater und Sohn: Eine psychologische Untersuchung*. Zurich and Freiburg im Breisgau, 1978

——, 'Leopold Mozart als Persönlichkeit', *Mozart-Jahrbuch 1987/88*, Salzburg, 1988, pp.107–14

Larsen, J.P., and Wedin, K., eds, *Die Sinfonie KV 16a 'del Sigr. Mozart'*. Odense, 1987

LaRue, J., 'Symphony (I/10/ii)', in *The New Grove Dictionary of Music and Musicians*, ed. S. Sadie, London, 1980, pp.449–52

Layer, A., *Die Augsburger Künstlerfamilie Mozart*. Augsburg, 1971

——, *Eine Jugend in Augsburg: Leopold Mozart 1719–87*. Augsburg, 1975

Leeson, D.N., and Levin, R.D., 'On the Authenticity of K.Anh.C 14.01 (297b), a Symphonia Concertante for Four Winds and Orchestra', *Mozart-Jahrbuch 1976/77*, Kassel etc., 1978, pp.70–96

——, 'Mozart's Thematic Catalogue', *Musical Times*, 114 (1973), pp.781–3

Le Huray, P.G., and Day, J. eds, *Music and Aesthetics in the Eighteenth and Early-nineteenth Centuries*. Cambridge, 1981

Lesure, F., 'L'Oeuvre de Mozart en France de 1793 à 1810', in *Bericht über den Internationalen Musikwissenschaftlichen Kongress Wien Mozartjahr 1956*, ed. E. Schenk, Graz, 1958, pp.344–7

Levin, R.D., 'Mozarts Bläserkonzertante KV Anh.9/297B und ihre Rekonstruction im 19. und 20. Jahrhundert', *Mozart-Jahrbuch 1984/85*, Kassel etc., 1986, pp.187–207

——, *Who wrote the Mozart Four-wind Concertante?*, New York, 1988

Liebner, J., *Mozart on the Stage*. London, 1972

Lippmann, F., ed., *Mozart und Italien*, Colloquium Rom, 1974. Cologne, 1978

Lorenz, A., *W.A. Mozart als Klavierkomponist*, Breslau, 1866

Luin, E.J., 'Mozarts Opern in Skandinavien', in *Bericht über den Internationalen Musikwissenschaftlichen Kongress Wien Mozartjahr 1956*, ed. E. Schenk, Graz, 1958, pp.387–96

Lüthy, W., *Mozart und die Tonartencharacteristik*. Strassburg, 1931; 2nd edn, Baden-Baden, 1974

Macartney, C.A., *The Habsburg Empire 1790–1918*. London, 1968

MacIntyre, B.C., 'Haydn's Doubtful and Spurious Masses: an Attribution Update', *Haydn-Studien*, 5 (1982), pp.42ff

——, *The Viennese Concerted Mass of the Early Classic Period*, in Studies in Musicology 89, Ann Arbor, 1984

Mahling, C.H., 'Mozart und die Orchesterpraxis seiner Zeit', *Mozart-Jahrbuch 1967*, Salzburg, 1968, pp.229–43

——, 'Bemerkungen zum Violinkonzert D-dur KV 271i', *Mozart-Jahrbuch 1978/79*, Kassel etc., 1979, pp.252–68

Mann, W., *The Operas of Mozart*. London, 1977

Marguerre, K., 'Forte und Piano bei Mozart', *Neue Zeitschrift für Musik*, 128 (1967), p.153

Marpurg, F.W., *Die Kunst das Clavier zu spielen*. Berlin, 1750; 4th edn Berlin, 1762, repr.1969

——, *Anleitung zum Klavierspielen*. Berlin, 1755; 2nd edn Berlin, 1765; repr.1969

——, *Versuch über die musikalische Temperatur*. Breslau, 1776

Massin, J. and B., *Wolfgang Amadeus Mozart*. Paris, 1959

Matthäus, W., *Johann André Musikverlag zu Offenbach am Main: Verlagsgeschichte und Bibliographie 1772–1800*. Tutzing, 1973

Maunder, R., *Mozart's Requiem: On Preparing a New Edition*. Oxford, 1988

Melkus, E., 'Zur Auszierung der Da capo-Arien in Mozarts Werken', *Mozart-Jahrbuch 1968/70*, Salzburg, 1971, pp.159–85

——, Über die Ausführung der Stricharten in Mozarts Werken', *Mozart-Jahrbuch 1967*, Salzburg, 1968, pp.244–65

Mendel, A., ed., *Studies in the History of Musical Pitch*. Amsterdam, 1968

——, 'Pitch in Western Music Since 1500: a Re-examination', *Acta musicologica*, 1 (1978), 1

Meude-Monpas, J.J.O. de, *Dictionnaire de musique*. Paris, 1787

Meusel, J.G., *Teutsches Künstlerlexikon oder Verzeichnis der Jetztlebenden teutschen Künstler*. Lemgo, 1778

Michtner, O., *Das alte Burgtheater als Opernbühne*. (Theatergeschichte Österreichs, Band III: Wien, Heft 1), Vienna, 1970

Mies, P., 'Die Artikulationszeichen Strich und Punkt bei W.A. Mozart', *Musikforschung*, 11 (1958), pp.428–55

Milchmeyer, J.P., *Die wahre Art das Pianoforte zu spielen*. Dresden, 1797

Mishkin, H.G., 'Incomplete Notation in Mozart's Piano Concertos', *Musical Quarterly*, 61 (1975), pp.345–59

Moberley, R.B., *Three Mozart Operas; Figaro–Don Giovanni–The Magic Flute*. London and New York, 1967

Mohr, A.R., *Das Frankfurter Mozart-Buch*. Frankfurt a.M., 1968

Moore, J., *A View of Society and Manners in France, Switzerland and Germany*. London, 1779

Morin, G., 'Wolfgang Amadeus Mozart und Schweden', in *Bericht über den Internationalen Musikwissenschaftlichen Kongress Wien Mozartjahr 1956*, ed. E. Schenk, Graz, 1958, pp.416-20

Mozart, L., *Versuch einer gründlichen Violinschule*. Augsburg, 1756. Eng. trans. E. Knocker as *A Treatise on the Fundamental Principles of*

Violin Playing. London, 1948

Münster, R., 'Authentische Tempi zu den sechs letzten Sinfonien W.A. Mozarts', *Mozart-Jahrbuch 1962/63*, Salzburg, 1964, pp.185–99

——, 'Mozarts "Tantum ergerl" KV 142 und KV 197', *Acta Mozartiana*, 10 (1963), pp.54–61; continued 12 (1965), pp.9ff

——, 'Mozart bearbeitet Cannabich', *Festschrift Walter Senn zum 70. Geburtstag* (Munich and Salzburg, 1975), pp.142–57

Murr, C.G., 'Entwurf eines Verzeichnisses der besten jetzt lebenden Tonkünstler in Europa', *Journal zur Kunstgeschichte und zur allgemeinen Litteratur*. Nuremberg, 1776

Nagel, W., *Goethe und Mozart = Musikalisches Magazin*, Heft 8. Langensalza, 1904

Nettl, P., *Mozart und die königliche Kunst: Die freimaurerische Grundlage der 'Zauberflöte'*. Berlin, 1932

——, *Mozart in Böhmen*. Prague, 1938

——, *Goethe und Mozart: Eine Betrachtung*. Esslingen, 1949

Neumann, F., *Ornamentation and Improvisation in Mozart*. Princeton, 1986

Niemetschek, F.X., *Leben der k.k. Kapellmeisters Wolfgang Gottlieb Mozart nach Originalquellen beschrieben*. Prague, 1798; 2nd edn 1808

Nissen, G.N. von, *Biographie W.A. Mozarts*. Leipzig, 1828; repr.1964 and 1972

Novello, M. and V., *A Mozart Pilgrimage: Being the Travel Diaries of Vincent and Mary Novello in the Year 1829*, ed. N. Medici di Marignano and R. Hughes. London, 1955, and 1975

Nowak, L., 'Wer hat die Instrumentalstimmen in der Kyrie-Fuge des Requiems von W.A. Mozart geschrieben? . . .', *Mozart-Jahrbuch 1973/74*, Salzburg, 1975, pp.191–201

Oldman, C.B., 'J.A. André on Mozart's Manuscripts', *Music & Letters*, 5 (1924), pp.169–76

——, 'Mozart's Scena for Tenducci', *Music & Letters*, 42 (1961), p.44

——, 'Dr. Burney and Mozart', *Mozart-Jahrbuch 1962/63*, Salzburg, 1964, pp.75–81

Ord-Hume, A.W.J.G., *Clockwork Music: an Illustrated Musical History of Mechanical Musical Instruments*. London, 1973

——, *Joseph Haydn and the Mechanical Organ*. Cardiff, 1982

Paumgartner, B., 'Zu Mozarts Oboen-Concert D-Dur', *Mozart-Jahrbuch 1950*, Salzburg, 1951, pp.24–40

Payer-von Thurn, R., *Joseph II als Theaterdirektor*. Vienna and Leipzig, 1920

Petri, J.S., *Anleitung zur practischen Musik*. Lauban, 1767; 2nd edn Leipzig, 1782

Pfannhauser, K., 'Mozart hat kopiert', *Acta Mozartiana*, 1 (1954a), Heft 2, p.21

——, 'Zu Mozarts Kirchenwerken von 1768', *Mozart-Jahrbuch 1954b*, Salzburg, 1955, pp.150–68

——, 'Mozarts Krönungsmesse', *Mitteilungen der Internationalen Stiftung Mozarteum*, 11 (1963), pp.3–11

——, 'Epilogomena Mozartiana', *Mozart-Jahrbuch 1971/2*, Salzburg, 1973, pp.268–312

Pizka, H., *Das Horn bei Mozart (Mozart and the Horn)*, Facsimile-Collection. Kirchheim bei München, 1980

Plantinga, L., *Muzio Clementi: His Life and Music*. London, 1977

Planyavsky, A., 'Mozarts Arie mit obligatem Kontrabass', *Mozart-Jahrbuch 1971/2*, Salzburg, 1973, pp.313–36

Plath, W., 'Der Stand der Neuen Mozart-Ausgabe', *Musica*, 14 (1960), pp.46–8

——, 'Beiträge zur Mozart-Autographie I: Die Handschrift Leopold Mozarts', *Mozart-Jahrbuch 1960/61*, Salzburg, 1961, pp.82–117

——, 'Über Skizzen zu Mozarts "Requiem"', in *Bericht über den Internationalen Musikwissenschaftlichen Kongress Kassel 1961*, Kassel etc., 1963, pp.184–7

——, 'Der Ballo des "Ascanio" und die Klavierstücke KV Anh.207', *Mozart-Jahrbuch 1964*, Salzburg, 1965, pp.111–29

——, 'Aus der Werkstatt der Neuen Mozart-Ausgabe', *Acta Mozartiana*, 12/3 (1965), pp.53–7

——, 'Überliefert die dubiose Klavier-Romanze in As KV Anh.205 das verschollene Quintett-Fragment KV Anh.54 (452a)?', *Mozart-Jahrbuch 1965/6*, Salzburg, 1967, pp.71–86

——, 'Zur Echtheitsfrage bei Mozart', *Mozart-Jahrbuch 1971/2*, Salzburg, 1973, pp.19–36 with discussion of the motet *Venti, fulgura, procellae*, pp.37ff

——, 'Ein "geistlicher" Sinfoniesatz Mozarts', *Die Musikforschung*, 27 (1974), pp.93–5

——, 'Mozart und Galuppi: Bemerkungen zur Szene "Ah non lasciarmi, no" KV 295a', *Festschrift Walter Senn* (Munich and Salzburg, 1975), pp.174–8

——, 'Beiträge zur Mozart-Autographie II: Schriftchronologie 1770–1780', *Mozart-Jahrbuch 1976/7*, Kassel etc., 1978, pp.131–73

——, 'Bericht über Schreiber und Schriftchronologie der Mozart-Überlieferung', in *Bericht über die Mitarbeitertagung in Kassel 29.–30.*

Mai 1981 (private printing, 1984), pp.69–70

Platoff, J., *Music and Drama in the 'Opera buffa'-Finale: Mozart and his Contemporaries in Vienna, 1781–1790*. Diss., University of Pennsylvania, 1984

Pohl, C.F., *Mozart in London*. Vienna, 1867

Quantz, J.J., *Versuch einer Anweisung, die Flöte traversiere zu spielen*. Berlin, 1752. Eng. trans. E.R. Reilly as *On Playing the Flute*, London, 1966

Radcliffe, P., *Mozart Piano Concertos*. London, 1978

Raeburn, C., 'Mozart's Operas in England', *Musical Times*, 97 (1956), pp.15–17

Rasmussen, M., 'Mozart, Michael Haydn, and the Romance from the Concerto in E-flat Major for Horn and Orchestra, K.447', *Brass and Woodwind Quarterly*, 1/1–2 (1966–7), pp.27–47

Rees, A., *Cyclopaedia*. 39 vols, London, 1819–20

Rehm, W., 'Ergebnisse der "Neuen Mozart-Ausgabe": Zwischenbilanz 1965', *Mozart-Jahrbuch 1964*, Salzburg, 1965, pp.151–71

——, 'Stand und Planung der "Neuen Mozart-Ausgabe" im Zeichen der Krakauer Quellen', in *Ars jocundissima: Festschrift für Kurt Dorfmüller zum 60. Geburtstag*, ed. H. Leuchtmann and R. Münster. Tutzing, 1984a, pp.267–76

——, '"Hundert Bände "Neue Mozart-Ausgabe"', *Mitteilungen der Internationalen Stiftung Mozarteum*, 32 (1984b), pp.85–90

——, 'Mozart-Miszelle: Bemerkungen zum Autograph des Schlusschors aus der "Grabmusik" KV42 (35a)', in *Festschrift Martin Ruhnke zum 65. Geburtstag*. Neuhausen-Stuttgart, 1986a, pp.321–5

——, 'Der Eingang im 3. Satz . . . ist authentisch! Mozarts Kadenzen-Autograph bringt Klarheit', *Mitteilungen der Internationalen Stiftung Mozarteum*, 34 (1986b), pp.35–40

——, 'Die neuen Gesamtausgaben', *Modern Music Librarianship: In Honor of Ruth Watanabe*, ed. A. Mann. New York and Kassel, forthcoming

Rellstab, J.C.F., *Anleitung für Clavierspieler*. Berlin, 1790

Riedel, F.W., 'Liturgie und Kirchenmusik', in *Joseph Haydn in seiner Zeit*, ed. G. Mraz, G. Mraz and G. Schlag (catalogue of the exhibition: Eisenstadt, Kulturabteilung des Amtes der Burgenländischen Landesregierung), 1982, pp.121–33

Rochlitz, F., 'Verbürgte Anekdoten aus Wolfgang Gottlieb Mozarts Leben: ein Beitrag zur richtigeren Kenntnis dieses Mannes, als Mensch und Künstler', *AMZ*, i (1798–9), cols 17–24, 49–55, 81–6, 113–17, 145–52, 177–83, 289–91, 480, 854–6 [854–5 re K.421 (417b)]; iii (1800–01), cols 450–52, 493–7, 590–96

Röhrig, F., 'Das religiöse Leben Wiens zwischen Barock und Aufklärung', in *Joseph Haydn in seiner Zeit, op. cit.*, pp.114–20

Rosen, C., *The Classical Style: Haydn, Mozart, Beethoven*. London, 1971; rev. edn 1976

Rosen, D., 'The Composer's "Standard Operating Procedure" as Evidence of Intention: The Case of a Formal Quirk in Mozart's K.595', *Journal of Musicology*, 5 (1987), pp.79–90

Rosenthal, C.A., 'Der Einfluss der Salzburger Kirchenmusik auf Mozarts kirchenmusikalische Kompositionen', *Mozart-Jahrbuch 1971/2*, Salzburg, 1973, pp.173–81

Rosenthal, H., ed., *Opera Annual 1955–56* (Mozart bicentenary number). London, 1955

Rothschild, F., *Musical Performance in the Times of Mozart and Beethoven: The Lost Tradition in Music*, part II. London, 1961

Rousseau, J.J., ed., *Dictionnaire de musique*. Paris, 1768; repr. 1969

Rushton, J., ed., *Don Giovanni*. Cambridge, 1981

——, ed., *Idomeneo*. Cambridge, forthcoming

Sadie, S., 'Mozart', in *The New Grove*, vol.12. London, 1980, pp.681–752. Rev. edn as *The New Grove Mozart*. London, 1982

——, *Mozart Symphonies*. London, 1984

Sagarra, E., *A Social History of Germany 1648–1914*. London, 1977

Saint-Foix, G. de, *Les symphonies de Mozart: Étude et analyse*. Paris, 1932. Eng. trans. L. Orrey. London, 1947

——, 'Les Éditions françaises de Mozart (1765–1801)', in *Mélanges de Musicologie offerts à M. Lionel de la Laurencie*. Paris, 1933, pp.247–58

Schenk, E., *Wolfgang Amadeus Mozart: Eine Biographie*. Zurich, 1955. Rev. edn as *Mozart: Sein Leben, seine Welt*, Munich, 1975. Eng. trans. by R. and C. Winston as *Mozart and his Times*, London, 1960

Schiedermair, L., 'A Musical Traveler: Giacomo Gotifredo Ferrari (1759–1842)', *Musical Quarterly*, 25 (1939), pp.455–65

Schinn, G.J., and Otter, F.J., *Biographische Skizze von Johann Michael Haydn*, Salzburg, 1808

Schlager, K.H. ed., *Wolfgang Amadeus Mozart: Verzeichnis von Erst- und Frühdrucken bis 1800*. Kassel, 1978 (offprint from *Répertoire Internationale des Sources Musicales A/I: Einzeldrucke vor 1800: Band 6: Montalbano-Pleyel*, Kassel, 1975)

Schmid, E.F., *Ein Schwäbisches Mozart Buch*. Lorch-Stuttgart, 1948

Schmid, M.H., 'Mozart und die Salzburger Kirchenmusik', *Mozart-Jahrbuch 1978/9*, Kassel etc., 1979, pp.26–9

Schmitz, H.-P., *Die Kunst der Verzierung im 18. Jahrhundert*. Kassel and Basel, 1955

Schneider, O. and Algatzy, A., *Mozart-Handbuch: Chronik–Werk-Bibliographie*. Vienna, 1962

Schönberg, A., *Style and Idea*, ed. L. Stein. London, 1975. Rev. and enlarged version of edn by D. Newlin, New York, 1950

Schubart, C.F.D., *Leben und Gesinnung*. Stuttgart, 1791–3

Senn, W., *Missa Brevis* K.140, Bärenreiter-Verlag 4736 (1959) with foreword

——, 'Das Menuett KV 122 (73t) – eine Komposition Mozarts?', *Acta Mozartiana*, 8 (1961a), pp.46–52

——, 'Mozarts Skizze der Ballettmusik zu "Le gelosie del serraglio" (KV Anh.109/135a)', *Acta Musicologica*, xxxiii (1961b), pp.169–92

——, 'Die Menuette KV 104, Nr.1 und 2', *Mozart-Jahrbuch 1964*, Salzburg, 1965, pp.71–82

——, 'Das wiedergefundene Autograph der Sakramentalitanei in D von Leopold Mozart', *Mozart-Jahrbuch 1971/2a*, Salzburg, 1973, pp.197–216

——, 'Der Catalogus Musicalis des Salzburger Doms (1788)', *Mozart-Jahrbuch 1971/2b*, Salzburg, 1973, pp.182–96

——, 'Mozarts Kirchenmusik und die Literatur', *Mozart-Jahrbuch 1978/9*, Kassel etc., 1979, pp.14–18

Singer, I., *Mozart & Beethoven: The Concept of Love in their Operas*. Baltimore, 1977

Smith, E., *Mozart Serenades, Divertimenti & Dances*. London, 1982

Solomon, M., 'Mozart's Zoroastran Riddles', *American Imago*, 42 (Winter 1985), pp.345–69

Sonneck, O., *Catalogue of Librettos Printed Before 1800 in the Library of Congress*. Washington, 1914

Spitzer, J., and Zaslaw, N., 'Improvised Ornamentation in 18th-century Orchestras', *Journal of the American Musicological Society*, 32 (1986), p.524

Staehelin, L.E., *Die Reise der Familie Mozart durch die Schweiz*. Berne, 1968

Staehelin, M. and Birsak, K., 'Konzertante Sinfonie KV 297b/ Anh. C 14.01', *Mozart-Jahrbuch 1971/2*, Salzburg, 1973, pp.56ff

Steblin, R., *A History of Key Characteristics in the 18th and Early 19th Centuries*. Ann Arbor, 1983

Steglich, R., 'Das Auszierungswesen in der Musik W.A. Mozarts', *Mozart-Jahrbuch 1955*, Salzburg, 1956, p.181

Steinpress, B., 'Russische Ausgaben der Mozart-Werke im 18. Jahrhundert', *Mozart-Jahrbuch 1962/3*, Salzburg, 1964, pp.292–8

Steptoe, A., 'Mozart, Joseph II and Social Sensitivity', *Music Review*, 43 (1982), pp.109–20

——, 'Mozart and Poverty: A Re-examination of the Evidence', *Musical Times*, 125 (1984), pp.10–12

——, 'Mozart, Mesmer and Così fan tutte', *Music & Letters*, 67 (1986), pp.248–55

——, *The Mozart Da Ponte Operas: The Cultural and Musical Background to 'Le Nozze di Figaro', 'Don Giovanni' and 'Così fan tutte'*. Oxford, 1988

Stevens, J.R., 'An 18th Century Description of Concerto First-Movement Form', *Journal of the American Musicological Society*, 24 (1971), pp.85–95

——, 'Theme, Harmony and Texture in Classic-Romantic Descriptions of Concerto First-Movement Form', *Journal of the American Musicological Society*, 27 (1974), pp.25–60

——, Review of 'Ratner, Leonard G.: Classic Music: Expression, Form and Style', New York, 1980, *Journal of Music Theory*, 27 (1983), pp.121–7

——, 'Georg Joseph Vogler and the "Second Theme" in Sonata Form', *Journal of Musicology*, 2 (1983), pp.278–304

Stowell, R., *Violin Technique and Performance Practice in the Late Eighteenth and Early Nineteenth Centuries*. Cambridge, 1985

——, 'Good Execution and Other Necessary Skills – The role of the concertmaster in the late 18th century', *Early Music*, 16 (1988), p.21

Subira, J., 'Un insospechado inventario musical del siglo XVIII', *Annuario Musical*, 24 (1969), pp.227–36

Sulzer, J., ed., *Allgemeine Theorie der schönen Künste*. Leipzig, 1771–4

Tenschert, R., *Mozart: Ein Leben für die Oper*. Vienna, 1941

Thieme, C., *Der Klangstil des Mozartorchesters*. Leipzig, 1936

Thies, H.A., *Mozart und München: Ein Gedenkbuch*. Munich, 1941

Thomson, K., *The Masonic Thread in Mozart*. London, 1977

Tischler, H., *A Structural Analysis of Mozart's Piano Concertos*. Musicological Studies, 10. Brooklyn, 1966

Toeplitz, U., *Die Holzbläser in der Musik Mozarts und ihr Verhältnis zur Tonartenwahl*. Baden-Baden, 1978

Tromlitz, J.G., *Ausführlicher und gründlicher Unterricht, die Flöte zu spielen*. Leipzig, 1791; repr. Amsterdam, 1973

Türk, D.G., *Klavierschule; oder Anweisung zum Klavierspielen für Lehrer und Lernende mit kritischen Anmerkungen*. Leipzig and Halle, 1789; 2nd edn 1802, repr. 1967. Eng. trans. R.H. Haggh as *School of Clavier Playing*, Nebraska, 1982

Tyson, A., 'Mozart's Truthfulness', *Musical Times*, 119 (1978), pp.938–9

——, 'A Reconstruction of Nannerl Mozart's Music Book (Notenbuch)', *Music & Letters*, 60 (1979), pp.389–400; repr. in Tyson, 1987, pp.61–72

——, 'Mozart's "Haydn" Quartets: The Contribution of Paper Studies', in *The String Quartets of Haydn, Mozart and Beethoven: Studies of the Autograph Manuscripts*, ed. C. Wolff. Cambridge, Mass., 1980, pp.179–90; repr. in Tyson, 1987, pp.82–93

——, 'The Date of Mozart's Piano Sonata in B flat, KV 333 (315c): the "Linz" Sonata?', in *Musik-Edition-Interpretation: Gedenkschrift Günter Henle*, ed. M. Bente. Munich, 1980, pp.447–54; repr. in Tyson, 1987, pp.73–81

——, 'The Origins of Mozart's "Hunt" Quartet, K.458', in *Music and Bibliography: Essays in Honour of Alec Hyatt King*, ed. O. Neighbour. London, 1980, pp.132–48

——, 'The Mozart Fragments in the Mozarteum, Salzburg: A Preliminary Study of Their Chronology and Their Significance', *Journal of the American Musicological Society*, 34 (1981), pp.471–510; repr. in Tyson, 1987, pp.125–61

——, 'The Two Slow Movements of Mozart's "Paris" Symphony K.297', *Musical Times*, 122 (1981), pp.17–21; repr. in Tyson, 1987, pp.106–13

——, 'The Dates of Mozart's Missa brevis KV 258 and Missa longa KV 262 (246a): An Investigation into his "Klein-Querformat" Papers', in *Bachiana et alia musicologica: Festschrift Alfred Dürr zum 65. Geburtstag*, ed. W. Rehm. Kassel, 1983, pp.328–39; repr. in Tyson, 1987, pp.162–76

——, 'Mozart's Use of 10-Stave and 12-Stave Paper', in *Festschrift Albi Rosenthal*, ed. R. Elvers. Tutzing, 1984, pp.277–89; repr. in Tyson, 1987, pp.222–33

——, 'New Dating Methods: Watermarks and Paper-Studies', in *Bericht über die Mitarbeitertagung in Kassel 29.–30. Mai 1981*, ed. D. Hannemann. Kassel, 1984, pp.49–65; repr. in Tyson, 1987, pp.1–22

——, 'Notes on the Composition of Mozart's "Così fan tutte"', *Journal of the American Musicological Society*, 37 (1984), pp.356–401; repr. in Tyson, 1987, pp.177–221

——, *Mozart: Studies of the Autograph Scores*. Cambridge, Mass., and London, 1987

——, 'Redating Mozart: Some Stylistic and Biographical Implications', in Tyson, 1987, pp.21–35

——, 'A Feature of the Structure of Mozart's Autograph Scores', in *Festschrift Wolfgang Rehm zum 60. Geburtstag*, ed. D. Berke and H. Heckmann. Kassel, etc., 1989, pp.95–105

——, 'Some Features of the Autograph Score of Don Giovanni: the contributions that they may perhaps make to our understanding of the order in which Mozart wrote much of it, and occasionally revised it', *Israel Studies in Musicology*, 5 (1990), pp.1–19

Valentin, E., 'Die goldene Spur: Mozart in der Dichtung Hermann Hesses', in *Festschrift Alfred Orel zum 70. Geburtstag*. Vienna, 1960; Augsburg, 1966

——, *Leopold Mozart: Porträt einer Persönlichkeit*. Munich, 1987

——, ed., *Neues Mozart-Jahrbuch*. Regensburg, 1941–3 Verchaly, A., ed., *Les influences étrangères dans l'oeuvre de W.A. Mozart*. Internat. Colloquium. Paris, 10–13 October 1956. Paris, 1958

Wagner, C., *Diaries*. Eng. trans. G. Skelton. 2 vols. London and New York, 1978–80

Wangermann, E., *From Joseph II to the Jacobin Trials*. London, 1959

——, *The Austrian Achievement 1700–1800*. London, 1973

Webster, J., 'Towards a History of Viennese Chamber Music in the Early Classical Period', *Journal of the American Musicological Society*, 27 (1974), pp.212–47

——, 'The Scoring of Mozart's Chamber Music for Strings', *Essays on Music of the Classic Era in Honor of Barry S. Brook*. New York, 1983, pp.259–96

Wedin, K., 'The Discovery of the Copy of K.16a and the Orchestral Music by Mozart Owned by the Odense Club', in *Die Sinfonie KV 16a 'del Sigr. Mozart'*, ed. J.P. Larsen and K. Wedin. Odense, 1987, pp.9–24

Wegele, L., *Der Augsburger Maler Anton Mozart*. Augsburg, 1969

Weisstein, U., *The Essence of the Opera*. New York, 1969

Whewell, M., 'Mozart's Bassethorn Trios', *Musical Times*, 103 (1962) p.19

Wilson, B.E., Review of Hans Günter Klein, *Wolfgang Amadeus Mozart: Autographe und Abschriften. Katalog*, Berlin, 1982, in *Notes*, 39 (1982/3), pp. 841–3

Wlassak, E., *Chronik des K.K. Hof-Burgtheaters*. Vienna, 1876

Wolff, C., 'Creative Exuberance vs. Critical Choice: Thoughts on Mozart's Quartet Fragments', in *The String Quartets of Haydn, Mozart and Beethoven: Studies of the Autograph Manuscripts*, ed. C. Wolff. Cambridge, Mass., 1980, pp.191–210

Wraxall, N., *Memoirs of the Courts of Berlin, Warsaw and Vienna*. Dublin, 1799

Würtz, R., *Das Mannheimer Mozart-Buch*. Wilhelmshaven, 1977

Wurzbach, C. von, *Mozart-Buch*. Vienna, 1869
Wyzewa, T. de, and Saint-Foix, G. de, *Wolfgang Amédée Mozart*. Paris, 1912–46; repr. 1979
Zaslaw, N., 'A Rediscovered Mozart Autograph at Cornell University', *Mozart-Jahrbuch 1971/2*, Salzburg, 1973, pp.419–31
——, 'Mozart's Tempo Conventions', *International Musicological Society Report of the Eleventh Congress*, Copenhagen, 1972, pp.720ff.
——, 'Toward the Revival of the Classical Orchestra', *Proceedings of the Royal Musical Association*, 103 (1977), p.179
——, 'Mozart's Paris Symphonies', *Musical Times*, 119 (1978), pp.753–7
——, 'The Size and Composition of European Orchestras, 1775–95', in *Haydn Studies: Proceedings of the International Haydn Conference Washington DC (1975)*, ed. J.P. Larsen, H. Serwer and J. Webster. New York, 1981, p.186
——, 'Leopold Mozart's List of his Son's Works', in *Essays on Music of the Classic Era in Honor of Barry S. Brook*. New York, 1983, pp.323–58
——, *Mozart's Symphonies: Context, Performance Practice, Reception*. Oxford, 1989
——, and Eisen, C., 'Signor Mozart's Symphony in A minor K.Anh.220 = 16a', *Journal of Musicology*, 4 (1985/6), pp.191–206
Zeileis, F.G., 'Bemerkungen zum Fragment von Mozarts Freimaurerkantate KV 429', *Mitteilungen der Internationalen Stiftung Mozarteum*, 33 (1985), pp.11–16

List of Illustrations

Measurements are given in centimetres then inches, height before width.

1 Anonymous portrait of Mozart, ?*c*. 1790. Drawing, 9 × 8 (3½ × 3⅛). Courtesy Albi Rosenthal. **2** Attr. Pietro Antonio Lorenzoni, Mozart as a boy, 1763. Oil painting, 83.7 × 64 (33 × 25¼). Internationale Stiftung Mozarteum, Salzburg. **3** Louis Carrogis de Carmontelle, Leopold Mozart with Wolfgang and Nannerl, 1777 (copy of 1763 portrait). Watercolour on paper, 32.6 × 20.1 (12⅞ × 7⅞). National Gallery, London. **4** Michel Barthélemy Ollivier, Tea at Prince Louis-François de Conti's residence in the 'Temple', 1766. Oil painting, 53 × 68 (20⅞ × 26¾). Louvre, Paris. Photo Bulloz. **5** Saverio della Rosa, Mozart in Verona, 1770. Oil Painting, 71 × 58 (28 × 22⅞). Private Collection. **6** Attr. Martin Knoller, portrait of Mozart, ?1773. Miniature on ivory, 5 (2) in diameter. Internationale Stiftung Mozarteum, Salzburg. **7** Anonymous portrait of Mozart, 1777. Miniature on ivory, 4 × 2.8 (1⅝ × 1⅛). Mozart Gedenkstätte, Augsburg. **8** Anonymous, Mozart as Knight of the Golden Spur, 1777. Oil painting, 75 × 65 (29½ × 25⅝). Internationale Stiftung Mozarteum, Salzburg. **9** Johann Nepomuk della Croce, the Mozart Family, 1780–81. Oil painting, 140 × 186 (55⅛ × 73¼). Internationale Stiftung Mozarteum, Salzburg. **10** Barbara Krafft, portrait of Mozart, 1819. Oil painting, 54 × 42 (21¼ × 16½). Gesellschaft der Musikfreunde, Vienna. **11** Hieronymous Löschenkohl, silhouette of Mozart, 1785. Engraving, 8.1 × 5 (3⅛ × 2). Historisches Museum der Stadt, Vienna. **12** Joseph Lange, portrait of Mozart published in *Biographie W.A. Mozarts nach Originalbriefen* by Georg Nikolaus Nissen, Leipzig, 1828. Lithograph. Photo courtesy Albi Rosenthal. **13** Leonard Posch, plaster medallion of Mozart, 1788/89. 8.2 × 6.9 (3¼ × 2¾). Kunsthistorisches Museum, Vienna. **14** Doris Stock, drawing of Mozart, 1789. Silver-point on ivory paste board, 7.5 × 6.2 (3 × 2⅜). Musikbibliothek der Stadt, Leipzig. **15** Joseph Lange, Mozart at the Pianoforte, 1789/90 (unfinished). Oil painting, 34.6 × 29.7 (13⅝ × 16¾). Internationale Stiftung Mozarteum, Salzburg. **16** Letter from Wolfgang to his cousin, 10 May 1779. British Library, London (Stefan Zweig Collection). **17** *God is our Refuge*, K.20, 1765. British Library, London. **18** *Apollo et Hyacinthus*, K.38, 1767. Staatsbibliothek Preussischer Kulturbesitz, Berlin. **19** String Quintet in B♭ major, K.174, 1773. Biblioteka Jagiellónska, Kraców (ex Preussische Staatsbibliothek, Berlin). **20** Concerto for Three Pianos and Orchestra, K.242, 1776. Biblioteka Jagiellónska, Kraców (ex Preussische Staatsbibliothek, Berlin). **21** Serenade in B♭ for 13 instruments, K.361, ?1781–2. Library of Congress, Washington DC. **22** Mass in C minor, K.427 (417a), composed 1782–3. Biblioteka Jagiellónska, Kraców (ex Preussische Staatsbibliothek, Berlin). **23, 24** Piano Concerto in C minor, K.491, 1786. Royal College of Music, London. **25** *Der Schauspieldirektor*, K.486, 1786. Pierpont Morgan Library, New York City. **26** Sketches for Piano Concerto in C major, K.503, 1786. Deutsche Staatsbibliothek, Berlin. **27** The first of the 6 German Dances, K.509, 1787. Staatsbibliothek Preussischer Kulturbesitz, Berlin. **28** Last page of the 'Lacrimosa' from the Requiem, 1791. Musiksammlung, Österreichische Nationalbibliothek, Vienna. **29** Final page of Mozart's thematic catalogue. British Library, London (Stefan Zweig Collection). **30** Mozart's signature dated 15 November 1791 on the first page of the *Kleine Freymaurerkantate*, K.623. Musiksammlung, Österreichische Nationalbibliothek, Vienna.

The Contributors

JOHN ARTHUR	Doctoral dissertation on Mozart's fragments and sketches (Christ Church, Oxford)
PHILIPPE A. AUTEXIER	Director of the Centre Mozart, Poitiers. Specialist on Mozart, Liszt, Bartók and masonic music
OTTO BIBA	Scholar; Director of the Archives, Library and Collections of the Gesellschaft der Musikfreunde in Wien, Vienna
MALCOLM BOYD	Lecturer in Music, University of Wales College of Cardiff
PETER BRANSCOMBE	Professor of Austrian Studies, University of St Andrews
DEREK CAREW	Lecturer in Music, University of Wales College of Cardiff
ESTHER CAVETT-DUNSBY	Publications on Mozart, Beethoven, Elgar and music theory from the 18th century to the present day. Forthcoming publication of 1985 doctoral dissertation on Mozart's variations
CLIFF EISEN	Professor, Department of Music, New York University. Forthcoming monographs include *New Mozart Documents* and *Mozart: the Salzburg Symphonist*, as well as an edited volume, *Mozart Studies*
PATRICK GALE	Novelist, critic and amateur musician
ROGER HELLYER	Wind player with Royal Shakespeare Company; position also held with Birmingham Conservatoire. Specialist in *Harmoniemusik*
AMANDA HOLDEN	Translator of several operas, including *Don Giovanni* and *La finta giardiniera*. General editor of forthcoming *Penguin Opera Guide*
CLEMENS HÖSLINGER	Librarian of Haus-, Hof- und Staatsarchiv, Vienna. Authority on Mozart and 18th-century music
DAVID HUMPHREYS	Lecturer in Music, University of Wales College of Cardiff
DAVID WYN JONES	Lecturer in Music, University of Wales College of Cardiff
ALEC HYATT KING	Superintendent of the Music Room, British Museum (1945–72). Music Librarian of the British Library (1972–6). Leading Mozart authority
ROBERT LEVIN	Concert pianist, musicologist, theorist; Professor of Piano at the Staatliche Hochschule für Musik, Freiburg im Breisgau
ELSE RADANT	Historian and researcher
WOLFGANG REHM	Co-editor of the Neue Mozart-Ausgabe. Programme Director of the Salzburg Mozartwoche
MICHAEL F. ROBINSON	Head of Music Department, University of Wales College of Cardiff
ALBI ROSENTHAL	Music historian and leading expert on musical bibliography and the study of autographs
JULIAN RUSHTON	Professor of Music, University of Leeds. Editor of Cambridge Opera Handbooks on *Don Giovanni* and *Idomeneo*
ANDREW STEPTOE	Professor of Psychology, University of London. Author of recent study of Mozart – Da Ponte operas
JOHN STONE	Writer on musical history and aesthetics; has made a special study of Mozart's operas
ROBIN STOWELL	Professor of Music, University of Wales College of Cardiff

EDITOR'S NOTE: As this book goes to press, the authenticity of the letter from Constanze Mozart, referred to on p.137, has been questioned, and the letter temporarily withdrawn from the Sotheby's sale.

INDEX

437

Mancelona Township Library
202 W State Street
P.O. Box 499
Mancelona, MI 49659